Japan and the United States in World Trade

WARREN S. HUNSBERGER

Japan and the United States in World Trade

Published for the
Council on Foreign Relations
by
Harper & Row, Publishers
New York and Evanston

JAPAN AND THE UNITED STATES IN WORLD TRADE

For information, address Council on Foreign Relations, 58 East 68th Street, New York 21

FIRST EDITION

Library of Congress catalog card number: 64-24790

Printed in the United States of America by Quinn & Boden Company, Inc., Rahway, N.J.

Published by Harper & Row, Publishers, Incorporated

The Council on Foreign Relations is a non-profit institution devoted to study of the international aspects of American political, economic and strategic problems. It takes no stand, expressed or implied, on American policy.

The authors of books published under the auspices of the Council are responsible for their statements of fact and expressions of opinion. The Council is responsible only for determining that they should be presented to the public.

For a list of Council publications see pages 493 and 494.

To
P, D, E, R

Preface

This study of Japan's foreign economic relations seeks to illuminate not only the Japanese side of the story but also American interests and the issues of American policy involved. Since Japan was opened to international intercourse in the nineteenth century there has never been a time when the United States was not important to Japan. The bitter battles of the Pacific war were one demonstration of the great importance Japan has acquired for the United States. Since then Japan has made a remarkable—probably unique—resurgence from defeat. The two countries have come to trade with each other, and to maintain many other business and nonbusiness contacts, to an extent far beyond previous imagination. In the process, they have encountered some notable problems. One that has caused particularly serious concern to the United States is the unprecedented volume of Japanese goods, mostly competitive with American, that Japanese producers have sought to sell in the United States. No other country has ever put so great a strain on American tolerance of competitive manufactures.

Japan in the 1960s is no longer a weakling, no longer an aggressor, but a strong and remarkably peaceful industrial nation. But what is Japan's place in international economic councils? What does Japan stand for? What contribution does or can Japan make to the great battles of our age? What influence can Japan exert on the struggle of poor nations everywhere to climb from traditional poverty to modern urban living—as only Japan in all of the non-Western world has done so far? What is Japan doing to make the international economy such that poor countries as well as rich can grow and prosper, or, more immediately, such that Japan itself can count on continued access to foreign markets for exports and imports? What can or should the United States do about Japan's role in these and other matters of American interest, including the many issues that arise out of direct business dealings between Japanese and Americans?

This study deals with these and related questions and their background. As work progressed, I found it necessary to investigate various historical and statistical questions, as well as certain policy matters, not initially considered essential. The resulting length and complexity of this book reflect the number and character of the issues involved.

To keep the text readable, I have where possible pushed technical details into tables, footnotes (including footnotes to tables), and appendixes. The style has been improved by the firm editing of skilled hands after having left mine. To assist readers and make the book as useful as possible for reference, there are not only the index but also numerous headings, subheadings and cross-references in the text. There is some repetition of points that are pertinent in more than one context. Part III and especially the two final chapters recapitulate certain material presented earlier and draw policy conclusions.

Because source materials in English—leaving aside those in Japanese and other languages—are so numerous, uneven in quality, and at times so frustrating to use, I am including an analytical bibliographic note. It does not list everything on the various subjects discussed in this book, but it should prove helpful to others interested in these matters. More than that, I have some hope that this statement about sources, along with comments on statistics in the appendixes and elsewhere, may induce the organizations concerned to make further improvement in the readily available information, which has grown notably fuller and generally better during the course of this study.

The manuscript was virtually completed by mid-1963. Statistics and other material are generally carried through 1962, but in some places this was not possible. Some updating and change took place during the editing process, especially as a result of my visiting Japan in July and August 1963, and a few further changes were made even later. Essentially, however, the presentation and the judgments herein remain as they were in the spring of 1963.

Since then Japan has continued to move rapidly, and significant changes have occurred in Japan's international economic position. Japan has become a full-fledged member of the Organization for Economic Cooperation and Development. On April 1, 1964, Japan at last shifted its status in the International Monetary Fund from transitional under Article 14 to regular under Article 8, thus assuming with some temporary exceptions the obligations of liberality and nondiscrimination that are basic to the philosophy and policy of IMF. Japan has also had some new and rather different experiences with its balance-of-payments cycle.

Much has also happened elsewhere. Peking and Moscow are making moves that suggest larger trade with Japan than previously seemed likely. Political and economic relations in Asia are given added uncertainty by grave deterioration of the situation in Viet-Nam, by General de Gaulle's initiatives there and his recognition of Communist China, by Sukarno's threat to the peace in his "confrontation" of Malaysia, and by other events. In the United States the assassination of President Kennedy and the different character of Lyndon Johnson's Presidency have so far had fewer economic implications for Japan than the greater-than-expected vigor of the American economy. The United Nations Conference on Trade and Development is taking place in Geneva as these words are written, and the "Kennedy Round" of tariff discussions in GATT has opened. These and many other new developments are likely to affect the circumstances in which Japan conducts its foreign economic relations.

Still, if I were writing the book in 1964, it would not be essentially different. What has happened since writing generally follows trends discussed herein. I do not see fundamental changes that warrant any substantial shift of interpretation or emphasis. Nor has the general character of the issues changed. Japanese thinking has advanced somewhat along lines previously evident, but as yet I see no basic change.

One question that might be asked more pointedly in 1964 than earlier is whether Japan, having demonstrated the capacity and will to pay its way internationally, may not now shift its focus of attention more toward domestic issues than at any time in the past generation. Domestic problems are accumulating and growing urgent—as any visitor to Tokyo can tell at once from the frantic efforts and confusion involved in preparing the city for the Olympic games taking place in October 1964. Vast investments are needed in many parts of the country in transportation facilities, in other public services, and in housing. Japan has yet to come to terms with large numbers of newly affluent people, with more and more cars and other twentieth-century machines in a society that is physically and psychologically unprepared for them. Rapidly expanding employment and rising wages are changing Japanese life. An economy that has always had a surplus of labor, and a plethora of little shops and service people to perform countless functions, must now adjust to the rapidly rising costs of such labor-intensive activities. Labor and employers are looking at each other with new eyes, but not yet with the new understanding needed for a successful transition from traditional paternalism to a new, more modern relationship. Outside of economics, Japan has a vast number of new situations and problems, from dangerous polarization and factionalism in politics to severe strains in family life.

A lesson that is illustrated repeatedly in this volume and remains pertinent in a changing Japan is the nation's capacity to work out solutions to its problems. Just as the many international economic problems that seemed hopeless a few years ago have yielded to the energy, skill, and enterprise of Japanese businessmen and economic managers, so may these other problems give way before concerted attack, assuming favorable circumstances. One cannot be sure; the Japanese genius in business, in art, and in other areas of previous success may not necessarily be matched—fully or soon—by genius in new endeavors. But for all one's doubts about unconquered difficulties and unsolved problems, one should keep in mind how often Japan's problems of yesterday have become Japan's achievements of today. There seems to be good reason to expect that as the new nation turns to new problems these too will in time provide new victories.

There is, of course, the danger that a shift of focus from international economic affairs to other urgent matters may lead to giving unsufficient attention to the balance of payments. The recent acceleration in the rise of consumer prices is a possible danger signal, but it has not yet been confirmed by any persistent increase in wholesale or export prices. It would not take much diversion from the stern tasks of continuing rapid export expansion to bring on a new crisis in the balance of payments. The very immediacy of this danger makes a dramatic failure in exports less likely than the possibility that export growth might prove so sluggish as to put severe pressure on Japan's newly adopted liberal policies toward foreign payments. I do not really expect a serious slowing down of export growth, however, unless some new difficulty of major proportions should arise. I feel, as this volume says in a number of contexts, that the Japanese have adequate opportunities for trade and other foreign economic transactions, that they will continue to exploit these opportunities energetically and skillfully, but that Japanese acceptance of liberal trading principles remains limited and needs to be deepened.

The origins of this study lie in the 1930s, when as a graduate student at Yale I first looked seriously at Japanese foreign economic relations. World War II and its aftermath gave me intermittent periods of work on Japan but little opportunity to write for publication. It was only in 1954, after several years of concern with other parts of the world and different kinds of problems from Japan's, that a return to academic life provided me renewed occasion for concentrated study of Japan. A visit to Asia in 1955 turned up strong evidence that Japan had not yet found a reliable means of paying for an adequate volume of imports, dependence on which had provided an important excuse for Japanese aggression, proved the basis of a successful Allied blockade of Japan during the Pacific war, and stimulated large American aid to Japan during the Occupation.

Specific work on the present volume began with a summer in Japan in 1958, financed by a grant from the American Philosophical Society. The Council on Foreign Relations has financed and assisted the rest of my work, by extending the 1958 trip to make it possible to visit a number of other countries in Asia, by granting me a year at the Council as Research Fellow, 1958–1959, and by providing many other forms of assistance since then. At the end of that year I had drafts of most of the chapters, but there remained some unanswered research questions and some gaps in the analysis of a fast-moving Japan and of its changing world environment, including in particular certain aspects of American policy. Completion of the book has proved unexpectedly difficult and slow, largely because of the speed of new developments and the other demands on my time.

A particularly valuable feature of the period in New York was the Study Group on Japanese-American Economic Relations, set up by the Council on Foreign Relations with Dr. August Maffry as Chairman. The other members of the group were: Solomon Barkin, A. Doak Barnett, Percy W. Bidwell, Eugene M. Braderman, Thomas W. Childs, Jerome B. Cohen, William Diebold, Jr., John Exter, Nevil Ford, Arthur B. Foye, George S. Franklin, Jr., W. Rogers Herod, Willem Holst, Milton C. Lightner, William W. Lockwood, David W. MacEachron, Clifford C. Matlock, Alfred C. Neal, James William Morley, J. Morden Murphy, the late John C. Orchard, Andrew Overby, John D. Rockefeller, 3rd, Howard S. Piquet, Willard L. Thorp, Raymond Vernon, and James Warren. James I. Nakamura prepared digests of the meetings. The group met eight times during the year, on three occasions with outside guests expert on the subject under discussion: R. Buford Brandis, Noel Hemmendinger, Sam Ishikawa, Mike Masaoka, William Sullivan, and Gengo Suzuki. For each meeting I prepared a paper raising questions and presenting background in a particular area. Several of these papers served as nuclei for corresponding chapters in the first draft of this book. Discussions in the group added much to my thinking and stirred me to several new lines of inquiry. However, the group as a whole and the individual members of it have no responsibility at all for what I say in this book.

That this book has even now reached print is in large part the result of assistance much greater and more varied than I can sufficiently acknowledge here. At the Council on Foreign Relations, Mr. William Diebold, Jr., Senior Research Fellow, and Mrs. Helena Stalson, Economist, have contributed far beyond the normal call of duty. Many others in Japan, in New York, in Washington and elsewhere have patiently provided information and contributed skilled effort to what for a while seemed an endless series of revisions and updatings of text and tables. To all the organizations and individuals who have taken an interest in this work and contributed information, documents, comment, labor, encouragement or sheer patience, I feel deep gratitude, even though I may never succeed in expressing it adequately. But for the shortcomings that this book will surely be found to contain, I myself take responsibility.

WARREN S. HUNSBERGER

Kuala Lumpur, Malaysia
May 1964

Contents

Part II
JAPANESE COMMODITY TRADE

Part III
POLICY NEEDS AND POSSIBILITIES

TABLES

CHARTS

Part I
Japan in the World Economy

Chapter 1

The United States and Japan

Japan in the early 1960s was a prosperous industrial country, an important factor in world trade, and a peaceful, cooperative ally of the United States. A decade ago, when Japan was newly independent after defeat and Occupation, it was by no means clear how, or even whether, a large population could earn a living within the narrow limits of the rugged islands to which Japan had been thrown back after losing an overseas empire. A decade before that, Japan and the United States were locked in a long, bitter war, started by Japan at least partly because, over the years, the idea had gained ground that foreign countries, and particularly the United States, would always restrict trade and immigration to a degree that would prevent the Japanese people from making a decent living in the world. And a decade earlier still, in 1930 and early 1931, Japan was suffering acutely from a depression imported from the United States and magnified by a stern deflationary policy that reflected efforts to follow what were deemed to be the financially orthodox policies of Western countries. Out of the social and political confusion of deep depression came the military forces' assertion of power that started the nation on a course leading in time to suffering, destruction, and, ultimately, surrender aboard the U.S.S. *Missouri* in Tokyo Bay.

That was the second time American warships had spelled an end to an established Japanese policy and marked the beginning of a new relation between Japan and the rest of the world. The squadron of ten "Black Ships" that Commodore Matthew Calbraith Perry, U.S.N., led to Japan in 1854 ended the country's isolation without bloodshed. Reluctantly the Japanese permitted trade to grow and granted foreigners privileges hitherto denied them. But for some time it was not clear how Japan should conduct itself toward the outside world so as to satisfy Japanese interests. The nearest and most obvious example of another country that had had to deal against its will with the intrusive

West was China, but the model was nothing to copy, only evidence of misfortunes to try to avoid. Japan succeeded in avoiding China's fate and seemed gradually not only to have come to some sort of terms with the outside world but to have found its own formula for economic growth and political development as well. But after the First World War there were setbacks that led to the sequence of depression, aggression, war, and defeat that made it necessary for Japan to start all over again in 1945.

The negatives were starkly clear: Japan was thrown back into its main islands; its population, more than double the 1854 size, was heavily dependent on foreign trade, but trade privileges were gone; all of Japan's neighbors had suffered at Japanese hands and none had reason to befriend Japan, or even to do ordinary business with her. Much of this book is concerned with how that bleak prospect was replaced by the pleasing one of the early 1960s. Of special concern will be the place of the United States in that process. Japan's principal antagonist in the war, the leader among the victors in the Occupation, the United States subsequently played the largest single part of any foreign country in Japan's recovery. How that happened, and what actions and policies it required of the United States, is another of the main subjects of this volume.

This is not, however, a history book. It deals with the present and looks to the future, analyzing the problems Japan's new position is likely to create in the decade ahead. Some of these problems and the policy alternatives they pose are essentially new phases of familiar issues while others arise for the first time. During the past decade and a half, relations between Japan and the United States depended largely on American recognition of a strong national interest in the welfare of Japan. That attitude will continue to be crucial in the future, but Japan's separate and independent judgment of its own interests will be more important than before. The implications of the new situation for the United States, and the policy questions presented to the American people, make up the focus of this book's conclusions and recommendations.

The chapters that follow deal very largely with trade, but they treat trade problems as part of the whole complex of American relations with Japan. Two main factors justify this emphasis. First, trade and other economic transactions make up a large part of the relations between the two countries. And second, Japan's strength, stability, and political health are closely linked with its economic welfare, which in turn depends heavily on foreign trade. Therefore, if American foreign policy calls for a strong and stable Japan, the United States must also be concerned about Japan's trade—across the Pacific and with other parts of the world as well.

The importance of economic affairs in the relations of the two countries is no recent development. In the mid-nineteenth century Japan, situated on the great circle route from California to the China coast, was viewed as a good stopping place for American ships and as a place of refuge from typhoons. Whalers, which in those days operated in many parts of the Pacific, also liked to make port from time to time. But the Japanese prohibited visits by American ships. Seamen shipwrecked on the Japanese coast were treated roughly. Only very limited foreign trade, with the Dutch and Chinese, was permitted. Americans and others who were excluded thought they could do a greatly profitable trade with Japan if they were allowed to. The movement toward the Pacific that came with the discovery of gold in California and the bringing of the Oregon Territory into the union helped make Americans feel their country should be the one to end Japan's isolation. After others had failed, Perry succeeded in 1854.

Since then a vast network of economic transactions has grown up between Japan and the United States. Though the last war and the events leading up to it cut ties and seemed to destroy some of the foundations of profitable and friendly economic relations, the postwar years have brought the exchange of goods and services and the financial and investment links to unprecedented levels. The United States is the largest factor in Japan's foreign trade, and Japan is the second largest trading partner of the United States. Economic relations on this scale have, of course, brought problems as well. For the United States the most difficult of these have arisen from the impact of a large volume of competitive imports in the domestic market.

Japanese–American economic relations have developed with such strength and vigor because of mutual advantage. But they have been fostered by national policy, too. In the immediate postwar years the United States helped Japan directly, with money and supplies; since then its aim has been to help keep open the possibility for Japan to earn its own way in the world by selling increasing quantities of goods abroad. These policies were not adopted without dispute and opposition—and often they have shown the marks of inevitable compromise in their imperfections and inadequacies. American policies favorable to Japan will be questioned again in the future. Since they will also continue to be of great significance to Japan, it is a matter of considerable importance to understand why the United States has so great an interest in Japan's prosperity and growth.

The value of American–Japanese relations to the economies of the two countries is only part of the story. Japan is important to the United States in other ways; as a friendly country, indeed an ally, it is a source of strength and cooperation in Asian and world affairs. With a functioning democracy, a private-enterprise economy, and an industrial, urban, middle-class society, Japan is not only a country with which Americans can do business but also one with which they can have far more comfortable relations than with totalitarian or statist countries. Though without great military power, Japan as an ally is an important part of the free world's political and military defenses against aggressive and expansionist communism, whether Russian or Chinese. Lying off the coast of Asia, between the Central Pacific and northern China, Korea, and the southern maritime province of Soviet Asia, Japan has great strategic importance. Except for the sprawling eastern reaches of the Soviet Far East, it is America's nearest trans-Pacific neighbor. It is a stable and mature member of the community of nations, willing to cooperate with the United States and anxious to prove that it can play a part in world affairs commensurate with its strength and experience. That part can be a very effective and constructive one. By producing, buying, and selling, by helping the economic development of other countries in Asia and elsewhere, by contributing to the strength, resources, and guidance of international organizations, and by setting an example of peaceful economic growth through relatively free methods, from which the masses of Japanese as well as the leaders benefit, Japan can make a major contribution to the progress of the free world in the decades to come.

But Japan can do none of these things unless two major conditions are met. In return for their efforts its people must be able to attain reasonable economic security and a rising standard of living. And Japan must be accepted by the rest of the free world as an equal, if relatively recent, member of the group of advanced industrial countries which have a major voice in major decisions—and carry their share of the political, military, and economic burdens that go with this responsibility. While many things need to be done to satisfy these two conditions, one that is of fundamental importance is that Japan should be able to trade relatively freely and in expanding volume with most parts of the world, for that is the economic prerequisite of Japanese prosperity and growth and the psychological prerequisite for calling forth a continuing responsible reaction from the Japanese people.

If these conditions are not met, the free world will not only lose some of the contribution Japan can make but may once again find Japan a problem, and perhaps a threat. The people, resources, skills, and position that make Japan an important country and, potentially, a major ally of the United States can also be turned to other ends. Disturbed and disaffected, Japan would be, at a minimum, a source of instability in Asia and of weakness for the whole free world. Mobilized on a narrowly nationalistic or pro-Communist basis, Japan's strengths would be a source of danger. Economic prosperity and expansion are not in themselves guarantees against this kind of perverted political development, but without them there is little chance for anything but undesirable results. A poor Japan, whose citizens' productive efforts yielded frustratingly meager results and who felt discriminated against by the countries of Western Europe and North America, would be highly vulnerable to Russian and Chinese pressure or to enticements from without and to serious damage from exacerbated political and social tensions within.

Even if the United States and the other countries of the free world follow policies that permit Japan to prosper and to develop internally and in its international position in a satisfactory fashion, it does not follow that Japan will become dependably docile or overwhelmingly pro-American. There is a remarkable amount of anti-American sentiment in Japan. Much of it springs from Marxist views which are widely held, and may be spreading, especially among industrial workers. Some anti-American feeling is a belated reaction by a proud and sensitive people to the continuing large American presence in Japan. Some is a reaction to economic and military dependence. Many Japanese are passionately pacifist and feel that American military forces in Japan serve not to defend the nation but rather to invite attack from powerful neighbors who might otherwise leave Japan alone. Nuclear weapons raise highly emotional issues in Japan, the only country thus far to feel their terrible blast in war. And there are, of course, many other grievances that Japanese feel, rightly or wrongly, about Americans and American policy.

Economic growth is not likely to eliminate these things. Closer and more numerous economic contacts may intensify some of them and create new frictions. Moreover, economic strength and a diversification of Japan's trade and financial relations among free world countries will increase Japan's sense of political independence. Almost inevitably there will be more occasions in the future than in the recent past when Japan and the United States will disagree in their diagnoses of problems and follow divergent policies. And when they are able to compromise or concert their action, concessions will have to be made by the United States as well as Japan. Just as the great economic growth of Western Europe has strengthened the free world but presented the United States with new problems, a Japan that doubled its national product between 1960 and 1970 would be a different force in the world.

It should be a welcome force and it is the task of American diplomacy, and the foreign and security policies on which it is based, to maintain harmonious relations and to make the most of the new advantage. Economic policy alone cannot do this, but without the right economic policies it cannot be done. The main responsibility politically and economically lies, of course, in Japan. But the Japanese alone cannot assure their economic welfare. At least as much as any major country, Japan depends on foreign trade. More than any other major country except Canada its foreign trade depends on the United States. So it falls to the industrial countries of the free world, and especially the United States, to follow those economic policies that will permit Japan to continue the economic growth it has so effectively achieved in the past decade and to lay what the lend-lease agreements called "the material foundations of the liberty and welfare of all peoples." This will not be something done *for* Japan, but for the common interest, and it will have to be done *with* Japan, which will itself be called on to assume greater responsibility for world affairs than in the past.

It is for these reasons that American economic policy, and especially trade policy, toward Japan has a significance greater than that which can be measured in dollars, yen, and percentages.

Chapter 2

Japan's Approach to Foreign Economic Policy

For all its phenomenal development during the past century, the Japanese nation has not established what either its own people or their neighbors would regard as generally satisfactory relations with foreign countries. A large part of the problem is economic. Through all the ups and downs of fortune, Japan has not until recently been able to count on exporting enough to pay for its reasonable import needs. Strict economy of foreign exchange earnings has been a necessity. Here we find an important reason why the Japanese people and their representatives often appear to lack confidence in international contacts. One can easily think of other probable reasons, including language difficulties, the relatively short history of modern Japanese foreign relations, the dominance during much of that modern history of exaggerated military nationalism, the sense of second-class status, and the lack of adequate standards for international conduct to guide an insular people used to following in their domestic life complicated rules that do not fit many international situations. But Japan's insecure balance of international payments has been a large element.

Japan's history is very different from that of Britain or the United States. There is virtually no indigenous tradition to support free trade, not even a tradition of freebooting more recent than the early seventeenth century. For more than two hundred years before Commodore Perry's arrival in 1853, the ruling Shogun had forbidden virtually all foreign commerce, although there was a small amount of authorized trade with the Dutch and Chinese and, in the years immediately preceding Perry's arrival, a significant growth in illicit trade, especially by restless groups in western Japan. The decision to open Japan to foreign trade, although it would have had to come in time anyhow, was not a voluntary one when it was made during Perry's second visit in 1854.

A PHENOMENAL FIFTY YEARS, 1868–1918: ECONOMIC POLICY SUBORDINATE TO POWER POLICY

Following Perry's visits and the subsequent stay of the American Consul General, Townsend Harris, the Japanese found themselves receiving a growing number of foreigners from various countries and carrying on a rising volume of trade, mostly on terms that many Japanese regarded as unfairly favorable to the foreigners. The rising opposition to the Shogun seized upon the issue. Discontent with foreigners and their activities in Japan contributed importantly to the end of the military dictatorship that hereditary Shoguns had exercised for centuries. Mutsuhito, a young Emperor, had just acceded to the throne. At the beginning of 1868 he proclaimed the Restoration of Imperial Prerogatives and took for his reign the name of Meiji. The men around him were mostly the successful clan leaders who had been principally responsible for the overthrow of the Shogun. At once they abandoned their opposition to foreign trade and foreign contacts and proceeded to lead Japan through a series of changes so dramatic and successful that the Meiji Era (1868–1912) remains an epoch in Japanese history and a phenomenon in the annals of economic development.

This about-face on the part of Japan's new leaders did not result from any basic change of attitude about the world outside Japan. These leaders had not come to like the foreigner nor had they abandoned their fierce loyalty to their own clans, country, and Emperor. Quite the reverse. The Emperor was to be exalted and the Japanese nation driven to many violent changes in the name of patriotism. What the Meiji leaders sought was to make Japan so strong, with the aid of foreign machines and methods, that foreigners would never again be able, as Perry had been, to impose their will upon Japan by force. Limited and short-lived opposition to this policy came from die-hards who wanted nothing to do with foreigners, even for patriotic, nationalistic purposes. Few, if any, voices were raised in favor of Western life, culture, or philosophy. It was Western military power and the factors contributing to it that interested the Meiji leaders.

This basic policy had already been articulated while Japan was negotiating its first formal treaty of amity and commerce. In 1858, during the course of negotiations with Townsend Harris, Lord Hotta, President of the Shogun's Council of Elders, submitted a memorial to the throne urging that Japan undertake to remedy any defects in matters in which the foreigner proved superior. Trade, shipping, and economic development should be stimulated and military preparations made. "The object should always be kept in view of laying the foundation for securing hegemony over all nations."[1] It is by no means certain how fully the early Meiji leaders at first shared this view. But the course Japan followed from 1868 to 1945 was certainly close to Hotta's recommendation.

What is remarkable about the Meiji period is not so much the nature of its goals, since the Meiji government was dominated by military men, as the success with which the goals were achieved. Japan successfully and rapidly mastered military, industrial, financial, and other Western techniques. By 1895, only a generation after the Restoration, Japanese forces proved their strength by defeating China. Ten years later another test was successfully passed in the victory over Russia. By this time Japan's rise to power had been recognized by Great Britain in the formation of the Anglo–Japanese Alliance of 1902. Korea was annexed in 1910. In World War I Japan profited both militarily and economically. German possessions in the Pacific were taken over. Japan also extorted various concessions from China, although after the war most of these were terminated under Allied pressure.

The fifty years from 1868 to 1918 were the formative period for modern Japan, a period of truly phenomenal growth and success. Some of the major features of Meiji economic policy had a lasting influence. The interests of the state were paramount, and these were conceived in terms of military power. Japan had lived for over two and a half centuries under a stern military dictatorship, and those who overthrew this dictatorship and led the new government were military men. Under their leadership many members of the new bureaucracy and of the new class of entrepreneurs that sprang up were former *samurai*, members of the military caste which had performed most of the administrative work during the feudal period. To these men loyalty to their lords, later to their bureaucratic superiors, was a highly regarded virtue, and Meiji Japan had in such men effective agents for carrying out national policy. The *samurai* contributed capital as well as administrative skills and leadership to the Meiji upsurge, investing much of their proceeds when feudal incomes were commuted and they received cash and government bonds.

Another source of capital and entrepreneurship was the merchant class, which had grown powerful during late feudal times despite its lowly legal status. Some of the greatest business names in Japan today come from merchant families who made a successful transition from feudal to modern business. Yet it was *samurai* rather than merchants who dominated Meiji Japan. There was no important business challenge to the government and little business sentiment to influence national economic policy until the government had put large resources into strengthening and enlarging a few favored firms and families. Thus there was no

[1] Quoted in Foster Rhea Dulles, *Forty Years of American-Japanese Relations* (New York: Appleton-Century, 1937), p. 12.

opposition to the government's entering business and no tradition to overcome about the proper spheres of public and private economic activity. In fact the paternalism that Japan inherited from its feudal past gave the government more of a sense of obligation in some matters than was common in the West, an obligation that was often discharged by assisting firms that encountered difficulty. Private employers, too, took much more responsibility toward their workers than was customary in the West before unions, social security, and other benefits became common.

Meiji policy toward international trade and related matters started from a position of extreme weakness. Initially, the Japanese were not sufficiently sophisticated in trade and exchange to avoid costly losses in their commercial dealings with foreigners. It is not particularly surprising that in port areas the prices of export goods soared, causing other prices to rise also, or that Japan had to export large sums of gold and silver to meet trade deficits and pay the fees charged by foreign merchants. Japan also incurred losses from arbitrage in precious metals. When trade was first opened, silver commanded a much higher price in terms of gold in Japan than was the case abroad. Consequently the export of Japanese gold, particularly to the China ports, yielded large profits for foreigners before the ratio in Japan came to conform to that abroad.[2] The sensitive, nationalistic, and ambitious Japanese leaders could hardly approve a system that resulted in unequal bargains at their expense.

Japan did not move very far toward theoretical or doctrinal free trade, which was being practiced by Britain, then the world's greatest trading nation and Japan's leading trade partner. A few doctrinaire free traders appeared in Japan, but even some of these later turned protectionist, and the influence of free-trade ideas was minimal. When a Western economic theory did attract a significant following, it was the theory of Friedrich List, the German economist who stressed protection of infant industries during industrialization.[3]

Large-scale tariff protection was not possible for Japan in the nineteenth century, because the "unequal" treaties with the United States and other Western powers severely limited Japan's tariff rates. Japan gained general tariff autonomy only in 1899, and then adopted a definite policy of protecting domestic industry. Few rates, however, exceeded 10 to 15 per cent until the general tariff revision of 1911; certain rates

[2] Hugh Borton, *Japan's Modern Century* (New York: Ronald Press, 1955), pp. 59–60.

[3] G. B. Sansom, *The Western World and Japan* (New York: Knopf, 1951), pp. 437–441.

continued to be bound by convention until 1923.[4] The tariff of 1911 embodied completely new rates, classifying goods according to their "essentiality." Much of the basic classification and nomenclature adopted then was retained until the tariff act of 1961. Raw materials were generally on the free list or given low rates. Semimanufactures, manufactures, and luxuries were assigned progressively higher rates. Outside this general scale, however, were rates designed to protect specific industries judged unable to survive otherwise. More and more were added as time went on. During the years immediately after 1911 the duties collected averaged about 20 per cent of the value of dutiable goods imported.[5]

Because in Meiji times the tariff was low, the government relied more on other measures to support new industries than might have been the case if tariffs could have been made protective. As it was, Japanese industry was stimulated by low-interest loans, dividend guarantees, bounties, technical assistance, and preference for government procurement, especially military procurement.[6] Many new factories and other enterprises were initially government-owned and some were also government-operated. Later most were turned over—at far below cost—to a few favored private owners; the enterprises that grew largest became known as *zaibatsu*, the huge combines in which a tremendous amount of wealth and power had become concentrated by the middle 1930s. Such firms were to some extent "chosen instruments" for the Meiji government, in shipping and foreign trade as well as domestic production, finance, and commerce.

By the end of World War I, Japan had achieved tremendous economic and military growth, just as the founders of the Meiji regime planned. And—also as planned—Japanese life, spirit, and goals retained a remarkably large part of their pre-Restoration character. In some ways the years 1918 and 1919 may be regarded as marking the peak of Japan's planned march to power. The 1920s were to bring trial and trouble.

THE UNCERTAIN 1920s: RAPID GROWTH, POLICY VACILLATION, AND DISASTER FOR LIBERAL FORCES

The 1920s were a period of mixed fortunes for Japan. During most of the decade economic growth continued rapidly, if unevenly. But in economic and political policy there were fierce conflicts, reflecting the spread of Western political thought and rising political influence of the *zaibatsu*, despite the opposition of the military. Leaders who wished to see Japan

[4] William W. Lockwood, *The Economic Development of Japan* (Princeton University Press, 1954), pp. 539–544.

[5] U.S. Tariff Commission, *Postwar Developments in Japan's Foreign Trade* (Washington: GPO, 1958), pp. 9–10.

[6] Lockwood, cited.

move away from military oligarchy and financial paternalism toward Western parliamentary democracy and financial orthodoxy gained prominence for a time, only to fall tragically as the 1930s opened with economic disaster that precipitated violent rejection of Western liberalism.

Over-all economic growth was even more rapid in the 1920s than in the decade that included World War I. Real national income is estimated to have risen by 74 per cent during the later decade as compared with 48 per cent during the earlier period.[7] Private enterprise accounted for the greatest part of this increase. The Japanese government participated in economic activity less than in the Meiji period. While the government operated tobacco, salt, and camphor monopolies for profit, and arsenals and naval dockyards as part of the military establishment, the only other direct state enterprises of importance were the national railways, some shipping activities, and the Yawata Iron Works, the dominant steel producer. Other government activities included participation in various colonial ventures, most notably the South Manchuria Railway Company, and in a number of special banks. Subsidies were provided to certain transportation activities, some kinds of chemical production, notably soda ash and dyestuffs, and some colonial exploitation, most notably sugar production in Taiwan and oil exploration and production in Southern Sakhalin.[8]

So the 1920s were, in Japan as in the United States and elsewhere, a time of relatively undiluted private enterprise. Yet, despite rapid growth and much private prosperity, the 1920s are not remembered happily. As before, workers and farmers shared very little in the fruits of economic growth. Although the greatest growth was in manufacturing, "Japanese industrialists . . . were inclined in subsequent years to look back on the whole decade as one of stagnation."[9] One reason is that there was a downward drift in prices sufficient to flatten out economic curves representing yen values. By contrast with generally rapid growth from 1890 to 1915, the curve of net national product in yen, for instance, rose steeply from 1915 to 1920, only to level off and then decline as the 1930s opened.[10]

Trouble began with the panic of 1920. Export orders suddenly dropped sharply, and prices collapsed, especially for silk and rice, the main cash crops of Japanese farmers. The government undertook measures to support rice and silk prices. Many firms, especially those producing for export, ran into financial difficulties. Some failed. In order to prevent even

[7] Kazushi Ohkawa and associates, *The Growth Rate of the Japanese Economy Since 1878* (Tokyo: Kinokuniya Bookstore, 1957), p. 32.

[8] G. C. Allen, *A Short Economic History of Modern Japan, 1867–1937* (London: Allen & Unwin, 1946), pp. 120–121; Lockwood, cited, Ch. 10.

[9] Allen, cited, p. 106. The following three paragraphs are based mainly on this source, pp. 93–96.

[10] Henry Rosovsky, *Capital Formation in Japan, 1868–1940* (Glencoe, Ill.: The Free Press, 1961), p. 5.

more bankruptcies, the government ordered a moratorium on certain bank credit. Largely as a result of government intervention, deflation in the 1920 crisis was less in Japan than in other countries. While domestic gold payments were not at this time resumed after their suspension during World War I, the government financed current balance-of-payments deficits by drawing on large gold holdings abroad accumulated during World War I. This use of gold supported the yen at near the prewar parity despite deficits. Its overvaluation stimulated imports more than exports, and gold reserves began to shrink.

A new disaster struck in September 1923, the Great Earthquake that shook and set fire to much of Tokyo and Yokohama, leaving vast destruction as well as a terrible death toll. Imports jumped as emergency needs of various kinds were met from abroad. The yen was allowed to fall and the initial drop in exports was soon reversed, but the trade deficit reached unprecedented levels. Again the government helped out financially, this time not only by freezing certain existing loans but also by guaranteeing new loans for reconstruction. As the yen depreciated, the possibility of Japan's return to the gold standard at prewar parity was made more remote.

New deflationary measures were adopted in 1925, and these looked so promising that speculators anticipated a return of the yen to gold and bid up its exchange value above what domestic prices justified. The high exchange rate hurt exports and the deflation reduced the ability of borrowers to pay their bank loans. The Banking Crisis of 1927 resulted basically from this situation. Precipitated by the revelation that the overextended Bank of Taiwan was insolvent after speculative ventures had failed, this crisis too postponed Japan's return to the gold standard while extending the period of declining foreign assets.

Throughout this period, many Japanese leaders sought cooperation with other nations and urged progressively more Western ways on Japan, including parliamentary democracy and the supremacy of civilian government over military forces. Japan joined the League of Nations and in 1922 at Washington agreed to naval limitation. Universal manhood suffrage was adopted in 1925, thereby increasing the electorate from 3 million to 13 million out of a population of 62 million. Political parties formed the governments that held office during the years 1918 to 1922 and 1924 to 1931, the fall of one being followed by the formation of a government by the opposition in normal parliamentary fashion. In 1930 Japan renewed its acceptance of naval inferiority to Britain and the United States in agreeing to the London Naval Treaty.[11]

[11] The discussion here and below of political developments in the 1920s and early 1930s is based mainly on Borton, cited, Ch. 16. See also Franz H. Michael and George E. Taylor, *The Far East in the Modern World* (New York: Holt, 1958), pp. 482–518.

Tariff policy moved toward more protection and rates were repeatedly raised. In 1924 duties of 100 per cent were imposed on 123 items classed as luxuries, including vegetables and fruits, beer, soap, perfume, many types of clothing, cutlery, watches, clocks, and phonographs. This move is partly explained by a desire to save foreign exchange and penalize extravagance in the wake of the earthquake, but in 1930 about a hundred items still retained the full 100 per cent rate, including all those mentioned. In the general tariff revision of 1926 many rates were raised, and increased protection was given to the woolen, rayon, and chemical industries and to wheat farming. Later, other rates were raised from time to time, such as those on iron and steel in 1927. That the Japanese tariff had an impact on imports of finished consumer goods seems clear. In the years after 1900 these goods (other than food) were consistently less than 10 per cent of total imports and in the period following the First World War the figure was hardly more than 5 per cent, a very low proportion for a rapidly expanding economy with a growing appetite for new things from abroad. Japanese protectionism was well developed before the Great Depression.[12]

Financial policy was generally weak and vacillating during the 1920s. Instead of carrying deflation far enough to make the prewar parity of $0.4985 feasible, or of adopting a new par value, or even (a very unlikely choice in the atmosphere of world finance in the 1920s) abandoning the objective of returning to gold, Japanese governments temporized and vacillated. It was not until mid-1929 that a clear decision was reached, with the accession to power of a conservative cabinet under Prime Minister Osachi Hamaguchi.

The new Finance Minister, Junnosuke Inouye, a banker and former Governor of the Bank of Japan, led a successful campaign for reduction in government expenditures and a balanced budget. In January 1930, Japan returned to the gold standard at the pre-1914 parity, just when the world depression was spreading financial and economic havoc. The years 1930 and 1931 saw Japan successfully lower costs of production, especially by "rationalizing" industry through technical and financial means. High-cost firms disappeared and unemployment spread.[13] But the social and political, as well as financial and economic, costs were ex-

[12] Allen speaks of Japanese duties as still moderate in 1929, citing the fact that customs receipts were only 17 per cent of the value of dutiable imports, but Lockwood calls Japanese tariffs in the 1920s "strongly protectionist" after 1922. Lockwood, cited, p. 543 and earlier; Allen, cited, pp. 122–123.

[13] For a defense of Inouye's policy see his *Problems of the Japanese Exchange, 1914–1926* (London: Macmillan, 1931). For an American comment very sympathetic to Inouye and his policy, but written before the abandonment of this policy, see Harold G. Moulton, *Japan: An Economic and Financial Appraisal* (Washington: Brookings Institution, 1931), Ch. 21.

tremely high. Foreign as well as Japanese observers reported intense suffering by many Japanese. This soon affected the balance of political power.

The liberal, democratic, internationalist, and financially orthodox trends of the 1920s had not gone unchallenged. Japanese army and navy leaders, whose predecessors in Meiji times had dominated the ruling oligarchy, repeatedly opposed moves toward liberalism and international cooperation. When military influence was insufficient to control policy, there were repeated acts of violence and insubordination by military groups, especially among young officers on the continent of Asia. In the minds of many Japanese, the army represented the nation and had patriotic motives, in contrast and opposition to allegedly selfish and corrupt politicians and the heartless profit-seeking of the *zaibatsu* and other wealthy industrialists, financiers, and merchants. These sentiments reflected the Japanese tradition that placed soldiers (*samurai*) high on the social scale, merchants very low. Military extremists made use of resentments aroused by the harsh financial restrictions to bring about the downfall of first the Hamaguchi Cabinet and then the interim Wakatsuki Cabinet. One of the first acts of the new government formed by Tsuyoshi Inukai in December 1931 was to take Japan off the gold standard and permit the yen to depreciate. The new cabinet put an end to the deflationary policies that had brought so much hardship and went on to sanction large increases in government expenditures and deficits.

The removal of Hamaguchi and Inouye brought an end to Japan's first serious experiment with political liberalism and party governments, and the economic policies associated with them. Economic disaster demoralized the people and brought down not only the government in power but also the prestige of a political system imported from the West. G. C. Allen says: "The collapse of 'American prosperity' discredited these new leaders and, indeed, parliamentary government as a whole." [14]

The phenomenal economic expansion that had started with the Meiji Restoration in 1868 had been checked. Japan's most vigorous and extreme effort to follow policies devised and favored in the West was defeated by the import from the West of its own greatest economic depression. In the circumstances, Japanese liberals who favored the freedom and democracy of such Western countries as Britain and the United States could not effectively resist the rise of militant nationalism. The militarists who sought a return to aggressive policies were able to command widespread support. As the expansionist policy became clearer and was more fully worked out in the years after 1931, it provided answers, convincing to many Japanese, to such questions as how to find

[14] Cited, p. 99.

employment for Japan's "surplus" population, how to obtain necessary raw materials for Japanese factories and outlets for their products. Most of all, the military imperialism of the period 1931 to 1945 offered the nation a mission into which the people of Japan could throw themselves with tremendous enthusiasm. Such a mission had been lacking in the 1920s, when the center of the stage was occupied by politicians, whom their opponents labeled as selfish and who were supported by businessmen, whose leaders were with some truth called monopolists. Democratic government and orthodox economics had failed in their most serious trial in Japan up to that time.

1932–1945: ECONOMIC CONTROLS DURING RECOVERY AND WAR

Voices favoring economic freedoms, private enterprise, and conservative economic policies were further stilled by the abandonment of such policies in other countries and by the success of financial expansionism in Japan. Under the brilliant leadership of Korekiyo Takahashi, as Finance Minister and the most powerful civilian cabinet member in the years 1932 to 1936,[15] Japan followed a policy of regulated "reflation." The country was led out of the depression by methods remarkably close to those espoused by the great British economist, John Maynard Keynes, but not fully expounded until the publication of his *General Theory of Employment, Interest and Money* in 1936, after Takahashi had disappeared from the scene.

The Takahashi policy was to promote economic recovery by devaluation of the yen, budget deficits, and credit expansion, but to keep inflation in check, mainly by carefully controlling the amount of credit made available for government and private uses. Excessive private credit expansion was prevented by government bond sales timed to use up any dangerous credit potential in the banking system.[16]

Inflationary pressures were kept in check by a number of factors. Takahashi's influence was great enough to limit the size of government deficits. Commercial banks continued to follow very cautious loan poli-

[15] Takahashi was out of the cabinet for four months in 1934.

[16] The method was to sell government bonds initially to the Bank of Japan and to permit the use of the proceeds by the government to expand bank deposits and thus the capacity of the banking system to extend credit. When the desired degree of ease had been reached, the Bank of Japan would dispose of bonds to the banks and, within the limited extent possible, to the public. During the period 1932 to 1936 the great bulk of all new government bonds were thus disposed of by the Bank of Japan, whose note issue rose only moderately. Meanwhile bank deposits rose but bank loans declined. Interest rates also declined. Frank M. Tamagna, *Civil Affairs Handbook, Japan, Section 5, Money and Banking,* U.S. Army Service Forces Manual 345–5 (Washington: Headquarters, Army Service Forces, November 1944), pp. 8–9.

cies. World prices of raw materials remained very low. Acute agrarian distress in Japan was exacerbated by a very sharp drop in the value of raw silk exports. Unemployment continued to be a serious problem, magnified by the flow of workers to factory areas from the silk districts. Real wages declined as workers' incomes rose less rapidly than prices.[17] Nevertheless, Japan's recovery from the depression was orderly, dramatically successful, and prompter than that of any other country.

The year 1932, which saw spreading economic chaos in Western countries, was for Japan a year of substantial economic recovery, even in exports. Industrial production in 1935 was 45 per cent above the low level of 1931.[18] Japanese prices and wages were kept in check so successfully that the advantages of yen devaluation continued for years. While the yen cost of dollars rose 75 per cent from 1931 to 1935, wholesale prices increased by only 33 per cent.[19] Exports were stimulated and imports held down. (See Table 3-2, p. 31.) The Capital Flight Prevention Law of 1932 marked Japan's entry into the extensive use of direct controls in the domestic and foreign economy which became progressively more important thereafter. As a result of yen depreciation and direct controls, tariffs fell into a secondary place as a means of limiting Japan's imports.[20]

Foreign tariffs on Japanese goods became very important, however, and were followed almost everywhere by other trade restrictions. More than 40 countries raised tariffs or imposed other new restrictions on Japanese goods during the world depression. This did not stop the remarkable growth of Japanese exports but, coming at a time of intense nationalistic excitement in Japan, the foreign trade barriers stirred deep feeling among the Japanese. In addition to serving the jingoistic and aggressive policies of the military clique, these foreign actions created impressions that survive today in the fear that is widespread in Japan that foreign countries simply will not buy Japanese goods in adequate volume.

By the beginning of 1936, however, the Japanese economy had about reached capacity production, and Takahashi's control over government spending was proving too restrictive for restless elements in the army. On February 26, 1936, a group of young officers succeeded in killing Takahashi and several other leaders. In the aftermath a number of the demands of the assassins were accepted by the new government under

[17] G. C. Allen, *Japanese Industry: Its Recent Development and Present Condition* (New York: Institute of Pacific Relations, 1940), pp. 89–97.

[18] Bank of Japan, *Economic Statistics of Japan*, 1959, p. 2.

[19] Same, pp. 259 and 269.

[20] A trade-protection law of 1934, however, empowered the cabinet to impose tariffs of 100 per cent in retaliation for foreign discrimination against Japanese shipping and trade; this authority was used against Canada in 1935 and Australia in 1936. U.S. Tariff Commission, cited, p. 10.

Koki Hirota. An expansion of government spending followed. In July 1937 the Japanese army started operations in China proper. A major war boom soon developed. Expenditures and prices rose, shortages appeared, and a growing array of direct controls were introduced to do—sometimes poorly—what had been done with remarkable success under less strained conditions by Takahashi's indirect controls. Thus recovery gave way promptly to a war boom with both open and suppressed inflation.

As the 1930s progressed, Japanese expansionists articulated their version of an argument Hitler and Mussolini were using to justify aggression. One Japanese put it as follows:

> We are like a great crowd of people packed into a small and narrow room, and there are only three doors through which we might escape, namely emigration, advance into world markets, and expansion of territory. The first door, emigration, has been barred to us by the anti-Japanese immigration policies of other countries. The second door, advance into world markets, is being pushed shut by tariff barriers and the abrogation of commercial treaties. What should Japan do when two of the three doors have been closed against her?
>
> It is quite natural that Japan should rush upon the last remaining door.[21]

In time, the Japanese began to refer to the large area they aspired to control as the Greater East Asia Co-Prosperity Sphere. This was to include not only Japan proper, its colonies, and all of China north of the Yangtse River, but also the rest of China, Southeast Asia, and ultimately eastern Siberia, India, and Australia. "The Southern region would supply raw materials and surplus food, while Manchuria and North China provided the materials and basis for a heavy industry complex. The rest of Asia would become a vast market, defended and integrated by Japanese planning, tools, skills and arms." [22]

The Pacific war resulted from Japan's audacious gamble for this huge empire. The attack on Pearl Harbor in December 1941 was far more successful than Japan's war planners had a right to expect. In the weeks that followed, Japanese forces seized a vast area from Alaska to Indonesia and Burma. Greater East Asia, except for the fringe areas not on Japan's timetable until a later war, was in Japanese hands.

The war plan called for capture of raw materials producing areas in the first phase, their exploitation in the second phase, and their defense

[21] Kingoro Hashimoto, as quoted in Ryusaku Tsunoda, Wm. Theodore de Bary and Donald Keene, *Sources of Japanese Tradition* (New York: Columbia University Press, 1958), p. 796. This statement comes from Hashimoto's *Addresses to Young Men,* International Military Tribunal for the Far East, International Prosecution Section, Document 487B, Exhibit 1290.

[22] Tsunoda, de Bary and Keene, cited, p. 801.

only in the third phase. The United States was expected to react far more slowly and with far less vigor than proved to be the case. The result was that Japan had time for only a limited exploitation of the "riches of the Indies" before losses of ships seriously reduced the capacity to carry things home. In the final war year, ending March 31, 1945, Japan lost more shipping tonnage than it had had in operation at the beginning of the year. In 1945 Japan was so short of raw materials that American bombs on several occasions destroyed factories that were already idle. By the summer of 1945 the modern economy of Japan had nearly ground to a halt, and the people were being subjected to extreme privation. Not only had Japan failed to solve the problem of obtaining necessary imports, but untold suffering had been brought on millions throughout a major portion of the globe.[23]

THE OCCUPATION PERIOD: CONTROLS UNDER FOREIGN RULE

The Allied forces that moved in to occupy defeated Japan, under General of the Army Douglas MacArthur, found the country facing economic collapse. The modern sector of the economy was most severely disrupted. Where factories had not been destroyed by bombing or made idle by the lack of imported raw materials, the dilapidated condition of plant and equipment, combined with the hunger, demoralization, and disorganization of the work force, kept production and efficiency low. Japanese mines, especially the coal mines, had been worked mainly by Koreans and Chinese, most of whom simply quit upon hearing the news of Japan's surrender. Transportation and commerce were widely disrupted. A substantial part of the domestic trade in the early days after surrender was black marketing. The overcrowded railways were further burdened by people from the extensively devastated and largely depopulated cities who were traveling to farm areas to get food by purchase or barter.

The farms continued to function, and many a farm household bulged with relatives who had fled the cities, often after having had their houses burned. Farm production, not extensively dependent on imported materials, had suffered less than mining, manufacturing, and other parts of Japan's modern economy. In this ability to rely once again on its farm-

[23] Based on Jerome B. Cohen, *Japan's Economy in War and Reconstruction* (Minneapolis: University of Minnesota Press, 1949), pp. 51, 104–110, 267, and elsewhere. Cohen makes it very clear by many illustrations throughout his study that Japanese economic mobilization, controls, and administration had many and serious weaknesses, but what concerns us here is not the weaknesses but the fact that modern wartime controls were adopted and maintained with sufficient success to keep the country effectively at war despite vast losses, and that surrender did not take place until the nation's economy was almost ruined.

ers, as in preceding crises, Japan was fortunate that its "dual economy" had a large rural segment that was not ruined by the war. But Japanese agriculture, despite the garden-size units and heavy reliance on hand cultivation, did suffer from shortages, especially of manufactured fertilizer. The rice crop declined from an average of 9.6 million metric tons in the years 1938–1942 to only 5.9 million tons in the particularly poor harvest of 1945, when bad weather was added to all the other factors reducing yields. Rice imports almost disappeared because of shipping shortages. Fishing had been severely curtailed as a result of the war, and the catch in 1945 was less than half the average for the ten years 1933–1942. Imports of sugar from Taiwan were sharply reduced. Although few actually died of starvation, the Japanese people were very hungry.

In the few weeks before Occupation controls were imposed on the defeated nation, the Japanese government made huge payments to military personnel, government suppliers, and others. At the same time depositors withdrew large sums in cash from the banks. The inflationary impact of the additional currency in circulation, added to the virtual breakdown of rationing and price controls during the confused months of August and September 1945, led to a situation that approached chaos.

The Occupation's policy on internal economic matters was at first to leave as much as possible to the Japanese. The hunger and other suffering were regarded as results of Japan's own actions at Pearl Harbor and elsewhere. The only controls, supervision, and aid contemplated were those necessary to keep disease and unrest within bounds. As it turned out, the Occupation almost at once had to take a hand in the restoration of coal mining, and aid soon became a major factor in other parts of the economy. But not until 1948, when the cold war had become a basic fact in U.S. policy calculations, did the Occupation undertake active efforts at checking the massive inflation and stimulating general economic recovery.[24]

Foreign contacts of any sort by the Japanese were completely prohibited from the start of the Occupation. This measure had the same purpose as the isolation of Japan imposed before 1854 by the Tokugawa Shogunate: to make control effective and unqualified. But fortunately for Japan, the isolation ordered in 1945 did not long remain complete. At first all international transactions were conducted by military and civilian officials of the General Headquarters, Supreme Commander for the Allied Powers (SCAP). Foreign trade and exchange controls were

[24] Cohen, cited, pp. 417–419; E. M. Martin, *The Allied Occupation of Japan* (Stanford: Stanford University Press, 1948), Ch. 6 and elsewhere; Sherwood M. Fine, "Japan's Postwar Industrial Recovery," *Contemporary Japan*, nos. 4–6, 1952, pp. 165–216, also separately published by the Foreign Affairs Association of Japan (Tokyo, undated), 52 pp.

more stringent than any the Japanese had maintained in the years before surrender. All foreign exchange received was at first kept in SCAP hands. Gradually the Japanese were permitted to assume more and more functions.[25] In December 1945 a Board of Trade was established as a Japanese government agency to handle export and import transactions, but without any access to foreign exchange. SCAP continued to hold all foreign currencies, receiving and making payments as necessary, but with no great regard for yen costs or prices. Thus transactions took place in which the yen prices and the foreign currency prices implied exchange rates that varied from a few yen to the dollar to over 600.

In time, limits were placed on the implied exchange rates allowed in import or export transactions. Progressive changes permitted private traders a growing role. In 1949 inflation was at last halted by a broad economic stabilization program guided by Joseph M. Dodge, a Detroit banker. As a result of this program, Japanese government expenditures dropped below receipts, subsidies were sharply cut, government marketing agencies (*kodan*) were reduced in number and in functions, and bank credit was subjected to the policy decisions of a Credit Control Board.[26] In April of that year, as part of the stabilization program, a single foreign exchange rate was established at 360 yen to the dollar, with consistent cross rates for other currencies. This rate has continued unchanged down to the present day. The Foreign Exchange and Foreign Trade Control Law of December 1, 1949 put Japan's foreign exchange funds in the custody of the Foreign Exchange Control Board (established in March 1949 in the Prime Minister's office). In 1950 a law was passed to encourage foreigners to invest in Japan by establishing their right to withdraw earnings and capital under certain conditions.

Tariffs were unimportant during the Occupation period and their collection was for a time suspended. The volume of imports was regulated by direct controls and by bilateral agreements with other countries that were short of foreign exchange.[27] Inflation made old specific tariff rates meaningless; so when a revised tariff was put into effect in 1951 it used almost entirely ad valorem rates. There was, however, no break with

[25] This account of the Occupation period follows generally that in "Postwar Development of Japan's Foreign Exchange System," Bank of Tokyo, *Semiannual Report*, September 1953 (Tokyo: Author, 1953), especially pp. 43–57. The Bank of Tokyo, successor to the prewar Yokohama Specie Bank, is Japan's leading foreign exchange bank.

[26] Jerome B. Cohen, *Japan's Postwar Economy* (Bloomington: Indiana University Press, 1958), pp. 86–89.

[27] At the end of 1950 about one-quarter of Japan's trade was covered by "open-account" agreements with some 20 countries and about 30 per cent by a payments arrangement with the sterling area. U.S. Tariff Commission, cited, p. 15. Bank of Japan, *Foreign Exchange Statistics Monthly*, December 1959, pp. 17, 20.

the traditional structure or protectionist character of Japanese tariffs. (See Chapter 5, p. 138.)

Japan's foreign economic transactions were beginning to look more normal, and trade was on the rise even before the Korean War gave the Japanese economy a powerful forward thrust.

THE JAPANESE OUTLOOK IN 1952

The San Francisco Peace Treaty became effective April 28, 1952. In international economic relations, as in other matters, the Japanese nation was again formally in full command of its own affairs. Although the Korean War boom had greatly enlarged Japan's earnings of foreign exchange, the demand for imports was far from satisfied. The newly sovereign government in Tokyo had very little leeway and not much inclination to change the patterns inherited from its predecessors, Japanese and American.

To the Japanese people the world economy in 1952 appeared no more hospitable than it had seemed before the war. They would still be required to strain to meet their needs from exiguous resources and to accommodate their economic policies to conditions shaped by nature, war, and other countries. As before, the international position was bound to have a great influence on Japan's domestic activities. The traditions of government control were deeply ingrained. They were reinforced by the strong sense of duty and habits of discipline of a people crowded into a few narrow islands where the harsh environment, with its destructive typhoons, floods, earthquakes, and fires, reduced the scope of individual action. For a people used to making a living by hard work, no relaxation in their strictly regulated way of life seemed warranted. Their goods still met resistance in foreign markets and the problem of paying for imports was intensified by the loss of the former colonies. For the immediate requirements of 1952, Japanese leaders had no alternative to cooperating with the United States, hoping that dollar income to Japan from Korean War activities would be large enough and last long enough for some other means to be found to balance the nation's international accounts without having to forgo needed food, fuel, or raw materials.

Those Japanese whose attention could be taken off the most immediate problems could find little encouragement in what they could remember of the past or see of the world around them. The 1920s had begun with the painful readjustments after World War I. There was no very convincing evidence to show that the aftermath of World War II would be much easier, especially for a defeated nation, despite the generous aid the United States had provided in Japan, in Europe, and elsewhere. Japanese Marxists were direly predicting a severe capitalist depression.

The victors had decisively terminated Japan's "co-prosperity" policy. But what was to take its place? Would foreign countries now buy Japanese export products and eschew the restrictions so widely imposed in the 1930s? As a matter of fact, restrictions on world trade in 1952 were far more numerous and severe than those of the prewar years. Would the United States, which loomed over the Japanese economy as an almost all-powerful giant and which was supplying far more imports than any other country, ever buy as much from Japan as it sold there? Those Japanese who could remember the 1920s or had read enough to know of the attempts then made in Japan to follow Western political and financial practices could find no encouragement in the failure of these policies.

The outlook in 1952 was indeed far from bright. The chapters that follow tell in considerable detail what happened to Japanese foreign trade and other international economic activities in the ensuing years. Standing at the dizzy heights of Japan's economic and commercial prosperity today, one finds it extremely difficult to recapture the gloomy feelings of a decade ago. But if we make the effort, we find strong reasons to explain the tenacious reluctance of Japan today to take large and rapid strides in the direction of liberal trade policies which are today's orthodoxy, at least in word even if not always and for all leading countries in daily deed.

Chapter 3

The Balance of International Payments

For any country that must make its living in large part from the world economy, the balance of international payments is a most important economic indicator. It records the nation's transactions with foreigners: what comes from abroad and how it is paid for.

Today's booming Japanese economy reflects phenomenal success in the nation's attempts to pay its way in the world. Despite severe constraints of space, resources, and apparent opportunities, Japan has managed to finance a rapidly, if unevenly, expanding flow of imports and at the same time accumulate a substantial volume of foreign assets. Now the nation is receiving, through exports and other sources, a sufficient flow of foreign currency to allow of wider policy choices than have been possible in the past.

To what extent, for instance, should quantitative controls be relaxed on commodity imports, or restrictions eased on other expenditures of foreign exchange? With relaxation, how far should Japan go in protecting domestic production by means of tariffs and other new measures? To what extent should the Japanese government make loans and grants, especially in countries in South and Southeast Asia, for purposes of economic development? What encouragement should be given to private Japanese capital to go abroad, either for developing sources of imports needed by Japan, or for other development projects in the less developed countries? These and related questions are subjects for earnest debate in Japan and the source of much pressure on the Japanese government by Japanese business interests, by the International Monetary Fund, by the United States government, and by others. Has Japanese policy been soundly conceived? Is American pressure wise and proper in its direction and emphasis?

In preparation for discussion of these questions, this chapter will examine the structure and component elements of Japan's balance of payments, and the changes that have taken place during the postwar period. After a section on the leading role of the United States in Japan's international economic transactions, attention will be directed to the sharp cyclical fluctuations in the balance of payments and in the flow of foreign exchange.

STRUCTURE OF JAPAN'S INTERNATIONAL PAYMENTS

Trade is naturally the largest factor in Japan's balance of payments. What Japan imports must be mainly crude materials, fuels, and foodstuffs. What Japan sells abroad are mostly manufactured goods. Very few of these are of completely Japanese origin; part of the value of most of them is represented by imports. Most of what Japan earns from foreign countries comes from the value the Japanese people add to the materials they import.

In addition to goods, Japan buys and sells services, including shipping, aviation, travel, insurance, government services, the use of capital (yielding or costing interest and dividends), and a number of lesser items. Japan is also involved in international capital movements, especially in loans, investments, and short-term transfers. Borrowing abroad increases what Japan can currently buy; lending abroad initially stimulates Japanese exports and also fosters development abroad, heretofore usually of sources of materials needed by Japanese industry.

Both before and after World War II the shape of Japan's balance of payments has been markedly affected by special circumstances. Before the war Japan had in parts of Asia special privileges that resulted in enlarged trade and investment and a significant flow of personal remittances to Japan. These privileges were lost, but in the postwar period Japan depended heavily on special sources of income from abroad, notably American aid and military procurement. Among the legacies of the war that affect the balance of payments are the reparations Japan is obliged to make to several Asian countries.

Before 1945

During the prewar period Japan was able not only to meet its current expenses abroad, but also to make substantial net foreign investments, especially in the colonies and China. A balance of payments for the year 1936 has been prepared on the basis of Japan's postwar boundaries, showing transactions with the former colonies, Korea and Taiwan, as well as with areas that were then regarded as foreign. While not strictly comparable with the postwar statistics that will be presented later in this chapter, the figures for 1936 do shed light on the structure of Japan's international economic relations. (Table 3-1.)

A very small import surplus in merchandise trade in 1936 was much more than offset by net income from services.[1] Large earnings from the Japanese merchant marine and income from Japanese investments abroad, supplemented by substantial personal remittances from Japanese living or working overseas and small net income from travel and insurance, yielded net receipts from goods and services of $110 million, after deduction of substantial net outpayments on account of government transactions and smaller net outpayments on merchandise trade and miscellaneous services. The $100-million increase in Japan's net international assets that remained after deduction of errors and omissions was made up of a rise in gold reserves ($23 million), an increase in private capital assets abroad ($48 million), and a decrease in both public and private liabilities to foreign countries ($30 million). Japan in 1936 not only paid its way but also significantly strengthened its international financial position.

This picture changes, however, upon closer inspection. During the 1930s a large proportion of all Japan's overseas transactions were not really international. They took place across what are now the boundaries of Japan, to be sure, but in 1936 Japanese political and economic control extended from Japan proper to the territories at the other end of these transactions. Korea and Taiwan were Japanese colonies in 1936 and Manchuria was firmly under Japanese control, as were a number of smaller areas. A substantial portion of Japan's trade with China proper enjoyed special privileges, particularly in the Treaty Ports such as Shanghai and Tientsin. Expansionist policies fostered heavy Japanese investment in these areas, and in the middle 1930s the flow of investment to Manchuria was especially heavy. Much of the flow of personal remittances by Japanese abroad came from occupied areas and was not convertible into foreign exchange.

[1] Merchandise debits and service credits are swollen by the inclusion in the figures for merchandise trade of all transportation and insurance costs related to imports, as a result of using c.i.f. valuations. All payments for import freights, whether paid to Japanese or foreign shipping companies, are included in the recorded value of imports, even though the only international transactions involved are the payments to foreign carriers. Then in the transportation account the import freights received by Japanese shipowners (even though domestic transactions) are shown among credits. Insurance is handled in the same way. Since the same addition is thus made to both sides of the balance of payments, the net payments on the commodity, transportation, and insurance accounts together are not affected. In present practice the listing of imports as well as exports at f.o.b. values eliminates all transportation and related costs from the commodity account. Then only international transactions are included in the transportation and other accounts. By either method of accounting, Japan's 1936 net payments on account of merchandise, transportation, and insurance come to a credit of $56.4 million.

TABLE 3-1. JAPAN'S BALANCE OF INTERNATIONAL PAYMENTS IN 1936

(In millions of dollars)

	Credit	*Debit*	*Balance*
Goods and services	**1,332**	**1,222**	**110**
Merchandise trade [a]	1,015	1,027	−12
Services	316	195	122
Transportation	96	32	64
Insurance	40	35	5
Travel	25	17	9
Investment income	94	43	50
Private remittances	39	2	37
Government transactions, n.i.e.	12	50	−37
Miscellaneous services	10	16	−6
Errors and omissions (net)			**−9**
Capital and gold movements	**−30** [b]	**71** [c]	**−100**
Private capital	−15	48	−63
Long-term	−2	26	−28
Direct investment	—	54	−54
Portfolio securities	9	23	−14
Other, including amortization	−11	−50	39
Short-term	−12	22	−35
Official and banking capital	−15	. . .	−15
Long-term	−15	. . .	−15
Short-term	. . .	. . .	. . .
Monetary gold	—	23	−23

[a] Exports at f.o.b. values, imports at c.i.f. values.
[b] Net changes in Japanese liabilities abroad.
[c] Net changes in Japanese assets abroad.

Notes: A dash (—) indicates that a figure is zero or less than $500,000.
Dots (. . .) indicate that data are not available.
Minor inconsistencies result from rounding.

Source: International Monetary Fund, *Balance of Payments Yearbook, 1938, 1946, 1947*, pp. 244–245.

Japan's small import surplus in 1936 hides a large export surplus with Korea, Taiwan, and China and a somewhat greater import surplus with other areas. Korea, Taiwan, and Manchuria were principal parts of what came to be called the Yen Bloc.[2] Japan's trade deficit with other areas had to be settled in foreign exchange, but the surplus with the Yen Bloc did not, for the most part, yield foreign exchange. This surplus was largely financed by long-term Japanese investment in Manchuria and elsewhere.

The contrasting record of Japan's trade with its colonies and China and with the rest of the world in the period from 1929 to the end of the war is set out in Table 3-2 in terms of yen. In Korea, Taiwan, and Mainland China Japanese military and political power, trade privileges, and expansionist policies made possible a rapid growth of trade, despite the efforts of many Chinese to boycott Japanese trade in reprisal for Japanese aggression in China. The yen value of Japan's exports to these neighboring areas rose every year from the low in 1931 through 1940. Imports were smaller, but their rise continued through 1942.[3]

A number of factors contributed to this growth. This trade was not subject to the normal hazards and limitations of international business dealings. Japanese authority, financial institutions, and currency controls applied, at least in large degree, at both ends of the transactions. In Korea, Taiwan, and much of China Japanese firms and individuals had a privileged status, very different from that of Japanese businessmen in competitive markets beyond Tokyo's jurisdiction. The prospects for profit were so favorable that both private and public Japanese corporations made heavy investments in these areas. Japanese government expenditures there generated large sales for Japanese firms.

Not all the privileges stemmed directly from political controls or governmental regulation. The vast interconnections of the *zaibatsu* and other large Japanese firms meant that much business between Japan proper and the controlled areas was conducted between branches of the same

[2] Warren S. Hunsberger, "The Yen Bloc in Japan's Expansion Program," *Far Eastern Survey*, November 9, 1938, p. 251. Until 1931 only the parts of the Japanese empire were joined by formal currency arrangements. But much of Japan's China trade had long been under Japanese control, in the Treaty Ports, in the Kwantung Leased Territory, and in the South Manchuria Railway Zone. After 1931 "Manchukuo" was added to the currency bloc, and after 1937 some other parts of China also, but the tie was not so close with the areas of China proper where Japanese-issued currency was circulated.

[3] It seems more than possible, in view of Japan's monopolistic and monopsonistic positions in occupied areas, that export valuations were higher, import valuations lower, than would have been the case if markets had been fully competitive. Thus the net outflow of resources from Japan may have been substantially less than the statistics indicate. And, of course, Japanese owners and creditors were enjoying a rapid increase in their net claims on the occupied areas, claims that might have proved very valuable to the Japanese concerned, had not the whole empire been lost.

TABLE 3-2. BALANCE OF TRADE OF JAPAN, 1929–1945
(In millions of yen)

	Exports (f.o.b.)			Imports (c.i.f.)			Balance of Trade		
Year	To Korea, Taiwan and China	To Other Areas	Total	From Korea, Taiwan and China	From Other Areas	Total	With Korea, Taiwan and China	With Other Areas	Total
1929	926	1,678	2,604	925	1,840	2,765	1	−162	−161
1930	749	1,122	1,871	743	1,263	2,006	6	−141	−135
1931	554	926	1,480	686	1,000	1,686	−132	−74	−206
1932	668	1,134	1,802	710	1,226	1,936	−42	−92	−134
1933	901	1,450	2,351	828	1,636	2,464	73	−186	−113
1934	1,137	1,652	2,789	998	1,972	2,970	139	−320	−181
1935	1,352	1,924	3,276	1,150	2,122	3,272	202	−198	4
1936	1,550	2,035	3,585	1,271	2,370	3,641	279	−335	−56
1937	1,804	2,384	4,188	1,420	3,345	4,765	384	−961	−577
1938	2,415	1,524	3,939	1,695	2,099	3,794	720	−575	145
1939	3,334	1,829	5,163	1,930	2,235	4,165	1,404	−406	998
1940	3,629	1,789	5,418	1,956	2,697	4,653	1,673	−908	765
1941	3,392	992	4,384	2,019	2,049	4,068	1,373	−1,057	316
1942	3,226	280	3,506	2,394	530	2,924	832	−250	582
1943	2,727	328	3,055	2,337	602	2,939	390	−274	116
1944	1,122 [a]	176	1,298	1,707 [a]	240	1,947	−585 [a]	−64	−649
1945 [b]	372 [a]	16	388	855 [a]	102	957	−483 [a]	−86	−569
Total	29,858	21,239	51,097	23,624	27,328	50,952	6,234	−6,089	145

[a] China only; no figures available for trade with Korea and Taiwan in 1944 or 1945.
[b] January–August only.

Sources: 1929—The Oriental Economist, *Foreign Trade of Japan, A Statistical Survey* (Tokyo: Author, 1935), pp. 2, 349, 359, 663.
1930–1945—Bank of Japan, *Economic Statistics of Japan*, 1959, pp. 241, 243.

organization. For instance, a Mitsui factory in Japan would be likely to purchase imported coal through Mitsui Bussan Kaisha, the huge trading firm that handled a very large part of all Japanese overseas trade; the coal might be mined by a Mitsui subsidiary in Taiwan, carried on a Mitsui ship, financed by the Mitsui Bank, and insured by one of the Mitsui insurance companies. In addition, both in the colonies and in China, Japanese firms engaged in a number of monopolistic practices that must have depressed buying prices, raised selling prices, and added greatly to profits.

Outside these areas of Japanese privilege, dealings were on a much different basis. Silk prices dropped sharply during the Great Depression and the value of Japan's silk exports declined from 781 million yen in 1929 to a low of 287 million devalued yen in 1934, that is, from $360 million to $85 million.[4] Still, Japanese manufacturers and exporters were able to offer such low prices that the value of Japanese exports to areas other than Korea, Taiwan, and Mainland China rose from the low point of 926 million yen in 1931 to a peak of 2,384 million yen in 1937. This was an important fruit of the Takahashi recovery referred to in the preceding chapter. Raw materials prices in world markets remained depressed, productive efficiency in Japan was high after the cost-cutting "rationalization" measures taken in 1930 and 1931, new facilities were adding to capacity as well as efficiency, and labor remained plentiful. These factors, combined with careful inflation-control measures, checked the upward trend of prices in Japan during the years 1933 to 1936. While Japanese exports were encouraged, the more rapid increase in import prices marked a deterioration of the terms of trade that added to Japan's balance-of-payments problems.[5]

After 1936 war shortages and larger budget deficits stepped up the pace of inflation in Japan. The wholesale price index jumped 21 per cent from 1936 to 1937, 70 per cent between 1936 and 1941. Abroad, barriers to Japanese goods increased. Exports to areas outside Japanese control declined after reaching a peak in 1937. Imports also declined after 1937 but to the end of the war remained well above exports. The large deficit in trade with these outside areas, exceeding a billion yen in 1940, made it necessary for Japan to ship large quantities of gold abroad during the years 1937–1941.

[4] Japan, Department of Finance, *The Thirty-Eighth Financial and Economic Annual of Japan*, 1938 (Tokyo: Government Printing Office), pp. 160–161.

[5] Between 1931 and 1936 Japanese wholesale prices increased by 38.5 per cent, the unit price index for exports by 22.7 per cent and that for imports by 77.9 per cent. Wholesale price index is taken from Bank of Japan, *Economic Statistics of Japan*, 1960, p. 273; export and import price indexes from *Japan-Manchoukuo Year Book*, 1940, p. 450; they exclude trade with Korea and Taiwan but include trade with China.

After 1941, having opened full-scale war in a huge area from Alaska to Indonesia and India, Japan carried on almost no trade except with areas controlled by its own forces. Although vast territories and tremendous populations were included within these areas, foreign trade came more and more to be confined to the "Inner Zone" of Korea, Taiwan, and the more accessible parts of Mainland China. Even here the volume of trade declined after 1940 for exports and after 1942 for imports.

At least until the late stages of the war (figures are incomplete for 1944 and 1945), Japan proper continued to export more to its controlled territories than it imported from them. All in all, therefore, Japan did not achieve one of the central economic purposes generally assumed to have motivated the imperialist policy, namely, to obtain from dominated areas a net inflow of real income.[6]

Perhaps in time, if Japanese domination had continued, China and Korea would have yielded returns that financially justified the large investments made during the years after 1931. As it was, in its overseas economic relations before 1945 Japan made very heavy net investments in the controlled areas while paying its way in dealings with the rest of the world. In the light of this record, and of Japan's tremendous military expenditures, the facts can be said to demonstrate conclusively the falsity of the Japanese claims of the 1930s that limited space, meager natural resources, and large population made control of nearby areas an economic necessity. If the large net flow of resources to controlled areas had been spent for peaceful purposes, Japan might have done a great deal more for its people's welfare.

Since World War II

No privileged trade or yen area complicates the balance of payments of postwar Japan, but the account now has some new and different special characteristics. With the prewar international payments structure completely destroyed and the modern sectors of the domestic economy virtually at a standstill, Japan was so helpless immediately after surrender that the principal occupying power fairly soon modified and later abandoned its initial policy of leaving recovery to the Japanese and began to provide food, medicine, fertilizer, petroleum, and other goods without asking if Japan could pay for them. United States aid had reached nearly $2 bil-

[6] Only with Taiwan did Japan achieve a surplus of imports over a long period (1914–1943). With Korea a series of small commodity import surpluses during most of the years 1918–1932 and a continuing flow of gold from Korean mines to Japan proper were much more than overbalanced by large export surpluses after 1932. With Manchuria likewise, a series of small import surpluses before 1931 were replaced by later large export surpluses. Oriental Economist, *Foreign Trade of Japan, A Statistical Survey* (Tokyo: Author, 1935), pp. 349, 359, 663, 665; Bank of Japan, *Economic Statistics of Japan,* 1959, pp. 241, 243.

lion when the outbreak of war in Korea in 1950 brought Japan an opportunity to earn vast sums by supplying goods and services to UN forces. Japan became the forward supply, staging, repair, and rest area for these forces. Foreign military expenditures, mostly American, soon provided Japan with more income than had ever been received from aid, and proved more lasting as well. Procurement by the United States for its own military forces and for assistance to Asian allies continued after the end of fighting in Korea. These dollars still flow to Japan in substantial volume. Total military expenditures through 1962 were nearly $6.5 billion.

These two "extraordinary" types of income have contributed decisively to the phenomenal postwar recovery of the Japanese economy. From 1945 through 1962 they brought Japan enough income to pay for nearly 20 per cent of its total imports of goods and services. Thanks to this income Japan was able to spend abroad much more than it earned from exports of goods and services, pay some reparations, and still accumulate a large balance of foreign assets and gold.

Japan's cumulative balance of payments for the whole postwar period through 1962 is summarized in Table 3-3. The figures there show that U.S. aid and military expenditures were the only major items to bring net revenue to Japan. What they brought in cumulated to $8.6 billion. This, along with a little other net income unaccounted for and listed as net errors and omissions, was used by Japan as follows: [7]

$4.9 billion to cover the net deficit on account of services.
$2.6 billion to meet the merchandise deficit.
$0.7 billion in payment of World War II reparations.
$0.5 billion to accumulate net assets abroad.

This is a very different payments structure from that of 1936. Instead of getting from the services account enough to pay for deficits in the goods and capital accounts, postwar Japan has its largest deficit in services, which is added to a large goods deficit and net outpayments on capital and reparations. Japan has received from the outside world far more than it has provided in commodities and in all the ordinary services except travel. Extraordinary income, supplemented by foreign capital, has made this possible.

[7] Totaling the balances of payments for the whole postwar period, as is done here, or making annual averages, as is done for four postwar periods in Table 3–9 below, provides useful information on the types of movements that took place and the orders of magnitude involved. Although a good deal of care has gone into preparation of these and related tables, the figures therein cannot be regarded as precise. Ways of recording some transactions have changed, and some adjustments have had to be made. Some figures are estimates, as in any country's balance-of-payments statistics. A technical discussion of Japan's international accounts will be presented in Appendix A, including annual figures for the balance of payments.

TABLE 3-3. JAPAN'S BALANCE OF INTERNATIONAL PAYMENTS: CUMULATIVE, 1945–1962
(In millions of dollars)

	Credit	*Debit*	*Balance*
Goods and services (ordinary)	**38,912**	**46,497**	**−7,585**
Merchandise trade, f.o.b.	33,992	36,629	−2,637
Services	4,919	9,868	−4,949
Transportation and insurance	2,730	6,585	−3,854
Travel	311	236	75
Investment income	460	924	−464
Government transactions, n.i.e.	188	243	−55
Miscellaneous services	1,229	1,881	−651
Extraordinary items	**8,614**	**672**	**7,942**
U.S. economic aid	2,160		2,160
U.S. military expenditures [a]	6,454		6,454
Reparations		672 [b]	−672
Errors and omissions (net)			**135**
Capital and gold movements (ordinary)	**4,313** [c]	**4,805** [d]	**−492**
Private capital	1,354 [c]	1,043 [d]	310
Long-term	1,066 [c]	1,031 [d]	36
Short-term	287 [c]	13 [d]	275
Official and banking capital	2,948 [c]	3,559 [d]	−612
Long-term	395 [c]	669 [d]	−274
Short-term	2,552 [c]	2,890 [d]	−338
Monetary gold	12	202	−190

[a] Includes small amounts spent in Japan by third countries, mostly during the Korean War, by units and personnel of the United Nations Command.
[b] Includes $177 million granted to Indonesia by cancellation of commercial debt at the time of the reparations settlement.
[c] Net change in Japanese liabilities abroad.
[d] Net change in Japanese assets abroad.

Note: Minor inconsistencies result from rounding.

Sources: 1945–1960—International Monetary Fund, *Balance of Payments Yearbook.* 1961–1962—Bank of Japan, *Balance of Payments of Japan,* 1961, 1962. See Appendix Table A-1 for detailed annual statistics.

MAJOR ELEMENTS OF THE BALANCE OF PAYMENTS

Each major type of international transaction has had a history of its own in the postwar period. Each has played a different and changing part in the totality of Japan's economic relations with the outside world. Net movements for each major item are shown by years in Table 3-4, which is based on detailed figures appearing in Appendix Table A-1.

U.S. Economic Aid

A large amount of aid for relief and economic recovery in Japan was supplied by the United States, mostly in the first five years, from appropriations for Government and Relief in Occupied Areas (GARIOA) and Economic Rehabilitation in Occupied Areas (EROA). Smaller amounts came from surplus property transfers and some other items. Food began to be shipped in soon after surrender, and after some delay raw materials for industrial operations. The value of U.S. aid rose to a peak in 1949. By that year the most essential needs had been met, and the Dodge stabilization plan signaled American determination to reduce the level of aid. Even before the Korean War began, the flow of supplies diminished, and by the close of 1951 it had virtually ended.

In the 1950s two new U.S. programs provided economic aid of a quite different kind. A limited technical assistance program, instituted by the International Cooperation Administration (ICA) in 1955 and terminated in June 1961, provided a total of $22 million for the productivity program which will be described in the next chapter. Shipments of agricultural surplus commodities totaled roughly $255 million since the end of the Occupation. The largest part of this amount, authorized in the mid-1950s, was sold for yen and the proceeds used for long-term loans to Japan for agricultural, industrial, and mining projects, with small sums going as grants for military use and for a hospital in Hiroshima. Under grant programs a substantial volume of agricultural commodities went for emergency assistance and at least some agricultural surplus was given each year to voluntary relief agencies for work in Japan.[8]

[8] Two sales agreements in 1955 and 1956 under Title I of the Agricultural Trade Development and Assistance Act of 1954 (PL 480, 83d Congress) resulted in total shipments of $146 million (market value) of whose yen proceeds $106 million was used for the benefit of Japan, almost all going into these loans. Under an earlier agreement, sale of agricultural surplus was authorized in the U.S. fiscal year 1954, under Section 550 of the Mutual Security Act of 1951 (PL 165, 82d Congress), as amended. The yen proceeds, equivalent to $47 million, went mostly for procurement programs of the U.S. military forces, but $9 million worth was allotted Japan as a military assistance grant. The aid to Japan from these sales agreements thus totaled $115 million. Under Title II of PL 480, $37 million (C.C.C. cost) was

TABLE 3-4. JAPAN'S BALANCE OF PAYMENTS: NET TRANSACTIONS BY MAJOR ITEM, 1945–1962
(In millions of dollars)

Year	*Goods*	*Ordinary Services*	*U.S. Military Expenditures* [a]	*U.S. Economic Aid*	*Reparations*	*Errors and Omissions*	*Ordinary Capital Transactions*	*Increase of Japanese Assets Abroad*	*Increase of Japanese Liabilities Abroad*
1945–1946	−220	−33	—	193	—	−3	63	51	114
1947	−267	−91	—	404	—	14	−60	42	−18
1948	−284	−121	19	461	—	27	−102	44	−58
1949	−195	−156	49	535	−18	−18	−196	198	2
1950	−1	−38	154	360	—	−17	−459	433	−26
1951	−292	−159	624	155	—	9	−338	371	33
1952	−413	−156	788	5	—	1	−225	364	139
1953	−792	−217	803	—	—	1	204	123	327
1954	−429	−224	602	—	—	18	33	124	157
1955	−55	−215	505	13	−24	−102	−123	329	206
1956	−131	−393	498	12	−20	14	20	230	250
1957	−402	−602	449	10	−76	5	615	−423	193
1958	369	−278	404	10	−241 [b]	72	−336	255	−81
1959	361	−311	381	—	−70	57	−418	895	476
1960	271	−471	413	—	−69	33	−176	856	680
1961	−559	−728	389	—	−86	19	963	195	1,158
1962	402	−759	377	—	−68	6	43	718	761
Total	−2,637	−4,949	6,454	2,160	−672	135	−492	4,805	4,313

[a] Includes small amounts spent in Japan by third countries, mostly during the Korean War by units and personnel of the United Nations Command.
[b] Includes $177 million granted to Indonesia by cancellation of commercial debt at the time of the reparations settlement.

Notes: A dash (—) indicates that a figure is zero or less than $500,000.
Minor inconsistencies result from rounding.

Sources: 1945–1960—International Monetary Fund, *Balance of Payments Yearbook.*
1961–1962—Bank of Japan, *Balance of Payments of Japan,* 1961, 1962.

Japan has not taken as much advantage of the opportunity to buy U.S. surpluses as some other food-importing countries. The most important reason is that with increased domestic agricultural production Japan would have had difficulty in satisfying the requirement that surplus disposal represent sales in addition to those that would normally take place. Also, since the last sales agreement in 1956 Japan has been well able to pay for normal imports.

Neither the technical aid nor the grant portion of agricultural deliveries imposes on Japan any obligation to repay. The loans made from part of the proceeds of agricultural sales are repayable in yen or dollars, as the Japanese prefer (p. 74). Although GARIOA aid was at first treated as a unilateral transfer, as the 1950s wore on the United States began to press for a settlement under which Japan would, over a number of years, repay some part of the total, just as the Germans had agreed to repay part of the aid given to them.

A settlement was reached in June 1961, signed the following January, and then approved by the Diet. Japan agreed to repay $490 million over a period of fifteen years, with interest at the rate of 2.5 per cent a year; for the first twelve years semiannual payments are to be slightly less than $22 million each. This settlement is substantially more generous than the German GARIOA settlement, under which Germany agreed to repay a billion dollars out of three billion advanced by the United States. The Japanese negotiation involved, first, a scaling down of the amount of American advances considered for repayment. The Japanese challenged certain aspects of the Occupation's records on aid and the $2.2 billion shown in the Japanese balance of payments was reduced to $1.8 billion as a basis for discussion. Secondly, the proportion to be repaid was set at only 27 per cent, well below the one-third of the German precedent. Thirdly, the American negotiators indicated the manner in which the proceeds of Japan's repayments would probably be spent, whereas German repayments are made in wholly unrestricted funds with no commitment as to their use. In an exchange of notes the United States indicated its intention, subject to appropriate legislation, to use $25 million of the repayments in Japanese–American educational exchange programs, and the rest as aid to less developed countries. The $25 million for educational

---

granted for emergency assistance in the U.S. fiscal years 1957 through 1962. Under Title III of PL 480, $26.4 million (C.C.C. cost) was granted to voluntary relief agencies for use in Japan between July 1, 1949 and June 30, 1961. (Of this, $2 million was authorized before June 30, 1954, and may already have been included in the aid figures shown in the balance of payments for the years 1949–1952.) Information from International Cooperation Administration, Office of Statistics and Reports, *Operations Report,* Data as of June 30, 1961 (Washington: Author, 1961), pp. 113 and 115; additional material directly from ICA and its successor, the Agency for International Development.

and cultural exchange can be paid in yen as part of the first two installments.[9]

Military Assistance

U.S. grants of military aid to Japan began soon after the San Francisco Peace Treaty went into effect; by June 30, 1962, grants under the Military Assistance Program (MAP) totaled $847 million and other military aid provided $886 million more.[10] These large sums do not appear in Japan's balance of payments, but the omission has only limited economic significance since Japan neither gains nor loses therefrom with respect to international trade and finance. Most military aid took the form of equipment and supplies delivered directly to Japan but not included in the trade statistics. A small part consists of the services of military personnel assigned as instructors or advisers. There is a small direct effect on the Japanese economy when these men spend their pay in Japan; such sums are included in the foreign military expenditures that appear in the published figures.

A reverse movement that is also omitted from the balance of payments is the expenditure by the Japanese government to support the American military establishment in Japan. During the Occupation, payments of this sort were large and were levied on the Japanese government, in the tradition of occupying armies, as costs of terminating the war. Now the limited Japanese contributions in the form of base rights and certain services are regarded as part of the Japanese defense effort. In neither case was any significant direct foreign exchange cost involved, although there were some indirect foreign costs.

Foreign Military Expenditures

Foreign military expenditures in Japan are not aid. The $6.5 billion indicated in the balance of payments as having been paid to Japan from 1948 through 1962 represented value received and was fully earned by the Japanese nation. The initial practice of charging the yen costs of the

[9] U.S. Department of State, *For the Press,* No. 18, January 9, 1962; *The New York Times,* June 10, 1961 and January 10, 1962; Consulate General of Japan, New York, *Japan Report,* June 15, 1961, pp. 3–4; *Prospectus,* dated October 3, 1961, contained in Registration Statement of the Japan Development Bank, U.S. Securities and Exchange Commission file no. 2-18854, covering $20,000,000 Guaranteed External Loan Bonds, dated September 15, 1961, p. 50.

[10] This other military aid included vessels, valued at $175 million, which were lent to Japan for an indefinite period and $540 million worth of matériel given to Japan out of stocks of the Department of Defense. In the MAP figure of $847 million is included the rehabilitation costs of certain equipment from excess U.S. stocks, but the original cost, totaling $171.4 million, was not included; actual value was presumably above the rehabilitation cost but below the original cost to the United States. Agency for International Development, *U.S. Foreign Assistance and Assistance from International Organizations, July 1, 1945–June 30, 1962* (Washington: Author, 1963), p. 63.

Occupation establishment to the Japanese government was modified in 1948 when the United States started paying for some of the services provided to American troops. These early payments were small, however, compared to the amounts spent after the Korean War began. During the war it was extremely advantageous to the United States and the United Nations to have facilities and goods provided by Japan. Most of the military equipment, such as jeeps and artillery shells, might have been brought from the United States but the costs would have been much higher. But a special advantage of the forward Japanese base was that so many services were readily and cheaply available there, from repairing ships and trucks to washing clothes or filling a thousand and one other requirements. Other countries than the United States also made some use of these advantages, and small sums were spent in Japan by units and troops of other countries that were participating in the defense of Korea under the United Nations.

After the end of the fighting in Korea in 1953, the level of foreign military expenditures in Japan declined gradually, but the sums remained important. The larger share of these expenditures has covered the costs of American troops and dependents living in Japan and in areas near enough to provide ready access by procurement officers to Japanese suppliers. So far as leaves and furloughs are concerned, Japan is a favored area for military personnel and their families stationed in Korea, Okinawa, Taiwan, and elsewhere, and for naval personnel from the Seventh Fleet and other ships that may be in the Western Pacific.

Japan has also been a favored source for American military procurement for third countries. Army, naval, and air forces have bought many kinds of goods and services in Japan for American military aid programs in Korea, Taiwan, Viet-Nam, and other countries. Partly because of Japan's location, partly because of favorable prices, and partly as a matter of policy to help support the Japanese economy, U.S. procurement organizations and procedures were developed to make military purchases in Japan. Although U.S. ground combat troops were all transferred out of Japan in 1958, U.S. army procurement in Japan has continued, with procurement personnel stationed there for the purpose. Table 3-5 summarizes expenditures for all years except 1948 and 1949, differentiating between military procurement, which involves appropriated funds, and yen sales, which represent individual or group expenditures with personal funds.[11]

[11] The figures in Table 3-5 have been compiled differently from those in the balance of payments. The principal, but not the only, reason for disagreements is exclusion of FOA/ICA/AID expenditures from the balance of payments, which includes them among commodities exported from Japan. This procedure is valid, not only statistically but also legally, since U.S. aid funds were paid, not directly to Japan, but to the aided country.

TABLE 3-5. JAPAN'S SPECIAL DOLLAR EARNINGS, 1950–1962

(In millions of dollars)

	Military Spending			*FOA/ICA/ AID*		
Year	*Yen Sales* [a]	*Military Procurement* [b]	*Total*	*Procurement* [c]	*Other* [d]	*Total*
1950	110	38	149	—	—	149
1951	228	337	566	—	26	592
1952	288	504	791	—	33	824
1953	323	456	779	8	22	809
1954	313	246	559	10	27	596
1955	287	194	481	65	11	557
1956	278	187	465	119	11	595
1957	259	155	414	126	9	549
1958	208	164	371	104	7	482
1959	210	131	341	111	19	471
1960	216	173	389	147	6	542
1961	183	187	371	74	1	446
1962	201	165	366	10	—	376
Total	3,103	2,937	6,040	774	172	6,988

[a] Yen sales are purchases of yen by civilian and military personnel of the U.S. military forces and by quasi-official organizations where funds do not come from the U.S. budget, such as post exchanges and service clubs.

[b] Military procurement represents expenditures from appropriated funds for goods and services for the U.S. forces, Japan; for U.S. forces elsewhere; and for military assistance programs.

[c] Procurement with U.S. foreign aid funds is in most ways ordinary export trade to Korea, Viet-Nam, and other countries. These exports are shown in Japan's commodity trade statistics and do not appear separately in Japan's balance of payments.

[d] Includes purchases in Japan by the U.S. General Services Administration, by the UN Korean Rehabilitation Agency (UNKRA), and by the U.S. military forces for construction work in Okinawa.

Notes: A dash (—) indicates that a figure is zero or less than $500,000.
Minor inconsistencies result from rounding.

Sources: All 1950 figures from U.S. Embassy, Tokyo.
FOA/ICA/AID figures for 1951–1959 from International Cooperation Administration, Washington.
All figures for 1960, 1961, and 1962 from Bank of Tokyo, *Weekly Review*, February 25, 1963, pp. 2–3.
All other figures from Bank of Japan, *Foreign Exchange Statistics Monthly*, December 1959, p. 105.

ICA and AID Procurement

Another special source of dollar income to Japan has been the purchase with U.S. foreign aid funds of Japanese goods for delivery to third countries, especially Korea and Viet-Nam, but also India, Cambodia, Taiwan, and many others. These purchases were started in 1953 under the Foreign Operations Administration (FOA), and continued under the successor agencies, the International Cooperation Administration (ICA), 1955–1961, and since November 1961 the Agency for International Development (AID). By the end of 1962, $774 million worth of Japanese fertilizers, textiles, steel products, machinery, and other goods had been purchased. (See Table 3-5.) These purchases do not appear separately in Japan's balance of payments but are part of commodity exports, not distinguished from other exports. Without ICA financing, however, the recipients might not have been able to buy the goods; certainly they would not have been able to pay in dollars for a comparable volume.

The Future of Special Dollar Income

Japan's special dollar income has declined much less than was expected several years ago. In 1955 the Japanese government officially assumed that this income would decline and disappear by 1960.[12] What happened instead was that the total of military and ICA expenditures rose in 1956 and then went down slowly until 1959, but in 1960 rose again. A serious cut was indicated in the November 1960 decision to limit both military and other spending abroad by the U.S. government as part of the program to deal with the persistent deficit in the U.S. balance of payments. But this has not affected much the level of military procurement or troop spending. What has been cut is procurement by countries receiving U.S. foreign economic aid, as shown in Table 3-5. As a result, Japan's total special dollar earnings dropped below $400 million in 1962 for the first time since 1950. Even at this somewhat reduced level, however, this continues to be a substantial source of Japanese earnings.

Whatever the future level of special dollar receipts, extraordinary income no longer plays the crucial part for Japan that it did in the first decade after the surrender. The sum of two items, military procurement and U.S. aid (without ICA procurement), has shrunk progressively in comparison with income from goods and services sold to foreigners, as the following figures, based on Table 3-9, show:

1945–1950	107 per cent
1951–1954	48 per cent

[12] Japan, Economic Planning Board, *Economic Self Support Five-Year Plan Tables* (Tokyo: Author, 1956, mimeographed), p. 15. (The Economic Planning Board was the predecessor of the Economic Planning Agency.)

1955–1957	18 per cent
1958–1962	9 per cent

Even this last figure is important, but Japan's economic vitality no longer depends on special dollar receipts.

Japanese Reparations

The Potsdam Proclamation calling on Japan to surrender included, in paragraph 11, the assertion that "Japan shall be permitted to maintain such industries as will sustain her economy and permit the exaction of just reparations in kind. . . ." An abortive effort was made during the first years of the Occupation to transfer industrial equipment from Japan as reparations in the hope of speeding the reconstruction and development of other countries that had suffered from Japanese aggression, while taking from Japan only excess capacity that would not be needed by a disarmed nation. Agreement on the exact amount of reparations that Japan should pay each claimant country was to come later. As it turned out, only a small amount of machinery from Japanese arsenals and certain laboratory equipment had been transferred when the program was halted by disagreements among the Allies and by the new American policy of stimulating Japanese economic recovery and self-support.[13] As a result, the only reparations transfer recorded in the balance of payments during the Occupation was $18.4 million in 1949.

The San Francisco Peace Treaty left the reparations problem to be settled through bilateral agreements between Japan and the claimant countries. From November 1955 to May 1958 agreements were signed obligating Japan to pay $1,012 million in reparations in kind to Burma, the Philippines, Indonesia, and Viet-Nam, and to write off a $177 million trade debt owed by Indonesia. A supplementary agreement with Burma was signed in January 1963, after years of Burmese pressure for increased payments. Table 3-6 presents the facts of the reparations program, showing total obligations of $1,329 million and payments through September 1962 totaling $559 million. Japan regarded the program shown in Table 3-6, plus some smaller war-connected claims totaling $120 million,[14] as constituting its total reparations burden.[15] But the problem has not dis-

[13] Jerome B. Cohen, *Japan's Economy in War and Reconstruction* (Minneapolis: University of Minnesota Press, 1949), pp. 419–427.

[14] This figure is less than the $672 million cumulative total of reparations payments indicated in the balance of payments through 1962. (Tables 3-3 and 3-4.) The $18.4 million of reparations recorded in 1949 is part of the explanation. The balance represents miscellaneous war-connected payments, mostly claims for property loss, mainly those covered in the $120 million agreed total.

[15] In addition to these obligated transfers, Japan agreed to facilitate and expedite private loans and investments in Burma, Indonesia, and the Philippines, and to make certain public loans to finance Japanese exports to Burma, as will be described in Chapter 4, pp. 96–97.

TABLE 3-6 JAPANESE REPARATIONS: PROGRAM AND PAYMENTS THROUGH SEPTEMBER 30, 1962

(Amounts in millions of dollars)

	Burma	*Philippines*	*Indonesia*	*Viet-Nam*	*Total*
Dates of agreement:					
Signed	Nov. 5, 1954	May 9, 1956	Jan. 20, 1958	May 13, 1959	
Effective	Apr. 16, 1955	July 23, 1956	Apr. 15, 1958	Jan. 12, 1960	
Scheduled completion of payments	Apr. 15, 1965	July 22, 1976	Apr. 14, 1970	Jan. 11, 1965	
Amounts payable:					
Total	200 [a] (340)	550	400 [b]	39 [c]	1,189 [d] (1,329)
Annual	20	25–30 [e]	20 [f]	10–4.5 [g]	75 (maximum)
Total payments through September 30, 1962	139.9	128.4	267.4 [b]	23	558.7
Balance outstanding, September 30, 1962	60.1 (200.1) [h]	421.6	132.6	16	630.3 (770.3) [h]
Proportion of total obligations already paid	70% (41%) [h]	23%	67%	59%	47% (42%) [h]

[a] Burma's long-standing claim to an increase in the total agreed upon in 1954 led, on January 25, 1963, to the initialing of a preliminary agreement stating that Japan would pay an additional $140 million to Burma in goods and services after the 1954 agreement is fulfilled in 1965. This supplement will be paid over a period of 12 years in annual installments. According to the Japanese foreign office, the additional grants will represent "non-repayable economic cooperation," not "true reparations." *The Japan Times Weekly*, February 2, 1963, p. 3.

[b] In addition to assuming an obligation to deliver $223,080,000 in reparations to Indonesia, Japan simultaneously canceled an accumulated trade debt of $176,914,000 owed by Indonesia as a result of previous open-account trade with Japan.

[c] In addition, Japan is obligated to provide Viet-Nam $7.5 million in government loans over a 3-year period, and $9.1 million in commercial loans. Although these are firm obligations, they are to be repaid to Japan and so seem better omitted from the list of reparations payments required.

[d] The supplementary agreement with Burma raises this total to $1,329 million.

[e] Annual payment is to be $25 million from July 1956 until July 1966, and $30 million from then until July 1976.

[f] Annual rate, April 1958 to April 1969; the balance of $3,080,000 to be paid by April 1970.

[g] Annual rate of $10 million, January 1960 to January 1963; $4.5 million from then until January 1965.

[h] Amount shown in parentheses includes additional deliveries to Burma stipulated in agreement signed January 1963.

Sources: Japan, Ministry of Finance; Japan, Ministry of Foreign Affairs; Embassy of Japan, Washington. Balance outstanding on September 30, 1962 from *Prospectus*, dated January 30, 1963, contained in Registration Statement of the Japan Development Bank, U.S. Securities and Exchange Commission file no. 2-21009, covering $22,500,000 Guaranteed External Loan Bonds, p. 69.

appeared. During the summer of 1963, for example, a clamor arose in Singapore for substantial Japanese payments in "atonement" for Japanese war atrocities. This "blood debt" issue was taken up for discussion with Japan by the newly formed government of Malaysia in September, but no agreement had been reached by the middle of March 1964.

Payments began in 1955 and by the end of September 1962, in addition to canceling the Indonesian trade debt, Japan had made deliveries valued at $382 million, a third of the agreed total, counting in the supplementary deliveries to be made to Burma. Combining all obligations as listed in Table 3-6, and all payments through September 1962, Japan had paid off 42 per cent of her total reparations debt. The country record ranged from 67 per cent in Indonesia to 23 per cent in the Philippines. The schedule called for annual transfers of about $75 million until 1963 and smaller payments thereafter. All these obligations are scheduled to be discharged by 1977, when the supplementary payments to Burma are due to be completed.

Some related problems are outstanding with other countries not receiving reparations. One of long standing with Thailand, a dispute over interpretation of the 1955 agreement compensating Thailand for currency issued by Japanese forces during World War II, was settled at the beginning of February 1962 when Japan acceded to the Thai request that the $26.7 million settlement be a grant rather than a credit.[16]

Closing the Gap in Commodity Trade

Although Japanese exports amounted to only $65 million between September 1945 and the end of 1946, American aid and a cotton credit made it possible to import $286 million worth of goods. From these very low levels trade rose irregularly, with exports increasing more rapidly than imports until by 1958 Japan achieved an export balance, which was maintained during the next two years. The pace of this improvement through 1962 may be seen from the rising value of exports as a percentage of imports:[17]

1945–1946	23
1945–1950	66
1951–1954	74
1955–1957	93
1958–1962	105

This closing of the trade gap is a success story of the first order. At the end of the war the foreign trade problem was clear and urgent, and

[16] *The Japan Times Weekly,* February 10, 1962, p. 3.

[17] These percentages are derived from balance-of-payments figures using f.o.b. values for exports and imports. Customs statistics (see Table 5-1 below), which show imports at c.i.f. values, indicate a surplus of imports in every postwar year.

the prospect dark. Two conditions were indispensable: adequate foreign sources of food and raw materials, and access to foreign markets for Japan's finished products. The loss of colonial sources of supply and the disappearance of prewar markets forced Japan to find new trading partners. Changes in world prices brought a change in the structure of Japan's trade. Commercial relationships, sometimes painfully established, were distorted by the imposition of artificial barriers to the movement of goods. And at many points political events accentuated the economic difficulties, most disastrously when the Chinese Communists gained control of the mainland. How Japan successfully accommodated itself to circumstances and what the future holds for Japanese trade are the subjects of later chapters.

Rising Services Deficit

Japan's exchange of services with the rest of the world has also grown but, unlike trade, has shown a generally growing deficit. Transportation, the largest service item, continues to account for large net outpayments.[18] Although the tonnage of Japanese trade carried aboard Japanese ships has grown, so has that carried in foreign bottoms. In 1962 the Japanese share was just over two-fifths of the total and much less than in the peak year of 1958, as Table 3-7 shows. Japan's transportation earnings grew from $41 million in 1951 to $355 million in 1961, largely as a result of the increase in tonnage. But transportation costs also have risen rapidly, reaching $830 million in 1961, and leaving a net outpayment for transportation of $476 million, which was exceeded only in 1957, when a great surge of payments resulted from speculative importing and ship chartering at high prices after the Suez crisis.

Air transportation was prohibited to Japan for a while after World

[18] The transportation account of the postwar balance of payments omits entirely the freights earned by Japanese ships in carrying Japanese imports, since payment of such freights is regarded as a domestic, not an international, transaction. Also omitted are freight charges for exports carried in foreign ships, since these are regarded as transactions not involving Japan. The transportation item in Japan's balance of payments shows mainly freights paid to foreign ships for bringing imports to Japan, freights received by Japanese ships for carrying Japanese exports, freights from service between one foreign country and another, passenger fares received and paid, and charter fees and port charges (both mostly outpayments). Since the tonnage of Japanese imports is many times the tonnage of exports—in 1960 and 1961 the ratio was almost eight to one—there is a strong tendency for the balance-of-payments outgo on account of shipping to exceed income, despite the higher rates charged on the kinds of things Japan exports than on the raw materials that move into Japan. In addition the expenditures of Japanese ships abroad far exceed those of foreign ships in Japanese ports. Fuel, usually the largest item of port costs, is normally bought outside of Japan by both Japanese and foreign vessels. Aviation transactions are handled similarly; their volume is very small in comparison with shipping transactions. The concepts and categories follow those prescribed by the IMF.

TABLE 3-7 THE JAPANESE MERCHANT MARINE AND ITS SHARE IN CARRYING JAPAN'S FOREIGN TRADE, 1934–1936 AND 1945–1962

Year	Merchant Fleet [a]		Exports [b]			Imports [b]		
				Carried Aboard Japanese Ships			Carried Aboard Japanese Ships	
	Number of Vessels	*Million Gross Tons*	*Total (million metric tons)*	*(million metric tons)*	*(per cent)*	*Total (million metric tons)*	*(million metric tons)*	*(per cent)*
1934–1936 av.	1,363	3.9	12.5 [c]	8.2 [c]	66.0	31.1 [c]	17.3 [c]	55.4
1945–1946 [d]	813	1.4	1.1	1.0	93.6	1.5	0.3	20.2
1947	869	1.5	1.8	1.4	81.7	4.5	0.4	8.1
1948	922	1.6	1.8	1.3	69.2	7.4	0.6	8.4
1949	994	1.7	2.3	0.8	29.6	12.8	1.5	11.4
1950	944	1.7	3.1	0.5	17.3	10.5	2.8	26.8
1951	1,017	2.3	3.6	1.0	26.6	20.7	6.8	32.6
1952	1,065	2.7	5.1	1.6	31.6	23.7	10.8	45.5
1953	1,067	3.0	5.0	1.9	37.7	31.3	13.5	43.0
1954	1,138	3.3	5.7	2.5	43.3	33.5	15.6	46.7
1955	1,181	3.4	7.7	3.4	43.5	36.7	19.1	52.1
1956	1,284	3.7	8.8	3.9	44.8	46.5	22.1	47.5
1957	1,455	4.4	8.4	4.2	49.3	58.7	25.1	42.8
1958	1,661	5.3	9.3	5.3	56.6	49.1	28.2	57.4
1959	1,856	5.9	10.1	5.4	53.6	65.0	35.0	53.8
1960	2,100	6.5	11.1	5.5	49.6	87.6	42.4	48.4
1961	3,067	7.3	15.4	6.6	43.0	118.5	47.5	40.1
1962	3,354	8.5	18.9	8.1	42.9	123.1	53.9	43.8

[a] Steel vessels of 100 gross tons or larger, as of the end of December. Through 1951 sunken vessels regarded as recoverable are included.
[b] Omits the very small movement of goods by air and parcel post.
[c] Not corrected to include trade between Japan proper and the colonies (Korea and Taiwan). Since Japanese ships carried virtually all this trade, its inclusion would increase the share carried in Japanese ships.
[d] September 1945–December 1946.

Sources: Bank of Japan, *Economic Statistics of Japan*, 1955, p. 246; 1960, p. 235. Japan, Ministry of Finance, *Monthly Return of the Foreign Trade of Japan*, January–December 1960, p. 380. Japan, Economic Planning Agency, *Japanese Economic Statistics*, April 1963, p. 45. Japan, Ministry of Transportation, *Nihon Kaiun No Genjo* (Present Situation of Japanese Shipping), July 1963, pp. 54–55.

War II. Now the Japan Air Lines is extending its international routes, and foreign exchange earnings from this company are rising. But the figures are still very small and are not usually shown separately in the balance of payments.

Japan's transportation deficit is likely to persist and even grow in the years ahead. Imports of bulk commodities from distant sources are expected to continue to grow rapidly, especially crude oil, ores, scrap metals, and coal. There seems no prospect of regaining the prewar pattern, when trade was carried predominantly in Japanese ships and a much higher proportion went to or came from nearby areas. And now that Japanese coal no longer serves as fuel for ships, both Japanese and foreign, fuel will cost progressively more as the Japanese merchant fleet expands.

Travel is an exceptional item in the service account because it yielded a surplus in every year from 1949 through 1959. Japan is something of a tourist paradise; the number of foreign visitors is rising progressively, from 103,000 in 1955 to 152,000 in 1958, 212,000 in 1960, and 280,000 in 1962. Visitors' estimated expenditures rose from $45 million in 1955 to $150 million in 1962.[19] This increase may be expected to continue. Business as well as tourist travel is becoming easier with the increased speed provided by jet planes. The number of passenger accommodations is growing rapidly. Western-style hotel rooms, although scarce, are increasing. Travel promotion is being stepped up. Holding the 1964 Olympic Games in Japan may well give a lasting boost to tourism. On the other side of this account, a rising number of Japanese are going abroad at Japanese expense, and this number is expected to grow further with liberalization of Japan's exchange regulations. Fear of the cost involved has led Japan, with special IMF permission, to continue to restrict Japanese "sightseeing" travel abroad, even after most other payments were freed in April 1964.

Travel outpayments were kept down after World War II by severe Occupation and Japanese restrictions on the use of foreign exchange for travel. Once these were relaxed Japanese spent much more on foreign travel. In 1960 the travel account showed debits twice as large as those of 1959, the previous peak year, and 1961 and 1962 showed further increases. Japanese are avid tourists, both within Japan and in the world at large. It is not yet evident how much a prosperous Japan would spend on foreign travel if all restraints were removed, but ap-

[19] Estimates of the Japanese Ministry of Transportation, as given in the Foreign Capital Research Society, care of the Bank of Japan, *Japanese Industry*, 1963 (Tokyo: Author, 1963), p. 154. It is not clear why such estimates are so far above the receipts indicated in the balance of payments. Apparently there is some underreporting in the channels that provide information for the balance of payments.

parently the ceiling is well above anything yet seen. The near future of the travel account seems unpredictable so far as the comparative increase of foreign travel in Japan and of Japanese abroad is concerned, but there is little doubt both will grow substantially during the 1960s.

Investment income is a service item of growing importance. In the postwar period outpayments have exceeded inpayments in every year since entries first appeared in 1947. Total recorded postwar outpayments came to $924 million by the end of 1962, inpayments to only $460 million. How does this happen, when the balance of payments shows accumulation during the postwar period of net foreign assets worth nearly $500 million? The answer lies in the nature of Japan's foreign assets and liabilities, and in relative costs of capital in Japan and abroad. Roughly half of all Japanese foreign assets are foreign exchange reserves, which are held in relatively liquid form and earn little. Nothing at all is earned by the capital contributions to the World Bank, the International Monetary Fund, and other international organizations, a total of $264 million at the end of September 1962.[20] The remainder of Japan's foreign assets earn varying amounts, often small, as in the case of certain credits granted in order to foster exports. Foreign capital in Japan, on the other hand, earns rates that vary from moderate interest on public loans to high rates of profit on the more successful equity investments. Japan's deficit on account of investment income seems likely to continue for some time, but as overseas investments grow this trend should be reversed, and in time income may exceed outgo.

Foreign technology is a closely related item, but one that does not appear separately in the balance-of-payments tables in this chapter, being included in miscellaneous services. Since Japan has so far exported very little technology but has imported a great deal, payments have been mainly outward. As Table 4-4 (p. 83) shows, gross payments for foreign technology were $124 million in 1961. This figure has risen rapidly in recent years, and promises to keep on growing with the continued use of foreign technology in the expanding Japanese economy.

Several other service items are also generating growing deficits. Among these are brokerage fees, reflecting Japan's expanding volume of international transactions; film rentals, which have been tightly controlled by the Japanese Ministry of Finance but which may increase with progressive liberalization; telecommunications fees; and management fees.

All in all, the continued rise in both credits and debits on account of services reflects expanding production and trade. The tendency for the services deficit to persist and even to grow is a matter of some significance, since this deficit must be covered by net inpayments elsewhere in the balance of payments. But the size of the services deficit is not large

[20] Bank of Tokyo, *Weekly Review*, December 10, 1962, p. 335.

relative to total movements of goods and services, and there is no reason at present to fear that it will prove embarrassing.

Accumulation of Foreign Assets and Liabilities

The cumulative movements from 1945 through 1962, as shown in balance-of-payments reports, brought Japan a total of $4.8 billion in foreign assets, as we saw above. (Tables 3-3 and 3-4.) Offsetting these were a cumulation of obligations to the extent of $4.3 billion, leaving a net increase of assets of $492 million.

These figures represent *changes* during the postwar period, not balances at the end of 1962. But Japanese foreign assets were very few in 1945, and consequently the $4.8 billion figure should be close to the total of Japanese assets abroad, long- and short-term, subject to omissions and errors in the reported balance-of-payments figures.[21] Japan's foreign assets today consist mostly of gold and foreign exchange reserves, other holdings of foreign currency, both long-term and short-term trade credits outstanding to foreigners, some long-term private loans and investments, and substantial capital subscriptions to the World Bank, the International Monetary Fund, and other international organizations.

Foreign liabilities are somewhat more complicated. In addition to the cumulative increase indicated in the balance of payments for the postwar period, Japan has some obligations still outstanding from the prewar period, the heavy burden of reparations and smaller obligations arising out of the war, and now also the GARIOA debt to the United States.

Capital movements and related matters will be discussed more fully in the following chapter but, to provide a rounded picture, here is the record of the official gold and foreign exchange reserves of Japan over the first twelve years of full independence (in millions of dollars): [22]

End of Year	*Reserves*	*End of Year*	*Reserves*
1952	979	1958	861
1953	823	1959	1,322
1954	738	1960	1,824
1955	769	1961	1,486
1956	941	1962	1,841
1957	524	1963	1,878

[21] In the compilation of these figures, assets are taken at their acquisition cost, and no allowance is made for later alteration of value. Some assets abroad have been recovered from the pre-surrender period, including not only real estate, such as the Japanese Embassy property in Washington, but also gold that had been held by the Supreme Commander for the Allied Powers. Net purchases of gold during the postwar years through 1962 are shown in the balance of payments as $190 million, but gold holdings at the end of 1962 were reported as $289 million. *International Financial Statistics* (IMF), September 1963, p. 167.

[22] Japan, Ministry of Finance, *Quarterly Bulletin of Financial Statistics,* various issues; for 1952–1955, *International Financial Statistics* (IMF); for 1963, Bank of Tokyo, *Weekly Review,* February 3, 1964.

The pattern is an interesting one. During the first seven post-Occupation years, reserves fluctuated at a level not much below that of 1952, except for a sharp drop in 1957 when the boom in Japanese production created a heavy drain on the balance of payments. From 1959 on the figures for reserves—much higher than before—reflect the strength and health of the Japanese economy. The accumulation is not as great as that of some European countries, and could hardly be regarded as excessive in view of the growing scale of Japanese international transactions and the rising level of Japan's demand liabilities and other short-term obligations to foreigners. Still, these figures suggest that Japan has achieved an international financial position compatible with the country's importance in world trade.

THE ROLE OF THE UNITED STATES

The United States looms large in Japan's balance of payments and has throughout the postwar period. For the period of the Occupation the United States dominated economic activities, domestic and foreign. The United States provided nearly two-thirds of Japan's imports but took less than a quarter of Japanese exports. The charge for ocean freight on imports was the main noncommodity item in Japan's payments to the rest of the world; much of the shipping was American, since imports came mostly from the United States and American vessels made up a large part of the world's merchant fleet. American aid was crucial to the balance of payments. During the 1950s the American share of Japan's foreign transactions declined, although remaining much larger than that of any other country. The fall was especially marked in commodity imports, as other sources of supply became available to Japan, but the United States continued to loom large in almost every item, especially in the capital account. Heavy American military expenditures kept Japanese–American bilateral transactions strongly favorable to Japan.

The Bank of Japan has provided detailed information on the bilateral transactions between Japan and the United States since the time of the Korean War. Table 3-8 summarizes the years 1952–1962; annual figures appear in Table A-4 in Appendix A.[23] As this table shows, Americans paid to Japanese more dollars than flowed from Japan to the United States during the eleven-year period, 1952–1962. The largest item of net

[23] These figures are even rougher approximations than most balance-of-payments figures, and it will be noted that some of them disagree with others in this volume. For instance, commodity exports to the United States at f.o.b. values are somewhat different in Table A-4 and Table 7-3. An additional complication in a bilateral account is that some of the transactions that seem to Japanese to be with residents of the United States may be carried out in behalf of residents of third countries, since American markets and the American dollar are recognized everywhere. The large error item in Table A-4, especially in 1959 and 1961, reflects some of these statistical problems.

TABLE 3-8. BALANCE OF PAYMENTS OF JAPAN WITH THE UNITED STATES: SUMMARY, 1952–1962

(In millions of dollars)

	Credit	*Debit*	*Balance*
Goods and services (ordinary)	**8,843**	**14,117**	**−5,274**
Merchandise trade, f.o.b.	6,731	10,968	−4,237
Services	2,112	3,149	−1,037
Transportation and insurance	830	1,398	−568
Travel	209	132	77
Investment income	332	494	−162
Private donations	341	17	324
Other	400	1,108	−708
Extraordinary items	**6,356**		**6,356**
U.S. economic aid to Japan	50		50
Procurement in Japan of U.S. economic aid goods and services for third countries	767		767
U.S. military expenditures in Japan [a]	5,539		5,539
Errors and omissions (net) [b]			**−574**
Capital movements (ordinary)	**3,010** [c]	**1,964** [d]	**1,046**
Private capital	1,113 [c]	233 [d]	880
Long-term	916 [c]	141 [d]	775
Short-term	197 [c]	92 [d]	105
Official and banking capital	1,897 [c]	1,731 [d]	166
Long-term	208 [c]	7 [d]	201
Short-term	1,689 [c]	1,724 [d]	−35
Monetary gold		**275**	**−275**
Multilateral settlements			**−1,279**

[a] Estimated by the Bank of Japan from figures showing total foreign military expenditures in Japan.
[b] Beginning in 1959, includes "regional adjustments."
[c] Net change in Japanese liabilities to residents of the United States.
[d] Net change in Japanese assets in the United States and claims on residents of the United States.

Source: Bank of Japan. See Appendix Table A-4 for detailed annual statistics.

flow, over $6 billion, came from extraordinary American outlays in Japan, mainly military expenditures and procurement of aid goods for third countries. Net capital flows from the United States to Japan added another billion dollars to the resources received by Japan from the United States. Even after adjustment for substantial errors and omissions these net credits amounted to $6,828 million. Of this sum, $4,237 million went to cover Japan's net commodity imports from the United States, another $1,037 million to cover the deficit in services. There still remained enough to permit Japan to buy from the United States $275 million of gold and to spend (or invest) $1,279 million in third countries.

The United States thus provided Japan all the dollars used in the United States and substantial additional sums used elsewhere. The totals cover not only Japanese purchases of goods, services, and gold but also increases in bank deposits. Most Japanese deposits abroad, including nearly all foreign exchange reserves, are in the United States. In Table 3-8, deposits are mixed with commercial credit under short-term official and banking capital. The slight excess of debits (increases in assets) over credits (increases in liabilities) shows that Japanese deposits in the United States (plus small extensions of credit by Japanese banks to American borrowers) grew a little faster than American short-term loans and credits to Japanese borrowers (plus small American deposits in Japan).

The figures in Table 3-8, despite statistical imperfections, should dispose conclusively of a misleading impression that because Japan buys more goods and services in the United States than it sells there it makes a net contribution to the international payments position of the United States. Instead, as this summary has shown, the United States has provided more dollars than Japan needed to finance its American purchases.

Fluctuations in the flow of bilateral payments have been marked, especially as they reflect Japan's cyclical booms and periods of financial restraint. In three years, 1954, 1957, and 1961, short-term official and banking capital showed reductions in Japanese claims on the United States, that is, reductions in Japan's foreign exchange reserves. In four of the twelve years shown in Table A-4, 1956, 1958, 1959, and 1960, multilateral settlements showed a net credit, that is, Japanese transactions with the United States produced deficits that were financed with dollars acquired from third countries. But the cumulative record for the period since the end of the Occupation is one that shows that the way the United States conducted itself and the policies it pursued have contributed in an important degree to Japan's international financial position.

FLUCTUATIONS IN THE BALANCE OF PAYMENTS

The great postwar improvement in the Japanese balance of payments has been marked by a series of fluctuations. Their character and the problems they have posed to the Japanese government are important to a full understanding of Japan's international economic position.

Foreign Exchange Movements Since 1950

The cyclical fluctuations are most easily visible in the statistics of Japan's receipts and payments of foreign exchange. (Charts 3–A and 3–B.) Although these figures have shortcomings as measures of the national balance-of-payments position,[24] they give the earliest indications of the rise and fall of balances abroad and of the nature and composition of receipts and payments of foreign currencies. It is on the foreign exchange statistics that the Japanese government relies for policy decisions. In times of crisis, it is the flow of foreign exchange that is crucial. The ability to make payments protects Japan's international financial standing; inability to provide foreign exchange would threaten it. Transactions not involving foreign exchange are not immediately pertinent. Whether credit on commercial bills is shortening or lengthening is important mainly as the foreign exchange position is affected. Loans and IMF drawings are sought primarily to improve the short-run foreign exchange position.

Chart 3-A shows total receipts and payments with the exception of short-term capital, for which data are inadequate.[25] The most striking feature of these movements is the contrast between a relatively steady and rapid rise in receipts and sharp swings in payments, resulting in alternating periods of surplus and deficit. The sharpest reductions in receipts, in 1952, 1958, and 1961, were small in comparison with the precipitous drops in payments in 1954 and 1957, which followed the impo-

[24] Although there are differences of coverage, valuation, and timing between the balance of payments and foreign exchange movements, the latter have tended to move fairly closely with the balance of payments, but generally at a somewhat lower level. In the current account, foreign exchange debits by years were lower than debits in the balance of payments for every year from 1952 through 1960; the gap widened in 1954 and 1955, narrowed again in 1957, and was wider again in the following three years. In merchandise debits, that is imports, the same relationship held generally, but the foreign exchange figures exceeded the balance-of-payments figures in 1953 and 1957. These relationships are shown and explained further in Appendix A. Balance-of-payments data in this section are taken from Appendix Table A-1; foreign exchange movements and reserves from Tables A-2 and A-3.

[25] Information on short-term capital is available only since April 1960 and only for net movements. These charts are essentially the same as those appearing in my report, *Japan in United States Foreign Economic Policy*, submitted to the Subcommittee on Foreign Economic Policy of the U.S. Joint Economic Committee, 87th Cong., 1st sess. (Washington: GPO, 1961), pp. 9 and 10.

sition of severe restrictions. It is clear that the task of Japanese policy has been to control a payments curve that shows a marked proclivity for rapid upward movement, but this task has been smaller than would have been the case if receipts had grown less rapidly and steadily. Japan's problem is thus very different from that of countries relying on exports of primary products which yield sharply different amounts of foreign exchange from one year to the next, amounts that for all too many poor countries rise distressingly little through the years.

Chart 3-B records the movements of the three major components of the totals, namely, goods, invisibles (meaning services, including special dollar receipts), and long-term capital. Merchandise trade is, of course, the most important. Fluctuations in the foreign exchange flows resulting from movements of goods were mainly responsible for the dramatic changes that occurred in Japan's foreign exchange position after 1950. The merchandise curves in Chart 3-B look remarkably like the curves for total movements in Chart 3-A, especially after 1956, when the surplus from invisibles, resulting mainly from special dollar income, was no longer large enough to hide merchandise deficits, as it tended to do in 1951–1954. Invisibles represented a declining share of total foreign exchange receipts as well as a declining surplus, which was very large in 1952 but disappeared in 1961. Long-term capital became significant only in recent years and is still the smallest of the three components.

Four Cycles in the Balance of Payments

Moving from foreign exchange figures to balance-of-payments data helps us distinguish four periods covering sharp changes in the postwar Japanese balance of payments. (Table 3-9.) After the initial period of grave shortages, severe controls, and large-scale American aid, ending at about the time of the outbreak of the war in Korea, the fluctuations have been of a cyclical character. Each cycle began when economic activity was expanding rapidly, domestically and in foreign transactions, then proceeded through successive phases of foreign exchange surplus, relaxed restrictions, renewed deficit, and finally imposition of new restrictions to remove the deficit by cutting foreign payments. The scale of activities grew from one period to the next, and the structure of the balance of payments changed significantly.

1945–1950. In the initial period, which covers all but the last 16 months of the Occupation, Japan's international economic relations were, as we have seen, dominated by Occupation controls and U.S. aid, which exceeded total exports and was large enough to pay for 70 per cent of total imports. These, in turn, were kept down to a level at which it was possible to accumulate a significant amount of foreign exchange. (Part of this consisted of clearing balances and other inconvertible as-

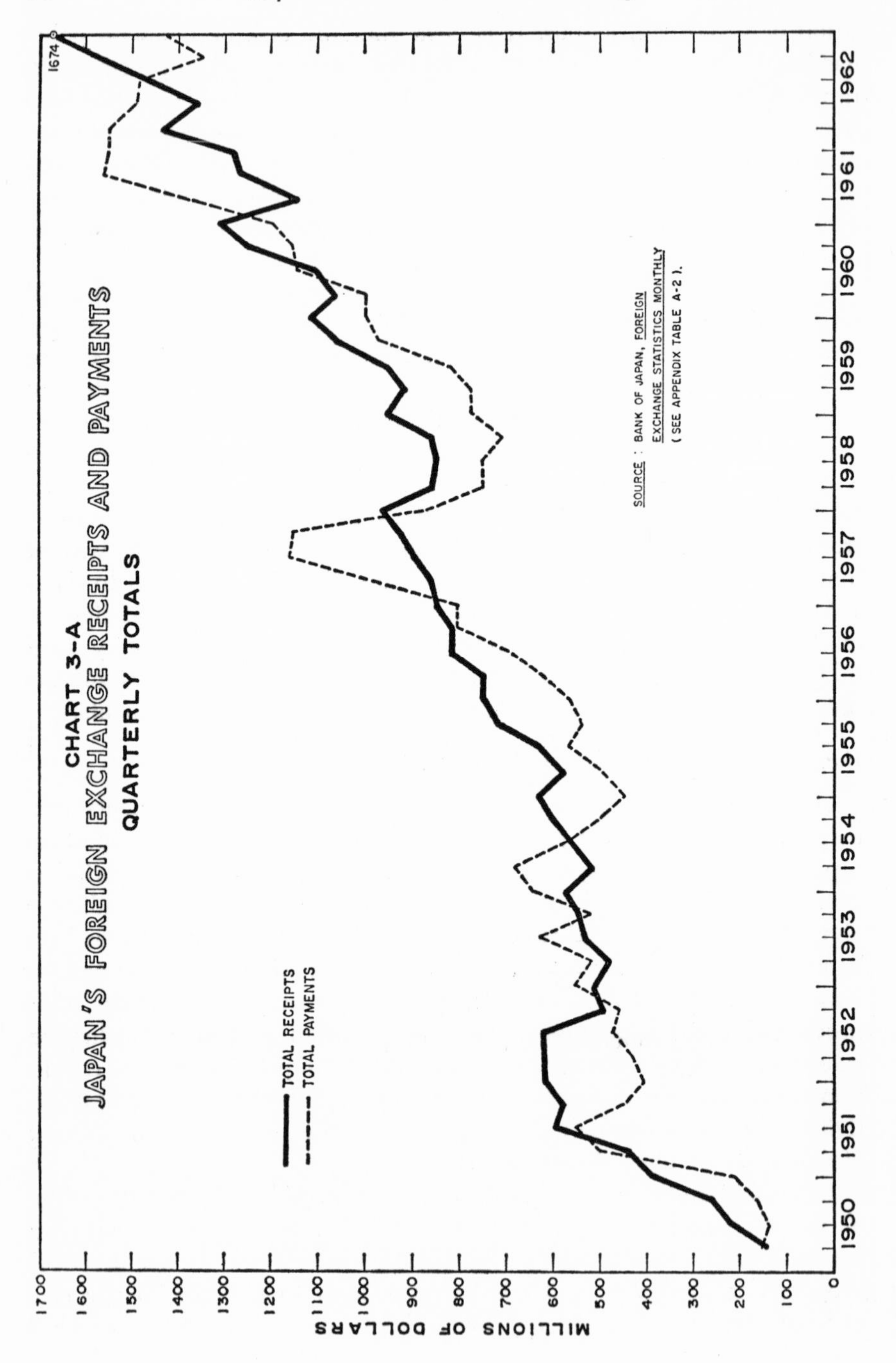
CHART 3-A
JAPAN'S FOREIGN EXCHANGE RECEIPTS AND PAYMENTS
QUARTERLY TOTALS
TOTAL RECEIPTS
TOTAL PAYMENTS
SOURCE: BANK OF JAPAN, FOREIGN EXCHANGE STATISTICS MONTHLY
(SEE APPENDIX TABLE A-2).
MILLIONS OF DOLLARS
1674
1700
1600
1500
1400
1300
1200
1100
1000
900
800
700
600
500
400
300
200
100
0
1950
1951
1952
1953
1954
1955
1956
1957
1958
1959
1960
1961
1962

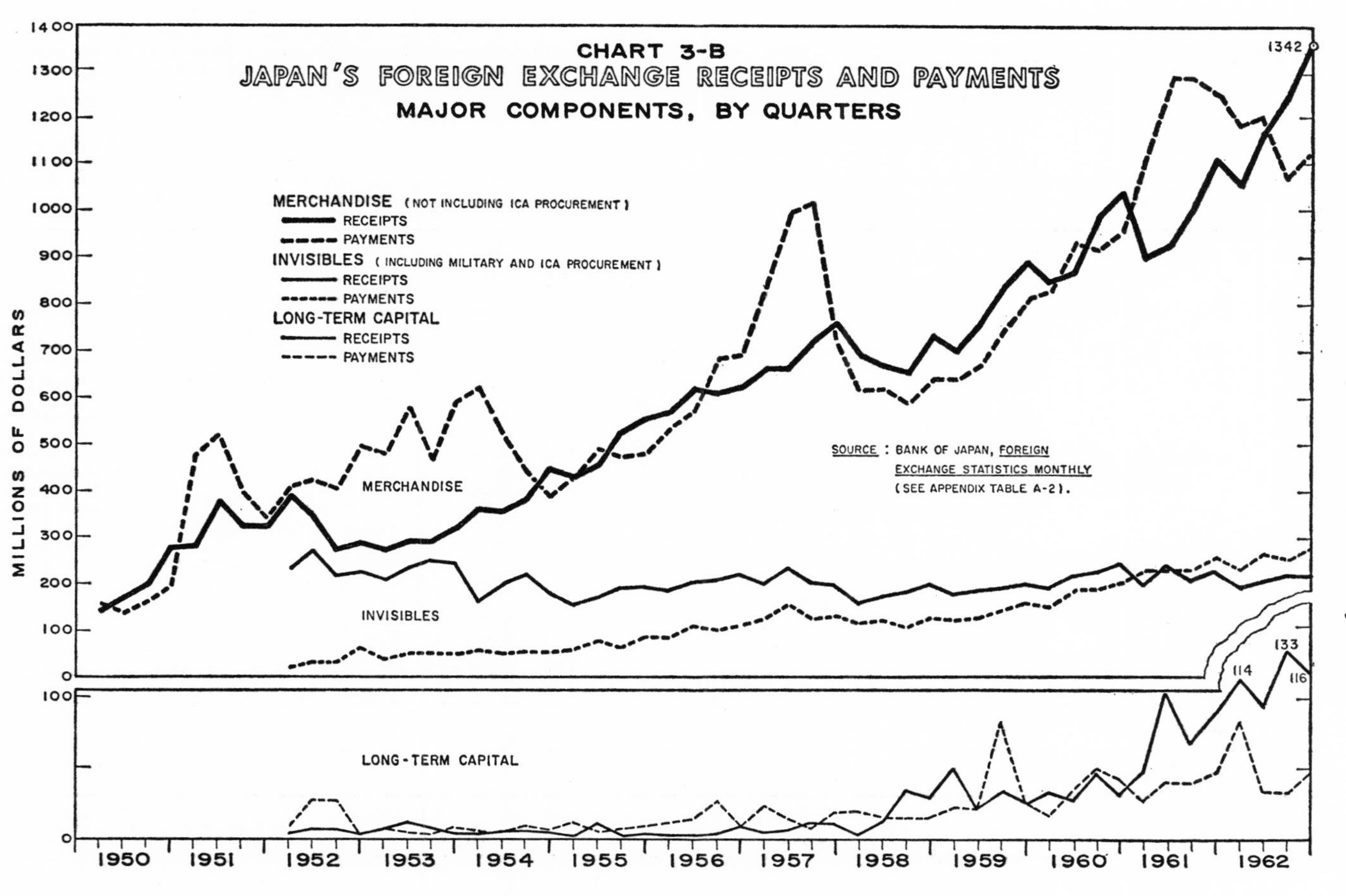
CHART 3-B
JAPAN'S FOREIGN EXCHANGE RECEIPTS AND PAYMENTS
MAJOR COMPONENTS, BY QUARTERS
MERCHANDISE (NOT INCLUDING ICA PROCUREMENT)
RECEIPTS
PAYMENTS
INVISIBLES (INCLUDING MILITARY AND ICA PROCUREMENT)
RECEIPTS
PAYMENTS
LONG-TERM CAPITAL
RECEIPTS
PAYMENTS
SOURCE: BANK OF JAPAN, FOREIGN EXCHANGE STATISTICS MONTHLY
(SEE APPENDIX TABLE A-2).
MERCHANDISE
INVISIBLES
LONG-TERM CAPITAL
MILLIONS OF DOLLARS
1342
133
116
114
1400
1300
1200
1100
1000
900
800
700
600
500
400
300
200
100
0
100
0
1950
1951
1952
1953
1954
1955
1956
1957
1958
1959
1960
1961
1962

TABLE 3-9. JAPAN'S BALANCE OF INTERNATIONAL PAYMENTS: ANNUAL AVERAGES FOR FOUR POSTWAR PERIODS
(In millions of dollars)

	1945–1950			*1951–1954*			*1955–1957*			*1958–1962*		
	Credit	*Debit*	*Balance*	*Credit*	*Debit*	*Balance*	*Credit*	*Debit*	*Balance*	*Credit*	*Debit*	*Balance*
Goods and services (ordinary)	**380**	**643**	**−264**	**1,551**	**2,221**	**−670**	**2,798**	**3,398**	**−599**	**4,458**	**4,798**	**−340**
Merchandise trade	350	531	−181	1,378	1,859	−481	2,447	2,643	−196	3,855	3,686	169
Services	30	112	−82	173	362	−189	351	754	−403	603	1,112	−509
Transportation and insurance	6	105	−99	75	263	−187	212	543	−331	352	669	−317
Travel	5	—	5	10	6	4	18	12	6	38	36	2
Investment income	—	2	−2	7	25	−18	25	68	−43	72	121	−49
Government transactions, n.i.e.	—	—	—	6	7	−1	27	17	9	17	32	−15
Miscellaneous services	19	5	14	75	62	14	69	114	−45	124	253	−129
Extraordinary items	**408**	**3**	**404**	**745**	**—**	**745**	**496**	**40**	**456**	**395**	**107**	**288**
U.S. economic aid	366		366	40		40	12		12	2		2
U.S. military expenditures [a]	41		41	704		704	484		484	393		393
Reparations		3	−3		—	—		40	−40		107 [b]	−107
Errors and omissions (net)			**1**			**7**			**−28**			**37**
Capital and gold movements (ordinary)	**3 [c]**	**144 [d]**	**−141**	**164 [c]**	**245 [d]**	**−82**	**216 [c]**	**46 [d]**	**171**	**599 [c]**	**584 [d]**	**15**
Private capital	1 [c]	—	1	30 [c]	13 [d]	17	91 [c]	42 [d]	49	191 [c]	173 [d]	18
Long-term	1 [c]	—	1	22 [c]	1 [d]	21	24 [c]	54 [d]	−30	181 [c]	173 [d]	8
Short-term	—	—	—	8 [c]	12 [d]	−4	68 [c]	−12 [d]	80	10 [c]	—	10
Official and banking capital	2 [c]	142 [d]	−140	131 [c]	230 [d]	−99	125 [c]	3 [d]	122	408 [c]	375 [d]	33
Long-term	1 [c]	—	1	−3 [c]	77 [d]	−80	35 [c]	1 [d]	34	61 [c]	72 [d]	−11
Short-term	2 [c]	142 [d]	−140	134 [c]	153 [d]	−19	90 [c]	2 [d]	88	347 [c]	303 [d]	43
Monetary gold	—	2	−2	3	2	1	—	1	−1	—	35	−35

[a] Includes small amounts spent in Japan by third countries, mostly during the Korean War by units and personnel of the United Nations Command.
[b] The total for the five years of $533.9 million includes $177 million granted to Indonesia by cancellation of commercial debt at the time of the reparations settlement.
[c] Net change in Japanese liabilities abroad.
[d] Net change in Japanese assets abroad.

Notes: A dash (—) indicates that a figure is zero or less than $500,000.
Minor inconsistencies result from rounding.

Sources: 1945–1960—International Monetary Fund, *Balance of Payments Yearbook.*
1961–1962—Bank of Japan, *Balance of Payments of Japan,* 1961, 1962.
(See Appendix Table A-1 for detailed annual statistics.)

sets.) Japan acquired only very small foreign liabilities because foreigners were not willing to lend or invest much in Japan under the conditions of the late 1940s.

1951–1954. The Korean War came at a time when U.S. aid to Japan was decreasing. The war provided a much better source of income and made it possible to terminate aid almost completely in 1951. Military orders and a rapid increase in export demand put Japan in the midst of its first postwar boom. This soon brought rising domestic demand which, combined with export and military demand, pressed hard against limited productive capacity. The results included rising prices and after 1951 a halt in export growth. Merchandise imports doubled between 1950 and 1951, stood still for a year, and then rose again in 1953. Exports stood still from 1951 to 1953.

Imports of services, too, doubled between 1950 and 1951; exports rose less strongly and then declined again. In 1953 payments for services were more than twice receipts. Foreign exchange reserves declined as the war boom's legacy of commodity deficits exceeded the special dollar income that had also started with the war in Korea. The gathering crisis was capped by a crop failure in 1953, the last such disaster to occur during the years covered in this study.

The Japanese government, which obtained full command of its affairs only in April 1952, finally took measures late in 1953 to correct the exchange deficit. These included severe restrictions on credit and on government expenditures. While both consumption and fixed investment continued to rise, the rate was slowed, and inventory investment declined. The rising flow of imports was checked early in 1954, and by mid-year the foreign exchange deficit turned to surplus.[26] Since the shortage of foreign exchange was mainly in sterling, Japan made a drawing in sterling from the International Monetary Fund and obtained additional sterling from London banks in dollar swap transactions.[27]

The austerity policy was an outstanding success. With domestic demand greatly reduced, Japanese producers began to look more vigorously for sales abroad. Lower costs permitted them to reduce prices and they found that they could compete in foreign markets with a growing number of products.[28] Exports began to rise again in 1954, while imports were

[26] In foreign exchange terms, imports of goods declined from a total of $2,101 million in 1953 to $1,962 million in 1954. (Appendix Table A-2.) But customs and balance-of-payments figures showed very slight import declines. (Table 5-1 and Appendix Table A-1.)

[27] Japan obtained $124 million in sterling from IMF but no more than $62.4 million of this was outstanding at any one time; the balance was repaid in 1955. P. R. Narvekar, "The 1954–55 Improvement in Japan's Balance of Payments," *Staff Papers* (IMF), November 1957, p. 143.

[28] Same, pp. 168–169; Hugh T. Patrick, "Monetary Policy in Japan's Economic Growth, 1945–1959," *Far Eastern Survey,* May 1959, pp. 68–69.

held in check. The improvement in the balance of payments was such that the year 1954 showed only a small deficit.[29]

1955–1957. The expansion under way at the start of the third cycle became by 1956 an unprecedented boom of such proportions that the Japanese nicknamed it *Jimmu Keiki,* the greatest prosperity since the nation's mythical founding by the Emperor Jimmu twenty-six centuries ago. The Suez crisis of the summer and autumn of 1956 gave added impetus. Japanese producers, who were already operating at capacity in many lines, expected serious shortages of shipping, raw materials, and, especially in South and Southeast Asia, of manufactured goods that Japan could supply. Producers increased their purchases of foreign goods, undeterred by inflated world prices and rising transportation costs. Traders brought in raw materials on speculation and chartered foreign vessels at peak rates. Instead of taking restrictive measures to control the "overheated" economy, the Japanese government for a number of months encouraged further expansion.

These events proved very costly. Income from military expenditures and ICA procurement fell behind outpayments for merchandise imports. By the spring of 1957 the loss of foreign exchange reserves reached emergency proportions. A debate over the cause and cure of the deficit was one of a number of factors that kept the government from acting.[30] Some preliminary steps showed no results, and at last in May 1957 the government adopted stern countermeasures. Credit was restricted, both by increasing its cost and also by rationing its volume. Government expenditures were abruptly curtailed. Imports were cut by administrative action, supplementing fiscal and monetary measures.[31] Again the government turned to the International Monetary Fund. In June 1957 a new drawing of $125 million, half of Japan's quota, was arranged.[32] This was only six months after Japan's gold and foreign exchange holdings had reached a record level.

As before, a sharp improvement came quickly. Foreign exchange deficits reached a peak in June, then declined for three months, after which followed a new period of surplus. Still, the year's deficit on current ac-

[29] It is because of this deficit that the year is grouped in Table 3-9 with those preceding instead of being put into the new period. If balance-of-payments figures were on a quarterly basis, at least part of 1954 would belong with the boom years that followed.

[30] One view was that the principal cause was speculative import of raw materials and that the proper policy was to let it run its course. The opposing view was that the basic cause was "overheating" of the economy from too rapid growth, the proper policy being disinflation, to check the rate of economic growth and strengthen foreign trade. Patrick, cited, pp. 69–70.

[31] Patrick, cited, p. 70; P. R. Narvekar, "The Cycle in Japan's Balance of Payments, 1955–58," *Staff Papers* (IMF), December 1961, pp. 392–400.

[32] *International Financial News Survey* (IMF), July 5, 1957, p. 1.

count in the balance of payments came to a record $615 million, three times that of 1953. The strength of the reversal could be measured in 1958 when recorded net receipts of foreign exchange (omitting short-term capital) reached the highest level of the whole postwar period, $511 million, a phenomenal improvement over the 1957 deficit of $533 million.

The crisis of 1957 is reflected variously in the balance of payments. For one thing the 1955–1957 period is the only one among the four shown in Table 3-9 during which Japan's net foreign assets shrank sharply. The trade balance improved and, in spite of a large increase in payments for services, the deficit for goods and services combined was actually somewhat lower than in the 1951–1954 period. But U.S. military expenditures had declined and there was a net deficit.

The restrictive measures of 1957, like those of 1953, consisted mainly of counterinflationary moves. Most reliance was put on credit controls, with fiscal adjustments carrying less burden. Exchange and import controls were used, but mainly to reinforce domestic monetary and fiscal measures. Credit control has been a particularly powerful weapon in postwar Japan, because bank credit has provided an unusually large proportion of the resources available to businessmen, and the banks have been "overloaned" to such an extent as to be heavily dependent on central bank credit. The Bank of Japan thus has had tremendous power, but its means are different from those of central banks in the industrial countries of the West. Open-market operations are hardly possible because there are very few government securities outstanding. Changes in reserve requirements were impractical in 1957, when laws calling for compulsory reserve requirements were just being enacted. Interest charges are a weapon, but the increases enforced by the Bank of Japan in 1957, from 7.3 per cent to 7.67 per cent in March and to 8.4 per cent in May, were important more as signals of official attitude than as effective controls in themselves. What had the greatest impact on the economy was the rationing of credit by the Bank of Japan through a severe form of what Americans call "moral suasion" or "window guidance," and Japanese call *madoguchishido*.[33] More formal and official sanctions were not necessary once the officials concerned made clear their determination to restrict credit. This is a typically Japanese way of meeting a problem. Finance Minister Takahashi had used it to a considerable extent in 1932–1935; in more recent years, the government has relied on persuasion to get cotton textile producers to control exports to the United States.

1958–1962. The three years following 1957 saw such prosperity in Japan that the wags who had named the earlier boom after the mythical

[33] Patrick, cited, pp. 65–68.

first emperor were hard put to it to find a nickname for the even better times in which Japan suddenly and unexpectedly found itself. A few tried the appellations *Iwato Keiki* or *Amaterasu Keiki,* after the sun-goddess from whom the first emperor supposedly sprang, but the tags did not stick. Perhaps it is just as well. Perhaps the failure to pin a label from the past is symptomatic of this period, when Japanese thoughts were concentrated mainly on the present and future.

The unprecedented boom showed both in the scale of international transactions and in their favorable trend. Commodity exports in the years 1958–1962 averaged more than ten times their annual level in 1945–1950. For the first time they exceeded imports (in f.o.b. terms) and contributed to covering the services deficit. During the first two of these years the export surplus on goods exceeded the services deficit and permitted the net income from extraordinary items to be used to increase Japan's net foreign assets. For the period as a whole, however, the net contribution of extraordinary items was much lower than before, not only because U.S. military expenditures were smaller but also because of the substantial outflow of reparations, including cancellation of Indonesia's trade debt in 1958.

Through most of 1960, prosperity seemed remarkably stable. Despite extremely rapid growth in gross national product—in real terms amounting to 19 per cent in 1959, 13 per cent in 1960, and 16 per cent in 1961—wholesale prices rose very little; the index for 1961 and 1962 was below that for 1956. The Tokyo consumer price index, however, rose in every year after 1955.[34] Labor grew scarcer than ever before, the rise in real wages gained speed, and some firms, especially small, marginal ones, found difficulty in getting new workers.

The balance-of-payments surplus dropped from $418 million in 1959 to $176 million in 1960. Current transactions were in deficit from the beginning of 1961, but heavy capital imports kept the foreign exchange balance from becoming negative until May 1961. In addition to continued long-term borrowing from the World Bank and other lenders, Japan received a large volume of new short-term capital, especially Euro-dollars, and other deposits attracted by Japan's high interest rates. The introduction in July 1960 of "free-yen accounts" permitting easy withdrawal of foreign funds helped. This step, representing a form of limited nonresident convertibility, was part of the process of liberalizing Japanese trade and payments.

From April 1960 through July 1961 there was a net inflow of $953 million, including not only deposits but "usance credits" and other

[34] Less than 1 per cent in 1956, in 1958, and in 1959, but 3 per cent in 1957, 4 per cent in 1960, 5 per cent in 1961, and 6.7 per cent in 1962. Bank of Japan, *Economic Statistics Monthly,* June 1963, p. 3.

short-term capital. The substantial part of this total in demand deposits, and so subject to rapid withdrawal, gave the Japanese authorities some concern especially after monthly deficits in the short-term capital account set in in August 1961. Japan's foreign exchange reserves reached an all-time high of $2,035 million at the end of April 1961. Then monthly deficits began which in August amounted to over a hundred million dollars net. The first part of September gave no signs of improvement, and late in that month the Cabinet acted.

As before, the delayed corrective measures were mainly monetary; the Bank of Japan took several steps to check the expansion of credit. Fiscal policy was given a supporting role. But this time, because of liberalization, less could be done than before to supplement monetary measures by direct limitations on imports and other expenditures abroad. Steps were also taken to strengthen Japan's ability to meet possible withdrawals from the free-yen accounts. Funds were borrowed in New York and a stand-by arrangement negotiated with the International Monetary Fund.[35]

When the balance of payments for 1961 was compiled, it showed a deficit half again as large as that of 1957. Japan's net claims on the world declined by $963 million, as compared with the 1957 decline of $615 million. The merchandise deficit of $559 million and the services deficit of $728 million were counteracted by only $304 million of net income from extraordinary items (and $19 million of errors and omissions). In official and banking capital, liabilities to foreigners rose by $898 million, assets abroad declined by $111 million. The resulting net deterioration of Japan's position by just over a billion dollars was counteracted slightly by an increase of $26 million in Japan's gold holdings and by $20 million of net increase in private Japanese assets abroad.

By year-end the tide turned in foreign exchange terms. Reserves rose and by summer Japan was exporting more than it was importing. Taking 1962 as a whole one finds the largest postwar surplus in merchandise trade but also the largest postwar deficit in services. In the capital account liabilities to foreigners rose much less during the year than in

[35] In November 1961 the Bank of Japan, as agent of the Ministry of Finance, arranged to borrow $200 million for one year from three commercial banks in the United States, the first such borrowing in the postwar period. Bank of Tokyo, *Weekly Review*, November 13, 1961, pp. 315–316; *International Financial News Survey* (IMF), December 8, 1961, p. 387. The one-year stand-by arrangement with the International Monetary Fund made in January 1962 permitted Japan to draw up to $305 million. Same, January 26, 1962, p. 21. In February seven American commercial banks lent $125 million for one year, with a guarantee by the Export–Import Bank. Formally a commercial credit to cover Japanese purchases of U.S. agricultural commodities, this loan, too, was a means of bolstering Japan's foreign exchange reserves. Export–Import Bank of Washington, *Eximbank Reports*, February 1962, p. 15.

1961 and assets abroad increased much more. By December 1962 foreign exchange reserves were 25 per cent higher than their low point a year before and nearly equal to the high levels of early 1961.

Lessons of the Crises

The three cycles since the end of the Occupation have some common characteristics closely related to Japan's international economic position. In each case the cyclical crisis was precipitated by weakness in the balance of payments, not by the action of domestic forces. Booming business sharply raised imports, with resulting net outflows of foreign exchange that led to severe countermeasures.

The Japanese economy "overheats" and imports spurt partly because the natural resource base is narrow and partly because bottlenecks appear at the peak of the business cycle. Imports provide the easiest source of additional supply. Substitution and transfer of resources within the economy are less possible than in the United States and other countries with larger, more diversified economies, less dependent on imported resources. Japan's problem has been that its balance of payments could not stand the pace of the country's phenomenal economic growth.

A second lesson of the crises is that there is no doubt that the Japanese authorities have the power and skill to check cyclical drains on foreign exchange reserves. The countermeasures promptly showed impressive results in each of the crises. This is significant evidence that Japan's dependence on international trade does not leave it a helpless orphan among nations; instead it supports the evidence of the record of growth that Japan is a modern industrial society with remarkable capacity to adjust to circumstances.

The principal instrument for checking foreign exchange loss in the crises has been credit policy. In the 1950s, with the unsatisfied demand for imports far greater than it is now, direct import and exchange controls were a powerful supplement to credit restraints. Fiscal policy has also been used and may in the future become more important than in the past. External assistance has helped to assure all concerned that Japan would not run out of foreign exchange. Three times the International Monetary Fund played a key role. Twice the help was in the form of actual drawings, which were repaid promptly. On the third occasion it was only a stand-by arrangement; no drawing was made, and the credit was allowed to lapse at its end in February 1963. Instead of using IMF funds, Japan drew on unprecedentedly large credits obtained from commercial banks in the United States—a further evidence of new economic strength.

The price of Japan's success in checking the drain on foreign exchange reserves has been the slowing down of business activity and growth.

TABLE 3-10. JAPAN'S GROSS NATIONAL PRODUCT AND MAJOR COMPONENTS, 1953–1958

(In billions of yen at 1954 prices)

	1953	*1954*	*1955*	*1956*	*1957*	*1958*
1. Gross national product	**7,171**	**7,379**	**8,190**	**8,696**	**9,328**	**9,576**
2. Consumption	**5,321**	**5,594**	**5,941**	**6,301**	**6,642**	**7,114**
Private	4,496	4,668	4,997	5,386	5,688	6,007
Government	825	926	944	915	954	1,107
3. Fixed investment	**1,492**	**1,508**	**1,509**	**1,830**	**2,224**	**2,470**
Private	913	930	888	1,231	1,568	1,696
Government	579	578	621	599	656	774
4. Investment in inventories	**455**	**307**	**666**	**606**	**656**	**−172** [a]
Private	437	314	509	490	769	−172
Government	18	−7	157	116	−113	—
5. Domestic absorption (2 + 3 + 4)	**7,267**	**7,408**	**8,116**	**8,737**	**9,522**	**9,412**
6. External balance (1 minus 5)	**−96**	**−29**	**74**	**−41**	**−194**	**164**

[a] All government investment in 1958 is shown as fixed.

Source: P. R. Narvekar, "The Cycle in Japan's Balance of Payments, 1955–58," *Staff Papers* (IMF), December 1961, p. 405.

Business failures have risen each time restraints have been applied. Stock market prices have dropped, more sharply in 1957 and 1961 than in 1953. General prices have declined somewhat.[36] In each case over-all economic growth was retarded but not stopped or reversed by the steps taken to bring foreign exchange outgo within income.

A more detailed account of the effects on the Japanese economy of the restrictive measures taken in 1953 and 1957 can be derived from Table 3-10. The adjustments were greatest in inventories, less in fixed investment, and virtually nil in private consumption. Total consumption rose steadily and rapidly between 1953 and 1958, despite some unevenness in the government's share. Total fixed investment also rose every year, but in 1954 the increase was small and in 1955 insignificant. Private fixed investment nearly doubled between the low point of 1955 and 1958. Inventory investments fluctuated sharply, with government and private inventory expenditures sometimes moving in opposite directions. The marked drop in inventory accumulation in 1954 was an important factor in that year's adjustment. The speculative boom of 1957 shows in the peak figure for private inventory investment that year. The decline in 1958 was the sharpest in any item shown in the table. The change of 941 billion yen between 1957 and 1958 equaled a tenth

[36] Bank of Japan, *Economic Statistics of Japan,* various issues; *The Oriental Economist,* various issues.

of the gross national product in 1957 and was large enough to cause the only decline in total domestic absorption (consumption plus investment) during the period. The external balance, which is the difference between gross national product and domestic absorption, was positive only in 1955 and 1958; in the other years shown, it was negative, indicating net contributions from abroad to the total of Japanese consumption and investment.[37]

THE FUTURE

Will Japan continue to be able to pay its way in the world economy? Must we expect an indefinite continuation of periodic crises like those that have been occurring at four-year intervals? These questions can be answered only in part, but what can be said is most favorable.

Japan has been paying its way since the outbreak of the Korean War, and there is no reason to expect that its capacity to do so will decline. But to continue the rapid increase in foreign earnings Japan must find markets. Much of the rest of this book is concerned with the problems Japan faces in earning and spending the foreign income it requires to provide for the consumption and investment needs of its people.

Cyclical deficits or crises in the balance of payments are unlikely to disappear in the future, but it does not seem necessary for them to be as severe as those of 1957 and 1961. In a private enterprise economy consumption and investment will fluctuate, and the methods so far devised for maintaining or regaining balance, either domestically or internationally, do not make adjustments fine enough to eliminate substantial swings between surplus and deficit. Economic and financial management in Japan is already of a high order, and this is an important factor in the successes that have been achieved. But there is room for improvement, especially in timing. Earlier action in 1957 could have checked speculative inventory buying, thus reducing the size of the foreign exchange deficit and the severity of the restrictive measures necessary to remove it. Again in 1961 the Japanese authorities waited longer than, in retrospect, seems desirable. In 1957 the delay stemmed from disagreement on the nature of the problem; in 1961 it was generally agreed that there was only limited inventory building but strong demand for consumption and fixed investment, but the Ikeda government delayed taking corrective measures because it was reluctant to check the rate of economic growth. Both factors may influence action in future crises as well,

[37] The direction of movement in the net foreign balance was the same as that indicated by the balance of payments, but the balance of payments shows a much larger net flow into Japan during the six years ($413 million compared with $122 million). The differences of coverage, concepts, and definition that explain this discrepancy are set out in the study from which Table 3-10 was taken.

but there is at least some ground for believing that the experience of the past decade will encourage the view that timeliness confers important advantages in dealing with this kind of problem. Japan has already been able to call on outside financial resources to help meet crises; a good record will keep this kind of aid available and moderate the impact of restrictions on Japanese growth.

Japan's balance of payments remains vulnerable, but there is no longer valid reason for the "poor Japan" view widely held a decade or so ago. At that time many observers, both Japanese and foreign, felt strong doubt that Japan could possibly earn enough abroad to cover a reasonable level of foreign expenditures. In fact, foreign income has been large enough to permit economic growth so rapid and vigorous that an American economist, who recently returned from his first visit, found the feeling of growth so pervasive that "you feel that if you don't watch out the place will run you down." To maintain continued rapid expansion in income from abroad is a leading aim of Japanese policy. But even if growth should be slower than the Japanese hope, the nation has the capacity to live within its external means.

Chapter 4

Capital and Technology

Foreign technology has made indispensable qualitative contributions to Japan's economy throughout the past century. Without products and productive processes that originated abroad, along with foreign scientific and managerial ideas, it is doubtful that Japan could support today's 96 million people. Most Japanese exports and a large proportion of the domestic products consumed in Japan are manufactured goods whose very nature, as well as the methods by which they are produced, rests on technical and cultural imports from other countries.

Foreign capital has been less vital, but nevertheless important, and can be measured by statistics more satisfactory than those for technology. Capital imports have enabled Japan to finance a significant volume of foreign expenditures and investments that could not have been made otherwise.

In Japan's balance of payments, foreign capital and technology are both important. The service deficit noted in the preceding chapter is to a significant degree the result of the growing payments of interest on foreign loans, dividends on foreign investments, and royalties and fees for the use of foreign technology. Though much smaller, Japanese investments abroad and the export of technology are also coming to be an appreciable element in Japan's international economic position and the growth of its foreign trade.

HIGHLIGHTS OF THE RECORD TO 1945

Little foreign capital went into Japan until nearly the end of the nineteenth century. To the normal difficulties any new country would have in attracting funds from abroad, Japan added acute suspicion of foreign loans and investments. By the end of the century the Japanese felt they had reached a point that permitted them to borrow abroad on terms that did not challenge their sovereignty and independence. The quick military victory over China in 1895 was achieved without foreign financial assistance, but heavy foreign borrowing through the flotation of bonds in the London market was undertaken in 1904–1905 to assist in financing the war against Russia.

Japan has paid its foreign debts scrupulously. The only default was a temporary suspension of payments during World War II.[1] Under Article 18 of the San Francisco Peace Treaty Japan recognizes the validity of prewar financial obligations, both private and public, to foreign owners or creditors. Japan has carried out its obligations under this provision and made settlement with nearly all holders of prewar bonds.[2]

Equity investment by foreigners in Japan has always been small. What there was in the early Meiji period went into trade, finance, and shipping; foreigners, especially the British, handled more than half of Japan's foreign trade until 1900 but have had a subordinate role since World War I. Foreign capital has never been very important in Japanese manufacturing. The Meiji government, concerned about national power, set up state enterprises and also gave financial support to private Japanese firms in a number of fields. After the military victory over Russia in 1905, there was little danger of foreigners gaining undue power in the country, but the Japanese continued to keep alien businessmen at arm's length.

Japan lagged behind older industrial countries in the development of new technical processes and, as a result, most of its technology has come from abroad. Japanese were early sent abroad to study and bring

[1] In the case of a disputed issue of 1912 in French francs, bondholders did not receive payment for a long period, but the issuer, the City of Tokyo, continued to make payments to the fiscal agent in Japan. A settlement agreement, signed November 5, 1960, was approved by the Tokyo Metropolitan Assembly on December 20, 1960, and by the Court of Appeal in Paris on January 18, 1963. On October 16, 1961, the City of Tokyo offered to purchase from the bondholders its outstanding French franc bonds in accordance with the payment terms of the agreement of November 5, 1960. As of November 30, 1962, approximately 91 per cent of the outstanding bonds had thus been purchased. *Prospectus,* dated January 30, 1963, contained in Registration Statement of the Japan Development Bank, U.S. Securities and Exchange Commission file no. 2-21009, covering $22,500,000 Guaranteed External Loan Bonds, dated February 1, 1963; p. 54.

[2] The offer to holders of all Japanese dollar bonds, municipal and corporate as well as government, was made on November 24, 1952, providing for full service on all bonds, but with each maturity extended by ten years. In addition to interest payments during such extended life, back interest was to be paid for the period December 22, 1942 through September 25, 1952, each payment to be made ten years after the date originally specified. "Arrears Coupon Strips" covering back interest were to be issued to each stockholder but are detachable from the bonds and are quoted separately in the market. By September 30, 1962, holders of 99 per cent of all outstanding dollar bonds had accepted this offer. Offers to holders of sterling and franc bonds, generally similar but extending some sterling maturities by fifteen years, were made on November 24, 1952 and February 28, 1957, respectively; acceptances at the end of September 1962 covered 99 per cent of all sterling bonds and 91 per cent of all franc bonds outstanding. *Prospectus,* dated January 30, 1963, cited, pp. 54, 55, and 65.

back both ideas and machines that would advance Japan's purposes. Foreign products and processes were imported and Western technicians employed, but almost always under Japanese control. Most of the industrially creative steps taken by Japan have involved the adaptation of this foreign technology to Japanese circumstances and, in some cases, the refinement of processes or equipment obtained from abroad. In the future more basic innovations may originate in Japan, as did the tunnel diode, an electronic device. Japan's technological lead in many fields over her Asian neighbors may well result in an expansion of Japan's presently small exports of technology.

Prewar export of Japanese capital reached impressive levels, as we saw in the preceding chapter. Despite limited capital resources Japan made major investments in neighboring areas, especially when they were under Japanese military and political control. Much smaller sums went to other areas. In several parts of the world, notably in the Philippines and several countries of Latin America, Japanese emigrants made significant contributions to local production, mainly in agriculture and some mining activities. In Davao in the Philippines, for instance, Japanese settlers developed abaca production to a high level before 1941. Aside from what went with investments and emigrants, little Japanese technology was exported before World War II.

FOREIGN CAPITAL AND TECHNOLOGY IN POSTWAR JAPAN

Japan's economic performance since 1945 would have been vastly different without foreign capital and foreign technology. Until 1950 American aid dominated the scene, but since then a series of less dramatic flows have contributed a great deal. These involve, in addition to imports of machinery and publications, many foreign patents, some foreign personnel, some equity investments, substantial commercial bank credit, and a good deal of public borrowing.

The inflow of capital to Japan, as measured by the cumulation of Japanese liabilities to foreigners, totaled $4.3 billion from 1945 through 1962.[3] The flow was extremely slow at first, consisting of little besides a U.S. cotton credit granted during the first postwar year and liquidated in the succeeding years. By the end of 1950 the cumulation of Japanese

[3] This figure is from the balance of payments, as summarized in Table 3-3. Although the balance of payments is the most complete record of capital movements available, the figure must be used with care. It does not include the $2.2 billion of U.S. aid or the relatively small amounts of private American donations and remittances to Japan. Nor is the $4.3 billion figure a measure of Japan's total liabilities to foreigners at the end of 1962, since it does not include prewar debts, reparations, or the GARIOA repayment, all of which are shown for September 30, 1962 in Table 4-1.

liabilities abroad was only $14 million. But then a significant inflow began and the cumulation reached $670 million by the end of 1954, $1,319 million by the end of 1957, $2,394 million by the end of 1960, and $4,313 million by the end of 1962. (Tables 3-3 and 3-4.)

Most of these liabilities have been short-term commercial ("usance") credits related to the flow of imports into Japan. Since the middle of 1960 Japan has also received deposits from abroad, attracted by high interest rates and the ready convertibility of free-yen accounts. Altogether, about two-thirds of Japan's outstanding obligations at the end of 1962 were short term, that is, of less than a year's duration. Such capital depends on import levels, on Japan's credit rating with foreigners, and on Japanese policy restrictions. It is to be expected that all three factors will contribute to future progressive expansion of the volume of these kinds of foreign short-term capital in Japan.

After the end of 1960 the cyclical crisis in Japan's balance of payments brought another kind of short-term capital import: bank borrowing to bolster Japan's foreign exchange reserves (pp. 63, 64). According to reports, the $200 million bank loan of November 1961 was secured by pledge of Japanese foreign exchange reserves. This transaction did not increase Japan's net assets abroad, but it did provide funds that could be spent without disturbing reserves on time deposit in the United States. In February 1962, seven U.S. banks provided $125 million to finance imports of agricultural products, secured not by Japanese pledge of specific assets but by a guarantee from the Export–Import Bank of Washington; this was an unusual form of credit, although not unprecedented, since a somewhat similar borrowing had been arranged in July 1957.[4]

Public Loans and Grants to Japan

The government has been the largest Japanese importer of foreign long-term capital during the postwar years, and throughout the modern era. The most massive capital import in Japanese history was the GARIOA and related assistance provided by the United States during the Occupation. Other foreign public capital was slow to enter postwar Japan, as we have seen (Tables 3-4 and 3-9), but in recent years the inflow has reached substantial proportions.

At the end of September 1962 the Japanese government had funded foreign obligations, both direct debts and guarantees, totaling a little over $2 billion. (Table 4-1.) Of this sum only about three-eighths, $784

[4] In that case the Bank extended $46 million of its own credits, participating banks $69 million, to make up a total of $115 million to finance purchases of American agricultural commodities. Export–Import Bank of Washington, *Statement of Terminated Credits,* July 1, 1960, p. 4.

TABLE 4-1. FOREIGN PUBLIC DEBT OF JAPAN, SEPTEMBER 30, 1962, INCLUDING OBLIGATIONS GUARANTEED BY THE JAPANESE GOVERNMENT OR PUBLIC CORPORATIONS [a]

(In millions of dollars)

Bonds issued or assumed by the Japanese government		156.9 [b]
Dollar bonds (prewar, 49.7; postwar, 27)	76.7	
Sterling bonds, prewar	79.9	
Franc bonds, prewar	0.3	
World Bank loans		373.1
ICA loans from the yen proceeds of agricultural surplus sales		104.6
Bonds guaranteed by the Japanese government		101.0
Nippon Telegraph and Telephone Public Corporation	38.5	
Japan Development Bank	37.5	
Deutsche Mark bonds	25.0	
Loans from the Export–Import Bank of Washington to Japanese firms, guaranteed by the Japan Development Bank		104.9
Other obligations of Japanese firms guaranteed by public corporations		68.7
Loans from U.S. suppliers	22.3	
Notes and bonds issued by a U.S. subsidiary of a Japanese firm	20.0	
Loans from a British supplier	26.4	
Credits received by a Japanese firm from U.S. banks		4.5
Total, excluding reparations and GARIOA		913.7
Reparations and other settlements from World War II		637.2 [c]
Total, including reparations		1,550.9
GARIOA settlement		490.0
Total, including reparations and GARIOA		2,040.9

[a] Funded debt only. In addition there was external floating debt of $325 million.

[b] In addition to this principal amount there was outstanding a total of $2.7 million in interest arrears from the period of wartime payment suspension that ended with the postwar settlements. These arrears are represented by specially issued coupon strips, each payment being due 10 years after the original interest due date.

[c] Japan's reparations obligation was tentatively raised by $140 million in January 1963 when a memorandum of agreement was initialed, calling for additional deliveries to Burma. The basis for this addition is the clause in the original Japan–Burma reparations agreement permitting Burma to reopen discussions if other reparations-receiving countries should receive better treatment than Burma. *The Japan Times Weekly*, February 2, 1963, p. 3.

Source: Prospectus, dated January 30, 1963, contained in Registration Statement of the Japan Development Bank, U.S. Securities and Exchange Commission file no. 2-21009, covering $22,500,000 Fifteen-year 6% Guaranteed External Loan Bonds, due February 1, 1978; pp. 63–69.

million, resulted from formal borrowing in the postwar period, as shown in the capital account of the balance of payments. The $490 million to be repaid on account of GARIOA aid represents part of a capital import, but that was shown separately in the balance of payments, and at the time no one knew how much repayment Japan would be obliged to make. Prewar bonds accounted for $130 million of debts outstanding in September 1962, and reparations and other World War II settlements for $637 million.

After U.S. aid the World Bank is the next largest source of Japan's postwar capital imports. Admitted to membership in August 1952, Japan has become the Bank's second largest customer, following India. By the end of 1961 Japan had obtained 24 loans totaling $482 million, of which $356 million had actually been drawn. No new loans were made in 1962, but total drawings on World Bank loans to Japan rose to $420 million by the end of the year. These borrowings have supported mainly electric power, steel, and transportation projects.[5]

Contrary to its usual policy of lending only to cover foreign-currency costs, the World Bank has permitted some of the funds lent to Japan to be spent on yen costs. As a result, loans for individual projects have been substantially larger than would otherwise have been possible. Japan imports far less of its finished equipment than do underdeveloped countries; so application of the normal rule would have cut considerably the proportion of the cost of each project that could be financed by the World Bank. To have borrowed as much under the normal rule, many more projects of comparable size would have been necessary, thus involving the Bank much further in the operation of the Japanese economy. The Bank was willing to waive the rule because Japan's debt-carrying capacity seemed great enough to warrant the foreign-currency obligations involved. Japan's national economic and financial management, governmental and private too, has thus been given a strong vote of confidence.

The International Cooperation Administration, predecessor of the Agency for International Development, made loans to Japan from the yen acquired by the U.S. government by sales of agricultural surpluses (p. 36). The equivalent of $106 million was allocated in 1955 and 1956 to economic development loans; nearly three-fourths of this has gone into industry and mining, most of the balance into agricultural activities.[6]

[5] International Bank for Reconstruction and Development, *Statement of Loans,* December 31, 1962. The original principal amounted to $487.9 million for all loans, but it is here reduced by $5.7 million for cancellations. Repayments of principal totaled $33.2 million, of which $3.3 million was repaid to the World Bank and $29.9 million was repaid to purchasers of portions of loans. The total of such purchases was $65.1 million. In the fall of 1963 the World Bank made its 25th loan to Japan, $75 million for highway construction. IBRD Press Release No. 63/43, September 27, 1963.

[6] Statistics and Reports Division, Agency for International Development, Washington.

Although a little of the original principal has already been repaid, the bulk of these loans run for 40 years and are repayable in either yen or dollars. The interest rate is 4 per cent when paid in yen, or 3 per cent when paid in dollars. Thus far the Japanese have preferred the lower interest rate and have met payments in dollars. Since there is every expectation that yen payments would correspondingly reduce Japan's dollar income from U.S. government purchases of yen to meet its expenditures in Japan, this choice appears to be financially prudent.

The Export–Import Bank of Washington is another large source of credit. The 54 loans and credits to Japan authorized from 1948 through 1962 totaled $1,185 million. Fifteen one-year cotton credits, together with a small credit for various agricultural commodities, made up $800 million of this total. The remaining third of the total authorized consisted of long-term loans that financed the export to Japan of aircraft and of equipment components for electric utilities, steel mills, automobile factories, and other industries. By December 31, 1962 all but $119 million of the authorized funds had been used (aside from small amounts that were canceled). Repayments had reduced Japan's outstanding indebtedness to $272 million.[7] The total credits Japan has had from the Export–Import Bank exceed those from the World Bank or any other governmental or intergovernmental agency. But most of the Export–Import Bank credits were for short periods while the World Bank's loans run for a number of years.

Public Bonds Issued Abroad

The Japanese government's re-entry into the New York bond market in 1959 was significant less for the $29 million of proceeds received from the first issue than for the fact that such borrowing had become possible. Before World War II, sale of Japanese bonds and debentures abroad had been the principal means of obtaining foreign capital, far more important than direct investment. The government was the principal borrower. Smaller amounts were borrowed by municipalities and corporations, mostly semigovernmental agencies.[8] The main source of borrowed funds was the London money market although Paris took some issues, and beginning in 1923 a number of corporate issues and two muni-

[7] The sharp difference between this figure and the $104.9 million shown in Table 4-1 is explained only partly by the difference in dates, more by the fact that the $272 million includes the loans made from the yen proceeds of agricultural surplus sales, for which the Export–Import Bank of Washington is technically the creditor (shown separately in the table). In addition, the $104.9 million figure does not include Export–Import Bank loans to Japanese firms that are not guaranteed by the Japan Development Bank. Export–Import Bank of Washington, *Statement of Terminated Credits,* July 1, 1961; *Statement of Loans and Authorized Credits,* December 31, 1962; *Cotton Credits Extended by Export–Import Bank of Washington,* December 31, 1961.

[8] Edwin P. Reubens, "Foreign Capital and Domestic Development in Japan," in Simon Kuznets and others, *Economic Growth: Brazil, India, Japan* (Durham, N.C.:

cipal issues were floated in New York. In addition a small volume of Japanese domestic bonds and debentures was bought by foreigners.[9] These sources of foreign capital dried up during the depression, and the 1959 borrowing was the first Japanese issue of bonds abroad after 1931.

By successfully selling this first postwar bond issue, the Japanese government signaled the re-establishment of its credit standing with investors, despite the lack of enthusiasm in the United States for foreign bonds after the defaults of the 1930s. But then over two years passed before a second issue was sold. The delay was the result mainly of the unfavorable state of the New York bond market. The second issue, sold in May 1961 by the Nippon Telegraph and Telephone Public Corporation with Japanese government guarantee, totaled $20 million, of which $15 million was 15-year bonds and the balance 3-, 4-, and 5-year bonds.[10]

During the four years ending February 1963, nine issues of bonds or debentures, all guaranteed by the Japanese government and totaling $168.5 million, were sold in the New York bond market. The 1959 bond issue of the Japanese government mentioned above, together with three issues from the Japan Development Bank, accounted for almost half of this total. A second issue sold by the Nippon Telegraph and Telephone Public Corporation in September 1962 brought its total to $38.5 million for the period. Three of the nine issues covered convertible debentures of private corporations totaling $40 million.[11] In March 1963 the Associated Press reported that Japan planned to sell an additional $100 million of government-guaranteed bonds in the United States to help finance industrial expansion.[12] By the early 1960s, then, Japan had firmly re-established its standing in the New York money market.

European capital is beginning to be tapped by Japanese bond sales. The first postwar bond issue in Europe by any Japanese borrower was issued in West Germany in February 1962. Fifteen-year bonds of the City and Prefecture of Osaka valued at DM 100 million ($25 million) were sold through a consortium of German banks.[13] A second issue, almost identical to this, was sold in March 1963.[14]

Duke University Press, 1955), pp. 222–227; William W. Lockwood, *The Economic Development of Japan* (Princeton University Press, 1954), pp. 253–260.

[9] Harold G. Moulton, *Japan: An Economic and Financial Appraisal* (Washington: Brookings Institution, 1931), pp. 488–495.

[10] *The New York Times,* May 3, 1961. *Prospectus,* dated May 2, 1961, contained in Registration Statement of Nippon Telegraph and Telephone Public Corporation, U.S. Securities and Exchange Commission file no. 2-17937, covering $20,000,000 Dollar Bonds [dated April 15, 1961]; p. 1.

[11] Information from files of the U.S. Securities and Exchange Commission, Washington.

[12] *The Wall Street Journal,* March 19, 1963.

[13] This issue is guaranteed by the Japanese government and will pay 6.5 per cent interest. *International Financial News Survey* (IMF), February 23, 1962, p. 59, from Bundesminister für Wirtschaft, *Tages-Nachrichten,* Bonn, February 12, 1962.

[14] Bank of Tokyo, *Weekly Review,* March 18, 1963, p. 69.

The proceeds of the government bond issue of 1959 went for hydroelectric power development, along with the proceeds of a $10 million World Bank loan made at the same time to the Japan Development Bank. The Nippon Telegraph and Telephone issue provided funds to expand the company's facilities, and the Japan Development Bank planned to use its proceeds for expanding thermal electric power facilities. Proceeds of the Osaka bonds sold in Germany are to be used to finance part of a large, five-year program of harbor equipment, land reclamation, and water supply.[15] The sums obtained from abroad are only a small part of the total supply of capital being used for these purposes, but the foreign capital is a useful supplement, reducing the pressure for domestic borrowing or inflationary financing. Perhaps the greatest advantage of the foreign bond issues for Japan so far has come from the resulting additions to foreign exchange receipts and reserves.

Foreign Investment in Japanese Private Enterprise

In the postwar period, as before, Japan has received far less capital through foreign private direct investment than from borrowing.[16] Until the Foreign Investment Law went into effect in June 1950[17] there was virtually no private investment. Subject to Occupation control, in default on prewar debts, and under the severe disability of grave balance-of-payments weakness, Japan was not attractive to foreign capital. The principal purpose of the new law was to establish rules that would attract foreign investment while still protecting Japan's interests.

The law provided that after a specific import of technology or capital had been approved by the Ministry of Finance, any earnings or patent royalties could be taken out of Japan without reference to foreign exchange controls. In a similar way the principal of validated foreign investments could be withdrawn from Japan, starting two years after the investment was made, but only at the rate of 20 per cent a year. The key to foreign investment under this law was, therefore, validation by the Ministry of Finance. Without validation an investment had no standing, and any attempt to withdraw earnings or capital would be subject to official decision at the time under the foreign exchange regulations. But once an investment had been validated, an absolute right of withdrawal was created, subject only to the rules of the Foreign Investment Law and

[15] Bank of Japan, *News Survey*, February 27, 1962, from *Nihon Keizai*, February 9, 1962.

[16] From 1896 to 1913, only 5.5 per cent of the foreign capital entering Japan was direct private investment. Another 9.5 per cent took the form of loans to Japanese corporations. National and municipal government borrowing absorbed 85 per cent of all foreign capital. Reubens, cited, p. 219.

[17] Law No. 163, May 10, 1950.

any further stipulations that might be made in the validation itself. Of course, no guarantee was made about whether the foreign capital would earn anything in Japan. Commercial risks remained with the lender or investor; the Japanese government simply guaranteed to convert yen into foreign currency.

Probably the main result of the law was to stimulate the inflow of foreign technology in Japan, a subject to be discussed later in this chapter. Capital inflows have been mainly of two sorts not dependent on the law: public borrowing and short-term commercial credits. But as the 1950s closed, the flow of private investment was quickening, stimulated by the spreading reputation of Japanese economic growth and by liberalization of the pertinent regulations. (Table 4-2.) Validated investments in the

TABLE 4-2. FOREIGN PRIVATE EQUITY INVESTMENTS IN JAPAN, 1950–1962

(In millions of dollars)

Fiscal Year (April–March)	*Total Investment*		*Investment Involving Management Participation*	
	Validated	*Effected*	*Validated*	*Effected*
1950	3.8	1.2	2.6	1.2
1951	13.3	11.9	11.6	11.3
1952	9.8	6.5	7.2	4.4
1953	4.3	7.0	2.7	5.8
1954	4.0	4.8	2.5	3.5
1955	4.3	3.3	2.3	1.5
1956	9.4	7.7	5.4	4.8
1957	12.1	11.2	7.3	6.5
1958	11.0	11.3	3.7	4.6
1959	27.1	26.8	14.6	14.3
1960	74.9	45.6	31.6	20.7
1961	116.1	128.6	40.2	38.1[a]
1962	164.7	149.7	22.6	N.A.
Total, 1950–1962	454.8	415.6	154.3	116.7[b]

[a] April–December 1961.
[b] 1950–December 1961.

Sources: 1950–1960—Foreign Capital Research Society, care of the Bank of Japan, *Japanese Industry,* 1961, p. 151. 1961–1962—Bank of Japan, *Economic Statistics of Japan,* 1962, p. 256; 1963, p. 277.

fiscal year 1962 reached $165 million, which was 15 times the amount approved four years earlier. In the 1950s a substantial proportion of these investments represented no cash payments by foreigners to Japan, but rather the assignment of patent rights, with or without provision of specialized machinery. Sometimes Americans or other foreigners were stationed in Japan in connection with such investments, especially those involving foreign participation in management. Such participation went with nearly a third of all foreign investment actually effected through December 1961.

American investors accounted for the greatest part of the validated investment involving participation in management, 74 per cent of the total as of March 31, 1961. British investors had 7 per cent; investors in Kuwait and Saudi Arabia, 6 per cent each; Canadian, German, and Dutch investors, 2 per cent each. These investments were heavily concentrated in the newly expanding industries where modern technology is of particular importance. Over a third (37 per cent) of the total value was in the petroleum industry, 28 per cent in chemicals, 18 per cent in machinery, especially electrical and electronic equipment manufacture, 8 per cent in rubber and leather production, and 5 per cent in metals. Investments in petroleum refining and marketing averaged well over a million dollars each, those in the chemicals and rubber and leather industries over half a million dollars each on the average. All others were much smaller in average size. Among the traditional industries with very little foreign equity interest was spinning and weaving, for which only eight cases were shown, totaling $870,000.[18]

This limited accumulation of foreign investments did not bring any significant degree of alien control in most sectors of Japanese business. In 1959 foreign holdings exceeded 5 per cent of total shares outstanding in only three industries. The entire list of manufacturing industries in which foreign shares were 1 per cent or more was: [19]

Industry	*Per Cent of Total*	*Industry*	*Per Cent of Total*
Petroleum	24.53	Instruments	2.69
Rubber products	15.67	Stone, clay, and glass	1.46
Nonferrous metals	9.14	Chemical fibers	1.00
Electrical equipment and appliances	3.72		

[18] Foreign Capital Research Society, care of the Bank of Japan, *Japanese Industry, 1961*, p. 153.

[19] These are percentages of shares of companies listed on the stock exchanges and nonlisted corporations with capital of more than 50 million yen. *The Oriental Economist*, June 1960, p. 318, from Japan, Ministry of Finance.

The concentration of foreign interests in oil refining has given large international companies an important influence in Japan. I have heard responsible Japanese officials refer to the foreign oil "monopoly." This term exaggerates the situation, but of no other industry could the complaint be made with even the slightest plausibility.

Foreign equity investments and loans increased sharply after mid-1959, when the Japanese authorities started relaxing the rules for approving capital imports. What is thought to be the largest direct loan ever obtained from abroad by a private Japanese firm was made in June 1960 when the Prudential Insurance Company of America made a 15-year loan of $30 million to the Kobe Steel Works.[20] Equity investments have included not only company connections but also purchases by foreigners of existing Japanese shares. Interest in Japanese securities has spread, especially in the United States. A sign of the times was the establishment in the United States in 1961 of the Japan Fund, Inc., for the specific purpose of investing in Japanese securities, primarily common stocks.[21]

Stock markets in Tokyo and elsewhere have recently become important attracters of foreign capital. In calendar year 1961, $47 million was invested through the market, a sum slightly larger than that for the whole period 1950–1959. In 1962 market purchases rose to $83 million. In 1963 they were $105 million. Thus the cumulative total of Japanese shares acquired through the stock market from 1950 came to $175 million at the end of 1962, $280 million at the end of 1963. In addition, substantial sums are being put into Japanese shares by foreigners through other means, $64 million in 1961, $42 million in 1962, and $131 million in 1963.[22]

Even so, total foreign private investment is small in comparison with other factors in the Japanese economy. Foreign capital has contributed to Japan fewer of the by-product benefits of management, know-how, and business connections than would be expected if equity investments had been larger. On the other hand, the highly nationalistic Japanese have been able to get the advantages of foreign capital without more than a minimum of foreign control in the operation of individual firms

[20] This loan was reportedly made without collateral but with the guarantee of five Japanese banks; the rate of interest is 7 per cent. Bank of Tokyo, *Weekly Review*, June 20, 1960, p. 166.

[21] A total of $25 million was sought by public sales of 2 million shares of the Japan Fund common stock at $12.50 a share. The president of the Japan Fund is Robert L. Garner, former president of the International Finance Corporation and former vice-president of the World Bank. *Prospectus*, dated April 13, 1962, contained in Registration Statement of the Japan Fund, Inc., U.S. Securities and Exchange Commission file no. 2-19166, covering 2,000,000 shares of common stock; pp. 1, 3, 16, and elsewhere.

[22] Bank of Tokyo, *Weekly Review*, March 5, 1962, p. 60; February 11, 1963, p. 34; February 10, 1964, p. 30.

and industries. As to foreign participation in the management or control of the Japanese economy, the end of the Occupation left Japanese in effective command; neither the requirements of the World Bank nor those of other creditors have significantly modified Japanese control. Foreigners have attempted to influence Japanese policy, mainly toward liberalization, as we shall see later (pp. 92, 138–139), but foreign capital has not been used as a lever.

Sales of Private Securities in the United States

An important new approach to foreign investors was made in 1961 when for the first time since World War II Japanese private securities were made easily available in foreign securities markets. American Depositary Receipts (ADRs), which had been used for some time as a means of permitting American domestic dealings in foreign securities, were first used for Japanese common stock when 2 million shares of Sony Corporation common stock (represented by 200,000 American Depositary Shares) were sold in New York in June 1961 for $3.5 million.[23] Under these arrangements the actual share certificates remain on deposit in Tokyo, but may be obtained on demand by the holder of an ADR representing American Depositary Shares. The arrangements save some legal formalities but the sale and transfer of the shares are still subject to the Japanese government's investment laws. By the spring of 1963 eight private issues of common stock had been placed on the New York market, totaling nearly $75 million. The great majority of these issues involved electrical or machinery companies including Tokyo Shibaura Electric, Kansai Electric Power, Honda Motor, and Mitsui.[24]

Postwar Imports of Technology

Postwar imports of technology have been of special importance to Japan because so much of the country's productive plant that survived the war was obsolete. Long heavily dependent on foreign technology, Japan had been isolated for a number of years during which technical progress was very rapid in Western countries, especially the United States. If Japanese products were to compete in world markets, much lost time had to be made up somehow. New processes had to be brought to Japan, modern machinery installed in place of worn-out and obsolete

[23] *The Oriental Economist,* September 1961, pp. 551–552. *Prospectus,* dated June 6, 1961, contained in U.S. Securities and Exchange Commission file no. 2-18035, covering 2,000,0000 shares of common stock (par value 50 Japanese yen per share), represented by 200,000 American Depositary Shares, Sony Corporation; p. 1.

[24] John B. Christensen, "Japanese Equity Financing with Special Reference to Issues in the United States," *Washington Law Review* (University of Washington), Spring 1963, pp. 105–106.

equipment, advanced methods adopted, and new products introduced such as nylon, plastics, and a multitude of electronic devices.

Only a limited amount of technical help was obtained from abroad during the early postwar years. Although the initial Occupation policy left economic recovery to the Japanese, they were not permitted to travel abroad, and foreign traders did not soon bring in much of the needed technology. The Occupation itself began early to render technical assistance, however. Then just before the outbreak of war in Korea, the new Foreign Investment Law provided means to assure foreigners that they would receive payment for technology provided to Japan through technical assistance contracts and investments that took the form of supplying patents and know-how. Table 4-3 summarizes by industry the 1,660 cases validated for import of technology up to the end of 1961. The fact that 354 cases, or 21 per cent of all contracts, were made in 1961, shows the fast pace at which foreign technology has recently been going into Japan. Again, as in the case of capital investments, the great bulk of movement has been in the heavy and chemical industries, machinery, chemicals, and metals, which together accounted for 85 per cent of the total. At the end of July 1961, 63 per cent of the 1,457 cases approved up to that time showed the source of technology as the United States; West Germany accounted for 9 per cent; Switzerland, 7 per cent; and other

TABLE 4-3. TECHNOLOGY IMPORT CONTRACTS, BY INDUSTRY, 1961 AND 1949–1961

Industry	*Number of Cases*		*Per Cent of Total*
	1961	*1949–1961*	*1949–1961*
Machinery	204	902	54.3
Chemicals	63	344	20.7
Metals and metal products	31	157	9.4
Spinning and weaving	18	81	4.8
Rubber and leather products	12	49	3.0
Petroleum	9	45	2.8
Glass and ceramic products	9	30	1.9
Paper and pulp	5	20	1.2
Construction	1	16	0.9
Other	2	17	1.0
Total	354	1,660	100.0

Source: Japan, Ministry of International Trade and Industry, *Boeki Hakusho* (Foreign Trade White Paper), 1962, p. 625.

European countries, 15 per cent.[25] The Japanese probably do themselves a disservice by using the phrase *technical assistance* for these contracts; it implies an element of donation outside normal commercial channels. In fact these contracts have been made on a strictly commercial basis; the foreign interests concerned are being paid in full for what they provide.

The results of this imported technology are spread widely in the form of more and better products, lower costs, and growing exports. There was a time when Japanese cotton cloth would shrink seriously on first washing, as the writer learned to his regret after having a white uniform made from Japanese material in the 1930s. One of the contracts covered by Table 4-3 applies to "Sanforizing," a process for preshrinking cloth. The Cluett-Peabody Company, originator and owner of the "Sanforizing" process, is among the large American importers of Japanese cloth, and Sanforized Japanese cloth now sells in markets nearly all over the world. Without foreign technology the postwar improvement in quality of many Japanese products could have taken place only slowly and to a limited degree. Japanese exports could not have fared so well, and Japan would be far less prosperous than now.

Cost of Foreign Capital and Technology

The amount Japan pays for foreign capital and technology is rising year by year. In 1961 the total came to $268 million, made up of the items shown in Table 4-4. No repatriation of capital is included. Less than half of the payment went for interest, including that on prewar government bonds floated abroad. World Bank loans cost relatively little in that year, the interest rates being low and some loans not yet having passed from the grace period into the period of service payments. "Other interest," including charges on short-term "usance" and other commercial credits, accounted for sizable payments. Patent royalties were an even more expensive item. Only a small amount was paid on equity capital (including some interest paid by subsidiaries and, of course, return on equity investment obtained by provision of foreign technology).

Japanese preference for borrowed capital instead of foreign equity investment is explained by Finance Ministry officials primarily on grounds of cost, since interest, especially from the World Bank, runs less than

[25] Foreign Capital Research Society, *Japanese Industry*, cited, p. 152. The numbers here and in Table 4-3 refer to individual contracts, which vary a great deal in size and in significance for the Japanese economy. In 1962 there were 278 new contracts, divided as follows: machinery (154), chemicals (71), metals and metal products (19), spinning and weaving (10), glass and ceramic products (10), petroleum (4), rubber and leather products (3), construction (1), and all other (6). Japan, Ministry of International Trade and Industry, *Boeki Hakusho* (Foreign Trade White Paper), 1963, p. 664.

TABLE 4-4. JAPAN'S FOREIGN PAYMENTS FOR CAPITAL AND TECHNOLOGY, 1961

(In millions of dollars)

Royalty payments for patents and copyrights				123.8
Payments for capital				144.0
Equity capital			27.4	
Direct investment capital		21.3		
Interest	2.0			
Dividends	11.7			
Undistributed corporate earnings	4.1			
Earnings of branches	3.5			
Other dividends (portfolio securities)		6.1		
Borrowed capital, etc.[a]			116.6	
Interest on loans from international agencies		15.3		
Interest on other government obligations		24.5		
Interest on deposits		1.7		
Other interest [b]		75.2		
Total payments for foreign capital and technology				267.8

[a] Includes interest and other payments on account of prewar loans and investments.
[b] Omits interest from subsidiaries, which is shown under direct investment capital.

Source: Bank of Japan, *Balance of Payments of Japan,* 1961, pp. 25, 29.

equity earnings. Previous restrictions on acquisition by foreigners of existing Japanese stocks and other equity securities were motivated largely by unwillingness to permit foreigners to share in the capital gains expected as undervalued issues rose in delayed recognition of extensive postwar inflation. Some of the opposition to foreign management within the Japanese economy results from nationalistic feeling, but more of the explanation probably lies in protectionist attitudes—existing firms objecting to competition and able to make the objection effective against foreigners.

The rapid rise in the inflow of foreign capital and technology reflects growing foreign interest and confidence in Japan as well as more receptivity in Japan to equity capital. It has become easier for foreigners to invest in Japan (see p. 92), and the prospect is that interest, dividends, and related payments will grow progressively during the years ahead. In time a peak may be reached at which the flow may level off, but that time is not yet in sight. Japanese capital and technology exports will probably continue to rise gradually, but it is too early to estimate how long it will be before income on this account may begin to catch up with payments.

PREDOMINANCE OF AMERICAN CAPITAL AND TECHNOLOGY

The United States is the source of the great bulk of the technology and capital that Japan has obtained from abroad since 1945. As we have seen, the United States accounted for nearly two-thirds of the technology contracts and almost three-fourths of the value of private equity investment. Of public loans and grants, practically all have come from the United States, except for World Bank loans, and the United States is the source of a large part of the Bank's funds. Commercial credits also originate overwhelmingly in the United States. Although the American share has shrunk somewhat in recent years with economic recovery in Europe and elsewhere, the United States remains much more important to Japan than all other countries combined.

Electronics is a field in which American technical contributions stand out most. Here 90 per cent of technology import arrangements approved through 1959 involved the United States, covering such things as television tubes, teletype equipment, radar, thermionic tubes, and transistors. Other products in which American sources dominate Japan's imports of technology include water turbines, turbo-generators, high-pressure steam boilers, gas turbines, transformers, petrochemicals, fertilizers, aviation gasoline and high-grade lubricants, certain chemical fibers, and a number of steel-mill processes.[26]

Table 4-5 shows the Japanese and American partners in 36 joint enterprises in which the American share is 40 per cent or more. In another 15 Japanese companies American ownership amounted to 20 to 39 per cent. Americans have acquired their equity more by supplying technology or equipment than by advancing funds, and while a few of the connections were established before World War II, most are recent. Through these investments, but much more through patent licensing and loans and sales of equipment, knowledge of American products and methods is spreading in Japan. By contrast, the inflow from other countries is very small.

Reasons for this predominant American role are not far to seek. The United States has the largest volume of available capital and technology of any country. In much of the postwar period Europe was preoccupied with reconstruction, integration, and relations with overseas dependencies. Geographically and in many other ways the United States has been more accessible to Japan than any other major industrial country. Japanese and Americans have been forced to become acquainted with each other as a result of World War II, the Occupation, the Korean War, and continuing tension between Communist and non-Communist forces throughout the world. Now the two peoples have a remarkable interest

[26] *The Oriental Economist,* June 1960, p. 318.

TABLE 4-5. JAPANESE–AMERICAN JOINT ENTERPRISES IN JAPAN, AS OF AUGUST 1962

Japanese Partner	*American Firm*	*American Firm's Shareholdings (Per Cent)*
IBM of Japan	International Business Machines Corp.	99
Tokyo Shibaura Electric Co.	Otis Elevator Co.	80
Toyo Carrier Engineering Co.	Carrier Corp.	75
National Cash Register Co. (Japan)	National Cash Register Co.	70
Nippon Typewriter Co.	Sperry Rand Corp.	70
Asahi Chemical Industry	Dow Chemical Co.	50
General Sekiyu Co.	Esso Standard Eastern, Inc.	50
Hitachi, Ltd.	Babcock & Wilcox Co.	50
Ishikawajima-Harima Heavy Industries	Foster Wheeler Corp.	50
Koa Oil Co.	California Texas Oil Corp.	50
Mitsubishi Chemical Industries	Monsanto Chemical Co.	50
Mitsui Petrochemical	Du Pont & Co.	50
Nippon Oil Refining	California Texas Oil Corp.	50
Nitto Chemical Industry	Union Carbide Corp.	50
Ricoh, Ltd.	Hamilton Watch Co.	50
Shin Mitsubishi Heavy Industries	Caterpillar Overseas	50
Showa Denko Co.	Du Pont & Co.	50
Sumitomo Group	Dunlop Tire & Rubber Corp.	50
Taito Co.	Charles Pfizer & Co.	50
Takeda Chemical Co.	American Cyanamid Co.	50
Yamatake-Honeywell Instrument Co.	Minneapolis-Honeywell Regulator Co.	50
Mitsubishi Oil Co.	Tidewater Oil Co.	49
Niigata Engineering Co.	Worthington Corp.	49
Nippon Electric Co.	Hughes Aircraft Co.	49
J. Osawa & Co.	Bell & Howell Co.	49
Tokyo Shibaura Electric Co.	United Engineering & Foundry Co.	49
Yoshitomi Pharmaceutical Industries	Wallace & Tiernan, Inc.	49
Teijin, Ltd.	Avisco International	48
Asahi Glass Co.	Owens-Corning Fiberglas Corp.	47.5
Nissan Chemical Industries	Rohm & Haas Co.	47.5
Kao Soap Co.	California Chemical Co.	45
Nippon Petrochemicals	California Chemical Co.	45
Ray-O-Vac Co. (Japan)	Electric Storage Battery Co.	43.3
Japan-Organo Co.	Degremont, Inc.	40
Mitsubishi Electric Manufacturing	General Precision, Inc.	40
Nippon International Rectifier	International Rectifier Corp.	40

Note: The Japanese and American firms listed here are partners in jointly owned enterprises in Japan, which are not named here.

Source: The Japan Times, Foreign Investment Supplement [1963], p. B-11; altered in the light of later information.

in one another, extending widely over commercial, financial, political, strategic, and cultural affairs. Of all the major countries of Asia, Japan offers the most congenial environment for American business enterprise. The rapidity and vigor of Japanese growth and the shortage of capital in Japan, with consequent high interest and profit rates, have provided particularly good opportunities. The large U.S. market has offered tremendous opportunities for Japanese exports and for Americans to help in the exploitation of these opportunities. American interest in teaming up with Japanese firms has risen as Japanese competitive power has grown and American firms have taken advantage of Japan's low production costs, and as Japanese foreign exchange controls and investment procedures have been liberalized.

One wonders, indeed, why American investments in Japan are not a good deal larger. Much of the answer lies in Japanese policy (which will be discussed in a section below). Another part of the explanation lies in the time it takes for American firms to decide to team up with Japanese. Both Japanese and American firms have in many cases been slow to see advantages in closer links. In the industries producing cotton textiles and textile machinery, for instance, protectionist feelings seem to have been an important deterrent to American firms, and Japanese cotton textile producers are already so far advanced they have not felt the need for American capital or technology nearly so much as have producers in fields where Japan is less advanced. In other industries, including electronics, company ties have been important as a means by which Japanese firms have obtained American technology and gained (although it is not publicly known how much) in reduced opposition by American producers to imports from Japan. The forces leading toward company tie-ups, with or without American participation in management of Japanese firms, do not appear likely to diminish unless restrictive government action is taken, for instance, in the form of increased American import barriers. At the same time European firms may increase their interest in Japanese connections, and the U.S. share of such arrangements may possibly decline somewhat during the coming years.

A blow to American predominance in supplying capital to Japan was struck by the United States itself in July 1963, when President Kennedy proposed an interest equalization tax on certain capital exports, especially foreign securities floated in the United States. This proposed measure would levy a variable tax aimed at making the American capital market less attractive to foreigners seeking capital, thus reducing the outflow of capital and the strain on the American balance of payments without a general increase in interest rates. The Japanese reaction was dramatic. Stock market prices fell. The Foreign Minister went to Washington in an unsuccessful effort to have Japan exempted from the proposed tax (as

Canada was). And there were widespread expressions of concern in Japan, not only about the cost of American capital, but also about a range of different matters, including possible new American import restrictions. Although Congress was slow to act on the equalization tax, in anticipation of it there was some reduction in the flow of American capital to Japan in the second half of 1963 and a little increase in Japanese borrowing from Europeans.

The Japanese–American Productivity Program

In addition to importing technology commercially, Japan has received a significant amount of technical assistance under the auspices of the U.S. government. During the Occupation, American technicians in many fields were sent to Japan to assist in economic rehabilitation, and Japanese leaders and technicians were brought to the United States, and in lesser numbers sent to other countries, to observe modern methods. At a time when private travel was largely impossible these U.S.-financed activities played a significant part in the technical rehabilitation of the Japanese economy.[27]

For three years after the Occupation ended in 1952 there were no government programs of technical assistance. Then in 1955 a new program was inaugurated, involving government and business in both Japan and the United States. The heart of the new program was the Japan Productivity Center (JPC), sponsored by the Japanese government and four businessmen's organizations. Modeled on the European Productivity Agency, JPC had been established in 1954 in recognition of Japan's weaknesses in export competition and in expectation of aid from the United States. The U.S. government financed the dollar costs of certain training by American universities in cooperation with Japanese universities, sending American technicians and technical literature to Japan and bringing many Japanese "productivity teams" to the United States for observation and discussion on relatively short trips of five to six weeks and "trainees" for longer periods for study. Some Japanese were sent to third countries for training. American business and labor organizations, universities, and other groups have contributed, mainly by receiving Japanese visitors, showing them American methods, and discussing production and management problems.[28]

This joint productivity program has supplemented in important ways

[27] The limited cost of these activities was not charged to Japan, either through inclusion in the GARIOA account or by adding to the heavy yen payments the Japanese were required to make for the support of Occupation forces in Japan.

[28] The total contribution of the U.S. government to this program from 1955 through June 30, 1961 was $12.1 million, including funds for training in Japan persons from other countries. Information from Statistics and Reports Division, Agency for International Development.

the commercial import of foreign technology by Japanese firms. While private contracts have been wholly industrial and the bulk of the activities of the Japan Productivity Center lie in the field of industry, some of the productivity program has concerned agriculture, labor, and other fields. Of 4,080 Japanese who had arrived in the United States from Japan by the end of June 1961 under this program, more than half (2,478) studied some aspects of industry, 602 were concerned with labor matters, 549 with food and agriculture, 250 with transportation, mainly civil aviation, 149 with atomic energy, and 52 with other fields.[29]

Financial support with U.S. foreign aid funds ended in June 1961. But the Japan Productivity Center continues as a Japanese enterprise, and teams continue to be sent to the United States to study, not only production processes but also personnel management, executive development, marketing, insurance, and banking. JPC has established a liaison office in Washington.

Labor has proved an especially important area of contact between Japanese and Americans. Many Japanese labor organizations, especially the largest federation, SOHYO, have strong leftist and anti-American tendencies. It is not surprising therefore that at first much of Japanese labor was distinctly cool to the productivity program, regarding it as not in labor's interest. Some unions did participate, nevertheless, and after a while even some SOHYO unions, with the result that American concepts of labor-management relations and of worker education began to make headway in Japan. The U.S. government regards this trend as healthy, and the Department of State, through its cultural exchange program, is now bringing Japanese labor leaders to the United States. In the twenty months following June 1961 about 160 of them came to the United States in this way. SOHYO, now divided into "left-wing" and "moderate" factions, provided nearly half of these leaders. What began as a productivity movement has continued and grown, with important results and continuing activities, political as well as economic.

JAPANESE POLICY TOWARD IMPORT OF TECHNOLOGY AND CAPITAL

Officially, Japanese policy strongly favors import of foreign technology and capital and has done so ever since the enactment of the Foreign Investment Law of 1950. Actually, technology is eagerly sought and widely accepted, although with some continuing control. The Ministry of International Trade and Industry continues to publish a periodic list of technology deemed especially desirable. The import of capital, however, is controlled to a considerably greater extent than technology, and there

[29] Same.

are important differences in the way various types of capital movements are regarded. There is a distinct preference for loans over equity investments, and public loans are favored over private borrowing, primarily because they cost less.

The Climate for Foreign Private Investment in Japan

"The Japanese have been determined and show every evidence of continued determination to prevent foreigners from obtaining a significant degree of ownership and control, particularly in important sectors of the economy."[30] So said the principal publication of the U.S. government on the subject of Japan's investment climate, published in 1956. Japanese sensitivities have moderated in many ways since then, but this statement appears to be still valid. The Japanese government and business community remain today far from ready to let such matters be decided by the forces of the market and of competition.

The Foreign Investment Law of 1950 has been the basis for very strict control over the commercial entry from abroad of technology, loans, and investments. To gain the valuable transfer privileges provided by the law a project must pass a severe test of advantage and acceptability to Japan. ". . . priority shall be given to those [contracts] which will most speedily and effectively contribute to an improvement of the international balance of payments,"[31] says the law. This emphasis was to be expected in 1950, but it was continued long after the Japanese balance of payments had improved.

Technology contracts are scrutinized just as closely as those for investments. For one thing, the Ministry of Finance is on the lookout for efforts by foreign patent owners to take advantage of Japanese firms by offering "second-hand" technology, by charging too much, or by setting other onerous terms. There is indeed some danger of sharp practice. Not infrequently foreign businessmen, today as in times past, try to squeeze the Japanese. This problem is, of course, not confined to international transactions or to Japan. Still, Japanese, especially small businessmen, frequently do not have enough information, particularly about circumstances outside of Japan, to bargain effectively. The government's approach reflects a responsible, even paternalistic attitude. Some foreigners attempting to exploit unsuspecting Japanese firms have been prevented from doing so. But probably the greatest advantage Japan has gained from intervention by the Finance Ministry has been improvement in the terms of some contracts.

[30] U.S. Department of Commerce, *Investment in Japan* (Washington: GPO, 1956), p. 1.

[31] Same, p. 120. Most of the law is presented in English in this publication, pp. 119–126.

This is not, however, the only aspect of capital or technology contracts the Finance Ministry examines. The Ministry is also concerned about contracts that would create "too much competition" within Japan. One contract in a given field might be sufficient, according to this view, and Japan might be handicapped if a competitor of a licensee in Japan were allowed to contract with a competitor of the licensor in the United States for rights on a competing product or process. As we shall see later, this is not the only instance in which the fear that competition is destructive leads to the conclusion that the government must keep firm control of international transactions.

A number of other Japanese laws and regulations affect—and often deter—foreign equity investment. License, regulatory, and tax laws are required under Article VII of the Treaty of Friendship, Commerce and Navigation between the United States and Japan [32] to apply equally to Americans and to Japanese; that is, Americans are entitled to national treatment in conducting business in Japan. The rule is hard to apply. Japanese local and national officials often have much authority and discretion. There are formal and informal steps that skillful Japanese can take to bend an official's judgment in one direction or another. Without any intentional or overt discrimination, an official might decide less favorably in the case of an American who was less skillful in justifying his project or in making friends and exercising legitimate influence in the Japanese milieu. And if there is a hint that higher officialdom is opposed to a projected activity of the foreigner, a great deal of quite legal interference can be created without providing the foreigner with any legal or practical basis for protest.

Taxes are a case in point, especially those on incomes earned by American businessmen stationed in Japan. Since Japanese incomes are far lower than American, and since the Japanese government must, if it is to get adequate revenue, set income tax rates so as to bear fairly heavily in those brackets where most of the incomes fall, the progression of rates is such that incomes at American levels are taxed much more heavily than in the United States. Add to this the wide discretion of tax collectors with respect to the amount of property taxes to be paid and the informal methods used to determine taxable value, and it is easy to see how an American might find himself in difficulties.

Another inhibition in the early 1950s was fear of unfair exploitation by foreign carpetbaggers. A number of Americans stayed on in Japan after serving in civilian or military posts in the Occupation. Some may have been able to exploit their former positions. Many Japanese believed

[32] Signed at Tokyo, April 2, 1953, entered into force October 30, 1953. The text is printed in full in same, pp. 133–139.

that was so and suspected these people of evading or violating Japanese law. This problem is no longer significant, but it gave rise to attitudes and regulations that linger on to the present day.

Liberalization of Capital and Technology Imports

The Treaty of Friendship, Commerce and Navigation of 1953 with the United States required a number of measures of liberalization. But because of their fear of foreign exploitation of a temporary situation the Japanese requested and the American government agreed to a three-year delay in putting the equal-treatment provision into force with respect to stock market purchases. In the early 1950s, Japanese security prices were low both because of the incompleteness of economic recovery and because the pre-1949 inflation had not been fully reflected in stock prices, primarily as a result of regulations limiting revaluation of business assets. This situation would provide unfair bargains for foreigners, the Japanese thought. Through most of the 1950s stock market prices rose extremely fast, outstripping dividend increases and cutting yields far below going rates of interest. National treatment for Americans was introduced in 1956.

As time passed and Japan recovered, both economically and psychologically, and as the balance of payments grew stronger, the need for stringent controls declined. The first major changes, in July 1959, made it easier to obtain government validation, which assured ultimate transfer of earnings and profits but left timing dependent on the state of the Japanese balance of payments. In the spring of 1960 the waiting period for the repatriation of capital used in validated purchases of shares was reduced to six months and in April 1963 it was abolished.

Under the Foreign Investment Law of 1950 Japanese officials have had a great deal of discretion in deciding whether to validate the purchase of stock, or any other foreign investment. A few broad rules were laid down. Certain fields, notably banking, transportation, insurance, and public utilities, were designated as "restricted" and tighter rules applied to them than to other industries. Validation was unlikely to be given for a purchase of more than 5 per cent of the outstanding shares of a restricted company before 1960, and 10 per cent afterwards. In other industries, in contrast, validation was virtually guaranteed for investments up to 8 per cent of the outstanding stock up to the spring of 1960 and 15 per cent afterwards. Validation was often granted for larger amounts and over the period of liberalization there was some easing of standards. Some American companies established wholly owned subsidiaries without validation; only in exceptional cases did the government validate foreign investments of as much as 50 per cent in joint ventures with Japanese. Investors could move somewhat more freely if they did not seek validation, but then the remittance of returns on capital would depend on government decisions made on a case-by-case basis, with no advance assurances.

The liberalization decrees of April 1963 abolished the distinction between validated and other investments for the future. Earnings and principal of all investments made after July 1963 were to be automatically eligible for remittance abroad. (New rules were to be worked out about earlier investments.) However all foreign investments would require government approval (which had not previously been necessary for investments made outside the validation procedure). The Japanese government's press release about the new measures said that direct investments "will in principle be approved unless they are deemed to have conspicuously adverse effects upon our national economy."[33] (For technical assistance contracts a cautious "provided conditions are proper" was added.) New and quicker procedures of examination and approval were promised. While the measures of April 1963 seemed to be further steps along the road Japan had been following since 1959 in freeing foreign investment, a publication of the U.S. Department of Commerce observed, "The extent to which the recent changes actually represent a liberalization of investment controls, however, can be determined only after the new rules have been implemented."

Although foreigners continue to object to the degree of government control over investment exercised in Japan, liberalization was perhaps the most important factor in the sharp rise that took place after mid-1959 in the amount of private capital going into the country. Naturally potential investors abroad were becoming deeply impressed with Japan's phenomenal economic growth and the consequent profit opportunities. On the Japanese side the official explanation for retaining administrative control over imports of capital and technology is concern with the balance of payments. Since the balance remains vulnerable, this is a valid concern, but as liberalization progresses, an underlying hostility to foreign activities is becoming clearer. "The closest care must be taken lest the industries of the nation should come under the control of foreign capital," says a leading Japanese bank.[34] There is evident reluctance to agree to any unnecessary sharing with foreigners of the benefits of the Japanese economy, in employment, income, and especially managerial functions. Foreigners, it is said, should not be allowed to "skim the cream" off profitable lines of business. This last may in reality be the strongest motive of all, stronger even than fears about the balance of

[33] Text in *International Commerce,* August 5, 1963, pp. 28, 29. Subsequent quotation from same.

[34] "Liberalization of Capital Transactions," *Monthly Review* (Mitsui Bank), March 1963, p. 3.

payments. In addition to the very human desire to keep good things to oneself and to run one's own affairs in one's own way, two contradictory business motives appear to be involved in the objection to foreign management.

First, there is confidence, based on Japan's impressive record to date, that Japanese businessmen can manage their affairs successfully and do not really need foreign managerial services. Unnecessary payments to foreigners—especially at the high salaries Americans command—are, on this assumption, a waste of scarce money. This confidence in Japanese management, while often soundly based, is sometimes unjustified. The leaders who understand least well the value of advanced managerial and marketing techniques can be expected to resist foreign management most vigorously. Yet their businesses may be the ones most in need of modern management.

The opposite reason for objecting to foreigners is fear that they may indeed have superior business capability and may use it to harm competing Japanese business. For several years the Singer Manufacturing Company's plan to join with a Japanese firm to make sewing machines was rebuffed by officials who failed to act on the validation application. The opposition in this case seems to have been based on fear of the Singer name and the company's proven competitive skills. This is a kind of protectionism that the outsider can readily denounce. But the official, whether in Japan, in the United States, or in any other country with representative institutions, has difficulty in denying the appeal of the citizen who feels hurt, especially if the other party is foreign.

Despite inhibitions, Japan is in the process of dismantling its system of exchange controls, including import licenses, controls over invisible transactions, and capital controls. In February 1963 the International Monetary Fund urged Japan to terminate its transitional status under Article 14 of the Fund Agreement and accept the full obligations of Article 8, which prohibits exchange restrictions for balance-of-payments reasons. The Japanese government accepted this recommendation and announced its intention to assume Article 8 status in 1964. After this shift, which took place at the beginning of April 1964, Japan was still permitted some restrictions, especially to prevent capital flight.[35] Other steps toward liberalization were entailed in Japan's becoming a member of the OECD. Eventually Japan will have to conform to the comprehensive OECD code for the liberalization of payments for services and

[35] The IMF permitted Japan temporarily to restrict the tourist travel of Japanese abroad and to continue the bilateral payments agreement with Korea. At the same time the IMF granted Japan a stand-by credit of $305 million, partly as a means of strengthening the yen against drains resulting from the decontrol of foreign exchange movements, partly as a protection in the face of some decline in Japan's foreign exchange reserves. Bank of Tokyo, *Weekly Review*, March 16, 1964, pp. 60–61.

other "invisible" transactions. In spite of these steps, many Japanese still have serious inhibitions about opening their economy wide to foreign investment.

EXPORTS OF JAPANESE CAPITAL AND TECHNOLOGY

Japan's vigorous economy can offer much to the underdeveloped areas in Asia and elsewhere. Japan has skilled technicians who can be of great help abroad. There is no large amount of capital available for export, but there is some, in fact more every year, and Japanese businessmen are keenly interested in establishing overseas branches and developing foreign sources of raw materials to be imported into Japan.

Loans and Investments

Japanese loans and investments abroad totaled $1,543 million at the end of 1962 and $1,853 million at the end of 1963, made up as follows: [36]

	1962	*1963*
	(in millions of dollars)	
Direct private investments	436	564
Deferred payment for exports	837	1,012
Subscriptions to international organizations	270	277
Total	1,543	1,853

These figures omit foreign exchange reserves, commercial and other short-term credits, and also the balance outstanding in favor of Japan in the clearing account with the Republic of Korea. The largest item, more than half of the indicated totals, is export credits, which are listed only when their term exceeds one year. The geographic allocation of these credits is as follows:

	1962	*1963*
	(in millions of dollars)	
Southeast Asia	258	335
Central and South America	284	281
Middle and Near East	98	52
Other areas	196	344
Total	837	1,012

The geographic distribution of direct private investments is somewhat different. Here are the figures:

[36] These and other figures in this paragraph come from Bank of Tokyo, *Weekly Review,* March 23, 1964, pp. 69–70. Some minor inconsistencies result from rounding.

	1962	*1963*
	(in millions of dollars)	
Southeast Asia	80	96
Central and South America	118	155
Middle and Near East	123	143
Other areas	115	170
Total	436	564

Paradoxically, one of Japan's largest single direct investments abroad in the postwar period is in the United States. A large rayon pulp mill costing $61 million has been built in Sitka, Alaska. There are some American loans to this project, but over two-thirds of the capital is Japanese. The investors include 9 rayon companies, 6 trading companies, 7 cotton spinning companies, 12 paper and pulp companies, 46 lumber companies, 4 insurance companies, 3 steel companies, and several others. The new mill can provide as much rayon pulp as the total imported into Japan in 1960.[37]

The purpose of about two-thirds of postwar Japanese investments abroad has been to develop sources of materials to be imported into Japan. In addition to Alaskan pulp, investments have been made in Chilean copper, oil in Indonesia and the Persian Gulf, and coking coal in West Virginia. Investments in other types of activities include cotton textile manufacture in Brazil and Hong Kong, small steel mills in Hong Kong and Singapore, a larger steel mill in Brazil, a tuna cannery and toothpaste factory in Malaysia, fishing facilities in Thailand, a whaling fleet based in Vancouver, shipbuilding in Brazil, department stores in the United States, Hong Kong, and Indonesia, a skyscraper in Taiwan, factories making radios, television sets, and sewing machines in Ireland, and a growing range of other activities that have reached a developed stage in Japan and are amenable to introduction or expansion elsewhere. Sometimes Japanese participation involves complete ownership and operation, sometimes joint ventures, sometimes Japanese credits. A substantial proportion of the total sum is represented by the value of offices abroad of Japanese banks, trading companies, and other firms.

Intergovernmental loans have become an important means of exporting Japanese capital. Japanese and American loans are helping to develop

[37] The Alaska Lumber and Pulp Company, Inc., is an Alaskan subsidiary of Alaska Pulp Company, Ltd., of Tokyo, which owns all of the $8.5 million of capital stock. The parent company issued $19 million of notes and bonds abroad, with government guarantee. The remaining funds for the venture were obtained in Japan. The mill, which started to produce pulp in 1960, has a rated capacity of 120,000 tons a year. Output is expected to go entirely to Japan, where it will meet most of present requirements for imported rayon pulp. Information from the Alaska Lumber and Pulp Company, Inc.

iron mining and transportation facilities in the state of Orissa in India. Japan participates in the international consortia for both India and Pakistan. Japan may be expected to play a growing part in the various arrangements by which advanced countries finance economic development abroad. It made a start in this direction in its reparations agreements with Burma, the Philippines, and Indonesia which called, not only for direct Japanese payments, but also for economic cooperation, mainly in the form of Japanese agreement to foster private loans and investments in those countries.

Japan's obligation was limited to facilitating the movement of private capital, over an unspecified period of time, up to an amount set out in each agreement: for Indonesia $400 million, the Philippines $250 million, Burma $50 million.[38] These figures make up a large total, but only a small amount of Japanese funds have actually moved under these agreements. Some Japanese activities in Burma fall into the category of "economic cooperation," but it is not certain that more investment and lending have taken place than would have without the agreement. It has been reported that some Japanese efforts have been rebuffed, each of the three governments asking that the proposed projects be considered ordinary reparations. This kind of action goes back to the bargaining that produced the agreements in the first place, when the Japanese agreed to expedite private loans and investments instead of accepting demands for larger reparations. It remains for the future to show how important these agreements will become for either Japan or the other three countries concerned.

The agreement initialed in January 1963, to settle the Burmese government's long-standing claim for additional reparations, has added a slightly different category of "economic cooperation." In addition to more reparations grants, the agreement provides that Japan will extend to Burma "ordinary yen credits" amounting to $30 million over a six-year period. These are to be suppliers' credits extended by the Export–Import Bank of Japan to Japanese exporters. Unlike the "economic cooperation"

[38] Paragraph 3 of a note from the Japanese plenipotentiary to the Indonesian plenipotentiary, dated January 20, 1958, the day on which the reparations agreement was signed, reads as follows:

> 3. The two governments shall facilitate and expedite the extension of loans [i.e., commercial investments, long-term loans, or similar credit arrangements] within the scope of pertinent laws and regulations. The facilitation and expedition the government of Japan is required to offer as to loans will be similar to those which are currently provided to those loans contracted between nationals of Japan and the government or nationals of the Republic of Indonesia and financed on an ordinary commercial basis by the Japanese banking institutions like the Export–Import Bank of Japan, within their available funds.
>
> The two governments shall jointly review from time to time the progress of the conclusion and performance of the loan contracts with a view to effecting the smooth operation of the present arrangement.

part of earlier reparations agreements, this portion of the agreement is in the form of a definite Japanese commitment, extending to the terms of the credits to be made—interest at six per cent and principal repayable in 15 years.[39]

Technology

Japanese exports of technology began very slowly after 1945 and have remained small but by no means insignificant. In 1961, for example, Japanese firms made 43 contracts to export technology, 19 of them with American firms.[40] Technology exports take a number of forms. Direct investments abroad usually involve technology and so do sales of machinery and equipment. Japanese consulting firms now offer a variety of technical services in foreign countries. Foreigners, mostly Asians, are coming to Japan in growing numbers for education and technical training, while Japanese technicians are serving in other Asian countries as part of the reparations program. A few Japanese technicians are stationed abroad and there are Japanese technical training centers in India, Pakistan, Afghanistan, Thailand, and Brazil. Under the Colombo Plan, which Japan joined in 1954, 347 Japanese experts had gone to other Asian countries by the end of March 1962.

Technical training of foreigners in Japan is mostly financed by the Japanese and U.S. governments. Under the Colombo Plan, a total of 646 trainees had been brought to Japan by the end of March 1962.[41] As part of American aid to other Asian countries the ICA sent to Japan over a thousand "participants" from Taiwan, the Philippines, Cambodia, Viet-Nam, Thailand, Indonesia, and elsewhere; this movement continued under the Agency for International Development. Both these groups are given training through a semigovernmental organization, Asia Kyokai, which has constructed a center in Tokyo where trainees can live and study. Agricultural and fishing techniques are the focus of a large part of such training, and in these fields Japan has a great deal to teach other Asians. Other fields of training include forest conservation, textile processes, handicraft industry, other small-scale manufacture, railroad operations, public health, and government administration.

The Asian Productivity Organization (APO) offers a particularly promising means for the export of technology from Japan. Established in May 1961 with headquarters in Tokyo and members from eight Asian

[39] *The Oriental Economist,* March 1963, pp. 134–135.

[40] Japan, Ministry of International Trade and Industry, *White Paper on Science and Technology* [in Japanese] (Tokyo: Author, 1962), p. 56. Even American textile manufacturers have imported Japanese machinery because of improvements in design (see pp. 276–277).

[41] *The Tenth Annual Report of the Consultative Committee of the Colombo Plan* (Kuala Lumpur: Acting Government Printer, 1962), p. 223.

nations,[42] this organization has as its Secretary-General Ichiro Oshikawa, vice-president of the Japan Productivity Center. With initial contributions from member countries matched by a U.S. grant and further supplemented by a special U.S. contribution to "working capital," the APO appears to be safely launched and capable of actively promoting technical interchange. Additional resources may be obtained from the International Labor Organization and the United Nations Special Fund. Japanese interest has been manifested in many ways, including a contribution to administrative expenses and much of the leadership necessary to bring APO into being. Japan has a great deal to offer through APO and is expected to give far more than it gets in technology. But if the organization succeeds and the other member nations come to look on Japanese leadership as constructive and helpful, then Japan may have gained politically far more than the relatively modest outlays in money and effort have cost.

THE FUTURE

Japan's unique position as the only highly industrialized economy in Asia means that Japan has a great deal that neighboring countries lack. In this age of rising aspirations Japan's lead can potentially be used for the benefit of economic development elsewhere. Japanese processes contain many exportable elements. Japanese technicians are numerous and skillful, despite occasional shortages in some lines. The continuing rapid growth of the Japanese economy makes progressively smaller the drain represented by exporting a given volume of capital.

How much capital of all kinds can Japan afford to export in the years ahead? The Japanese tend to think that their country cannot export much. They cite the traditional shortage of capital, high interest and profit rates, and the growing volume of foreign capital now flowing into Japan on both long and short term. The outside observer must agree that these and other signs indicate limited ability to release capital for export. But that is not the whole story. Japan's phenomenal recent rates of saving and investment have caused many observers to wonder not about Japan's capacity to create capital but about whether much of the new production capacity is not destined to lie idle. The credit restraints imposed in 1961 because of the balance-of-payments crisis led to a sharp cut in fixed investment in 1962, with the result that production of steel and a number

[42] India, Japan, and the Philippines were co-sponsors. Other member nations represented at the first meeting of the Governing Body in Tokyo, May 22–27, 1961, were the Republic of China, the Republic of Korea, Nepal, Pakistan, and Thailand. Information on APO is from *Productivity, The Bulletin of the Japan Productivity Center* (Tokyo), No. 25, June 1, 1961.

of other products ran well below full capacity, and sales in some cases were below production, leading to growing stocks of finished goods.

Such excess capacity represents a waste of resources, in Japan as in any other country. One way to avoid this situation in the future would be to increase consumption and decrease the relative importance of investment in the economy. *The Economist* in September 1962 surmised that a shift of 5 to 10 per cent of gross national product toward consumption would be desirable but pointed out that Japanese habits and institutions make it unlikely that so big a change would occur in a short period of time.[43] A reduction in Japanese investment in fixed capital might lead to increased Japanese investment abroad. The capital-goods-producing capacity is now in existence. Where it is not used for domestic private investment, or public investment for much-needed overhead capital, it could reasonably be used to produce machinery and equipment for export, even if the return were to be long delayed.

The same reasoning could be used to support pleas for more Japanese grant aid to developing countries. Japan has unprecedented capacity to perform in many directions. In certain past periods, notably during World War I and the 1930s, Japan made large foreign investments, many of which were lost for political or military reasons. Now Japan can again afford large capital exports, this time without unduly depressing income levels within Japan. Hopefully most such investment would prove sounder than the politically motivated Nishihara loans to China in World War I [44] and more profitable in the long run than the huge investments made before 1945 in Taiwan, Korea, and Manchuria. Japan could afford to export substantially more capital as government grants than is now in prospect. The likelihood is that Japanese leaders will gradually come around to this view, although not without a good deal of prodding from the United States and other countries, especially in meetings of the Development Assistance Committee of the Organization for Economic Cooperation and Development.

As an importer of capital Japan has an appetite that promises to remain large in the foreseeable future. Even if domestic savings continue at their recent extremely high levels, foreign capital will be a very useful supplement. Capital cost is one reason; foreign capital is cheaper than Japanese. Foreign exchange problems are another reason; Japan can make good use of all the foreign exchange that can be obtained, especially on long-term arrangements.

[43] September 1, 1962, p. 815.

[44] When China defaulted the Japanese government had to make good on its guarantees to private lenders. Lockwood, *The Economic Development of Japan*, cited, p. 42. Moulton, *Japan: An Economic and Financial Appraisal*, cited, pp. 210, 283, 534.

Hunger for capital in Japan arises mainly from economic growth. At best, each advance in output requires some new capital. New machinery and buildings and other facilities must be built. Larger inventories must be maintained, of raw materials, goods in the process of production, and finished products. But in addition Japan now must undertake a growing volume of capital projects of the overhead type, and these are going to be very expensive. Perhaps the best example of what this may involve is transportation.

Japanese transportation facilities are seriously overloaded. Traffic is jamming. New automobiles are being produced far faster than the narrow, often crooked city streets can absorb them. Even the high accident rate does not keep total vehicle numbers within manageable limits. The capital expenses that may be in prospect for relieving congestion in Tokyo and other cities are almost frightening to contemplate, but they are inescapable.

Highway transportation outside the cities has long been grossly inadequate, and something is now, at last, being done about it. After years of discussion, vast highway projects have been started. The most dramatic is a superhighway connecting Kobe, Osaka, Kyoto, Nagoya, and Tokyo, for which the World Bank approved four loans that came to a total of $205 million. In time it is expected that the highway will be extended northward from Tokyo and westward from Kobe. Other highways will have to be constructed, to feed this main line and to provide improved local connections. In Japan's mountainous terrain major highways are extremely expensive, involving large cuts and fills, many bridges, and not a few tunnels. The danger of earthquakes requires heavy construction that adds further to the cost.

Railways too are overcrowded. Operation is remarkably efficient, so traffic cannot be increased without adding new lines. A major new railroad is now under construction between Tokyo and Osaka, called the New Tokaido Line in honor of the ancient highway it generally parallels. The fastest passenger trains on this double-tracked, electrified line are to cover the full 310 miles from Tokyo to Osaka in exactly three hours. This compares with at least six and one-half hours at present and is faster than air travel, because of the time taken between city and airport at each end of an air trip. Bridges, tunnels, and other structures, including elevated tracks along much of the route and a subway at the Tokyo end, help make the total estimated cost of building this railway nearly $550 million. A World Bank loan of $80 million granted in 1961 will cover about 15 per cent of the total.

Ports and harbors are also bottlenecks. The handling of maritime cargo has not shared the modernization of so much of the Japanese economy. Pier space is scarce. A large portion of general cargo and some bulk cargoes are handled by lighters, requiring much stevedoring labor, which has become scarce. Storage facilities in port areas are limited. In the booming times of 1961 ships frequently had to wait weeks to unload.[45] The Japanese government has large plans for port improvement, but fortunately the cost will be relatively small compared with building roads and railways.

It seems most unlikely that the volume of capital imports into Japan in the years ahead will be enough to meet needs such as those just cited. As in the past, the bulk of Japan's new capital will probably come from domestic sources. But the country's capacity to service foreign debt is rising rapidly, and so are the opportunities for foreign lenders and investors in Japan.

Japan has now outgrown dependence on the World Bank for new capital. The Bank indicated in 1961 that it intended to terminate lending to Japan but relented temporarily in view of the acute crisis that developed in Japan's balance of payments. Now Japanese borrowers can get enough in the capital markets of the United States and Europe to make it seem wise to the World Bank to reserve its lending for needier and weaker borrowers than Japan. This change means that capital will cost somewhat more. Still, it confirms what many other economic indicators are showing: Japan is no longer a weakling, no longer in need of special help, but a leading industrial nation, capable of fending for itself in world markets for capital as well as for goods and services.

[45] One report put the average delay in Osaka port at 20 days. *The New York Times,* June 30, 1961. Tokyo was the most congested of all ports, with an October report putting the number of waiting ships at an average of nearly 50. "In extreme cases, some tramp steamers wait three months before they can unload cargo." *The New York Times,* October 9, 1961.

Part II
Japanese Commodity Trade

Chapter 5

Japanese Imports

To get imports is the main object of Japanese foreign trade. Though exports usually occupy the center of public attention in Japan, they are basically not ends in themselves but means by which the Japanese nation provides itself with imports. Commodities account for about four-fifths of Japanese expenditures abroad, and about half the remainder goes for transportation and insurance directly associated with imports of goods.

POSTWAR GROWTH OF IMPORTS

Japan could not possibly have risen rapidly from its economic prostration in 1945 without foreign goods. The first very small flow of imports was paid for with a U.S. cotton credit, U.S. aid, and funds obtained by shipping abroad what little could be found that was suitable for export. Table 5-1 shows the record through 1962. In the first sixteen months through December 1946, imports amounted to no more than $306 million, and exports were only a third of that low level. Since then both exports and imports have risen irregularly but, in the better years, very rapidly. Imports did not reach their 1934–1936 dollar value until 1950, and exports the next year.[1] Higher postwar prices meant that the physical volume of trade was still far below the prewar level. Imports regained their prewar quantum only in 1956, but have since risen even more rapidly than import values, as the prices of imports have been

[1] The average for the years 1934–1936 is used frequently in this study as a basis for prewar comparison, especially for commodity trade. These years were the last before war began in China, which distorted Japanese trade as well as other economic activities. The trade figures for 1934–1936 used in this study have been adjusted to conform to Japan's postwar boundaries, except as may be indicated in particular cases. (Unattributed data on trade statistics in this chapter come from the tables herein or from standard sources cited in the Bibliographic Note.)

TABLE 5-1. JAPAN'S FOREIGN TRADE BALANCE, 1934–1936, 1945–1962

Year	Imports (c.i.f.) Value (millions of dollars)	Imports (c.i.f.) Change from Previous Year (per cent)	Exports (f.o.b.) Value (millions of dollars)	Exports (f.o.b.) Change from Previous Year (per cent)	Excess of Imports (millions of dollars)	Exports as Per Cent of Imports
1934–1936 av.	955		933		23	97.6
1945–1946 [a]	306		103		203	33.7
1947	526	71.9	174	68.9	352	33.1
1948	684	30.0	258	48.3	426	37.7
1949	905	32.3	510	97.7	395	56.4
1950	974	7.6	820	60.8	154	84.2
1951	1,995	104.8	1,355	65.2	641	67.9
1952	2,028	1.7	1,273	−6.1	755	62.8
1953	2,410	18.8	1,275	0.2	1,135	52.9
1954	2,399	−0.5	1,629	27.8	770	67.9
1955	2,471	3.0	2,011	23.4	461	81.4
1956	3,230	30.7	2,501	24.4	729	77.4
1957	4,284	32.6	2,858	14.3	1,426	66.7
1958	3,033	−29.2	2,877	0.7	157	94.9
1959	3,599	18.7	3,456	20.1	143	96.0
1960	4,491	24.8	4,055	17.3	437	90.3
1961	5,810	29.4	4,236	4.5	1,575	72.9
1962	5,637	−3.0	4,916	16.1	721	87.2
Postwar total	44,782		34,307		10,480	76.6

[a] September 1945 through December 1946.

Note: Minor inconsistencies result from rounding.

Sources: 1934–1936—Calculated from yen figures in Bank of Japan, *Economic Statistics of Japan*, 1960, pp. 245, 247, adjusted to include Japan's trade with Korea and Taiwan, and converted to dollars at exchange rates shown on p. 263.
1945–1962—Bank of Japan, *Economic Statistics Monthly*, March 1963, p. 2.

declining. (Table 5-6.) The following figures show changes in the physical volume of imports: [2]

Quantum Index of Imports
(1934–1936 = 100)

1950	37	1957	143
1951	55	1958	117
1952	61	1959	148
1953	83	1960	186
1954	86	1961	243
1955	90	1962	240
1956	114		

[2] Converted from 1953 and 1960 bases. Bank of Japan, *Economic Statistics of Japan*, 1960, p. 244; 1962, p. 253.

Japan's exports by value have risen more rapidly than imports, though here too the movement has been irregular.[3] The first four years of the Occupation, down to the end of 1949, were the hardest. In this period exports totaled only 43 per cent of imports. During the Korean War boom and its aftermath, 1950–1954, exports came to 65 per cent of imports (they were 84 per cent in 1950). In the years 1955–1957, the average was 74 per cent, despite the very large imports of 1957. For the three following years the figure reached 94 per cent, only to fall back to 73 per cent in 1961. Then it rose again to 87 in 1962. As the scale of Japanese trade rises in the years ahead and special dollar income declines, we can expect to see this percentage fluctuate at generally high levels, probably at times exceeding 100. If exports should prove insufficient and the figure tends to decline very far, the pressure will be strong to reimpose import restrictions to protect the balance of payments.

COMMODITY COMPOSITION OF IMPORTS

Raw materials, fuels, and foodstuffs dominate Japanese imports. As Table 5-2 shows, raw materials (including soybeans) account for nearly half the total value of imports. Coal and oil make up nearly a sixth of the total and foodstuffs an eighth. In recent years crude petroleum has been contending with raw cotton for the position of Japan's largest import item. The race is now going to petroleum; in the future oil imports seem certain to rise continually (pp. 126–127) while the growth of cotton imports is uncertain at best. After fuel and cotton, the major imports in the early 1960s were iron and nonferrous ores, metal scrap, lumber, raw wool, wheat, and machine tools.

Japanese industry lives largely by processing foreign raw materials. The textile industry, the country's largest manufacturing employer, heads the list of users of imports. Cotton, wool, and small amounts of other materials like wood pulp and chemicals going to textile makers account for about a sixth of Japan's imports. The second largest industrial user of imported materials is the iron and steel industry. Its iron ore, scrap, coking coal, and other items account for another sixth of all imports; these commodities are rising fast in import volume. In some years, notably 1957 and 1961, imports have been swelled by significant quantities of pig iron.

Machinery, chemicals, and other production goods make up roughly a fifth of total imports. Ranging from steam turbines, machine tools, and steel plates to electronic computers, fertilizer, and chemicals, these

[3] In Table 5-1 and throughout this chapter import value figures include freight and insurance costs, i.e., are valued c.i.f. They differ, therefore, from the balance-of-payments figures used in Chapter 3, which show imports as well as exports f.o.b. The excess of imports consequently looks larger here, and in no postwar year have exports exceeded imports on this basis.

TABLE 5-2. JAPAN'S IMPORTS BY COMMODITY, 1954, 1957, 1960, 1961, 1962

Commodity	1954		1957		1960		1961		1962	
	Million Dollars	*Per Cent of Total*	*Million Dollars*	*Per Cent of Total*	*Million Dollars*	*Per Cent of Total*	*Million Dollars*	*Per Cent of Total*	*Million Dollars*	*Per Cent of Total*
Food, beverages and tobacco	**653.8**	**27.3**	**574.1**	**13.4**	**547.2**	**12.2**	**667.4**	**11.5**	**740.5**	**13.2**
Wheat	168.0	7.0	163.3	3.8	176.9	3.9	179.4	3.1	180.9	3.2
Rice	250.9	10.5	48.2	1.1	19.6	0.4	16.6	0.3	23.8	0.4
Barley	51.1	2.1	56.4	1.3	0.1	0.002	0.0	0.0	0.0	0.0
Corn	14.4	0.6	36.5	0.9	81.0	1.8	107.0	1.8	133.7	2.4
Sugar	107.9	4.5	161.2	3.8	111.2	2.5	122.3	2.1	118.4	2.1
Animal feedstuffs	0.1	0.0	10.0	0.2	17.8	0.4	44.2	0.8	34.8	0.6
Unmanufactured tobacco	0.5	0.0	4.6	0.1	13.6	0.3	21.0	0.4	32.3	0.6
Other	60.9	2.6	94.0	2.2	127.0	2.8	177.0	3.1	216.6	3.8
Raw materials, except fuel	**1,125.9**	**47.0**	**2,010.0**	**46.9**	**2,169.2**	**48.4**	**2,748.7**	**47.4**	**2,361.9**	**42.0**
Hides and skins (except furs)	19.8	0.8	28.4	0.7	41.3	0.9	58.3	1.0	51.1	0.9
Soybeans	66.5	2.8	93.4	2.2	107.4	2.4	128.8	2.2	132.7	2.4
Other oilseeds	30.3	1.3	47.7	1.1	78.4	1.8	68.7	1.2	73.0	1.3
Crude rubber and latex	40.9	1.7	89.7	2.1	143.0	3.2	111.5	1.9	108.9	1.9
Logs and lumber	48.0	2.0	79.0	1.8	170.3	3.8	260.4	4.5	313.6	5.6
Pulp and waste paper	24.3	1.0	41.4	1.0	31.0	0.7	35.4	0.6	35.6	0.6
Raw wool (sheep's and lambs')	130.8	5.5	257.6	6.0	257.2	5.7	325.4	5.6	290.8	5.2
Raw cotton and linters	411.6	17.2	424.5	9.9	423.8	9.5	517.0	8.9	382.0	6.8
Phosphate rock	24.5	1.0	40.2	0.9	32.4	0.7	35.7	0.6	32.8	0.6
Crude salt	16.0	0.7	29.2	0.7	21.0	0.5	22.3	0.4	25.0	0.4
Iron ore and concentrates	66.2	2.8	205.7	4.8	213.7	4.8	301.8	5.2	318.2	5.7
Iron and steel scrap	43.9	1.8	284.5	6.6	229.7	5.1	387.5	6.7	179.2	3.2
Nonferrous metal ores and concentrates	25.2	1.1	126.3	3.0	155.5	3.5	171.1	2.9	161.9	2.9
Nonferrous metal scrap	35.8	1.5	76.4	1.8	74.3	1.7	94.9	1.6	52.1	0.9
Other	142.0	5.9	186.1	4.3	190.3	4.2	230.1	4.0	204.9	3.6
Mineral fuels and lubricants	**267.2**	**11.1**	**679.8**	**15.9**	**741.6**	**16.5**	**932.0**	**16.1**	**1,041.3**	**18.5**
Coal	62.9	2.6	174.5	4.1	141.2	3.2	188.2	3.2	201.5	3.6
Crude petroleum	134.0	5.6	323.5	7.6	465.0	10.4	538.7	9.3	620.5	11.0
Heavy oil	43.1	1.8	142.9	3.3	93.6	2.1	148.5	2.6	158.6	2.8
Lubricating oils and greases	4.5	0.2	11.9	0.3	19.5	0.4	25.0	0.4	30.1	0.5
Other	22.7	0.9	27.0	0.6	22.2	0.5	31.6	0.5	30.6	0.5

Fats and oils	**23.9**	**1.0**	**36.8**	**0.9**	**38.0**	**0.9**	**38.3**	**0.7**	**31.3**	**0.6**
Beef tallow	18.8	0.8	27.1	0.6	25.4	0.6	28.3	0.5	20.6	0.4
Other	5.1	0.2	9.8	0.2	12.7	0.3	10.0	0.2	10.7	0.2
Chemicals	**63.9**	**2.7**	**183.4**	**4.3**	**265.2**	**5.9**	**336.0**	**5.8**	**300.4**	**5.3**
Inorganic chemicals	0.1	0.0	11.7	0.3	19.1	0.4	27.1	0.5	21.8	0.4
Organic chemicals	13.9	0.6	34.8	0.8	50.4	1.1	60.4	1.0	75.3	1.3
Medicinal and pharmaceutical products	0.8	0.0	11.0	0.3	17.0	0.4	26.9	0.5	27.0	0.5
Potassic fertilizers	0.0	0.0	33.2	0.8	37.2	0.8	45.9	0.8	32.0	0.6
Synthetic plastic materials	5.4	0.2	24.4	0.6	34.8	0.8	43.2	0.7	35.2	0.6
Other	43.7	1.9	68.3	1.6	106.6	2.4	132.5	2.3	109.1	1.9
Manufactured goods classified by material	**61.5**	**2.6**	**462.6**	**10.8**	**257.2**	**5.7**	**389.7**	**6.7**	**295.1**	**5.2**
Pig iron	0.3	0.0	92.5	2.2	55.3	1.2	116.9	2.0	83.3	1.5
Steel plates, sheets, shapes, rails, etc.	7.7	0.3	156.4	3.7	29.6	0.7	21.2	0.4	9.0 [a]	0.2
Other iron and steel	3.5	0.1	56.0	1.3	2.7	0.1	18.2	0.3	19.9	0.4
Nonferrous metals	25.6	1.1	100.1	2.3	104.1	2.3	148.9	2.6	100.0	1.7
Other	24.4	1.0	57.6	1.3	65.5	1.5	84.6	1.5	82.9	1.5
Machinery and transport equipment	**177.1**	**7.4**	**288.4**	**6.7**	**402.7**	**9.0**	**599.2**	**10.3**	**767.3**	**13.6**
Power-generating machinery	9.8	0.4	26.1	0.6	31.5	0.7	36.4	0.6	71.3	1.3
Office machinery	13.5	0.6	19.0	0.4	52.9	1.2	84.9	1.5	104.4	1.9
Machine tools and other metal-working machinery	25.2	1.0	48.9	1.1	84.8	1.9	168.7	2.9	187.1	3.3
Machinery for conveying, mining and road construction	9.6	0.4	13.7	0.3	10.1	0.2	13.0	0.2	14.9 [a]	0.3
Textile machinery	9.9	0.4	17.6	0.4	15.6	0.4	19.3	0.3	26.8	0.5
Electrical machinery and appliances	13.1	0.5	21.2	0.5	34.2	0.8	41.0	0.7	79.5	1.4
Automotive vehicles and parts	28.0	1.2	16.3	0.4	13.3	0.3	16.8	0.3	19.8	0.4
Aircraft and parts	12.8	0.5	13.9	0.3	43.9	1.0	49.6	0.9	64.9	1.2
Other	55.3	2.3	111.7	2.6	116.5	2.6	169.6	2.9	198.6	3.5
Miscellaneous products and transactions	**23.8**	**1.0**	**44.4**	**1.0**	**63.4**	**1.4**	**87.5**	**1.5**	**90.4**	**1.6**
Scientific, etc., instruments and apparatus	8.4	0.4	21.2	0.5	28.8	0.6	40.9	0.7	32.2	0.6
Other	15.3	0.6	23.2	0.5	34.6	0.8	46.6	0.8	58.2	1.0
Total imports of foreign goods	**2,397.0**	**100.0**	**4,279.5**	**100.0**	**4,484.5**	**100.0**	**5,798.8**	**100.0**	**5,628.0**	**100.0**
Re-imports	**2.4**	**0.1**	**4.1**	**0.1**	**6.6**	**0.2**	**11.6**	**0.2**	**8.5**	**0.2**
Total imports, including re-imports	**2,399.4**	**100.1**	**4,283.6**	**100.1**	**4,491.1**	**100.2**	**5,810.4**	**100.2**	**5,636.5**	**100.0**

[a] Because of the extensive reorganization of the components of this item in 1962, coverage differs somewhat as between 1962 and earlier years.

Notes: See Appendix B for definitions of commodity groupings in terms of code designators. The customs statistics underlying this table are described in the Bibliographic Note.
Minor inconsistencies result from rounding.

Sources: Calculated from yen figures in Japan, Ministry of Finance, *Monthly Return of the Foreign Trade of Japan*, January–December issue, 1954, 1957, 1960, 1961; *Trade of Japan* (Monthly Return), January–December 1962.

TABLE 5-3. JAPANESE IMPORTS BY ECONOMIC CLASSES, 1946–1961

(In per cent)

Year	*Food-stuffs*	*Crude Materials*	*Fabricated Basic Materials*	*Finished Products*	*Other*
1946	40.8	49.5	4.9	4.6	0.2
1947	52.7	19.7	10.3	16.8	0.5
1948	47.9	24.3	8.1	18.7	1.0
1949	43.1	34.0	11.7	10.0	1.2
1950	33.5	42.0	6.3	18.1	0.1
1951	27.7	58.4	7.3	6.5	0.1
1952	32.1	52.1	6.6	9.1	0.1
1953	27.8	48.7	10.4	13.0	0.1
1954	29.7	46.7	10.3	13.1	0.2
1955	29.0	47.4	11.5	12.0	0.1
1956	20.2	58.5	10.7	10.5	0.1
1957	15.1	54.3	16.0	14.5	0.1
1958	19.7	53.5	9.0	17.6	0.2
1959	15.1	58.6	10.3	15.8	0.2
1960	13.9	58.6	11.9	15.4	0.2
1961	12.6	57.1	12.8	17.3	0.2

Source: Bank of Japan, *Economic Statistics of Japan,* 1961, p. 249.

items contribute qualitatively to the Japanese economy far more than their value might suggest. Japan now has very modern factories, largely as a result of importing the most advanced machinery and technology from wherever new processes and products are to be found.

Food is a less important part of Japan's imports than it used to be, especially in the years immediately after World War II. From more than half of total imports in 1947 the share of foodstuffs declined to a third in 1950, a fifth in 1956, and an eighth in 1961. (Table 5-3.) [4] Mean-

[4] The categories in Table 5-3, which reflect uses in Japan, are different in some respects from those in Table 5-2, which reflect an international compromise on statistical treatment. Soybeans, for instance, are listed in Table 5-2 among raw materials, but in Table 5-3 among foodstuffs, since Japanese food uses of soybeans exceed other uses. Other commodities presenting the same problem include peanuts and salt, both of which are included among raw materials in Table 5-2. Peanuts, like soybeans, are listed among foodstuffs in Table 5-3, but salt is included there partly among foodstuffs and partly among crude materials. Live animals, on the other hand, are all listed under "other" in Table 5-3 and in "food, beverages and tobacco" in Table 5-2. For details see *Statistical Classification of Commodities for Japanese Foreign Trade* (Tokyo: Japan Tariff Association, annual).

while Japanese agriculture has progressively increased yields on the limited acreage that can be cultivated.

Imports are evidently a serious business for Japan. There is very little waste or luxury here, few indications of imports that could be reduced or eliminated. Even if one goes behind the categories shown in Table 5-2 and scrutinizes the record of individual products, there is little to be found, at least until recent import liberalization, that is not a strict necessity. And when something appears in the list of imports that Japan is not compelled by circumstances to buy abroad, the volume imported is likely to be extremely small. Such items include prototypes of articles to be manufactured in Japan and products bought for some special purpose, such as catering to tourists. Only 2.6 per cent of total imports during the fiscal year 1959 were listed as manufactured goods other than machinery, and this figure is expected to rise to no more than 6 per cent in the last year of Japan's ambitious, ten-year, income-doubling plan.[5]

JAPAN'S DEPENDENCE ON IMPORTS

Japan relies on imports for all of its cotton, wool, natural rubber, bauxite, phosphate rock, nickel, and abaca. (Table 5-4.) These seven commodities account for nearly a fifth of Japan's imports. Imports provide more than 90 per cent of total supplies of crude petroleum, tin ore, sugar, and iron ore. In addition, more than half Japan's consumption of soybeans, wheat, and salt comes from abroad. All these products together accounted for 45 per cent of Japanese imports in 1960 and 40 per cent in 1961. This share would be even larger if particular specialties were shown separately, like lauan logs for plywood.

There are no apparent prospects of expanding domestic production of most of these goods on any large scale.[6] Only soybeans and wheat are already produced in significant quantities, which could not be enlarged except at high cost, in both money and displacement of other crops. Slow increase in output is possible as yields continue to rise, but it is more likely that rising demand for these products and liberalization of imports will lead to a decline in the share provided from local production.

These basic products could be dispensed with only at severe cost to

[5] Japan, Economic Planning Agency, *New Long-Range Economic Plan of Japan (1961–1970): Doubling National Income Plan* (Tokyo: The Japan Times, 1961), p. 80. The Japanese fiscal year runs from April 1 of the year named through March 31 of the following year.

[6] The minerals are lacking and there are no apparent possibilities of producing large quantities of cotton or tropical products. Production of wool in quantity would probably raise costs so high as to eliminate its major present uses, especially manufacture for export.

Table 5-4. Japan's Dependence on Imports of Certain Commodities, Selected Years

(Imports as a percentage of the sum of domestic production and imports, quantity basis)

	1934–1936 av.[a]	*1950*	*1954*	*1957*	*1960*	*1961*
Foodstuffs						
Rice	18.6[b]	5.7	13.6	2.9	1.6	1.0
Wheat	24.5	52.9	60.6	66.1	63.4	59.6
Barley	0.9	18.9	38.0	43.0	0.0	0.0
Soybeans	69.8	37.8	57.4	63.7	73.6	
Sugar	87.7	92.5	95.2	91.7	89.9	
Textile fibers						
Cotton	100.0	100.0	100.0	100.0	100.0	100.0
Wool	100.0	100.0	100.0	100.0	100.0	100.0
Rayon pulp	81.4	24.0	26.7	21.9	29.3	28.7
Metals						
Iron ore	93.4	64.0	81.0	89.1	92.1	94.9
Bauxite	100.0	100.0	100.0	100.0	100.0	100.0
Nickel	100.0	100.0	100.0	100.0	100.0	100.0
Tin ore	87.2	64.8	94.9[c]	85.0	93.2	93.3
Fuels						
Crude oil	93.5[d]	81.0	95.2	97.6	98.1	98.2
Coal	11.1	2.1	7.4	11.1	14.0	17.0
(Coking coal)		9.4	28.4	33.2	39.4	
Other						
Phosphate rock	100.0	100.0	100.0	100.0	100.0	100.0
Salt	65.0	60.6	80.2	70.6	72.7	73.9
Abaca	100.0	100.0	100.0	100.0	100.0	100.0
Copra	100.0	100.0	100.0	100.0	100.0	100.0
Crude rubber	100.0	100.0	100.0	100.0	100.0	100.0

[a] Imports from Japanese dependencies are included.

[b] Changed from source figure of 8.6 which is patently too low and appears to be a typographical error. The figure of 18.6 given here was calculated from E. F. Penrose's tables on rice production and imports, in E. B. Schumpeter and others, *The Industrialization of Japan and Manchukuo, 1930–1940* (New York: MacMillan, 1940), pp. 151–152. A round figure of 19 is given in Japan, Economic Planning Board, *Economic Survey of Japan* (1955–1956), p. 49. Figures provided by the Embassy of Japan, Washington, from Ministry of Agriculture and Forestry, *Foodstuff Statistics*, 1958, p. 58, show 18.7 per cent if rice exports are ignored, and 14.5 per cent if exports are allowed for.

[c] 1955.

[d] Includes heavy oil.

Sources: 1934–1936, 1950, 1954, 1957—Japan, Ministry of Foreign Affairs, *Statistical Survey of Economy of Japan* (Tokyo: Author, various years); Embassy of Japan, Washington, from Japanese official sources.
1960–1961—Same; and Japan, Economic Planning Agency, *Handbook of Economic Statistics* (in Japanese), 1963, p. 212, from Ministry of International Trade and Industry.

production in Japan. But not much of the rest is dispensable either, whether because of qualitative factors, as in the case of coking coal or of the most advanced machinery; because of limited domestic supply, as in the case of iron and steel scrap; or because increasing domestic production would be too expensive, as in the case of animal feedstuffs and many other items. Japan's import dependence thus is not a matter of marginal supplies or small price changes. Imports are essential to maintain the modern sector of the Japanese economy. Without them Japan's major industries, textiles and steel, would shrink severely with drastic effects on exports, domestic production, and employment.

Any continued severe reduction in Japanese imports, such as was experienced during World War II, would seriously affect both the quality and the quantity of what Japan produces. Levels of production and consumption would decline, and Japan would retrogress toward more primitive methods. It would probably be an exaggeration to say, as some observers have, that the Japanese people "would starve" if imports were stopped or severely curtailed. But, as experience during World War II clearly indicated, they might go very hungry, and the quality of their diet would suffer seriously as sugar and other components were lost, and as fertilizer production declined for lack of imported ingredients.

Such negative approaches as these, focusing attention on the dangers inherent in heavy dependence on imports, are customary among both Japanese and foreign observers of the Japanese economy. But this is only one side of the picture. The things Japan imports are, for the most part, available in ample quantities and cheaply. In fact, cotton, wheat, and some other products are exported at subsidized prices from the United States. In an era when much of the world may be blown to bits on no more than a few minutes' notice, can Japan be regarded as particularly unfortunate and vulnerable because it must import a great deal? Most countries must depend on foreign sources for many things. Japan is one country among many in an interdependent world, not a unique case. It is true that Japan's import dependence is great, but it is also true that this dependence is in some ways less than it used to be.

Japanese imports since 1950 have varied between 13 and 19 per cent of national income. (Table 5-5.) This ratio is remarkably small in view of Japan's great need to rely on foreign sources of primary products. Moreover, the ratio is significantly lower today than in the prewar period, and in recent years, as in the 1930s, there have been marked cyclical fluctuations. The factors influencing changes in Japan's import dependence are numerous, as the rest of this section shows.

TABLE 5-5. JAPANESE IMPORTS AS A PERCENTAGE OF NATIONAL INCOME, 1930–1939, 1946–1962

Year		*Year*	
1930	17.5	1946	1.1
1931	16.1	1947	2.1
1932	17.1	1948	3.1
1933	19.9	1949	10.4
1934	22.7	1950	10.3
1935	22.7	1951	17.0
1936	23.5	1952	14.7
1937	25.6	1953	15.4
1938	19.0	1954	14.4
1939	16.4	1955	13.6
		1956	15.7
		1957	18.6
		1958	13.1
		1959	13.4
		1960	14.1
		1961	15.3
		1962	13.1

Note: The percentages for the years 1946–1950 are approximate only. They were calculated from national income figures for fiscal years, beginning April 1, and import figures for calendar years, except for 1946, when import figures also included September–December 1945. All other figures apply to calendar years.

Source: Calculated from Bank of Japan, *Economic Statistics of Japan*, 1962, pp. 252 and 302; *Economic Statistics Monthly*, August 1963, p. 152. The prewar percentages have been adjusted to include imports from Korea and Taiwan.

Cyclical Elements in Import Dependence

Prominent peaks in the ratio of import value to national income occurred in 1937 and 1957, lesser peaks in 1951, 1953, and 1961. Five major price and demand factors are at work, and these explain most of the fluctuations involved.

In the first place, Japanese producers need a growing proportion of imported raw materials and semimanufactures when industrial expansion outstrips the domestic supply of such things as iron ore, pig iron, and metallic scrap. Increased purchases can come only from abroad when Japanese domestic production has reached its limit.

The second factor is the common business practice of accumulating inventories of raw materials and partly finished products when demand is rising. In such times producers tend to fear shortages and rising prices more than surpluses; the result is efforts to keep on hand the materials and parts necessary to cover a longer period of production. In slack times, by contrast, the burden of overstocking seems a more serious hazard, and the greater ease of procuring what is needed makes it prudent to adjust buying more closely to current needs, or to reduce inventories of raw materials and goods in process. In the first nine months of 1957 Japan was importing materials substantially in excess of current needs, but in 1958 imports fell below current consumption. The tendency to accumulate inventories was much less marked in 1961. The usually heavy dependence of Japanese production on bank credit during the postwar period has contributed to inventory fluctuations. Not only are banks less willing to extend credit when repayment prospects are less certain but, as we have seen in Chapter 3, Japan's countercyclical policy measures have relied heavily on limiting bank credit.

A third factor is the long lead time between placing import orders and the delivery in Japan of the commodities concerned. Transportation to Japan from Atlantic or Gulf ports of the United States normally takes about a month, which must be added to the delay between receipts of orders and shipment of goods by American suppliers, and any delays along the way, for instance, in congested Japanese ports. The businessman in Japan cannot, of course, expect immediate delivery of imports in case of sudden need. Nor can he ordinarily decide to do without ordered commodities that are on the high seas and, if he has chartered shipping to carry his cargo, it is expensive not to fill the ships.

The fourth factor, import prices, has had an uneven effect on import values. From a peak in 1951 the trend of import prices has been strongly, if irregularly, downward, as will be shown presently in the discussion of the terms of trade. The price paid by Japanese users of imports reflects not only goods' prices abroad but transportation charges involved in getting things to Japan. Ocean freight rates and ship charter rates fluctuate cyclically. The following figures show import freight costs as a percentage of c.i.f. values: [7]

1952	16.4	1957	21.1
1953	14.3	1958	15.4
1954	14.4	1959	14.8
1955	17.0	1960	15.4
1956	19.6	1961	16.6

[7] Bank of Japan, *Balance of Payments of Japan*, 1955, p. 37; 1959, p. 60; 1960, p. 65; 1961, p. 65.

Fifth, Japan's limited ability to finance imports has repeatedly led to the imposition of official import restrictions before other cyclical forces have worked themselves out. As we have seen, recent business cycles have shown themselves most sharply in the balance of payments and in the level of foreign exchange reserves. Restrictions on expenditures abroad have been the first object of Japanese countercyclical policy when economic growth has outrun available resources. Then when declining imports and rising exports have brought improvement in the foreign exchange position, restrictions have been relaxed and imports have again risen, not only in monetary terms but also in relation to total national income.

These cyclical factors are to some extent inherent in Japan's economic and geographic position and are unlikely to change greatly in the years ahead. What can be hoped for is that the severity of the swings will be moderated, perhaps through earlier exercise of monetary restraints when imports rise too fast. If the fluctuations in import demand can be made less severe, then perhaps the factor of limited ability to make foreign payments will become less important in determining Japanese policy. In 1961 the crisis was less severe than in 1957, and so were the countermeasures. If steps are taken earlier during the next economic upswing, then perhaps the restraint on payments can be even milder.

Import Prices and the Terms of Trade

Relatively low import prices are one of the important reasons why imports do not loom larger in relation to national income. During the ten years following the San Francisco Peace Treaty, prices of Japanese imports dropped to a marked degree. (Table 5-6.) The high prices of the early Korean War period had declined significantly by 1952, but by 1962 the index of Japanese import prices went down another 27 per cent. In fact, the 1962 index was less than two-thirds the high average for 1951. This decline in import prices took place in two stages. After 1951 the index declined for three years, then remained remarkably steady for four years, only to fall sharply in 1958 and a little further in 1959. Then there was stability again for three years before the small decline in 1962.

Domestic prices in Japan have, for the most part, not been going down. The wholesale price index has moved irregularly but within a narrow range, and in 1962 it was slightly above its 1952 level. The Tokyo consumer price index (1952 = 100) stood at 138.3 in 1962.[8] Thus while import prices fell by more than a quarter, wholesale prices showed no long-

[8] Bank of Japan, *Economic Statistics Monthly,* December 1962, p. 3; December 1963, p. 3. Before the wholesale price index was revised at the beginning of 1963, it showed an increase of 5 per cent from 1952 to 1962.

TABLE 5-6. JAPAN'S TERMS OF TRADE, 1950–1963 (1960 = 100)

Year	*Export Prices*	*Import Prices*	*Terms of Trade*
1950	96.2	118.8	81.0
1951	137.7	150.2	91.7
1952	112.3	134.6	83.4
1953	106.5	121.4	87.7
1954	102.4	116.6	87.8
1955	102.8	117.4	87.6
1956	107.3	117.3	91.5
1957	103.9	117.6	88.4
1958	94.5	103.8	91.0
1959	98.4	100.4	98.0
1960	100.0	100.0	100.0
1961	99.2	100.9	98.3
1962	97.9	98.6	99.3
1963	100.2	101.4	98.8

Source: Bank of Japan, *Economic Statistics Monthly*, January 1963, p. 3; January 1964, p. 3. (Figures from the second issue have been adjusted to the base of 100 for 1960.)

range decline, and Tokyo consumer prices went up by nearly 40 per cent. Declining import prices reflected mainly surpluses in the markets for primary commodities. The fluctuations in Japanese wholesale prices were a response to the powerful demand of a rocketing economy, to rising wages, and to some other factors, such as continuing high interest rates and the oligopolistic character of many Japanese markets. Consumer prices are much more affected by rising incomes and wages and only remotely related to import prices.

Export prices dropped by about 13 per cent between 1952 and 1962, about half the decline of import prices. The lag in the decline of export prices as compared with import prices has given Japan progressively more favorable terms of trade. In 1962 a unit of exports would buy 19 per cent more imports than in 1952.

The physical volume of imports that can be bought with a ton of exports is now between two and three times as large as in 1934–36. Then a metric ton of exports would pay for an average of 2.4 tons of imports; in 1960 the figure was 7.1 and in 1961, 5.6. This change reflects the progressively more advanced manufactures exported by Japan, while imports remain mainly commodities in crude form. This is much of the reason why it was financially possible for imports to be two and one-half times their prewar tonnage while exports did not reach their prewar tonnage until the end of the 1950s. In every year after 1946 the total tonnage of imports that could be bought with total exports rose, from only 500,000 metric tons in 1945–46 to 30 million tons in 1955 and to 79 million tons in 1960. In 1961 the 15.4 million tons of exports were worth as much as 86 million tons of the goods imported.[9] This rising trend results from increases in the volume of exports, combined with changes in the unit values of exports and imports.

Sharp Decline in Dependence on Food Imports

Food accounted for over half Japan's total import costs in 1947, over a quarter as late as 1955, but only an eighth in 1961. (Table 5-3.) This rapid decline was mainly a reflection of the swelling volume of total imports, but the dollar value of food imports for human consumption actually declined a little after 1955, despite the gradual rise in Japanese population and the very rapid rise in incomes.[10] Part of the explanation lies in the limited increase in food consumption during the years of unprecedented prosperity. Intake per capita rose only from 2,143 calories, with 65.1 grams of protein a day, in 1956, to an estimated 2,209 calories and 68.2 grams in 1962.[11] Another part of the explanation lies in the rapid expansion of the fish catch and the consequent large increase in that form of food, especially important for its high protein content. But most of the increase in fishery production has gone into exports, not domestic consumption.[12]

More of the explanation for lagging food imports lies in the extraordinarily rapid growth of agricultural production in Japan, despite the virtual impossibility of expanding acreage under cultivation. The general index of the Ministry of Agriculture and Forestry shows an increase

[9] Figures derived from Table 5-1 and from export and import tonnages given in Table 3-7.

[10] Table 5-2 shows total imports of food, beverages, and tobacco at $653.8 million in 1954, of which $0.1 million consisted of animal feedstuffs. The figures were a little higher in 1955, partly as a lingering result of the unusually short crop of 1953. The largest subsequent import level was that of 1962, but that year's $740.5 million of imports included $34.8 million of animal feedstuffs.

[11] Lester R. Brown, *The Japanese Agricultural Economy* (Washington: U.S. Department of Agriculture, Economic Research Service, ERS-Foreign-7, June 1961), p. 24.

[12] Japan has long been the world's leader among fishing nations, but postwar production has grown rapidly. From a level in 1945 that was only 85 per cent as high as that of 1935, Japanese fishermen had increased their catch nearly threefold in the fifteen years to 1960. Figures from an index of the Ministry of Agriculture and Forestry in Japan, Office of the Prime Minister, *Japan Statistical Yearbook*, 1961, p. 197.

in total crop production of almost 80 per cent between 1935 and 1960. A large element in this growth is the impressive increase in rice production. But increases have been notable in other products too, in wheat, potatoes, fruits, vegetables, and livestock, while in silk cocoons a sharp decline from prewar levels has occurred.[13]

Self-Sufficiency in Rice

The rice story is most illuminating. Rice accounts for nearly half of all food calories consumed by Japanese.[14] Per capita consumption has declined since the 1930s by a third, from about 12 kilos a month to about 8. Roughly half of the calories lost in this decline have been replaced by wheat, mainly in bread and noodles, the other half by meat, milk, and fats, an important nutritional improvement.[15]

Before and immediately after World War II a substantial part of the rice consumed in Japan was imported. In the 1930s most imports came from Korea and Taiwan, where the production of Japanese-style rice had been developed as part of Japanese colonial policy. In the three years, 1934–36, 18.6 per cent of the rice consumed in Japan was imported.[16] In the immediate postwar years imports never supplied more than 13.6 per cent of rice consumption (in 1954, following the particularly poor crop of 1953). Since then imports have been very small, and in the past several years hardly significant at all.

By the late 1950s Japanese rice production had reached record levels. The war reduced fertilizer supplies and disrupted production. The 1945 crop was disastrous. In the years following, planting, production, yields, and harvests were comparable to those of the early 1930s. Following the bad crop of 1953, the smallest since 1945, new measures were taken to stimulate rice production. By 1955, when the weather proved particularly favorable, yield per hectare rose 29 per cent and total production 36 per cent above 1954. Other rich harvests followed but the 1955 record was not surpassed until 1960. In that year, though the area planted was only 3 per cent above the 1930 level, production was 28 per cent higher, thanks to a 24 per cent increase in yields.[17]

These remarkable increases in production and productivity over

[13] Same; Brown, cited, p. 12; and estimates by the Economic Research Service, U.S. Department of Agriculture, based on reports of the agricultural attaché in the American Embassy, Tokyo.

[14] Brown, cited, p. 25. The rice favored in Japan is a special glutinous variety (*Japonica*).

[15] Seiki Nakayama, "The Rice Diet," *Japan Quarterly*, April–June 1961, p. 230 and elsewhere.

[16] E. F. Penrose, "Rice Culture in the Japanese Economy," in E. B. Schumpeter and others, *The Industrialization of Japan and Manchukuo, 1930–1940* (New York: Macmillan, 1940), pp. 151–153 and elsewhere. See also Table 5-4.

[17] *Japan Statistical Yearbook*, 1961, cited, pp. 11, 90, and 201.

levels that were already the highest in Asia sprang from technical improvements, stimulated by strong incentives and supported by various institutional advances. The land reform imposed during the Occupation increased the stake of individual farmers in high productivity and production. Price supports gave an added incentive. The government Food Bureau pays farmers prices that, after addition of milling and handling costs, are well above the prices at which it sells to consumers. The losses it incurs in selling domestic grain—most of the marketed rice and about a third of the wheat purchased by Japanese consumers—are made up by substantial net income from sales of imported wheat. The price of wheat in Japan is far above the world price.[18]

Japanese rice culture is highly labor-intensive even today. The postwar technical improvements, like those of the earlier years of the modern era, have been largely biological and chemical. Though machinery is doing more and more work—pumping, threshing, and spraying—the increase in tractors and cultivators has not yet displaced many draft animals in plowing and other heavy operations. A good many processes, especially seeding, transplanting, and harvesting, depend mainly on the bent backs, strong arms, and skilled hands of rural men and women. Plots are still too small for efficient use of some kinds of machinery. An era of intensive mechanization may be just ahead, however, as labor becomes scarce on the farms. One frequently hears stories about girls not wanting to marry farmers, at least unless they have many labor-saving devices and comforts. Heavy and skilled use of fertilizer, imaginative seed-bed techniques, and successful chemical campaigns against weeds, pests, and plant diseases have been responsible for most of the increases in rice production. Plastic film over seed-beds protects against weather and insects, and hastens growth. New chemicals that kill weeds not only increase yields and reduce hand labor, but permit more flexibility in crop selection and the timing of planting. Interplanting of crops and multiple cropping are highly developed to get maximum use of the soil for as many months of the year as weather permits. In some parts of Japan crops can be grown throughout the year.

Behind these progressive improvements stand a country-wide extension service with some 12,000 extension workers, a persistent and successful national research program, and almost universally literate farmers who give remarkable attention to detail and painstaking care to their work. Typhoons may still destroy standing crops just before harvest, but growth cycles have been adjusted so as largely to avoid the most dangerous seasons. Droughts, too, may damage rice, but water control is gradually improving, so that one area is progressively less likely to lack

[18] Based mainly on Brown, cited, especially pp. 17–24.

irrigation when a nearby area has more than enough water. Credit, marketing, handling, and transportation have improved, partly as a result of the better economic position and credit rating of farmers and partly because of institutional advances such as the postwar reconstitution of farmers' cooperatives, ending their role as agents of authoritarian control and making them representative of the farmers themselves. Credit is still scarce and there are other problems, but the growth of domestic output in rice and other agricultural products is solidly based on a whole series of technical, institutional, and economic improvements wrought since World War II.

Changes in Japan's Industrial Structure

The rapid growth of Japanese industry since World War II has brought important structural changes. Heavy industry has grown more than light; the effect on import dependence is mixed, but for the most part heavy industries, especially machinery, generate more income with imports of a given value than do light industries, notably textiles. At the same time, in all industries there has been a tendency toward higher degrees of processing, higher quality, and more complicated products, all changes that magnify the value added to a unit of imports.[19]

The leading manufacturing industries in 1955, as measured by value added to purchased materials, were machinery, textiles, food products, and chemicals. In the years that followed, machinery led all others in rate of growth, while textiles and other light industries grew much less rapidly. Chemicals, metals, and other more modern and heavy industries came in between. Since the value added by manufacture is on the whole greater in these more rapidly growing industries, the shift toward them tends to reduce Japan's raw materials costs in relation to final value of production.

A related development is shown in Table 5-7. Between the early 1950s and the early 1960s import costs fell from about 20 per cent of the price of Japanese exports as a whole to a figure near 15 per cent. Most of the decline is explained by the lower import prices already discussed, but technological changes have also played a part. The figures for major industrial sectors moved rather diversely. Foodstuffs, textiles and, less clearly, chemicals showed the most progress. Iron and steel, nonferrous metals and machinery moved in the other direction. Nevertheless the import cost of exports remains much lower for machinery and chemicals than for textiles.

[19] In establishments with 30 or more employees, value added per employee in 1961 was as follows (in thousand yen): textiles, 500; chemicals, 1,470; iron and steel, 1,185; machinery, 932; all manufacturing industries, 864. From census of manufactures, Bank of Japan, *Economic Statistics of Japan*, 1962, p. 222.

TABLE 5-7. IMPORT COSTS OF JAPANESE EXPORTS, BY COMMODITY GROUPS, 1952–1961
(Direct import cost as a percentage of f.o.b. price)

	1952	*1953*	*1954*	*1955*	*1956*	*1957*	*1958*	*1959*	*1960*	*1961*
All exports	19.0	21.1	22.9	21.2	18.5	17.1	16.4	15.7	15.3	15.5
Foodstuffs	15.0	15.8	8.8	7.6	6.2	6.4	6.1	5.5	6.3	6.9
Textiles	31.1	33.8	36.2	32.3	26.2	23.9	22.4	20.0	20.1	18.9
Iron and steel	19.0	19.3	15.8	14.5	27.6	27.2	20.9	23.4	25.5	28.0
Nonferrous metals	20.8	35.4	22.0	23.8	32.0	27.1	28.2	32.1	42.5	38.0
Machinery	4.1	5.7	7.9	9.9	9.6	10.8	9.0	10.7	8.6	10.4
Chemicals	13.2	3.5	7.7	9.2	12.6	8.3	8.0	4.8	7.0	10.3
Other	11.1	18.3	14.2	15.4	15.8	12.3	19.2	18.1	15.4	15.8

Source: Japan, Economic Planning Agency, *Economic Survey of Japan* (1961–1962) (Tokyo: The Japan Times, 1962), p. 389.

The reduction in the import cost of textile exports from over 30 per cent to less than 20 per cent in the course of a decade is explained in large part by a shift from natural fibers to synthetics. Nylon, orlon, and the other new "test-tube" fibers can be produced in Japan with a foreign exchange cost that goes very little beyond the fee to patent owners abroad (not covered in Tables 5-7 and 5-8). Table 5-8 shows the sharp contrast between the relatively high import content of cotton and wool manufactures and the very low import content of rayon and nylon.

Other Factors Reducing Import Dependence

A factor working to limit the physical volume of imports is production in Japan of raw materials formerly imported. This development is far less spectacular than the rise in food self-sufficiency because, in total, Japan's dependence on imported raw materials and fuels is rising. Still there are cases of decreasing reliance on imports, most notably, perhaps, the increased production of rayon pulp, which in 1961 was six times the 1936–38 average and nearly three times the average at the beginning of the 1950s.[20] Prewar imports of sulphate of ammonia and of soybean cake for fertilizer are now displaced by sulphate of ammonia made in Japan from domestic materials. The present small imports of soybean cake go to feed cattle.

A second and closely related change is a shift toward importing products at an earlier stage of manufacture, thus reducing import cost in relation to the value of the final product. For instance, instead of importing pig iron from Manchuria, as in the 1930s, Japan now imports more ore and produces most of its own pig iron, using coke made from a mix-

[20] Bank of Japan, *Economic Statistics of Japan,* 1961, p. 227.

TABLE 5-8. IMPORT COSTS OF SELECTED JAPANESE EXPORT PRODUCTS, 1961
(Direct import cost as a percentage of f.o.b. price)

Product	Import cost
Textiles and clothing	
Cotton yarn, #20	70.6
Cotton yarn, #40	60.6
Cotton fabric, #2023 sheeting	71.9
Cotton handkerchiefs	39.3
Cotton shirts	28.0
Cotton blouses	24.5
Woolen yarn	58.9
Woolen fabric, carded	36.6
Woolen sweaters	23.9
Rayon filament yarn	12.1
Rayon fabric	5.8
Spun rayon yarn	4.8
Spun rayon fabric	4.5
Nylon stockings	0.0
Miscellaneous products	
Cameras, 35 mm.	0.9
Umbrellas	5.0
Artificial flowers	8.1
Fountain pens	0.6
Metal toys, electric type	3.3
Tennis shoes	20.5
Rubber boots	21.4
Automobile tires, 7.50–20.12P	23.9
Automobile tubes, 7.50–20.12P	40.8
Plywood, lauan	62.7
Gasoline	47.8
Tuna fish, albacore, canned	0.9

Product	Import cost
Metals and machinery	
Pig iron, cast	49.0 [a]
Steel billets	30.9
Steel bars	37.7
Galvanized iron wire, BWG #8	25.4
Galvanized iron sheet	22.6
Tin plate	19.3
Aluminum sheet	11.8
Titanium sponge	1.8
Diesel engines	2.3
Cotton looms	7.3
Home sewing machines	7.2
Electric motors	6.9
Electric transformers	11.4
Electric insulators	3.6
Radio receivers, transistor	10.6
Radio receivers, other	1.9
Tape recorders	0.4
Locomotives	17.8
Bicycles	10.1
Autobuses	3.5
Tank ships	16.5
Cargo ships	15.4

[a] 1959.

Source: Japan, Economic Planning Agency, *Economic Survey of Japan* (1961–1962) (Tokyo: The Japan Times, 1962), pp. 390–395.

ture of imported and domestic coal. Even before the war, Japan vigorously pushed the development of oil refining. Then the motive was military more than financial, but nowadays Japan imports mostly crude oil and only a few petroleum products, including heavy oil and some specialties, such as bearing oil and lubricating oils.

A third factor is improvements in technology that reduce the amount of crude material consumed per unit of output. Dramatic evidence of this kind of progress can be found in the decreased amounts of raw materials needed for making pig iron. The following figures show consumption in kilograms per metric ton of pig iron produced in blast furnaces:[21]

	1952	*1955*	*1959*
Iron ore	1,593	1,574	1,539
Imported ore	877	785	750
Coke	883	711	632
Manganese ore and slag	26	12	8
Open-hearth slag	88	111	84
Iron and steel scrap	85	56	32
Limestone	368	246	143
Other	16	15	3

Since coking coal, manganese, and scrap, as well as iron ore, are imported in substantial quantity, it is evident that these savings are an important factor in reducing the steel industry's dependence on imports, as well as in reducing costs and making the industry more competitive. Iron and steel scrap comes mostly from abroad, but Japan's use of pig iron (which has a lower proportion of import cost) in steel-making is rising faster than the consumption of scrap. In 1951 half as much pig iron as scrap was used, while in 1960, after blast furnaces had begun to catch up with steel-making, the ratio had risen to 89 per cent.[22]

As the value added by manufacture rises and import cost declines in relation to export proceeds, Japanese trading and industrial activity produces larger amounts of foreign exchange for each unit of turnover. To earn a million dollars in foreign exchange by exporting cotton cloth, Japan has recently had to export and import a total of $6.1 million.[23] On the other hand, camera exports of $1,009,000 were sufficient to earn a million dollars in foreign exchange, since to produce that quantity involved only $9,000 in imports, a total turnover of $1,018,000. Thus to generate a given amount of net foreign exchange earnings through the manufacture of cotton cloth required six times as much foreign trade turnover as did cameras.

These factors that have reduced Japan's import dependence are in part the natural result of economic and technological changes and the expansion of the Japanese economy. In part they result from international developments and Japanese policies. For instance, domestic pro-

[21] Japan Iron and Steel Federation, *Statistical Year Book for 1960* (Tokyo: Author, 1961), p. 71.

[22] Same, p. 6.

[23] Figures apply to 1961 and come from the same source as Table 5-8. Foreign exchange earnings from exports of #2023 sheeting were 28.1 per cent of export prices received. Foreign sales of $3.56 million were therefore necessary to yield $1 million. To produce this volume called for imports of $2.56 million.

duction of a number of products, notably rice, has been stimulated by the fact that Japan's trade with Asian countries, artificially boosted in prewar years, contracted after the war, partly for political reasons. The chronic shortage of foreign exchange has curtailed imports and encouraged the search for measures to reduce import dependence. Protectionism, expressed in exchange controls and quantitative restrictions as well as high tariffs, has played an important part in keeping out foreign products and stimulating home production. More coal is produced in Japan than would be needed if oil imports were not limited. Subsidies are paid for the growing of rice, wheat, and soybeans. In addition to affecting trade and production directly, these measures stimulate technological changes that reduce the amount of imports needed per unit of output.

Factors Increasing Import Dependence

Opposing these factors that work to reduce Japan's dependence on imports are others pushing in the opposite direction. The better deposits of some domestic mineral resources, like copper and iron ore, may gradually be exhausted; as wages rise other deposits will become too expensive to work. Imported substitutes tend to displace some Japanese commodities, as petroleum is displacing coal under steam boilers. As the economy expands, it will, of course, require more materials; in many cases Japanese production cannot expand much, if at all. As the Japanese economy and balance of payments grow stronger, Japan may be willing as well as able to buy a growing volume of consumer goods from abroad and to admit competitive cotton yarns and other semimanufactures.

As the economy expands and the population increases, more of everything is needed. Japan will have to continue to import some of its food—in time, perhaps, a higher proportion than in the recent past, as consumption rises and nonagricultural activities encroach on land now devoted to crops. While improved utilization of materials and a continued shift toward industries with high value added by manufacture reduce dependence on imports as measured by some standards, great expansion of Japanese industrial production will inevitably require large increases in imports. In what may prove to be an optimistically low projection, the income-doubling plan puts imports in fiscal year 1970 at 16.7 per cent of national income, as compared with an average of 14.1 per cent in the fiscal years 1956 through 1958.[24]

Energy illustrates the relation between economic expansion and increased reliance on imports. Japan consumed about twice as much

[24] Japan, Economic Planning Agency, *New Long-Range Economic Plan of Japan (1961–1970): Doubling National Income Plan,* cited, p. 80.

energy in fiscal year 1959 as the annual average of the period 1934–36. The Economic Planning Agency expects that during the 1960s energy consumption will grow at the same rate as national income, 7.8 per cent a year, thus doubling in a decade. The use of imported fuels is expected to rise much faster. They supplied 34 per cent of all energy consumed in fiscal 1959 but are expected to supply 59 per cent in fiscal 1970.[25]

The domestic energy sources that provided two-thirds of 1959 consumption were mainly coal and hydro power. Firewood and charcoal, the traditional fuels of Japan, provided only 4 per cent of consumption, while another 1.6 per cent came from domestic petroleum, natural gas, and lignite. These minor sources are expected to expand faster than consumption but to remain very small. Only a small contribution is expected from nuclear energy by 1970.

The future of domestic energy supply rests, therefore, on the rate at which production of coal and hydro power expands. Japanese coal deposits are large (estimated at 818 billion tons), but the quality is low. Many seams are small and so situated as to make mining extremely difficult; extensive faulting causes discontinuities and adds to problems of flammable gas and pit water.[26] Because of these difficulties, Japanese coal is very expensive, and a major shift from coal to heavy oil as a fuel for steam boilers is under way. Technical improvements in mining may give some help in reducing prices. The income-doubling plan anticipates an increase in coal production of about 20 per cent by 1970, and a decline in the share of domestic coal in total energy consumption from 32 per cent in 1959 to 18 per cent in 1970. Favorable economic developments in the 1960s might make it difficult to justify any increase at all in domestic coal production. Most of the coal produced in Japan will continue to be burned under boilers. To make coke for the steel industry Japanese coal must have a heavy admixture of high-grade coking coal from abroad. The volume of coal imports, mainly of heavy coking grades, is expected to be more than four times as large in 1970 as in 1960.

Hydroelectricity, which now provides over a quarter of Japan's energy consumption, is expected to expand faster than coal production but only by 49 per cent in eleven years. As a result this source will provide only a fifth of energy consumption in 1970. Japan has already tapped its best hydro sources, and major new ones are becoming difficult to find;

[25] Figure for 1934–36 from Japan, Economic Planning Agency, *New Long-Range Economic Plan of Japan* (*FY 1958–FY 1962*) (Tokyo: Author, 1957), p. 98. Later figures from the EPA's *New Long-Range Economic Plan of Japan* (*1961–1970*)*: Doubling National Income Plan,* cited, pp. 11, 90–93, on which most of this discussion of Japan's future energy balance is based. These projections are used here as representing the result of careful and informed judgments although, like previous projections, they may prove wrong.

[26] Foreign Capital Research Society, care of the Bank of Japan, *Japanese Industry,* 1960, p. 27.

so the decline in the relative contribution of falling water to Japan's power supply is likely to go on.

The largest increase will come in the use of petroleum, practically all imported. Crude oil and products imports, which accounted for 29 per cent of 1959 energy consumption, are expected to reach 49 per cent by 1970. That means increasing Japan's largest import item to 3.6 times its 1959 tonnage, while the value of all imports together is going up to 2.5 times the 1959 level. It would take a great many import savings elsewhere in the economy to make up for such a massive increase. The long-range prospect is that this and other increases will exceed import savings, and that the share of Japan's national income going for imports will gradually rise through the years. The increase could become rapid if import prices rose sharply.

JAPANESE IMPORT POLICY

Prospects are excellent for Japan to get the large and expanding flow of imports it needs to keep the economy healthy and growing. The goods are available, and on favorable terms. Rising export income puts Japan in a progressively stronger position to buy.

Japan's import position has been much helped by the plentiful, and even surplus, supply of cotton, wheat, petroleum, and other primary products in world markets. While the relatively low prices of recent years may not last, there is at least no special reason for Japan to expect sharp price increases. Agricultural subsidy and price-support programs, notably in the United States, seem likely to continue to generate surpluses which will generally assure importing countries of adequate supplies on relatively favorable terms. Iron and steel scrap has been easily and relatively cheaply available in the United States, because of slack conditions in the steel industry here. Another price-reducing factor, international competition, is for the first time becoming of major importance in world markets for petroleum, which will constitute a growing fraction of Japan's import bill. Coal of high quality is plentiful in the United States, but usable coking coal is also increasingly available elsewhere, notably in Australia and Soviet Asia, and perhaps in time in Communist China. Other developments may, for longer or shorter periods, make some commodities scarcer or more expensive; events in Cuba, for instance, have had an effect on Japan's sugar supply. For still other commodities, such as iron ore, new sources will have to be developed as Japanese demand grows.

Japan's dependence on imports cannot be escaped, but when all the factors are weighed realistically it does not look like a crippling handicap. In today's frighteningly explosive world, Japan's vulnerability as a result of import dependence is only one fact among many, and Japan is only one of many vulnerable countries. For the immediate future, at any rate, the prospects of Japan's meeting its import needs on reasonably favorable terms are excellent. The Japanese can do much to keep the outlook like this. Their treatment of imports is an element of major significance in Japan's future economic position.

Import Projections for 1970

All the conflicting factors affecting Japan's import dependence had to be examined by the authors of the import projections in the income-doubling plan. (Table 5-9.) The most noteworthy feature of these projections is the anticipated shift of imports away from foodstuffs and even raw materials, toward finished and semifinished products. Foodstuff im-

TABLE 5-9. JAPAN'S IMPORT PROJECTIONS FOR 1970

(Values in millions of dollars)

	Fiscal Year 1959		*Fiscal Year 1970*		*Percentage Increase*	
Item	*Value*	*Per Cent of Total*	*Value*	*Per Cent of Total*	*Total*	*Annual*
Foodstuffs	499	12.6	804	8.1	61	4.4
Raw materials	1,995	50.2	3,789	38.3	90	6.0
Textiles	778	19.6	1,131	11.4	45	3.4
Chemicals	81	2.0	94	1.0	16	1.4
Iron and steel	390	9.8	901	9.1	131	7.9
Nonferrous metals	155	3.9	53	5.8	270	12.8
Agriculture, forestry	350	8.8	599	6.1	71	5.0
Miscellaneous	241	6.1	491	5.0	104	6.7
Mineral fuel	693	17.4	1,863	18.8	169	9.4
Semifinished products	312	7.8	1,093	11.1	250	12.1
Finished products	471	11.8	2,330	23.6	395	15.6
Machinery	366	9.2	1,735	17.5	374	15.2
Miscellaneous	105	2.6	595	6.0	467	17.1
Other items	6	0.2	12	0.1	100	6.5
Total imports	3,976	100.0	9,891	100.0	149	8.6

Source: Japan, Economic Planning Agency, *New Long-Range Economic Plan of Japan (1961–1970): Doubling National Income Plan* (Tokyo: The Japan Times, 1961), p. 80.

ports are projected to decline from one-eighth to one-twelfth of total imports, despite a 61 per cent increase in value. Raw materials will drop from half to about three-eighths of total imports, despite a 90 per cent increase in value, which itself is moderate in view of the projected trebling of manufacturing production. Mineral fuel imports are expected, as we have seen, to expand faster than total imports. The small group of semifinished imports will show even more rapid expansion, rising from about 8 to about 11 per cent of total imports. The greatest expansion of all is expected in imports of finished products, which are projected to double their share of the total, from about 12 per cent to about 24 per cent. Machinery is expected to remain the largest part of this last group and to constitute 17.5 per cent of 1970 imports. Here we have vivid evidence that Japan's economic planners expect trade with developed areas to increase at a greater rate than trade with areas that produce only primary products. The development of ultramodern facilities in Japan is evidently far from finished, despite the tremendous volume of investment in recent years. Japan's continuing—even growing—dependence on the most advanced foreign technology and machinery should give reassurance to Americans who fear that Japanese trade may be harmful to the American economy.

Another striking feature of the import projections is the increase in the small item of miscellaneous finished products, from 2.6 per cent to 6.0 per cent of the total, indicating a structural shift in imports with liberalization. The figures are small, but the doubling of this little item is of special significance for Japanese import policy. It suggests a willingness to import some things Japan could probably produce at home at higher cost. If so this represents a shift from the traditional attitude that Japan's international economic position is so vulnerable that the country should avoid using scarce foreign exchange for luxuries and concentrate on the maximum import of essentials.

Traditional Avoidance of Unnecessary Imports

This basic approach is manifested in thousands of ways that strike the eye of the foreign visitor, especially the American. Away from Western-style eating places he will find meat and dairy products much less plentiful than in the United States. At his breakfast he may miss citrus fruits and bananas. On the streets and in the countryside he will see straw rope used for many purposes that would seem to be better served by twine or rope made from heavy fibers. In his shopping he will probably be impressed with the esthetic quality and delicate handling of the wrappings on his packages, which will probably be tied with paper string. These do beautifully, especially if the package is then covered and carried in a silk—or rayon or nylon—*furoshiki* of attractive design.

Traditional ways of packaging are far less costly, especially in terms of imports, than heavy cardboard, thick wrapping paper, and twine of cotton, jute, sisal, or hemp.

Rice is usually handled in bags of woven straw, as it has been for centuries. Straw makes less tight and sturdy bags than burlap, cotton, or paper, but the bags, made in very small plants in parts of Japan where rice straw of the right quality is available, cost no foreign exchange and their manufacture provides a by-employment for farmers. It is high time Japan shifted to the use of sturdier bags that do not let rice grains spill out. Paper bags have already displaced straw for ammonium sulphate, but the government Food Bureau, which has a monopoly of rice marketing, is not yet ready to use them for rice. One problem is the lighter weight of paper bags. At present, rice is handled in units of 60 kilograms including the bag. Paper bags would require shifting to a slightly different unit, either gross or net, and a decision on this question has not been reached. Meanwhile, Japan pays a price, in mild inconveniences and some loss of rice in handling, for a traditional method that requires no foreign exchange, while paper bags would involve a small foreign exchange outlay for imported pulp.

On the streets of Tokyo and other large Japanese cities the visitor encounters a dismaying congestion of vehicles of many types. The bicycles, motor bicycles, scooters, and motorcycles, the distinctive Japanese three-wheel trucks, and vehicles of four or more wheels in all sizes have crowded most hand-carts and horse-drawn vehicles from the streets. Although the rapid spread of petroleum-powered vehicles represents a national commitment to continuing and increasing imports of oil, most of the vehicles themselves are being produced domestically. The Japanese motor vehicle industry has been given strong protection by high import duties and strict quantitative limitations on the number of foreign vehicles permitted entrance.

The total effect of habit, personal economy, conservation of foreign exchange, and protective measures in Japan has been that even in recent years little has come in from abroad that could be produced in Japan, whether manufactures, minerals, or farm products. Japanese policy has sought to reduce import dependence to the practical minimum. Japanese authorities have been most reluctant to permit much consumption of anything that involves what seems to them an unnecessary expenditure of foreign exchange. Domestic production of rice and wheat is subsidized, and more expensive Japanese coal is favored by checking imports of coal and oil. The general policy goal during the 1950s was to maximize domestic production in certain fields where imports would thus be reduced, and to confine import purchases mainly to commodities having the maximum effect on Japanese production and economic growth.

Factors Retarding Relaxation of Import Restrictions

Although the balance of payments has improved greatly in the past decade, a number of forces have remained at work to keep Japanese import policy in its former mold. The projected import increases in the new ten-year growth plan allow for some liberalization of restrictions but not, it would appear, very much, if by 1970 imports are to be kept to the projected one-sixth of national income. With high and rising dependence on imported supplies of petroleum, coking coal, iron ore, and a number of other materials, there remains a good deal of apprehension in Japan about the country's ability to pay its bills. The degree to which barriers are relaxed will depend in part on export income and in part on the psychological mood of the Japanese, especially businessmen and government leaders.

Protectionism is another powerful factor. Import controls imposed to conserve foreign exchange have permitted the establishment in Japan of many plants with costs higher than those abroad. These businesses depend on continued protection for their profits or even their survival. The resulting political pressure has recently been a powerful force holding back the liberalization of Japanese import policy.

A third factor heretofore has been the widespread underemployment of labor in Japan, a continuing reflection of the fact that boom times have not yet spread to all parts of the Japanese economy. Where many have been without any remunerative employment, or have had to work at archaic and relatively unproductive tasks or for extremely low wages, there is some economic as well as social and political justification for continuing certain activities, such as coal mining, beyond the point where price considerations suggest shifting to imports. This not only gives miners employment but saves foreign exchange that can be used to buy raw materials, the processing of which will give employment to others. Recent prosperity has created serious labor shortages for the first time during peace. While this phenomenon can be expected to recur, it will be limited by the unusually large numbers of new entrants joining the labor force in the mid 1960s. Even when new workers find many jobs available, the habit of Japanese employers to take on employees only at the bottom of the scale makes it most difficult for a middle-aged miner or other worker to find a satisfactory new job if he should be displaced. It will probably take a long time to eliminate the thousands of forms of make-work to which Japanese offices, shops, factories, and other organizations have become accustomed.

The fourth strong force for limiting Japanese imports is not economic so much as psychological, mainly a yearning for security. A people subject to earthquakes, typhoons, floods, and fires that at times reach devastating proportions cannot expect complete physical security. Dependence on foreign sources of supply for many necessities increases vulnerability, as the Japanese found out when lack of imports reached extreme proportions during the war, touching everyone, especially in the form of severe food shortages. It is not surprising, therefore, that there is strong pressure in Japan to maximize food production.

In addition to limiting total imports, the Japanese government has been deeply concerned, during a large part of the postwar period, with the place of origin of imports, because of the inconvertibility of its own and many other currencies. The United States, having the hardest currency, was, in effect, the import source of last resort, to be used only if other countries could not supply on reasonably favorable terms, as they often could not. By purchasing from some of these countries Japan was able to make larger sales to them, so discrimination not only saved dollars but also promoted exports. In 1958 the Minister of International Trade and Industry questioned the idea that Japan should buy a country's goods just because they are cheap and proposed instead that Japan should favor purchases in countries that make its own sales easy.[27] Discrimination against dollar goods had been wholly removed by the end of 1960, but it is still of interest to Japan to maximize purchases from various exchange-short countries, especially in Asia, as a means of making possible larger Japanese sales to them.

Japanese investments in raw materials production abroad are growing. They are a second force for directing import orders to particular sources. For instance, it seems unlikely that oil produced in the Japanese concession in the Persian Gulf, pulp from the Alaskan mill built by the Japanese, and iron ore from Malayan and Indian mines into which substantial amounts of Japanese capital have been sunk will be allowed to go unsold while Japan imports similar commodities from other sources. A contest has been going on with foreign oil companies in Japan. They want to use their own oil, but the Japanese want to bring in more from new Japanese-controlled wells in the Persian Gulf. As Japanese investment grows in raw materials production overseas, this factor is likely to become more important in Japanese import policy. Interconnections among Japanese firms would probably be enough, even without government controls, to direct many import orders to those sources in which there is a substantial Japanese investment.

[27] Tatsunosuke Takasaki, as quoted in U.S. Board of Governors of the Federal Reserve System, *Far Eastern Economic Developments*, July 28, 1958, p. 1.

Import Control Techniques

Since 1952 as before, the principal method used to restrict total Japanese imports and to discriminate against certain sources such as dollar countries has been direct import licensing. Although the issuing of licenses has become progressively freer and many exceptions have been permitted, especially in recent years, the basic system remains legally the one inherited from the Occupation in 1952.[28] In principle nothing may be bought from abroad without permission from the government. Permission has been limited first of all by basic decisions made semiannually in the foreign exchange budget, which sets limits on the amounts of foreign exchange to be made available for particular uses.

Within these limits the Ministry of International Trade and Industry (MITI) exercises wide discretion in issuing licenses. The procedure for licensing imports has been very detailed for most items. A Foreign Exchange Fund Allocation (FA) system has required case-by-case consideration of applications for licenses, which when granted provide both import authority and a right to purchase the necessary foreign exchange. Under the FA system quotas are set up in considerable detail by commodity, in some cases also by country. These quotas are allocated among Japanese import firms, usually on the basis of past import volume. Under the FA system MITI has exercised not only detailed control over Japanese imports but also a good deal of guidance and even initiative in importing. MITI import notices start the import process within the foreign exchange budget, and their nature and timing have been important means of government control. MITI stipulates the commodities for which license requests will be received during a stated period, often short. Other means of guidance are the deposits that must be made on application and the various limitations put on licenses or applications for them, such as those limiting the amount of goods for which an individual importer may apply.

A second system of licensing imports, Automatic Approval (AA), is much freer and simpler. Subject to total import quotas for individual commodities and sometimes also to limitations on source, applications for licenses to import AA items are granted automatically, as the title

[28] Based on the Foreign Exchange and Foreign Trade Control Law of 1949 (Law No. 228), most of the text of which is presented in English translation in U.S. Department of Commerce, *Investment in Japan* (Washington: GPO, 1956), pp. 141–143. See also IMF, *Twelfth Annual Report on Exchange Restrictions* (Washington: Author, 1961), esp. pp. 208–209, and other reports in this series. This law is to be revised in connection with the further liberalization associated with Japan's shift to Article 8 status in the IMF. The principal change is reported to be abolition of the foreign exchange budget, but it is not immediately clear that licensing of imports will effectively stop. Bank of Tokyo, *Weekly Review*, February 17, 1964, p. 38; February 24, 1964, p. 43; March 16, 1964, pp. 60–61.

suggests. (There are, however, certain administrative restrictions, including discrimination against firms that have previously violated license regulations.)

A third procedure, introduced in November 1959, is called Automatic Fund Allocation (AFA). An intermediate step between the other two systems, AFA in practice permits automatic approval and allocation of exchange for requested imports. Like FA, the AFA procedure requires application to MITI, while AA permits foreign exchange banks to issue both import licenses and foreign exchange without prior MITI action. In the foreign exchange budget for October 1960–March 1961, 42 per cent of imports fell under AA, 2 per cent under AFA, and the remaining 56 per cent under FA.[29] In contrast, the budget for April–September 1963 allocated 66 per cent for AA imports, 12 per cent for AFA, and 22 per cent for FA.[30]

As long as the present law stands, the Japanese government is legally free to take administrative action to tighten controls by shifting particular items to FA from AFA or AA treatment and restricting the issuance of import licenses.

In addition to these general import controls, bilateral trade and payments agreements have been an important feature of Japanese trade policy, especially in the earlier years of the postwar period. Often these agreements have amounted to barter arrangements, with provisions for keeping trade between Japan and the other partner in approximate balance. Usually the agreements have stipulated that credit balances exceeding a specific sum should be settled in certain specified currencies. These agreements have helped Japanese sales in countries that could not pay in convertible currency and have permitted imports without having to give up foreign exchange. In the early postwar years this sort of trade was very attractive and important to Japan. In 1950, 25 per cent of all imports came in under these open-account arrangements. The figure dropped to 13 per cent in 1952 but rose to 25 again in 1955 and then fell rapidly after many currencies had become convertible and Japan found itself in a much easier payments position. In 1961 only 1.5 per cent, and in 1962 only 0.4, of imports came in on open account.[31] At the beginning of 1963 Japan had only one remaining agreement of this sort, with Korea.

[29] *The Oriental Economist,* December 1959, p. 711; U.S. Department of Commerce, "Licensing and exchange controls . . . Japan," *World Trade Information Service,* pt. 2, no. 61-27, April 1961, pp. 1–2.

[30] Bank of Tokyo, *Weekly Review,* April 1, 1963, p. 81.

[31] Bank of Japan, *Foreign Exchange Statistics Monthly,* December 1959, p. 20; December 1962, pp. 2, 6.

Liberalization since 1958

Until the late 1950s restrictive import policy had strong justification in Japan's weak balance of payments. Few, if any, Japanese had given much thought to extensive liberalization before the announcement at the end of 1958 of external convertibility for the pound sterling and several other European currencies. After that, however, it was not long before the question was raised of relaxing restrictions on Japanese commodity imports and other international expenditures.

Foreign pressure was more significant than domestic in bringing change. While the Japanese government held back, foreign demands for liberalization increased. They were particularly strong at the meetings of the World Bank and International Monetary Fund in October 1959 and at the GATT meeting in Tokyo a few weeks later. The United States government in particular pressed Japan to remove discrimination against dollar imports and to ease restrictions against all kinds of imports. Finally, nearly a year after the major European moves toward convertibility, the Japanese government undertook a serious study of the problem of freeing trade and payments from direct quantitative controls. No basic decision was taken until June 1960. Before then only limited moves were made, mostly steps that might have been taken in any case as booming prosperity replaced the financial crisis of 1957—larger foreign exchange budgets, eased administrative arrangements, and shifts of individual items from more restrictive to less restrictive treatment.

In June 1960 the cabinet adopted a "Plan for Trade and Exchange Liberalization." By this action the government approved the principle of liberalization and proposed to apply it on a broad front. Four stages of liberalization were laid out for commodity imports: (1) Imports were to be liberalized as quickly as possible for certain raw materials and finished products that raised no serious problems, notably mineral ores, pig iron, cotton and silk manufactures, optical goods, and textile machinery. (2) Imports of commodities that Japan could sell on a competitive basis abroad or that do not compete in the domestic market were to be liberalized within three years. Among these commodities were synthetic fibers, wool manufactures, plate glass, special steels, and some machinery. (3) Commodities that would not be removed from the quota list for more than three years included products of industries in which technical development is being fostered, for example, machine tools, automobiles, heavy electrical equipment, some fertilizers, metals, and forestry products. (4) The fourth group consisted of items whose "liberalization appears to be difficult for a fairly long period of time," including rice and wheat, dairy products, vegetable oils, and most fruits.[32]

A particular import product is regarded as liberalized if it is allowed to enter Japan under either AA or AFA treatment. (See pp. 133–134.) Thus the law and philosophy of control are not changed, for in principle all imports continue to require licenses. In practice, however, AA items do not have to wait for licenses, and licenses for AFA items are easy to get through foreign exchange banks. The progress of liberalization can thus be measured by the share of AA and AFA imports in total imports, but the calculation can be misleading because items that are most effectively barred are given the least weight.

The Japanese use 1959 as the basis of calculation so the importance of liberalizing any particular item is measured by its share in imports in that year. Items that were important then, like raw cotton or crude petroleum, carry heavy weight in measuring liberalization. Items whose import was small in 1959 carry little weight. And items not imported at all in 1959 do not affect the liberalization calculation, no matter how much or little of them is later permitted entry, or on what terms. By this standard of measurement, 40 per cent of Japanese imports were already liberalized as of April 1960. The policy decision in June called for raising this figure progressively to 80 by the end of March 1963 (or to 90 per cent if coal and petroleum products should have been liberalized by then). The schedule was advanced in an announcement made during the annual IMF consultations in mid-1961, setting the target definitely at 90 per cent liberalization by September 30, 1962. The actual record is as follows:

	Per Cent		*Per Cent*
October 1960	44	April 1962	73
April 1961	62	October 1962	88
October 1961	68	April 1963	89

Thus the target was almost met: only 12 per cent of Japan's 1959 imports remained unliberalized in the autumn of 1962, and this was reduced to 11 per cent in April 1963. Discrimination in treatment of different sources of imports ended with the termination of dollar discrimination in October 1960.

Since liberalized items can be imported without quantitative limit,

[32] This discussion of liberalization is based mainly on *The Oriental Economist,* May 1960, pp. 237–244; August 1960, pp. 448–449; September 1961, pp. 523–524; and November 1962, pp. 632–637; *Fuji Bank Bulletin,* September 1960, pp. 10–16; Bank of Tokyo, *Weekly Review,* July 4, 1960, pp. 180–184; Bank of Tokyo, *Semi-annual Report,* June 1960, pp. 17–28, December 1961, pp. 20–25; International Monetary Fund, *Annual Report on Exchange Restrictions,* 1962 and earlier issues; and conversations with officials of the U.S. and Japanese governments and the International Monetary Fund.

the importance of the foreign exchange budgets has declined sharply. Enough foreign exchange is provided to cover payments for imports of liberalized items, whatever amount comes in. The budget is controlling only for items not liberalized. Consequently the foreign exchange budget has shifted progressively from being a major instrument of exchange control to becoming an index of official expectations about imports and other transactions involving expenditures abroad.

Another, and perhaps more meaningful, measure of Japan's remaining quantitative controls is given in a new negative list of the products whose import into Japan remains subject to specific approval under the FA system. This list, as issued on October 11, 1962,[33] is described as containing 262 items, but many of these are subdivided. Among the items listed are rice, sugar, common salt, several fruits in fresh form, soybean oil, peanut oil, coal, coke, heavy oil, nitrogenous fertilizers, urea, lauan logs, cotton yarn, woolen yarn, synthetic fiber yarns and fabrics, bed linen, face powder, safety razor blades, typewriters, cash registers, digital computers, steam boilers (of capacity between 650 tons and 1,100 tons an hour), turbines, electric generators, and various other kinds of machinery. Deletions from the negative list had brought down the official number of items thereon to 182 by the end of February 1964.[34]

There was some fear in Japan early in 1963 that liberalization might have gone too fast and too far. In the United States, on the other hand, disappointment was expressed at continued import restriction. The liberalization process consists simply of removing direct quantitative controls; it does not entail tariff changes. But what both sides are discussing basically is the extent to which market forces are to control Japanese imports. Japanese who fear foreign competition are prominent among these who contend liberalization has been too rapid. Among the foreigners who argue it has not gone far enough many would like to sell in Japan but find the barriers still prohibitive.

An illustration of the Japanese protectionists' point is found in what happened when soluble coffee was liberalized in July 1961. Nescafé took the lead among foreign brands in making what *The Oriental Economist* calls "a big dent" in the Japanese market.[35] A case on the other side is razor blades. In anticipation of liberalization, the Gillette company in the United States made a sales arrangement with a Japanese

[33] Japan, Ministry of International Trade and Industry, Import Notice No. 2, Notification No. 529, dated October 11, 1962, pp. 41–50.

[34] Bank of Tokyo, *Weekly Review*, March 9, 1964, pp. 55–56.

[35] November 1962, p. 633. Total imports of soluble coffee in 1960 had been $161,000. After liberalization, imports jumped to $7.1 million in July–December 1961 and $7.6 million in January–June 1962. Figures from Japan, Ministry of Finance, *Monthly Return of the Foreign Trade of Japan*, 1961 issues, and *Trade of Japan* (Monthly Return), 1962 issues.

firm. But failure of razor blades to be included in the 88 per cent liberalization achieved by October 1962 made these plans premature. Fountain pens and ball-point pens, especially American pens, appeal strongly to Japanese, as to many others all over the world. Immediately after they were liberalized at the beginning of October 1962, pens began to flow into Japan in sharply increased quantities, especially from the United States. In November 1962 the inflow was slightly larger than the total for 1961. And in December imports almost doubled over November. Altogether, imports in 1962 reached $646,000, compared with $154,000 in 1961.[36]

The Tariff

Tariffs were not significant to Japan during the Occupation, either as commercial policy measures or as sources of revenue. Their collection was suspended for several years and the volume of imports was regulated by direct controls and by trade and payments agreements with other countries. In 1951 a completely revised tariff was put into effect, using ad valorem rates almost exclusively and dropping most of the specific duties whose former rates had become virtually meaningless as a result of the three-hundredfold inflation during the Occupation and before.[37] The 1951 tariff constituted no break in Japanese tariff traditions, however, despite the new rates. The classification continued to follow that of the 1911 tariff as amended in subsequent years. About a fifth of the items listed, mainly raw materials, were permitted duty-free entry. Rates of less than 15 per cent applied to about a quarter of all dutiable items; another quarter were subject to a 15 per cent duty. On the remaining half of dutiable items, rates ranged from 15 to 50 per cent and were intended to protect domestic production of plastics, clothing, watches, automobiles, machinery, and luxuries such as jewelry, cosmetics, perfumes, and alcoholic liquors.[38]

The Japanese knew when they adopted the 1951 tariff that it would not displace quantitative import controls. The Occupation had pressed for generally low tariffs, partly to accord with the broadly liberal philosophy of the United States government and partly as a matter of public relations in a period when the United States was attempting to help Japan regain standing in international affairs. The Japanese themselves had felt severely inhibited about erecting tariff barriers as high as they might

[36] United States–Japan Trade Council, from figures in *Monthly Return of the Foreign Trade of Japan,* 1961 issues, and *Trade of Japan* (Monthly Return), 1962 issues.

[37] The wholesale price index of the Bank of Japan (1934–1936 average = 100) rose from 232 in 1944 to 350 in 1945, then to 24,681 in 1950, and 34,253 in 1951. Bank of Japan, *Economic Statistics of Japan,* 1961, p. 279.

[38] U.S. Tariff Commission, *Postwar Developments in Japan's Foreign Trade,* Report No. 201, Second Series (Washington: GPO, 1958), pp. 10–11.

have liked, especially because of the difficulties Japan could expect in seeking admission to GATT. But as soon as the discussion of liberalization began in 1959, Japanese began talking about the need for higher tariffs.

Six months after the Cabinet adopted its liberalization plan, the Tariff Council, an advisory group representing businessmen as well as government officials, received from the Ministry of Finance a detailed proposal for revising the tariff. With few changes this became the tariff that was promulgated on March 31, 1961, to take effect in June. The new Law No. 26 changed not only the rates but the tariff classification, increasing the list of items from 940 to 2,183. Of these, 1,550 showed no change in rate under the new tariff, 380 were given lower tariff rates, and 253 were raised in rate.[39]

The philosophy of the new rates is very simple. As *The Oriental Economist* says, "The ultimate aim . . . is no doubt the adequate protection of domestic industry in connection with the trade liberalization." Where rates were left unchanged or lowered, there was no intention to permit foreign goods to displace Japanese goods to any great degree. The items in these categories were the goods Japan already obtained mainly by importing, for instance, crude petroleum (for which the rate remained 10 per cent), or "goods with much international competitive power," such as radio receivers. (The rate dropped only from 40 to 35 per cent for radio receivers with sound reproduction, thus retaining a high degree of protection even though Japan is a large exporter.) *The Economist* of London came to the conclusion that "Japan has the highest level of tariffs of all the main industrial countries." [40]

As if to make protection sure, the new law gives large discretionary powers to the Ministry of Finance to check imports. If an increase in imports seriously threatens a domestic industry the Ministry may take emergency steps, chiefly raising tariff rates and imposing tariff quotas. In October 1962 the Finance Minister established an emergency tariff division, under the Tariff Council, to decide on the steps to be taken under these powers. In April 1963, new provisions were made effective permitting the government to raise tariffs as a countermeasure against countries that impose emergency or other restrictions affecting Japanese exports.[41]

[39] *The Oriental Economist,* February 1961, p. 91. Except as otherwise indicated, this description of the 1961 tariff is based on this source. Rates in the next paragraph are taken from the draft tariff as translated by the American Embassy in Tokyo.

[40] *The Economist,* August 18, 1962, p. 645.

[41] *The Japan Times Weekly,* April 6, 1963, p. 8.

CONCLUSION

The Japanese nation is not yet psychologically ready to put full reliance on market forces to meet import requirements. These needs have never been so well met as in recent years, when quantitative controls have been diminishing in importance. The Japanese economy stands out in the whole non-Western world as the leading example of successful private enterprise. But the Japanese people remember their hunger during the blockade of World War II, and Japanese businessmen are used to many forms of open and disguised control outside of competitive market forces. Free trade does not attract many followers in Japan. As Peter F. Drucker put it, "Japan is thoroughly mercantilist. It is, indeed, the one example of successful mercantilism which combines governmental direction with entrepreneurial vigor, and aggressive competition abroad with protectionism and imposed price stability at home." [42]

Imports are kept down by a number of measures that raise costs. High prices for rice, wheat, sugar, and some other foodstuffs stimulate domestic production and reduce import demand. Although many products have been freed from import licensing, quantitative restrictions continue to be important. Petroleum imports are formally liberalized but the government "suggests" to refiners what crude oil they should use, thus providing a market for the Japanese-owned oil produced in the Persian Gulf and at the same time protecting the market for high-cost domestic coal. If the powers of the petroleum industry law were invoked these suggestions could become orders. Tariffs are another hurdle for imports; a substantial number of tariff increases were put into effect in order to protect Japanese producers after the relaxation of quantitative controls. In addition, the Ministry of Finance has been given large discretionary powers to increase tariff rates in cases where increased imports threaten serious injury to domestic production.

Still, the import liberalization that Japan has put into effect is a substantial achievement, despite its limitations. Suppressing deep misgivings, Japan is moving fairly rapidly away from the forms of direct control that have prevailed since 1945 and that go back in many cases to 1932. Once again, as in the 1920s, Japan is feeling its way toward new modes of behavior as part of the process of adjusting to the world environment. The steps taken so far cannot, however, be regarded as irreversible. If, as in the early 1930s, Japanese fortunes should suffer serious setbacks, new leaders could be expected to introduce new protective measures. The nature of such measures would be determined mainly by a pragmatic view of Japanese interests. The limits on protection

[42] "Japan Tries for a Second Miracle," *Harper's Magazine*, March 1963, p. 74.

and restriction would be not so much adherence to the principles of liberal trade as concern for retaliation by other countries against Japanese trade.

The present position, then, is one in which Japanese import policy moves reluctantly to accommodate Japanese practice to the preachings of the United States and other foreign countries and international organizations. If Japanese prosperity continues, and if liberal trade policies seem to contribute to this prosperity, the moves will continue and Japanese gradually may come to accept more and more of the liberal trade philosophy. In the short run, however, we should not expect a conversion in principle but, at best, a liberal policy resulting from circumstances that make such conduct beneficial to Japan.

Chapter 6

Japanese Exports

As the main source of income from abroad, exports are the key to Japan's ability to pay its way in the world economy. They are, indeed, much more than just an economic key. Both domestic politics and foreign policy are deeply affected by attitudes related to exports. Fears that the world may not accept enough goods to permit Japan to meet its reasonable needs persist widely among a people highly conscious of dependence on world trade and of past difficulties. Given continued rapid economic growth in the years ahead, such fears can be expected to subside, permitting, although not assuring, more liberal and constructive Japanese policies at home and abroad. On the other hand, if such fears should be strengthened by events, then the effects would spread far beyond the economic problems—such as import shortages, unemployment, business failures—that would result from an export lag. Extremism within Japan would be likely to grow. Japanese could not be expected to be very cooperative with other countries while harboring resentments on account of their trade barriers. Although export success and economic prosperity cannot by any means guarantee political stability, there appear to be strong reasons to expect that, if exports are comfortably adequate during the next decade or two, Japan is likely to make further startling economic progress and become an important force for peace, for accelerated development in Asia, Africa, and elsewhere, and perhaps also an impressive example of healthy democracy in Asia.

POSTWAR REVIVAL AND GROWTH OF EXPORTS

During the early period after surrender Japan's export problem seemed nearly hopeless. The overseas territories, which provided a large share of the raw materials for Japanese exports, were lost. Factories had been crippled. The urban population had been largely dispersed as a result of bombings. Efficiency was low. Transportation, communications, power, and other services were severely impaired. The whole modern economy was disorganized. The Occupation had a prior claim on goods and services. The economic "purge" contributed to further disorganization by removing many business leaders from their positions, by splitting up the large *zaibatsu* combines, and by other measures aimed at reform rather than recovery. As part of the Occupation's control policy, Japanese businessmen were forbidden to have foreign contacts, so they could not easily start the process of discovering, selecting, and obtaining new technology, promoting business, or even procuring materials and equipment. All transactions with foreigners were the monopoly of Occupation agencies. Even if Japanese businessmen had had goods to offer abroad, foreign hostility would have seriously limited export sales.

Other immediate major difficulties could be foreseen. A revival of Japanese exports would require new industries and a new type of export structure. No longer would Japanese producers have an assured market in areas under Japanese control. Not for some years, at least, could a large flow of Japanese capital equipment to other Asian areas be financed by Japanese investment. Although Japanese goods of the old type could be expected to find markets for a while in a world of almost universal shortages, in time the American economy would be reconverted and European production would recover, and Japanese goods would have to compete against the products of up-to-date American and European technology and mass-production methods.

As the postwar world took shape, additional problems for Japanese exports appeared. Mainland China fell under the unified control of powerful and hostile leaders. New Asian nations began to produce domestically, behind protective walls, cotton textiles and other things formerly imported from Japan. More and more of Japan's former markets were lost or challenged. Export recovery could not, therefore, be based simply on re-establishing contact with former customers, rebuilding factories in their prewar form, and selling the same kinds of things to the same countries as before.

The expectations were too gloomy. The United States government proved to be realistic, flexible, and surprisingly generous in modifying its original Occupation policies. The Japanese nation, to its great credit, overcame circumstances and vigorously, skillfully, and with great adaptability attacked and solved the seemingly hopeless export problem.

Today Japan is again a leading export nation. But the road has not been smooth. Until the mid-1950s exports lagged behind the rest of the Japanese economy. Japanese economists regard exports as the principal limiting factor in postwar economic growth. Yet, as we look back at the expansion of exports since 1945, as shown in Table 6-1, it is difficult

TABLE 6-1. MEASURES OF JAPANESE EXPORT GROWTH, 1934–1936, 1945–1962

Year	Exports: Quantum Index (1953 = 100)	Exports: Value (millions of dollars)	Exports as Per Cent of Imports	Japanese Exports as Per Cent of World Exports
1934–1936 av.	243.0	933	97.6	4.6
1945–1946 [a]		103	33.7	
1947		174	33.1	0.4
1948	16.6	258	37.7	0.5
1949	39.1	510	56.4	0.9
1950	78.1	820	84.2	1.4
1951	87.1	1,355	67.9	1.8
1952	92.4	1,273	62.8	1.7
1953	100.0	1,275	52.9	1.7
1954	133.3	1,629	67.9	2.1
1955	174.1	2,011	81.4	2.4
1956	207.9	2,501	77.4	2.7
1957	231.5	2,858	66.7	2.8
1958	239.9	2,877	94.9	3.0
1959	284.9	3,456	96.0	3.4
1960	324.1	4,055	90.3	3.6
1961	346.4	4,236	72.9	3.6
1962	414.5	4,916	87.2	4.0

[a] September 1945 through December 1946.

Sources: Quantum index, except for 1948 and 1949, from Japan, Ministry of Finance, *Monthly Return of the Foreign Trade of Japan*, January–December 1958, p. 384; January–December 1961, p. 376; *Trade of Japan* (Monthly Return), January–December 1962, p. 499. Figures for 1948 and 1949 derived from an index based on 1934–1936 av. = 100, published by Japan, Economic Counsel Board (now Economic Planning Agency), *Economic Survey of Japan* (1953–1954), p. 169.

Value and ratio of exports to imports from Table 5-1.

Share of world trade calculated from United Nations, *Yearbook of International Trade Statistics, 1953*, 1954.XVII.3 (New York: Author, 1954), and *International Financial Statistics* (IMF). Figures for 1934–1936 calculated from data in *Statistical Yearbook of the League of Nations, 1938/39* (Geneva: Author, 1939), pp. 211 and 219, including trade with Korea and Taiwan as part of Japan's foreign trade.

to regard the pace as slow. From 1946 through 1951 the value of exports grew very rapidly, between 48 and 98 per cent annually. (Table 5-1.) In the next two years export quantum rose slowly, but because of sharply declining prices, export value remained below the 1951 level. Factory production in Japan was continuing to expand, but most of the increase went to the domestic market and foreign military users. Then the picture changed. Between 1953 and 1957 the value and volume of exports more than doubled. The recession year of 1958 saw virtually no growth, but in the next four years the level rose by another 70 per cent.

Exports have also grown impressively in relation to imports. In the grim days of 1945 and 1946 exports covered only a third of the landed costs of Japanese imports. In 1959 the ratio of exports to imports reached its postwar peak of 96 per cent. In terms of physical volume, Japanese exports have recovered more slowly. Although increasing every year since 1948, the quantum index passed the average of 1934–1936 only in 1959. Another lag is shown in Japan's share of total world exports as measured by value. Although the share has risen in every postwar year except 1952 and 1953, it was still in 1962 well below the prewar level. It is not necessary, however, to sell any particular physical volume of exports or to reach the prewar share of world trade. What is necessary is that export proceeds be sufficient to meet that part of Japan's reasonable foreign-currency needs that is not covered otherwise. The postwar record has been good enough to enable Japan to lead the world in the rate of economic growth.

WHAT JAPAN SELLS ABROAD

Few countries have a higher concentration of manufactured goods in their exports than Japan. In 1960, 85 per cent of Japan's exports fell into classifications officially labeled "manufactured," including machinery.[1] But most of what Japan exports in other categories, such as food, is also processed or partly processed. Crude products made up only 4.6 per cent of Japanese exports in 1960. All the rest were to some degree manufactured; of the total, 70 per cent were finished goods.[2]

Table 6-2 shows the main export goods, as reported in the trade returns. The manufactures cover a very wide range: locomotives and leather goods, plywood and pearls, bicycles, buses and binoculars, toys

[1] Unattributed data on trade statistics in this chapter come from the tables herein or from standard sources cited in the Bibliographic Note.

[2] Crude foodstuffs were 1.7 per cent; raw materials, 2.9 per cent; prepared foods, 4.8 per cent; manufactures for further processing, 19.8 per cent; finished manufactures, 70.4 per cent. Japan, Ministry of Finance, *Monthly Return of the Foreign Trade of Japan*, January–December 1960, p. 8. These shares have changed to only a limited degree since 1949. Bank of Japan, *Economic Statistics of Japan*, 1962, p. 251.

TABLE 6-2. JAPAN'S EXPORTS BY COMMODITY, 1954, 1957, 1960, 1961, 1962

Commodity	*1954* Million Dollars	*1954* Per Cent of Total	*1957* Million Dollars	*1957* Per Cent of Total	*1960* Million Dollars	*1960* Per Cent of Total	*1961* Million Dollars	*1961* Per Cent of Total	*1962* Million Dollars	*1962* Per Cent of Total
Food, beverages and tobacco	**134.7**	**8.3**	**183.2**	**6.4**	**267.6**	**6.6**	**265.1**	**6.3**	**353.9**	**7.2**
Fish and fish products	74.2	4.6	122.1	4.3	174.7	4.3	162.7	3.9	245.2	5.0
Mandarin oranges (preserved)	8.8	0.5	18.2	0.6	25.2	0.6	23.7	0.6	23.7	0.5
Tea	13.6	0.8	5.0	0.2	5.6	0.1	4.7	0.1	5.3	0.1
Monosodium glutamate	10.0	0.6	9.7	0.3	11.9	0.3	13.6	0.3	14.9	0.3
Other	28.1	1.7	27.3	1.0	50.2	1.2	60.3	1.4	65.3	1.3
Raw materials, including fuel, fats and oils	**101.9**	**6.3**	**127.5**	**4.5**	**169.5**	**4.2**	**184.7**	**4.4**	**201.3**	**4.1**
Lumber	20.7	1.3	21.4	0.8	24.6	0.6	23.0	0.5	21.9	0.4
Raw silk	46.9	2.9	41.8	1.5	50.5	1.2	46.2	1.1	53.7	1.1
Synthetic fibers	0.5	0.0	4.6	0.2	11.4	0.3	16.6	0.4	29.9	0.6
Petroleum products	0.9	0.1	2.6	0.1	15.8	0.4	18.7	0.4	18.0	0.4
Fats and oils	13.0	0.8	30.3	1.1	30.0	0.7	34.7	0.8	24.3	0.5
Other	20.0	1.2	26.8	0.9	37.3	0.9	45.7	1.1	53.5	1.1
Chemicals	**78.9**	**4.8**	**125.9**	**4.4**	**169.2**	**4.2**	**188.7**	**4.5**	**246.6**	**5.0**
Inorganic chemicals	8.7	0.5	15.9	0.6	25.6	0.6	29.0	0.7	31.9	0.7
Organic chemicals	6.6	0.4	7.9	0.3	12.5	0.3	16.8	0.4	64.1	1.3
Medicinal and pharmaceutical products	9.1	0.6	13.6	0.5	16.8	0.4	20.5	0.5	25.0	0.5
Manufactured fertilizers	37.0	2.3	64.0	2.2	59.5	1.5	63.2	1.5	55.1	1.1
Synthetic plastic materials	4.4	0.3	9.6	0.3	32.0	0.8	30.7	0.7	47.2	1.0
Other	13.1	0.8	15.0	0.5	22.9	0.6	28.5	0.7	23.3	0.5
Manufactured goods classified by material	**941.5**	**57.9**	**1,413.7**	**49.6**	**1,853.5**	**45.9**	**1,833.4**	**43.5**	**2,093.0**	**42.8**
Rubber manufactures	7.7	0.5	26.2	0.9	29.9	0.7	42.8	1.0	54.4	1.1
Wood manufactures	32.3	2.0	69.4	2.4	84.2	2.1	80.0	1.9	93.5	1.9
Plywood	25.5	1.6	55.0	1.9	62.6	1.5	58.7	1.4	67.6	1.4
Paper, pulp and manufactures	14.2	0.9	33.1	1.2	51.2	1.3	62.5	1.5	52.1	1.1
Textiles	549.8	33.8	814.5	28.6	923.6	22.9	877.3	20.8	931.2	19.0
Woolen yarn	26.3	1.6	21.2	0.7	14.9	0.4	13.9	0.3	24.6	0.5
Cotton yarn	23.6	1.5	27.2	1.0	52.4	1.3	33.1	0.8	25.9	0.5
Other yarn and thread	29.3	1.8	45.8	1.6	51.5	1.3	60.4	1.4	67.4	1.4
Cotton fabrics	252.3	15.5	316.8	11.1	351.4	8.7	347.7	8.3	341.3	7.0
Silk fabrics	13.6	0.8	32.3	1.1	52.2	1.3	34.4	0.8	48.0	1.0

Manufactured goods classified by material (cont'd)										
Woolen and worsted fabrics	16.8	1.0	44.6	1.6	54.5	1.3	37.4	0.9	50.4	1.0
Synthetic fiber fabrics	109.3	6.7	243.0	8.5	215.9	5.3	216.2	5.1	206.0	4.2
Cordage and manufactures, including fishnets	4.1	0.3	11.6	0.4	23.0	0.6	22.8	0.5	33.1	0.7
Blankets, sheets, towels, etc.	22.0	1.4	31.0	1.1	35.3	0.9	38.1	0.9	37.2	0.8
Floor coverings	9.2	0.6	12.1	0.4	27.4	0.7	26.4	0.6	32.7	0.7
Other textiles (excluding clothing)	43.3	2.7	28.9	1.0	45.1	1.1	46.9	1.1	64.6	1.3
Nonmetallic mineral manufactures	69.2	4.3	116.4	4.1	145.2	3.6	141.5	3.4	187.0	3.8
Cement	19.0	1.2	38.5	1.3	24.6	0.6	25.7	0.6	25.9	0.5
Tiles and other clay construction materials	2.2	0.1	4.9	0.2	14.5	0.4	17.0	0.4	23.2	0.5
Glass and glassware	9.9	0.6	14.7	0.5	24.5	0.6	25.1	0.6	24.2	0.5
Pottery	34.8	2.1	51.1	1.8	67.6	1.7	57.2	1.4	65.4	1.3
Gems, jewelry, etc.	18.4	1.1	28.5	1.0	52.9	1.3	63.2	1.5	42.8	0.9
Pearls	7.2	0.5	16.8	0.6	30.5	0.8	35.8	0.8	41.8	0.9
Costume jewelry	6.9	0.4	10.1	0.4	19.6	0.5	23.9	0.6	21.7	0.4
Iron and steel products	166.4	10.2	209.5	7.4	388.1	9.6	380.0	9.0	531.4	10.9
Nonferrous metals and products	41.8	2.6	41.5	1.5	25.6	0.6	27.8	0.7	34.5	0.7
Metal manufactures	40.8	2.5	72.4	2.5	147.8	3.7	152.5	3.6	176.7	3.6
Wire nails of iron and steel	4.6	0.3	6.4	0.2	20.6	0.5	19.4	0.5	23.5	0.5
Hand tools and implements	3.2	0.2	6.4	0.2	20.0	0.5	21.9	0.5	25.4	0.5
Cutlery	3.7	0.2	14.6	0.5	23.6	0.6	20.1	0.5	27.5	0.6
Other	0.9	0.1	2.2	0.1	5.1	0.1	5.8	0.1	0.0	0.0
Machinery and transport equipment	**202.3**	**12.4**	**629.6**	**22.0**	**928.3**	**23.0**	**1,119.4**	**26.6**	**1,232.6**	**25.2**
Internal combustion engines (excluding aircraft engines)	4.7	0.3	6.5	0.2	14.3	0.4	16.9	0.4	20.2	0.4
Office machinery	0.4	0.0	0.7	0.0	11.0	0.3	24.6	0.6	4.3	0.1
Industrial machinery (including for mining and construction)	91.5	5.6	112.8	4.0	172.7	4.3	241.3	5.7	276.4 [a]	5.7
Conveying, mining and road machinery	1.4	0.1	7.7	0.3	12.5	0.3	26.4	0.6	26.1 [a]	0.5
Textile machinery	45.5	2.8	32.5	1.1	48.4	1.2	57.9	1.4	73.4	1.5
Sewing machines	31.6	1.9	47.8	1.7	54.7	1.4	55.1	1.3	59.3	1.2
Ball and roller bearings and parts	1.8	0.1	5.9	0.2	7.5	0.2	15.1	0.4	22.7	0.5
Electrical equipment	23.0	1.4	77.7	2.7	273.9	6.8	337.0	8.0	425.5	8.7
Heavy electrical equipment	5.7	0.4	9.3	0.3	21.7	0.5	26.0	0.6	33.2	0.7
Electric light bulbs	3.6	0.2	9.0	0.3	12.4	0.3	14.0	0.3	15.2	0.3
Radio receivers	0.1	0.0	10.9	0.4	138.7	3.4	151.0	3.6	176.9	3.6
Insulated wire and cable	2.2	0.1	17.5	0.6	15.0	0.4	14.7	0.3	14.6	0.3

TABLE 6-2. (cont'd)

Commodity	1954		1957		1960		1961		1962	
	Million Dollars	*Per Cent of Total*	*Million Dollars*	*Per Cent of Total*	*Million Dollars*	*Per Cent of Total*	*Million Dollars*	*Per Cent of Total*	*Million Dollars*	*Per Cen of Total*
Machinery and transport equipment (cont'd)										
Automotive vehicles and parts	6.4	0.4	29.4	1.0	107.4	2.7	138.3	3.3	173.7	3.6
Bicycles and parts	6.9	0.4	8.6	0.3	14.9	0.4	14.1	0.3	14.1	0.3
Ships and boats	52.0	3.2	351.7	12.3	288.1	7.1	283.0	6.7	235.2	4.8
Other	17.4	1.1	42.2	1.5	46.0	1.1	64.2	1.5	83.5	1.7
Miscellaneous products and transactions	**166.5**	**10.4**	**369.0**	**13.0**	**658.8**	**16.3**	**622.0**	**14.8**	**784.4**	**16.0**
Clothing	56.0	3.4	142.5	5.0	220.0	5.4	191.0	4.5	204.2	4.2
Underwear and nightwear [b]	6.8	0.4	27.3	1.0	39.6	1.0	30.6	0.7	46.6	0.9
Outerwear	6.1	0.4	41.2	1.4	66.3	1.6	54.3	1.3	76.6	1.6
Gloves [c]	6.1	0.4	14.6	0.5	27.6	0.7	20.6	0.5	20.5	0.4
Shawls, comforters and mufflers	19.6	1.2	23.5	0.8	36.6	0.9	32.9	0.8	31.0	0.6
Footwear	3.5	0.2	14.5	0.5	72.1	1.8	62.3	1.5	84.6	1.7
Optical, scientific, etc. instruments	19.0	1.2	49.4	1.7	92.5	2.3	106.4	2.5	127.7	2.6
Binoculars	5.5	0.3	12.3	0.4	15.7	0.4	13.2	0.3	14.9	0.3
Cameras and parts	5.4	0.3	17.0	0.6	36.5	0.9	45.4	1.1	35.3	0.7
Sporting goods	0.8	0.1	7.5	0.3	16.5	0.4	17.2	0.4	23.1	0.5
Toys	31.4	1.9	61.5	2.2	90.0	2.2	83.3	2.0	92.1	1.9
Other	55.8	3.4	93.7	3.3	167.7	4.2	161.8	3.8	252.7	5.2
Total exports of Japanese goods	**1,625.8**	**100.0**	**2,849.1**	**100.0**	**4,039.8**	**100.0**	**4,213.3**	**100.0**	**4,890.0**	**100.0**
Re-exports	**3.5**	**0.2**	**9.0**	**0.3**	**14.8**	**0.4**	**22.2**	**0.5**	**26.1**	**0.5**
Total exports, including re-exports	**1,629.3**	**100.2**	**2,858.1**	**100.3**	**4,054.5**	**100.4**	**4,235.6**	**100.5**	**4,916.2**	**100.5**

[a] Because of the extensive reorganization of the components of this item in 1962, coverage differs somewhat as between 1962 and earlier years.
[b] Includes all shirts.
[c] Baseball gloves and other gloves for use in sports are included with gloves, not with sporting goods.

Notes: See Appendix B for definitions of commodity groupings in terms of code designators. The customs statistics underlying this table are described in the Bibliographic Note.
Minor inconsistencies result from rounding.

Sources: Calculated from yen figures in Japan, Ministry of Finance, *Monthly Return of the Foreign Trade of Japan*, January–December issue, 1954, 1957, 1960, 1961; *Trade of Japan* (Monthly Return), January–December 1962.

and tape recorders, sewing machines and sporting goods, cameras and cutlery. In the early 1960s, seven important groups of commodities accounted for 60 per cent of the total: textiles, iron and steel, electrical equipment, industrial machinery, fish, ships, and clothing.[3] (See Table 6-3.) During the seven years from 1954 to 1962 a significant amount of shifting took place among Japan's leading exports. The largest export of all, textiles, has lost relative position rapidly as other products have risen, most notably electrical equipment, which in 1954 was not even one of the first ten groups. The leading export products deserve individual comment.

Textiles have been Japan's largest export for a long time. Although their share has been declining, no other category of exports reached even half their value until 1962. Nearly 40 per cent of the total is made up of cotton fabrics, which in 1934 displaced raw silk from its traditional position as Japan's largest individual export.[4] (In 1957, ships took the lead over cotton fabrics, but lost it in 1960.) Fabrics of synthetic fiber, mainly rayon, are a strong second, followed by yarns and fabrics of wool, silk, and other fibers.

The range of textile products Japan exports is very wide, including many yarns and fabrics of new fibers and of mixtures. Hong Kong, Taiwan, India, Pakistan, and some other newly industrializing countries are now producing a number of cotton and rayon goods cheaply and well enough to compete successfully with imports from Japan, in some cases without protection. Still, the range of competition is fairly narrow. Japan is advancing rapidly in textile technology and leads the world in some branches.

Clothing as a leading Japanese export is a postwar development. Though knitted goods, especially underwear, and a small volume of West-

[3] Groupings like these must be used with caution; they are inevitably arbitrary because they include diverse items, much more so, for instance, than Japanese imports which consist in large part of recognizable bulk commodities. If textiles had been treated as several groups instead of one, as is frequently done in reports of Japanese trade, iron and steel products would have been Japan's first export in 1962, followed by electrical equipment and cotton fabrics; if all machinery and equipment were lumped together, they would have made a group nearly one-third larger than textiles. The groupings used here are believed to reflect adequately the realities of Japanese export trade, despite the difficulties created by the curious practice in the Japanese customs statistics of simply omitting totals for large statistical divisions and subdivisions.

[4] Raw silk, which is not part of textiles as presented in Tables 6-2 or 6-3, went mainly to the United States, where most of it was made into women's hosiery. The depression severely cut consumption and prices. The Pacific war removed first the silk from the American market and then the market from the silk, for by 1945 American women had adopted nylon stockings. Japanese exports of raw silk have for ten years fluctuated between $38 million and $50 million, except for the recession year 1958, when exports yielded only $22 million. Synthetic fibers are a very small export, since most exported synthetic leaves Japan in the form of yarn, fabric, or made-up goods.

TABLE 6-3. JAPAN'S LEADING EXPORT PRODUCTS, 1954, 1957, 1960, 1961, 1962

	1954		*1957*		*1960*		*1961*		*1962*	
Rank	*Commodity*	*Per Cent of Total*	*Commodity*	*Per Cent of Total*	*Commodity*	*Per Cent of Total*	*Commodity*	*Per Cent of Total*	*Commodity*	*Per Cent of Total*
1	Textiles	33.8	Textiles	28.6	Textiles	22.9	Textiles	20.8	Textiles	19.0
2	Iron and steel	10.2	Ships	12.3	Iron and steel	9.6	Iron and steel	9.0	Iron and steel	10.9
3	Industrial machinery	5.6	Iron and steel	7.4	Ships	7.1	Electrical equipment	8.0	Electrical equipment	8.7
4	Fish	4.6	Clothing	5.0	Electrical equipment	6.8	Ships	6.7	Industrial machinery	5.7
5	Nonmetallic mineral manufactures	4.3	Fish	4.3	Clothing	5.4	Industrial machinery	5.7	Fish	5.0
6	Clothing	3.4	Nonmetallic mineral manufactures	4.1	Fish	4.3	Clothing	4.5	Ships	4.8
7	Ships	3.2	Industrial machinery	4.0	Industrial machinery	4.3	Fish	3.9	Clothing	4.2
8	Raw silk	2.9	Electrical equipment	2.7	Metal manufactures	3.7	Metal manufactures	3.6	Nonmetallic mineral manufactures	3.8
9	Nonferrous metals and products	2.6	Metal manufactures	2.5	Nonmetallic mineral manufactures	3.6	Nonmetallic mineral manufactures	3.4	Metal manufactures	3.6
10	Metal manufactures	2.5	Wood manufactures	2.4	Automotive vehicles and parts	2.7	Automotive vehicles and parts	3.3	Automotive vehicles and parts	3.6
11	Manufactured fertilizers	2.3	Manufactured fertilizers	2.2	Instruments (optical, scientific, etc.)	2.3	Instruments (optical, scientific, etc.)	2.5	Instruments (optical, scientific, etc.)	2.6
Total, listed items		75.4		75.5		72.7		71.4		71.9

Note: Percentages represent commodity shares by value.

Source: Table 6-2.

ern-style dresses and other garments were exported before World War II, the total was not very large. Since the war clothing exports have increased rapidly, from $56 million in 1954 to an average of over $200 million in the early 1960s. Japanese exports of footwear (not included in the figures for clothing) have had an even better record proportionately, rising from $3.5 million in 1954 to $85 million in 1962.

Iron and steel shipments jumped above two million tons in 1960, after having risen more slowly than Japan's other exports during most of the 1950s. In a period when the Japanese steel industry was rapidly expanding, modernizing, and reducing production costs, exports first fluctuated considerably from year to year and then rose fairly rapidly but not as quickly as production until 1962, as the following figures show: [5]

Year	*Steel Ingot Production*	*Exports of Iron and Steel Products*
	(in thousands of metric tons)	
1952	6,988	1,633
1953	7,662	843
1954	7,750	1,187
1955	9,408	1,989
1956	11,106	1,291
1957	12,570	1,002
1958	12,118	1,690
1959	16,629	1,609
1960	22,138	2,313
1961	28,268	2,303
1962	27,546	3,873

The explanation for the lag in exports in relation to production lies in the rise in domestic demand. Construction, machinery, shipbuilding, motor vehicles, and a growing list of consumer articles have provided a rapidly expanding market for steel products within Japan. Like Britain, the United States, and other industrialized countries, Japan exports much steel indirectly, in the form of ships, machinery, and other finished products. The Japanese steel industry continues to expand its capacity rapidly, as well as to strengthen and modernize production processes. It was the lag in this demand, particularly in the machinery industry, that led to a drop in steel production in 1962 that would have been even greater if it had not been for a two-thirds increase in exports, much of it to the United States where Japanese iron and steel sales nearly doubled.

Electrical equipment exports, the third group in 1962, were nearly

[5] Production figures from Bank of Japan, *Economic Statistics of Japan,* 1962, p. 206; export figures, same, p. 245.

twenty times as large as in 1954. The range of products in this category is very great, from large motors, generators, and transformers through meters and communications equipment to wire, batteries, and Christmas tree lights. Radios are the largest item; mostly transistor sets, they accounted for nearly half the value of Japanese electrical equipment exports in the early 1960s. The growth in sales of radio receivers is phenomenal, from practically nothing in 1954 to $177 million in 1962. Vacuum tubes, condensers, transistors, and other radio equipment have also been exported in rapidly growing quantities. The production of television receivers is something new for Japan, but exports rose from $63,000 in 1956 to $2.9 million in 1960, $6.1 million in 1961, and $17.6 million in 1962.

Industrial machinery, including equipment for mining and construction, the fourth export group, has risen in pace with total Japanese exports and, after lagging a while, held about the same share, a little under 6 per cent, in 1962 as in 1954. This group includes a large number of types of products—pumps, industrial trucks, cranes, bulldozers, woodworking machinery, textile and sewing machines, air conditioners, and ball and roller bearings. During the 1950s there was a shift in export emphasis from textile and sewing machines to other types of industrial machinery. Japan has come a long way in these products of advanced engineering.

Fishery products are traditional Japanese exports, which have grown in value and volume, but less rapidly than other exports. Japan is the world leader in fishing. The growth in catch and export is the result of the expanding use of modern methods and equipment for finding, catching, packing, and exporting fish, and of the extension of Japanese fishing operations to all productive parts of the Pacific Ocean where Japanese fishermen are allowed access and also to the South China Sea, the Indian Ocean, Antarctic waters, and elsewhere. Fishery operations might be expanded further if Japan could find a favorable settlement of some of its international fishing disputes.[6]

Some of Japan's smaller exports are related to her fishing activities, notably fish and whale oil and pearls, mostly from pearl farms in Japanese waters but partly taken in international waters off the Philippines and elsewhere. Together these products yielded some $61 million in exports in 1961.

Ships were Japan's second largest export for a while in the 1950s, but

[6] In recent years friction with American and Canadian salmon fishing interests has been minimized mainly by Japanese restraint. Since 1945, without the privileges won in 1905 to bolster their bargaining position, the Japanese have been seriously restricted in access to Russian waters and in the size of the catch permitted. The same problem now eixsts with South Korea and to a lesser extent with China, both of which claim sovereignty in waters extending far out from the coastline. Occasional difficulties have also arisen with Australia, the Philippines, and other countries.

by 1960 they had dropped to third and in 1962 to sixth place, as the industry remained below the previous export peak and other exports continued to grow. Japan is the world's leading shipbuilder, both in total construction and also in exports. Welding, unit construction, and other modern techniques have made Japanese yards very rapid and efficient builders. Costs are probably the lowest in the world.[7] Most of the ships built in Japanese yards are exported. These are, in many cases, large vessels, including the biggest supertankers in the world.

Nonmetallic mineral manufactures include pottery, cement, glass, tiles, graphite products, and other things. Although the increase in these exports from $69 million in 1954 to $187 million in 1962 was substantial, it represented a rate of growth lower than that of total exports. Nearly half the total is pottery, a traditional Japanese product that has found growing markets abroad. In 1957 Japan was the world's principal exporter of cement, the next largest component. Sales have been lower since then, principally because of the expansion of production in Korea and Taiwan, with Taiwan entering export markets.

The other three groups listed in Table 6-3, metal manufactures, automotive vehicles, and instruments, are representative of new Japanese industry with modern facilities and methods, competitive products, and rapid growth. A decade ago few observers of the Japanese scene expected to see automobiles and related products playing a leading part in an export boom. Optical goods and other instruments we are more used to, having felt the initial impact of high-quality products from this source before 1955.

The smaller export items that made up the remaining third of Japan's exports in 1962 are spread throughout the commodity groups shown in Table 6-2. No single item accounted for as much as 2 per cent of exports in 1962, but in total these products represent a large and growing source of income. One expects to find tea among Japan's exports but petroleum products are something of a surprise. Most of this is gasoline, which Japanese refineries produce in larger quantities than Japan needs, while at the same time other refinery products, especially low-sulphur heavy oil needed in the steel industry, have to be imported. Chemical exports of many kinds have sold in growing volume in recent years, including fertilizers, plastics, dyestuffs, and industrial chemicals. Plywood is another postwar phenomenon of Japanese exports. Shipments rose from $3 million in 1952 to almost $70 million in 1962. The range of "miscellaneous products" that Japan exports seems to grow all the time. It extends literally from abacuses to zippers, includes pipes for smoking and for

[7] In calculating subsidies for U.S. shipbuilders, the U.S. Maritime Administration treats Japan as the cheapest alternative producer. Information from Maritime Administration, Washington.

plumbing, and provides the world with simple table mats and complex microscopes.

DOMESTIC FACTORS IN EXPORT GROWTH

Three essential elements were responsible for Japan's economic recovery after World War II. The tremendous contribution of U.S. policy has already been mentioned. Other forces, circumstances, and events beyond Japanese control have also, on balance, proved very advantageous, such as the Korean War and the growth of world markets. Japanese performance, the third element, has, in total, been very effective indeed. Among its ingredients have been some domestic factors that importantly affect Japan's export success.

Japan's Resource Limitations

"The fundamental problem of the Japanese nation can be expressed in the simple terms of too many people, too little land and too few natural resources." These words were spoken in 1952 by Joseph M. Dodge who in 1949 had successfully led the American program for economic stabilization in Japan.[8] Mr. Dodge was not alone in his pessimism, either then or at other times, for observers of Japan's economy have more often than not taken a very gloomy view of the country's position and prospects. Like Dodge, others have emphasized the limitation of area and resources. The large and, until recently, fast-growing population has usually been regarded as a major part of the problem. A classic statement of the pessimistic view of Japan's position and prospects was made over thirty years ago by an American geographer in concluding a careful and informed study of Japanese industrialization, the most thorough published in English up to that time. He said:

> The weakness of Japanese industry is more than immaturity. It lies deeper and is more fundamental. It is the result of the poverty of the country and of other factors that cannot be altered easily or quickly. They are factors so vital that they seem certain to put their permanent mark on Japanese industry. Though there undoubtedly will be further development, Japan cannot hope to become a manufacturing nation of major rank. Her successful industries will necessarily be restricted to a limited number.
>
> A country's strength or weakness in industry, realized or potential, depends in the final analysis upon its strength or weakness in capital, mechanical skill, raw materials, power, labor, and markets. In none of these basic elements is the position of Japan entirely satisfactory. Much of the present industrial development has been accomplished through the offsetting of natural handicaps by the vigorous enterprise of a paternalistic government

[8] Address in New York, February 2, 1952, as quoted in Jerome B. Cohen, *Japan's Postwar Economy* (Bloomington: Indiana University Press, 1958), p. 11.

in the liberal use of subsidies and through the fortuitous circumstance of a great war, but an industrial structure must have a firmer foundation if it is to prosper and continue to grow.[9]

In the light of what we have learned from the phenomenal growth of the 1950s, it is clear that such pessimistic views exaggerated the importance of Japan's deficiencies in physical resources and underestimated the human resources. We now know that Japan has the workers, managers, and institutions required to produce enough to pay for adequate imports of commodities, technology, and capital. Japan also has the habits, institutions, and discipline to create large amounts of capital through saving. This combination of indigenous and imported resources makes the Japanese economy one of the wonders of the contemporary world.

Part of the problem of judging the resource endowment of Japan or any nation lies in the difference between tangible geographic and economic facts that can be seen, even counted, and the intangibles of human strengths and weaknesses, of social, political, and economic institutions. Raw materials deficiencies can be measured and recorded in very specific terms, as is done, for instance, in Tables 5-4 and 5-8 above. But there are no such specific measures of Japan's ability to organize, direct, and operate industrial activities. Japan's human resources have overcome raw materials deficiencies while some other countries, for instance Indonesia, have been unable as yet to achieve satisfactory economic development despite vast natural resources.

How has the scarcity of raw materials in Japan been overcome? To produce steel, for instance, Japan must import four-fifths of its iron ore, mostly from Asia, and a quarter of its coking coal, mostly from Hampton Roads ports on the east coast of the United States. It must also import substantial quantities of scrap. How, then, is it possible for Japan to export steel not only to Asian countries but also to the United States and Europe? The basic reason is that most of the price of steel products, even in Japan, is domestic rather than foreign cost. If Japan exports pig iron, direct import costs are 49 per cent; for steel billets the figure is 31 per cent. But for more finished steel products the import ingredient is much lower: galvanized iron wire, 25 per cent, galvanized iron sheet, 23 per cent, and for more highly fabricated products such as steel ships, machinery, radios, or cameras still less. (See Table 5-8.) Japan's advantages, especially in low labor costs, come to outweigh its import dependence.

The great distance many Japanese imports must be carried is not as serious a disadvantage as many people suppose. Sea transportation is

[9] John E. Orchard, *Japan's Economic Position: The Progress of Industrialization* (New York: McGraw-Hill, 1930), p. 242.

relatively cheap, and many Japanese goods can be profitably sold abroad despite the costs of two long sea voyages, one for the raw materials, the other for the finished products. The average freight cost of all imports, including ore and fuels, has varied between 14 and 21 per cent of total c.i.f. value. For some products freight costs are far lower. For instance, cotton textiles that are used in New York after being made in Japan of cotton purchased mostly in New Orleans have behind them total hauls by ship of more than 20,000 statute miles. The ocean freight costs on Japan's cotton imports usually amount to between 4 and 5 per cent of total landed cost. For wool, which is of high unit value and most of which travels the relatively short distance from Australia to Japan, the figure varies between 1 and 4 per cent. For goods of lower value per ton, of course, freight costs bear more heavily. For coal and iron ore the share of freight has varied in recent years between about half and two-thirds of the total landed cost, and for crude petroleum between one-third and a half. Freight costs are being cut by specialized ships such as huge ore carriers, supertankers, and special craft such as tankers to carry liquid petroleum gas. Japanese exports have a high value per unit of weight and the cost of carrying them abroad is further limited by the fact that ships which come to Japan full and down with import cargoes can seldom get a full load outbound; so the marginal cost of carrying additional cargo from Japan is very low.

The net effect of Japan's peculiar resource endowment has not, therefore, been to stifle production for export but simply to direct it into certain channels—just as accepted trade theory would suggest, and despite many gloomy predictions. Light manufactures, mainly textiles, sundries, and light machinery, dominated the export list, but with recent advances Japanese manufacturers have shown that they can manufacture some heavy products, especially ships, more cheaply in Japan than elsewhere. Heavier goods remain, however, in a minority position among Japanese exports. Steel exports are important and increasing, but there are many heavy steel products Japan cannot yet produce as cheaply as countries can that are more favorably situated in relation to raw materials. Even in cotton textiles, one of Japan's largest exports, Japanese producers cannot successfully compete in the American market in a number of kinds of cloth. (See Chapter 9.) As in trade almost anywhere, Japanese exports reflect the strong points in the domestic economy and the market opportunities that have been found. The export structure that results is changing, and today Japan finds itself facing both high-income markets, where sales are mainly of labor-intensive consumer goods, and low-income markets, where Japan sells machinery and other capital goods, some of which are also labor-intensive. (See Chapter 7.)

Low Prices of Japanese Exports

There have been times when Japanese products have found buyers abroad mainly because Japan had goods to sell during a period of shortage. Among Japan's exports immediately after the Meiji Restoration in 1868 were raw silk and silkworm eggs for which the market was particularly strong because of a silkworm disease in Europe.[10] During World War I the withdrawal of European supplies from markets in Asia presented Japan with a strong demand for goods without much regard for quality or price. During the Korean War, again, world-wide shortages gave Japanese exporters rich opportunities before Japan's export industries had become fully competitive with the best American and European goods. One of the major factors in Japan's shipbuilding boom from 1955 to 1957 was a world shortage of shipping and of shipbuilding capacity.

Usually, however, Japanese products must sell competitively. While quality or distinctive characteristics of style or use underlie some Japanese exports, historically low price has been the predominant feature in making Japanese goods attractive abroad. Wood-block prints and other examples of Japanese art, kimonos or happi coats, and hibachi find markets abroad as distinctively "Japanese" products, but they constitute only a small part of the country's exports. High quality, as well as low price, was important in making Japanese silk dominant in the American market in the interwar years. In quality it was better and more dependable than Chinese silk, while in price it tended to be cheaper than European silk.

Japan's advantages in the production and export of silk played an important part in the country's modernization. Cocoons were raised on farms where a great deal of surplus labor was available for the time-consuming tasks involved. Reeling was progressively modernized but did not require large amounts of capital, and it was not necessary to make violent adjustments in production, processing, and marketing methods. Thus a traditional process developed into a modern one without major upheaval, meanwhile employing a great deal of labor, earning a great deal of foreign exchange, generating capital, and providing Japan the essential element, time, in which to develop other export industries, especially factory production.[11]

[10] G. C. Allen, *A Short Economic History of Modern Japan, 1867–1937* (London: Allen & Unwin, 1946), pp. 32–33.

[11] The share of raw silk in Japan's total exports fluctuated as follows (in per cent):

1868–1872	38	1901–1910	26
1873–1880	35	1911–1920	21
1881–1890	36	1921–1930	31
1891–1900	30	1931–1933	20

These figures, which carry the record through the last year when silk was the leading

Export of factory products came harder and more slowly. Japan was offering goods for which there was already an established market. Japanese cotton cloth, toys, bicycles, Christmas tree ornaments, rubber shoes, and the rest were not initially superior to Western products in quality, design, or workmanship, nor were they often of distinctive character. What sold them was a low price.

Only too often quality and workmanship were well below those of American or European products. I bought some Japanese rubber-soled shoes in Singapore in 1933 for the equivalent of 20 cents in U.S. currency. They looked good enough, but on the second wearing one of them lost its rubber sole. Such shoddiness in Japanese goods was, however, not universal then and is very rare today. The quality of postwar Japanese goods is generally much better than it used to be. Still, enough poor merchandise has been made in Japan and sold abroad to create a reputation that still hurts the sale of Japanese goods, especially in the United States, and tends to lower the price that can be charged. Though the stage has passed when Japan could hope to enter foreign markets only by selling goods cheaply, the heritage is still alive. Seldom have Japanese goods been sold at prices above those of similar foreign products solely on the basis of higher Japanese quality. To sell abroad, Japanese producers have frequently felt they had to ask low prices, except in times of scarcity.

Low Japanese Wages and Labor Costs

One of the principal elements in Japan's ability to export at low prices has been the willingness of Japanese workers to accept low wages. This is an old bone of contention for foreign competitors. Japanese wages are certainly lower than American and Western European wages.[12] Until per

---

export, are adjusted to include Korea and Taiwan as foreign countries throughout, but no price adjustment has been made. The Oriental Economist, *Foreign Trade of Japan, A Statistical Survey* (Tokyo: Author, 1935), pp. 2, 5, 462, 577.

In 1929, nearly 40 per cent of all farm families in Japan raised silkworms as a subsidiary occupation. G. C. Allen, "The Traditional Trades: The Structure of the Silk and Pottery Industries," Chapter 14 in E. B. Schumpeter and others, *The Industrialization of Japan and Manchukuo, 1930–1940* (New York: Macmillan, 1940), pp. 512–513.

[12] Precise comparison of Japanese wages with those in other countries is extremely difficult, mainly because of the complexities of the Japanese wage structure, numerous and valuable fringe benefits, Japanese living patterns and costs, and the knotty problem of conversion from one currency to another. In general, wage differentials, while great, are narrower than the published wage statistics in Japan and the United States would suggest. (Some earnings are given on p. 284.) But for present purposes precise international comparison is unnecessary. A comparison for 1957 between wage rates of manufacturing production workers in Japan and those in the United States was prepared by the U.S. Department of Labor. The average for the United States was about ten times that in Japan, but many fringe benefits, which are more important in Japan, were unavoidably omitted from the comparison. U.S. Department of Labor, Bureau of Labor Statistics, "Employment, Wages, and Foreign Trade," in *Foreign Trade Policy*, compendium of papers collected by the staff of

capita production in the Japanese economy as a whole approaches that of the more advanced industrial countries, Japanese real wages must inevitably be generally lower. But lower wages do not necessarily mean lower costs, and despite Japan's lower wages it remains true, as we have seen, that costs of producing many products are higher in Japan than abroad. That is one reason why Japan buys so much equipment in the United States and other industrial countries, and also why recent moves toward liberalization of Japanese import policy have been made so reluctantly.

By accepting normal Japanese wages instead of unrealistically attempting to get, say, American wages, Japanese workers can expect to produce certain products more cheaply than foreign producers can, despite higher materials costs and despite overhead costs that in some cases are higher in Japan than abroad. In the case of shipbuilding, for instance, Japan was found in 1957 to have the highest materials costs in the world.[13] But Japanese workmen and executives work longer hours for much lower wages and salaries, and Japanese shipyards are much less inhibited by restrictive labor practices than British and American yards.

The lowest wages in Japan are paid to temporary workers and those employed by very small-scale producing units. Small units produce a good deal of the clothing now being exported. For some products of large factories, individual processes are performed by small units, for instance, the hand-sewing of decorations on wool gloves or the finishing of fabrics. Those who operate their own workshops, often with only family labor, have in the past usually had to take what they could get, having literally no alternative means of livelihood in most cases. Very high levels of skill and workmanship are to be found in many of Japan's small-scale enterprises. Often skills handed down through generations are used to turn out products that cannot be matched by machine methods. But the average worker in a small-scale enterprise produces and

---

a subcommittee of the House Ways and Means Committee (Washington: GPO, 1957), pp. 774, 779, and elsewhere. The Japanese government has published figures for 1960 that suggest some narrowing of the wage gap between Japan and the industrial countries of the West. Hourly wages in manufacturing are shown as 13.2 per cent of those in the United States. Japan, Ministry of Foreign Affairs and Ministry of Labor, *Wage Problems in Japan,* 1962, p. 13. Still later comparisons raise the Japanese figure to 16.5 per cent of the American, a level very little below that of Italy and about half the British rate. *The Times* (London), June 17, 1963. A brief, clear summary of problems involved in international comparisons of wages is contained in N. Arnold Tolles and Betti C. Goldwasser, *Labor Costs and International Trade* (Washington: Committee for a National Trade Policy, 1961).

[13] A study made by W. G. Weston, Ltd., reported in *The New York Times,* April 23, 1957, showed Japanese materials costs to be 63 per cent higher than Britain's. In Germany shipbuilding materials were found to cost 3 per cent more than in Britain; in the United States, 9 per cent; in Belgium, 15 per cent; and in Italy, 59 per cent.

earns far less than regular employees of large-scale enterprises who also have a high degree of job security.[14] For the tiny independent operators the main problem is to keep going. Many fail, but failure provides no additional opportunity to work elsewhere and most small enterprisers who fail just start in again as best they can. With rapidly expanding employment opportunities elsewhere in recent years, workers have not been available for small firms in traditional numbers. Now a new squeeze on small proprietors comes from labor scarcity and rising wages. Gradually the number of small firms will decline with continued prosperity.

Wages have been rising rapidly in recent years and may be expected to continue to rise as further economic growth brings both continued increases in productivity and some shortages of labor. The cash earnings of regular workers, as reflected in the Labor Ministry's index for establishments with 30 or more regular workers, doubled in the ten years, 1952 to 1962. Since consumer prices were also rising, the increase in real wages came to only a little over 50 per cent.[15] Employment too has been going up fast. The index shows an increase of over 80 per cent in ten years. The sharpest increases have occurred in construction and wholesale and retail trade. Differentials in wage increases have not been sharp from one industry to the next, but construction wages have increased somewhat faster than those in other major industries.

If economic growth during the 1960s should even approach Prime Minister Ikeda's goal of doubling the national income in ten years, then further large increases in employment and wages may be expected. Both are much needed. Japan has in prospect an unusually large increase in workers as a result of the high birth rates of the years just after World War II, and there are vast pools of underemployed and persons working at such relatively unremunerative occupations as farming on too small plots and small-scale manufacturing and shopkeeping. The poorest fam-

[14] The Japanese Ministry of Labor has published the following figures to show the great, but narrowing, differences in manufacturing wages, according to size of establishment (figures are percentages of wages in the largest establishments):

Number of employees	*1958*	*1961*
500 or more	100.0	100.0
100–499	69.7	74.5
30–99	54.7	61.7
1–29	43.6	49.3

Source: Japan, Ministry of Foreign Affairs and Ministry of Labor, *Wage Problems in Japan,* 1962, p. 24, from Ministry of Labor, *Monthly Labor Survey.*

[15] These figures leave out a large number of workers, both temporary workers and workers in smaller shops. Bank of Japan, *Economic Statistics of Japan,* 1961, pp. 301–302, and *Economic Statistics Monthly,* February 1963, pp. 130–132. The figures on employment in the rest of this paragraph come from the same sources and apply to the same establishments.

ilies in Japan still get extremely little, despite the country's prodigious growth.

In large sectors of the economy the introduction of labor-saving methods has made little progress so far. To get labor from where it is to where it may be needed, however, will be difficult, not only because of the frictional problems present in any economy but also because of a number of peculiarly Japanese practices, especially the employer's virtual guarantee of job security for regular workers and the tradition that these regular workers stay with the same firm for life. One fact that is significant for export costs is that very small-scale establishments, which offer the lowest wages and fringe benefits, had particular difficulty in finding new workers during the boom of 1960 and 1961, and even the large companies found they had to offer more benefits in order to attract labor.[16]

For the present, as in the past, low labor costs are a leading factor in Japanese export success, along with modern technology and efficient management. As real wages rise with economic growth in the years ahead, some export products are likely to become noncompetitive, especially as newly developing countries begin to offer in export markets such things as certain textiles and clothing, which are mainly the product of labor working with a limited amount of machinery. Hong Kong is already far advanced in the production of clothing for export. But Japanese manufacturers should be able to produce on fully competitive terms many new products too advanced for the newer countries. Electrical appliances and electronic devices and other machinery seem especially likely prospects. Low wages will thus gradually become less of a factor in Japanese export success as Japanese industrial maturity advances and real income rises.

Technical Development and Efficiency

Without technical efficiency low wages cannot be converted into low labor costs. Without technical development it is not possible to meet the quality standards required in many foreign markets, especially the high-income markets of America, Europe, Australia, and New Zealand. High technical proficiency is a prominent feature that sets Japan apart from the less developed countries. Technical advance and performance have done

[16] A. M. Rosenthal, "Help-Wanted Sign Goes Up in Japan," *The New York Times*, June 25, 1961, sec. 1; Japan, Economic Planning Agency, *Economic Survey of Japan* (1960–1961) (Tokyo: The Japan Times, 1961), pp. 31–33; and Shuzo Watano, "Fear of Inflation Justifiable." *The Oriental Economist*, November 1960, pp. 619–622. Mr. Watano, editor of *The Oriental Economist*, feels that the need for shifting workers from primary to secondary and tertiary production in the 1960s is likely to be so great under Prime Minister Ikeda's economic growth plan that, unless special steps are taken to expedite transfers, undue wage increases may occur, to the detriment of Japanese exports.

much to make possible Japan's phenomenal postwar recovery and present prosperity.

In Japan today the technical level in much of the modern sector of the economy, including factories producing for export, is very high. Starting sometimes from a piece of ground covered with nothing but ashes and a little wreckage, or in recent years often reclaiming industrial sites from the sea, Japanese manufacturers have brought into being many completely modern factories, taking remarkably full advantage of the best technology the world had for sale. Some of Japan's new cotton textile mills are as efficient as those anywhere. New iron and steel facilities are technically very efficient, as are power-generating plants, automobile factories, cement plants, and many others.

To operate these plants Japan has a wealth of human talent, including technicians and university graduates in rapidly growing numbers. Military service and the administration of occupied areas in Asia no longer draw in large numbers of capable young Japanese. The universities are turning out many more graduates than in the years before 1945 and there are far more scientists and engineers.[17] As industry employs these young people, the Japanese economy benefits. Despite increasing pay, Japanese technicians cost very much less than Western technicians; so many plants use more highly trained people than comparable foreign plants can afford, despite spreading shortages of engineers and of certain kinds of technicians. For example, a prominent manufacturer of transistor radios and other electronic products employs in its main plant 4,000 persons, of whom 650 are engineers.[18]

These new developments have had progressively more effect on the Japanese economy, especially since the mid-1950s. Excellent quality-control staffs and equipment have made the quality and dependability of goods produced in modern factories often as high as that to be found anywhere. Japan's progress in making complicated scientific, precision, and optical goods of high quality and performance is also due in no small part to the increased use of skilled people in much of Japan's manufacturing industry.

Nevertheless, Japan has not yet matched the highest levels reached abroad in some industries. As Table 5-2 above shows, Japan imports large quantities of power-generating machinery, office machinery, electronic computing equipment, machine tools, heavy electrical equipment, large aircraft, and numerous other manufactured goods. It is to be expected that in the years to come Japan will succeed in bringing a progres-

[17] Japan, Ministry of Education, *Demand and Supply for University Graduates, Japan* (Tokyo: Author, 1958), pp. 10, 12, 68–69, and elsewhere.

[18] William M. Freeman, "Sony, Expanding, Thinks Smaller," *The New York Times*, October 22, 1961, sec. 3.

sively wider area of its production nearer to the level of the most advanced countries. The editor of *The Oriental Economist* says: ". . . even with the big operations the output per capita is generally much lower than in Western countries. With the small and marginal operations the gap is incomparably greater." [19] In sum, Japan, whose many technical advances have made possible greater prosperity than anyone expected, has a long way still to travel in the same direction. This promises to be a very productive journey, as was suggested by our review of Japanese imports of technology in Chapter 4.

Japanese Institutions and Business Practices

The island people of Japan have an ancient and highly developed civilization. The amalgam of their customs and institutions, absorbed in large part from China through the centuries, and imported from the West in modern times, contains many elements that strongly influence Japanese capacity to export. Stern attention to duty; austere habits of living; extraordinary capacity for administration in large as well as small units; great skill to adopt, adapt, and absorb new technology and new ideas and to make new products; highly developed social, political, and economic institutions and public services; and an unusual degree of political stability give Japan unique opportunities for profitable foreign commerce.

Human and institutional resources are, in fact, Japan's greatest asset. With these providing the drive, direction, and operating skills, the Japanese economy is able to squeeze a remarkably large amount of capital out of heretofore severely limited production, and to obtain from abroad the raw materials and other things not available in the narrow, rugged, and in some ways barren islands of Japan. By prodigious energy, pragmatic acceptance of reality, and persistent exploitation of opportunities, the Japanese people have repeatedly outperformed other Asian peoples in modern economic activity and surprised the world with unexpected success. Not only in production but also in selling export products, the Japanese can be counted on to press their interests vigorously; their trade missions can be found in remote Africa as well as in America, Europe, Russia, and China. That Japanese goods of many kinds turn up in unexpected places is often a simple reflection of Japanese zeal in pushing sales.

On the other hand, Japanese ways are by no means wholly in tune with those of foreigners, and Japanese producers and traders are often slow to discover and fill the needs of foreign customers, actual and potential. The very traits that facilitate adapting foreign ways to Japanese life

[19] Watano, cited, p. 621.

sometimes become a handicap when the problem is to adapt Japanese or foreign things to foreign needs, for the circumstances abroad that have created established products or that now generate new opportunities are often unknown to the Japanese. It is in the Japanese setting that Japanese successes have mostly been achieved. Abroad, a Japanese individual or export product has frequently seemed notably out of place and ill-adapted to the environment.

What is the problem? Why should Japanese islanders, to whom external economic relations are essential, have difficulty in dealing with foreigners? In part the answer seems to be that the Japanese people have not yet turned much of their very substantial ability toward understanding other peoples. In part the explanation seems to lie in several specific problems. One is the often noticed discomfort of Japanese in foreign situations, especially in societies with looser patterns of interpersonal relations than those followed in Japan.

Language is another barrier. Since English has been the language of commerce in Japan for a century and nearly all Japanese study English in school, one would not expect to find this a serious difficulty. Most Japanese in important trade positions can read English reasonably well and many understand sufficient spoken English for ordinary needs, but English as written or spoken by Japanese is often an imprecise and clumsy tool, even for those who have spent years in English-speaking countries. While individuals can be found who are thorough masters of English and other languages, these persons are relatively few, even in the foreign branches of the Japanese government and business firms. The same criticism could, of course, be directed at Americans with a good deal of validity, but they have the tremendous advantage that their own language is used in major centers all over the world. For Japanese, as for the peoples of most countries smaller than Japan, to deal with foreigners almost always means to deal in a foreign language.

Insufficient understanding of foreign cultures seriously handicaps the Japanese in communicating with foreign peoples. For example, among Japanese designers, producers, and sellers of export products, one often finds surprisingly little appreciation of how the products are used, why they are used, and of the environment into which they must fit. A member of one of the official U.S. trade missions to Japan told on his return of a meeting at which a Japanese manufacturer had brought out a small lacquer box and asked what Americans might possibly use it for. He explained that he had been selling many such boxes to buyers in the United States. The American at once recognized it as a cigarette box and wondered both how any one could miss the identity of such a common object—the Japanese know cigarettes—and how any producer could make a product without learning at the start how it was intended to be used. This lack of understanding is most extreme among very small producers, some of whom live in small rural communities and do not know well the habits even of metropolitan Japanese.

Some Japanese are extremely effective in bargaining with foreign businessmen. But other Japanese stationed abroad often arrive with far too little command of the local language, mix too little with local people, and stay there too short a time. Consequently in many cases they return home without necessary insights or the ability to judge the foreign people or to bargain with them in a fully effective manner.

A promising move toward correcting part of this situation was made late in 1958 with the establishment in Tokyo of the Institute of Asian Economic Affairs. Now a "semigovernmental" organization with strong financial support, the Institute engages in a wide variety of research on Asian countries, including field studies by staff members. This organization has already published some important works and promises to meet a number of the broad research needs for Japan's economic relations with Asia.[20]

Large Japanese industrial and trading firms could improve their organizations and personnel for the tasks of selling Japanese goods in highly competitive foreign markets. Small producers will probably have to rely for some time to come on trading firms or foreign buyers for designs, specifications, and manufacturing instructions. The bigger organizations, however, have some drawbacks resulting from their size. Bureaucratic tendencies are well developed. In most companies promotion depends less on skill in negotiating with foreigners than on other criteria, such as seniority. Firms with branches abroad would find it useful to employ people who had spent an important part of their youth in a foreign country and thereby learned things that come less easily, if at all, to Japanese who go abroad only after graduating from college. But the importance of a Japanese college degree for acceptance in the hierarchical system of Japanese big business is so great that an acquaintance of mine firmly, although reluctantly, denied his son's request to be sent to the United States to college. The father himself had attended college abroad and felt that his lack of a Japanese alma mater had severely limited his career.

A common Japanese trait is the tendency to follow an acknowledged leader. This often results in vigorous efforts by all firms in any category to keep up with others to hold or gain a particular share of the market. When a product sells well it frequently happens that a number of firms

[20] Information about the Institute is given in a pamphlet, *Institute of Asian Economic Affairs*, 1961. An impressive publication of the Institute is *Asian Trade Statistics, Statistics on Foreign Trade between the Asian Countries and Industrial Nations Classified by Commodities* (Tokyo: Author, 1961), 503 pp. plus large folding matrix tables.

will rush to "jump on the bandwagon" and cash in on the proven market. This is a commercial manifestation of the fads so common in Japan. As a result, the rise of Japanese production in lines that are succeeding is at times extremely rapid. The boom may be destroyed by overproduction, price cutting, and a decline in the market, as foreign distributors lose on inventories and drop the product as soon as possible. Sales below cost may lessen not only dealer interest but also customer willingness to pay more normal prices later.

Often the Japanese manufacturer who suddenly undertakes production for export of a new product does so in complete innocence of climbing aboard a bandwagon, since he is simply acting on orders received. The small producer with no direct contacts abroad, with a great need for business, probably with a loan due at the bank or to some other creditor, perhaps also having inadequate means to pay his help, is seldom in a position to ask many questions about firm orders. If he does not accept the order, an equally needy small enterpriser down the street or in the next village will be eager to take it.

Unused capacity and financial instability often stimulate fierce competition that is commonly regarded in Japan as destructive. Because of the cut-throat competition traditional among small producers, they will accept orders that promise to cover little more than out-of-pocket costs. Such firms probably stay in business only because the small producers have nowhere to turn. Labor, which is most of what they have to offer, has usually been plentiful and cheap. The paternalistic labor-employer relation permits some depression of wages and extension of working hours in hard times.

Less readily understandable are some forms of competition among larger firms, including price competition in export markets. Whereas in the oligopolistic automobile industry in the United States competition has traditionally taken other forms than price cutting, the handful of Japanese trading companies competing with each other in the sale of cotton textiles in New York sometimes resort to price competition in circumstances from which no one seems to gain but the American purchaser. While an American may be pleased to see Japanese business houses accepting what appear to be less than maximum obtainable prices, the business motives of these Japanese are at times baffling to their American customers.

Observers have cited several factors to help explain this kind of price competition among the large, established Japanese firms operating in foreign markets. First, the trading companies act as brokers for manufacturers, receiving a fixed percentage on gross sales, and price is often a far less important consideration than volume. Here we see the other side of the picture of the trading company driving down the price of the small producer. Apparently the large producer in Japan is often subjected to the same treatment.

Second, Japanese trading companies, especially the largest ones, earn the bulk of their income from import trade. The main reason for this, aside from the simple fact that Japan's imports exceed exports, is that more of the arrangements for trade are handled by foreigners in the case of exports than of imports. The trading firms are staffed with commodity specialists, skilled in handling large transactions involving a relatively small number of bulk commodities, bought often in highly organized markets in which price is the controlling factor. The export trade comes to be looked upon as less important and tends to be handled as though here too price were the main variable.

A third factor working toward price competition has been Japanese exchange and trade controls. They have often made export volume more important than price since, in any export with a small import cost, a sale involving loss in terms of yen probably still yields a net income in terms of foreign exchange. During the early 1950s, when foreign exchange was extremely scarce and controls very tight, this factor was important, especially in cases where high profits could be made through linked transactions (see pp. 170–171).

Fourth, a bias toward volume is imparted by the forces that give Japan a "bicycle economy," in which the great desideratum is to maintain a certain amount of forward motion. The paternalistic habit is still to keep permanent employees on the payroll whether or not they can be kept busy or income justifies their wages. Such practices sharply lower the point at which a Japanese firm gains by closing down. In firms where many of the workers live at the plant, either in dormitories or in other company houses, it would pay a firm to operate if income covered raw materials costs, power, and relatively little else. Even below this point, the high cost of paying traditional, contractual, or legal severance wages serves as a bar to disbanding a work force except in the face of a long-lived loss of sales. Of course, if the firm failed, there might be no choice. But in Japan large firms seldom fail; merger or operation by creditors tends to minimize the loss of jobs.

Finally, Japanese price cutting appears at times to be not just misjudgment of the American market, as some American businessmen contend, but a generally rational effort to push Japanese export goods, not for maximum immediate profits, nor only for market development in the American sense of enlarging acceptance and demand, but for purposes of maintaining the relative standing of a given firm in relation to other Japanese firms, or a given branch office in relation to others in the firm. More attention may be paid by large Japanese firms to their market share than is the case with similar firms in the United States.

Japanese sentiment, especially among large businessmen and government officials, tends to favor regulation, price fixing, allocation of orders, and other supervised or concerted action. Voluntary business associations are a common device for adopting, administering, and policing such controls. Another less formal means is the tie between a small manufacturing firm and a large trading firm which will bring orders, provide capital, and assist and supervise in other ways. But the large trading firm seldom does much to protect the prices received by its small suppliers. In fact, the trading firm is often the one to beat down the prices. Another means of checking excessive competition is, of course, direct government intervention. This is a widely used means of maintaining export prices, but the object is less to keep small firms alive than to protect the export market by guarding against restrictive actions by importing countries.

In the late 1930s I was extremely skeptical of Japanese assertions that competition among exporters explained why Japanese cotton textiles and other manufactured goods were being offered in the United States at large discounts below American prices when small discounts seemed to me more likely to maximize Japanese dollar income. Regarding the *zaibatsu* as cartelist and monopolistic, I found this reasoning particularly unconvincing. Now I am more inclined to accept it, both for the prewar years and for the present. It is true that the large Japanese manufacturing and trading firms act in concert to a large extent, and that Japan has no traditional objection to monopolies or cartels. The short experience of moving against them under the Occupation has largely been rejected.[21] But competition of certain kinds flourishes and reflects characteristic Japanese vigor. The Japanese mixture of the tendency to combine and the drive to compete is different from the American mixture, but both elements are strongly represented in Japanese business.

Because their ways are very different from those of Americans, Japanese often appear to be fumbling, and so give their business contacts abroad an impression of weakness. Among persons consulted in the course of the present study those most scornful of Japanese business methods and acumen were foreigners who worked very closely with Japanese representatives. When one pulls back and looks at Japanese export activities from a greater distance, however, they often seem much more impressive than when viewed at close range. The Japanese nation has achieved so much in so many lines, including the development of exports to rather forbidding markets, that impressions of weak Japanese performance need to be treated with great care. Despite many appearances of clumsiness

[21] G. C. Allen, *Japan's Economic Recovery* (New York: Oxford University Press, 1958), Chapter 9, especially pp. 143–144.

the Japanese are obviously succeeding in the task of rapidly expanding their export sales. It seems clear that Japanese efforts have had a great deal to do with this growth, even though much of the credit goes to American commercial initiative, a subject that will be discussed more fully in Chapter 8. Despite such drawbacks as those just discussed, Japanese methods and institutions contain a great deal that is helpful, and the positive factors seem far more important than the negative. And in the years ahead it is likely that Japanese concerned with exports will devote much more attention than has yet been given to attacking the weaknesses that still impede them.

JAPANESE EXPORT POLICY

The basic objective of Japanese export policy is very simple: to maximize real income from exports. Therefore, the Japanese government aims to have the level of total exports rise as fast as is consistent with continued growth and amicable relations with important customers. The methods used run the gamut from basic measures affecting the growth and health of the Japanese economy and of export goods and their competitiveness in world markets, through diplomatic steps aimed at clearing away general impediments, to specific measures intended to foster the sales of particular products in particular foreign markets.

Government and business are both deeply involved in Japanese export policy. Japan is the outstanding Asian example of successful private enterprise, but still the government has such pervasive power and influence in economic affairs that frequently the outside observer wonders whether important developments reflect private or government initiative. Often there is no significant difference, for there is a wide area of effective consensus between business and political leadership on export matters as well as other issues. Not only do the two groups cooperate in the dominant conservative party (the Liberal-Democratic Party), but business leaders often hold cabinet positions.[22]

Partly because there is so little difference of opinion on basic matters and partly because there are fewer direct conflicts of interest, export policy is politically less difficult than import policy. Most questions relate to tactics. At some point, however, export policy, like import policy,

[22] "Close, informal association between executives and officials is typical of the basic industries. . . . Throughout the key industries there is much consultation and joint planning. It is not always clear who is controlling whom. The balance of power is apt to depend on whether the company is in debt to a governmental agency and therefore vulnerable to pressure." William W. Lockwood, " 'The Socialist Society': India and Japan," *Foreign Affairs*, October 1958, p. 127.

must face the basic question of how far Japan will go in relying on the world market and accepting imports as one of many means of promoting exports.

Management of the National Economy

The government policies that influence exports most profoundly are those aiming at general growth, modernization, and rising productivity. These have been remarkably successful. National government budgets have been balanced, thanks to stiff taxes, the lack of large military expenditures, and the rapid expansion of the tax base with the growth of production and incomes. Business taxes, while not light, have taken a smaller share of business income than in the United States. Inflationary pressures have been kept under such generally effective control, and productivity in Japan has risen so much by international standards, that Shigeto Tsuru in 1960 called the yen undervalued.[23]

The management of the Japanese economy affects exports to a great extent. The record of the post-treaty years is generally excellent but is marred mainly by the tardiness of measures to meet the foreign exchange crises of 1953, 1957, and 1961. We have seen in Chapter 3 that before restrictive measures were adopted domestic consumption or speculation in raw materials stimulated imports and deterred exports. The task of Japanese economic management is to stimulate maximum economic growth without such severe crises in the future. The authorities in Tokyo have been remarkably successful in meeting the past crises, once it was decided that action was necessary. It is to be hoped that fiscal and monetary measures will be taken at an earlier stage in the future.

Export Promotion

In addition to following general policies that favored exports, the Japanese government has through the years promoted exports in a variety of specific ways. Imports needed to manufacture export goods have been given priority in the allocation of import licenses and foreign exchange. Before the war, and again for a time afterwards, various "link systems" were used to stimulate exports by granting import privileges to firms that sold goods abroad. Some links gave the exporter permission to import the raw materials used in producing the export; for instance, by exporting cotton or woolen manufactures a firm gained the right to import the raw fiber. For a while, beginning in 1953, import licenses were sometimes

[23] Speaking before the Association for Asian Studies in New York in April 1960, he suggested that 300 yen might be a reasonable dollar equivalent, instead of the official 360, even though 360 had been a realistic rate in 1949 when it was adopted as part of the Dodge stabilization program. The 300 figure has since been mentioned from time to time by other economists in Japan.

given for more than the amount of raw material needed for the export involved. This gave added stimulus to exports, so much so that exporters or manufacturers of export goods were at times willing to cut prices drastically in order to increase the volume sold abroad.[24]

Another kind of link gave exporters of high-cost Japanese goods the privilege of importing unrelated goods that were scarce in Japan and on which a large profit could be made. In 1953 and 1954 links between ships and sugar or bananas were especially common for a while. A substantial boost was given the Japanese shipbuilding industry at a time when it needed orders but had difficulty offering competitive prices. Foreigners complained that this was an export subsidy, and at the International Monetary Fund's recommendation Japan abolished this type of link at the end of 1954.

A third kind of link relates not to imports at all but to products subject to export controls, notably sewing machines. An extra share of the total export quota is allocated to producers who meet standards of quality, price, or completeness. Still another device used in the 1950s was the exchange retention system, under which 5 per cent, later 3 per cent, of total export proceeds could be used by exporters for certain purposes for which they would not otherwise be able to get foreign exchange licenses, for instance, office expenses abroad, travel, advertising, and certain commodity imports. This system was abolished in 1960 when Japan liberalized some of its foreign trade and exchange regulations.

A less direct but still significant form of assistance has been the government's measures to guarantee the convertibility into foreign exchange of royalties and other payments for approved imports of foreign technology and foreign capital, much of which, especially the technology, has gone into export industries. As Japan's balance-of-payments position has improved and exchange regulations have been progressively liberalized, specialized devices of this sort, aimed at giving exchange privileges, have become less important.

Among other export promotion activities of the Japanese government, financial assistance has probably been the most significant. Substantial tax concessions are offered for most export production or sales. For instance in 1956 and 1957 exporters were permitted to deduct from their taxable income 80 per cent of the net income derived from export sales or 1 per cent of the f.o.b. value of export sales, whichever was lower. In addition, manufacturers were permitted to deduct 80 per cent of net income derived from goods exported or 3 per cent of the sales price of goods

[24] Except as otherwise noted, this account of Japanese export promotion is based on information from the American Embassy, Tokyo, and from the Ministry of International Trade and Industry.

exported, whichever was lower.[25] It has been estimated that in 1956 these tax concessions totaled about 0.8 per cent of Japan's total export sales, that is $20 million.

Financing of exports is also assisted by the government. Since 1947 export advance bills, covering a period of three to six months between receipt of an export order and the time goods are shipped abroad, have been available to large, well-established firms at interest rates below those on domestic short-term credit. The period between shipment and actual receipt of payment from abroad is covered principally by the export time bill, which has been in use since 1953. Normally drawn for three months but often renewed, these bills carry interest according to the world market rate for similar bills in the foreign currencies in which they are drawn, which is much cheaper than commercial yen credits in Japan. This short-term financing is available for all exports. A borrower deals with his own bank which rediscounts the bills at the Bank of Japan where interest rates for the system are set.

Long-term export financing is provided by the Export–Import Bank of Japan (established in 1950), directly or in cooperation with commercial banks. At the end of March 1962, the export credits outstanding totaled $464 million, of which 44 per cent financed ship exports. Other loans went for steel products, electrical and textile machinery, railroad rolling stock, and other capital goods. Loans are for one to ten years, occasionally as long as fifteen. They are supposed to be made only when commercial bank credit cannot be obtained and the loan is necessary to make the sale. Rates of interest are much below commercial bank rates, at times only half.[26]

The government also insures several types of export risk for which private insurance is not available. General export insurance covers risk of loss from war, revolution, and sudden changes in foreign import and exchange regulations. Other insurance covers the danger that foreign firms may default on their contracts. Sometimes insurance is issued on exports put on consignment in order to make possible shipments without firm orders. One can also insure promotional expenditures overseas against

[25] In accordance with the Special Taxation Law (No. 15 of September 1, 1946), manufacturers and exporters get not only the concessions mentioned here but also the right to deduct from earnings for tax purposes 80 per cent of export earnings or 5 per cent of gross sales, whichever is lower, in cases of exports of industrial plants and equipment.

[26] Loan figures from the Bank's Washington representative. Earlier figures and other information can be found in *Export–Import Bank of Japan, Functions and Operations* (Tokyo: Author, 1960); *Export–Import Bank of Japan, What It Is and How It Works* (Tokyo: Author, 1957); Export–Import Bank of Japan, *Annual Reports; The Export–Import Bank of Japan Law,* Law No. 268 of 1950, as amended by Law No. 122 of 1957 (Tokyo, 1957).

loss resulting from the actions of foreign governments. Financial institutions can also insure their export trade financing.

Public relations, advertising, and other export promotion activities are handled by JETRO, the Japan Export Trade Promotion Agency, an independent government corporation.[27] The government provided JETRO's capital of 2 billion yen ($5.6 million) and annually appropriates about half of JETRO's operating expenses. Almost as much is provided by prefectural and city governments and business, mostly through trade associations. Sales of publications and fees charged for certain services provide some additional income. Of the budget of $9.2 million for fiscal year 1962, $4.9 million came from the national government.

With continuing status and sizable funds, JETRO carries a heavy load of export promotion. Its officially stated functions are credit inquiries, market research, collecting of catalogs and samples, answering inquiries from Japanese and other foreign traders, maintenance of trade centers abroad, exhibiting Japanese goods at trade fairs abroad, other overseas publicity work, and issuing trade publications. JETRO is thus charged not only with telling the world about Japanese goods but also with bringing information about foreign markets to Japanese manufacturers, especially the small producers who are not well placed to learn about foreign markets on their own.

As the financing of JETRO shows, prefectural governments, municipal governments, and a wide variety of business organizations support or conduct trade promotion activities. The prefectural governments of Tokyo, Kanagawa, Aichi, Hyogo, and Osaka, and in addition the city of Osaka, offer export insurance that supplements the national insurance so that transactions covered by both national and other insurance are protected to almost 100 per cent of possible losses. Tokyo and Osaka also subsidize trade fairs, commercial missions, trial manufacture of export commodities, and certain design and research activities.

To what extent does all this activity subsidize Japanese exports? The national government pays out money to JETRO and forgoes revenue by tax concessions. So far export insurance premiums have exceeded loss payments, so the government is not out of pocket. (From another point of view, however, one could argue that reduced interest rates constitute an element of subsidy provided by the government.) Cheaper credit is a benefit for exports, but not one that burdens the treasury or the taxpay-

[27] Originally the Japan Export Trade Research Organization, a semiofficial agency established in 1951, before the end of the Occupation, JETRO was renamed the Japan External Trade Recovery Organization in 1954. The acronym was found to be so well established that it was kept when the body was given its present organization in July 1958. A general description is contained in the leaflet, *JETRO, Its Character and Activities* (Tokyo: Author, 1963).

ers. In any case trade promotion activities such as those of JETRO are quite common abroad, and the U.S. Department of Commerce, for instance, is doing similar work.

What has been accomplished by Japanese export promotion activities? Japanese sales have certainly expanded in the United States and other areas where the bulk of JETRO activities are concentrated, but it is impossible to know how much JETRO contributed to this result. Certainly advertising, public relations, trade fairs, and other activities have ensured that a growing number of people in various countries would hear about Japanese goods. One must assume that some customers have been recruited in this fashion.

A number of persons who are involved in these activities, or are close enough to them for observation, were consulted during the present study. Their impressions are not uniform. Apparently there is a good bit of variation from one case to another in the quality of Japanese public relations and advertising and in the results. American and other non-Japanese observers of Japanese public relations work would probably agree that Japanese efforts are constructive and at times important stimulants to Japanese exports and that the cumulative effect of such efforts should increase with time and with growing Japanese effort and skill in this direction. Most would also observe, however, that up to now the most successful Japanese promotional efforts have been those in which expert guidance or assistance has been obtained from nationals of the country to which the sales are made. More will be said on this subject in Chapter 8 with reference to Japanese sales in the American market.

Another way in which the Japanese government has aided export sales is by supporting or requiring "orderly marketing" procedures. Not entirely euphemistic, this is an expression that denotes mostly negative measures taken to prevent an increase in foreign barriers to the import of Japanese goods. The main aim has been to avoid particularly rapid sales increases or the expansion of sales beyond the point that will be tolerated by politically powerful groups in foreign countries. Export quotas, minimum standards of quality, and minimum-price limitations are the most important measures, which will be discussed in the following chapters.

Detailed discussion of the Japanese government's role in the country's export successes runs the danger of doing less than full justice to the initiative, imagination, and effort of private business, both Japanese and foreign. The motive power driving Japanese goods abroad has been private. Japanese government policies have contributed mainly in promoting economic growth and modernization in Japan and in holding down inflation. Specific measures have assisted exports, especially credit, insurance, and "orderly marketing" activities. But there is doubt about the effectiveness of Japanese government sales promotion activities abroad, and it is fortunate for Japanese exports that these activities have not had to carry much of the load.

EXPORT PROSPECTS

Exports will probably continue to be the single most important limitation on the Japanese economy in the 1960s, much as was the case in the 1950s. This prospect results not from any likelihood of poor export performance, but rather from the tremendous growth pressure of the economy. If growth were occurring at a more moderate pace, export growth at present and likely rates would probably provide ample income for most, if not all, foreign expenditures.

The plan for doubling national income during the 1960s cannot succeed if exports do not increase rapidly. In fact, if the value of imports is to rise faster than national income, as is contemplated, if despite declining special dollar income from the United States government Japan is to pay her obligations, including interest, dividends, royalties, reparations, and GARIOA payments, then exports will have to rise not only faster than national income but faster than imports as well. The plan projections seem to accept this logic and call for annual export increases averaging 10 per cent a year throughout the decade. Imports are projected to rise 9.3 per cent a year and national income 7.8 per cent.[28]

Table 6-4 summarizes the export projections by commodity groups. The planners contemplate a continuation of the shift that has been taking place toward heavy industrial and chemical products, which are projected to rise from 38 to 54 per cent of total exports. But the most rapid increase is expected not in this category but in light machinery, which includes many electrical appliances, optical goods, and other products whose export has been growing especially fast in recent years. Textiles (and clothing) are expected to lose ground relatively and drop to about 19 per cent of total exports. Still, in dollar values this group of exports is projected to rise by 5.3 per cent a year. In almost any other context this would seem like a rapid increase. Nonindustrial exports also are expected to decline relatively, making up only 5 per cent of total exports in 1970.

To push out into foreign markets each year an additional 10 per cent of Japanese goods, and include in this growth annual increases of 16 per cent in light machinery and 14 per cent in heavy machinery and transport equipment, will require more and better export design, production, and promotion, as well as continued reduction in costs. Japan can

[28] Japan, Economic Planning Agency, *New Long-Range Economic Plan of Japan (1961–1970): Doubling National Income Plan* (Tokyo: The Japan Times, 1961), p. 11.

TABLE 6-4. JAPAN'S EXPORT PROJECTIONS FOR 1970

(Values in millions of dollars)

Item	*Average of Fiscal Years 1956–1958*		*Fiscal Year 1970*		*Percentage Increase*	
	Value	*Per Cent of Total*	*Value*	*Per Cent of Total*	*Total*	*Annual*
Industrial products	**2,402**	**88.9**	**8,859**	**95.1**	**269**	**10.5**
Heavy	1,015	37.6	4,983	53.5	391	13.0
Machinery and transportation equipment	603	22.4	3,450	37.0	472	14.3
Metals, metal products	292	10.8	1,040	11.2	256	10.2
Medical, chemical goods	120	4.4	493	5.3	311	11.5
Light	1,387	51.3	3,876	41.6	180	8.2
Textiles and apparel	879	32.5	1,723	18.5	96	5.3
Foodstuffs	206	7.6	547	5.9	166	7.8
Light machinery	56	2.1	400	4.3	612	16.3
Other	246	9.1	1,206	12.9	390	13.0
Nonindustrial products	**299**	**11.1**	**461**	**4.9**	**54**	**3.4**
Total exports	**2,701**	**100.0**	**9,320**	**100.0**	**245**	**10.0**

Source: Japan, Economic Planning Agency, *New Long-Range Economic Plan of Japan (1961–1970)*: *Doubling National Income Plan* (Tokyo: The Japan Times, 1961), p. 77.

produce the goods and there seems no reason to doubt its power to keep prices competitive. Nor is there doubt about effective design or technology and high efficiency of production, what with the continuing purchase of technology projected in the plan, the increasing and progressively more successful Japanese technical training and research activities, the growing number of Japanese traveling and studying abroad, and the recent phenomenal amount of investment in new equipment of advanced design. There need not be difficulty with export promotion either. Japanese firms and industrial associations can employ qualified foreign specialists for sales and public relations functions, supplementing Japanese personnel. The government should have to give fewer tax benefits than in the 1950s, while foreign exchange problems and devices to give special privileges should hopefully be no part of the scene. Credit, too, should not pose difficulties.

The export projections seem reasonably consistent with other parts of the income-doubling plan, although one might question the small margin by which export growth is projected to exceed growth in imports. The basic question is whether during the decade the pressures on Japan will, like those of 1961, create a strong tendency to exceed targets. This happened with earlier plans and again seems a real possibility. In that case the export projections are too modest and Japan's export task even greater.

The strong prospect is for growth, and the trend in Japanese industry and exporting is toward more highly fabricated, more "sophisticated" products. The questions begin with the rate of economic growth the Japanese will try to achieve and the exports needed for it.[29] Next there are questions about inflation control and the general management of the economy, especially of cyclical swings. Then there are the questions of how well the Japanese will promote their exports. The record so far suggests that promotional tasks will be performed gradually better, but it is not certain that cyclical crises will be handled better and exports stimulated more consistently and steadily than in the past. No doubt the Japanese government will continue to help exporters in meeting marketing problems and in adapting to problems encountered abroad, as illustrated by the use of quality, price, and quantity controls on various export products. Gradually better performance may be expected in both government and private efforts to promote exports. How foreign governments will react to a growing flow of Japanese exports cannot be predicted firmly, but most of the signs are hopeful for Japan. The trend is toward reducing barriers, not raising them, except as newly developing countries attempt to protect new industries. Two other questions are how Japan will treat foreign goods and how effective Japanese representatives will be in bargaining to lower both Japanese and foreign trade barriers. Here again the signs are generally hopeful for Japanese trade expansion.

Some of the problems and issues concerning trade relations with particular foreign areas will be discussed in the following chapter. But before turning to them, the observer of Japanese trade should perhaps take note again of the unexpected extent to which Japanese effort has solved problems in the past, both before and after World War II, despite allegedly impassable barriers placed in Japan's way by nature or by foreign governments. Japan is no helpless orphan in a world economy of com-

[29] Since the rate of export growth from the base period (FY 1956–58 average) through FY 1962 was over 13 per cent at current prices and even higher at constant prices, Japan could meet the 1970 targets with growth during the remainder of the 1960s slower than the 10 per cent a year projected in the plan. What seems more likely in view of Japan's recent record is that the targets will be increased. Here is evidence of the great dynamism of the economy and also of the nature of Japanese economic planning, which sets targets but does not control the thousands of firms and millions of individuals who make up the Japanese economy.

mercial giants. A hundred years ago, when such a characterization contained some truth, Japan succeeded in meeting its trade problems, both by taking advantage of Japanese capabilities and of the goods and services offered by foreigners on a competitive basis and also by undertaking Japanese activities, including, for instance, building the Yokohama Specie Bank into a foreign exchange institution conducting business nearly all over the world.

So long as the international atmosphere remains favorable it is in Japan that the main answers will have to be found to Japanese export problems. Will a reasonable amount of the nation's genius for hard work, for organization, for creative adaptation, and for solving problems continue to be devoted to the stimulation of exports—from general economic policies, through specific measures like the design, production, and quality control of export products, to the newer and subtler aspects of export promotion and "orderly marketing"? If so, Japan's export prospects are bright indeed. Inside Japan they could be clouded by adverse political developments or by anything else that would—perhaps by reducing private incentives—divert attention and energy away from the job of expanding Japanese sales abroad. So far no clouds are evident. What can be seen instead is Japan's great capacity for production and trade, and the likelihood that Japanese exports will continue their steep rise—unless the rest of the world puts new barriers in the way.

Chapter 7

The Geography of Japan's Foreign Trade

The limited natural resources of Japan's island economy and the high skills of its numerous and vigorous people determine much of the character of Japanese exports and imports. The trade problems that Tokyo faces can be seen partly in an analysis of these characteristics like that of the last chapter, and partly by an examination of the geographical patterns of Japan's commerce which show both how widely the country trades and something of the opportunities, or lack of them, that it has to expand its imports from and exports to various parts of the world. This chapter examines these geographical elements, first in terms of the general pattern, then with regard to the special problems of Japan's relations with certain parts of the world—notably her Asian neighbors. From this review there emerges some indication of the place of the United States in Japan's foreign trade and of the American interest in Japan's trade with other areas. Both must be taken into account in the formulation of American policy toward Japan.

"DUALISM" IN JAPANESE TRADE

Japanese often speak of a "dualism" in their country's exports. About half go to Asia, Africa, and Latin America, where per capita income is generally lower than in Japan. The other half go to Europe, Australia, New Zealand, the United States, and Canada, where per capita incomes are higher than in Japan.[1] For the most part the two groups of countries

[1] Exports to Liberia are here counted in the latter group because the ships which make up most of the trade are bought by owners in the high-income group of countries. The share of high-income countries rose from 27 per cent in 1934–36 to 38 per cent in 1953 and 53 per cent in 1959 but fell back to 49 per cent in 1960 and 46 per cent in 1961, before rising to 53 per cent again in 1962. This section owes

take different kinds of things from Japan. According to Saburo Okita's calculation the low-income countries were in the late 1950s taking at least 70 per cent of Japan's exports of railroad rolling stock, chemical fertilizer, rayon yarn, textile machines and parts, spun rayon yarn, iron and steel, cotton fabrics, and copper. On the other hand, the high-income countries were taking 70 per cent or more of Japan's exports of ships, raw silk, blouses, plywood, cultured pearls, silk fabrics, canned fish, fish and whale oil, toys, linens, cameras, and radios.

Capital-intensive products are prominent among Japan's sales to low-income countries and labor-intensive products in the exports to wealthier markets. Except for textiles, which are of major importance in sales to both groups, the exports to low-income countries emphasize capital goods, while the high-income countries take more consumer goods. Partly because they are capital-intensive, many exports to the underdeveloped countries come from the big Japanese enterprises, while many of the goods in the latter group come from small or medium-sized producers.

Some Japanese economists with whom I have discussed this dualism argue that the exports to the low-income countries are particularly good for Japan because they stimulate large-scale industry, which is regarded as better than small-scale industry, where productivity and wages are far lower. These Japanese seem to feel that Japan's exports to the United States and other high-income countries are less advantageous to Japan's economic progress, while the exports to the underdeveloped countries represent the wave of the future. Once in a conversation in Tokyo a Japanese shifted from Japanese–American trade, which we had been discussing, to Japan's Asian trade with something like these words: "Now the really important part of our trade is with Asia." Okita does not go so far but says "it is desirable for Japan's export trade to increase the weight of capital-intensive products by developing heavy industries." He adds that it is "also necessary for Japan to promote the export of labor-intensive commodities in order to increase employment as well as to acquire more foreign exchange." One could go further and add a point that will be discussed in the following chapter: Japan's exports to the United States involve less foreign exchange cost per unit than the average of all Japanese exports.

Other trading nations also find important differences between high-income and low-income markets for exports. The peculiarity of Japan's position is that it stands between the two groups in its income level

much to Saburo Okita's *Postwar Structure of Japan's Foreign Trade* (mimeographed), April 1959, pp. 16–17. Mr. Okita was then Director of the Planning Bureau of the Economic Planning Agency (EPA) in Tokyo. Among the published sources where dualism in both the domestic economy and foreign trade is discussed is EPA, *Economic Survey of Japan* (1956–1957) (Tokyo: Author, 1957), pp. 22–28.

and is distinct from each. Changes in the domestic economy as well as the progress of development abroad are likely to have an important effect on the pattern of trade. Japanese sales have been growing more rapidly in the high-income countries, and the long-range forecasts of Japanese trade suggest that this trend may go on for some time. These countries are taking an increasing variety of Japanese goods and are providing important markets for such modern and profitable industries as electronics and optical goods. Textiles are likely to decline in importance among Japanese sales to underdeveloped countries, thus tending to heighten the concentration on capital goods. But at the same time rising living standards in these countries will create an added demand for cheap consumer goods that may well be reflected in increased Japanese exports.

On the import side, there is no dualism to parallel that of Japanese exports, beyond the obvious grouping of imports around crude materials at one end of the scale and highly specialized manufactures at the other. Japanese importing is big business; most bulk commodities and practically all capital goods are usually handled by large trading companies. The users are mainly large textile, steel, or flour mills, petroleum refineries, chemical plants, and so forth. Where goods are bought depends on availability and price, with price playing a much larger role in purchases of bulk commodities than of machinery, airplanes, and other products of modern specialized technology.

The bulk of Japanese imports are primary products, as we saw in Chapter 5. Many come from the less developed areas, which are, of course, incapable of providing specialized machinery or most of the other secondary products imported by Japan. These are supplied by the industrial countries, many of which have very little to export in the line of raw materials, fuels, and foodstuffs. A dualism in Japanese imports could thus be said to exist but it is of limited significance since the United States, which is by a wide margin the largest source of Japanese imports of manufactured goods, is also much the largest provider of the primary products imported into Japan.

A significant kind of dualism may possibly emerge in the future, however, and if or when it does, Japan will have advanced far beyond the economic and policy confines of a few years ago. The new dichotomy would arise if Japan became able and willing to import large quantities of things that are not the strict necessities that make up almost all present imports. The signal of the change would be imports in volume of goods that Japanese could manufacture quite adequately, but that were being bought abroad because they were cheaper. And if the cheapness stemmed from lower labor costs than those in Japan, the new dualism would be pushed even further. In the past manufactured consumer goods have been well below 5 per cent of Japan's total imports,[2] and virtually none have come from "low-wage" countries. The present liberalization program will increase the flow of these goods but, as we saw in Chapter 5, the income-doubling plan calls for imports of finished manufactures other than machinery to rise to only 6 per cent of the total in 1970. Within such severe limits, what will come in seems likely to consist mainly of branded products from high-income countries rather than competitive goods from Korea, Taiwan, Southeast Asia, India, Pakistan, or other low-income countries. Before Japan could take manufactured goods in large quantities from low-wage producers, Tokyo would have to move much further toward the elimination of protectionism than has yet been contemplated. Some of the problems Japan would face will be discussed in Chapter 11.

It is unlikely, then, that a dualism will emerge in Japanese imports comparable to the pattern that can be discerned in exports. The export dualism is itself undergoing some changes, as we have seen. Even the present neat balance of exports, about half to high-income and about half to low-income countries, is unlikely to last, since sales to high-income countries are growing more rapidly than to the others. The official ten-year projections call for a further rise in the relative importance of the high-income countries both as suppliers of imports and markets for exports of Japan. The planners foresee a further departure from the dualism of the recent past in the growth of exports of heavy goods to the high-income countries.

Japanese policy does not seem to be guided by the view referred to above that the low-income markets are better for Japan than the wealthier countries. Clearly, the government planners are aware of the tremendous opportunities the high-income markets offer to Japan. Many other Japanese, however, still show some of the traditional fear of foreign tariffs and sensitivity to insults from the most advanced countries. These people think of Japan as the economic leader of Asia and are apt at the same time to exaggerate the economic significance of the underdeveloped countries for Japan and to underestimate the resistance to Japanese leadership in these countries. To be sure, Japanese trade meets resistance in the advanced countries as well, but of a different sort. The rewards for overcoming these obstacles in the high-income markets are substantial. The record of recent years suggests that Japan in the course of the 1960s can win a new place, not only in the markets of Europe and North America, but in the councils of the economically strong countries of the free world.

[2] Japan, Economic Planning Agency, especially *New Long-Range Economic Plan of Japan (1961–1970): Doubling National Income Plan* (Tokyo: The Japan Times, 1961), p. 80.

The simple fact of the matter is that for a country like Japan trade with all the world is important. Expectations of a relative shift in Japan's trade toward the advanced countries do not mean that the underdeveloped countries are unimportant as suppliers and markets, any more than the persistence of obstacles to low-wage exports in high-income markets—especially in Europe, but also in Australia, North America, and elsewhere—means that Japan should reduce its efforts to expand sales there. Dualism, a helpful concept for analysis, throws light on Japan's position in the world at a certain moment of time. But there is nothing inevitable about it that tells us what Japan's trade will look like in the future. It is a useful reminder, though, of the differences in the markets of poor and rich countries and of the differing capabilities of the Japanese economy in relation to them. The potentialities, and some of the obstacles to taking full advantage of them, are explored in the pages that follow.

THE GEOGRAPHICAL PATTERN OF TRADE

Japan trades nearly everywhere. But there has always been a high degree of concentration in a few major areas. Recently the United States and Canada together have accounted for about a third of Japan's trade and Asia for another third, with the remainder spread widely over other parts of the earth. (Tables 7-1 and 7-2.) This is in sharp contrast with the previous pattern. In 1934–1936 most of the trade of the area that is now Japan was with Asia, which accounted for nearly two-thirds of exports and a half of imports. Korea, Taiwan, and Mainland China provided the largest part of this trade. In those days the United States supplied another quarter of Japan's imports and took about a sixth of the exports, leaving only a fifth of the exports and a quarter of imports for all other markets. Right after the war the United States was for a time almost the sole supplier of imports; its share declined from 97 per cent in the sixteen months after surrender to 32 per cent in 1962. In exports, however, the 1950s saw a decrease in the share taken by Asia and a rise in that going to the United States and Canada.[3]

Asia

China, Taiwan, and Korea took 42 per cent of Japan's exports in 1934–1936 and only 6 per cent in 1962. The sharp decline resulted mainly from Japan's loss of military and political control in those territories and the subsequent events there. The share of the rest of Asia in Japanese exports is higher now than it was before the war, but not all countries have

[3] Unattributed trade statistics in this chapter come from the tables herein or from standard sources cited in the Bibliographic Note.

TABLE 7-1. GEOGRAPHIC DISTRIBUTION OF JAPAN'S IMPORTS, 1934–1936, 1950, 1960, 1962

(Values in millions of dollars)

Region and Country of Origin	1934–1936 av. Value	1934–1936 av. Per Cent of Total	1950 Value	1950 Per Cent of Total	1960 Value	1960 Per Cent of Total	1962 Value	1962 Per Cent of Total
Asia	**494.4**	**51.7**	**315.5**	**32.6**	**1,407.1**	**31.3**	**1,614.1**	**28.6**
China	102.0	10.7	39.3	4.0	20.7	0.5	46.0	0.8
Korea [a]	136.4	14.3	15.7	1.6	18.6	0.4	28.5	0.5
Taiwan	92.0	9.6	35.8	3.7	63.5	1.4	61.4	1.1
Ryukyus	0.0	0.0	0.7	0.1	26.1	0.6	41.1	0.7
Hong Kong	0.7	0.1	0.8	0.1	23.0	0.5	18.9	0.3
Thailand	1.5	0.2	43.4	4.5	72.3	1.6	71.7	1.3
Malaya	20.6	2.1	39.0	4.0	193.6	4.3	186.2	3.3
Singapore	0.0	0.0	0.5	0.1	13.5	0.3	22.7	0.4
Burma			17.6	1.8	13.4	0.3	16.3	0.3
India	93.6	9.8	17.4	1.8	99.5	2.2	93.1	1.7
Pakistan			38.4	4.0	31.7	0.7	28.5	0.5
Indonesia [b]	24.6	2.6	13.3	1.4	70.3	1.6	91.2	1.6
Philippines	7.6	0.8	22.5	2.3	158.9	3.5	183.9	3.3
British Borneo	3.2	0.3	0.9	0.1	77.5	1.7	76.0	1.3
Persian Gulf region [d]	0.3	0.0	20.6	2.1	411.2	9.2	570.3	10.1
Other Asia	11.8	1.3	9.6	1.0	113.3	2.5	78.2	1.4
U.S.S.R. [f]	**8.1**	**0.8**	**0.7**	**0.1**	**87.0**	**1.9**	**147.3**	**2.6**
Europe	**93.7**	**9.8**	**38.5**	**4.0**	**448.5**	**10.0**	**766.9**	**13.6**
EEC countries	47.3	5.0	21.1	2.2	209.1	4.7	344.0	6.1
United Kingdom	21.7	2.3	6.2	0.6	99.1	2.2	145.8	2.6
Latin America [g]	**20.2**	**2.1**	**68.8**	**7.1**	**310.1**	**6.9**	**476.8**	**8.5**
Mexico	2.4	0.3	16.5	1.7	102.9	2.3	127.8	2.3
Africa	**24.9**	**2.6**	**26.3**	**2.7**	**163.9**	**3.6**	**218.1**	**3.9**
Australia and Oceania	**65.1**	**6.8**	**84.4**	**8.7**	**405.4**	**9.0**	**493.1**	**8.7**
Australia	59.4	6.2	76.9	8.0	343.7	7.7	435.5	7.7
Northern America [h]	**252.0**	**26.4**	**433.6**	**44.9**	**1,756.0**	**39.1**	**2,064.1**	**36.6**
Canada	17.4	1.8	15.4	1.6	203.7	4.5	255.0	4.5
United States [i]	234.5	24.6	418.2	43.3	1,545.4	34.4	1,809.0	32.1
Total imports [j]	**955.4**	**100.0**	**967.2**	**100.0**	**4,491.1**	**100.0**	**5,636.5**	**100.0**

Notes and sources: See Table 7-2, below.

Table 7-2. Geographic Distribution of Japan's Exports, 1934–1936, 1950, 1960, 1962

(Values in millions of dollars)

Region and Country of Destination	1934–1936 av. Value	1934–1936 av. Per Cent of Total	1950 Value	1950 Per Cent of Total	1960 Value	1960 Per Cent of Total	1962 Value	1962 Per Cent of Total
Asia	**593.5**	**63.7**	**383.1**	**46.3**	**1,500.9**	**37.0**	**1,674.4**	**34.1**
China	169.5	18.2	19.6	2.4	2.7	0.1	38.5	0.8
Korea [a]	159.1	17.1	18.1	2.2	100.1	2.5	138.1	2.8
Taiwan	61.7	6.6	38.0	4.6	102.2	2.5	118.6	2.4
Ryukyus	0.0	0.0	0.0	0.0	94.6	2.3	133.8	2.7
Hong Kong	13.6	1.5	53.3	6.4	156.0	3.8	192.4	3.9
Thailand	10.7	1.1	43.1	5.2	117.5	2.9	148.5	3.0
Malaya	0.5	0.1	4.4	0.5	31.7	0.8	38.7	0.8
Singapore	16.5	1.8	13.3	1.6	87.0	2.1	105.0	2.1
Burma	}	}	16.3	2.0	64.5	1.6	53.4	1.1
India	} 74.7	8.0 }	20.7	2.5	108.7	2.7	119.4	2.4
Pakistan	}	}	55.6	6.7	59.0	1.5	57.3	1.2
Indonesia [b]	41.6	4.5	46.3	5.6	110.2	2.7	115.3	2.3
Philippines	13.1	1.4	21.3	2.6	154.5	3.8	120.0	2.4
Viet-Nam [c]	1.1	0.1	2.1	0.2	61.5	1.5	60.1	1.2
Persian Gulf region [e]	7.7	0.8	6.5	0.8	100.6	2.5	98.2	2.0
Other Asia	23.7	2.5	24.5	3.0	150.1	3.7	137.0	2.8
U.S.S.R. [f]	**6.9**	**0.7**	**0.4**	**0.0**	**60.0**	**1.5**	**149.4**	**3.0**
Europe	**76.2**	**8.1**	**99.7**	**12.0**	**495.0**	**12.2**	**844.9**	**17.2**
EEC countries	30.7	3.3	40.5	4.9	174.6	4.3	274.4	5.6
United Kingdom	36.4	3.9	26.0	3.1	120.5	3.0	192.3	3.9
Latin America [g]	**31.2**	**3.4**	**47.3**	**5.7**	**303.9**	**7.5**	**353.7**	**7.2**
Africa	**54.6**	**5.8**	**73.8**	**8.9**	**351.8**	**8.7**	**335.2**	**6.8**
Australia and Oceania	**26.4**	**2.8**	**30.0**	**3.6**	**199.3**	**4.9**	**180.0**	**3.7**
Australia	20.2	2.2	23.4	2.8	144.1	3.6	138.5	2.8
Northern America [h]	**150.8**	**16.2**	**194.0**	**23.4**	**1,203.4**	**29.7**	**1,525.2**	**31.0**
Canada	3.1	0.3	14.7	1.8	119.2	2.9	126.2	2.6
United States [i]	147.7	15.9	179.3	21.7	1,082.9	26.7	1,400.2	28.5
Total exports [j]	**932.6**	**100.0**	**827.8**	**100.0**	**4,054.5**	**100.0**	**4,916.2**	**100.0**

[a] Republic of Korea only, except for 1934–1936.
[b] Republic of Indonesia for postwar years: for 1934–1936, all of Netherlands India.
[c] South Viet-Nam only in 1960 and 1962; for other years, French Indo-China.
[d] Postwar years: Iran, Iraq, Bahrein, Saudi Arabia, Kuwait, and Trucial Oman and Qatar; in 1934–1936, Iran only.
[e] Iran, Iraq, Saudi Arabia, and Kuwait; in 1960 and 1962 also Bahrein and Trucial Oman and Qatar.
[f] Data on Japanese trade with the U.S.S.R. are also included in the totals for Asia and Europe through 1960; in 1962 all U.S.S.R. trade is included in the total for Europe.
[g] All of the Western Hemisphere, except Northern America, as defined in the following note.
[h] Figures for 1960 and 1962 cover Greenland, Canada, St. Pierre and Miquelon, continental United States, and Alaska. Figures for earlier years include continental United States and Canada only. Hawaii is excluded in all years except 1962.
[i] Forty-eight states only, except in 1962, when Alaska and Hawaii are included.
[j] In some years total includes a very small amount of trade with "special areas," mostly within Japanese territorial waters.

Note: Dollar values converted from yen figures at exchange rates given in Bank of Japan, *Economic Statistics of Japan*, 1962, p. 259.

Sources: 1934–1936 and 1950: Bank of Japan, *Economic Statistics of Japan*, 1961, pp. 251–254, with some figures from Japan, Ministry of International Trade and Industry.
1960 and 1962: Japan, Ministry of Finance, *Monthly Return of the Foreign Trade of Japan*, January–December 1960, and *Trade of Japan* (Monthly Return), January–December 1962.

participated uniformly in this growth. Hong Kong, the Persian Gulf region, the Philippines, Thailand, Malaya, and Singapore have risen in importance while India, Pakistan, Burma, and Indonesia have declined somewhat, though remaining very important. Textiles, especially cotton fabrics, and capital goods are the main items Japan sends to the rest of Asia.

About a seventh of Japan's exports to Asian countries in the late 1950s were paid for not by the recipient countries but by the Japanese government as reparations or by the United States as economic aid. Reparations deliveries totaled $70 million in 1959, $64 million in 1960 and $86 million in 1961. (Appendix Table A-1.) They went mainly to Burma, the Philippines, and Indonesia, representing a significant share of Japanese exports to those countries. Purchases in Japan with funds provided by the International Cooperation Administration (ICA) paid for exports mainly to Korea, Viet-Nam, Taiwan, Pakistan, and Cambodia. They were substantially reduced by measures the United States took to meet its balance-of-payments problems.[4]

On the import side, too, Asia has become much less important to Japan than it was. From over half in 1934–1936, Asia's share of Japan's imports fell to less than one-third in the early 1960s. Again, as with exports, the principal drop was in imports from Korea, Taiwan, and China. These areas provided just over a third of Japan's total imports in 1934–1936, but only 2.4 per cent in 1962. From the other end of Asia Japan's imports have increased sharply, because of the rapidly expanding use of petroleum. The Persian Gulf area provided 10 per cent of Japan's imports in 1962, in contrast to only 0.03 per cent in 1934–1936. Other Asian areas showed much smaller changes.

The elimination of the prewar pattern of Japan's Asian trade is probably final, corresponding to fundamental political changes and some major economic shifts as well. But there is nothing inevitable about the trade pattern of recent years. In Japan much attention focuses on some possibilities that are discussed later in this chapter: expanding trade with Communist countries and Europe, and Japan's assuming a

[4] During U.S. FY 1961 expenditures in Japan of ICA funds totaled $132 million, of which $124 million was for Asian countries, divided as follows, in millions of dollars: Korea, 44; Viet-Nam, 32; Republic of China, 28; Pakistan, 10; Cambodia, 5; India, 3; others, 2. ICA, *Operations Report,* Data as of June 30, 1961 (Washington: Author, 1961), p. 94. The next year, fiscal 1962, the total dropped to $25 million, of which $22 million for Asia was divided as follows: Viet-Nam, 7; Korea, 6; Republic of China, 6; others, 3. Agency for International Development, *Operations Report,* Data as of June 30, 1962 (Washington: Author, 1962), p. 54. The Japanese government reported that reparations payments to Asia east of Iran covered $55 million of Japanese exports in 1959, and $47 million in 1958, while ICA funds paid for $109 million and $98 million respectively. Japan, Ministry of International Trade and Industry, *Foreign Trade of Japan,* 1960, p. 149.

greater place in the foreign economic relations of the developing countries of South and Southeast Asia.

Taiwan. While the old pattern of colonial trade has been altered, Japan has retained closer commercial ties with Taiwan than with the other territories formerly under its control. Despite the relatively small size of the island and its limited exportable surplus, Taiwan sold more to Japan in the early 1960s than did Mainland China or Korea. As before, sugar was the most important product and there were also smaller quantities of fruit, salt, coal, and other items. But rice, which was second only to sugar until 1960, dropped to a very low level in that year, as Taiwan's rice surplus virtually disappeared, immediately as a result of bad weather, but more fundamentally because population has grown faster than rice production. Rising Japanese incomes provide a growing demand for Taiwan's sugar, fruit, and minor products. The ostracism of Cuba has made Taiwan Japan's main supplier of sugar and for the time being virtually guarantees a market for all the sugar Taiwan can export.

The future of Japan's trade with Taiwan—if political or military developments do not interfere—appears to depend mainly on the price at which Taiwan can supply sugar and on the quantities of coal and fruit it can export. As part of its development program Taiwan will make an effort to increase exports of goods that Japan imports, but it is doubtful that this will offset the disappearance of rice exports. Population growth and economic development in Taiwan will have important trade effects. To improve the trade balance Taiwan will try to export many goods competitive with Japanese products, such as textiles, clothing, and cement. Some of the things now imported from Japan will be produced domestically. Capital goods will be needed and Taiwan hopes to attract more foreign investment. Japanese capital appears to be more welcome there than in most other areas that were once under Japanese control. While the outcome of these mixed forces is uncertain, Taiwan may well be unable to hold its present share of Japanese trade.

As Taiwan gradually proves capable of producing factory products good enough and cheap enough for the Japanese market, and as the Japanese permit entry of such goods, Taiwan's exports to Japan may regain lost ground. Japanese reluctance to buy may be overcome by the inability or unwillingness of Taiwan to continue financing large net imports from Japan. These economic factors could easily become lost in political acrimony, however, especially over Japanese relations with Peking.

Korea. Before 1945 Japan had developed Korea as a source for a large and diversified flow of imports. Only the United States supplied more to Japan in the years 1934–1936. Half or more of what Japan purchased from

Korea was rice, mostly of the particular glutinous kind favored by the Japanese and cultivated in Korea as a part of Tokyo's colonial policy. Silk, soybeans, fertilizers, fish, minerals, and mineral products were the other principal imports. Japan provided to Korea mainly manufactured goods, but also some coal and certain foodstuffs, including wheat flour and fruit. On balance, as we saw in Chapter 3, the net flow of trade was from Japan toward Korea, except during the 1920s.[5]

Since the ending of Japanese control in 1945 Korea has been afflicted by partition, occupation, and war. Hostility to Japan has proved both deep and lasting. Such trade as moves between Japan and Korea is almost exclusively with the Republic of Korea in the south.[6] This trade has had a stormy record, punctuated by Korean embargoes and unsuccessful attempts to establish normal relations. Syngman Rhee, the autocratic president of the Republic of Korea from its founding in 1948 until his overthrow in the student-led revolution of April 1960, was particularly bitter against Japan and intransigent in his dealings. The various leaders who have held office since Rhee have appeared to be more interested in coming to terms with Japan, but political relations have been far from normal or smooth. In addition there are very serious economic obstacles. Korea has not yet been able to produce very much for export. Rice, marine products, and a few minerals seem to have the greatest potential, but the rapid increase in the Korean population raises some doubt about how much food the country can export.

The possibilities of Japan's providing goods for the needs of South Korea are far better, provided some means of payment can be found. United States aid and military expenditures are the principal sources of funds with which Korea can pay for imports. Japan is the nearest, cheapest, and generally best source for much of what Koreans must get from abroad. Despite all its difficulties with the Rhee regime, Japan succeeded in exporting a wide variety of goods to Korea. Since Rhee's departure Japanese sales have more than doubled, from $62 million in 1959 to $138 million in 1962. Though procurement in Japan with American aid funds has been restricted, Korea has been able to finance imports, mainly with funds obtained from exports and from American military spending in Korea. The prospect seems to be for Japan to continue to dominate that part of Korea's import trade not tied to U.S. sources. As political relations

[5] The Oriental Economist, *Foreign Trade of Japan, A Statistical Survey* (Tokyo: Author, 1935), pp. 578–634.

[6] The Communist People's Republic of Korea in the north has mineral products Japan might import, and could, of course, make use of many things from Japan. But what North Korea can export is limited by the demands of its own economic program and by its trade obligations inside the Communist bloc. South Korea's bitter resentment of any Japanese contact with North Korea inhibits Japan's efforts to develop that trade.

improve between Tokyo and Seoul, Japanese investments may be expected to add further to the flow of trade.

China and Southeast Asia present Japan with large trade opportunities and also serious problems. These two areas will receive special attention later in the chapter.

Europe

Europe's share in Japan's foreign trade has only recently grown to exceed its prewar level of just under 10 per cent of total trade. In 1962 Europe supplied 13.6 per cent of imports and bought 17.2 per cent of exports. Europe provides Japan mostly machinery and other products of advanced technology, along with some fertilizer, fish oils, and raw materials. Japan needs new types of machinery and stands to gain from strong European competition with the United States, the present principal supplier of this kind of import. No great change in the pattern seems likely to occur, though the rapid expansion of European production, coupled with gains from economic integration, may enable European producers to take part of the Japanese market away from U.S. suppliers.

Textiles, fish, and ships lead the list of what Japan sends to Europe, but many other products are also sold. The United Kingdom, West Germany, Italy, Switzerland, and the Netherlands have been the principal customers, taking over half of Japan's 1962 sales to Europe. Scandinavia and other West European countries account for most of the remainder. Purchases by Communist countries in Europe have been very small. One might suppose that by increasing its sales efforts Japan could do about as well in Western Europe as it has done in the United States, for these markets are in many respects similar, and in recent years the Western European economy has been growing more rapidly. In fact the Japanese look on the European market with feelings of hope, based on rising European incomes and convertible currencies, mixed with fear that integration will leave Japanese exports at a disadvantage and that European governments will continue to resist the entry of many kinds of Japanese goods. The hopeful factors have recently been in the ascendant, for Japanese sales to Europe in the early 1960s had a remarkably good record. But the future depends in large part on the willingness of Europeans to open their markets wider to Japanese goods, a matter to be looked at more closely later in this chapter.

Latin America

Of substantially more importance in Japanese trade since World War II than before, Latin America is an area where some Japanese hope trade expansion will be particularly rapid in the years ahead. This region, with approximately 200 million population, accounted for 8.5 per cent of

1962 imports and 7.2 per cent of exports, as compared with 2.1 and 3.4 per cent respectively in the years 1934–1936. Japan is less important in Latin American trade than Latin America is in Japanese trade. For Latin America as a whole Japan accounted for less than 4 per cent of total exports or imports throughout the 1950s, although for individual countries Japan's importance was greater, especially as a buyer.

The leading import item, raw cotton, comes mainly from Mexico, but also from Central America, Brazil, Peru, and Argentina.[7] Sugar follows, coming much less from Cuba than before the days of Fidel Castro and more from Brazil, which in 1961 was not far short of Taiwan, Japan's principal supplier. Other Latin American sources of sugar are the Dominican Republic, Argentina, Ecuador, and Peru. Other leading imports from Latin America are corn, ores (mainly iron and copper), and wool. Among exports the leading item is machinery (including radios and ships), followed by textiles and metal products. The distribution of trade among countries is very uneven. While Japan has an import surplus with the area as a whole—exports amounted to 63 per cent of the value of imports in 1950–1961—the balance of trade varies sharply from one country to another.

Mexico is much the largest source of imports. Nearly a quarter of all Japanese imports from Latin America in 1961 consisted of Mexican cotton, which made up nearly all of the $135 million worth of imports from Mexico. The $67 million of imports from Peru were half iron ore, the rest mainly other ores and metals and some cotton. Argentina provided $65 million, mostly wool, wheat, and corn. Brazil's $61 million was made up nearly half of sugar and a quarter of raw cotton, followed by iron ore and then coffee. Chile provided principally iron ore and some copper ore, Cuba almost entirely sugar. Raw cotton and some cotton seed were mainly responsible for putting El Salvador and Nicaragua next in order of import supply, the figure for Nicaragua being a substantial $17 million. No other Latin American country provided Japan as much as $10 million worth of imports in 1961.

Brazil stood out as the leading market in 1961, taking $86 million worth of Japanese goods, mostly machinery and steel products. Sales to Argentina amounted to $41 million, also mainly machinery and steel. Venezuela, on the other hand, took more textiles, radios, and other consumer products than capital goods. Exports to Panama nominally included a 26,000-ton tanker, four cargo vessels totaling 18,000 gross tons, besides a variety of manufactures, mostly consumer goods that were actually shipped to Panama. At the head of the long list of manufactured goods sold in Mexico were 3,682 passenger cars, the most Japan sold

[7] The discussion of commodity trade is based on figures for 1961.

to any foreign country. Other Latin American nations which bought more than $10 million worth of Japanese goods in 1961 were Chile, Colombia, Peru, and Cuba.

The future of Japanese trade with Latin America is promising, although by no means certain. Latin American demand is great. The Alliance for Progress promises to provide much of the capital for development and is attempting to induce the social and institutional reforms necessary for continuing growth. Although Alliance funds originating in the United States are not eligible for spending elsewhere, the Latin American countries can usually buy from Japan with foreign exchange they have earned. Still, chronic shortages of foreign exchange seriously limit the capacity of Latin American countries to import, and prominent among the imports restricted in times of exchange shortage are consumer manufactures, in which Japan tends to have the greatest competitive advantage. By increasing imports from Latin America, Japan can somewhat alleviate this situation, but the possibilities for bilateral balancing of trade do not appear very great. Japanese investments, such as those in the Usiminas steel plant in Brazil, can also do much to promote trade. Political and social upheavals are enough of a hazard in Latin America to remove the possibility of simple predictions. Still, barring upheavals that block trade, Japan's export prospects appear very good.

Africa

The smallest of the continents as a trading partner of Japan, Africa provides some cotton, iron and steel scrap, corn, phosphate rock, wool, oilseeds, and various minerals. Recently Africa's share of Japanese imports has been a little above the prewar level. More trade flows the other way. A large part of the explanation lies in the emergence of Liberia as the largest listed buyer of Japanese ships. Apart from this rather special trade—the ships are registered in Liberia but owned elsewhere—Japanese sales to Africa now represent a slightly larger share of total exports than in 1934–1936. Textiles and clothing account for about three-fourths of sales, with various other goods, including iron and steel, radios, tea, and textile machinery, making up the rest.

Within the African continent the places where Japan trades are scattered unevenly, and the trade with individual areas or countries tends to be very unbalanced. The Republic of South Africa is Japan's leading trade partner in Africa, providing mainly corn, wool, iron and copper ores, pig iron, and asbestos. Japan's $81 million of imports from there in 1961 made up 43 per cent of purchases from the whole continent. As an outlet for Japanese goods South Africa is far less imposing. In 1961 Japanese exports amounted to $49 million, mainly textiles, machinery, clothing, and sundry goods.

Liberia was second in Japanese trade with Africa in 1961 by virtue of $96 million of Japanese ships going to Liberian registry. But other exports were only $5 million, imports $6 million.

Nigeria also is a large buyer of Japanese exports without selling much in return. But in this case the exports actually go to the African country. They consist mainly of textiles, clothing, and limited quantities of other consumer goods.

The three countries just mentioned each accounted for more than $80 million of trade in both directions in 1961. No other African country accounted for half as much. Egypt, Ghana, Kenya, the Central African Federation (the Rhodesias and Nyasaland), and the Sudan, all carried on trade of $20 to $40 million with Japan.

During the 1950s Africa's place in Japanese trade rose substantially, mainly because of the boom in sales of ships for Liberian registry. These sales hit a peak in 1957 and then declined somewhat, turning upward again in 1961. Presumably this trade will continue unless there is a slump in shipping or some change in the circumstances that make Liberian registry attractive for ships owned elsewhere. The future of the rest of Japan's trade with Africa depends on political and economic developments in that continent. African countries with exports to offer during the 1960s will find Japan a potential purchaser of primary products, including minerals, fibers, and tropical foods. Japan is likely to continue to want such specialties as Egyptian cotton and Moroccan phosphate. Japanese policy may well seek larger imports from Africa as a means of expanding Japanese exports there.

On the export side, Japan has much to offer African countries, ranging from cheap consumer goods to capital equipment. The pace of economic development and the character of public policy will determine whether African countries are able and willing to buy. Aside from ship sales, Japan's substantial export surplus with Africa could grow rapidly if import controls were relaxed and traditional trade ties with Europe weakened. A triangular trading relationship might evolve with a number of African countries running export surpluses with their main customers in Europe and North America to offset import surpluses with Japan—and perhaps in time also with India and the more advanced African countries. At present many of the African territories still have preferential tariff relations with Britain or the European Economic Community. But if circumstances are favorable Japan—with goods to sell—can reasonably expect to play a growing part in the foreign trade of developing Africa.

Australia and New Zealand

Australia and New Zealand, along with the islands in the Pacific, provide nearly a tenth of Japan's imports. Australia alone was the second largest national supplier in the early 1960s, sending principally wool but also significant quantities of coal, wheat, metals, ores, and scrap. The trade is important and has good prospects for expansion. Political conditions are favorable: Japan is no longer feared as she was before World War II. Economically there are several favorable factors. Japan's woolen mills now produce goods of excellent quality, and unless synthetic fibers or barriers against Japanese exports of woolen goods interfere, Australia and New Zealand can expect to find a growing market in Japan. There have already been some years, including 1961, when Japan was the principal buyer of Australian wool. Since Japanese eating habits are shifting away from former extreme reliance on rice, fish, and soybeans, toward such Western foods as wheat, barley, meat, and dairy products, Australian and New Zealand farmers may sell more in Japan despite competition from the United States and Canada. Mineral products, too, seem to have a bright future. The Pacific islands provide phosphate rock and other minerals. Japanese imports of Australian coal have grown to large proportions. American coal is of higher quality but must be carried much farther to reach Japan.

Japanese exports to the region are far below imports, in 1962 only 36 per cent as high. Both Australia and New Zealand have a tradition of anti-Japanese protection and for a long time refused to grant Japan equal treatment under GATT. Now, however, the trend is toward liberalization. Japanese sales to Australia trebled between 1957 and 1960; they fell sharply in 1961 but then rose again in 1962. Japanese regard this trade as particularly important and hope for a further large expansion of exports. The major Japanese exports have been textiles, but in some recent years there have been large sales of metal products, especially iron and steel. Many other products, including chemicals, cameras, radios, and toys, have reached significant volume. Further growth appears to depend on reduction of import barriers. Australia's agreement in July 1963 to disinvoke Article 35 of GATT is a hopeful sign. Australia and New Zealand are high-income countries, capable of sharply increasing their purchases from Japan, as the United States and other high-income countries are doing. Unlike most high-income countries, Australia and especially New Zealand have only limited industrial sectors, and protectionist pressure against imports may be less pervasive than, say, in Europe. The geographic propinquity and economic complementarity of these areas and Japan offer promising prospects for mutually profitable interchange on a rapidly expanding scale.

Canada

Canada has become an important partner in Japanese trade only in recent years. A leading seller of wheat and several other principal

Japanese imports, Canada is now also a leading buyer of Japanese exports. Like the United States, which accounts for almost ten times as much Japanese trade, Canada consistently sells more than it buys from Japan. Canada is like the United States also in some of the kinds of goods exchanged and in some of the policy problems caused by the competition of Japanese exports.

Wheat is the principal commodity Japan imports from Canada, which in some years has been Japan's leading supplier of the grain. In 1961 nearly 40 per cent of Japan's imports from Canada were made up of wheat, and the rest largely of scrap iron and steel, iron ore, linseed and other oilseeds, asbestos, coal, aluminum, and other metals. Clothing leads the list of Japanese exports to Canada, followed by machinery, metal products, textiles, and a wide range of other things. Transistor radios suddenly became prominent in 1959. Footwear has become important only in recent years. Toys, plywood, and fish products are also sold in significant quantities.

As a producer of large quantities of farm, forest, and mineral products, and an importer of many manufactured products, Canada has an economy largely complementary to Japan's, so there is a sound basis for expanding reciprocal trade in the years to come. This basis would be strengthened if the United Kingdom entered the European Economic Community under conditions that reduced the preferences that in the past have favored Canadian–British trade. Japanese goods are becoming progressively better adapted to Canadian tastes. At the same time Japanese enterprises are showing interest in developing copper, iron ore, and other Canadian resources to supply part of Japan's growing needs.

This complementarity does not, however, prevent serious problems from arising between the two countries. Canadian producers of textiles and other products have protested against Japanese competition so vigorously that Japan has imposed "voluntary" quotas on exports to Canada of stainless steel flatware and a number of textile products. As in the United States, the strength of the producers' protest is primarily the result of the impact of imports on certain groups and areas such as the small textile towns in Quebec. As former Prime Minister Diefenbaker put it, "The difficulties which have arisen in Canada as regards trade, result not from the total level of imports from Japan but from a concentration in particularly sensitive lines such as textiles and other consumer products." [8]

This problem, like many others in Canadian–Japanese trade relations, parallels problems that arise between Japan and the United States. Con-

[8] John Diefenbaker, "Trade Pacts Benefit Canada, Japan," *World* (Washington), December 20, 1961, p. 21.

sequently much of what is said in this volume with respect to the United States applies in some degree to Canada as well. Indeed, problems relating to the competition of Japanese export products have in some cases spread from the United States to Canada. Despite the relatively short distance between Japan and Canada across the Pacific Ocean, most of what Japan sells in Canada is carried through the Panama Canal to the Atlantic Ocean, and a good deal is unloaded in New York. Canadian sales have, thus, been in significant degree an extension of sales in the United States, new products appearing in Canada only after they have had some experience in the Eastern seaboard area of the United States.

Canadian policy toward Japanese exports is liberal. According to Mr. Diefenbaker, "It is generally agreed that Japanese goods enjoy freer access to the Canadian market than to the market of any other industrialized country in the world." There seems a good prospect for Canada to grow even more important in Japanese trade in the future than in the recent past.

The United States

The United States is far and away Japan's largest trading partner. The huge trade, nearly a third of Japan's total overseas commerce since surrender, has been very lopsided, with Japan buying twice as much as it sold. (See Table 7-3.) [9] But the period of extreme imbalance has passed, and in recent years exports to the United States have increased more rapidly than imports. At the low point in 1947, Japan sold in the American market only 4 per cent of its purchases here. This figure rose gradually to more than 90 per cent in 1959 but has since been lower. As Japa-

[9] Table 7-3 omits Japan's trade with Puerto Rico in all years and that with Alaska and Hawaii for the years before 1962. With none of these areas was Japan's trade large, as the following figures (in millions of dollars) show:

	Alaska		*Hawaii*		*Puerto Rico*	
Year	*Imports*	*Exports*	*Imports*	*Exports*	*Imports*	*Exports*
1954	0.004	0.017	1.8	5.8	0.3	0.2
1957	1.5	0.027	3.7	7.8	2.9	2.1
1960	6.9	1.3	1.3	17.5	0.5	5.7
1961	15.4	0.49	1.1	15.4	0.6	5.8
1962	n.a.	n.a.	n.a.	n.a.	0.3	10.2

Sources: Japan, Ministry of Finance, *Monthly Return of the Foreign Trade of Japan,* January–December issue, 1954, 1957, 1960, 1961; *Trade of Japan* (Monthly Return), January–December 1962; *Trade of Japan* (Annual Return), 1961 and 1962. Japan's main import from Alaska is rayon pulp from the Japanese mill at Sitka opened in 1960. From Hawaii and Puerto Rico Japan imports mainly iron and steel scrap. To Hawaii Japan exports fish and other marine products, textiles, and a long list of other things. To Puerto Rico Japan's leading exports are fish and other marine products, motorcycles, some textiles, and some radios.

TABLE 7-3. JAPAN'S BALANCE OF TRADE WITH THE UNITED STATES, 1934–1936, 1945–1962

Year	*Imports from United States*			*Exports to United States*			*Excess of Imports*		*Exports to U.S. as Per Cent of Imports from U.S.*
	Million Dollars c.i.f.	*Per Cent Change from Previous Year*	*Per Cent of Japan's Total Imports*	*Million Dollars f.o.b.*	*Per Cent Change from Previous Year*	*Per Cent of Japan's Total Exports*	*Million Dollars*	*Per Cent of World Import Excess*	
1934–1936 av.	235		24.6	148		15.9	87	378.2	63.0
1945–1946 [a]	298		97.4	77		74.8	220	108.4	25.8
1947	481	61.4	91.8	20	−74.0	11.5	461	131.0	4.2
1948	442	−8.1	64.6	66	230.0	25.6	376	88.3	14.9
1949	575	30.1	63.5	79	19.7	15.5	496	125.6	13.7
1950	428	−25.5	43.9	179	126.6	21.8	249	161.7	41.8
1945–1950	**2,224**		**65.5**	**421**		**22.6**	**1,802**	**117.9**	**18.9**
1951	695	62.4	34.8	185	3.4	13.6	510	79.6	26.6
1952	768	10.5	37.9	229	23.8	18.0	539	71.4	29.8
1953	758	−1.3	31.4	227	−0.9	17.8	531	46.8	29.9
1954	847	11.7	35.3	277	22.0	17.0	570	74.0	32.7
1955	772	−8.9	31.2	449	62.1	22.3	323	70.1	58.2
1951–1955	**3,840**	**72.7** [b]	**34.0**	**1,367**	**224.7** [b]	**18.1**	**2,473**	**65.7**	**35.6**
1956	1,064	37.8	33.0	543	20.9	21.7	521	71.5	51.0
1957	1,618	52.1	37.8	597	9.9	20.9	1,021	71.6	36.9
1958	1,054	−34.9	34.7	680	13.9	23.7	374	238.2	64.6
1959	1,113	5.6	30.9	1,031	51.6	29.8	82	57.3	92.6
1960	1,545	38.9	34.4	1,083	5.0	26.7	463	105.9	70.1
1956–1960	**6,394**	**66.5** [b]	**34.3**	**3,934**	**187.8** [b]	**25.0**	**2,461**	**85.1**	**61.5**
1961	2,079	34.6	35.8	1,051	−3.0	24.8	1,028	65.3	50.6
1962	1,809	−13.0	32.1	1,400	33.2	28.5	409	56.7	77.4
Postwar total	**16,346**		**36.5**	**8,173**		**23.8**	**8,173**	**78.0**	**50.0**

[a] September 1945 through December 1946.
[b] Change from previous five-year period.

Notes: Excludes trade with Alaska and Hawaii through 1961, with Puerto Rico in all years. Minor inconsistencies result from rounding.

Sources: 1934–1936 and 1951–1961 calculated from yen figures in Bank of Japan, *Economic Statistics of Japan*, 1961, pp. 251 and 253, converted at exchange rates shown on p. 269.
1945–1950 from Japan, Economic Stabilization Board (predecessor to present Economic Planning Agency), *Japanese Economic Statistics*, December 1951, Sec. II, p. 11. The small difference in 1950 imports as reported here and in Table 7-1 reflects an unexplained inconsistency in the sources used.
1962 from Japan, Ministry of Finance, *Trade of Japan* (Monthly Return), January–December 1962.
Percentages of Japan's total imports and exports calculated with data from Table 5-1.

nese exports to the United States were rising, the recovery of production in other countries made it possible for them to supply things Japan had been able to get only from the United States in the immediate postwar years when this country supplied over 60 per cent of the total. The two chapters that follow will deal in detail with Japan's exports to the United States; here we are concerned only with what Japan buys from this country.

The range of Japan's purchases in the United States is enormous. This country is Japan's largest source of primary products and also of manufactures. Table 7-4 shows the record for selected years. Nearly two-thirds of the total consists of raw materials (including fats and oils), foodstuffs, and fuel. Of these the United States provides roughly a third of all that Japan imports. But of manufactures, especially chemicals and machinery, more than half of all that Japan imports comes from American suppliers. These figures were lower in 1962, when import suppression measures affected mainly Japan's bulk imports, and for all commodity groups except foods, purchases from the United States dropped more than those from other sources. Among individual commodities, iron and steel scrap is the largest import of all, followed by raw cotton, soybeans, and coal. The United States usually provides more than half of Japanese imports of each of these items.

The emergence of scrap iron and steel as the leading import from the United States reflects the tremendous growth of Japan's steel industry to its present position of fourth in the world, following the United States, the U.S.S.R., and West Germany. In 1961 a contributing factor was the low level of American steel production, which reduced domestic demand for scrap and permitted Japan to obtain here three-quarters of the year's total scrap imports. In that year, the United States sold more scrap than cotton to Japan (as it did in 1959 when sales of soybeans also exceeded those of cotton). Whether cotton will be permanently displaced from it traditional position as the largest Japanese import from the United States remains to be seen. Although the value of the cotton sales rose substantially between 1954 and 1961, the relative importance of cotton declined (from 20.4 to 12.6 per cent), largely because textile production in Japan has not kept pace with other burgeoning industries. Cotton exports receive special U.S. government support, first in the credits given annually by the Export–Import Bank of Washington to finance Japanese purchases (see p. 74), and secondly in the price differential that has made the cost of cotton for foreign purchasers lower (now 8½ cents a pound less) than the price which domestic mills must pay.

The subsidy, which is by far the more significant factor, was not enough to prevent a decline in the American share of Japan's cotton imports,

Table 7-4. Japan's Imports from the United States, by Commodity, 1954, 1957, 1960, 1961, 1962

Commodity	Value (millions of dollars)					Per Cent of Total Imports from U.S.					U.S. Share of Total Japanese Imports (per cent)				
	1954	*1957*	*1960*	*1961*	*1962*	*1954*	*1957*	*1960*	*1961*	*1962*	*1954*	*1957*	*1960*	*1961*	*1962*
Food, beverages and tobacco	**187.7**	**149.4**	**122.2**	**160.2**	**223.3**	**22.2**	**9.2**	**7.9**	**7.7**	**12.4**	**28.7**	**26.0**	**22.3**	**24.0**	**30.2**
Wheat	83.1	93.9	63.0	52.9	60.0	9.8	5.8	4.1	2.5	3.3	49.4	57.5	35.6	29.5	33.2
Barley	13.6	12.1	0.0	0.0	0.0	1.6	0.7	0.0	0.0	0.0	26.7	21.4	0.0	0.0	0.0
Corn	5.8	17.0	11.2	29.8	59.6	0.7	1.1	0.7	1.4	3.3	40.4	46.6	13.8	27.9	44.6
Unmanufactured tobacco	7.7	3.5	12.5	16.3	24.1	0.9	0.2	0.8	0.8	1.3	83.8	76.9	91.5	77.7	74.6
Other	77.5	22.9	35.5	61.2	79.6	9.2	1.4	2.3	2.9	4.4	18.9	7.3	12.9	17.0	20.2
Raw materials, except fuel	**356.9**	**672.2**	**701.7**	**974.3**	**630.1**	**42.2**	**41.6**	**45.5**	**46.9**	**34.9**	**31.7**	**33.4**	**32.3**	**35.4**	**26.7**
Hides and skins (except furs)	12.6	17.8	24.6	35.9	38.0	1.5	1.1	1.6	1.7	2.1	63.4	62.8	59.6	61.6	60.2
Soybeans	56.2	69.6	103.0	122.1	116.0	6.6	4.3	6.7	5.9	6.4	84.6	74.5	95.9	94.8	87.4
Other oilseeds	2.6	4.6	12.6	8.7	8.2	0.3	0.3	0.8	0.4	0.5	8.7	9.6	16.0	12.7	11.2
Synthetic rubber	1.7	8.9	28.4	25.7	26.1	0.2	0.6	1.8	1.2	1.4	89.0	79.5	84.6	81.5	81.6
Logs and lumber	9.9	13.7	24.4	70.0	66.5	1.2	0.8	1.6	3.4	3.7	20.6	17.3	14.3	26.9	21.0
Pulp and waste paper	9.2	21.8	20.5	19.8	34.0	1.1	1.3	1.3	1.0	1.9	37.7	52.5	66.1	55.9	80.4
Raw cotton and linters	172.3	215.0	217.8	262.1	125.0	20.4	13.3	14.1	12.6	6.9	41.9	50.7	51.4	50.7	32.7
Phosphate rock	13.5	28.4	21.4	23.4	20.6	1.6	1.8	1.4	1.1	1.1	55.0	70.5	66.0	65.4	62.8
Crude salt	0.5	1.8	3.3	4.5	4.8	0.1	0.1	0.2	0.2	0.3	3.1	6.2	15.6	20.1	19.2
Iron ore and concentrates	6.3	25.3	12.8	14.8	12.7	0.8	1.6	0.8	0.7	0.7	9.6	12.3	6.0	4.9	4.0
Iron and steel scrap	14.7	199.4	155.4	289.5	131.6	1.7	12.3	10.1	13.9	7.3	33.4	70.1	67.7	74.7	73.4
Nonferrous metal ores and concentrates	3.3	11.5	9.6	12.0	3.0	0.4	0.7	0.6	0.6	0.2	13.0	9.1	6.2	7.0	1.9
Nonferrous metal scrap	30.3	29.5	48.0	63.6	29.1	3.6	1.8	3.1	3.1	1.6	84.7	38.7	64.6	67.0	55.9
Other	23.9	24.8	20.2	22.3	14.5	2.8	1.5	1.3	1.1	0.8	7.7	4.7	3.6	3.5	2.6
Mineral fuels and lubricants	**85.4**	**221.3**	**178.0**	**207.8**	**202.6**	**10.1**	**13.7**	**11.5**	**10.0**	**11.2**	**32.0**	**32.6**	**24.0**	**22.3**	**19.5**
Coal	52.2	134.9	91.6	110.3	112.7	6.2	8.3	5.9	5.3	6.2	83.1	77.3	64.8	58.6	55.9
Crude petroleum	1.0	7.0	9.2	10.3	7.5	0.1	0.4	0.6	0.5	0.4	0.7	2.2	2.0	1.9	1.2
Heavy oil	15.3	56.8	46.3	45.9	43.9	1.8	3.5	3.0	2.2	2.4	35.6	39.7	49.4	30.9	27.7
Lubricating oils and greases	4.0	9.7	16.5	22.5	23.1	0.5	0.6	1.1	1.1	1.3	88.2	81.9	84.7	90.2	76.7
Other	12.9	12.9	14.5	18.8	15.4	1.5	0.8	0.9	0.9	0.9	56.8	47.7	65.2	59.4	50.3
Fats and oils	**19.0**	**23.8**	**29.9**	**29.0**	**20.2**	**2.2**	**1.5**	**1.9**	**1.4**	**1.1**	**79.3**	**64.6**	**78.6**	**75.7**	**64.5**
Beef tallow	18.1	22.0	23.0	25.5	16.6	2.1	1.4	1.5	1.2	0.9	96.4	81.3	90.8	90.2	80.6
Other	0.8	1.8	6.8	3.5	3.6	0.1	0.1	0.4	0.2	0.2	16.1	18.3	54.1	34.6	33.6

Chemicals	**36.4**	**96.7**	**148.5**	**178.6**	**158.9**	**4.3**	**6.0**	**9.6**	**8.6**	**8.8**	**57.0**	**52.7**	**56.0**	**53.2**	**52.9**
Organic chemicals	10.1	23.8	35.8	38.3	42.3	1.2	1.5	2.3	1.8	2.3	72.7	68.5	71.0	63.4	56.2
Potassic fertilizers	0.0	13.9	16.3	16.2	15.9	0.0	0.9	1.1	0.8	0.9	0.0	41.9	43.8	35.2	49.7
Synthetic plastic materials	4.1	19.4	26.9	32.6	24.1	0.5	1.2	1.7	1.6	1.3	75.1	79.3	77.3	75.4	68.5
Other	22.2	39.6	69.4	91.6	76.6	2.6	2.4	4.5	4.4	4.2	49.8	43.5	48.6	49.1	48.5
Manufactured goods classified by material	**23.1**	**236.7**	**76.7**	**119.1**	**69.1**	**2.7**	**14.6**	**5.0**	**5.7**	**3.8**	**37.7**	**51.2**	**29.9**	**30.7**	**23.4**
Pig iron	0.0	61.2	1.7	14.6	6.6	0.0	3.8	0.1	0.7	0.4	6.0	66.2	3.0	12.5	7.9
Steel plates, sheets, shapes, rails, etc.	4.1	72.5	17.9	9.9	4.0 [a]	0.5	4.5	1.2	0.5	0.2 [a]	53.1	46.4	60.3	46.5	75.5 [a]
Other iron and steel	1.9	36.9	1.0	9.0	7.5	0.2	2.3	0.1	0.4	0.4	54.9	65.9	37.1	49.8	31.8
Nonferrous metals	6.7	41.2	38.4	59.4	19.9	0.8	2.5	2.5	2.9	1.1	25.0	39.7	32.4	36.4	49.9
Other	10.4	24.9	17.8	26.1	31.1	1.2	1.5	1.2	1.3	1.7	44.6	46.2	34.8	37.1	37.6
Machinery and transport equipment	**123.2**	**188.7**	**247.3**	**354.2**	**449.9**	**14.6**	**11.7**	**16.0**	**17.1**	**24.9**	**69.6**	**65.4**	**61.4**	**59.1**	**58.6**
Power-generating machinery	6.9	23.2	23.8	29.1	63.6	0.8	1.4	1.5	1.4	3.5	70.1	88.8	75.4	79.9	89.2
Office machinery	11.5	16.1	30.6	56.0	61.3	1.4	1.0	2.0	2.7	3.4	85.7	84.9	57.9	66.0	58.7
Machine tools and other metal-working machinery	15.1	28.5	46.2	89.6	94.5	1.8	1.8	3.0	4.3	5.2	59.9	58.4	54.5	53.1	50.5
Machinery for conveying, mining, and road construction	7.3	10.4	5.7	6.5	6.3 [a]	0.9	0.6	0.4	0.3	0.3 [a]	76.8	75.7	56.6	49.8	42.3 [a]
Textile machinery	6.7	5.1	3.7	5.1	8.7	0.8	0.3	0.2	0.2	0.5	67.8	29.2	24.0	26.6	32.5
Electrical machinery and appliances	8.5	15.8	27.0	29.7	59.4	1.0	1.0	1.7	1.4	3.3	64.5	74.2	79.1	72.4	74.7
Automotive vehicles and parts	19.5	12.4	10.1	12.4	13.4	2.3	0.8	0.7	0.6	0.7	69.5	76.3	75.7	73.8	67.7
Aircraft and parts	11.5	13.1	40.9	40.5	51.1	1.4	0.8	2.7	2.0	2.8	89.7	94.2	93.3	81.8	78.7
Other	36.3	64.1	59.3	85.2	91.6	4.3	4.0	3.8	4.1	5.1	65.6	57.4	50.9	50.2	46.1
Miscellaneous products and transactions	**14.7**	**27.7**	**38.7**	**53.6**	**51.5**	**1.7**	**1.7**	**2.5**	**2.6**	**2.9**	**61.8**	**62.2**	**60.7**	**60.4**	**57.0**
Scientific, etc., instruments and apparatus	5.6	15.4	19.6	28.7	22.9	0.7	1.0	1.3	1.4	1.3	66.6	72.9	68.0	70.3	71.1
Other	9.1	12.2	19.1	24.9	28.6	1.1	0.8	1.2	1.2	1.6	59.1	52.4	54.4	52.1	49.1
Total imports of foreign goods	**846.4**	**1,616.5**	**1,543.1**	**2,076.8**	**1,805.6**	**100.0**	**100.0**	**100.0**	**100.0**	**100.0**	**35.3**	**37.8**	**34.4**	**35.8**	**32.1**
Re-imports	**0.6**	**1.4**	**2.3**	**2.6**	**3.3**	**0.1**	**0.1**	**0.1**	**0.1**	**0.2**	**23.0**	**34.0**	**34.4**	**22.3**	**38.8**
Total imports (including re-imports)	**846.9**	**1,617.9**	**1,545.4**	**2,079.4**	**1,809.0**	**100.1**	**100.1**	**100.1**	**100.1**	**100.2**	**35.3**	**37.8**	**34.4**	**35.8**	**32.1**

[a] Because of the extensive reorganization of the components of this item in 1962, coverage differs somewhat between 1962 and earlier years.

Notes: Trade with Alaska and Hawaii is included for 1962, omitted for earlier years. See Appendix B for definitions of commodity groupings in terms of code designators. The customs statistics underlying this table are described in the Bibliographic Note.
Minor inconsistencies result from rounding.

Sources: Japan, Ministry of Finance, *Annual Return of the Foreign Trade of Japan*, January–December issue, 1954, 1957, 1960; *Trade of Japan* (Annual Return), 1961; and Table 5-2. 1962 figures provided by Japan, Ministry of Finance, Customs Bureau, Business Section.

from 51 per cent in 1960 and 1961 to 32 per cent in 1962. The effect of the 1962 drop was particularly sharp because Japan's total cotton imports fell from $511 million to $377 million. American cotton fared badly in other markets as well. The U.S. Department of Agriculture suggests as causes a decline in consumption in importing countries, reduction of cotton inventories, and increasing competition from record production abroad of cotton and man-made fibers.[10] But this listing fails to pinpoint what seems to have been the key factor so far as Japan at least is concerned. That is the reported higher prices of American cotton, even after the export subsidy. If this is indeed the main factor, lower prices may be able to stimulate exports of American cotton and the place of cotton in American sales to Japan may prove better in the future than in the immediate past.

Manufactured goods, including chemicals, machinery, and instruments, make up a third of Japan's purchases from the United States. In 1961 the United States provided nearly a third of Japan's imports of general manufactures and over half the imported chemicals and machinery. The American share of Japanese imports of some items runs very high: in 1961, 82 per cent for aircraft and parts, 80 per cent for power-generating machinery.

In the future the United States may supply a smaller share of Japanese imports. The Japanese are shifting to other sources of supply in Asia, Australia, and Latin America, as they have already done in the case of cotton. Rapidly increasing imports of petroleum, mainly from the Middle East, Indonesia, and other sources, now including Soviet Russia, are another factor in pushing down the U.S. share. European manufacturers may supply a larger share of Japanese machinery imports in the years to come. A large-scale expansion of trade with Mainland China would be another force in the same direction.

Despite these developments, the United States is likely to remain the best source of many Japanese imports and there seem no reasons to expect violent change. As Japan liberalizes its import policy, American exporters of manufactured products are likely to benefit more than those of other countries, partly because of the effect on Japanese tastes of years of demonstration by Americans stationed in Japan, and partly because American businessmen know the country far better than do their competitors from Europe and elsewhere. These factors could, of course, be nullified by high prices if American goods should cease to be fully competitive, or if American exporters should lag behind foreign competitors in sales efforts in Japan.

[10] U.S. Department of Agriculture, Economic Research Service, *The Cotton Situation*, CS-206, May 1963, p. 5.

DOING BUSINESS WITH CHINA

China is a huge, powerful, and very close neighbor of whose presence the Japanese people are deeply and continuously conscious. It is also the country with which Japan has been trading longer than with any other. China is the source of Japan's writing and much else in its civilization. China is an area where Japanese imperialism had both great successes and great failures and where, for a time after 1937, Japanese traders did more business than anywhere else outside the main home islands. Most of all, China today poses the largest, and to many Japanese the most urgent, unsolved problem of Japanese foreign relations, economic, political, and cultural. In approaching questions related to China, even China under Communist control, Japanese begin with a feeling of friendliness and confidence that differs markedly from their attitudes toward other nations, especially Russia.[11]

Loss of the China Trade

China was Japan's largest overseas market in 1934–1936 and second to Korea as a source of imports. (Tables 7-1 and 7-2.) The exports were in large measure capital goods, representing Japanese investments, especially in Manchuria; another part was consumer goods for Japanese on the mainland, as well as for the Chinese population. In 1935 two-thirds of Japan's imports from China were soybeans, oil cake (for fertilizer), oilseeds, raw cotton, coal, pig iron, and iron ore.[12] Thereafter manufacturing expanded vigorously on the mainland. In 1940, I observed not only coal mining and extraction of oil from shale in Manchuria, but also steel production there and cotton textile production in Shanghai. Many other plants were also in the planning or building stage and some, notably textile mills in Tsingtao, had been destroyed by the Chinese in the fighting. The expansion of manufacturing was intended mainly to supply the local market, but in the late 1930s the Japanese also imported fertilizer and pig iron from Manchuria.

Immediately after the war resumption of commercial relations was out of the question. The end of Japanese military and political control in China meant the severance of nearly all prewar economic bonds. Neither country was in a position to supply even a small part of the other's needs. Civil war raged in China until the Communist victory in 1949 put a government in firm control of the whole mainland area for

[11] C. Martin Wilbur, "Japan and the Rise of Communist China," in Hugh Borton and others, *Japan between East and West* (New York: Harper, for the Council on Foreign Relations, 1957), especially pp. 223–227.

[12] Mitsubishi Economic Research Bureau, *Japanese Trade and Industry, Present and Future* (London: Macmillan, 1936), p. 544.

the first time in over a century. No Chinese government, of course, would have had any reason to want to revive the previous trade, designed and shaped as it had been to serve Japanese aims. The Communist government has been implacably hostile to the dominant conservative forces in Japan as well as to the United States, to Japanese–American cooperation, and especially to American military bases in Japan. On the Japanese side, the Occupation, the Korean War, relations with Chiang Kai-shek, and American pressure for trade controls at first prevented and then restrained approaches to Peking. Since 1958 the Japanese have been held back also by awareness of the difficulties of attempting to trade with China under existing conditions.

Political relations between the two countries are limited. Neither Communist nor Nationalist China was present when the Japanese peace treaty was signed at San Francisco, since the Allies could not agree on which regime should represent China. Japan agreed with the United States to recognize Chiang Kai-shek's government but restricted recognition to the territory actually controlled, then or in the future, by the regime on Taiwan.[13] Despite strong pressure within Japan to recognize the Peking regime as well, no Japanese government has made serious moves in that direction.

The problem of establishing even a reasonably satisfactory modus vivendi between Japan and China remains, and the Japanese people are widely and deeply uneasy about this problem. Even within the ruling Liberal-Democratic Party there is sentiment in favor of expanding trade and other contacts with Mainland China, at the cost, if necessary, of American displeasure and of greater concessions to Peking than have yet been seriously contemplated by the Japanese government. The Socialist opposition advocates going even further and at once.

The Resumption of Trade

Some trade has taken place between Japan and Mainland China in every year since the People's Republic was established in October 1949. Table 7-5 shows the record. The contraction of trade from 1950 to 1952 resulted from the Korean War, Chinese intervention, and the controls imposed by UN action which, as applied to Occupied Japan in December 1950, severely limited exports to China. Trade reached its lowest level in 1952, the year Japan regained its independence. Pressed by the United States, Japan continued to control exports to China after the Korean armistice. Nevertheless, trade expanded substantially and reached a peak in 1956. Japanese purchases were much larger than sales. Soy-

[13] This discussion of Japan and Communist China has drawn heavily from A. Doak Barnett's *Communist China and Asia* (New York: Harper, for the Council on Foreign Relations, 1960), Chapter 10.

TABLE 7-5. JAPAN–CHINA TRADE, 1950–1962

(In millions of dollars)

Year	*Imports from China*	*Exports to China*	*Excess of Imports*	*Total*
1950	39.3	19.6	19.7	58.9
1951	21.6	5.8	15.8	27.4
1952	14.9	0.6	14.3	15.5
1953	29.7	4.5	25.2	34.2
1954	40.8	19.1	21.7	59.9
1955	80.8	28.5	52.3	109.3
1956	83.6	67.3	16.3	150.9
1957	80.5	60.5	20.0	141.0
1958	54.4	50.6	3.8	105.0
1959	18.9	3.6	15.3	22.5
1960	20.7	2.7	18.0	23.4
1961	30.9	16.6	14.3	47.5
1962	46.0	38.5	7.5	84.5

Source: Bank of Japan, *Economic Statistics of Japan,* 1961, pp. 251–253; Bank of Japan, *Economic Statistics Monthly,* March 1963, pp. 105–106.

beans, rice, salt, and coking coal were the main imports; fertilizers, textiles, and machinery the main exports.

The conduct of this trade was complicated by the fact that on the Chinese side it was handled by official or semiofficial groups, while the Japanese negotiators had no formal official status, not because of Japan's private enterprise economy but because Japan does not have diplomatic relations with the Peking regime. A series of so-called "private trade agreements" provided the framework for trade after June 1952. The fourth and largest of these agreements was signed in March 1958. Months of bargaining had gone into it, mainly about peripheral matters, especially whether a Chinese trade mission in Japan would be permitted to fly the flag of the People's Republic of China. Two months later, in May 1958, China abruptly imposed an embargo on Japanese goods, though still permitting a reduced volume of exports to Japan, mainly via Hong Kong. The immediate occasion for this action was an incident in a department store: a young Japanese pulled down a Communist Chinese flag at a stamp show, and Japanese authorities who handled the case charged the youth with destroying furniture, not insulting a foreign flag.[14]

[14] *The Oriental Economist,* June 1958, p. 291.

China's effort in early 1958 to use trade bargaining for political purposes differed only in detail, but not in basic character, from its earlier conduct. As C. Martin Wilbur said in 1957, "China has exploited the lure of trade to the hilt."[15] Japanese expectations were aroused by glowing descriptions of the large opportunities for trade with China, with figures as high as a billion dollars a year in both directions.[16] But always before very much trade could move there were conditions for Japan to fulfill—recognition of Peking or some steps in this direction, reduction of the restrictions that Japan applied to China trade in cooperation with other free world countries, or violation of them, provision of restricted items in return for Chinese acceptance of items the Japanese are most eager to sell.

For two years after 1958 trade remained dormant. Small quantities of Chinese goods trickled into Japan, but almost nothing Japanese went to China. Meanwhile talk of China trade never ceased in Japan, and before long groups of Japanese were again making trips to Peking to discuss trade. In November 1962 a mission headed by Tatsunosuke Takasaki, former Minister of International Trade and Industry, concluded in Peking a new "private trade agreement" covering a five-year period. The annual volume of trade called for was "about $100 million" in both directions, which is not much higher than actual trade in 1962, and below the level of 1955 through 1958. Japan was to provide steel products, chemical fertilizers, agricultural chemicals, and industrial plants, and to import coal, iron ore, soybeans, and corn.[17] In August 1963 it was learned that the Japanese government had approved the sale to China by the Kurashiki Rayon Company of a $20 million synthetic fiber plant. Payment was to be made over a period of five years. Again Japanese interest in the China trade was spurred; new studies and explanations were undertaken, but still the amounts discussed as possible for 1963 and 1964 were no higher than the levels of the mid 1950s.

Trade Controls and Japanese Attitudes

The trade controls, which have been such a prime target of Chinese propaganda and which have been subject to great controversy in Japan, were put into effect before Japan regained its independence of action in 1952. Beginning in 1950 a group of leading non-Communist countries have coordinated their strategic controls over trade with Communist areas through a Consultative Group (CG) and its Coordinating Committee (COCOM). Export of arms, ammunition, implements of war,

[15] Cited, p. 215.
[16] Same, p. 237; *The Oriental Economist,* April 1958, p. 213.
[17] *The Oriental Economist,* December 1962, p. 682.

and atomic energy materials to Communist areas is prohibited. Less complete and rigid restrictions are maintained on a wide range of goods including metal-working, chemical, petroleum, power-generating, transportation, and general industrial equipment; electronic and precision instruments; metals, minerals, and their manufactures; chemicals and petroleum products; rubber and rubber products. Large shipments of these items are considered dangerous, but there is room for some discretion by national governments in the application of the rules.

When Japan joined CG and COCOM in September 1952, a special group called CHINCOM (China Committee) was organized to extend and increase the controls that had already been in effect against Communist China and North Korea. The CHINCOM embargo list was substantially larger than the COCOM list, including about 200 additional items. In August 1954 the COCOM list was revised and reduced but no changes were made in the China list. By then several members of COCOM–CHINCOM were already relaxing their controls on China trade while Japan felt pressed by the United States to apply the rules quite rigorously. In 1957, however, Japan joined most of the members in completely removing the differential between the two lists, despite opposition from the United States, which still has a virtual embargo on all trade with Communist China and North Korea.[18]

From the beginning the Japanese found the restrictions particularly irksome and adhered to them reluctantly. This attitude came not only from the feeling that the controls were economically damaging at a time when Japan already had grave trade problems, but also from a complex of emotional factors related to China, to Japan's newly regained sovereignty, to hopes for reducing American dominance in Japan, and to widespread Japanese lack of realism about the cold war. Because the rules for trading with China were stricter than those for trade with the U.S.S.R. and its European satellites, the Japanese felt that they were sacrificing more potential trade than the Western European countries were. Moreover, when European governments made use of the discretion accorded them under CHINCOM rules to expand their exports to China, the Japanese resented the American pressure they held responsible for their own government's strict application of the rules.

When he was Minister of International Trade and Industry in 1956, Tanzan Ishibashi said: "It is true that Japan is highly desirous of promoting trade with Communist China, but many hurdles, COCOM restrictions on exports for instance, stand in the way. Japan has been working hard

[18] Mutual Defense Assistance Control Act of 1951 Administrator, *The Strategic Trade Control System, 1948–1956,* Report to the Congress (Washington: GPO, 1957), and other reports to Congress by the Administrator.

for the alleviation or removal of such restrictions." [19] Many Japanese felt that the limitations were discriminatory: [20]

> Although Japan is remaining apprehensive of and faithful to the COCOM regulations, Western European countries are practically ignoring them as they export generators, 3½ ton trucks, and 10,000 ton class ships to Communist China. Why is it that Japan is unable to export even wooden vessels, which are regarded as strategic goods, while European countries that are part of the Free World can export 10,000 ton class ships?

Trade with China is a subject of very wide interest in Japan and is connected in Japanese minds with other matters, such as American trade restrictions and U.S. government expenditures in Japan. The Director of the Economic Affairs Bureau of the Foreign Ministry told a visiting group from the U.S. Congress in December 1956: [21]

> There has also been a strong public desire in Japan for the expansion of trade with Communist China. I would like to stress that Japan, as a member of the community of free nations, has not the slightest intention of modifying its policy of cooperation with the free world. However, I feel constrained to add that movements for restriction of imports from Japan in the United States have already caused considerable restlessness on the part of the Japanese industry, and that if actual import restrictions were put into effect, such a fact would most assuredly play into the hands of the vocal minority of the anti-American segment of our people.

Four years later, at the end of 1960, following the Washington decision for "orderly cessation" of foreign aid procurement in Japan and other industrial countries and substantial reductions in military spending there, the Socialist opposition immediately renewed its clamor for large-scale trade between Japan and China. The Japanese government, while officially denying that it had been influenced by the American action, was reported to be "taking the initiative in resuming our trade with Communist China," with a view to reaching at least double the previous high level.[22]

[19] Tanzan Ishibashi, "Trading with China," *The Oriental Economist,* August 1956, p. 397.

[20] *Mainichi* (Tokyo and other cities), September 9, 1956, p. 1.

[21] Statement of Morio Yukawa, *Administration and Operation of Customs and Tariff Laws and the Trade Agreements Program,* Hearings before a subcommittee of the House Committee on Ways and Means, 84th Cong., 2d sess., pt. 4, Digests of Conferences Held in Europe, November 26 to December 13, 1956, and Japan, December 4 to 6, 1956, and Statements and Documents Received (Washington: GPO, 1957), p. 2010.

[22] United Press International dispatch from Tokyo, December 6, 1960, *The Washington Post,* December 7, 1960.

Great Expectations and Small Accomplishments

The setback of May 1958 was a shock to many Japanese. Even before then, the observations of Japanese businessmen and other Japanese who had visited China had reduced some of the exaggerated hopes about the Communist regime and shown what it is like to deal with China's ruthless rulers. In one way or another a large number of Japanese, in the words of one of them, "have had their eyes opened."

Still, within Japan relations with China are a political issue that generates serious strife. A good bit of illusion persists. Japanese hopes for large and profitable trade with China seem to be related to a yearning for the good old days of Japanese privilege and the dream of "four hundred million customers." No regime in China could be expected to tolerate trade that smacked of former unequal dealings with industrial countries, least of all with Japan, at whose hands China suffered so much. Nor could a developing China be expected to give consumer goods a high priority in the allocation of scarce foreign exchange. What China needs most from abroad is machinery, and in any open competition Japan would have opportunities similar to those it finds in other developing areas, perhaps somewhat enlarged by proximity. But many Japanese seem to expect more. In 1955 the head of a Japanese mining company indicated to me that he was seriously hoping the Peking government would permit his firm to exploit certain mineral resources in China. Japanese investments could indeed help Chinese development, just as Japan developed Manchuria. But those days are gone, and it would be a most remarkable reversal of Communist policy to admit Japanese private investment in the extraction of minerals for export.

The attitude of many Japanese toward China trade seems to rest on the questionable assumption that "Economic ties between Japan and the Chinese continent are bound to grow closer whether the two parties concerned like it or not." [23] This view not only accepts a false principle—economic determinism—but at the same time fails to evaluate realistically the Communist movement and Communist trade policy. The economic factors favoring trade between Japan and China are very powerful, but they are not enough in themselves to determine either nation's policy, especially not that of Communist China. At a minimum, Peking demands more deference from Japan, and preferably recognition, as the price of trade. Even if Japan could accept these terms, and the Chinese were to permit trade to resume, the flow thereafter would be completely subject to Peking's whim, and a new embargo might be imposed at any time. The one element that seems inevitable about the China trade is its uncertainty under the Communists. By its actions Peking has made it

[23] Ishibashi, cited, p. 396.

clear that dependability is definitely not a feature that can be included in any future trade package. Dependability is something the Japanese want very badly.

A false assumption many Japanese have made is that their country is compelled to trade with Mainland China because Japan cannot find adequate export outlets elsewhere. Japan's whole postwar record shows that this so-called "necessity" is, to say the least, not pressing. In the 1950s Japan imported more from China than it sold there. Tanzan Ishibashi, a leading enthusiast for China trade among Japanese conservatives, himself put this point in proper perspective when he was Minister of International Trade and Industry in 1956: "If economic ties strong enough to support the existence of Japan could be formulated with countries other than Communist China, Japan might not necessarily stick to the Communist China area."[24] Only a serious deterioration in Japanese trade with the rest of the world would give validity to the assumption that China trade is a necessity.

The Japanese "seem quite confident of their ability to understand the Chinese and to handle them."[25] The Chinese seem not to share this view of Japanese ability. In any case it is perfectly clear that if Japan is to seek an expansion of trade with the mainland, the chances of making satisfactory arrangements are better if Japan is in the strong economic position of recent years than if it feels driven to the "inevitable" trade with China because Japanese goods cannot find markets in the rest of the world. But Japanese traders are not interested only in the inevitable; they want to make the most of every profitable opportunity. The assumption that China provides great opportunities explains part of the constant pressure in Japan to try to buy and sell more on the mainland.

Is this assumption valid? Dismiss illusions about old trade patterns and a privileged position for Japan. Assume that political obstacles to trade are somehow largely removed on both sides and that Japan has some reason to believe that Peking will refrain from sudden interruption of trade. Suppose, finally, that Japan's economic position is strong enough to ensure a reasonably satisfactory trade bargain. What then are the potentialities of Sino–Japanese trade?

In the short run it looks as if a ceiling on trade would be set by China's severely limited ability to pay and Japan's limited willingness and ability to extend credit. Large credits would be difficult in view of the capital shortage in Japan, and risky because of political factors. Chinese ability to pay is limited mainly by grave shortages during the continuing economic crisis, to say nothing of large prior commitments

[24] Same, p. 397.
[25] Wilbur, cited, p. 225; see also Barnett, cited, p. 279.

for both goods and foreign exchange. Peking would have to want Japanese goods very much to be willing to take the great trouble needed to find enough products to ship to Japan to expand trade rapidly.[26]

The short-run situation is complicated by the economic emergency that began in 1959 and developed into the most serious setback the Chinese Communists have suffered since coming to power. Food is not the only shortage, for agricultural raw materials have been scarce and human energy and vitality have been so weakened that industrial production and political and administrative discipline have been damaged, apparently on occasion breaking down completely. Although the U.S.S.R. has agreed to postponement of large deliveries of food and raw materials due in payment of previous Russian loans to China, many other goods as well appear to be extremely scarce. Large food imports are being obtained, and the burden on foreign exchange reserves is very severe.

The food emergency of recent years seems to be easing, and the Communist regime seems likely to stay firmly in power. Other specific shortages can be made up in the course of time. Given time (probably at least five years) and an interest in Peking in expanding trade with Japan, the main limitations on Japanese–Chinese trade would be Chinese physical resources and their development. Although our information on what lies underground in China is far from complete, we know enough to conclude that surpluses, even above China's own rapidly rising requirements, could be generated of coking coal, magnesia clinker, and certain other mineral products. How much exportable surplus could be produced by Chinese agriculture is another question for which the answer is far from clear. Soybeans are moving to Japan in limited quantities, and there may well be a continuing flow of other oilseeds, wheat, wool, and additional agricultural products. But it is doubtful how much the Chinese will be able to provide of these commodities. One would be rash to anticipate very large movements.

China seems a most unlikely source for the capital equipment Japan will be importing in the years ahead, since Japan's need will continue to be for things that represent the most advanced technology, and China is hardly likely in the foreseeable future to originate such things. China might, however, provide light manufactured goods requiring labor cheaper than Japan's will be. China will probably be able to provide

[26] The basic elements described by George Waldstein in 1954 are still valid, currently in exaggerated degree. He found that China simply did not have available for export any large quantities of the goods Japan most wanted to import. "Showdown in the Orient," *Harvard Business Review*, November–December 1954, pp. 113–120. For a consistent conclusion in a later study, see T. J. Hughes and D. E. T. Luard, *The Economic Development of Communist China, 1949–1960* (2d ed.; New York: Oxford University Press, 1961), p. 137.

substantial quantities of textiles and handicrafts of many kinds, as well as Chinese porcelain, and probably many electronic products among a lengthening list of export goods. For such things to be bought in quantity by Japan would require a revolution in Japanese policy and economic structure. China's vast size would mean that the adjustment problems involved in Japan might reach unmanageable proportions. While the logic of Japan's growth as an industrial power calls for gradually more imports of simple and cheap manufactures, it is difficult to foresee a vast flow of such goods being accepted from Communist China.

The long-run prospects for Chinese exports to Japan, then, appear to depend mainly on minerals, given favorable political dispositions in Tokyo and Peking. To develop the necessary Chinese export surpluses will require capital investment beyond that going into domestic development, or transfer to Japan of export products that have been going to other Communist countries. Japan could provide much of the equipment needed for development, and might even finance part of it on long-term loans.

How large might Japan–China trade become? I asked this question of a number of persons, mainly Japanese and American businessmen, economists, and officials, in 1955 and the largest sum mentioned by any of them was $200 million a year in both directions. More recently much larger figures have been mentioned, going all the way up to $1 billion a year in both directions. That figure could be reached if China could provide Japan with $500 million worth of minerals and other products a year and were willing to spend the proceeds in Japan. Such a level would be somewhat more than three times the postwar peak reached in 1956, and just over 5 per cent of the $9.9 billion of imports projected for 1970 in Japan's income-doubling plan.[27] This volume of trade seems not unreasonable economically, although it is not by any means certain what commodities might make up the total. The fundamental barrier to achieving this or possibly an even higher level of trade is not economic but political.

The one possible development that might reasonably lead to a significant degree of political cooperation between Tokyo and Peking would be the Socialists' accession to power in Japan, a possibility that is real but apparently not immediate. The Socialists have led the political campaign for Japanese recognition of the Peking regime. They want Japan to move away from its present alignment with the United States. No doubt a Socialist government would take steps in these directions, but how far

[27] The plan calls for 5.2 per cent of all *exports* to go to Communist countries in 1970. Presumably imports would not be very far from the value of exports, or a little under $500 million. Japan, Economic Planning Agency, *New Long-Range Economic Plan of Japan (1961–1970): Doubling National Income Plan,* cited, p. 77.

it would go is uncertain. Even if Peking did not make demands that caused a Socialist government in Tokyo to demur, Japan would still have to face the consequences of what it might do. Loss of trade with Taiwan might not seem too great a price, but if trade with the United States and other major buyers and suppliers were endangered, even the Socialist leaders might draw back. (Perhaps this is one reason why many Socialists regard Japan as too dependent on U.S. trade.) In any case, the matter is highly speculative. Much of present Socialist talk seems unrelated to what Japanese leaders—of Socialist or any other stripe—would feel they should do when actually in power.

Japan is now economically strong enough to resist blandishments from the Chinese Communists. That is to say, economic considerations do not force Japan to pay Peking's price for the expansion of trade. If Japanese prosperity continues, this room for decision will remain. At present it is Peking that creates the main obstacle to trade. If the Chinese Communists show a desire to trade on more reasonable political terms, they will find a response in Japan. The United States and the other major trading nations of the free world can have an influence on that response; what policies would be wise to adopt is a question that is discussed in Chapter 12. In any case it is to be hoped that, whatever the circumstances, the Japanese prove to be right in their feeling that they can "handle" trade with China. For if they are not right, a high cost may be borne not only by Japan but by the United States and other countries as well.

A NEW PHENOMENON: GROWING TRADE WITH THE U.S.S.R.

Another giant neighbor, the U.S.S.R., was only a tiny factor in Japanese trade until 1957. Trade was already expanding when, in December of that year, the two countries signed a treaty of commerce and navigation valid for five years. The expansion continued, as Table 7-6 shows.[28] It was most marked in Japan's trade with the Asian part of the Soviet Union but in 1960 and 1961 imports from Soviet European ports rose sharply, in part as a result of purchases of oil ($16 and $27 million in 1960 and 1961 respectively). Other imports from that area in 1961 included pig iron, some other metals, various ores, coal, and chemicals.

[28] The separate figures for the Asian and European parts of Soviet Russia reflect the way Japanese statistics reported this trade before 1962. Beginning in 1962 the published statistics show total figures for all of Russia, with no regional breakdown. All trade with Russia is now included in the continental total for Europe. In Tables 7-1 and 7-2, the U.S.S.R. is listed between Asia and Europe, because the respective portions of Japan's trade are also shown in the totals for Asia and Europe. In 1960 and 1961 over a third of the indicated imports from "Other Asia" shown in Table 7-1 consisted of purchases from Soviet Asia.

TABLE 7-6. JAPAN'S TRADE WITH THE U.S.S.R., SELECTED YEARS
(In millions of dollars)

Year	Asian U.S.S.R. Imports	Asian U.S.S.R. Exports	European U.S.S.R. Imports	European U.S.S.R. Exports	Total U.S.S.R. Imports	Total U.S.S.R. Exports	Total U.S.S.R. Balance	Total U.S.S.R. Total
1934–1936 av.	0.0	0.0	8.1	6.9	8.1	6.9	−1.2	15.0
1950	0.7	0.4	0.0	0.0	0.7	0.4	−0.3	1.1
1954	2.2	0.0	0.1	0.0	2.3	0.0	−2.3	2.3
1955	2.0	1.6	1.1	0.5	3.1	2.1	−1.0	5.2
1956	2.2	0.7	0.7	0.1	2.9	0.8	−2.1	3.7
1957	10.8	5.7	1.5	3.6	12.3	9.3	−3.0	21.6
1958	18.4	15.6	3.8	2.6	22.2	18.1	−4.1	40.3
1959	26.9	19.3	12.6	3.8	39.5	23.0	−16.5	62.5
1960	40.0	42.6	47.0	17.3	87.0	60.0	−27.0	147.0
1961	58.4	55.0	87.0	10.4	145.4	65.4	−80.0	210.8
1962 [a]					147.3	149.4	2.1	296.7

[a] 1962 trade figures not available for Asian U.S.S.R. and European U.S.S.R. separately.

Note: Minor inconsistencies result from rounding.

Sources: 1934–1936 and 1950—Japan, Ministry of International Trade and Industry.
1954–1961—Japan, Ministry of Finance, *Monthly Return of the Foreign Trade of Japan*, January–December issues.
1962—Japan, Ministry of Finance, *Trade of Japan* (Monthly Return), January–December 1962.

Japanese exports to European U.S.S.R. remained very small and were made up of various manufactures, notably machinery and steel. In the larger and more nearly balanced trade with the Asian part of the Soviet Union, Japan's leading export items in 1961 were machinery, ships, steel (including a large order of stainless steel pipe), and synthetic fibers and yarn. Japan's imports were mainly logs, pulpwood, raw cotton, crude and heavy oil, coal, potassium chloride, and pig iron.[29]

In 1958 and 1959 annual trade and payments agreements supplemented the broader treaty of commerce and navigation. A three-year agreement signed in March 1960 called for rapid expansion of trade. Russia agreed to increase her purchases of industrial equipment, ships, steel products, and other things, and Japan agreed to accept deferred payments. Japanese exports reached their target under this agreement in 1960 but fell a little short in 1961, despite heavier extension of export credit by Japan to the U.S.S.R. than to any other country. Japanese imports far exceeded the targets in both years, producing the large deficits shown in Table 7-6. Targets for 1962 were revised sharply upward in a protocol signed

[29] Details from Japan, Ministry of Finance, *Trade of Japan* (Annual Return), 1961.

in February 1962.[30] Another agreement was signed in Tokyo in February 1963, calling for total trade of about $670 to $700 million in the three years ending with 1965.[31] This would be a substantially lower level than that actually achieved in 1962.

The Commodity Structure of Soviet–Japanese Trade

Soviet oil has become the largest commodity in trade between Japan and the U.S.S.R. From Japan's point of view low sulphur content gives Baku oil an important advantage over Persian Gulf oil.[32] The price, too, is low—but how much lower than Persian Gulf oil when delivered in Japan is hard to discover. As the demand for petroleum products grows in the years ahead, Japan's interest in Soviet oil is likely to increase, and there is every reason to believe that the U.S.S.R. will have the oil to export. There is talk of a pipeline to carry crude from Irkutsk to the Vladivostok area on the Pacific Ocean. If the price continued to be low the attraction of such a nearby source would be very great to Japanese oil importers, despite the closing of Soviet Pacific ports by ice in winter.

There are, however, considerations that may make Japan go slow in buying Russian crude petroleum. One is the rapidly expanding potential of the Japanese-owned and managed Arabian Oil Company in Kuwait. This enterprise represents a large Japanese investment and the government has an interest in importing petroleum from a Japanese-controlled source, less subject to interruption than foreign-controlled sources, especially through arbitrary action such as the Soviet government might take at any moment. Most of all, though, the Japanese government must be concerned not to jeopardize other important trade or political ties for the sake of Soviet oil. To date it has encountered some difficulties but not enough to deter increased purchases.

American, British, and Dutch oil companies, which have an interest in a large part of Japan's refining capacity, prefer to sell their own crude. By the allocation of import quotas the Japanese government could assure the use of Japanese or Soviet oil. The removal of quantitative import controls over petroleum in late 1962 as part of the liberalization policy would have deprived the government of this weapon, but a new Petroleum Industry Law was passed giving the government power to control various aspects of the petroleum industry.

The U.S. government, too, has presented Japan with some problems about the import of Soviet oil.

[30] Bank of Tokyo, *Weekly Review*, March 12, 1962, pp. 67–68; "Japan–Communist Bloc Trade," *The Oriental Economist*, April 1962, pp. 190, 192.

[31] *The Japan Times Weekly*, February 16, 1963, p. 3.

[32] "Japan–Communist Bloc Trade," *The Oriental Economist*, cited, p. 190.

> The Department of Defense, as a matter of policy, seeks to avoid purchasing products of Soviet origin. In recent years the Department has become increasingly concerned as such petroleum products are offered more widely in world markets.
>
> A case in point has been the Idemitsu Kosan Company of Japan. This company initially made purchases of Soviet crude oil which were so small in quantity as to be insignificant. However, over the period of the last few years, purchase of Soviet crude by Idemitsu has increased substantially.[33]

As a result, in December 1961 the Department announced that it would refrain from purchasing jet aircraft fuel from Idemitsu Kosan, the largest Japanese importer of Soviet oil. The defense purchases involved were small, and Soviet oil reportedly formed only 30 per cent of Idemitsu's imports, but the decision of the U.S. government, based undoubtedly on political even more than balance-of-payments reasons, was an indication of problems Japan would have to face in shaping its oil import policy.

Other raw materials and semimanufactures make up most of the rest of Japan's imports from the U.S.S.R. The 1961 trade included not only the pig iron, coal, chemicals, forest products, potassium, and raw cotton already mentioned, but also small quantities of platinum, chromium, palladium, tin, lead, manganese ore, aluminum, steel billets, asbestos, wheat and wheat bran, hog bristles, benzol, vaccines, and machinery. As with oil, there is little doubt that the trade could expand substantially if both countries wanted it to. Transportation could be a problem and, if the sources of supply are to be in Asiatic Russia, production capacity might also have to be expanded.

Soviet machinery and other manufactures have not yet found a significant market in Japan, but it may well be that Soviet equipment would on occasion offer advantages to Japan in price or quality. Japan may also gain from Soviet competition with Western suppliers. On the other hand, machinery purchases could entail more risks for Japan than raw materials do. For instance, a sudden stoppage of trade by the Kremlin could prove acutely embarrassing if Japan were dependent on Soviet replacement parts.

Manufactured products make up Japan's exports to the U.S.S.R. They move in substantial variety, including synthetic fibers, steel pipes, and machinery, notably ships. Japan can provide larger quantities of these goods and can widen the range of products, if the Russians are willing to buy and no other impediments prevent the sales. Japan's ability to provide consumer goods is clear. But Japan is also a potential supplier of tremendous importance to the Soviet Union for equipment to expand basic facilities, especially in the Soviet Far East. The Soviet willingness to

[33] U.S. Department of Defense, Office of Public Affairs, Press Release No. 1477-61, December 21, 1961.

import this kind of thing is uncertain. Pipeline steel and equipment provide a case in point. For several years Soviet inquiries have encouraged Japanese producers to hope for large orders in connection with the talked-of pipeline to bring Soviet petroleum from the interior to the Pacific coast.[34] No Japanese firm had actually been given an order by the time, in August 1962, that Premier Khrushchev received a visiting delegation of top Japanese businessmen at his vacation home on the Black Sea and offered to build such a pipeline if the Japanese would provide the equipment.[35] This project would mean large orders for the Japanese producers involved. Mr. Khrushchev's reminder at a time when Japanese industry was operating below capacity must have whetted the appetites of his visitors. A year later, however, the contract was still hanging fire. There is room for a large volume of trade in this and other possible projects, especially in the Soviet Far East, where real costs of equipment produced in the U.S.S.R. may be far above those for Japanese equipment. In this, as in so many of the trade questions, what is in doubt is Soviet intentions. After years of uncertainty the Japanese believe that there are indications of a greater Soviet willingness than ever before to let the exchange of goods grow. Part of the evidence lies in the promotional activities of both countries.

Trade Promotion

Promotional activity has been growing, along with the volume of trade. The largest Japanese Industrial Sample Fair ever held was in Moscow in the summer of 1960, with 10,000 items exhibited. A Soviet Commerce and Industry Fair was held in Tokyo the following summer. When Russian Deputy Premier Anastas I. Mikoyan attended the exhibit in Moscow, his presence could, according to one Japanese journal, "be taken as a sign of the importance attached by the Kremlin to the Japan Trade Fair." [36] By attending the Soviet fair in Tokyo a year later, Mr. Mikoyan became the highest Russian official to visit Japan in the twentieth century, but he antagonized many Japanese by his political propaganda, especially against the Japan–U.S. Security Treaty.[37] Commercially the

[34] For example, in 1960 Nippon Kokan (the Japan Steel and Tube Corporation) was asked about 250,000 tons of oil pipe of 20- and 28-inch diameter. The company was just then building the only plant in Japan that could produce such pipe, and its capacity was to be 7,000 tons a month. "Soviet Trade Hopes and Fears," *The Oriental Economist*, October 1960, p. 555.

[35] *The Washington Post*, August 23, 1962.

[36] "Soviet Trade Hopes and Fears," *The Oriental Economist*, cited, p. 552.

[37] In the first such statement of its kind ever issued by a ruling party in Japan concerning a visiting foreign dignitary, the Liberal-Democratic Party called Mr. Mikoyan's activities interference with Japanese internal affairs. Statements to the same effect were made less publicly by the Japanese Foreign Office. A. M. Rosenthal, "Mikoyan Rebuked on Japan Threat," *The New York Times*, August 18, 1961.

fair seems to have had only slight direct results. Japan continues to import mainly crude and semimanufactured materials from the U.S.S.R., although visitors to the fair saw not only models of sputniks and of advanced scientific apparatus but also a good deal of machinery of sorts that Japanese might be able to use. Russian consumer goods were reported as less impressive.[38]

A major Japanese initiative to promote trade was taken in the summer of 1962, when a delegation of Japanese businessmen representing leading firms went to the Soviet Union. During the mission's visit long-term contracts were reportedly signed for $96 million[39] worth of Japanese ships—an amount that would fulfill Japanese shipbuilders' hopes that have been aroused repeatedly over several years by Soviet inquiries. The prominence of the mission's members reflected both active interest by the business community and tolerance by the government, which was in contrast with earlier feelings that Soviet trade was not sufficiently promising to outweigh Japanese feelings of hostility toward Russia and fear of U.S. displeasure.[40]

Some Unanswered Questions

More than promotional activity led the Japanese to feel in the summer of 1962 that Russian interest in an expansion of trade had reached unprecedented heights. The U.S.S.R.'s recent expansion of trade with other parts of the non-Communist world and the state of Sino-Soviet relations suggested that perhaps this time the Kremlin was serious. The Japanese, too, had reasons to be interested in the possibilities. Perennial concern over treatment of their exports in the United States and worries over the future of Japanese trade with the European Economic Community combined with the aftermath of Japan's 1961 measures to check the severe deficit in the balance of payments, all made for a willingness to explore the possibilities of more trade with the Soviet Union.

But the discussions of mid-1962 could not solve all the problems. Most

[38] *The Oriental Economist,* September 1961, p. 535.

[39] Payment was to be 30 per cent down, with the balance due over six years. *International Commerce* (U.S. Department of Commerce), November 12, 1962, p. 11. The contracts covered 12 tankers of the 35,000-ton dead-weight class, 5 freighters of the 12,000-ton class, and 28 other ships, including 10 crane boats.

[40] These feelings had not by any means disappeared. "There is some nervousness among Japanese business men that a growth of trade with the Soviet Union might cost Japan special consideration in Washington. But the journey to Moscow by the eighteen Japanese executives reflects a basic decision by important segments of Japanese business to forget its political distaste for the Soviet Union and seek Soviet markets." A. M. Rosenthal, "Tokyo Trade Mission to Visit Soviet Next Month," *The New York Times,* July 25, 1962. A list of the members of the group, as planned in June 1962, is given in *The Oriental Economist,* July 1962, p. 395.

of those that remain are in some degree political; not all can be solved by Japan and the Soviet Union alone. For instance, when Japanese firms produce under American or other foreign licenses, the agreements covering patents may forbid export to the U.S.S.R.[41] The export of other types of equipment may be prevented by international controls on sales to Communist countries (pp. 204–206). These controls are, however, limited enough so that they should not significantly affect the volume of Japanese exports to the U.S.S.R.

The largest problems and unanswered questions relate to Soviet policy and intentions. We take for granted by now the Communist habit of using trade for political purposes. In August 1962 Khrushchev coupled his offer of trade to the visiting delegation of Japanese businessmen with denunciation of the United States, boasts about Soviet achievements, and a prediction that the United States would ultimately be compelled to expand its trade with the Soviet Union.[42] Although this kind of talk was milder and less offensive to the Japanese than Mikoyan's denunciation of the Japan–U.S. Security Treaty while on an official visit to Japan, the remarks are both part of normal Communist practice.

But so far the Kremlin has not made political demands on Japan as the price for expanding trade in any way comparable to the repeated Chinese demands for diplomatic recognition. There is less inclination in Japan to accede to Soviet than to Chinese political terms. Among the basic reasons are Japan's long-standing hostility to Russia, memory of the last part of World War II when instead of granting Japan's request for mediation the U.S.S.R. attacked Japan, and the fact that the U.S.S.R. is a major power and antagonist in the cold war. This resistance is reinforced by Japanese economic growth, which reduces the pressure to pay a political price for trade. Still there appears to be some naïve hope in Japan that the Kremlin will put political considerations aside and trade on the basis of economic considerations alone.[43] This seems to be a case of wishfully attributing one's own outlook to the other side.

Another problem of Soviet–Japanese trade is the Soviet demand for long-term commercial credit. The amount of credit demanded seems unnecessary considering the heavy Japanese import surplus in trade with the U.S.S.R. If such demands are for bargaining purposes, and contracts are actually made on terms like those reported for ships, then there need be no problem. In 1961 the Export–Import Bank of Japan

[41] Some patent exchanges between Japan and the Soviet Union were reported after a Soviet patent delegation visited Japan in the autumn of 1961 and a delegation from the Japanese Patent Office visited the Soviet Union in July 1962. *The New York Times*, July 22, 1962, Section 1.

[42] *The New York Times*, August 23, 1962.

[43] See, for example, *The Oriental Economist*, September 1961, p. 535.

advanced more money to the Soviet Union than to any other country.[44] Japan has too little capacity to export capital and too many claims on what is available to justify continuation of this emphasis. If the U.S.S.R. persists in asking for extra-generous credit terms, then one will have to conclude that the Russians are less interested in Japanese trade than in international politics. The Japanese hope—and expect—that the recent promising growth of their trade with the U.S.S.R. will not end in another situation in which Japan is the creditor and trade is cut off because of inability to collect on accumulating debts.

The greatest problem of all is the risk that Japan will become so dependent on Soviet trade that it would be subject to serious political pressure by threats to terminate sales or purchases. At the levels of trade that can now be foreseen, the risk is not very great, but it is something the Japanese must take into account. Among the reports that have circulated about the possible Soviet pipeline to the Pacific is the suggestion that the Russians repay large Japanese long-term equipment credits in oil. It would be difficult to think of a more effective way for the Russians to acquire leverage over the Japanese. Given the nature of the Soviet government, the fear must persist that trade may be abruptly terminated, in part or altogether. Japanese self-interest requires preparation of defenses against such action. One defense is to avoid becoming too large a creditor, but basically the problem is one of limiting dependence on Soviet trade. It is no different from the problem of limiting dependence on trade with China and other Communist states. Essentially this is a question of assuring a thriving Japanese trade with the free world.

JAPAN AND SOUTHEAST ASIA

The Japanese dream of military domination over what came to be called the Greater East Asia Co-Prosperity Sphere vanished with defeat, but the co-prosperity part of the dream is still alive. Many observers, and not just the Japanese, have discerned a natural complementarity between Japan, which can supply industrial products, and the countries of southern and eastern Asia, which are exporters of raw materials. A booming two-way trade has been envisioned which, in the minds of some, has been identified as being close to the solution of Japan's basic trade problems. At a minimum, it has been argued, the enlargement of Japan's role in Asian development would relieve the problem—disturbing for Japanese and others alike—of the growing pressure to find markets for

[44] The amount of the Bank's outstanding export credits to the U.S.S.R. was $37.7 million at the end of March 1962, as compared with $2.7 million and $50,000 one and two years earlier, respectively. Information from the Washington representative, Export–Import Bank of Japan.

Japanese manufactures in the industrialized countries of North America and Europe.

As we have seen, East Asia, particularly China, is failing to play the role in Japanese trade pictured in this view. What about South and Southeast Asia? In 1934–1936 Southeast Asia—the area from Afghanistan to the Philippines[45]—provided 16.4 per cent of Japan's imports. (Table 7-7.) In 1961 and 1962 the share of Southeast Asia was only 15 per cent, but this was exceptionally low for the postwar period; in 1959 and 1960 Southeast Asia provided 18 per cent of Japan's imports and from 1952 through 1956 between 19 and 22 per cent, substantially more than before the war. As a market for Japanese exports, Southeast Asia has also been more important in recent years than before the war. In 1934–1936, 19 per cent of Japan's exports went to Southeast Asia, and in 1961 and 1962 it was nearly 25 per cent (it had been as high as 36 per cent in 1952). The balance of trade varies greatly from country to country, but with the area as a whole Japan has a substantial export excess.

The population of Southeast Asia is perhaps 800 million, scattered over a wide area of mainland and islands and subject to some fifteen sovereign Asian governments plus a few European powers in the remaining colonial possessions. More than half of the people are in India, and more than half of the rest live in Pakistan and Indonesia, but Japanese trade by no means follows the population pattern. India, even with the addition of Goa, was behind the Philippines in 1961 and 1962 and was not far ahead of Malaya and Thailand. These four, together with Hong Kong, Indonesia, and Singapore, accounted for more than three-fourths of Japan's Southeast Asian trade in the early 1960s. The new Malaysia, the amalgamation of Malaya, Singapore, Sarawak, and Sabah, would on the basis of 1962 figures become Japan's largest trading partner in Southeast Asia. In 1961 and 1962 Malaya was Japan's largest supplier in the region, shipping nearly $200 million worth of iron ore, rubber, latex, tin, and minor products. Singapore and British Borneo together provided another $100 million. Of the four territories, only Singapore was a large importer of Japanese goods.

Imports from Southeast Asia

To appraise the significance of the present level of Japan's imports from Southeast Asia, and to estimate the possibilities of expansion, requires an examination by commodity. Southeast Asia provides little or no wool, wheat, soybeans, or machine tools to Japan. Apart from these products,

[45] Comprising the countries shown in Table 7-7, the area includes both southern and southeastern Asia, as Americans usually label them, but this book follows the Japanese practice of calling both together *Southeast Asia.*

TABLE 7-7. JAPAN'S BALANCE OF TRADE WITH SOUTHEAST ASIAN COUNTRIES, 1962
(In millions of dollars)

	Japanese Imports	*Japanese Exports*	*Balance*	*Total*
Philippines	183.9	120.0	−63.9	303.9
India [a]	124.1	120.5	−3.6	244.6
Malaya	186.2	38.7	−147.5	224.9
Thailand	71.7	148.5	76.8	220.2
Hong Kong	18.9	192.4	173.5	211.3
Indonesia	91.2	115.3	24.1	206.5
Singapore	22.7	105.0	82.3	127.7
Pakistan	28.5	57.3	28.8	85.8
British Borneo	76.0	4.0	−72.0	80.0
Burma	16.3	53.4	37.1	69.7
South Viet-Nam	3.9	60.1	56.2	64.0
Ceylon	7.3	32.4	25.1	39.7
Cambodia	3.1	16.0	12.9	19.1
North Viet-Nam	13.0	3.4	−9.6	16.4
Other [b]	2.2	10.5	8.3	12.7
Total Southeast Asia	849.0	1,077.5	228.5	1,926.5
Share of Japan's total	15.1%	21.9%		18.3%
Share in 1934–1936 [c]	16.4%	18.9%		17.7%

[a] Including Goa and other former Portuguese possessions now a part of India.
[b] Afghanistan, West New Guinea, Laos, Maldive Islands, Portuguese Timor, Macao, Nepal, Bhutan.
[c] Calculated from figures of the Japanese Ministry of International Trade and Industry.

Note: Minor inconsistencies result from rounding.

Source: Japan, Ministry of Finance, *Trade of Japan* (Monthly Return), January–December 1962, pp. 11–12.

however, the region had a share in supplying Japan's leading imports in 1961.[46]

Crude petroleum has become Japan's leading import. In 1934–1936, British Borneo and the Netherlands East Indies provided about a sixth

[46] In the pages that follow the products are listed roughly in the order of their import value in 1961, as shown in Table 5-2. There were 17 products of which total Japanese imports exceeded $100 million. Percentages refer to values when not otherwise labeled. Unattributed statistics come from Japan, Ministry of Finance, either the *Monthly Return of the Foreign Trade of Japan,* January–December 1961, pp. 60–71, or *Trade of Japan* (Annual Return), 1961.

of Japan's imports; in 1961 their share was 14 per cent. It seems very likely that in the future Japanese demand will rise more rapidly than Southeast Asian supplies and that the already heavy reliance on oil from other sources will grow. Nor is the region likely to exceed its present limited importance as a supplier of *coal*. Anthracite from North Viet-Nam is the largest item in the present trade. Heavy coking coal, for which Japan's needs are growing, is hardly to be found in Southeast Asia outside India.

Until 1926 more than half of Japan's *raw cotton* came from British India. Thereafter the proportion declined as purchases of American cotton rose. During the 1930s the two suppliers competed for the leading position but since the war India, Pakistan, and Burma together have provided only a small share of Japan's cotton imports. In 1961 the figure was 7.2 per cent. Much of the shift is due to the fact that Japanese mills now spin a larger proportion of fine yarns than formerly and require the higher quality and longer-staple cotton grown in the United States and Mexico, which now supply the bulk of Japan's needs, or the extra-long staple produced mainly in Egypt.[47]

Japan obtained 9 per cent of its *iron and steel scrap* imports from Southeast Asia in 1961, compared with 14 per cent in 1960. The share may decline further in the future as Japanese consumption grows while the new steel mills being built in Southeast Asia raise demand for scrap there faster than they add to the supply. As a supplier of *iron ore*, however, Southeast Asia is well placed. The region provided 59 per cent of Japan's 1961 imports, mainly from Malaya, India (including Goa, a major supplier in its own right), and the Philippines. Proportionately, this is only a little more than before the war, but the tonnages are several times as great.[48] Although Southeast Asia's 1961 share of Japan's iron ore imports was below the 72 per cent of 1960 and the 81 per cent of 1959, the decline may not continue. Japan is investing heavily in Southeast Asian iron mining.[49] The region's resources are rich. Even though India will be consuming far more iron ore at home as it completes new blast furnaces, Japanese imports from India will probably grow greatly unless Mainland China should send much larger shipments than seem

[47] Keizo Seki, *The Cotton Industry of Japan* (Tokyo: Japan Society for the Promotion of Science, 1956), pp. 108 and 328.

[48] In 1936, Korea provided 6 per cent of Japan's iron ore imports by weight, China 31 per cent, and Southeast Asia 57 per cent. Imports in that year were 4 million metric tons but in 1961, 21 million metric tons. E. B. Schumpeter and others, *The Industrialization of Japan and Manchukuo, 1930–1940* (New York: Macmillan, 1940), p. 256; Japan, Ministry of Finance, *Annual Return of the Foreign Trade of Japan*, 1935–1936, p. 97; Japan, Ministry of Finance, *Monthly Return of the Foreign Trade of Japan*, January–December 1961, p. 65.

[49] Up to $50 million. Foreign Capital Research Society, care of the Bank of Japan, *Japanese Industry*, 1960, p. 34.

likely. The Japanese steel industry also buys *pig iron* from Southeast Asia in years of boom and shortage, but in 1961 the region's share was only 3.5 per cent.

Japan's *logs and lumber* now come mainly from Southeast Asia; in 1961, 53 per cent, in 1960, 70 per cent. This is a result of the postwar development of a large Japanese plywood industry using hardwood, mainly Philippine lauan, along with smaller quantities from British Borneo. These hardwoods have displaced the softwoods from North America that provided most of Japan's prewar wood imports. (The United States is still a leading source of Japan's wood imports, second in 1961, third in 1960.) Timber resources in Southeast Asia can apparently be exploited on a large scale for a long time to come. Increasing quantities are likely to be sold to Japan where the demand, for domestic consumption and processing for export, is rising fast.

Nonferrous metal ores from Southeast Asia flow to Japan in substantial quantities. The region supplies a major part of Japan's bauxite (84 per cent, nearly all from Malaya, Indonesia, and British Borneo), manganese ore (66 per cent, mostly from India), and chrome ore (67 per cent, principally from the Philippines). The Philippines also supplied 29 per cent of Japan's 1961 imports of copper ore and concentrates. India supplied some zinc ore, and varying amounts of other ores also came from the region. The prospects for expansion seem very good. The related trade in *nonferrous metals* is much smaller and is virtually confined to tin, mostly from Malaya and in small quantities from Indonesia.

Crude rubber comes to Japan almost exclusively from Southeast Asia, especially Malaya, with smaller quantities coming from Thailand, British Borneo, Ceylon, Indonesia, and elsewhere. Until 1957 Indonesia was a large second source of imports, but since then has provided very little. Use of rubber in Japan is expanding rapidly as a result of increasing production of automobiles and tires, rubber shoes, bicycle tires, and a great many other things. Most of this is natural rubber which supplied about 68 per cent of consumption in 1961.[50] While the use of both imported and domestically produced synthetic rubber is likely to increase, it is probable that imports of natural rubber from Southeast Asia will continue to grow.

Corn is becoming important in Japan, especially as an animal feed, and most of what is consumed comes from abroad. The United States is the leading supplier, with most of the rest coming in varying amounts from the Republic of South Africa, Thailand, and Argentina. Small quantities come also from Cambodia, Burma, Viet-Nam, Malaya, and the Philippines. The Philippines and, to a small extent, Indonesia also provided some of Japan's imported *sugar*. In 1960 the two countries sup-

[50] Same, 1962, p. 141.

plied 3.5 per cent but in 1961 Indonesia provided none, and the share of the Philippines fell to 0.3 per cent.

Rice is no longer one of Japan's major imports, as we saw in Chapter 5. Domestic production has risen so rapidly that imports in 1961 amounted to only $16 million, or 7 per cent as much as in 1954, when Japan was importing to make up for the poor crop of 1953, its last bad harvest. Southeast Asia remains the main source of this reduced supply of imports. Although Southeast Asian rice is not of the type most favored for kitchen use in Japan, the region was the source of most of the rice Japan has imported during the postwar period. Korea had no surplus for export and Taiwan provided only small quantities. This condition may well continue through the 1960s.

Southeast Asia was not in 1961 the principal source of any of the other import items shown in Table 5-2. The region does, however, provide substantial quantities of oilseeds and crude salt. Among products not shown separately in Table 5-2, most of Japan's abaca comes from the Philippines, most jute from Pakistan, and most palm oil from Indonesia and Malaya.

The somewhat surprising conclusion of this review is that Southeast Asia is the principal foreign supplier of only 4 of the 44 individual import categories listed in Table 5-2—iron ore, logs and lumber, rice, and crude rubber. The first two of these are leading Japanese imports, the other two much smaller. The area is also the main source of some lesser products, notably bauxite, manganese ore, chrome ore, and abaca, and is an important secondary supplier of a wide range of commodities. But there are many things that Japan must import which Southeast Asia cannot provide in quantity, while the things Southeast Asia can provide in quantity are often needed in Japan in only limited volume.

Can the situation be changed so that Southeast Asia produces and exports more of what Japan requires? Swelling sales of petroleum, rubber, logs, and iron ore show what can be done. Japanese loans and investments in iron mines illustrate a means of hastening development. The heart of the question, though, is what the rate of growth will be. Can Southeast Asia keep pace with the expansion of Japan's total imports? It is by no means clear. If recent trends continue, the area may fall behind. For Southeast Asia to grow more important as a supplier to Japan will probably require accelerated development in the production of the things Japan wants.

Exports to Southeast Asia

Southeast Asia is Japan's largest market for cotton cloth exports. Other significant exports are cotton yarn, rayon yarn and fabrics, spun rayon yarn (but not fabrics), steel rails (in some years), certain kinds of steel sheets, tin plate, textile machinery, agricultural machinery, heavy electrical machinery, electric fans, railway rolling stock, automobiles, bicycles, cement, and chemicals, especially fertilizers and pharmaceutical products.

Despite substantial net imports in trade with Malaya, British Borneo, and the Philippines, Japan's exports to Southeast Asia as a whole exceeded imports from there in 1962. The export excess arose mainly from trade with Hong Kong, Singapore, Thailand, South Viet-Nam, and Burma. Reparations contributed to the net exports to Burma and U.S. aid to the net exports to South Viet-Nam. Hong Kong, Singapore, and Thailand are able to finance net imports through their multilateral trade, paying Japan in convertible currency they earn in trade with other countries.

In exporting to Southeast Asia, the Japanese are hampered by the resentment and fear of their country that has not disappeared even after the passage of nearly two decades since World War II. These feelings largely account for restrictions on travel and residence by Japanese, especially in Indonesia and the Philippines, which have long been a detriment to trade. A competent official of one Southeast Asian government told me that imports from Japan were being closely watched; if they should at any time reach "too high" a level, quiet steps would be taken to check them.

Another, more surprising, reason why trade has not grown faster has been the slowness of Japan to press vigorously into Southeast Asian markets after World War II. Until recently Japanese put remarkably little attention, initiative, and capital into cultivating Asian markets. Surprisingly few trained and experienced specialists have been assigned to Japanese embassies, although until late in the 1950s it was impossible, or very difficult, for private Japanese firms to get permission to station people in many parts of Southeast Asia. At home in Japan the big firms and the universities have been slow to train specialists who would have adequate knowledge of the area and its languages though today some Japanese are being trained in Southeast Asia (p. 165). Altogether, one finds in Asia much the same general weaknesses in Japanese trade promotion that exist in the American market (see Chapter 8). The matter of language, for instance, is difficult; English is frequently used between Japanese and Southeast Asians, and sometimes neither party to a conversation is comfortable in its use.

Japanese efforts to gain ground are hampered in some countries by Commonwealth trading arrangements that give tariff preferences to British goods. Long-standing business ties between Asian and European countries may also be an obstacle. And, of course, Japanese goods are sometimes unable to compete in price, quality, or special characteristics.

But there is little doubt that the main brake on the expansion of Japanese trade in Southeast Asia is the limited purchasing power of the countries of the region. A number of them have chronic shortages of foreign exchange, notably India, Indonesia, and Pakistan. The use of American aid funds to pay for Japanese goods has been sharply curtailed. World Bank loans and other kinds of aid by international agencies will probably continue to finance some Japanese exports, as they have in the past, especially to India, the World Bank's largest borrower. Japanese grants, loans, and investments, hitherto a small factor, may be expected to grow in the years ahead. Reparations are not yet all paid off. Still, the main increase in Southeast Asian ability to pay for imports must come through economic development and rising export earnings.

Economic growth is taking place in Southeast Asia and that in itself is linked with the expansion of trade with Japan. But in gaining a larger share of Japanese trade Southeast Asia is seriously hampered by limitations on productive capacity and purchasing power, and especially by limitations on capacity to finance imports. Law and order are far from secure in many areas. Administrative weaknesses are compounded by political instability. While some of the countries are rich in natural resources, almost all are short of capital. In most countries of the region the essential human resources of leadership and enterprise are inadequate to the need, and most of the institutions and skills necessary for rapid economic growth have not yet been developed. In the past it was common to think that resource-poor Japan was unfortunately situated compared to some Southeast Asian countries. The record shows that the opposite is true. Japan clearly has what it takes to make a modern economy and to raise incomes rapidly. The countries of Southeast Asia for the most part have not yet demonstrated anything like an equal capability.

Development brings with it new problems for Japan's trade with Southeast Asia. One of them is protection of domestic production, a policy being followed by developing countries everywhere. Southeast Asian countries are already restraining imports by tariffs and other measures aimed at preserving the home market for domestic interests, including new high-cost manufacturing establishments. These measures are apt to fall particularly heavily on imports of consumer goods, especially textiles, which Japan might otherwise sell in larger quantities. Developing countries are likely to favor imports of capital goods in the sale of which Japan often cannot outdo European and American suppliers.

Japan also has to reckon with the likelihood that in time there will be a recurrence of competition from Communist China. Chinese goods made inroads in several countries of Southeast Asia during the middle 1950s; in 1958 these advances were particularly marked, aided by widespread price cutting. Both Japanese and Indian exports suffered, especially cotton textiles. Many Japanese linked this drive with the Chinese embargo of May 1958 on trade with Japan and interpreted it as an attempt to harm Japan as well as to sell goods and gain power and prestige for Communist China. Fortunately for Japanese exports, the Chinese drive subsided at the end of 1958, when the mainland's economy stumbled and fell in the attempted "Great Leap Forward." But Communist China remains a potentially strong competitor. The country badly needs foreign exchange, especially because it has had to pay for exceptionally large food imports. When it can again export in volume to Southeast Asia, China may be expected to use trade not only to earn exchange but also as a tool for the advancement of political interests. The Chinese minorities in Southeast Asia, although suffering various forms and degrees of discrimination, may prove effective instruments for the promotion of Chinese trade. Finally, Peking has extended aid to other countries, indicating an interest that may express itself in more trade as well.[51]

Prospects

Despite all these problems and difficulties, there is a powerful emotional appeal for many Japanese in the idea of closer trade relations between their country and the southern rimlands of Asia. In reality, this relation is hardly likely to come to dominate the foreign trade of either party. Both Japan and the southern areas need and want trade with third areas too much for that. There is, however, a basis for a very substantial expansion of Japanese trade with Southeast Asia, to the benefit of all.

To bring it about will require a great deal more Japanese initiative and effort than has recently been given to the realization of this dream. Japanese trade promotion, exploitation of Southeast Asian natural resources with Japanese capital and technology, and adaptation of manufactured goods to the particular needs of the people of the region will probably have to be mixed with a good deal more patience than most enthusiasts have shown in the past. Time is an important ingredient, although it is by no means sure that Communist and other threats will allow as much time as may be needed for orderly progress. Asian economic growth can very likely be accelerated, and Japanese trade can both gain and contribute much.

The prospects for Japanese trade in Southeast Asia have been estimated by both the Japanese Economic Planning Agency (EPA) and the United Nations Economic Commission for Asia and the Far East (ECAFE). If

[51] For an informed account of Communist Chinese trade see A. Doak Barnett, cited, Chapter 9. His discussion of aid and of trade with Southeast Asia is on pp. 238–245.

the estimates made in these studies prove to be even approximately correct, Japan will, during the next decade, become a more important market for the exports of the Southeast Asian countries than it has been, but Southeast Asia's share of Japan's foreign trade will fall.

The ECAFE study projects the industrial countries' demand for primary products from Southeast Asia to 1975.[52] For Burma, Taiwan, and South Viet-Nam, exports to Japan are expected to increase less rapidly than to the rest of the world; for Thailand the pace is about even, but for the rest sales to Japan are expected to increase more than to North America and Western Europe. For Malaya and Singapore, Indonesia, Cambodia, India, and the Philippines the projected rate of increase of sales to Japan is at least double that to the other industrialized areas. But in comparing the projections with those for Japanese imports from all areas, ECAFE estimated that only India, Indonesia, and Cambodia would increase their shipments of primary products to Japan at a faster rate than the annual 4.4 per cent projected for Japan's total imports of foodstuffs, raw materials, and fuels between 1955 and 1975.

The more recent EPA projections point to a similar conclusion in estimates of the composition of Japan's imports from 1961 to 1970. (Table 5-9.) The sharpest import increases of all are expected to come in finished and semifinished products, while imports of raw materials as a whole rise less rapidly. Specific commodities, like iron ore and petroleum, will rise very rapidly, but Southeast Asian countries will have to compete for a share of Japan's purchases of these as well as of various other products of which Japan's imports will rise less rapidly. EPA's conclusion is that trade with Southeast Asia will grow less rapidly than Japan's total trade, and that as a consequence this area will account for a smaller proportion of Japanese trade than today.[53]

There are some broader implications in the ECAFE study. Its projections are based on the proposition that "The import capacity of most primary exporting countries of the ECAFE region has largely depended and will probably continue to depend in the foreseeable future, on the export prospects *of agricultural and mineral products* to the industrial countries."[54] The highest rates projected for exports of primary products to the industrial nations as a whole were just under 3 per cent a year for

[52] This study was prepared before Japan's income-doubling plan was announced, and the figures underlying the projections for Japan may be substantially too small. But it is not the specific figures that are significant for our interest but the conclusions cited and the general relationships to be expected. UN Economic Commission for Asia and the Far East, *Economic Survey of Asia and the Far East, 1959,* 60.II.F.1 (Bangkok: Author, 1960), p. 91 and elsewhere.

[53] *New Long-Range Economic Plan of Japan (1961–1970): Doubling National Income Plan,* cited, pp. 76–77, 79.

[54] *Economic Survey of Asia and the Far East, 1959,* cited, p. 89. (Italics added.)

Indonesia and Malaya and Singapore. Such rates are far from encouraging for Southeast Asian economic development. As ECAFE concludes, "the prospects . . . do not seem bright." [55]

This suggests that developing countries will not be able to satisfy their desire for rapid economic expansion if they have to confine their exports to primary products, as the ECAFE study assumed. The missing element for satisfactory economic growth may well be the export of factory products in large volume. Some of the Southeast Asian countries are already producing textiles and a few other products for export. Other countries and other products will follow. Like cheap Japanese goods before them, these products encounter difficulties in the rich markets of advanced countries, not least in Japan. If the advanced countries would permit imports of factory goods from Asian countries as they reached the point of being able to undersell domestic producers with their higher wage levels, then the prospects for economic development in Southeast Asia would brighten dramatically. Only if Japan, too, were prepared to carry its liberalization policy as far as that would there be much prospect of expanding imports—and correspondingly exports—from Southeast Asia far beyond the general orders of magnitude projected. Of course the estimates may well prove wrong, but their main implication is accepted as valid, even if the specific projections prove to be no more than half of actual magnitudes.

There is no escaping the conclusion of the foregoing analysis that, even on the most optimistic assumptions, Japan and Southeast Asia cannot satisfy their needs by a great intensification of trade between them. Complementary as they are, both Japan and developing countries, in Southeast Asia and elsewhere, need to trade with the rest of the world also and not just with each other. Although Southeast Asia's export prospects may be better in Japan than elsewhere, as the ECAFE study suggests, Japan alone could not possibly use the bulk of the rubber, copra, tin, abaca, and other products the Southeast Asian countries have to export. While American and other foreign aid could be used to enlarge Japan's sales to Southeast Asia, that is becoming less of a reality and more pressure is being felt for Japan itself to give larger aid. Japanese concern with freer access to the American and European markets cannot properly be turned aside by suggesting that Japan should trade with her "natural" partners in Asia. Nature has not arranged things to make that trade large enough.

[55] Same, p. 92.

JAPAN, EUROPE, GATT, AND THE OECD

Europe is a large, rich, and potentially rewarding region for Japanese traders. Heretofore a series of separate, though interlocked, economies, Western Europe is now the scene of an historic transformation toward economic and political unity. This transformation was abruptly checked in January 1963 when General de Gaulle vetoed the British application for membership in the European Economic Community (EEC). But this action does not now appear to mean cessation or reversal of the historic process. A major question for Japan is what these European developments will mean for Japanese exports.

Japanese trade with Europe has been relatively limited in the past. Except for a few scattered years during the nineteenth century, when Britain held the leading position among Japan's trading partners, Japan has bought and sold far more in the United States than in Europe. There are some obvious reasons for this: geography, the ability of the United States to be Japan's main supplier of food and raw materials, and the special relationship that Japan and the United States have had in the postwar years. It was natural that trade relations between Japan and Europe should be of minor importance when both faced vast but generally similar problems in recovering from World War II, lacked foreign exchange for anything but the most necessary imports, were hard pressed to export, and—short of dollars—relied to a great extent on American aid.

Then, however, both Japan and Western Europe became unprecedentedly prosperous and experienced extraordinarily rapid economic growth. Europe became a good market for Japanese fish, textiles, and ships, while Japan bought mainly machinery, chemical products, and scrap metals. The value of trade more than doubled between 1958 and 1962. But important trade barriers remained, and the attitudes behind them raise questions about the future.

Japanese are much concerned to take advantage of the expanding market in Europe but fear two possibilities. One is that the Common Market will exclude Japanese goods to an excessive extent. The other is that producers within the market will become so efficient that Japanese producers will be unable to compete with them even in third markets, let alone at home in Europe.

So far Japan has felt the promise of European resurgence more than the dangers. Europe has accounted for a rising share of Japanese trade since 1956, as shown in Table 7-8, in conformity with the trend noted at the beginning of this chapter for advanced countries to become more important in Japanese trade. And there is a long way to go, if Japan and the European trade authorities can agree not to interfere seriously. Not

TABLE 7-8. JAPAN'S BALANCE OF TRADE WITH EUROPE, 1934–1936, 1950–1962

(Values in millions of dollars)

Year	Japanese Imports	Japanese Exports	Balance	Total: Value	Total: Per Cent of Total Japanese Trade
1934–1936 av.	93.7	76.2	−17.5	169.9	9.0
1950	38.5	99.7	61.2	138.2	7.7
1951	159.5	146.2	−13.3	305.7	9.1
1952	139.2	178.9	39.7	318.1	9.6
1953	200.8	118.6	−82.2	319.4	8.7
1954	192.8	146.3	−46.5	339.1	8.4
1955	175.0	205.8	30.8	380.8	8.5
1956	231.5	250.3	18.8	481.8	8.4
1957	391.9	326.6	−65.3	718.5	10.1
1958	268.7	333.3	64.6	602.0	10.2
1959	364.6	375.0	10.4	739.6	10.5
1960	448.5	495.0	46.5	943.5	11.1
1961	666.6	551.9	−114.7	1,218.5	12.1
1962 [a]	766.9	844.9	78.0	1,611.8	15.3
Total, 1950–1962	4,044.5	4,072.5	28.0	8,117.0	10.7

[a] Includes Japanese trade with Asian U.S.S.R.

Source: Bank of Japan, *Economic Statistics of Japan*, 1962, pp. 239–242; figures for total Japanese trade from Table 5-1.

all of the growth results from European economic integration. In fact, while Japan's 1962 trade with the six countries of the European Economic Community was 3.6 times its 1954 value, the figure for trade with all of Europe was nearly 5 times, partly because of the recent jump in trade with the Soviet Union. Yugoslavia and the Soviet European satellites have played a smaller part. But the United Kingdom and the smaller non-Communist countries have contributed a good deal, trading about four times as much with Japan in 1962 as they did in 1954. (Table 7-9.)

Europe's competitive power disturbs some Japanese, but its significance can easily be exaggerated, especially by persons who do not fully understand the nature of comparative advantage and mutual trade. Of course European producers can make certain things better or cheaper than Japanese producers can. But at the same time there are also many things that Japanese producers can make better or cheaper. Because both Japan and Western Europe have undergone phenomenal economic growth and modernization during the past ten years or so, their cost relationships have been shifting continually. While the list of things in which Japan has a competitive advantage over Europe changes, Japanese fears of inability to compete, either in Europe or in third markets, are less well grounded today than ever before.

Actually, protectionist sentiment and policy create the greatest problem in expanding Japanese sales to Europe. European producers, for all their vigorous and successful adaptation to the circumstances of recent years, both within the Common Market and outside it, fear cheap, low-wage goods from Japan. There is nothing new in this attitude. In 1956, J. E. Meade found the United Kingdom

> influenced by memories of the nineteen-thirties when many existing lines of trade and production were disrupted by a sudden incursion of cheap Japanese products, sold in many cases by means of questionable commercial devices which misled customers about the origin, content, or quality of the goods, which relied upon the copying of other traders' designs, and which involved export subsidies of one kind or another.[56]

At least in part because of this attitude, Japan can expect a difficult time as it negotiates with the EEC to reduce the level of the Community's common external tariff on Japanese goods. Unfortunately for Japan, it has only a limited amount of bargaining power since it may seem to Europeans to provide only a small market for European exports. In the early 1960s, for instance, Japan took less than one per cent of the exports of the EEC countries taken together; only for West Germany did exports to Japan exceed one per cent, and only by a small amount.[57] Partly for that reason Japan must look to international agreements and the agencies they create for help in trying to open European markets to its exports. By far the most important of these is the General Agreement on Tariffs and Trade (GATT).

The General Agreement on Tariffs and Trade

When Japan applied in July 1952 to become one of the Contracting Parties to GATT, a number of members, not only in Europe but elsewhere as well, held back. The United States pressed the case, and in October 1953 Japan was admitted to provisional membership. Soon

[56] J. E. Meade, *Japan and the General Agreement on Tariffs and Trade,* the Joseph Fisher Lecture in Commerce, given in Adelaide on August 8, 1956 (Adelaide, Australia: Griffin Press, 1956), p. 14.

[57] OECD, *Overall Trade by Countries, Statistical Bulletins, Foreign Trade,* Series A, June 1963.

TABLE 7-9. JAPAN'S BALANCE OF TRADE WITH INDIVIDUAL EUROPEAN COUNTRIES, 1962

(In millions of dollars)

Grouping and Country	*Japanese Imports*	*Japanese Exports*	*Balance*	*Total*
Europe, total	**766.9**	**844.9**	**78.0**	**1,611.8**
Non-Communist countries	**603.7**	**663.3**	**59.6**	**1,267.0**
European Economic Community	344.0	274.4	−70.0	618.4
West Germany	212.9	104.2	−108.7	317.1
Netherlands	41.1	49.2	8.1	90.3
France	46.3	23.0	−23.3	69.3
Italy	28.9	53.8	24.9	81.8
Belgium-Luxembourg	15.0	44.0	29.0	59.0
European Free Trade Area	245.3	320.9	75.6	566.2
Austria	5.2	4.4	−0.8	9.6
Denmark	9.6	24.6	15.0	34.2
Norway	9.3	11.0	1.7	20.3
Portugal	4.6	1.1	−3.5	5.7
Sweden	16.9	36.8	19.9	53.7
Switzerland	53.9	50.7	−3.2	104.6
United Kingdom	145.8	192.3	46.5	338.1
Other non-Communist countries	14.2	68.2	54.0	82.4
Greece	3.0	33.2	30.2	36.2
Spain	8.3	14.4	6.1	22.7
Ireland	0.5	9.0	8.5	9.5
Other	2.4	11.6	9.2	14.0
Communist countries	**163.4**	**181.5**	**18.1**	**344.9**
U.S.S.R.	147.3	149.4	2.1	296.7
Satellites	15.6	16.8	1.2	32.4
East Germany	4.7	0.4	−4.3	5.1
Czechoslovakia	4.1	3.6	−0.5	7.7
Rumania	3.5	6.4	2.9	9.9
Bulgaria	1.5	1.7	0.2	3.2
Poland	1.5	2.7	1.2	4.2
Hungary	0.2	2.0	1.8	2.2
Albania	0.1	0.01	−0.1	0.1
Yugoslavia	0.5	15.3	14.8	15.8

Note: Minor inconsistencies result from rounding.

Source: Japan, Ministry of Finance, *Trade of Japan* (Monthly Return), January–December 1962.

thereafter 24 of the Contracting Parties, including the United States, granted Japan at least some of the benefits of membership, the most important of which was most-favored-nation treatment. As a result of negotiations undertaken in Geneva in February 1955 Japan exchanged tariff concessions with 17 nations before being formally admitted to full membership on September 10, 1955. Although all 34 Contracting Parties approved Japan's accession to the agreement, 14 nations invoked Article 35 which entitled them to withhold from the new member some or all of the privileges of membership, especially by refraining from negotiating tariff reductions.[58] Japan has since put forth a good deal of effort toward getting rid of this discrimination, which has never been applied so extensively or stubbornly to any other new Contracting Party. For some time there was only limited progress, but later most of the major countries in the 1955 list withdrew their action. Others, as they have joined GATT, invoked Article 35 against Japan so that at the end of May 1963 ten countries were applying it.[59] This second list is far less imposing than the first; the ten countries accounted for less than 6 per cent of world imports in 1962.[60]

The effect of this form of discrimination on Japanese exports is difficult to judge. Some of the invoking countries have imposed quantitative controls on imports from Japan, and some have used discriminatory tariff duties. But the resulting limitation of Japanese sales seems to have been less in some cases than that experienced in certain countries, notably Italy, that have not taken advantage of Article 35. The motive behind the use of the clause has in most cases apparently been one of precaution: the governments concerned thereby gained greater freedom to restrict Japanese goods without transgressing GATT rules. The United Kingdom and some others granted Japan most-favored-nation treatment in tariff matters but imposed quantitative restrictions on the import of Japanese goods. The reservations of France and the United Kingdom applied also to their dependent overseas territories. These two countries, plus Benelux (Belgium, Netherlands, and Luxembourg), were the invoking countries most important to Japan's trade. All withdrew their

[58] Meade, cited, pp. 14–15; U.S. Tariff Commission, *Postwar Developments in Japan's Foreign Trade* (Washington: GPO, 1958), pp. 13–14. The 14 countries were Australia, Austria, Belgium, Brazil, Cuba, France, Haiti, India, Luxembourg, the Netherlands, New Zealand, Rhodesia, South Africa, and the United Kingdom. *The Oriental Economist*, October 1955, p. 519. They accounted for 34 per cent of world imports in 1955. *International Financial Statistics* (IMF), September 1959, pp. 17 and 19.

[59] Australia, Austria, Haiti, Nigeria, Portugal, Rhodesia and Nyasaland, Sierra Leone, South Africa, Tanganyika, and, temporarily, Cambodia. (Information from the Japanese Embassy, Washington.) Australia, the most important of these markets, stopped invoking Article 35 in May 1964.

[60] *International Financial Statistics*, June 1963, pp. 37 and 39.

formal applications of the article in 1963, but reserved the right to maintain or impose restrictions on imports of certain sensitive articles made in Japan.

Several factors are involved in this withholding from Japan of trade benefits generally shared and agreed upon among GATT members. General protectionist feeling that has been successfully countered in relation to the trade of Western countries often remains especially strong regarding Japan. Most Japanese exports compete directly with much European production. The United Kingdom has inclined to favor low-wage areas of the Commonwealth, giving them privileges withheld from Japan. A residue of political resentment against Japan may be an element in Australia. But the strongest force of all behind most discrimination against Japanese goods appears to be their low prices and the familiar low-wage argument associated with them.

One of the explanations frequently given for not removing barriers to imports of Japanese goods is the fear that a sudden spurt of cheap manufactures will seriously disrupt markets and damage domestic producers who have not been given the time to adjust themselves to the new competition. At the fifteenth semiannual session of the GATT Contracting Parties, held in Tokyo in October and November 1959, C. Douglas Dillon, then American Under Secretary of State, proposed that an effort be made "to find means to alleviate the adverse effects of such abrupt invasions of established markets while continuing to provide steadily enlarged opportunities for trade." [61] GATT proceeded to establish a committee to which countries could report cases of market disruption. Several studies were undertaken and efforts made to work out lines of agreement that would be satisfactory to both exporting and importing countries. Since mid-1961, however, concern about this sort of problem has concentrated on cotton textiles. The results of this work were embodied in an international cotton textile agreement which operates under GATT supervision. (See Chapter 9.)

Restrictions on Japanese Exports

Without regard to the market disruption procedure, European countries, and others as well, take measures to shut out goods which they say are cheap because of the low wages paid in producing countries. Japan and Hong Kong have been the principal targets of these restrictive measures, but India and Pakistan have also been affected. Similar complaints about China and East European states apply to dumping by Communist state-trading agencies as well as to low wages. The GATT secre-

[61] GATT, *Restrictions and Other Measures Relating to the Problem of Market Disruption,* L/1164 (Geneva: Author, May 17, 1960), p. 3.

tariat's list of the methods being used, in late 1959 and early 1960, to hold down imports of low-wage goods ran the gamut of tariff measures and included the familiar import quota and licensing devices as well.[62] Another device that has recently assumed unusual significance is the export quota imposed for purposes of "orderly marketing," that is, to forestall the importing country's imposing import restrictions. The United States and Japan between them seem to have invented this device but the technique has spread. Table 7-10 gives a partial list of the use of export quotas in early 1960 to restrain Japanese exports to several countries. Other exporters have used them too. Hong Kong, India, and Pakistan restrict exports of cotton textiles to the United Kingdom. Denmark has bilateral agreements affecting not only Japan but other East Asian and Eastern European countries.[63]

How much have Japanese exports been reduced as a result of these restraints? It is impossible to say, not only because we cannot know what exports would have been under other conditions, but also because the Japanese government has never published full details about the restraints being imposed. The list in Table 7-10 includes only what the Japanese call the principal products affected. Even with respect to these products the rules applied with regard to permitted quantities, qualities, and prices are not published. What is more, the nature and terms of restraints can vary whenever the Japanese government, or in some cases the private organization imposing the controls, chooses to change them, subject sometimes to consultation with foreign countries.

Japan's reason for accepting these restraints is simply that no better alternative seems available. These measures—distasteful as they are to eager Japanese businessmen—appear to the Japanese government as probably less damaging to exports than the destructive measures that importing countries might take in angry response to unchecked flows of competitive goods. On the surface these trade restraints seem to hurt Japan's exporters and producers. But it can be argued that if the use of these export restraints avoids even stricter foreign import restrictions then Japan is selling as much abroad as it can with safety. An optimistic estimate would be that in the end Japan would gain in total export volume by gradual expansion. To argue that Japan gets less is tantamount to saying that Japanese negotiators guessed wrong, or allowed them-

[62] Same, pp. 22–23. Import restrictions: discretionary licensing, global quotas, single country quotas (in some cases resulting from agreement with the government or industry of the exporting country). Export restrictions: general export quotas, quotas on exports to a particular country (in some cases resulting from agreement or consultation with the importing countries). Customs tariffs: increases in maximum duty rates, increases in most-favored-nation rates, minimum specific duties, sliding duty rates, antidumping duties, tariff quotas.

[63] Same, p. 8.

TABLE 7-10. PRINCIPAL JAPANESE PRODUCTS SUBJECT TO EXPORT RESTRAINT, EARLY 1960

Destination	*Product*	*Kind of Export Restraint*	
		Price	*Quantity*
Canada	Stainless steel table flatware	x	x
	Cotton piece-goods	x	x
	Spun rayon made-up goods [a]		x
	Woolen knitted made-up goods		x
United States	Frozen tuna, albacore	x	x
	Frozen tuna, loins and discs	x	x
	Tuna, yellow fin	x	
	Frozen tuna, swordfish		x
	Canned tuna [a]		x
	Plywood (including veneer and paper core)	x	x
	Wood screws	x	
	Iron pipe fittings	x	
	Clinical thermometers	x	
	Transistor radios	x	
	Stainless steel table flatware	x	x
	Porcelain and earthenware dinner sets	x	
	Umbrellas		x
	Silk faille, plain and mixed		x
	Cotton piece-goods	x	x
	Woolen fabrics	x	x
	Silk scarves and mufflers	x	x
	Woolen knitted goods		x
	Woolen hooked rugs		x
	Paper cups		x
Switzerland	Cotton piece-goods		x
	Woolen knitted wear and sweaters		x
	Cotton made-up goods (blouses and sports shirts)	x	x
Denmark	Cotton piece-goods	x	x
	Woolen yarns		x
	Spun rayon, rayon cloth		x
	Cotton made-up goods		x
	Spun rayon made-up goods		x
	Woolen knitted made-up goods		x
Benelux	Cotton piece-goods	x	x
Australia	Cotton piece-goods	x	x
	Woolen knitted goods		x
	Man-made fiber piece-goods		x

[a] Quality controls also applied.

Sources: Embassy of Japan, Washington; GATT, *Restrictions and Other Measures Relating to the Problem of Market Disruption*, L/1164 (Geneva: Author, May 17, 1960), pp. 35–36.

selves to be pushed too far. In some cases Japan may have accepted second-best solutions in interests of political harmony.

The most severe criticism of these restraints is one based on grounds of principle: the "voluntary" restraints violate the spirit of liberal trade and of the GATT, of which both Japan and most European countries, as well as Canada and the United States, are Contracting Parties. This issue will be explored further in Chapter 10 after a fuller examination in the next two chapters of the application of export quotas to Japanese sales to the United States, especially of cotton textiles.

The export restraints forced on Japan, the frequent denial of most-favored-nation treatment, and other obstacles all have made Japan, as it were, a second-class member of GATT. Economically, and perhaps even more politically, the rectification of this situation is a major part of the unfinished business of finding Japan's proper place in the free world economy. While GATT itself seems to offer the best framework of principles and procedures for meeting Japan's trade needs, bilateral negotiations are likely to be essential to progress. In this regard Japan made important steps forward in 1962 and 1963.

New Trade Treaties

The United Kingdom's invocation of Article 35 denied Japan fully equal treatment in all of Britain's dependent overseas territories as well as in the United Kingdom. After independence, several, including Nigeria, continued this treatment. Yet Japan's trade with the British territories has prospered. The United Kingdom, long Japan's best customer in Europe, has accorded most-favored-nation tariff treatment. Nigeria buys more Japanese goods than any other African country (if we omit the ships nominally exported to Liberia). Ghana, Kenya, and other British or former British territories are good customers of Japan. British quantitative restrictions on imports of some Japanese goods have been embodied in annual trade agreements after discussion with the Japanese. There are also substantial British tariffs on a number of Japanese products. Still British discrimination and other handicaps imposed on Japan have been limited and Japanese exports have had more scope than in many other countries.

Nevertheless when serious negotiations for a treaty of commerce and navigation were undertaken in 1962 one of Japan's central aims was to end British use of Article 35.[64] For their part, the British showed con-

[64] "In fact the biggest goal of Japanese economic diplomacy has been to have its trading partners stop applying the particular GATT article." Mitsuru Yamamoto, "Anglo–Japanese Treaty Marks New Era in Ties," *The Japan Times Weekly*, November 24, 1962, p. 4. The discussion that follows is based mainly on *The Economist*, August 18, 1962, pp. 642 and 645; *The Japan Times Weekly*, August 25, Septem-

cern over alleged Japanese export subsidies and over a number of "sensitive" products, notably Japanese woolen manufactures. At one point in the negotiations the word spread that the Japanese representatives were resisting a British request to extend most-favored-nation treatment and other benefits to the exports of all British territories, including Hong Kong. Agreement was reached before long, despite the fact that several previous efforts had proved abortive, beginning in 1955. The Anglo–Japanese Treaty of Commerce, Establishment and Navigation was signed in London, November 14, 1962 and went into effect in April 1963 upon the exchange of ratifications in Tokyo. In the main the treaty followed the general pattern. In addition, Britain acceded to the Japanese demand for termination of Article 35 discrimination. But the price to Japan was high. Japan accepted two kinds of quantitative restrictions on Japanese exports to the United Kingdom. In a protocol attached to the treaty there was a list of British quantitative controls to be continued at rising levels of trade during 1963, 1964, and 1965. Another protocol enumerated certain "voluntary" controls the Japanese government agreed to maintain on exports to the United Kingdom. This latter list consisted of textile products and transistor radio and television receiving sets and parts. The British list included cigarette lighters, cutlery, sewing machines, fishing tackle, binoculars, microscopes, and certain toys.

Thus Japan gained formal removal of discrimination but not immediate full access to the market of the United Kingdom. The two governments endorsed the principle of "orderly marketing," and in its name Japan accepted limitations on exports. But these limitations do not have to last long. The British list is to disappear after 1965. The Japanese list contains no specific commitment on the duration of export controls. Thus the treaty appears to represent a compromise that permits expansion of trade in the future but does not prohibit quantitative restrictions that are consistent with GATT.

Somewhat similar treaties have since been signed by Japan with France, in April 1963, and Benelux, in May 1963. They, too, provide for withdrawal of Article 35 treatment, but permit quantitative limitations on purchases of sensitive Japanese export goods.[65]

At more or less the same time, Japan at last began to make progress in its efforts to become a member of the Organization for Economic Cooperation and Development (OECD, the successor to the Organization for European Economic Cooperation). Like GATT and the trade treaties this association of Japan with the advanced countries of West-

ber 1 and November 24, 1962; *The Oriental Economist,* December 1962, p. 682; conversations with officials of the Japanese Embassy, Washington; and the texts of the Anglo–Japanese treaty and appended documents.

[65] *International Financial News Survey* (IMF), May 24, 1963, p. 184.

ern Europe and North America would assure some measure of liberalization and equal treatment on both sides. But its special importance for Japan—which was already a member of the Development Assistance Committee of the OECD, the body that tries to coordinate aid policies—was as a further mark of acceptance and fuller participation in the responsible handling of the free world's economic problems.

CONCLUSION: JAPAN GREATLY NEEDS THE AMERICAN MARKET

This survey of Japanese foreign trade by geographic areas is not complete, since no close look has been taken at Japan's largest export market, the United States of America. If it lacked that market, Japan would be in a far worse position than it is in earning its way in the world economy.

The non-Communist countries of Asia, as we have seen, offer a reality that falls far short of the old dream of a nearly self-contained Asian zone under Japanese leadership. Under present circumstances these countries are unable to provide many of the basic foodstuffs and raw materials Japan must import, to say nothing of the new technology and machinery that makes Japanese industry modern and efficient. Nor do they earn enough from their sales to the rest of the world to be able to buy from Japan in the huge quantities necessary to bring about a sharp increase in their share of Japanese trade. Japan can do much to foster development in Asia, but it will take time both to enlarge Japan's role in this respect and also to make the Asian countries much larger markets for Japanese goods. Much the same is true of the rest of the underdeveloped world; large growth potentials are linked with difficult problems. It is not to be expected that Japanese trade with these areas will grow as rapidly as total Japanese trade. Japanese planners are on sound ground in expecting the share of these low-income areas in Japan's trade to decline during the next decade, while the volume of trade increases.

Communist China and Russia might well provide Japan with many things not available in other Asian countries. But Communist regimes are notoriously unreliable trading partners, and though many Japanese badly want to normalize economic relations with the mainland, the government is likely to proceed cautiously. Fortunately for Japan, more trade with China and Russia is not a dire necessity; so the bargaining position is strong. There is some chance of very large trade with these countries, but even with maximum development that is likely during the 1960s, Japan's trade with these Communist giants and their brood of smaller fry seems most unlikely to reduce drastically the importance of the United States in Japanese trade.

Europe, Australia, New Zealand, and Canada stand today as Japan's most promising markets outside of the United States. In 1961 these areas supplied 25 per cent of Japanese imports and bought 19 per cent of exports. In 1962 the figures rose to 27 and 23 per cent respectively. These high-income areas could, if they were willing, buy a great deal more from Japan. Although Europe can offer only a limited volume of the primary products that constitute the bulk of Japanese imports, these areas also produce many things Japan could buy. The future of this trade depends mainly on policy. Will these countries buy Japan's low-wage manufactures? And will Japan buy from Europe things that compete with Japanese production? If so, trade can grow greatly.

We turn now to the United States as a market for Japanese exports. We have already seen that as a supplier of imports for Japan, the United States provides more raw materials, more foodstuffs, and more manufactured goods than any other country. It is also true that the United States is Japan's principal reserve source for many things when Japanese demand is unusually great. In the next chapter we shall see how important the American market is for Japan both at present levels of trade and for its growth potential. The many and difficult problems of the American market will also be examined in the next and subsequent chapters, in a case study of cotton textiles and then in an examination of United States policy.

Chapter 8

The United States Market for Japanese Goods

The United States is Japan's biggest market by far, taking in recent years between 25 and 30 per cent of total exports. In 1959 for the first time this country took more than a billion dollars' worth of Japanese goods. During the next two years the volume was about the same, and then a sharp increase in 1962 brought the level to about $1.4 billion. Most of this tremendous volume has developed since 1954, when the figure was only $277 million, 17 per cent of Japan's total exports. Trade is the greatest economic nexus between the two countries. Its size and character and the factors making for and against its expansion raise major questions of policy in Washington and Tokyo. All other questions of future United States economic policy toward Japan take second place behind the treatment of imports.

This situation is not new. It has existed most of the time since the beginning of the Meiji era. The United States' percentage share of Japanese exports and imports in each decade since the Japanese began keeping trade statistics in 1873 was: [1]

	Exports	*Imports*
1873–1880	30.2	6.6
1881–1890	37.6	8.8
1891–1900	31.5	13.5
1901–1910	29.2	15.5
1911–1920	28.0	26.8
1921–1930	35.0	23.7
1931–1940	15.2	25.0
1945–1950	22.6	65.5
1951–1960	22.8	34.2

[1] Figures for 1873 through 1930 from The Oriental Economist, *Foreign Trade of Japan, A Statistical Survey* (Tokyo: Author, 1935); 1931–1940 from Bank of Japan,

The 1930s, which would seem the natural base for measuring changes from prewar to now, prove to be unrepresentative so far as Japanese exports are concerned. Japan's dependence on the U.S. market was markedly less than at other times because of the sharp decline in the price of raw silk and Japan's heavy exports to occupied areas of Asia. Until the Great Depression the United States took more than a quarter, at times over a third, of all Japanese exports. This record contrasts with that for Japanese imports, of which the United States supplied very little at first but then a progressively larger share through World War I, after which there was a small, temporary decline.

After 1945 Japan had so little to sell that until the end of 1949 exports to the United States averaged only $60 million a year, including accumulated stocks of raw silk. A general rise in Japanese exports to the United States began in 1950, bringing sales to an average of $219 million a year in 1950–54, $567 million in 1955–58, and $1,141 million in 1959–62. (Table 7-3.)

WHAT JAPAN SELLS IN THE UNITED STATES

Japan ships a great many different things to the United States. The detailed list in the Japanese customs return for 1961 takes 96 printed pages.[2] The condensed list in Table 8-1 gives an idea of the range. That table also gives a picture of the postwar growth of Japanese sales to the United States since it compares the figures for five years: 1954, just before the most rapid growth set in; 1957 when sales had already more than doubled; and the three latest years for which detailed statistics were available when this book went to press. (Annual figures are shown in Table 7-3 for other postwar years.) The third group of columns in Table 8-1 gives an indication of the importance of the American market for Japan's sales abroad.

The structure of trade shown in Table 8-1 is very different from that of prewar years. Then raw silk dominated the picture. In 1913 it accounted for 68 per cent of the value of all Japanese exports to the United States. For more than twenty years thereafter its share never dropped below 60 per cent, and in 1925 it was 84 per cent.[3] After 1945 silk never

Economic Statistics of Japan, 1960, pp. 245 and 247; postwar figures from Table 7-3. Prewar figures have been calculated from published yen figures, without adjustment for price changes, but adjusted to include trade with Taiwan and Korea in total Japanese foreign trade.

[2] Japan, Ministry of Finance, *Trade of Japan* (Annual Return), 1961, Country by Commodity (Export) (Tokyo: Japan Tariff Association, 1961), pp. 1793–1888.

[3] Calculated from Mitsubishi Economic Research Bureau, *Japanese Trade and Industry, Present and Future* (London: Macmillan, 1936), p. 592, and Japanese official trade statistics.

regained predominance. A number of products now outrank it in Japan's exports to the United States. For many of them, the United States is Japan's most important market, as it continues to be for silk.

One of the most striking features of the postwar growth of trade has been the surge to importance of a number of products in the years after 1954. In 1962 Japan sold in the United States $92 million worth of radios, about half its total radio exports. Footwear sales reached $55 million in 1962, which was 65 per cent of total exports. Neither product accounted for as much as a million dollars of Japanese sales in the American market in 1954. Other less dramatic examples of rapid growth are woolen fabrics, metal manufactures, outerwear, and sporting goods. In each of these categories 40 per cent or more of total 1962 exports went to the United States. Of cameras, another growth product, the United States took 38 per cent. It is evident from these and other figures in Table 8-1 that the United States has played a very important part in the rise of new products among Japanese exports.

Textiles have traditionally been the largest group in Japanese exports to the United States. However, electrical equipment, in which radios are the largest item, is running a close second. Next come iron and steel products and clothing, both of which have shown tremendous growth, followed by metal manufactures and fish. The American share of Japan's total exports is over a third in the case of all these products except textiles and iron and steel. In the case of a number of the smaller exports listed in Table 8-1 the share going to the United States is much higher, reaching 88 per cent in the case of floor coverings in 1962. The United States is clearly a powerful factor in the life of many a Japanese manufacturer.

The role of the United States in Japan's dual export structure is also reflected in Table 8-1. Products of light industry predominate and they go mainly to consumer use in the United States. The Bank of Tokyo analyzed 1957 exports to the United States and concluded that 77.4 per cent were light-industry products, including foodstuffs, textiles, nonmetallic mineral products, and miscellaneous products. Only 19.1 per cent were classed as chemical and heavy-industry products, including metal products, machinery, and vehicles.[4] The increases in Japan's exports to the United States since 1957 have not changed this situation much. Although sales of iron and steel products rose greatly and automobiles passed bicycles, the bulk of the increase was in light goods. Looking at the products in terms of their use, the Bank of Tokyo concluded that, in 1957 and 1958, 84 to 85 per cent of Japanese exports to

[4] A final 3.5 per cent were not assigned to either of these categories. "Japanese Exports to the United States," Bank of Tokyo, *Semiannual Report,* October 1958–March 1959 (Tokyo: Author, 1959), p. 25.

TABLE 8-1. JAPAN'S EXPORTS TO THE UNITED STATES, BY COMMODITY, 1954, 1957, 1960, 1961, 1962

Commodity	*Value (millions of dollars)*					*Per Cent of Total Exports to U.S.*					*U.S. Share of Total Japanese Exports (per cent)*				
	1954	*1957*	*1960*	*1961*	*1962*	*1954*	*1957*	*1960*	*1961*	*1962*	*1954*	*1957*	*1960*	*1961*	*1962*
Food, beverages and tobacco	**42.9**	**63.0**	**73.1**	**81.5**	**102.1**	**15.5**	**10.6**	**6.8**	**7.8**	**7.4**	**31.9**	**34.4**	**27.3**	**30.7**	**30.1**
Fish and fish products	38.2	55.0	57.7	63.7	81.2	13.8	9.2	5.4	6.1	5.9	51.4	45.0	33.0	39.1	33.1
Mandarin oranges (preserved)	0.4	2.5	6.2	8.2	8.6	0.2	0.4	0.6	0.8	0.6	4.8	13.7	24.6	34.4	37.2
Other	4.3	5.5	9.2	9.7	12.3	1.5	1.0	0.9	0.9	0.9	8.4	12.8	13.0	12.3	17.3
Raw materials, including fuel, fats and oils	**42.4**	**39.2**	**46.9**	**51.0**	**52.7**	**15.4**	**6.6**	**4.3**	**4.9**	**3.8**	**41.7**	**30.7**	**27.7**	**15.0**	**26.2**
Lumber	4.9	6.4	8.2	7.1	8.4	1.8	1.1	0.8	0.7	0.6	23.7	29.9	33.3	31.1	38.4
Raw silk	27.5	21.3	24.7	25.0	25.8	10.0	3.6	2.3	2.4	1.9	58.7	51.0	48.9	54.2	48.0
Petroleum products	a	a	4.3	5.7	3.4	a	a	0.4	0.5	0.2	a	a	27.2	30.4	18.9
Fats and oils	3.3	3.7	2.4	5.1	6.5	1.2	0.6	0.2	0.5	0.5	25.6	12.2	8.0	14.7	26.7
Other	6.7	7.7	7.2	8.1	8.6	2.4	1.3	0.7	0.8	0.6	33.6	24.6	19.3	13.0	10.3
Chemicals	**3.5**	**5.4**	**16.9**	**21.1**	**28.2**	**1.3**	**0.9**	**1.6**	**2.0**	**2.0**	**4.5**	**4.3**	**10.0**	**11.2**	**10.8**
Inorganic chemicals	0.5	0.9	7.4	9.5	8.8	0.2	0.2	0.7	0.9	0.6	5.3	5.6	28.9	32.8	25.7
Medicinal and pharmaceutical products	1.7	1.8	2.2	1.9	3.1	0.6	0.3	0.2	0.2	0.2	18.3	13.2	13.1	9.2	12.4
Synthetic plastic materials	0.1	0.8	2.6	3.4	5.8	a	0.1	0.2	0.3	0.4	1.5	8.3	8.1	11.0	12.3
Other	1.4	1.9	4.6	6.3	10.5	0.5	0.3	0.4	0.6	0.8	2.4	2.2	13.0	5.8	6.8
Manufactured goods classified by material	**95.4**	**243.3**	**434.8**	**400.1**	**560.9**	**34.6**	**41.0**	**40.4**	**38.4**	**40.4**	**10.2**	**17.4**	**23.7**	**22.1**	**27.1**
Rubber manufactures	0.1	0.3	1.2	1.9	2.5	a	0.1	0.1	0.2	0.2	1.2	1.1	4.0	4.5	5.3
Wood manufactures	19.0	52.5	58.4	56.6	68.6	6.9	8.8	5.4	5.4	4.9	59.0	75.6	69.4	70.7	73.4
Plywood	16.3	44.2	45.5	44.7	53.3	5.9	7.4	4.2	4.3	3.8	63.9	80.4	72.7	76.1	78.8
Paper, pulp and manufactures	0.6	3.6	7.3	5.9	3.8	0.2	0.6	0.7	0.6	0.3	4.1	10.9	14.3	9.5	7.3
Textiles	38.3	87.4	146.1	121.5	173.5	13.9	14.7	13.6	11.7	12.5	7.0	10.7	15.8	13.9	18.5
Woolen yarn	2.0	2.2	4.9	3.3	7.5	0.7	0.4	0.5	0.3	0.5	7.7	10.2	32.9	24.0	30.5
Other yarn and thread	0.7	1.1	3.7	3.6	4.6	0.2	0.2	0.3	0.3	0.3	1.1	1.6	3.6	3.8	4.9
Cotton fabrics	10.5	17.7	22.0	23.4	33.0	3.8	3.0	2.0	2.2	2.4	4.2	5.6	6.3	6.7	9.7
Silk fabrics	5.0	22.1	36.0	20.8	31.2	1.8	3.7	3.3	2.0	2.2	36.4	68.4	69.0	60.6	65.0
Woolen and worsted fabrics	1.9	18.9	25.8	15.3	26.5	0.7	3.2	2.4	1.5	1.9	11.2	42.4	47.3	40.9	52.6
Synthetic fiber fabrics	0.3	1.4	8.2	8.5	15.0	0.1	0.2	0.8	0.8	1.1	0.3	0.6	3.8	4.0	6.4
Blankets, sheets, towels, etc.	5.4	9.2	10.5	12.0	12.1	2.0	1.6	1.0	1.2	0.9	24.4	29.8	29.7	31.4	32.5
Floor coverings	7.4	9.6	24.5	24.0	28.7	2.7	1.6	2.3	2.3	2.1	80.6	79.7	89.6	90.7	87.8
Other	5.2	5.1	10.6	10.7	14.9	1.9	0.9	1.0	1.0	1.1	12.1	12.7	15.6	15.3	19.9
Nonmetallic mineral manufactures	24.0	43.3	70.7	66.9	80.0	8.7	7.3	6.6	6.4	5.8	31.3	32.5	40.1	37.5	42.5
Tiles and other clay construction materials	0.3	1.7	8.4	9.7	13.8	0.1	0.3	0.8	0.9	1.0	14.7	34.5	57.9	57.3	59.5
Glass and glassware	3.0	4.3	9.1	8.9	9.2	1.1	0.7	0.8	0.9	0.7	30.7	29.2	37.1	35.7	37.9
Pottery	16.3	27.1	37.7	29.5	36.5	5.9	4.5	3.5	2.8	2.6	46.8	53.0	55.8	51.6	55.8

Pearls	4.0	9.5	14.1	16.7	18.7	1.5	1.6	1.3	1.6	1.3	54.5	56.5	46.3	46.8	44.7
Iron and steel products	2.7	11.9	71.7	69.2	135.7	1.0	2.0	6.7	6.7	9.8	1.6	5.7	18.5	18.2	25.5
Nonferrous metals and products	3.5	16.7	10.1	11.1	11.5	1.3	2.8	0.9	1.1	0.8	7.7	40.1	39.3	39.8	33.3
Metal manufactures	7.2	27.5	68.6	66.4	82.6	2.6	4.6	6.4	6.4	5.9	17.6	38.0	46.4	43.5	46.7
Wire nails of iron and steel	1.4	4.0	14.3	16.2	20.7	0.5	0.7	1.3	1.6	1.5	29.9	62.9	69.5	83.7	88.1
Cutlery	1.3	9.7	11.9	7.7	11.6	0.5	1.6	1.1	0.7	0.8	36.0	66.2	50.4	38.2	42.2
Other	[a]	0.2	0.6	0.5	2.7	[a]	[a]	0.1	[a]	0.2	0.6	8.1	11.7	8.9	25.2
Machinery and transport equipment	**24.7**	**50.0**	**150.0**	**182.6**	**226.4**	**8.9**	**8.4**	**13.9**	**17.5**	**16.3**	**12.2**	**7.9**	**16.2**	**16.3**	**18.4**
Textile machinery	[a]	0.2	0.9	1.7	1.3	[a]	[a]	0.1	0.2	0.1	0.1	0.6	1.9	2.9	1.8
Sewing machines	6.2	21.7	22.4	23.5	26.6	2.3	3.6	2.1	2.3	1.9	19.7	45.4	41.0	42.6	44.9
Electrical equipment	2.4	26.1	106.4	121.7	153.4	0.9	4.4	9.9	11.7	11.1	10.3	33.6	38.8	36.1	36.0
Electric light bulbs	2.0	6.1	8.1	8.4	8.1	0.7	1.0	0.8	0.8	0.6	54.9	67.8	65.4	59.7	53.3
Radio receivers	[a]	5.3	69.3	74.6	91.5	[a]	0.9	6.4	7.2	6.6	21.7	48.7	49.9	49.4	51.7
Automotive vehicles and parts	[a]	0.2	4.1	6.3	19.1	[a]	[a]	0.4	0.6	1.4	0.4	0.6	3.8	4.6	12.1
Bicycles and parts	[a]	0.2	3.2	2.3	2.4	[a]	[a]	0.3	0.2	0.2	0.5	2.0	21.5	16.6	17.0
Ships and boats	15.8	0.2	1.1	2.1	4.8	5.7	[a]	0.1	0.2	0.3	30.4	0.1	0.4	0.8	2.0
Other	0.2	1.4	11.9	25.0	18.8	0.1	0.2	1.1	2.4	1.3	0.8	1.7	8.4	10.7	7.1
Miscellaneous products and transactions	**67.1**	**192.9**	**355.0**	**304.5**	**416.6**	**24.3**	**32.5**	**33.0**	**29.3**	**30.0**	**38.7**	**50.7**	**55.1**	**44.9**	**53.1**
Clothing	18.0	73.4	116.9	87.1	103.1	6.5	12.3	10.9	8.4	7.4	32.2	51.5	53.1	45.6	50.5
Underwear and nightwear [b]	0.6	12.8	17.7	10.2	14.2	0.2	2.1	1.6	1.0	1.0	9.0	46.9	44.7	33.5	30.5
Outerwear	1.9	27.4	44.8	33.9	47.5	0.7	4.6	4.2	3.3	3.4	31.2	66.5	67.5	62.5	62.8
Gloves	4.3	11.1	23.1	16.9	16.7	1.5	1.9	2.1	1.6	1.2	69.9	76.0	83.8	81.7	81.5
Footwear	0.7	5.9	48.4	38.2	55.4	0.3	1.1	4.5	3.7	4.0	20.6	40.7	67.1	61.3	65.5
Optical, scientific, etc. instruments	6.9	23.3	36.1	38.3	49.0	2.5	3.9	3.4	3.7	3.5	36.1	47.1	39.0	36.0	38.4
Binoculars	3.9	7.6	6.9	5.8	6.7	1.4	1.3	0.6	0.6	0.5	70.9	61.8	44.0	44.2	45.0
Cameras and parts	1.3	9.6	13.5	16.9	20.8	0.5	1.6	1.3	1.6	1.5	24.0	56.5	37.0	37.1	38.2
Sporting goods	0.4	5.1	11.2	10.8	14.7	0.2	0.9	1.0	1.0	1.1	52.4	68.7	67.8	62.9	63.6
Toys	17.1	37.3	54.3	48.1	57.2	6.2	6.3	5.0	4.6	4.1	54.6	60.7	60.3	57.8	63.7
Costume jewelry	4.6	7.0	13.6	17.3	15.2	1.7	1.2	1.3	1.7	1.1	66.1	69.3	69.5	72.2	72.0
Other	19.3	40.9	74.5	64.7	122.0	7.0	6.9	6.9	6.2	8.8	34.5	43.1	56.0	33.4	52.1
Total exports of Japanese goods	**276.1**	**593.8**	**1,076.6**	**1,040.8**	**1,387.1**	**100.0**	**100.0**	**100.0**	**100.0**	**100.0**	**17.0**	**20.8**	**26.6**	**24.7**	**28.4**
Re-exports	**0.7**	**2.8**	**6.2**	**10.2**	**13.1**	**0.2**	**0.5**	**0.6**	**1.0**	**0.9**	**18.7**	**30.8**	**42.0**	**45.6**	**50.2**
Total exports (including re-exports)	**276.7**	**596.6**	**1,082.9**	**1,051.0**	**1,400.2**	**100.2**	**100.5**	**100.6**	**101.0**	**100.9**	**17.0**	**20.9**	**26.7**	**24.8**	**28.5**

[a] Less than $500,000 or 0.05 per cent.
[b] All shirts are included with underwear rather than outerwear.

Notes: Trade with Alaska and Hawaii is included for 1962, omitted for earlier years. See Appendix B for definitions of commodity groupings in terms of code designators. The customs statistics underlying this table are described in the Bibliographic Note. Minor inconsistencies result from rounding.

Sources: Japan, Ministry of Finance, *Annual Return of the Foreign Trade of Japan*, 1954, 1957, 1960, 1961; 1962 figures provided by Japan, Ministry of Finance, Customs Bureau, Business Section.

the United States were for consumption and 15 to 16 per cent for production. (All radios and household sewing machines were assigned to the consumption-goods category, and no distinction was made between durable and nondurable consumer products.)

Japan's exports to the United States are chiefly labor-intensive goods. Thus this trade contributes more to keeping Japanese workers employed than if capital-intensive goods predominated. It is because clothing, certain textiles, radios (especially the tiniest transistor sets), binoculars, cameras, pearls, raw silk, and many other Japanese products require a high proportion of labor that they can be produced more cheaply in low-wage Japan than in the United States. Since American wages are about the highest in the world, Japan's comparative advantage in labor-intensive products is greater with respect to the United States than to other countries.

In the years ahead this wage advantage may be expected to decline gradually with rising employment and wage rates in Japan. As time goes on, Japanese producers of one product and then another can be expected to find themselves unable to sell in the American market against new competition from developing countries where wages are still lower than in Japan. These changes do not take place all at once, however, and for a long time to come Japan can be expected to benefit substantially from large exports of labor-intensive goods to the United States. Many of these goods are made in small plants. Older workers in these plants have very little chance of finding other employment, and they need opportunities such as are offered by the American market.

To produce the things sold to the United States costs Japan less in foreign exchange than to produce the general run of exports. The list of sales to America includes a high percentage of things that, like fish, pearls, and silk, contain relatively little imported material [5] and, at the other end of the scale, highly fabricated products like cameras and radios for which the imported raw material cost is low compared to sales value of the finished product. (Table 5-8.) The most important Japanese exports that have a foreign exchange cost exceeding the general average (which in 1961 was 15.5 per cent) are cotton and woolen fabrics, iron and steel, and nonferrous metals and various metal products. Although the United States was the third largest market for Japan's

[5] Silk (raw, fabrics, handkerchiefs, scarves, and shawls), pearls, fish, ceramic and metal toys, spun rayon fabrics, sewing machines, pottery, optical and scientific instruments, and radios, making up a third of exports to the United States in 1959, involved Japan in direct import costs of only 2.6 per cent of f.o.b. export value. The United States took 53 per cent of total exports of these items. Calculated from trade returns, using direct import cost figures from Japan, Economic Planning Agency, *Economic Survey of Japan* (1959–1960) (Tokyo: The Japan Times, 1960), pp. 328–333. Some figures for 1961 may be found in Table 5-8.

exports of cotton fabrics in 1962, it took only 10 per cent. But 25 per cent of Japan's exports of iron and steel products went to the United States, which took an even larger proportion of woolen manufactures, metal manufactures, and nonferrous metals, as well as plywood. Nevertheless, it is clear that the foreign exchange cost of what Japan sends to the United States is well below the average of what is sent elsewhere.

Another factor that makes exports to the United States especially interesting to Japan is that American commercial initiative, which has been responsible for a large part of the flow of blouses, cigarette lighters, sewing machine components, toys, and many other products, has brought new ideas, products, and techniques to Japanese producers (pp. 250–252).

Taken all together, these considerations show that the significance of the American market for Japan is greater than the 25 to 30 per cent share would indicate. The United States market is clearly the largest, richest, and most promising source of the export earnings Japan needs to finance its ambitious plans for economic growth. Although the growth of the United States economy has been disappointingly slow in recent years, the opportunities it offers are very great. No other market anywhere can compare in importance for Japan.

MARKETING JAPANESE PRODUCTS IN THE UNITED STATES

Although rich, the United States is a difficult market. A country of about 190 million people with the highest per capita income of any large nation in history offers fabulous rewards for businessmen, American and foreign, who succeed in attracting customers. Japanese traders, like others from Europe and elsewhere, have found in recent years that there is room in the United States for a large volume of imports of manufactured goods of many kinds. But despite booming sales, Japanese businessmen are acutely aware of their difficulties in exporting to the United States. The basic one is that most of what they have to sell competes with American products. The decline of raw silk reduced the importance of the only leading product that faced no competition from American industry. Under present circumstances, a large increase in Japanese sales of almost anything will fairly soon be felt by American competitors, unless the economy here is expanding very rapidly.

In the past the Japanese have often found it difficult to know how to respond to the complaints coming from American competitors. In the free society of the United States, the producer whose interests are affected—actually or even potentially—complains publicly and makes various kinds of approaches to the federal government in Washington and, if he chooses, to his state and local governments as well. A single industry, even a single firm, can cause repeated headlines, both in the

United States and in Japan. Few Japanese know how to interpret such moves, and there is a tendency on the part of the Japanese press to exaggerate public statements, even at times to regard an industry's plea for import restrictions as meaning that such restrictions are about to be put into effect. The complexities of the U.S. government's procedures are a factor in these misunderstandings, and it is not surprising that most Japanese cannot follow fully the maneuvers involved in attempts to limit imports into the United States. Nor is it strange that many Japanese seem to overrate the importance of U.S. import barriers as a factor in Japanese sales.

Japanese manufacturers and merchants encounter many other difficulties as well, relating to customer tastes and preferences, changing patterns of demand, channels and methods of marketing, price practices, and other factors. During the postwar period, these problems have been solved in progressively greater degree, partly by a growth in Japanese awareness of the possibilities and the development of skills in grasping opportunities, but even more as a result of the commercial initiative of Americans who have gone to Japan to seek out sources of supply.

Japanese, among others, have long had an uneasy feeling that the United States market, although rich, was undependable because of the instability of the American economy. At its extreme this fear is related to the Marxist expectation that a "crisis of capitalism" in the form of a deep depression will cut American demand and lead to increased import barriers, which will cut not only Japan's exports to the United States but also its sales elsewhere as the reduction of U.S. imports of primary products lessens the ability of the countries producing them to buy from Japan. Nothing like this has happened, but the smaller fluctuations that have occurred in the postwar period are still seen by many Japanese as an indication of the undependability of the American market. The record in Table 7-3 shows that since 1951 the American market has absorbed the exports faster than other countries. The year-to-year fluctuations in sales to the United States have been large, but not more so than for other markets taken together. Because of its great wealth, the lack of any periods of sharply declining consumer incomes since World War II, and the general American policy of liberal trade, the United States market has not fulfilled the gloomy Marxist prophecies. Instead, Japanese goods have found progressively expanding outlets here.

However, evidence frequently crops up of Japanese lack of knowledge or understanding about the American market, its needs, opportunities, and many special features. Some of the difficulties are comparable to those encountered by Japanese in many markets (pp. 163–169). This problem has been stressed repeatedly by the United States trade missions that went to Japan annually for a number of years, beginning in 1955. For instance, the report of the 1959 mission says:

> One thing which struck the Mission rather forcefully was the apparent lack of information on the American market, distribution channels, and characteristics of the market.
>
> During the tour through northern Japan as well as at the Trade Information Center, hundreds of businessmen were counseled on a wide variety of products ranging from native giftware showing great creative, manual, and artistic skill to excellent machined metal products and components, hand tools, wood products, food items, and miscellaneous household and consumer goods of many types and character.
>
> Although the Northern Honshu area was once prominent in the linen trade, due to changing styles and demands in the United States this trade has dropped off and the manufacturers were unaware of the reason, having made little or no effort to find out. Rather there was a tendency to assume that U.S. restrictions were responsible for present limited demand. The same applied to Japanese mink pelts. The producers were unaware of the constantly changing styles which caused changes in demand, nor were they aware that their skins were noncompetitive with the higher-quality American mink. They too thought that their lack of business was due to some kind of restrictive action in the United States. These two examples are only a few of the many misconceptions uncovered.[6]

Low Prices of Japanese Goods

A major feature of Japanese marketing in the United States, as elsewhere, is the low price at which Japanese goods are offered. It is seldom indeed that a Japanese product commands a higher price than competitive goods of equal merit, and usually the Japanese article is priced significantly lower. The reasons include not only low cost of production but also tradition and reputation, and the methods used to promote sales of Japanese goods. In cases where price elasticity for Japanese goods is high, low prices are an effective means of getting for Japan larger net income from exports to the United States than could be obtained otherwise.[7] But repeated cases have been observed in which the price of a Japanese product seems excessively low, not only for immediate earnings but also for purposes of long-run market development. It seems clear that Japanese producers and traders have at times relied too heavily on price when other forms of competition might have yielded more advantage.

The importance of price as a means of competition in Japan, especially among small firms, is greater than in the United States, where branded

[6] "U.S. Trade Mission to Japan Makes Report," *Foreign Commerce Weekly*, July 22, 1959, p. 20.

[7] In terms both of profits for the producers and of foreign exchange earnings for the Japanese nation.

products have reduced the importance of price as a competitive force in many markets. The organizational structure and operating habits of Japanese trading firms put great emphasis on price competition in buying imports, where price is necessarily the controlling factor in many transactions, and these methods are carried over to exports to a greater extent than appears necessary. In bulk purchases of commodities such as cotton and wheat, Japanese traders have developed a high degree of skill in obtaining the best terms. Selling of the wide variety of finished products Japanese producers send to the United States often calls for different methods, but Japanese trading firms have been slow to learn many of the techniques by which American sales departments not only promote volume but also obtain prices above the minimum. In effect, Japanese exporters tend to assume a given schedule of total demand and attempt to maximize their own sales volume, while Americans frequently attempt to change the demand schedule so that more will be bought without lower prices. Still, it is frequently the American importers who lay great stress on price in placing orders in Japan. While these pressures for low prices do not nowadays often result in shoddy goods, as used to happen, especially in the 1930s, the American public still tends to associate Japan with low quality, and the very low prices of many Japanese goods appear to contribute to a continuation of these American attitudes.

Another factor tending to depress export prices is the weakness of many Japanese firms, especially the smallest, producing for the export market. With very limited financial resources, but with obligations to workers and creditors, small firms have often been willing to accept very low prices in order to get business. Some American businessmen in Japan have insisted to the writer that they have seen cases where small producers, probably not knowing their costs very well, have quoted prices that would not cover out-of-pocket costs.

American Commercial Initiative and Imports from Japan

Among the numerous achievements of the Japanese nation there have not been many successes in establishing large-scale rapport with other peoples. Marketing difficulties in the United States reflect this weakness, as well as the more mundane business problems anyone, American or foreign, encounters in doing business in the United States. Still the booming Japanese sales of recent years clearly show that, whatever the difficulties have been, they are being overcome with resounding success for a widening range of products. Much of the credit for this success goes to Americans. They have gone a good deal more than halfway in efforts to assist Japanese producers in adapting to American consumer demand. American buyers and importers in substantial and growing numbers go to Japan hunting for goods that would be salable in the United States. These buyers know the American market, or more usually segments of the American market, as Japanese producers do not. When buyers are interested, exports do not depend upon Japanese learning American tastes and the methods of appealing to them.

American businessmen did not wait for Japanese producers to turn out a better mouse trap before beating a path to the doors of their factories, large and small. The Americans went, sought out possible Japanese producers, told them what to produce, and frequently took the responsibility for the whole process. In many cases the Americans brought designs, specifications, and production methods, so that the Japanese producer needed only to follow specific directions. As a result, blouses, shirts, children's playclothes, "car coats," toys, trinkets, sewing machine heads, camera components, and many other things have been contracted for in Japan by American manufacturers and merchants. Many of the Japanese producers could not themselves have originated such designs. Indeed some did not even understand fully what they were producing or how it was used in the United States. For good or ill, American commercial initiative in substantial degree has taken the place of Japanese in stimulating sales in the United States.

By and large this American initiative has been of tremendous advantage to Japan. Reportedly, some Americans have ordered textiles and other products made to stolen designs, leading innocent Japanese, usually very small producers, into difficulty with the design owners and giving rise to publicity unfavorable to Japanese products generally, but such practices are now infrequent. Americans have often pressed their Japanese suppliers for very low prices, thus not only serving to hold down Japanese wages and profits, especially in very small firms, but also in the past sometimes sacrificing quality and long-range market development for immediate sales. But for the most part American buyers have insisted on quality and in a growing number of cases have taken the initiative in building up market demand by standing behind the products concerned. Many Japanese products today reach American consumers with the guarantee of a reliable American firm—department store, mail order house, or other merchant or manufacturer. The Japanese origin is not always clear to the purchaser, especially when a Japanese component is embodied in a product assembled in the United States, labeled with an American name, and guaranteed like other products of the American producer.

Without this promotional work, which Japanese businessmen are not yet able to do so well, their goods would probably be selling here in significantly lower volume. A drawback for Japanese businessmen is that they do not have direct contact with the ultimate consumer of many products and have less control of their export business than they would like. Under the present arrangements there is always the possibility that American buyers may go elsewhere with their orders. There is also the understandable desire of Japanese firms to employ more of their own people in exporting. Some efforts are being made by manufacturers, trading firms, and other organizations to handle more marketing operations themselves and there will probably be progressively more moves in this direction in the future. Until now, however, few Japanese firms have made marked progress although some of them, like Sony Radio, have become widely and favorably known. Understanding the American market is not easy for a foreigner, and Japanese firms need to employ American specialists before they can expect to displace American firms in marketing activities. One American middleman expressed to me strong confidence in his prospects for continuing to handle imports from Japan even though, in his case, there is no design problem. He reported that at one point several years ago some of his Japanese suppliers had tried to do their own selling in the United States, only to return to him ruefully when business fell off rapidly after mishandling.

Japanese Goods as "Low-End" Items

Without direct access to the ultimate consumer of certain products, especially in the case of many "sundry" goods, Japanese producers and exporters have had to accept such sales opportunities as were offered them by middlemen. Buyers for department or chain stores or large jobbing firms play a key part in this process and to a large degree determine what is put before the customer. Often the buyers find a place for Japanese supplies at the low end of the price line. Japanese goods are often to be found in "economy" stores, in bargain basements, or in "special low-price offers," or as premiums. While some Japanese radios and other products are advertised as such and are known to be of high quality, other Japanese goods have been unable to gain admittance to "good stores." Sometimes an American manufacturer will use Japanese products for the cheapest articles in his line and his own production for the rest, with or without distinction by brand.

In the case of baseball gloves, the Tariff Commission found in 1961 that imports, nearly all Japanese, mostly compete with domestically produced gloves in the lower-price ranges, \$1 to \$6, less in the middle-price range, \$6 to \$9, and virtually not at all in the highest-price range, above \$9. The Commission decided that American producers were being injured by imports.[8] In the case of plastic raincoats, however, the

[8] U.S. Tariff Commission, *Baseball and Softball Gloves, Including Mitts,* Report to the President on Escape-Clause Investigation No. 7-97, under the Provisions of Section 7 of the Trade Agreements Extension Act of 1951, as Amended, TC Pub-

Tariff Commission found no injury to the domestic industry despite a sharp increase of imports, because the foreign raincoats, nearly all Japanese, were sold at prices low enough to create a new market. In the words of the Commission, "a considerable part of the imports flow through a distribution system not utilized by domestic producers and most of the imports are sold in a price range much below the price range of the bulk of the domestic production." [9]

When Japanese products enter the American market at the low end of the price line, will they stop there or can they find wider opportunities? Some spokesmen for Japanese exports feel the possibilities are severely limited, especially by the need to sell to middlemen. But there seems no fundamental reason why, in the course of time, Japanese goods cannot move up the price line, especially in expanding markets where the American merchant or manufacturer must choose between increasing imports and increasing production in the United States. If the Japanese goods are better buys, the consumer may eventually make himself heard. Economic friction may be unusually great at this point in the marketing chain, however, and it is clear that the chances for Japanese goods may depend on the ultimate consumer's eagerness for them.

American Attitudes Toward Japanese Goods

Whether the salesmen are Japanese or American, they have to take account of consumer resistance resulting from unfavorable opinions about Japanese goods, about Japan, or about the desirability of stimulating American imports from Japan. In the past political animus of various sorts played a part. A traditional assumption of poor quality has not yet been entirely destroyed by the generally good postwar Japanese performance. Some interesting data on these matters are contained in a report published in 1959 based on 75 interviews in each of four cities: Philadelphia, Atlanta, Denver, and Omaha.[10]

A majority of those who responded approved in general terms of increasing imports into the United States, largely because foreign countries would in turn buy from the United States and because importing foreign goods reduces the likelihood of war. Two-thirds of the respond-

---

lication 15 (Washington: Author, May 1961), pp. 10, 26, 31, and elsewhere; *Baseball and Softball Gloves, Including Mitts,* Report in Response to the President's Request for Information Supplemental to the Report on Escape-Clause Investigation No. 7-97, TC Publication 44 (Washington: Author, December 1961), pp. 10–11 and elsewhere.

[9] U.S. Tariff Commission, *Plastic Film Raincoats,* Report on Escape-Clause Investigation No. 7-94, under the Provisions of Section 7 of the Trade Agreements Extension Act of 1951, as Amended (Washington: Author, March 1961), p. 21.

[10] Daniel Yankelovich, Inc., *Strengthening the Japanese Trade Position in the United States: A Pilot Study* (Washington: United States–Japan Trade Council, 1959). The report says nothing about differences in the replies among the four cities.

ents, however, thought the United States should be more selective than it was about the countries from which it imports. And here Japan stood near the bottom of a list of twelve countries from which the respondents would encourage imports (only Spain and Russia stood lower). Only 29 per cent favored encouraging imports from Japan while the favorable response for other countries ranged from 61 per cent for Canada and 51 per cent for England, through Mexico, France, Switzerland, Germany, the Netherlands, Sweden, Italy, Spain, and down to Russia with 8 per cent. In the same list Japan stood second among countries from which respondents would limit imports into the United States. Seventy-nine per cent favored limiting imports from Russia, 36 per cent Japan, 25 per cent Germany, 22 per cent Spain, 14 per cent Italy, and 11 per cent or less expressed themselves as favoring a limitation on imports from any of the other seven countries. Japan clearly did not stand well as a trading partner with this particular sample of American consumers.

The 29 per cent who favored encouraging imports from Japan had generally favorable impressions of Japan, its people, and its export products; among these people there was also a widespread readiness to accept more imports from all sources. The opposite views predominated among the 36 per cent who favored limiting imports from Japan. A majority of this group thought poorly of the quality of Japanese goods and of the Japanese people; 58 per cent thought imports from Japan harmful to the American economy; and 31 per cent showed evidence of resentment against Japan on account of World War II.

Strong evidence appeared that Japanese products are not well known. Only ten kinds of products were mentioned by as many as 5 per cent of respondents when asked what goods they associate with Japan. These items and the percentage of respondents mentioning each are listed below:

Toys	56	Blouses	14
Dinnerware	28	Sewing machines	11
Cameras	21	Shirts	10
Knickknacks	15	Transistor radios	9
Cigarette lighters	14	Costume jewelry	7

The list leaves out such important products as fish, raw silk, textiles of all kinds, pearls, binoculars, clothing other than blouses and shirts, iron and steel products, and other producer goods. The comments made by respondents about Japanese goods included approval and disapproval in varying degrees, but the majority held views that failed to take account of the generally high quality of many Japanese goods today. Only cameras received predominantly favorable comment in this respect.

The survey was sufficiently detailed to bring out the fact that many of the answers about Japanese products reflected views formed long ago. Some respondents, particularly older people, regarded Japanese goods as "cheap junk" or poor imitations of American products. This was especially true of toys. Apparently younger Americans hold these views to a lesser extent. Related to the stereotype of poor quality is a view of the Japanese people as tradition-bound, working mainly by hand, and unaccustomed to machines and complex modern technology.

This survey was financed by a group interested in fostering Japanese exports to the United States and has been used to guide its promotional efforts. Particular significance probably lies in the fact that the 29 per cent who favored encouraging imports from Japan also showed themselves better informed about Japanese goods than the other respondents. It is not clear to what extent knowing more about Japan has disposed people more favorably toward Japan and Japanese products or, conversely, to what extent favorable disposition leads to knowledge, but the positive correlation suggests strongly that promoters of Japanese goods have an opportunity among the 71 per cent who are not so well informed.

Japanese contacts with the American market have obviously been very rewarding during recent years. The rising volume of sales shows no signs of having yet exhausted the appetite of American consumers for Japanese products. In fact, the evidence of American ignorance about Japanese products and Japanese ignorance about the American market suggests strongly that there is much room for further rapid expansion of Japanese sales in the United States, as Japanese and Americans overcome their ignorance. The main dangers that might interfere with such expansion are a severe check to American demand, such as would result from deep economic depression, and interference with sales by means of import barriers. The former, like war, remains a hazard, although, unlike war, it is something the United States government has the power to deal with by domestic means. In any case, what the United States government does, or fails to do, about recessions will be only incidentally, if at all, influenced by the progress of Japanese sales in the American market. Quite the contrary is true of what may be done about import barriers.

AMERICAN POLICY TOWARD IMPORTS FROM JAPAN

As in virtually every foreign market, Japanese goods entering the United States must not only overcome ordinary business and consumer resistance but also hurdle barriers erected by governmental action. The tariffs, quotas, and other import restrictions sought by American producers as a defense against foreign competition are much feared by Japanese exporters.

For three decades now, American commercial policy has aimed at the reduction of barriers to international trade, thus modifying the protectionism that has marked much of American history, especially the early 1930s. Since 1934 Congress has delegated much power over the tariff to the President, and rates of duty have been substantially lowered. American law and policy make it possible, however, to maintain and impose very severe restrictions even without new legislative action (and, of course, Congress retains the constitutional power to intervene at any time and impose new barriers). Nevertheless, neither protectionist pressures nor legal possibilities have led to many sharp new limitations on imports from Japan since the end of the war. Indeed, Japanese goods have received far more liberal treatment in the United States than in any other of Japan's major export markets, with the exception of Hong Kong (and possibly Canada, p. 195). The Japanese are by no means confident that this liberality will continue in the face of recurrent campaigns against their goods by American employers and labor unions.

Past Treatment of Japanese Goods

As the leader of the mid-nineteenth-century effort by Western nations to open Japan to foreign trade, the United States would have been most inconsistent to place severe limits on imports of Japanese goods. Nor was there much of a problem until Japan began to offer manufactured goods for export. Most of what Japan sold here did not for some time compete with American products. Raw silk, which still made up more than half of the total even in the 1930s, has always been on the free list, as have tea, pyrethrum, and a few other Japanese products. During the depressed decade before the attack on Pearl Harbor, however, Japanese manufactured goods began to press more strongly on the American market, led by cotton textiles, toys, and miscellaneous products, many of them very cheap and often of low quality. The Hawley-Smoot tariff of 1930 had raised duties on a number of these products, and further restrictive steps were taken during the 1930s.[11] During the depression it was easy to call up the specter of cheap Japanese goods flooding the market.

The Reciprocal Trade Agreements program, inaugurated in 1934, reduced tariff rates progressively through bilateral agreements. No agree-

[11] In discussing the tariffs raised by many countries against Japanese goods in the 1930s, William W. Lockwood went so far as to say: "In the United States, for example, as quickly as cheap manufactures from Japan offered any competitive threat to even a small segment of an American industry, they were apt to be shut off promptly." *The Economic Development of Japan* (Princeton University Press, 1954), p. 542.

ment was made with the increasingly militaristic government of Japan, but through the workings of the most-favored-nation provision Japanese goods entered the United States at the reduced rates negotiated with other countries. It was American policy in those days to extend these concessions to almost all countries; moreover, under the 1911 Treaty of Commerce with Japan the United States had an obligation to grant most-favored-nation treatment to Japanese goods. Nevertheless, because of the way products were selected and defined in making tariff concessions, Japan's benefits from the program were kept to a minimum.[12] In January 1940, U.S. denunciation of the commercial treaty became effective, and a period of economic warfare preceded the Japanese attack on Pearl Harbor in December 1941.

Since September 1945 Japanese goods have continuously received most-favored-nation treatment in the United States. This means that many Japanese products have come in at much lower rates than in the 1930s, since American tariffs have been greatly reduced in the postwar period, mostly by tariff bargaining. Price increases have also reduced the burden of specific duties. This has had significance for Japan because silk and other free-list exports gave way to manufactured goods, mostly competitive and subject to import duty. Whereas in the years 1934–1936 only 31 per cent of U.S. imports from Japan were dutiable, the percentage in 1960 was 93.[13] In addition to the reduced rates applied under the most-favored-nation clause, Japan benefited from duty reductions on its products made in direct tariff bargaining with the United States under the General Agreement on Tariffs and Trade (GATT) (pp. 258–259). How much the lower tariff rates may have contributed to the sharp increases in Japanese sales to the United States in the middle and late 1950s is a matter not yet satisfactorily analyzed.

Article 12 of the peace treaty obliged Japan to grant, for four years, most-favored-nation treatment to each of the Allies that gave such treatment to Japan. That left it up to each Allied government to decide what to do. The United States granted Japan most-favored-nation treatment and proceeded to negotiate a new Treaty of Friendship, Commerce and Navigation which became effective in the fall of 1953.[14] In the same year,

[12] In 1940, Tariff Commissioner Manuel Fox said: ". . . I do not know of any country that has received as little direct benefit from the trade agreements as Japan. Not more than 3 per cent of our imports from Japan have received the benefit of concessions granted in the trade agreements." *Extension of Reciprocal Trade Agreements Act,* Hearings before the House Committee on Ways and Means, 76th Cong., 3d sess., on H. J. Res. 407 (Washington: GPO, 1940), p. 629.

[13] U.S. Department of Commerce, Bureau of Foreign Commerce.

[14] Signed in Tokyo, April 2, 1953, entered into effect October 30, 1953. U.S. Department of State, *Treaties and International Acts Series,* 2863 (Washington: GPO, 1954). The history of American Japanese commercial treaties begins with the one negotiated by Perry and signed in 1854. Three years later a commercial and consular treaty was signed that had been negotiated by Townsend Harris. His

under U.S. sponsorship Japan became a provisional member of GATT. During the first half of 1955 Japan and 17 Contracting Parties carried on bilateral tariff negotiations, preparatory to Japan's accession to full membership, which went into effect on September 10, 1955. Although some other countries invoked Article 35 to withhold some of the benefits of GATT from Japan (p. 233), the United States treated her as a full member from the beginning.

Concessions to Japan as a Member of GATT

In the 1955 GATT negotiations the United States reduced its tariffs on a number of Japanese goods. Their import value in 1953 was $81 million, 31 per cent of total imports from Japan in that year. In addition the United States bound its existing tariff treatment of a number of goods, that is, agreed not to raise the duty on them or take them off the free list. Imports of these bound goods in 1953 came to $53 million, 20 per cent of U.S. imports from Japan. Altogether, therefore, half of what Japan had sold in the United States in 1953 benefited from the new tariff concessions.

Reductions of duty, running from very small amounts to 50 per cent, were granted on, among other things, herring, mandarin oranges, chinaware, simple microscopes, prism binoculars, Christmas tree bulbs, rattan and related manufactures, pearls, toys, silk fabrics, gloves, some footwear, certain rubber manufactures, and certain cotton manufactures. The last included cotton velveteens,[15] cotton towels of certain types,[16]

principal treaty, proclaimed in 1860, superseded the 1857 treaty and part of Perry's treaty. The Treaty of Commerce and Navigation proclaimed in 1895 replaced all that had gone before and itself gave way in 1911 to another treaty which remained in force until January 1940, six months after the U.S. had denounced it. Texts of these treaties and of related conventions and other documents are published in William M. Malloy, compiler, *Treaties, Conventions, International Acts, Protocols and Agreements between the United States of America and Other Powers*, v. 1, Senate Document No. 357, 61st Cong., 2d sess. (Washington: GPO, 1910), pp. 996–1047; v. 3, Senate Document No. 348, 67th Cong., 4th sess. (Washington: GPO, 1923), pp. 2712–2728.

[15] The Department of State called the reduction on velveteens "very moderate." On plain-back velveteens the rate was reduced from 31¼ per cent to 25 per cent ad valorem. On twill-back velveteens the rate had been 25 cents a square yard with a minimum of 22½ per cent and a maximum of 44 per cent equivalent ad valorem; the only change was to lower the maximum to 30 per cent. Despite these reductions American producers later received increased protection as a result of the Treasury's decision, effective January 14, 1955, prohibiting the entry of velveteen as waterproof fabric (at 12½ per cent ad valorem) unless designed to afford protection against water to the extent expected in raincoats. Much of the import of velveteen before then had entered as waterproof fabric. U.S. Department of State, *General Agreement on Tariffs and Trade: Analysis of Protocol (including Schedules) for Accession of Japan; Analysis of Renegotiations of Certain Tariff Concessions Negotiated at Geneva, Switzerland, February–June 1955*, Publication 5881, Commercial Policy Series 150 (Washington: GPO, 1955), p. 70.

[16] Other than of pile fabrics. On Jacquard-figured towels the reduction was from 22½ cents a pound, with a maximum of 35 per cent and a minimum of 20 per cent

certain types of cotton cloth, mostly of low count, and several other categories of cotton manufactures. The cotton cloth concession applied to that 10 per cent of total United States cotton cloth imports in 1953 for which no trade agreement concessions had previously been made in negotiations with other exporting countries.[17] The other cotton manufactures included table damask, cotton blankets, sheets and pillowcases, table and bureau covers, etc., various kinds of wearing apparel, floor coverings, fish nets, etc.[18]

Bindings at existing duty rates affected principally fresh or frozen swordfish, canned tuna in brine, crab meat, more expensive microscopes, and sewing machines of popular types. Bindings in duty-free status applied mainly to raw silk, silk waste, fresh and frozen tuna, scallops (except fresh), certain oysters, and certain other shellfish.

During the GATT negotiations the United States made small additional concessions to third countries to induce them to grant concessions on Japanese goods. In return for these, as well as for concessions made directly, Japan made tariff concessions to the United States. Another round of GATT tariff negotiations took place in Geneva during the first half of 1956. Japan received a few small concessions, both by direct negotiation with the United States and by application to Japan of U.S. concessions made to third countries; they applied to fish-liver oils, wood manufactures, certain floor coverings, hemmed or hemstitched silk handkerchiefs and woven mufflers, silk wearing apparel (except blouses), and certain paper and toys. Japan gave the United States concessions in return.[19]

During GATT tariff negotiations in 1961, the United States made only minor additional reductions.[20] During the earlier part of these negotia-

ad valorem, to a flat rate of 20 per cent ad valorem. The rate on these had previously been reduced under GATT from the Hawley-Smoot rate of 40 per cent. On "the more important" item, the non-Jacquard-figured towels, of which imports from Japan were significant (about $700,000 in 1954), the reduction was from 25 per cent to 20 per cent ad valorem. Same, pp. 70–71.

[17] A series of cloth constructions are included, each with a different rate and rate reduction. These items fall in paragraph 904 of the tariff classification. Most of the reductions were in the neighborhood of 25 per cent. Same, pp. 69–70 and 93–94.

[18] Rate reductions varied from about 11 per cent to the 50 per cent maximum reduction allowed under the Trade Agreements Act, as amended to that time. Same, pp. 94–97.

[19] U.S. Department of State, *General Agreement on Tariffs and Trade: Analysis of United States Negotiations: Sixth Protocol (including Schedules) of Supplementary Concessions, Negotiated at Geneva, Switzerland, January–May 1956,* Publication 6348, Commercial Policy Series 158 (Washington: GPO, 1956), pp. 109 and 159.

[20] They affected imports from Japan amounting to $18.9 million in 1960. Bindings affected another $4.5 million. U.S. Department of State, *General Agreement on Tariffs and Trade: Analysis of United States Negotiations; Supplement to Vol. I: Concessions Exchanged with Japan; 1960–61 Tariff Conference, Geneva, Switzerland* (Washington: Author, 1961), p. 1.

tions, Japan renegotiated—upward—certain concessions formerly given, mainly on soybeans and polyethylene, and in return granted new concessions on a number of products, including bourbon whiskey, fountain pens, and wheel tractors.[21] Several factors help explain the relative meagerness of these results. Japan was prosperous as never before but disinclined to reduce tariffs. In fact there was pressure to raise them to counter the increase in competitive imports that would otherwise tend to result from the removal of quantitative restrictions under the liberalization program (p. 139). In the United States, enough imports had entered in the late 1950s to stir up a good deal of protectionist feeling. Slackness in the U.S. economy and deficit in the balance of payments restrained tariff cutting. The Kennedy Administration had not yet formulated its new trade policy and the President had only limited bargaining power left under the old legislation.

The President's Power to Lower or Raise Tariffs

In reducing the tariff on Japanese goods the President has been using authority originally granted him in the Trade Agreements Act of 1934. By the late 1950s the President's powers were circumscribed and the amount by which a duty could be cut was rather small. Before tariff concessions could be negotiated extensive public hearings were required, providing a forum for all those opposed to reductions in rates. The principle that tariff concessions should not seriously injure domestic producers was written into the law and endorsed by a whole series of policy statements. Before negotiations the Tariff Commission was required to determine a "peril point" below which a duty could not be reduced "without causing or threatening serious injury to the domestic industry producing like or directly competitive articles."[22] If the President wished to ignore the Tariff Commission's findings and make a larger concession, he was required to explain his action to Congress. If a concession already made led to such a flow of imports as to cause or threaten serious injury, the "escape clause" could be invoked. The Tariff Commission then investigated complaints of injury, with power to recommend that the President withdraw, suspend, or modify the concession, raise the tariff to a maximum of 50 per cent above the high Hawley-Smoot rate, or impose new restrictions, including import quotas or tariffs up to 50 per cent ad valorem on articles not otherwise subject to duty. Should the President not accept the Tariff Commission's recommendation for an increase in

[21] Same, *Vol. II: Compensatory Renegotiations,* pp. 31–33; U.S. Department of State, Press Release No. 206, "Renegotiation of Certain Tariff Concessions by Japan," April 12, 1961. It is customary for a GATT member country that withdraws or reduces a concession to compensate the principal exporting country with new concessions, duly negotiated.

[22] Sec. 3, par. (a), *Trade Agreements Extension Act of 1951* (65 Stat. 72).

import restrictions, he was required to explain to Congress, which could overrule him. Imports could also be restricted in the interests of national defense.

The Trade Expansion Act of 1962 significantly altered a number of these provisions but left the President with power to increase restrictions. It also granted him broad new authority to reduce tariffs by agreement with foreign countries. In general the amount of reduction permitted was 50 per cent of the level on July 1, 1962. In three cases, however, the President is empowered to go further and even eliminate duties altogether: products on which the rate of duty is already 5 per cent or less, tropical products, and products on which 80 per cent or more of free world exports is accounted for by the United States and the European Economic Community together. This last provision, by far the most important of the three, was written on the assumption that Britain—and probably other nations as well—would become members of the European Economic Community.[23] General de Gaulle's veto of January 1963 made it unlikely that Britain would become a member of the EEC for some time. Unless the Trade Expansion Act is amended, the provisions for complete tariff removal will apply to few manufactured products. Still, there will be room for a good deal of tariff cutting, under the 50 per cent provision, in bargaining by the United States with a smaller EEC and with Britain, Canada, and Japan as well. Since the United States will apply the most-favored-nation clause to its concessions, Japan has a direct interest in the whole range of these negotiations.

The President's ability to cut tariffs is limited in a number of ways by the new Act, and he retains discretion to withhold products from tariff bargaining. If Congress wishes to reverse his rejections of recommendations by the Tariff Commission to raise barriers, only a simple majority of the full membership of each house is required in contrast to the former requirement of two-thirds of those present. The peril-point

[23] In that case a large number of manufactured goods would have qualified for tariff removal, including the following broad categories of considerable interest to Japan: photographic and cinematographic supplies, except cameras; glass; metal-working machinery; road vehicles, except motor; agricultural machinery, including tractors; musical instruments, sound recorders, and parts; power-generating machinery, except electric; miscellaneous chemicals, including plastics and insecticides; materials of rubber; office machinery; industrial machinery, except power-generating and metal-working; articles of rubber; electrical machinery. The sample list was prepared by the Department of Commerce on the basis of 1960 statistics. Britain, Norway, Denmark, Ireland, and Greece were added to the Six to determine the Community's exports. (Testimony of Secretary of Commerce Luther M. Hodges, in *Trade Expansion Act of 1962,* Hearings before the Senate Committee on Finance, 87th Cong., 2d sess. (Washington: GPO, 1962), p. 45.) Trade within the enlarged Community and within the Communist bloc was not included in the global total. As passed, the law also called for omission from the calculation of all trade between Communist countries and the rest of the world.

and escape-clause rules have been altered in ways that may give the President more freedom of action than he had before, especially if an important innovation of the 1962 legislation proves effective: readjustment assistance.

This provision would provide help to firms and workers injured by increased imports resulting from tariff concessions. This is the first formal recognition by the United States that it may be in the national interest to sacrifice domestic production to imports in some cases because of the greater advantages to be gained by permitting trade than by protecting producers who cannot survive in open competition. This is a crucial principle in international trade. If this new provision of law is used to increase tariff reductions by the United States then the chances are good that foreign tariff reductions will also be larger.

This principle is important for Japan because it promises to enlarge the opportunities for Japanese exports, both in the United States and in other countries where import barriers may be lowered. But the principle is important also in putting the Japanese on notice that their country too will be asked to admit competing goods that may injure domestic producers. As long as the United States has held to the philosophy of not permitting increased imports to injure domestic production, the American voice in international trade and tariff discussions has been muffled and American bona fides in calling for lower tariffs and increased world trade have been subject to some doubt. If readjustment assistance makes it possible for the United States to permit substantially more competitive imports than would otherwise be acceptable, then it will help not only foreign countries but also American exports and contribute to the potential influence of the United States for further world trade liberalization.

With regard to Japan, American acceptance of the idea of adjustment may be especially important in relation to the escape clause and other devices that have been used to check imports after tariffs have been lowered. The Japanese are highly sensitive to these qualifications to the American commitment and show a great deal of nervousness about them. While the escape clause remains in the new legislation, acceptance of the idea of adjustment would imply a different use of it from that of the past, and one much more welcome to the Japanese.

All in all, the Trade Expansion Act of 1962 is a strong mandate to the President to lower import barriers and, in so doing, to induce foreign countries to do likewise. To follow the mandate will not be easy. It will require vigorous leadership, not only to set a new direction but to carry through a long series of specific measures, some of them politically difficult.

AMERICAN REACTION TO RAPIDLY INCREASING IMPORTS FROM JAPAN

The setting in which most of the debate about American trade restriction has taken place is one of a great flow of imports from Japan. In each year, 1954 through 1960, Japanese sales in the United States rose, both in absolute value and also in relation to imports from other countries. There was a small decline in 1961 and a sharp rise again in 1962. As the figures in Table 8-2 show,[24] Japan's share of U.S. imports rose from 2.1 per cent in 1952 to 8.3 per cent in 1962. In 1952 twelve other countries sold more in the United States than Japan did, but in the early 1960s only Canada exceeded Japan as a source of U.S. imports.

Every item and group listed in Table 8-2 shared in the great increase from 1952 to 1962 with the single exception of raw silk. The rates of growth are phenomenal in many cases and are greatest, of course, for the late-comers, which scarcely appeared in the statistics for earlier years. Of the major categories of imports shown, machinery increased the most—to 23 times the 1952 volume—led by radios and parts. Rubber manufactures also rose phenomenally, especially rubber footwear. Plywood, mandarin oranges, leather goods, and industrial chemicals, four very diverse items, had 1962 sales 20 to 50 times those of 1952. Miscellaneous manufactures, led by photographic equipment and toys, rose to nine times the starting level. Glassware sales were notable among nonmetallic mineral products. Textiles, the largest group, grew less rapidly than total exports, but includes a number of products that, as we shall see in Chapter 9, rose very rapidly indeed, at least for a while. Leading items were blouses and shirts among cotton articles, as well as woolen fabrics and wearing apparel of synthetics.

In addition to the increases shown in Table 8-2 there has also been a great expansion in sales of certain goods still sold in relatively small quantities and not appearing in the table. At the end of 1957, such products included: nails, automobiles, fireworks, cigarette lighters, watch bracelets, shovels, spades, scoops, photo and scrap albums, surface-coated or embossed paper, and body-support garments.[25]

[24] This table is based on American import statistics which would never exactly correspond, except by chance, with the Japanese export statistics on which Table 8-1 is based. Both tables record values f.o.b. port of departure, but the delay of about a month between leaving Japan and arriving in the United States and the varying systems of classification prevent exact correspondence. Further divergence is caused by transshipments and by delays in entry through customs as a result of storage in customs bond, sometimes for months on end.

[25] This listing comes from a valuable collection of statistics on specific items imported into the United States from Japan in the years 1954 through 1957, in a report prepared by the United States–Japan Trade Council for the use of the Japa-

TABLE 8-2. UNITED STATES IMPORTS FROM JAPAN, 1952–1962

(In millions of dollars, f.o.b. Japan)

Commodity	1952	1953	1954	1955	1956	1957	1958	1959	1960	1961	1962	1962 as Multiple of 1952
Foodstuffs	**28.8**	**44.3**	**47.1**	**48.9**	**61.8**	**68.3**	**72.6**	**88.1**	**79.1**	**81.2**	**95.6**	**3**
Fish, including shellfish	23.1	37.5	40.5	42.6	54.2	59.6	64.5	75.7	64.1	64.0	76.2	3
Tuna	14.0	24.0	30.4	29.1	27.4	30.8	37.3	38.7	37.0	39.6	49.6	4
Crabmeat	2.2	4.0	2.9	4.7	5.3	6.2	6.1	7.9	5.5	5.8	4.7	2
Mandarin oranges, canned	0.35	1.2	0.8	1.7	2.4	2.7	2.2	5.8	6.8	8.2	9.1	26
Animal and vegetable products, inedible	**13.1**	**13.9**	**14.4**	**17.0**	**16.9**	**20.9**	**35.8**	**82.0**	**125.0**	**106.7**	**118.3**	**9**
Leather, rawhide, and parchment manufactures	0.88	1.1	1.1	2.8	3.7	5.3	10.2	15.3	19.3	22.8	35.7	41
Leather footwear	0.88	1.1	1.1	2.1	2.4	2.7	6.2	6.2	6.7	8.8	12.4	14
Rubber manufactures	1.2	1.7	1.4	1.8	2.1	4.5	13.1	54.0	94.1	72.8	66.9	56
Rubber footwear						2.6	8.3	39.1	76.8	58.1	45.2	17 [a]
Textile fibers and manufactures	**81.0**	**81.9**	**95.5**	**158.3**	**203.8**	**189.9**	**201.2**	**266.0**	**279.2**	**238.8**	**294.5**	**4**
Cotton manufactures	11.8	19.4	25.5	59.6	84.1	65.7	71.7	76.9	73.4	69.7	100.5	8
Wool manufactures	5.3	5.8	7.6	17.0	30.5	34.4	41.5	55.6	67.6	57.2	67.5	13
Woolen fabrics	0.23	0.4	1.3	4.8	10.2	13.6	19.1	18.1	24.9	22.7	31.6	137
Wool wearing apparel	3.6	3.5	3.6	6.6	14.3	14.5	13.9	21.5	22.4	14.6	14.7	4
Carpets and carpeting	1.4	1.9	2.6	5.4	5.7	6.2	7.9	15.1	19.6	19.1	21.0	15
Silk and manufactures	54.1	43.7	45.8	57.0	62.6	61.8	55.2	77.8	75.6	59.1	62.1	1
Raw silk	30.3	23.4	27.2	31.8	30.2	23.0	13.4	21.8	20.5	19.5	16.0	1
Silk manufactures	21.6	18.8	18.0	23.6	30.1	36.7	40.5	54.1	49.6	34.3	37.5	2
Synthetic fibers and manufactures	1.7	2.8	3.7	6.3	7.0	8.6	11.2	29.0	33.5	27.6	35.9	21
Wearing apparel of synthetics	0.53	1.2	2.0	4.3	4.5	5.7	6.3	17.6	19.0	13.6	13.1	25
Wood and paper	**10.4**	**19.2**	**32.3**	**52.2**	**65.9**	**73.5**	**77.4**	**108.7**	**97.3**	**85.3**	**101.3**	**10**
Plywood	1.1	6.9	16.7	27.6	33.9	44.4	44.2	59.3	50.3	44.0	53.7	49
Nonmetallic mineral products	**18.1**	**19.6**	**23.1**	**30.7**	**42.2**	**44.8**	**55.3**	**70.7**	**83.5**	**79.6**	**91.2**	**5**
Glass and glass products	2.1	2.0	2.0	3.6	6.6	5.4	6.5	11.1	11.4	12.7	13.3	6
Glassware	1.9	1.9	1.8	2.4	4.6	4.5	4.2	5.4	5.7	6.8	7.4	4

Clay and clay products	12.1	13.3	16.4	20.3	26.8	29.0	31.4	40.7	50.3	41.6	49.7	4
Chinaware	4.8	5.1	6.7	7.6	9.1	9.8	10.6	12.4	13.4	12.1	15.1	3
Floor and wall tiles						1.5	2.6	5.6	8.6	9.4	13.5	9 [a]
Pearls and parts, not strung or set	3.4	3.8	4.3	6.2	7.9	9.4	10.3	13.0	13.8	16.2	18.3	5
Metals and manufactures	**45.0**	**43.0**	**18.9**	**45.2**	**70.9**	**77.5**	**95.4**	**173.2**	**191.8**	**171.0**	**248.9**	**6**
Steel-mill products	29.6	21.4	3.2	13.1	10.0	7.8	30.6	83.4	90.8	86.4	146.3	5
Jewelry and precious metals	6.2	6.3	6.4	8.7	10.0	10.2	10.7	17.2	20.7	19.3	19.9	3
Machinery and vehicles	**10.3**	**10.0**	**9.7**	**16.4**	**23.6**	**39.4**	**56.7**	**116.4**	**143.3**	**176.8**	**238.6**	**23**
Electrical machinery, etc.	0.64	1.0	2.2	3.0	8.1	16.0	28.2	74.0	102.1	124.2	173.7	271
Radio apparatus and parts		0.008	0.017	0.23	2.5	6.0	16.0	55.2	71.4	85.0	98.3	11,988 [b]
Transistors									54.5	61.9	64.1	[c]
Sewing machines and parts	9.2	8.5	7.2	12.5	13.5	19.7	21.8	28.3	21.8	21.3	25.5	3
Chemicals and related products	**2.9**	**4.4**	**2.5**	**3.1**	**3.9**	**3.9**	**7.7**	**17.3**	**15.6**	**18.6**	**18.8**	**6**
Industrial chemicals	0.59	0.7	1.0	2.4	2.5	2.0	5.1	12.1	9.9	12.2	10.4	18
Miscellaneous manufactures	**17.0**	**23.5**	**32.6**	**43.7**	**58.8**	**83.9**	**72.0**	**95.6**	**111.7**	**118.0**	**146.0**	**9**
Photographic goods	1.5	1.5	1.2	2.6	5.1	8.9	8.6	10.1	14.4	17.2	24.2	16
Cameras				2.1	4.5	8.5	8.2	9.7	11.9	14.5	21.0	10 [d]
Scientific and professional instruments	4.4	4.6	4.6	6.4	7.6	9.8	11.8	14.5	16.5	15.3	17.2	4
Prism binoculars	3.0	2.8	2.7	4.5	4.8	5.6	5.6	6.1	5.9	4.9	5.4	2
Dolls, toys, and sporting goods	4.7	8.1	10.2	15.9	23.6	27.4	27.3	39.5	45.8	45.3	59.7	13
Total imports from Japan												
Imports for consumption	**226.6**	**259.7**	**276.1**	**415.7**	**547.5**	**602.2**	**674.0**	**1,018.0**	**1,126.5**	**1,075.9**	**1,353.2**	**6**
General imports	**229.3**	**261.5**	**279.0**	**431.9**	**557.9**	**600.5**	**670.8**	**1,028.7**	**1,148.7**	**1,054.7**	**1,357.6**	**6**
General imports as a percentage of total U.S. imports	2.1	2.4	2.7	3.8	4.4	4.6	5.2	6.8	7.6	7.2	8.3	4

[a] 1962/1957.
[b] 1962/1953.
[c] Not listed as such until 1960.
[d] 1962/1955.

Note: Where no import figure is shown, the item concerned was not then separately reported in trade statistics.

Source: U.S. Department of Commerce, Bureau of Foreign Commerce and Bureau of the Census.

American Producer Protest Against Japanese Goods

As might be expected, the most vigorous protests by American producers have been about the imports that increased fastest and about those that have captured a substantial share of the total U.S. market. Almost every item in Table 8-2 for which the figure in the last column is over 10, indicating a ninefold or larger increase in sales to the United States between 1952 and 1962, has been the object of public complaint, notably cotton textiles, woolen fabrics, plywood, and radios. Mandarin oranges are an exception. Although imports in canned form in 1962 were 26 times the 1952 level, the total is still small in the American market for citrus fruit, and no protests seem to have been made.[26]

There have also been complaints about a number of imports which have risen less markedly, such as tuna fish, binoculars, and sewing machines. Imports of these last two items had risen substantially by 1952 and the subsequent increase was proportionately not as great as that of other products. Other items that have caused protest are too small in total value to be included in the table.

The way the American system operates, protests by producers are the usual starting point for action to restrain imports. Producers' protests have, in part, a psychological or public-relations aim. The business group is calling attention to itself and its interests. Whatever the specific issues, the general theme of such appeals is virtually always the same: foreigners are harming an American industry by "unfair" competition based on low wages; it is the duty of the American nation and its leaders to limit or stop such foreign action. For example, here is the full text of an advertisement published in *The New York Times:*[27]

> OPEN LETTER TO: HON. DWIGHT D. EISENHOWER, PRESIDENT OF THE UNITED STATES, MEMBERS OF CONGRESS.
>
> SUBJECT: JAPANESE INVASION OF AMERICAN MARKETS.
>
> The umbrella frame and the umbrella industry in the United States respectfully invite your attention to the following facts which are vitally affecting our industries and all the people who work in our plants.

nese trade mission that visited the United States and Canada in the autumn of 1958. *Commodity Analysis of United States Imports from Japan, 1954–1957* (Washington: United States–Japan Trade Council, 1958; processed).

[26] Fresh mandarins, however, have been excluded by administrative action of the Department of Agriculture, which explained that it wanted to prevent introduction into the United States of a citrus plant disease. The Japanese have contended that Japanese mandarins do not involve any danger of this sort. Vigorous bargaining has been reported over the possibility of removing the Department of Agriculture prohibition in return for a Japanese *quid pro quo*. Information from the United States–Japan Trade Council, Washington, September 1962.

[27] September 20, 1959, sec. 3, p. 13. Underscoring in original; variations in type size not shown, however.

1. In 1958 the Tariff Commission, after full hearings, recommended that the tariff on umbrella frames be restored to the former 60%. The President rejected this recommendation.

2. In the past ten years imports of Japanese umbrellas and frames skyrocketed from a trickle to an avalanche. In 1958, Japan accounted for 60% of the United States market.

3. Based upon imports of umbrellas and umbrella frames for the first five months of 1959, 75% of the United States market will have fallen into the hands of the Japanese this year.

4. In 1954, there were six umbrella frame manufacturers in the United States. As a result of Japanese competition, three have gone out of business—there are only three left. During the same period many umbrella manufacturers have gone by the wayside. Hundreds of employees were left out of jobs. Why? American industry pays high wages while Japanese industry pays low wages, 10 cents to 15 cents an hour.

5. The flood into this country of Japanese goods, produced by very low cost labor, is menacing the very existence of many American industries.

You members of Congress are charged by the Constitution with the protection of American industry.

It is your duty—take no one's word—investigate . . . and then enact appropriate legislation.

We invite the management and labor of all threatened industries to join with us.

THE UMBRELLA FRAME ASSOCIATION OF AMERICA, INC.
ASSOCIATION OF UMBRELLA MANUFACTURERS AND SUPPLIERS, INC.
C/O MORTIMER EISNER, ESQ., 24 BRANFORD PLACE, NEWARK 2, NEW JERSEY

While the announced aim is usually to induce governmental action, the campaign of protest may have other, perhaps more immediate results. American customers or dealers may be persuaded to buy less of the imported goods (though there is also the danger of advertising their lower price). The widespread negative attitudes of Americans about Japanese products (pp. 253–255) were probably based in part on such complaints and on news stories in the same vein. The complaint may frighten the foreign producer or exporter, or the American importer, into holding down shipments. Sometimes the protest is primarily a call to action for the American producing interests involved, including the labor unions. Or it may serve as evidence that a trade association is vigorously pursuing the interests of its members.

As a call for governmental action, protests will stress the injury imports are supposedly doing to American producers, because proof of the allegation has a chance of bringing public assistance in the form of new restrictions on foreign goods. Usually the industry will try, by assertion or implication, to show that damage to itself also hurts the public interest. A reduction in prices resulting from imports will be viewed not as a benefit for the buyers or as a step to check inflation, but as a loss to the producers and therefore to the national economy. Foreign goods, it seems, are always "unfairly low-priced." National security may be invoked; then the contention is that the United States must be able to produce these goods within its borders in case foreign supplies should be cut off. Dependence on imports is regarded as weakness, as though a future war would create the shipping and other problems of the last one. Mutual economic dependence among allies is not an American interest that finds expression in industry protests.

Employment and wages are usually discussed without reference to the possibility that workers might find employment, perhaps at better pay, in another industry. In fact, many industry protests seem to be written by persons wholly innocent of the concept of comparative costs. Their logic is about as follows: Industry is good, since it gives employment and pays wages and profits (and produces usable articles); an industry is threatened; therefore the threat must be removed. Usually the assumption is made, but not expressed, that the only alternative to their present employment for the workers in question is economic disaster.[28] A lawyer representing a protesting American producer group wrote to me: "In the many years that I have been confronted with tariff problems, I have never yet been able to have explained to me how the U.S., with its high wage levels, social security and fringe benefits, can gain any advantage from opening its markets to a flood of imports produced at the low wage scale prevailing in many foreign countries."

When protests against imports recognize the possibility that American workers, management, and capital might move to other productive activity, they stress the difficulties and costs of such moves and usually go on to ask for governmental action to make them unnecessary. To be sure, it is not economically advantageous (to say nothing about noneconomic considerations) to permit production to be devastated by foreign competition without regard to the possibilities of alternative employment and the difficulties and costs of attempting rapid shifts in production and employment. The sound alternative will usually be not to resist the shift altogether but to find ways of spreading it over a period of time and perhaps of cushioning its impact by other measures.

It is, of course, quite proper in our system for producer groups, whether management or labor, to pursue their own interest by protesting against

[28] "American hardwood plywood producers just *can't* compete with imported plywood priced duty-paid at less than the cost of production of a comparable American panel—that is, not until our U.S. workers decide to work for Japanese wages. . . ." (Italics in original.) *Import of Foreign Plywood: What It Means to You and Your Family* (Washington: Hardwood Plywood Manufacturers Committee, 1957), p. 4.

imports from Japan or elsewhere. To be effective under escape-clause procedures, as they operated before enactment of the Trade Expansion Act of 1962, no broader appeals to national interest were necessary. In such actions the Tariff Commission was concerned only with whether the industry in question was being seriously injured or threatened with serious injury and, if so, what action to recommend. Its proposals for curtailing imports were judged by the same standards. "It is not within the Commission's functions to appraise the effects on foreign countries or on our international relations that might follow from the President's action upon the Commission's recommendations." [29] These matters were left to the President. Under the new law the standards to be applied by the Tariff Commission and the President are altered—for instance, injury is more narrowly defined and must be shown to result "in major part" from import competition—and the range of possible action has been broadened, by permitting the use of adjustment assistance, but it will remain true that the producer's aim will be to plead his own cause and claim it parallels the national interest.

In the voluminous literature of protest against competitive imports, foreign policy considerations have entered only recently, and there has not been much time for the deficit in the U.S. balance of payments to be used as an argument for protection. But some protesters are sophisticated enough to see that they must counter the argument that political relations with other countries require that the United States buy as well as sell goods. They speak then as if imports were a burden to be shared by the nation at large, like taxes or military service. According to this argument, it is unfair to make a few industries, especially weak ones that happen to be exposed to severe foreign competition, bear the whole burden; it should instead be borne in part by stronger industries.

That these protectionist arguments are in large part economically fallacious does not greatly weaken their political effectiveness. What is pertinent is that such views have widespread support and play a role in American policy. The no-injury principle is a monument to such ideas and has made the producer protests harder to resist than if the national welfare had a more prominent place in law and policy on foreign trade.

Escape-Clause Actions Against Japanese Goods

The effects of producer protests can be seen clearly in escape-clause investigations by the Tariff Commission.[30] Of the 131 escape-clause in-

[29] U.S. Tariff Commission, *Screen-Printed Silk Scarves*, Supplementary Report to the President on Escape-Clause Investigation No. 19 under the Provisions of Section 7 of the Trade Agreements Extension Act of 1951 (Washington: Author, 1954), p. 2.

[30] Section 7 of the Trade Agreements Extension Act of 1951, as amended, established a statutory escape-clause procedure. It provided that the Tariff Commission,

TABLE 8-3. MAJOR ESCAPE-CLAUSE INVESTIGATIONS CONCERNING JAPANESE GOODS, THROUGH JUNE 1962

Commodity	*Date Investigation Initiated*	*Japan's Rank as Supplier*	*Export Quota by Japan?*	*Tariff Commission Finding*	*Presidential Action*
Bonito and tuna, not in oil	Dec. 28, 1951	1		No injury	—
Screen-printed silk scarves	Aug. 25, 1952	1		Injury	Recommendation rejected
Wool gloves and mittens	Apr. 12, 1954	1		No injury	—
Hardwood plywood					
1st investigation	Sept. 16, 1954	1		No injury	—
2nd investigation	Jan. 5, 1959	1	Yes	No injury	—
Velveteen fabrics	Jan. 26, 1956	1	Yes	Injury	Recommendation rejected
Cotton blouses	Feb. 21, 1956	1	Yes	None [a]	—
Cotton pillowcases	Mar. 6, 1956	1	Yes	No injury	—
Certain cotton cloth (gingham)	June 12, 1956	1	Yes	None [a]	—
Toyo cloth caps	Apr. 5, 1957	1		None [b]	—
Stainless steel table flatware	Apr. 18, 1957	1	Yes	Injury	Tariff quota imposed, Nov. 1, 1959
Umbrella frames	Apr. 25, 1957	1		Injury	Recommendation rejected
Clinical thermometers	May 29, 1957	1		Injury	Tariff raised, May 21, 1958
Certain carpets and rugs [c]					
1st investigation	Jan. 22, 1958	2		No injury	—
2nd investigation	Feb. 13, 1961	2		Injury	Tariff raised, June 17, 1962
Hand-made glassware	Nov. 12, 1958	4 [d]		No injury	—
Cotton typewriter ribbon cloth	Jan. 11, 1960	3	Yes	Injury	Tariff raised, Sept. 22, 1960
Plastic raincoats [e]	Sept. 29, 1960	1	Yes	No injury	—
Tennis rackets [e]	Oct. 20, 1960	f		None [b]	—
Baseball and softball gloves [e]	Oct. 31, 1960	1	Yes	Injury threatened	Recommendation rejected
Ceramic tile [e]	Nov. 10, 1960	1	Yes	Injury	Recommendation rejected
Sheet glass [e,g]	Nov. 17, 1960	2		Injury	Tariff raised, June 17, 1962
Rolled glass [e]	Nov. 25, 1960	2		Split [h]	—
Umbrellas and umbrella frames	June 16, 1961	1		None [a]	—

[a] No finding by Commission; application withdrawn at applicant's request.
[b] Investigation terminated by the Commission without formal findings.
[c] The reports are entitled, "Wilton, Brussels, Velvet and Tapestry Carpets and Rugs."
[d] Although 4th in rank in terms of value, Japan was first in terms of quantity entered.
[e] Escape-clause action which was initiated as a consequence of "peril-point" determinations.
[f] Exact rank as supplier not known.
[g] The report is entitled, "Cylinder, Crown and Sheet Glass."
[h] Split decision among Tariff Commissioners; therefore no recommendation submitted to the President.

Sources: U.S. Tariff Commission, especially *Investigations under the "Escape Clause" of Trade Agreements* (10th ed.; Washington: Author, 1958; 14th ed., April 1961; preliminary statistics in 15th ed., March 1962), and individual reports on the escape-clause actions concerned.

vestigations completed or terminated by the Tariff Commission between 1947, when they began, and mid-1962, 24 cases involved Japan as a principal or significant supplier. Table 8-3 summarizes these investigations. During the fiscal year, ending June 1961, 9 out of 23 cases involved Japan as the principal or significant supplier. Six of these were not initiated by producer petition but as a result of "peril-point" investigations.[31] As compared with Japan's share of total U.S. imports, which had not reached 10 per cent even at its peak in 1962, Japan is a very prominent supplier of goods involved in escape-clause proceedings. In fact Japan's prominent position in 18 per cent of all cases is higher than the share of any other country. An increase in escape-clause investigations followed the sharp rise in imports from Japan in 1959. The commodities included in Table 8-3 range from items in which trade is very small, such as clinical thermometers and umbrellas, to leading Japanese export items, notably tuna fish, plywood, clothing, and cotton goods. In all but five of the cases listed, Japan was the principal supplier of imports, and in the case of household glassware Japan was the first supplier in quantity terms, although fourth in value terms.

In nine of the 24 investigations listed in the table the Tariff Commission found serious injury to American industry. In the case of baseball gloves and mitts, it found a threat of serious injury. Thus in a total of 10 out of 24 cases, the Tariff Commission recommended to the President that concessions granted to Japan be withdrawn or modified. The President acted to reduce imports—always by increasing tariffs—in only five cases: cotton typewriter ribbon cloth, clinical thermometers, stainless steel table flatware, certain carpets and rugs, and sheet glass. Before accepting the recommendations of the Tariff Commission on the last two cases, the President requested further study and investigation. The volume of trade in these five commodities amounted to approxi-

---

upon the request of the President, upon resolution of either House of Congress, upon resolution of either the Senate Committee on Finance or the House Committee on Ways and Means upon its own motion, or upon application by any interested party (including any organization or group of employees), must promptly conduct an investigation to determine whether any product on which a trade agreement concession had been granted was, as a result, in whole or in part, of the customs treatment reflecting such concession, being imported in such increased quantities, either actual or relative, as to cause or threaten serious injury to the domestic industry producing like or directly competitive products.

[31] These six investigations resulted from peril-point determinations in accordance with Section 3 of the Trade Agreements Extension Act of 1951 as amended in 1958, which provided that if in the course of any peril-point investigation the Tariff Commission found—with respect to any article on the President's list upon which a tariff concession had been granted—that an increase in duty or additional import restriction was required to avoid serious injury to the domestic industry producing like or directly competitive articles, the Commission must promptly institute an escape-clause investigation with respect to that article under the procedure of Section 7.

mately $22 million in 1960, or only 2 per cent of Japan's total exports to the United States in that year.

There were reports that in the case of clinical thermometers the President acted less out of deference to the domestic producers than to give a small sop to other protectionist forces, which were chafing at their lack of success in escape-clause actions. The economic stakes in this case were small. Imports of unfinished clinical thermometers (blanks), the chief kind imported, came to $82,000 in 1955, $268,000 in 1956, and $136,000 in the first half of 1957. In 1956, the only year for which such information is available, about six-sevenths of the imports came from Japan. Domestic production of blanks was estimated at $1,250,000 in 1956.[32] By withdrawing the tariff concession the President doubled the duty from 42½ per cent to 85 per cent ad valorem. Japanese export quotas—some of them imposed to avoid American import restrictions—have influenced the outcome of some escape-clause actions. When the President in January 1957 rejected the Tariff Commission's recommendation that imports of velveteen be restricted, he referred to the Japanese export quotas. In March 1962, in the cases involving baseball gloves and mitts and ceramic tile, the President stated in his letter to Congress that the decision against raising tariffs was in part determined by the voluntary quotas on exports established by the Japanese manufacturers. Because Japan imposed quotas on exports of cotton blouses and gingham cloth, these proceedings were dropped before the Tariff Commission made any finding of injury. Its report on plywood, where no injury was found, mentioned the Japanese export quota.

Thus the full impact of escape-clause actions upon Japanese imports into the U.S. market cannot be judged solely by the formal decisions of the President. Investigations involving 22 commodities resulted in five restrictive actions by the United States and 10 by Japan (counting stainless flatware in both lists). Additional commodities have been subjected to Japanese export quotas, as indicated in Table 7-10, without any formal escape-clause action having first been started in the United States. This interrelation of Japanese and American restrictions is one of the significant peculiarities of trade relations between the two countries and one which raises some key long-run policy problems that will be discussed in Chapter 10.

[32] Japan supplied $232,144 and Mexico $35,979 in 1956. U.S. Tariff Commission, *Clinical Thermometers, Finished or Unfinished,* Report to the President on Escape-Clause Investigation No. 63, under the Provisions of Section 7 of the Trade Agreements Extension Act of 1951, as Amended (Washington: Author, 1958), Tables 8 and 9.

Other Moves to Limit Imports from Japan

Those Americans who want to limit imports from Japan have called for more and different kinds of restrictions. National security is often invoked, although the only use of the national security clause of the Trade Agreements Act (left unchanged in the Trade Expansion Act of 1962) has been to impose an import quota on crude oil. The textile industry invoked this clause unsuccessfully when it called for extensive import quotas in May 1961 (p. 336). The operation of the Buy American Act has sometimes made it impossible for foreign suppliers to sell certain equipment to the American government, on grounds of security. But in one case the Panama Canal Company was authorized in 1960 to award a contract for towing locomotives to a Japanese firm because the OCDM held that this would not damage national security.[33] Using the discretion granted it under Buy American rules, the Bureau of Reclamation in August 1960 accepted only one of three low bids for turbines by Hitachi, Ltd., a leading Japanese firm. The public explanation was that the "interests of the Bureau" would not be served by simultaneous award of three large contracts to the same foreign firm pending demonstration that the technical standards set in the Bureau's specifications could be met satisfactorily.[34]

A whole series of actions affecting Japan have been undertaken in the field of customs administration. Some of these have protective results, and often protective purposes, at least on the part of some of the interests involved. Tariff classification by act of Congress has also been used to raise duties on Japanese goods. For instance, in September 1958 certain footwear from Japan, containing both rubber and leather, was transferred from the classification at the lower rates applying to leather shoes to that for rubber-soled shoes, which carried a higher tariff. An earlier case affecting velveteens has been mentioned above.

The Antidumping Act has been invoked against Japan without much success. After a protracted investigation the Treasury decided in December 1955 that Japanese plywood was not being dumped.[35] In a series of cases involving imports of wire rods from a number of countries, the Treasury held that there was dumping from Western Europe but not Japan while the Tariff Commission took the view that the main source of damage to the domestic industry was the large quantity of cheap (but not dumped) wire rods from Japan, not the smaller amounts

[33] *The New York Times,* May 12, 1960. The OCDM (Office of Civil and Defense Mobilization) became the Office of Emergency Planning in September 1961.

[34] "Reclamation Awards Contracts for Turbines for Four Powerplants," U.S. Department of Interior, *Information Service,* Press Release, August 12, 1960.

[35] *The New York Times,* December 22, 1955; *International Financial News Survey* (IMF), January 20, 1956, p. 227.

dumped by Europe, so no antidumping action was taken. Even so, antidumping procedures can be something of a deterrent to Japanese exports. They raise the costs and increase the risks of foreign trade.

In addition to administrative measures and legal proceedings, congressional action is a possibility that attracts those who want to reduce imports from Japan. There has always been some congressional support for increased tariffs, import quotas, or other forms of restriction. Cotton textiles have frequently been the subject of sympathetic attention on Capitol Hill. Plywood, tuna, and screws have also been subjects of bills in Congress aimed at checking imports from Japan. But submission of a bill or delivery of a speech in Congress, even the holding of lengthy committee hearings, does not necessarily lead to legislation, and in recent years Congress has not often or seriously interfered with the power delegated to the Executive in the Trade Agreements Act.

HOW SERIOUS ARE THE BARRIERS?

What is the net effect of all these measures, and threats of measures, on imports into the United States from Japan? The usual Japanese view is that the barriers are serious, actually and potentially. It has long been assumed by many Japanese that the United States simply would never accept enough Japanese goods to meet all Japan's reasonable needs for dollars. The word "boycott" is frequently used, undoubtedly reminding older Japanese of genuine boycotts encountered in China before 1937 and in the United States during the years just before the attack on Pearl Harbor. Other Asians have at times expressed the same pessimistic view of the American readiness to accept Japanese goods.[36]

Japan's expectations—or at best fears—of being rebuffed in the American market have many and varied manifestations. Japanese headlines proclaiming a move by an American interest to restrict imports from Japan are frequent, prominent, and in many cases so worded as to suggest that the proposed restriction is almost a fact. Japanese businessmen, officials, and university economists show a remarkable awareness of protectionist moves in the United States, but often fail to show equal understanding of the procedures necessary before demands can result in actual import restrictions. For example the following statement comes from a report of the Bank of Tokyo:

> . . . Japanese exports to the United States are mostly light industrial products, the greater part of which are manufactured by medium and small

[36] For example, the following statement is taken from *Pakistan Horizon*, September 1958, p. 186. "The United States, in spite of its being a large export-import market for Japan, is too tariff-conscious and protectionist to offer a satisfactory outlet to Japan's industries, especially its textiles."

> industries that are competing with each other. Therefore, these export products are featured by the instability of prices and sudden rush of certain lines into the United States market. Because of this the interests in the United States are pursued by uneasiness, and accordingly any advance in Japanese exports to that country poses a grave threat to their livelihood, causing them to launch movements to restrict imports from Japan. A survey by the Japanese Embassy in the United States reveals that export items amounting to 65 per cent of the total value of Japanese exports to the United States in 1957 have met with or are facing American movements to restrict imports from Japan, and that other commodities equal to 10 per cent of the total value are likely to experience such movements.[37]

When a draft of Table 8-3 was shown to an official of the Ministry of International Trade and Industry in December 1959 with a query as to whether Japanese understood how few escape-clause applications had actually resulted in increased restrictions against Japanese goods, the reply was about as follows: "But the record of recent years is no guarantee about the future, and we are afraid of what American protectionists are planning right now." This remark was made at the end of a year when Japanese sales in the United States had risen by the extraordinary figure of 50 per cent, to exceed a billion dollars for the first time.

How justified are such Japanese fears? And how seriously do U.S. import barriers impede Japanese export growth? The evidence of this chapter is that Japanese fears are greatly exaggerated. Formal import barriers are only one of a number of factors limiting Japanese sales in the American market, and yet these sales have been booming phenomenally. This does not sound like a "boycott" or provide grounds for gloom about the future. Rather, when the sharp rise since 1952 is viewed along with evidence of the expanding ability of Japanese goods to compete on grounds of quality as well as price, the very limited formal restrictive steps taken thus far, the vast numbers of Americans not yet aware of the bargains that many Japanese products represent, the rudimentary character of much Japanese marketing activity, as well as the continued growth of the American economy, there seems to be ample room for further rapid expansion of Japanese sales here in the years ahead.

The question arises again: how much do Japanese export quotas hold back trade? As we saw in the preceding chapter (p. 235), available information about the quotas and about movements of quota items is insufficient for a detailed answer. According to Japanese estimates, 40 per cent of exports to the United States were subject to quantitative control at the end of 1962. American estimates put the figure a bit lower, about a third of the total. But these quotas have not by any means stifled trade expansion, as Table 8-2 shows. The sharp increases in American

[37] Bank of Tokyo, *Semiannual Report,* October 1958–March 1959, cited, p. 34.

purchases of Japanese goods during the past decade have applied to every product listed in that table, except for raw silk, which was not subjected to export restraint. In fact, all but one of the major categories and two-thirds of the individual items showed all-time records in 1962. One can therefore reach some general conclusions about the effects of Japanese export quotas. They have certainly not kept sales down to low levels. What quotas have done in the main is to slow down sales expansion. How great the retarding effect has been we do not know, except in the case of cotton textiles, which will be discussed in the chapter that follows. In that case, and perhaps in others as well, a rising level was caused to drop, after which further sales growth was held back by quotas. For all or most other quota products, however, the allowed volume has expanded more nearly in pace with the growth of demand.

Altogether, the record of Japanese sales in the United States since the peace treaty went into effect in 1952 does not justify Japanese fears of American reluctance or refusal to take large and growing quantities of Japanese goods. So far, aside from cotton textiles, the articles whose sale in the United States has been restricted by either Japan or the United States do not comprise a large part of total Japanese sales here, and the restrictions have not been severe. The American bite, in the form of trade restrictions, has been far less severe than the bark of American producers protesting against imports.

The fact is that Americans are buying Japanese goods of more and more kinds and in progressively (even if irregularly) rising quantities. New products are finding satisfied customers. A few years ago cameras and binoculars, then blouses and plywood forced themselves on our attention because of sales successes. Then it was woolen cloth, then radios, then men's suits. There has been trouble about some of these products, but one of the most interesting developments has been the decision by some producers to import Japanese machinery for making cotton goods. A mill in North Carolina was equipped with spinning machinery made in Japan. "It's beautiful stuff," said the mill superintendent. "We're getting better quality yarn, and we're saving labor." The same manufacturer in Osaka sold equipment to one of the larger American manufacturers—Berkshire Hathaway—who wanted to test it to keep up with advancing technology. Then it was announced that the Saco-Lowell Shops of the Maremont Corporation had obtained from Toyobo-Showa Textile Engineering Company, Ltd., a license to manufacture a continuous automated spinning system for the manufacture of cotton yarn.[38]

The purchase of Japanese machinery by American manufacturers is

[38] *Time,* September 12, 1960, p. 102; *The New York Times,* January 5, 1961; *New York Herald Tribune,* March 7, 1962 (cited in *Harvard Business Review,* March–April 1963, p. 89).

an interesting and probably hopeful development. Still the cotton textile story is a disturbing one in several ways. Here is a case where a major Japanese industry's sales expansion has been effectively choked off by quantitative restrictions, despite past strong American objections to the use of such restrictions. If this pattern of restrictions were to spread, Japan's export prospects would darken rapidly, not only in the United States but in all markets to which the restrictionist policies spread. Because of its significance for many policy questions, the case of cotton textiles will be examined in the next chapter.

Chapter 9

Cotton Textiles in Japanese–American Relations

Cotton textiles, for years Japan's leading export to the United States, have caused friction between the two countries far beyond what the actual volume of trade might suggest. Out of this friction have come trade restrictions that are central to the economic relations of the two countries and that are being extended to other products, and other countries. On the future of these restrictions and the policies behind them may depend, to an important degree, the development of political and economic relations between Japan and the United States. Moreover, the Japanese–American experience raises questions about United States policy toward newly industrializing countries of the world and, indeed, about the policies of other advanced countries toward Japan and toward the developing countries. Though more than cotton textiles are involved, a case study of that important industry will clarify some of the issues.

THE JAPANESE COTTON TEXTILE INDUSTRY

When the Lord of Satsuma established a steam-powered spinning mill in Kagoshima in 1867, Japan's modern textile industry began.[1] By 1887 the country had about as many spindles as a fair-sized English cotton mill.[2] For decades Japan continued to import yarn and cloth in large quantities but became a net exporter of yarn after 1896 and of cloth in 1909. In 1934 cotton cloth displaced raw silk as Japan's largest export and held that position until 1957. Ever since World War I, Japanese cotton goods have been produced mostly on Japanese-made machines and

[1] Keizo Seki, *The Cotton Industry of Japan* (Tokyo: Japan Society for the Promotion of Science, 1956), p. 14.

[2] G. C. Allen, *A Short Economic History of Modern Japan, 1867–1937* (London: Allen & Unwin, 1946), p. 65.

these too are exported—even to the United States (see p. 276). From 1933 on, except for World War II and its aftermath, Japan has been the world's largest exporter of cotton fabrics, even though its sales have been continuously interfered with by import restrictions abroad.

The Place of Cotton Textiles in Japanese Industry and Trade

At the time of surrender Japan had only 2.6 million operable cotton spindles, compared with 12.3 million in 1937. Weaving equipment suffered less in the war, but badly enough; the number of looms fell from 355,000 in 1937 to 134,000 in 1946. In rebuilding the industry the Japanese have modernized it almost completely and introduced the latest technological developments. Neither production nor exports, however, regained the 1937 peak. Some major export markets were lost while domestic consumption of cotton goods gave ground to other fibers. Nevertheless, cotton manufacturing remained the largest component of the Japanese textile industry which, as a whole, employed more workers than any other manufacturing industry.[3] Over a third of a million persons were employed in cotton textile mills at the end of 1956. They equaled 6.2 per cent of all manufacturing workers in establishments of four or more and generated one-twentieth of the total value added in Japanese manufacturing in that year.

As heavy industry has grown in Japan over the last thirty years, the relative importance of light industries, and especially textiles, has declined. The cotton textile industry's share of production has fallen more than most and, except for a brief period during the early postwar years, it has accounted for less of Japan's textile output than before the war. (Table 9-1.)

As exports, too, cotton textiles have declined in importance, though they remain near the top of the list of Japan's foreign exchange earners. In the 1930s, cotton textiles led Japan's great export boom. After the surrender in 1945, the Occupation authorities obtained raw cotton on credit and paid for it by taking Japanese cloth for export. For a time cotton textiles constituted an even larger share of total exports than before the war. Cotton goods did not keep pace during the export expansion of the 1950s, however, and by 1962 were less than one-tenth of Japanese exports, by value, even when the expanding sales of cotton clothing are included. (Table 9-2.)

[3] 1960 figures. In total shipments, however, the textile mill products industry (defined in footnote to Table 9-1) was second after food and related products; in value added, textiles came fourth after chemicals and allied products, electrical machinery, and other machinery. This 1960 information applies to establishments having four or more workers and comes from the Ministry of International Trade and Industry's Census of Manufactures. Bank of Japan, *Economic Statistics of Japan, 1962*, pp. 221–222.

TABLE 9-1. POSITION OF TEXTILES IN JAPANESE MANUFACTURING PRODUCTION, SELECTED YEARS

Year	*Textile Production as Per Cent of All Manufacturing Production*	*Cotton Textile Production as Per Cent of Total Textile Production*
1931	21.1	40.7
1937	19.2	36.9
1940	11.9	27.3
1946	23.9	39.9
1949	22.3	48.3
1952	26.7	36.9
1955	17.5	34.8
1958	13.8	35.3
1959	13.3	31.9
1960	12.4	30.7
1961	11.2	29.4
1962	10.9	26.9
1970 [a] (projected)	8.3	

[a] Fiscal year.

Notes: Calculated by weighted industrial production index on the basis of value added in 1955 for years before 1955 and of 1960 for 1958–1962. The figures here relate to "textile mill products," omitting "apparel and other finished products made from fabrics." Textile mill products include not only yarn and cloth but also certain made-up goods that are normally produced in textile mills and certain knitted goods like hosiery, underwear, and outerwear. The industries allied to textiles include the "garment" or "needle trades." These terms are not peculiar to Japan but are used in the United States and elsewhere as well.
The division between textiles and finished products is widely used in production statistics but does not always hold in trade statistics; the user of such statistics is warned to pay attention not only to labels but also to footnotes in cases where variations in definition may be significant.

Sources: All Japan Cotton Spinners' Association. Figures come from the Ministry of International Trade and Industry, except for 1970 figure which comes from Japan, Economic Planning Agency, *New Long-Range Economic Plan of Japan (1961–1970): Doubling National Income Plan* (Tokyo: The Japan Times, 1961), p. 87.

TABLE 9-2. JAPANESE EXPORTS OF COTTON TEXTILES, SELECTED YEARS

	1934–1936 (av.)	*1947*	*1950*	*1956*	*1957*	*1958*	*1959*	*1960*	*1961*	*1962*
Exports of cotton textiles [a]										
Value (million $)	202.7 [b]	103.1	239.0	357.7	416.7	369.4	391.5	487.0	459.7	474.4
Per cent of total exports	21.7	59.4	28.9	14.3	14.6	12.8	11.3	12.0	10.9	9.6
Exports of cotton cloth (million sq. yds.)										
Asia	1,895	242	701	765	801	633	630	629	623	590
Europe	74	83	206	133	226	160	141	185	190	139
Africa	485	34	119	90	133	134	142	214	252	277
United States [c]	46	6	23	123	82	97	97	87	98	128
Other W. Hemisphere	260	0.4	44	94	126	98	112	136	114	142
Australia and Oceania [d]	88	12	11	57	101	124	141	173	134	172
Total	2,849	377	1,103	1,262	1,468	1,245	1,263	1,424	1,411	1,448

[a] Yarn and thread, cloth, and made-up goods, including clothing.
[b] Includes, in the exports to Taiwan, textiles other than cotton.
[c] Includes Hawaii in 1962 only.
[d] Includes Hawaii in all years except 1962.

Sources: All Japan Cotton Spinners' Association, from the following sources: Japan, Ministry of Finance, *Annual Return of the Foreign Trade of Japan;* Government General of Korea, *Table of Trade and Shipping for 1936;* Ministry of Colonial Affairs, *Statistics on Colonial Affairs,* 1936; Economic and Scientific Section, General Headquarters, Supreme Commander for the Allied Powers.
Cloth export figures for 1947 from Keizo Seki, *The Cotton Industry of Japan* (Tokyo: Japan Society for the Promotion of Science, 1956), pp. 392–396.
Japan, Ministry of Finance, *Monthly Return of the Foreign Trade of Japan,* various years.
1962 figures from Japan, Ministry of Finance, Customs Bureau.

Japan sends much smaller quantities of cotton textiles abroad than it did before the war. The yardage of cotton cloth exported in the early 1960s was half that of 1934–36. Most of the decline, as Table 9-2 shows, was in sales to Asia and Africa, that is, to underdeveloped countries that were the largest prewar markets. In 1934–36, Asian countries took two-thirds of Japan's cotton cloth exports; in 1960, less than half. Korea and China which took over 500 million square yards of cotton cloth in prewar years bought only 144,000 square yards in 1960. The lands that are now the independent states of India, Pakistan, Burma, and Indonesia took 870 million yards before the war and 140 million in 1960. In Africa and Latin America also, sales fell substantially. The growth of domestic production in developing countries, foreign exchange difficulties, new competition—some of it from Communist China—and the loss of Japanese hegemony in eastern Asia, all contributed to this decline. Though it lost its largest markets, Japan gained substantially in sales to Europe, North America, Australia, and New Zealand. The goods these countries take are often priced higher than those sold to underdeveloped countries, although even here there are wide variations in the degree of finishing, from grey goods to prints.[4]

When Australia displaced Hong Kong as Japan's largest market (by value) for cotton cloth exports in 1959, the dominance of high-income markets was highlighted. Some Asian, African, and Latin American countries, where demand is rising faster than domestic textile production, are taking increasing amounts of Japanese cotton goods. In underdeveloped markets as a whole, however, the expansion of cotton goods production, usually behind tariff walls, seems likely to continue to limit Japanese sales. The result may not be a simple shrinkage in sales. There may well be substantial shifts in the kinds of textiles imported by low-income countries as they industrialize. Japan's yarn exports are much higher than they were before the war and these sales, along with those of garments and certain types of cloth, may sustain or even increase Japanese textile efforts for a time. But the longer-run future of Japan's sales of cotton textiles seems to depend on markets in the more developed areas.[5] North America, Europe, and other highly industrialized areas can obtain many textile products from Japan substantially more cheaply than they can

[4] The average value per square yard for cotton cloth sold to the United States in 1961 was 86 yen, Australia 110 yen, New Zealand 134 yen, Hong Kong 94 yen, the Philippines 88 yen, Thailand 81 yen, Indonesia 63 yen. Calculated from Japan, Ministry of Finance, *Monthly Return of the Foreign Trade of Japan,* January—December 1961, pp. 25–28.

[5] The fourteen countries with the highest per capita income in 1953 bought 14.4 per cent of Japan's cotton cloth exports by volume in that year. But five years later these same countries took 32.6 per cent of a substantially larger total. I am indebted to the All Japan Cotton Spinners' Association for these calculations.

produce them at home. Whether Japan will be able to take advantage of these opportunities depends very largely on the import policies of the industrialized countries.

The future of Japanese cotton textiles is very uncertain. Technological change is rapid and widespread. New fibers are being substituted for cotton and new products are displacing textiles in many uses. In the Japanese economy costs and employment conditions are changing rapidly. Newly industrializing countries are gradually becoming competitive in textiles. It seems more than likely that, in time, part of Japan's present production and export of cotton manufactures may have shifted to other textiles and to nontextile products, and that new suppliers will be able to undersell Japanese producers, especially in the coarser grades of yarn and cloth and in many made-up articles. The Japanese themselves seem to be less pessimistic, at least concerning the 1960s. Although they expect a continued decline in the relative importance of textiles in the economy, the plan for doubling national income during the decade projects absolute increases in both production and exports. (The plan does not deal with cotton textiles separately.) It is estimated that textile production in fiscal year 1970 will be more than double the level of fiscal year 1959 and that textile exports will be 60 per cent higher. Since these projected increases will be smaller than those for other products, textile production is expected to decline from 13 per cent of total manufacturing output in 1959 to 8.3 per cent in 1970, and exports of textiles and clothing together from 29.5 to 18.5 per cent of total exports.

"Cheap Labor"

In the industrialized countries there is frequent complaint from textile producers that Japanese goods gain their competitive advantages because Japanese wages are so low. A typical statement is this: "Japanese textile workers' hourly earnings were only one-tenth of the aggregate hourly earnings of textile workers in the U.S. . . . When it is further noted that labor costs constitute a substantial part of the total costs in textile production, it is apparent that the U.S.-foreign country earnings differential gives the latter a cost differential which could not be overcome even by the most efficient technology." [6]

There is no doubt that wages in Japanese cotton mills are far below those paid in the United States.[7] But the question here concerns the position of the textile industry in the Japanese economy. As Table 9-3

[6] William F. Sullivan, secretary of the Northern Textile Association, statement submitted to a subcommittee of the Senate Committee on Interstate and Foreign Commerce, in *Problems of the Domestic Textile Industry*, Hearings, 85th Cong., 2d sess. (Washington: GPO, 1958), pt. 1, pp. 267–268. (Hereafter cited as Pastore Subcommittee Hearings.)

[7] Exact comparison is not easy, however. (See Chapter 6, pp. 158–159.)

TABLE 9-3. AVERAGE MONTHLY CASH EARNINGS FOR REGULAR WORKERS IN JAPANESE TEXTILE MILLS, 1961

(Values in yen, for plants employing 30 or more workers)

	Cash Earnings						Ratio of Women's Earnings to Men's (per cent)
	Men		*Women*		*Total*		
	Value	*Ratio (per cent)*	*Value*	*Ratio (per cent)*	*Value*	*Ratio (per cent)*	
Cotton spinning	39,108	125	12,439	100	17,861	72	32
Cotton and spun rayon weaving	27,117	87	11,043	89	14,352	58	41
Textile mill products	28,531	91	11,384	91	16,109	65	40
Apparel and other finished products	24,070	77	9,694	78	13,655	55	40
All manufacturing	31,218	100	12,472	100	24,786	100	40

Source: All Japan Cotton Spinners' Association, from Japan, Ministry of Labor, Division of Labor Statistics and Research.

shows, men in the cotton spinning industry earn more than (and women as much as) the average in all manufacturing. In weaving and in all textiles together, however, both men and women receive less than the average levels in all manufacturing industries. For apparel workers the differential is greater, and earnings of both men and women are under 80 per cent of those for all manufacturing.[8]

In the United States also, textile wages are below the average, in fact further below than in Japan. In March 1962 average weekly wages in the American textile industry were 71 per cent of those for all manufacturing industries, well below the 91 per cent for Japanese men and women textile workers taken separately, as shown in Table 9-3. For apparel and other finished textile products the percentage in the United States was 64, as compared with 77 for men and 78 for women in these industries in Japan.[9] In one branch of Japanese textiles—cotton spinning—women were as well paid as the average of all women in manufacturing in 1961, and the relatively few men were getting a quarter more than the average for men in manufacturing generally.

Workers in other large modern Japanese textile mills also receive relatively good wages and are well treated in other respects. So far as working conditions are concerned, Canadian textile men, after observations in

[8] Total earnings for men and women averaged together are much lower in relation to the average in all manufacturing industries than for either men or women taken separately. This phenomenon, which holds true in all the textile and apparel groups shown in Table 9-3, is explained by the composition of the labor force in the textile industry. Women, most of whom do the least skilled work and usually stay in the factories only until marriage, are paid only about 40 per cent as much as men, who include the most highly skilled technicians and supervisory personnel. Even for equal work a Japanese woman would receive less than a man, especially if he were married. The proportion of women in the textile and apparel industries is more than double that in Japanese manufacturing generally. This fact contributed to the increase in the disparity between textile wages and all manufacturing wages in 1962. In that year the ratios of men's wages in the various branches of cotton textiles to men's wages in all manufacturing remained fairly constant; but women's wages in other manufacturing increased more than in cotton textile manufacturing. (U.S. Bureau of Labor Statistics, from Japan, Ministry of Labor, *Year Book of Labor Statistics, 1962* [Tokyo: Author, 1963], pp. 84–86, 104–105.) In considering these relationships, one must bear in mind that the figures here and in Table 9-3 apply only to regular workers and only to factories with payrolls of 30 or more; temporary employees and smaller plants are excluded.

[9] U.S. figures from U.S. Bureau of Labor Statistics, *Employment and Earnings*, May 1962, Table C-7. This averaging of men's and women's wages for the United States (necessary because of the nature of the available information) but not for Japan is justified by the fact that such wide differentials between men's and women's wages as occur in Japan are not common in the United States. For instance, in August 1960, men, who made up three-fifths of the 255,500 production workers in U.S. cotton manufacturing operations through the clothroom, had average earnings of $1.49 an hour, women $1.40 an hour or 94 per cent as much as men. U.S. Bureau of Labor Statistics, *Wage Structure: Cotton Textiles, August 1960*, BLS Report No. 184 (Washington: GPO, May 1961), p. 1.

1955, said: "Working conditions in big new mills . . . approach the ideal from the physical viewpoint. They provide ample space, controlled atmosphere, adequate lighting and excellent cleanliness and sanitation. Nor does the length of the working day or the amount of work expected of the operatives appear in any way excessive. Discipline appears no more and no less than is necessary in any large, complex, industrial organization." [10] Conditions are far less favorable in small shops, in textiles and other industries as well, but since 1955 the number of workers enjoying working conditions like those described here has multiplied rapidly.

Certainly low wages and low labor costs contribute to Japan's advantages as an exporter of cotton textiles. But wages are much higher and working conditions far better than in the early days of the industry. There is at present little or no basis for charges like those made in the 1930s that workers in the textile industry were so poorly treated as to make Japanese exports of cotton textiles a form of "social dumping." Wage rates in the cotton textile industry in Japan compare better with the general wage scale of the country than do wages in the American cotton textile industry. These facts will not put an end to demands for limiting imports so as to "protect American jobs" but they help put the issues in a reasonable perspective.

Structure and Control of the Industry

As American officials learned in the course of their efforts to persuade Hong Kong to limit textile exports to the United States, not every foreign industry is either so organized or so inclined that "voluntary" restraints are acceptable or workable. In Japan restraints are not only possible but in fact traditional. A few large firms can exercise a great deal of influence, in the past at times control, over the whole textile industry, and to a more limited extent the clothing industry. Cartel-like arrangements are a tradition. The interrelations of the cotton textile industry and the government bolster controls and ensure their enforcement.

The producers of cotton textiles in Japan vary from huge, ultramodern, integrated firms at one end of the scale to tiny, family-size, specialist enterprises at the other end. This diversity dates back to long before World War II. Spinning is the most highly concentrated process and the largest spinning firms, the "Big Ten," dominate the whole cotton textile

[10] *The Textile Industry in Japan*, Report of a Visit by a Group of Three from the Canadian Textile Industry to Japan in October–November 1955 (Toronto: Primary Textiles Institute, 1956), p. 48. Japanese textile men, for their part, make a point of the favorable treatment their workers receive. See, for instance, All Japan Cotton Spinners' Association, *Labour Situation of the Cotton Spinning Industry in Japan* (Osaka: Author, 1958); Takejiro Shindo, *Labor in the Japanese Cotton Industry* (Tokyo: Japan Society for the Promotion of Science, 1961), especially Chapters 3–6.

industry, as well as a substantial proportion of the synthetic textile industry.[11]

At the end of 1958 the spinning sector of the cotton textile industry comprised 145 firms. The Big Ten companies operated 55 per cent of the country's spindles, while the 45 smallest spinning firms accounted for only 2.3 per cent of the total. Spinning companies also weave on a large scale and had 21 per cent of all operable looms at the end of 1958.[12] They concentrate largely on the mass production of relatively few types of cloth, notably shirting, poplin, and broadcloth. Large quantities of these mass items are also made by the independent weavers, large and small, who produced 71 per cent of Japan's cotton cloth in 1957 and 1958. Most of the narrow cloth for Japanese-style clothing is made in small shops, which are also well adapted for a number of other products, including yarn-dyed fabrics such as gingham, toweling, and Jacquard-figured fabrics. Processes that are not well done by machine, like pile cutting in the production of velveteen, can also be efficiently handled by relatively small, independent firms, using much hand labor.

Mass operations in knitting and finishing are carried on by the big spinning weavers but they often contract with smaller firms for this work. Small firms also carry on finishing, and even a significant amount of weaving, for trading companies who often provide the yarn or cloth, dyes, designs, patterns, and sometimes working capital as well. The small firm in such cases performs only a very restricted range of operations, perhaps only one. This joining of large and small firms is very common in the export trade, not only in textiles, but in clothing and other light industries.

The small firm is in many cases only a family. What it has to offer is the time and skill of the members rather than facilities, organization, and contacts. Such cottage producers, working at piece rates, do much hand work, as in sewing decorations on clothing. With simple machinery, such as sewing machines, family enterprises often perform important parts of the production process. Labor has been so plentiful until recently that these tiny units, using workers who cannot find other employment, accept very low returns for their work. Because workers in such shops get the lowest wages, large firms find it profitable to put out work that might otherwise be performed in modern factories, with their greater investment in facilities for employee welfare as well as production, and their continuing obligations to regular workers. In textiles, as in other parts

[11] Most of the Big Ten used to have other interests as well, including pharmaceuticals, chemicals, cosmetics, foodstuffs, paper, plywood, bicycles, and machinery, but the Occupation required them to drop these activities.

[12] All Japan Cotton Spinners' Association, *Monthly Report of the Japanese Cotton Spinning Industry*, March 1959, p. 23.

of the Japanese economy, cottage industries are now under pressure as a result of expanding employment and higher wages. Young people entering the job market now have more and better opportunities elsewhere, and this form of production can be expected to shrink gradually in the years ahead.

There is a widespread feeling in Japan that intense competition, especially where there are many small units, is destructive and that large firms, cooperating with the government, should dominate or, if necessary, control an industry to keep it orderly and prosperous. During the panic of 1920 spinning companies which had accumulated large reserves from high wartime profits helped prevent widespread bankruptcies among cotton weavers, trading companies, and less fortunate spinners. Increasingly in the years before 1945, the Japanese government was involved in the textile industry's activities as instigator or even as administrator of control arrangements. When the war in China began to interfere seriously with the Japanese economy after 1937, many controls were applied to increase cotton goods exports and curb home consumption. The All Japan Cotton Spinners' Association, founded in 1882, played a key role in the application of these controls until 1942 when it was dissolved in the trend toward progressively more direct government control.[13] Later it was re-established under the Occupation.

During its long prewar life the Association made technical contributions and also played an important part in controlling production of yarn, thereby indirectly limiting the production of cloth.[14] When there was a tendency for prices to drop below cost the spinners, acting through their Association, would agree to curtail production. Various methods of enforcing these decisions were applied during eleven periods totaling seventeen of the sixty years from the establishment of the Association to 1942. "The Japanese industry used these controls in a most adept and skillful manner," says Keizo Seki, one of its leaders, contending that in spite of some difficulties these methods were more effective in Japan than in other countries.[15]

Much of the Association's strength during prewar years derived from agreements that ensured practically universal membership. Steamship companies carrying raw cotton to Japan from India agreed to give a rebate of one-third of the freight charge to members, through the Asso-

[13] Seki, cited, especially pp. 25–29, 37–48, 62–70, and Chapter 8.

[14] The Association helped the textile industry by its studies of raw materials supplies, transportation, and fiber-testing methods. It supported improved trade practices and inspection techniques and "played a spectacular part in the many countermeasures required at times when markets were disrupted. . . ." Same, p. 62.

[15] Same, p. 68. Seki was chairman of the board of the Toyo Spinning Company, one of Japan's leading firms, when he published his study of Japan's cotton textile industry in 1956.

ciation, and gave no rebate to nonmembers. Agreements between the Spinners' Association and the Federation of Japan Cotton Yarn Merchants' Associations and with the Japan Cotton Traders' Association provided that members of each would deal only with firms belonging to the Spinners' Association. The result was an effective monopoly, but Seki denies there was any monopoly pricing. He says: "Although these agreements between the *Boseki Rengokai* [All Japan Cotton Spinners' Association] and various business organizations appear to be extremely arbitrary, their chief purpose was to establish well-mannered, fair business practices with emphasis on improving trade and promoting better business practices among the parties concerned. In other words, these may be termed stabilizing measures for the general economy centered on the accumulation of large capital." [16]

This method of indirect controls operated by the industry itself, with varying degrees of government encouragement, began to give way by mid-1938 to direct government controls that changed often, and rapidly grew more stringent. The military leaders who dominated the government felt that domestic need for cotton goods required only a low level of production, so even before Pearl Harbor output and trade fell sharply. A series of enforced amalgamations reduced the number of producing units, first in spinning, then in weaving, and finally in the finishing processes. Much cotton spinning and weaving equipment was scrapped for metal, and many cotton mills were converted to war production, especially of aircraft or chemicals. Spun rayon (staple fiber) provided a large share of textile needs. Some producing equipment was shipped from Japanese factories to Korea, China, Taiwan, and Southeast Asia.[17]

At the end of the war the Occupation authorities subjected the greatly reduced cotton textile industry to strict controls, to ensure that the most urgent needs were filled. The American policy of dismantling the *zaibatsu* had only a limited effect on the cotton textile industry. Firms were required to dispose of their shares in nontextile companies. But no cotton spinning company was required to dissolve. Occupation policy did, however, restrict the activities of the reconstituted All Japan Cotton Spinners' Association. Article 3 of the Anti-Monopoly Law of 1947 "prohibited concerted action to fix prices, to restrict output . . . to control purchases or sales by exclusive contract, when the effect on competition was more than negligible." [18] Seki expresses a fairly typical Japanese view when he says:

[16] Same, p. 69.
[17] Same, pp. 388–390.
[18] T. A. Bisson, *Zaibatsu Dissolution in Japan* (Berkeley: University of California Press, 1954), p. 183.

> It cannot be denied that this law weakened the Japanese economy whose very foundations had already been considerably uprooted by the war. Belated recognition has recently been made of the fact that such programs are obstructing stabilization of the economy and the general trend is now toward reform or amendment of their provisions.[19]

Many of the effects of the Anti-Monopoly Law did not long survive the Occupation. The head of the Association told a U.S. House of Representatives subcommittee in December 1956 that he represented virtually all of the important units of the complex cotton textile industry:

> For the record, my name is Kojiro Abe, of Osaka. While I am the president of the Toyo Spinning Co., one of Japan's oldest and largest, I am appearing today as the chairman of the All Japan Cotton Spinners' Association. I have also been asked to represent the Japan Cotton Weavers' Association, the Japan Cotton Textile Exporters' Association, and the Japan Textile Products Exporters' Association.
>
> The All Japan Cotton Spinners' Association was organized in 1882. We have a current membership of 129 cotton spinners, which represents without a single exception every cotton spinning company in the nation.
>
> The Japan Cotton Weavers' Association was organized in 1928. Its membership includes 60 member associations, representing 15,600 separate and independent weaving companies.
>
> The Japan Cotton Textile Exporters' Association was organized in 1921. It currently lists 146 members who, in 1955, exported 93 per cent of all the Japanese cotton cloth into the United States.
>
> The Japan Textile Products Exporters' Association was formed in 1934. It has 417 members who exported more than 95 per cent of all cotton made-up goods to the United States in 1955.[20]

What Mr. Abe had to say about these associations and their purposes was very simple:

> The present and principal function of trade associations in Japan is to assure effective implementation of the voluntary export adjustment measures.
>
> Our associations are not cartels for monopoly, or for profit, but rather organizations purely for the purpose of enforcing the voluntary self-adjustment measures approved by the membership.

Surely such old, established organizations must have more to do than just enforce "self-adjustment measures." But such measures are imposed in Japan, and enforcement is largely in the hands of the trade associations. The All Japan Cotton Spinners' Association exercises a large amount of control over the level of production, much as in prewar days. The

[19] Seki, cited, p. 69.

[20] Statement submitted to a subcommittee of the House Committee on Ways and Means, in *Administration and Operation of Customs and Tariff Laws and the Trade Agreements Program,* Hearings, 84th Cong., 2d sess. (Washington: GPO, 1957), pt. 4, p. 2083. The second quotation comes from p. 2096.

foreign exchange controls assisted the Association in such control, since the Association exercised a powerful influence in the allocation of licenses for import of raw cotton, even to the point of squeezing out uncooperative firms. Still, new firms have appeared in the postwar period, the control of the Association has been weakened considerably, and liberalization of Japanese imports is weakening the control still further.[21]

The cotton textile trade associations have shown that they can enforce controls on direct exports to the United States. In doing so, they have had the support of the Japanese government. With full power to control all exports, the Ministry of International Trade and Industry (MITI) polices cotton textile exports in detail. It uses its powers especially to see that the agreements are carried out, even by recalcitrants who may be among the small minority not members of the Associations.[22] It may be a matter of doubt how far MITI could go in direct opposition to a strong view of the organizations, but MITI and the Foreign Office have accepted quota levels well below what the associations have thought reasonable. Perhaps the Japanese government went a good deal further than the U.S. government in taking a position disliked by its domestic industrial leaders.

In any case, as noted earlier, it is often not clear to the outsider when the locus of initiative and leadership in Japan is in the large firms and when it is in the government. Certainly the government leads and controls much more than in the United States. No traditions place limits of principle on its role. Perhaps it is an inheritance from the feudalism that still existed a hundred years ago that in Japan paternalism, leadership, and control at the top are much more practiced and accepted than in the American economy, with its long, strong tradition of private initiative. Within the Japanese cotton textile industry the large firms lead and the small ones follow. There is no accepted antitrust doctrine in Japan and if it were not for American antitrust laws much of the trade between the two countries would probably be arranged by direct agreement between Japanese and American producers. In this, as in other matters, the limits on government control and on cartel arrangements in the cotton textile industry are mostly the result of circumstances, not principle.

[21] "Past and Present of the Textile Industry," The Industrial Bank of Japan, *Survey of Japanese Finance and Industry,* March/April 1961, pp. 4–10.

[22] "Under the export-import transaction law . . . [MITI] has specified that no cotton yarn or fabric may be exported without their approval of the terms of the sales contract." Sam Ishikawa, secretary, and Mike Masaoka, Washington representative, the American Importers of Japanese Textiles, Inc., "The Importation of Cotton Textiles from Japan," in U.S. House, Committee on Ways and Means, *Foreign Trade Policy,* compendium of papers collected by the staff for the Subcommittee on Foreign Trade Policy (Washington: GPO, 1957), p. 923.

JAPANESE COTTON TEXTILE EXPORTS TO THE UNITED STATES [23]

Japanese cotton textiles began to enter the United States as early as 1887, with the shipment of 35,000 yards of cotton drills.[24] Until World War II the Japanese cotton goods sold here were mostly of the lower grades and simpler constructions, and they arrived in modest quantities. Only in 1937 did the shipments of cotton cloth exceed 100 million square yards, as Table 9-4 shows. After 1945 this trade resumed very slowly, and sales of Japanese cotton cloth in the United States did not pass 25 million square yards until 1953. Then a sharp rise set in, affecting not only cloth but many other products as well.

Rapid expansion of production had put Japan in a position to meet the demands of the American market. Anti-inflationary measures adopted in the autumn of 1953 may well have helped after the end of the year. The effect of U.S. tariff concessions has been the subject of much debate, but Japanese shipments of cotton textiles had begun to increase in 1954 and 1955, before the tariff reductions of 1955 and the smaller reductions in 1956 took effect.[25] A large inflow followed in late 1955 and 1956; in the latter year the value of shipments was seven times the 1952 level. While it is impossible to say how much tariff reductions may have contributed, it is clear that the tariff levels were not so restrictive as to prevent substantial sales of a wide range of textile products. The rapid increase stopped only when Japan imposed export quotas. In 1957 sales fell in every category shown in Table 9-4, except tablecloths and napkins (and they fell sharply in 1958). Later increases had not, by 1961, brought shipments up to the 1956 levels in any of the categories shown in Table 9-4.

Japan's Share in American Consumption of Cotton Goods

Japan is a larger source than any other country of U.S. imports of textiles, apparel, and related manufactures. It has long been the principal source of imports of cotton manufactures, but has never filled as much as 2 per cent of the American market. Not until the mid-1950s did the raw cotton content of U.S. cotton goods imports from all sources exceed 2 per cent of domestic mill consumption of raw cotton. By 1960, that figure had reached 5.6 per cent but in 1961 it dropped to 4.2 per

[23] Unless otherwise noted, the cut-off date for this section is 1961.

[24] Kojiro Abe, *The Story of the Japanese Cotton Textile Industry* (Osaka: All Japan Cotton Spinners' Association, Japan Cotton Textile Exporters' Association, Japan Textile Products Exporters' Association, 1957), p. 3.

[25] At least some of the 1955 shipments appear to have gone into customs bond in anticipation of duty reductions. *The New York Times,* December 4, 1955.

TABLE 9-4. JAPAN'S COTTON TEXTILE EXPORTS TO THE UNITED STATES: CLOTH AND SELECTED MADE-UP ARTICLES, 1932–1941, 1947–1961

Year	*Cloth (million sq. yds.)*	*Knitted Underwear (1,000 doz.)*	*Blouses (1,000 doz.)*	*Handker-chiefs (1,000 doz.)*	*Table-cloths* [a] *(1,000 lbs.)*
1932	1.6	180	—	52	N.A.
1933	7.5	177	—	149	N.A.
1934	17.4	116	—	787	N.A.
1935	48.3	137	—	3,537	1,313
1936	73.4	409	—	4,912	2,980
1937	123.8	101	—	2,375	2,448
1938	16.1	41	—	1,079	170
1939	71.5	63	—	1,957	1,080
1940	50.1	N.A.	—	N.A.	N.A.
1941	47.7	N.A.	—	N.A.	N.A.
1947	5.8	N.A.	—	—	12
1948	11.9	1	—	—	11
1949	5.0	N.A.	—	36	63
1950	22.9	N.A.	—	615	676
1951	1.6	N.A.	—	257	105
1952	6.5	83	—	73	69
1953	33.2	149	5	281	82
1954	49.5	168	171	319	110
1955	140.2	621	3,996	1,362	258
1956	122.5	859	2,010	2,645	450
1957	81.8	488	1,564	1,328	470
1958	97.3	574	1,547	1,162	110
1959	97.1	500	1,566	1,114	105
1960	87.3	354	1,284	1,045	174
1961	98.2	237	1,079	998	221

[a] Including napkins in postwar years.

Sources: 1932–1956—Kojiro Abe, *The Story of the Japanese Cotton Textile Industry* (Osaka: All Japan Cotton Spinners' Association, Japan Cotton Textile Exporters' Association, Japan Textile Products Exporters' Association, 1957), pp. 73–74, based on Ministry of Finance statistics, except for blouses, 1953–1955, for which figures come from Japan Textile Products Exporters' Association. 1957 and 1958—All Japan Cotton Spinners' Association from statistics of the Ministry of Finance.

1959–1961—Japan, Ministry of Finance, *Monthly Return of the Foreign Trade of Japan*, January–December issue, 1959, 1960, 1961; *Annual Return of the Foreign Trade of Japan*, 1959, 1960, 1961.

cent.[26] In 1961 about a third of the imports by value came from Japan.

As Table 9-5 shows, U.S. imports of cotton manufactures and of other fabrics, apparel, and related products increased substantially between 1957 and 1960. Because Japanese exports were subject to quota, the increased inflow of cotton goods came mainly from other sources, and Japan's share declined. But among imports of other textiles and textile products, Japan's sales rose faster than the total, especially in wool manufactures and synthetics, but also in silk manufactures. Consequently, Japan's share of total U.S. imports of all textiles and related products was about the same in 1960 as in 1957, roughly a third. In 1961 imports declined more from Japan than from other sources, but Japan remained the largest supplier.[27]

Hong Kong was the most notable source outside of Japan, becoming in the late 1950s for the first time a significant factor in U.S. textile markets. In 1960 and 1961 Hong Kong was second to Japan as a supplier of U.S. textile imports, not only of cotton goods but also of all fabrics, apparel, etc., having leaped ahead of the United Kingdom, Italy, and other traditional suppliers. Some other countries made smaller gains up through 1960, but in several cases these shrank or disappeared in 1961. Other suppliers that came into prominence included Spain, Portugal, and Egypt.

The relation of imports to domestic production varies greatly among individual products. In one case—velveteens—imports have exceeded production in the United States, and in some years imports from Japan alone have been larger than the output of the single firm then making velveteens in the United States. In no other case were imports as much as half of American production. In most cases Japan is the principal foreign supplier, but the share of the domestic market taken by Japan is very small. Table 9-6 shows production and imports of every category of cotton manufactures (except a few subgroups) for which adequate information is published.

Why, with its modern facilities and low wages, does Japan not sell far more cotton manufactures in the United States? And why has the increase in sales by other producing countries not been greater? Trade restrictions are a large part of the answer, and more will be said about

[26] U.S. Department of Commerce, Bureau of International Programs, "U.S. imports of textiles, apparel, and related manufactures and comparisons with U.S. production and exports, 1957–61," *World Trade Information Service*, pt. 3, no. 62–24, Table 5.

[27] Besides providing 31 per cent of all fabrics, apparel, etc., and 34 per cent of all cotton goods imported in 1961, as shown in Table 9-5, Japan supplied 29 per cent of woolen manufactures, 62 per cent of silk manufactures, and 57 per cent of man-made fiber manufactures. These figures reflect values, rather than physical volume. Same, Table 3.

them later. On grounds of price, quality, and service alone, Japan and other countries could probably provide a good deal more than they have heretofore. But in addition to restrictions there are purely economic factors that limit the size of the trade. It seems unlikely that, even without barriers, Japanese cotton textiles could ever dominate the American market. Distance, the long lead time between placing an order in Japan and delivery of finished products in the United States, established commercial relations, the vagaries of fashion, and many special factors constitute economic obstacles to large-scale imports of a number of cotton products. A prominent factor is cost.

Costs of Production in Japan and the United States

Cost may be less favorable to Japan than is sometimes thought. As indicated in Chapter 6 (pp. 154–156), Japan has a number of serious disadvantages in producing for export. Capital is more expensive in Japan than in the United States. Fuel and energy cost substantially more, flat land is at a great premium, and industrial water is becoming scarce in some parts of the country. Technology at times costs more. Japan's competitive advantage in the manufacture of cotton goods lies mainly in lower wages, modern facilities, excellent management, and the special competence some Japanese firms have developed in mixing different grades of raw cotton and in producing constructions of particular merit or unique qualities. Only where these advantages outweigh the disadvantages can Japanese cotton goods undersell American domestic products.

Over what portion of the American market have Japanese cotton textiles a cost advantage? The whole market, American producers tend to think. Japanese contend that the portion is not very large, pointing out that competition comes not only from American producers but also from countries with lower wage levels than Japan's, and citing the failure in some years to meet quotas allowed. A firm answer would require cost studies that have not been made and may be impossible. Table 9-7 is based on figures for 1959 provided by the All Japan Cotton Spinners' Association. It shows that jobbers in the United States were then selling Japanese broadcloth and velveteen at less than the price asked at American mills. On the other hand, Japanese corduroy and denim would have cost more than the American mill price and no sales were being made.[28] The Japanese believe that to sell denim they would have to offer a price so much below that asked by American mills that, according to their calculations, even complete removal of the American duty would leave them priced out of the American market. Corduroy, however, might just

[28] In 1937, however, Japanese corduroy was coming into the United States to such an extent as to be made the subject (along with velveteen) of a special quota agreement between Japanese and American producers. See pp. 316–317.

TABLE 9-5. TEXTILE IMPORTS INTO THE UNITED STATES, BY SOURCE, 1954–1961

(In millions of dollars)

	1954	*1955*	*1956* [a]	*1957* [a]	*1958*	*1959*	*1960*	*1961*
Cotton manufactures	**80.3**	**124.2**	**154.3**	**136.2**	**150.0**	**201.3**	**248.3**	**203.3**
Japan [b]	25.5	60.3	84.1	65.8	71.7	76.7	74.1	69.4
(per cent of total)	(32)	(49)	(55)	(48)	(48)	(38)	(30)	(34)
Hong Kong	0.1	0.3	0.7	5.8	17.4	45.8	63.5	47.0
Philippines [c]	12.5	13.7	13.1	11.3	10.7	12.0	13.3	12.9
India			1.3	0.7	0.9	4.4	8.8	2.5
Other Asian countries			0.9	1.0	2.7	7.6	11.9	9.6
Asia total			100.1	84.6	103.4	146.4	171.7	141.4
Italy	7.7	8.2	8.5	8.4	8.4	10.7	11.5	11.1
West Germany			6.3	5.8	6.4	7.2	8.4	9.1
United Kingdom	8.4	10.0	11.5	9.6	9.9	9.7	8.3	7.1
France			5.6	5.6	4.5	5.6	8.3	6.7
Switzerland			6.1	5.4	5.9	6.8	7.6	6.2
Spain			0.3	0.3	0.4	1.6	7.2	3.2
Belgium			5.9	6.7	5.3	6.4	6.3	6.3
Portugal			0.0	0.1	0.3	1.0	5.2	2.3
Other European countries			4.2	3.6	3.8	3.8	4.4	5.7
Europe total			48.4	45.5	44.9	52.8	67.2	57.7
Egypt			0.4	0.5	0.3	0.3	5.9	1.0
All other sources			2.0	2.2	1.8	2.1	9.4	4.2
All fabrics, apparel, etc.	**302.9**	**397.4**	**480.5**	**472.1**	**477.1**	**629.9**	**732.2**	**661.5**
Japan [b]	62.1	116.6	162.7	156.2	179.2	232.1	241.6	203.0
(per cent of total)	(21)	(29)	(34)	(33)	(38)	(37)	(33)	(31)

Hong Kong	0.8	1.7	3.2	10.1	24.3	61.1	94.2	81.4
India			14.5	14.6	10.5	16.5	23.7	27.5
Philippines [c]			18.6	17.8	18.5	20.1	21.6	22.8
Other Asian countries			6.1	8.8	8.5	14.4	19.5	17.5
Asia total			205.1	207.5	241.0	344.2	400.6	352.2
Italy	23.6	31.8	40.5	41.1	41.8	60.1	77.6	73.2
United Kingdom	70.4	80.3	83.4	73.0	63.8	69.5	70.2	63.3
Belgium and Luxembourg	23.8	27.1	29.9	30.5	27.4	32.8	33.5	34.4
France			22.3	21.0	18.3	21.4	27.0	24.4
West Germany			15.7	15.4	15.4	18.9	21.4	20.5
Switzerland			13.9	13.3	12.8	14.9	16.1	15.3
Netherlands			8.7	9.0	10.2	10.0	9.7	12.2
Portugal			0.3	0.9	2.3	4.0	9.0	7.9
Spain			0.5	0.6	0.9	2.3	8.9	4.7
Other European countries			12.7	12.2	11.5	15.0	14.7	15.2
Europe total	172.2	206.5	227.9	217.0	204.4	248.9	288.2	271.1
Mexico			16.0	16.6	19.2	21.4	21.3	22.7
All other sources			31.7	29.7	31.8	36.8	43.4	38.2

[a] Totals in 1956 and 1957 include estimates for entries valued $250 or less which are not available by country.
[b] Slight discrepancies between the figures here and corresponding figures in Table 8-2 reflect differences shown in the sources used. The explanation is the continuing process of revision of Bureau of the Census figures and differences in the dates used by the different sources.
[c] Includes handkerchiefs, gloves, and other wearing apparel produced on a contract basis from materials owned by U.S. establishments.

Note: Data include fabrics, apparel, and related manufactures. For details on coverage, etc., see source.

Source: U.S. Department of Commerce, Bureau of International Programs, "U.S. imports of textiles, apparel, and related manufactures and comparisons with U.S. production and exports, 1954–59," *World Trade Information Service*, pt. 3, no. 60-26, August 1960, pp. 2, 6; "U.S. imports . . . 1957–61," pt. 3, no. 62-24, Table 3.

TABLE 9-6. UNITED STATES PRODUCTION, IMPORTS, AND EXPORTS OF SELECTED COTTON MANUFACTURES, 1954–1961

Group and Commodity	*Unit*	*1954*	*1955*	*1956*	*1957*	*1958*	*1959*	*1960*	*1961*
I. Cotton cloth, all types									
Production	million sq. yds.	10,764	10,973	11,031	10,268	9,605	10,296	10,091	9,802
Imports	million sq. yds.	73	133	188	122	143	240	455	254
Imports from Japan	million sq. yds.	48	100	143	87	105	99	90	90
Imports as per cent of production	per cent	0.68	1.21	1.70	1.19	1.48	2.33	4.51	2.59
Japan's share of total imports	per cent	66	75	76	71	73	41	20	35
Exports	million sq. yds.	599	538	507	548	501	472	437	467
Imports as per cent of exports	per cent	12	25	37	22	29	51	104	54
A. *Ginghams*									
Production	million sq. yds.	182	250	217	223	256	256	265	241
Imports	million sq. yds.	6	36	83	46	50	43	61	47
Imports from Japan	million sq. yds.	4	33	77	43	47	36	38	38
Imports as per cent of production	per cent	3.3	14	38	21	20	17	23	20
Japan's share of total imports	per cent	67	92	93	94	94	84	62	81
B. *Velveteens*									
Production	thousand sq. yds.	4,322	4,246	N.A.	N.A.	N.A.	N.A.	N.A.	N.A.
Imports	thousand sq. yds.	5,157	8,600	8,324	4,254	4,157	4,675	4,900	4,488
Imports from Japan	thousand sq. yds.	3,145	6,796	6,898	3,163	2,797	3,026	3,087	2,662
Imports from Italy	thousand sq. yds.	1,999	1,672	1,410	1,087	1,232	1,590	1,753	1,797
Imports as per cent of production	per cent	119	203	N.A.	N.A.	N.A.	N.A.	N.A.	N.A.
Japan's share of total imports	per cent	61	79	83	74	67	65	63	59
II. Made-up goods									
A. *Sheets and pillow cases*									
Production	thousands	211,752	211,000	223,000	229,000	262,344	243,000	249,000	N.A.
Imports	thousands	1,337	11,738	4,923	5,035	7,648	5,990	5,444	6,109
Imports from Japan	thousands			4,900	4,860	6,391	5,128	4,970	5,306
Imports from Hong Kong	thousands				152	1,236	842	389	256
Imports as per cent of production	per cent	0.63	5.6	2.2	2.2	2.9	2.5	2.2	N.A.
Japan's share of total imports	per cent			99.5	97	84	86	91	87
B. *Table damask*									
Production	thousand pounds	6,004	5,991	6,854	8,028	7,509	7,280	8,571	7,776
Imports	thousand pounds	4,434	5,096	5,251	4,244	4,444	4,509	4,015	3,874
Imports from Japan	thousand pounds	3,534	4,208	4,258	3,324	3,511	3,459	2,949	2,993
Imports as per cent of production	per cent	74	85	77	53	59	62	47	50
Japan's share of total imports	per cent	80	83	81	78	79	77	73	77
C. *Handkerchiefs*									
Production	thousand dozens	20,941	21,700	21,900	21,300	20,800	20,800	20,600	N.A.
Imports	thousand dozens	3,429	4,247	5,453	6,135	7,506	6,721	6,707	5,798
Imports from the Philippines	thousand dozens	1,398	1,705	2,032	2,777	2,970	3,179	3,130	2,816

Imports from Japan	thousand dozens	614	1,107	1,908	1,825	2,933	1,754	1,526	1,201
Imports from Switzerland	thousand dozens	952	978	1,046	1,050	1,194	1,375	1,492	1,465
Imports as per cent of production	per cent	16	20	25	29	36	32	33	N.A.
Japan's share of total imports	per cent	18	26	35	30	39	26	23	21
III. Woven apparel									
A. *Blouses*									
Production	thousand dozens	6,569	10,066	10,800	12,500	12,400	14,400	14,200	14,200
Imports	thousand dozens					3,147	4,134	4,276	2,258
Imports from Hong Kong	thousand dozens					935	1,971	2,209	746
Imports from Japan [a]	thousand dozens	189	2,810	2,010	1,564	2,135	2,127	1,871	1,309
Imports as per cent of production	per cent					25	29	30	16
Japan's share of total imports	per cent					68	51	44	58
B. *Men's and boys' shirts*									
Production	thousand dozens	27,190	29,235	30,200	27,200	27,800	29,500	29,600	30,400
Imports (chiefly sport shirts)	thousand dozens	211	550	1,226	1,387	1,502	2,218	2,084	1,961
Imports from Hong Kong	thousand dozens	0	1	28	450	529	1,161	989	877
Imports from Japan	thousand dozens	210	548	1,190	925	967	1,048	859	646
Imports as per cent of production	per cent	0.78	1.9	4.1	5.1	5.4	7.5	7.0	6.5
Japan's share of total imports	per cent	99.5	99.6	97.1	67	64	47	41	33
Exports (chiefly dress shirts)	thousand dozens	282	291	369	316	241	217	233	197
C. *Men's and boys' slacks and shorts* [b]									
Production	thousand dozens			9,600	10,000	10,100	12,400	12,700	11,900
Imports	thousand dozens					333	818	1,283	885
Imports from Hong Kong	thousand dozens					170	578	1,012	560
Imports from Japan	thousand dozens					161	231	238	244
Imports as per cent of production	per cent					3.3	6.6	10.1	7.4
Japan's share of total imports	per cent					48	28	19	28
D. *Nightwear, woven*									
Production	thousand dozens			9,900	9,500	9,900	10,800	10,600	10,900
Imports	thousand dozens					172	504	609	397
Imports from Hong Kong	thousand dozens					126	478	572	346
Imports from Japan	thousand dozens					41	21	29	19
Imports as per cent of production	per cent					1.7	4.7	5.7	3.6
Japan's share of total imports	per cent					24	4.2	4.8	4.8
IV. Knit goods									
A. *Gloves, knit fabric*									
Production	thousand dozen pairs	3,600	4,200	4,200	4,000	3,500	3,800	3,600	3,400
Imports	thousand dozen pairs	448	704	865	892	862	944	1,003	956
Imports from Japan	thousand dozen pairs	112	245	356	362	342	428	391	332
Imports from Hong Kong	thousand dozen pairs	3	13	24	49	99	119	181	205
Imports from the Philippines	thousand dozen pairs	199	253	258	157	166	134	163	158
Imports from West Germany	thousand dozen pairs	66	114	125	123	155	152	143	105
Imports as per cent of production	per cent	12	17	21	22	25	25	28	28
Japan's share of total imports	per cent	25	35	41	40	40	45	39	35

TABLE 9-6. (cont'd)

Group and Commodity	Unit	1954	1955	1956	1957	1958	1959	1960	1961
IV. Knit goods (cont'd)									
B. *Polo shirts and other knit shirts*									
Production	thousand dozens			28,900	29,900	29,800	33,400	33,100	34,100
Imports	thousand dozens					1,288	1,702	2,291	1,704
Imports from Hong Kong	thousand dozens					115	351	1,079	615
Imports from Japan	thousand dozens					1,088	1,280	979	782
Imports as per cent of production	per cent					4.3	5.1	6.9	5.0
Japan's share of total imports	per cent					84	75	43	46
V. Miscellaneous									
A. *Floor coverings*									
Production	thousand sq. yds.	N.A.	N.A.	N.A.	N.A.	34,454	N.A.	N.A.	N.A.
Imports	thousand sq. yds.	5,258	5,467	4,870	5,313	4,172	3,349	2,397	2,060
Imports from Japan	thousand sq. yds.	3,347	3,976	3,617	3,561	3,099	2,111	1,460	1,498
Imports from Belgium	thousand sq. yds.	1,565	1,366	992	1,542	798	903	789	427
Japan's share of imports	per cent	64	73	74	67	74	63	61	73
B. *Quilts or bedspreads, woven*									
Production	thousands	8,400	9,400	10,300	10,200	9,900	11,200	10,300	10,400
Imports	thousands	630	988	1,052	918	1,010	1,019	965	956
Imports from Japan	thousands	141	433	464	400	515	542	500	528
Imports from India	thousands	174	286	315	202	326	283	250	268
Imports as per cent of production	per cent	7.5	11	10	9.0	10	9.1	9.4	9.2
Japan's share of total imports	per cent	22	44	44	44	51	53	52	55

[a] Blouse imports from Japan have been shown separately in U.S. imports only beginning in 1958. The figure here for 1954 comes from the National Association of Blouse Manufacturers (New York). The figure for 1955 is an estimate based on a special report of the Bureau of the Census. The 1956 and 1957 are Japanese figures for exports to the United States.

[b] Excluding dungarees.

Notes: Statistics of cotton textile production and trade lack a uniform basis in coverage, definition, and measurement, especially for the earlier years shown in the table; hence many of the figures have been arrived at by indirect methods. Cloth production figures, for instance, have had to be converted from linear yards to square yards, those for table damask from linear yards to pounds. Where possible, but not always, import statistics apply to imports for consumption.

Source: U.S. Department of Commerce, Bureau of International Programs (before 1961 Bureau of Foreign Commerce), "U.S. imports of textiles, apparel, and related manufactures and comparisons with U.S. production and exports, 1954–59," *World Trade Information Service*, pt. 3, no. 60-26, Table 1; "U.S. imports . . . 1957–61," pt. 3, no. 62-24, Table 1.

TABLE 9-7. COST OF REPRESENTATIVE COTTON CLOTH CONSTRUCTIONS IMPORTED INTO THE UNITED STATES FROM JAPAN

(In cents per linear yard)

	40" Broadcloth $\left(\frac{c\ 40 \times 40}{136 \times 60}\right)$	*36" Velveteen* $\left(\frac{6\frac{1}{2} \times c\ 40}{73 \times 288}\right)$	*36" Corduroy* $\left(\frac{16 \times 20}{44 \times 134}\right)$	*35/36" Denim* $\left(\frac{16 \times 16}{73 \times 58}\right)$
Mill price in Japan	19.68	83.18	37.93	32.257
Shipping charges in Japan	0.75	2.51	1.2	0.75
F.o.b. price	20.43	85.69	39.13	33.007
Ocean freight and insurance	1.5	6.75	5.3	3.5
Entry charges at U.S. port	0.6	1.5	1.0	1.0
Import duty: rate	17% of f.o.b.	25% + 1.25¢/yd.	50% of f.o.b.	25% of f.o.b.
amount	3.47	26.25	19.57	8.25
Landed cost	26.0	120.19	65.0	45.757
Importer's selling price	27.5 to 28.25	125.0 to 130.0	68.0	48.0
Jobber's selling price		137.5 to 142.5	75.0	
Assumed maximum price of Japanese cloth			55.0 to 57.0	35.5 to 36.25
Mill price of U.S. cloth	28.75 to 30.0	145.0 to 155.0	60.0 to 62.0	39.0 to 41.0

Source: All Japan Cotton Spinners' Association, December 1959

be able to sell if the 50 per cent duty were removed, even if the price had to be as much below the American price as the Japanese assume. The other two cloths sell competitively despite the tariff.[29]

These figures illustrate the three categories of Japanese goods in relation to the American market—those that can leap over present tariffs, those that are now stopped by the tariff, and those that could not at present costs and prices meet American competition even without a tariff. What we do not know is how much of American production would be subject to effective competition from Japanese cotton goods if tariffs were lowered or removed, or even if they were left at present levels and were the only restrictions on Japanese goods. It is unlikely that Japanese cotton products could sweep aside all American competition, even if there

[29] One may, perhaps, question the assumption that Japanese cloth need sell for significantly less than domestic cloth, especially when importers were selling broadcloth at only slightly below the minimum U.S. mill price. Memories of a time when Japanese cloth was of inferior quality enter into the matter, and established relations between American producers and customers constitute a barrier, to be sure. Still, the Japanese assumption may only reflect an acceptance of weak marketing arrangements. Later developments seem to disprove the gloomy judgment on corduroy, which was sold in the 1930s and has begun to flow into the United States again, becoming in 1963 an object of limitation. See p. 332.

were no import duties or quotas and if time were allowed in which to increase Japan's productive capacity.

Competition from third countries is a factor of growing significance to Japanese ability to sell in the United States. Hong Kong and other suppliers have been doing particularly well. By contrast with some of these countries, Japan has high wages, in some cases high labor costs and high total costs. Table 9-8 summarizes some results of a study of international comparisons in production costs of certain common constructions of cotton cloth in 1960. Japan had lower *production* costs than the United States for all of the four constructions listed. Selling and other nonproduction costs might change the comparison somewhat. For India, only two constructions are reported on, and these also show lower production costs than in the United States. As between Japan and India, the cheaper construction, sheeting, had slightly lower production costs in India, but for the more expensive fabric, print cloth, India's production costs were 14 per cent higher than those of Japan. Among the major elements making up the cost, raw cotton cost most in the United States and least in India, while labor cost was highest in the United States and lowest in Japan, although wage rates in Japan are much higher than in India. Other production costs were highest in India, lowest in Japan. Production per man-hour was by far the highest in the United States, but wage differentials were even greater.

As the years go by and economic growth brings greater efficiency in India and further wage increases in Japan, the competitive situation for cotton textiles is likely to move in favor of India. The equipment used in the Indian cotton textile industry is now far behind the ultramodern Japanese facilities, and a good deal of new investment is needed. In India I have been told forcibly how hard it is for producers there, not only of textiles but of many other things as well, to meet the high quality standards of the American market. As Indian industry matures, it can be expected to gain a progressively greater ability to meet these standards. As to costs, workers' skill may increase more rapidly than wages, in view of India's vast army of unemployed and underemployed. Thus India may be expected, in her own way and at her own pace, to follow Japan and other industrial countries up the ladder of industrial performance to higher qualities, more advanced and complicated products, and more product per man-hour. Other developing countries will also be in the race with India, Japan, and other traditional suppliers for foreign textile markets.

Japan has already shown what an industrially strong country can do to provide ever more satisfactory textile products in an ever broader range. Japan could, if permitted, compete successfully in the United States in a far wider range of cotton products than during the 1930s. As

TABLE 9-8. PRODUCTION COSTS OF SELECTED COTTON FABRICS IN THE UNITED STATES, JAPAN, AND INDIA, 1960

(In cents per linear yard)

	Sheeting [a]	*Print Cloth* [b]	*Broad-cloth* [c]	*Gingham* [d]
United States				
Cotton	8.4	8.7	11.8	10.4
Labor	3.9	5.6	9.1	12.0
Other production costs	2.3	4.1	5.3	11.2
Total	14.6	18.4	26.2	33.6
Japan				
Cotton	7.8	8.3	10.3	9.0
Labor	1.7	2.5	3.2	4.6
Other production costs	1.9	3.8	4.9	8.5
Total	11.4	14.6	18.4	22.1
India				
Cotton	5.6	7.0		
Labor	2.5	3.8		
Other production costs	3.2	5.9		
Total	11.3	16.7		

[a] Construction 44 by 40 threads per inch; yarns carded white, warp 20 single, filling 18 single; width 40 inches; weight 4.25 linear yards per pound.

[b] Construction 80 by 80; yarns carded white, warp 40 single, filling 40 single; width 39 inches; weight 4.00 linear yards per pound.

[c] Construction 136 by 60; yarns combed white, warp 40 single, filling 40 single; width 40 inches; weight 3.65 linear yards per pound.

[d] Construction 90 by 60; yarns combed, 50 per cent colored, warp 40 single, filling 40 single; weight 4.35 linear yards per pound.

Note: The costs reflected here apply only to production up to the gray cloth stage, omitting finishing, sales, and other costs. The costs shown here are for a few plants selected as representative in each country. The American plants are all highly modern and efficient, as are all of the Japanese plants covered except the one producing print cloth. The Indian plant reflects medium costs.

Source: U.S. Department of Commerce, Business and Defense Services Administration, *Comparative Fabric Production Costs in the United States and Four Other Countries* (Washington: GPO, 1961), pp. 5, 19, 21, and elsewhere.

time goes on, India and other industrializing countries can be expected to expand and extend their competitive power. As a result Japan will in the future find itself increasingly pressed by competition from newer sources, especially in the coarser grades and less highly processed goods. Here again, therefore, Japan stands between the newly industrializing countries on the one hand and the most industrialized on the other. Japan's future, if foreign markets remain open, lies in continuing to climb up the industrial ladder, keeping ahead of those below who may be clutching at Japan's heels.

Impact of Japanese Cotton Goods on the U.S. Market

Although they are so small a percentage of total American production, imports of cotton textiles from Japan have had a serious impact on some segments of the U.S. market. The principal reason is that Japanese sales have been concentrated in a few main categories, most notably ginghams and velveteens among fabrics, and pillowcases, shirts, and women's blouses among made-up goods. Imports have filled a much higher share of domestic demand for these products than for cotton textiles generally. The result has at times been to reduce U.S. output of these items.

Velveteen fabrics offer the clearest example. Imports from Japan were important before World War II, amounting to a little over a quarter of apparent U.S. consumption in 1939. After the war imports were at first very small. Italy became an important supplier in 1950, and from 1951 to 1953 more Italian than Japanese velveteens were imported into the United States. In 1954 and 1955, however, the flow of Japanese velveteens increased very rapidly, passing imports from Italy and, in 1955, exceeding sales of domestic velveteens. From less than 10 per cent of apparent U.S. consumption in 1949, imports from all countries came to nearly half of apparent consumption in 1954 and two-thirds in 1955 and 1956. The market was growing rapidly. From 1949 to 1955, apparent U.S. consumption rose from 4.8 to 12.8 million square yards. Sales by American producers in the latter years were slightly below the 1949 level.[30] Table 9-6 shows the record for imports from 1954 on.

Ginghams had a somewhat similar experience, although domestic producers fared better and imports never supplied such a large share of the American market. Production in the United States rose irregularly from 1951 to 1955, fell in 1956, but recovered in succeeding years. Imports from Japan were small until 1954, when a rapid rise began. This developed into a spurt of imports after June 1955. By this time most U.S.

[30] U.S. Tariff Commission, *Cotton Velveteen Fabrics,* Report to the President on Escape-Clause Investigation No. 49 under the Provisions of Section 7 of the Trade Agreements Extension Act of 1951, as Amended (Washington: Author, 1956), pp. 29 and 30.

imports of ginghams came from Japan. Total imports accounted for no more than 4 per cent of apparent consumption in 1953 and 1954, but in 1955 and 1956 jumped to 13 and 28 per cent, respectively. After the imposition of reduced quotas in 1957, the proportion declined.[31]

Women's blouses are a Western garment that Japan never used to export or even produce in quantity. But some enterprising American importers visited Japan with samples, and in 1953 for the first time 5,000 dozen blouses are recorded as having left Japan for the United States. (Table 9-4.) This figure grew to 171,000 dozen in 1954 and in 1955 skyrocketed to 4 million dozen.[32] In 1956 shipments dropped to 2 million dozen but were still nearly 12 times the 1954 level. Domestic production rose from 6.6 to 10.8 million dozen. (Table 9-6.) The percentage increase in Japanese sales was much greater than that of American producers, however, and the share of the market filled by Japan rose, because 1954 imports had been very small. Between 1956 and 1960 both imports and domestic production grew, but Hong Kong became the first foreign supplier. In 1961, imports fell and Hong Kong dropped behind Japan.

At the same time as imports into the United States of cotton goods and of other textiles and clothing showed a strong tendency to rise, exports first failed to increase and then showed some decline. In 1960 imports of cotton cloth exceeded exports for the first time since 1878.[33] The number of square yards imported in 1954 had been only 12 per cent of the amount exported. During the next four years this figure fluctuated between 22 and 37 per cent, then jumped to 51 in 1959 and 104 in 1960 before falling back to 54 in 1961. By value, cotton cloth imports have not yet come up to exports; in 1960, the peak year, they reached only 64 per cent.[34]

[31] In August 1956 a quota of 70 million square yards was announced for the calendar year 1956. This was cut back to 35 million yards in the quotas adopted in January 1957.

[32] There is a substantial discrepancy in the 1955 figures shown in Tables 9-4 and 9-6. Japanese sources show exports to the United States of 4 million dozen blouses against 2.8 million dozen estimated by the U.S. government. However, since the latter cites Japanese export data for 1956 and 1957, the fluctuation during these years was probably more accurately reflected in the Japanese figures.

[33] Secretary of Commerce Luther H. Hodges' address at the Annual Meeting of the American Cotton Manufacturers' Institute, March 24, 1961. Department of Commerce Press Release, March 24, 1961, p. 5.

[34] The figures for cotton manufactures as a whole (imports as a per cent of exports) are:

	By Volume	*By Value*
1954–1957	34	50
1960	106	108
1961	75	91

Source: U.S. Department of Commerce, "U.S. imports of textiles . . . 1957–61," cited, and an earlier report for 1954–59.

THE AMERICAN COTTON TEXTILE INDUSTRY

Although the amounts involved do not seem alarmingly large by objective standards, imports of Japanese cotton textiles stirred strong American reactions and posed major policy problems for the United States for most of the 1950s. Complaints by American cotton textile producers began almost as soon as Japanese textiles reappeared in quantity on the American market. These manufacturers regarded the rising Japanese imports as sales taken away from them, often, in fact, as sales that would not have been made except for the expensive promotional effort of American producers. They soon began to register vigorous protests, individually and through their trade associations. Textile and apparel unions before long added their own complaints. Consumers, characteristically, were virtually silent. Some business interests have opposed the call for restrictions, although for the most part acting less vigorously than the textile producers. Export groups have expressed some opposition to import restrictions. Raw cotton producers at first opposed restrictions but in 1959 joined the textile representatives in seeking import quotas under the Agricultural Adjustment Act. The principal opposition to restrictions has come from American importers, from the Japanese themselves, from other trade groups, American civic organizations, and economists.

The arguments, agitation, pressures, and counterpressures produced a series of proposals for the protection of the American industry, and some for its improvement. Most of the demands put forward for new American trade barriers were, in the end, turned aside but perhaps only because the Japanese themselves restricted exports to the United States. By the early 1960s the problem had gone beyond that of competition from Japan alone and the United States government had broadened the area of its response and taken the lead in creating a multilateral agreement regulating trade in cotton textiles. Before then, enough had been done and said to show rather clearly the character of the problem and its policy implications. It is with these matters, in rather condensed form, that the present section is concerned.

The Industry's Problems

Although efforts to check imports, and especially imports from Japan, were prominent features of the cotton textile industry's public activities throughout the 1950s, the industry's troubles stem from more than foreign competition. For one thing, the demand for cotton goods in the United States is declining. This results from changing habits regarding clothing, home furnishings, and other matters and growing competition from paper, synthetic fibers, and plastics. Consumption of cotton declined from 28.9 pounds per capita in 1940 to 22.1 pounds in 1961, while the consumption of all fibers together began and ended this period at a little less than 36 pounds per capita.[35]

Another source of difficulty for the industry is a continuing world-wide tendency toward overcapacity in spinning, weaving, and finishing. The rapid expansion of plant in foreign countries during the postwar period has been important to this development. Developing countries all over the world initiate or expand textile production at an early stage. Hong Kong, India, Korea, Pakistan, and Taiwan, as well as Japan and European countries, are all now exporting cotton textiles to the United States. Communist China has rapidly increased its capacity but at present is only a threat so far as exports are concerned. Taking the world as a whole, new equipment comes into being faster than the old disappears.

The age of much of the plant and equipment in the American cotton textile industry is a third major handicap. By contrast with the ultra-modern factories of Japan and the new capacity installed in recent years elsewhere, much of the machinery being used in the United States is obsolete. The president of the American Textile Machinery Association, an interested party, put the figure as high as 75 per cent in 1958.[36]

A fourth problem is that the structure and management of the American textile industry, particularly its cotton goods segment, are weak in a number of ways. There are some sharp contrasts with organization and management in the Japanese cotton textile industry. A textile labor spokesman who is one of management's sharpest critics said: "Fractionalized by traditional individualism, management in the industry has made only the most tentative and preliminary efforts at reorganizing itself for the new era. . . . Several ventures at establishing technical research institutions have left as residues modest institutions supported by few concerns which cannot tackle the competitive challenge sounded by other industries. Economic and marketing research are for the most part limited to a few individual companies. Less than a handful make serious investments in these fields." [37]

A fifth and particularly serious problem for the industry is that declining employment has accompanied a fairly rapid increase in productivity per worker, while the continuing shift of textile production from New England to the South has added to the total number of workers displaced.

[35] Consumption has fluctuated a great deal from the depression lows (18.7 pounds of cotton, 21.8 pounds of all fibers in 1932) to the wartime highs (40.2 pounds of cotton, 49.5 pounds of all fibers in 1942), to postwar lows (21.4 pounds of cotton, 33.5 pounds of all fibers in 1958). U.S. Department of Agriculture, Economic Research Service, *The Cotton Situation,* March 1962, p. 37.

[36] Statement of James H. Hunter in Pastore Subcommittee Hearings (1958), cited, pt. 1, p. 101.

[37] Statement of Solomon Barkin, Director of Research, Textile Workers Union of America, in same, p. 289.

Despite the allegation of obsolete equipment quoted above, the productivity of production workers rose by 44 per cent between 1947–1949 and 1958 while the number of workers dropped by 30 per cent.[38] The workers displaced in this reduction and in the migration of the industry have in many cases had great trouble finding other employment. The loss of a textile job is often more damaging than one might expect in the United States, even during a period of general economic growth; the age of workers is likely to be high, many are married women for whom moving elsewhere may be out of the question, and some closed mills are in regions without much alternative employment. A number of textile districts have for years been listed as labor-surplus areas. A study made in New England in 1954 showed the seriousness of the problem of displaced workers. It examined the consequences when five textile mills were closed and the work force in a sixth permanently reduced. (Four were cotton mills.) More than a year after four of the shutdowns, less than half of the persons who could be found were employed.[39] Thirty per cent of the men and 52 per cent of the women had had no employment since lay-off. Eight per cent of the men and 15 per cent of the women had withdrawn from the labor force. Age constituted a serious barrier to finding new jobs and 43 per cent of those still unemployed were 56 or over. A marked reluctance to move to new areas was another factor that kept people unemployed.

Already facing these difficulties, the American cotton textile industry has found cause for complaint in a series of governmental policies. Over and above the question of limiting imports, the industry has felt itself put at a disadvantage by measures that seemed to offer considerable help

[38] U.S. Department of Commerce, Business and Defense Services Administration, *Comparative Fabric Production Costs in the United States and Four Other Countries* (Washington: GPO, 1961), p. 8.

[39] It seems likely that former workers who were not found had been more successful in finding other employment than those who were found. William H. Miernyk, *Inter-Industry Labor Mobility: The Case of the Displaced Textile Worker* (Boston: Bureau of Business and Economic Research, Northeastern University, 1955), pp. 7 and 12–13. A later report, prepared for the U.S. Department of Commerce, gives the results of textile mill closings in eight communities during the 1950s. A total of 30,000 workers lost jobs in textiles, but it is not made clear how many jobs had related to cotton textiles, probably a minority. In a summary the report states: "Many older workers were unable to find new jobs; many younger men left their home communities to find employment elsewhere. Long periods of unemployment were common, and many displaced textile workers were forced to seek assistance from relatives or public assistance agencies, or eventually to take lower paying jobs in other industries. Emigration and lower paying jobs for women had the effect of changing the character of the labor in some communities, raising the average age of workers and increasing the proportion of women." U.S. Department of Commerce, *Economic Effect of Textile Mill Closings, Selected Communities in Middle Atlantic States,* prepared by George Perazich and W. T. Stone of Galaxy, Inc. (Washington: GPO, 1963), p. 2.

to its foreign competitors. The trouble started with so basic a matter as the price of cotton. U.S. farm policy establishes price supports that raise the cost of raw cotton to American mills, but not to foreign buyers who benefit from U.S. export subsidies. There are no countervailing duties to equalize this difference when the United States imports cotton manufactures. U.S. government procurement policies, permitting large textile purchases abroad, especially for military and foreign aid purposes, were also the object of repeated complaints by domestic producers until measures taken to protect the U.S. balance of payments substantially changed the situation.

Another complaint has been that American foreign aid money has been used to build up cotton textile manufacturing industries abroad, thus not only destroying some of the export markets for American textiles but also promoting import competition in the United States. This complaint does not apply to Japan, for no American grant money has gone into Japanese cotton textile industry capital facilities. To be sure, in addition to an advance of surplus raw cotton by the U.S. government to make possible the start of operations after surrender, the Export–Import Bank of Washington has extended a series of annual cotton credits, facilitating Japanese purchase of American raw cotton. But these credits are more in the nature of export promotion for raw cotton than aid to foreign manufacturing.

On top of all this, the American cotton textile industry felt that its "own" domestic market was being taken away by the incursion of foreign sellers. Since the cotton textile industry is beset by so many troubles, it is hard to say with any precision how much of its difficulty is attributable to imports. On only two occasions—up through June 1962—has the Tariff Commission found that imports from Japan were causing serious injury to segments of the domestic industry: in the case of velveteens in October 1956 and in the case of cotton typewriter ribbon cloth in June 1960, both by unanimous votes.[40] Taking the industry as a whole, we must say that only a small part of production has been displaced by imports. What can be concluded readily, however, is that the adjustments made necessary by imports are much more difficult than they would be if the cotton textile industry were expanding rapidly, or if the manufacturing firms had diversified interests and were gradually shifting emphasis from cotton goods to new products with expanding markets. In recent years alternative uses for cotton textile capital, labor, and man-

[40] Table 8-3, above; U.S. Tariff Commission, *Cotton Velveteen Fabrics*, cited, p. 3; U.S. Tariff Commission, *Investigations under the "Escape Clause" of Trade Agreements* (Washington: Author, 10th ed., 1958), p. 43; (13th ed., 1960), p. 27. In the only other escape-clause case in which the Commission acted, that of cotton pillowcases, November 1956, the Commission by 3–2 vote found no injury. Same, 10th ed., p. 44.

agement have not been easy to find. A procession of displaced workers before a committee under the chairmanship of Senator Pastore (see below) made their distress vividly clear. Because many cotton mills are in areas of high unemployment, any reduction of cotton textile employment tends to have a magnified effect. The long life of textile equipment and the very low rate of depreciation heretofore permitted by the income tax authorities make it difficult for investments to be amortized rapidly in a shrinking market.

Though one can argue that an equal expenditure of talent and energy on other problems would have produced more constructive results, it is not surprising that the industry should have concentrated its attention on foreign competition in the home market. Imports provide a convenient target. They are a visible source of difficulty and seem easier to cope with than some of the other problems facing the industry. So the producers have concentrated a great deal of effort on appeals for protection and thereby posed serious policy problems for the United States government.

Proposals for Protection

The industry's campaigns took many forms and had numerous targets. They began almost as soon as imports of cotton goods from Japan began to expand substantially. In 1954, for example, there were vigorous pleas to the Tariff Commission regarding peril points during the public hearings in preparation for the tariff negotiations before Japan's admission to GATT. Producers appeared at the congressional hearings on the Trade Agreements Extension Act of 1955. In addition, approaches were made repeatedly to individual Congressmen, to executive agencies in Washington, to the White House, and also to state governments. Escape-clause proceedings before the Tariff Commission were instituted in 1956 by U.S. producers of velveteens, ginghams, pillowcases, and blouses and later by makers of other products as well. In 1955, as was later announced, "the Executive Branch of the U.S. Government began an intensive study of the problem with a view to finding a resolution which would provide appropriate safeguards for the domestic industry within the framework of established U.S. foreign trade policy." [41]

Early in 1956 the state legislatures of South Carolina and Alabama passed laws requiring retail stores handling Japanese imports to display large signs saying "Japanese Textiles Sold Here." Similar legislation was considered but defeated in Georgia. The Japanese government protested that these laws violated the Treaty of Friendship, Commerce and Naviga-

[41] News release issued by the Departments of State, Commerce and Agriculture, Department of State Press Release No. 25, January 16, 1957.

tion of 1953[42] and the State Department pressed the Department of Justice on the matter. These laws were not enforced, perhaps because of protests by Secretary of State Dulles and other federal officials. As a consequence the Department of Justice did not undertake formal proceedings against the states.[43]

The Senate, in a July 1956 resolution, declared itself "gravely concerned over the acute distress existing in segments of the domestic textile industry and the greatly increased importations of foreign textiles and textile products."[44] During 1956 and 1957 the Boggs Subcommittee of the House Committee on Ways and Means explored the textile problem in studies and hearings and held some sessions in Japan.[45] In 1958 the Senate again expressed its concern about textiles and established a special subcommittee of the Senate Committee on Interstate and Foreign Commerce under Senator Pastore of Rhode Island to investigate problems of the domestic industry.[46] After hearings in Washington, New York, New England, and the South, the subcommittee issued a report in February 1959. Further hearings were held two years later and a supplementary report issued. The Pastore Subcommittee's report of 1959 supported a number of the views expressed by U.S. producers.[47] Regarding the export quotas Japan had meanwhile established (see below) as uncertain and inadequate, the subcommittee recommended that the United States impose import quotas that would restrict imports "within limits which will not further endanger existing capacity." It proposed subquotas for specific categories, "so that . . . no one branch of the domestic textile industry will feel the full impact" of imports. The subcommittee further recommended immediate removal of the price differential that permits foreigners to buy U.S. cotton at prices lower than those charged to American mills. If this could not be done at once, cotton goods imports should be subjected to an interim tariff high enough to offset the difference between world and U.S. prices of raw cotton. The subcommittee also urged "more realistic interpretation of the current peril-point provision of the Trade Agreements Act and faster action on escape-clause cases brought before the Tariff Commission."

The Pastore Subcommittee also supported the objections of the U.S.

[42] Department of State Press Release No. 199, April 17, 1956.

[43] Information from files of the Department of Justice.

[44] Senate Res. 236, 84th Cong., 2d sess., July 18, 1956.

[45] See *Foreign Trade Policy,* compendium of papers, cited, pp. 821–1027, and Hearings, 85th Cong., 1st sess. (Washington: GPO, 1958); also *Administration and Operation of Customs and Tariff Laws . . . ,* Hearings, cited, especially pp. 1979–1983, 2034–2037, 2080–2115.

[46] Senate Res. 287, 85th Cong., 2d sess., May 6, 1958.

[47] *Problems of the Domestic Textile Industry,* Senate Report No. 42, by a special subcommittee of the Interstate and Foreign Commerce Committee, 86th Cong., 1st sess. (Washington: GPO, 1959), pp. 24–28.

textile industry against the use of American aid to develop textile industries abroad, urging that "careful study be made of the long-run consequences of further expansion of world textile capacity before additional grants be made to other countries to expand their own textile production for the international market." And the subcommittee urged more rapid depreciation of new equipment for tax purposes. As a result of these recommendations, an interdepartmental committee on textiles was established in the executive branch, but no new legislation passed the Congress.

Earlier the textile industry's campaign had produced only very meager results so far as specific U.S. policy measures were concerned. The tightening of the escape clause and the national security clause in renewal of the Trade Agreements Act in 1955 and again in 1958, although not related specifically to the cotton textile industry, increased the possibilities for protection. President Eisenhower's decision in August 1960 to withdraw the tariff concession on cotton typewriter ribbon cloth raised the duty on that small item.[48] But other escape-clause actions failed and the industry seemed uninterested in filing many applications. What it wanted, it repeatedly made clear, was import quotas imposed by the U.S. government. [49] This position was held both before and after Japan imposed export quotas (see below). The industry's view was shared by others, as the passages just quoted from the Pastore report show. A Senate motion that would have imposed rigid and nondiscretionary quotas failed to pass by only two votes in 1956.[50]

At least twice the cotton textile producers sought a quota by asking the Secretary of Agriculture to use his power under Section 22 of the Agricultural Adjustment Act. The purpose of the provision is to prevent

[48] U.S. Tariff Commission, *Cotton Typewriter Ribbon Cloth,* Report to the President on Escape-Clause Investigation No. 7-85 under the Provisions of Section 7 of the Trade Agreements Extension Act of 1951, as Amended (Washington: Author, 1960); Public Information for Release August 24, 1960, "White House Statement concerning the President's Action on Cotton Typewriter Ribbon Cloth."

[49] See especially testimony by Robert C. Jackson, executive vice-president of the American Cotton Manufacturers' Institute, appearing on November 12, 1958, Pastore Subcommittee Hearings, cited, pp. 1250–1255. Mr. Jackson held a position equivalent to that of Dr. Claudius T. Murchison twenty years earlier (see pp. 314–316) and used as part of his presentation a new memorandum from Dr. Murchison justifying import quotas. Same, pp. 1253–1254.

[50] As an amendment to Section 22 of the Agricultural Adjustment Act of 1933 it was proposed that "(g) Whenever the Secretary of Agriculture determines that there is, or that there is likely to be, a surplus of any agricultural commodity in the United States, no such commodity *and no product thereof* shall be permitted to be entered or withdrawn from warehouse for consumption during any calendar or marketing year in excess of the annual average quantity . . . during the three calendar years immediately preceding such calendar or marketing year. . . ." (Italics added.) The amendment was defeated 45 to 43, with 8 Senators not voting. *Congressional Record,* v. 102, pt. 8, June 28, 1956, pp. 11222 and 11233.

imports from interfering with domestic agricultural programs—such as price supports—and, according to the Under Secretary of Agriculture, "also to prevent substantial reduction in the amount of the domestically produced commodity processed in the United States." [51] A petition presented by the American Cotton Manufacturers' Institute in December 1955 was denied. True D. Morse, the Acting Secretary of Agriculture, pointed out that in 1955 imports of cotton products were equivalent to less than one per cent of the U.S. cotton crop that year, and less than one and one-half per cent of the consumption of cotton by U.S. mills. Cotton goods exports, he said, exceeded imports by the equivalent of 400,000 bales of raw cotton annually. Japan, the principal source of U.S. cotton textile imports, was also the largest customer for U.S. raw cotton. The U.S. cotton textile industry operated at a relatively high level in 1954 and 1955. "We are advised, and it is generally known, that Japan is instituting controls on the quantity, quality and prices of goods exported to the United States." The Acting Secretary then suggested that "if certain sectors of the domestic textile industry are suffering from, or threatened with serious injury from imports, the so-called escape clause of the Trade Agreements Act offers an avenue through which relief may be obtained."

A second attempt to obtain quotas under Section 22 was made in 1959, this time with the support, and in the name, of the National Cotton Council, an organization of cotton dealers and ginners. The occasion for the new petition was the planned increase of the cotton export subsidy from 6.5 to 8 cents a pound in August 1959 and the progressive expansion that had occurred in imports of cotton manufactures from countries other than Japan, notably Hong Kong, Korea, India, Taiwan, and Pakistan. This time the appeal was recommended by the Secretary of Agriculture and became the subject of an investigation by the Tariff Commission, which decided, largely on technical grounds, that imports of articles containing cotton were not threatening the cotton export subsidy program, the only program to which the Tariff Commission addressed itself.[52]

Although these efforts failed, the demands for protection for the American cotton textile industry led to two very important results. The first was Japan's imposition of export quotas on sales of cotton goods to

[51] Quoted from Acting Secretary of Agriculture True D. Morse's letter, dated February 6, 1956, to A. K. Winget, President, American Cotton Manufacturers' Institute (ACMI) as printed in Pastore Subcommittee Hearings, cited, pp. 1259–1260. The ACMI petition is reproduced in same, pp. 1260–1264. Statistical and other material to support the petition is reproduced on pp. 1264–1276.

[52] U.S. Tariff Commission, *Articles Containing Cotton,* Report to the President on Investigation No. 22-22 under Section 22 of the Agricultural Adjustment Act, as Amended (Washington: Author, 1960), p. 2.

the United States, a step the Japanese took in order to avoid the restriction of imports they thought the U.S. government would otherwise impose. The second result, which grew in part out of the first, was the negotiation in the early 1960s of an international agreement regulating a large part of the world's trade in cotton textiles. While neither of these results altogether satisfied the American cotton textile industry, both did something to alleviate its position and neither would have come about had it not been for the strong reaction to the growth of Japanese sales of cotton goods to the United States in the mid-1950s.

JAPANESE EXPORT QUOTAS

The conflict between rising imports of cotton textiles and growing American opposition to them resulted in Japanese capitulation early in 1957. The character of this surrender reflects some of the many forces at work, especially the determination of American producers to secure more severe restrictions on imports than seemed likely to result from escape-clause actions, the political influence of management and labor in the geographically extensive textile industry, and the readiness of the Japanese, when convinced that restrictions of some sort were inevitable, to take action of their own instead of waiting for the United States to impose additional import barriers. None of these factors was entirely new. Indeed, the postwar developments had some marked prewar parallels.

Prewar Quotas

The first time Japanese cotton textiles came into the American market in such rapidly increasing quantities as to provoke strong reaction from the U.S. industry was in the 1930s, especially after the yen began to depreciate at the end of 1931. Japanese exports of cotton cloth to the United States rose from 1.6 million square yards in 1932 to 124 million square yards in 1937. (Table 9-4.) Although the prices were low the quality of this cloth and of other cotton products was high enough to evoke compliments from Dr. Claudius T. Murchison, president of the Cotton Textile Institute, Inc.:

> The Japanese have learned well modern methods of textile manufacturing. The days of their apprenticeship, when they were building up an industry from the cast-off machinery of Western nations, are over. There is no better textile machinery in the world than is now found in Japan. There is nowhere a finer mastery over the mechanical and chemical processes incident to the weaving and finishing of cloth and in no country are business organization and administration, from the standpoint of industry as a whole, more shrewdly devised to meet the trading requirements of a chaotic world.[53]

[53] *The New York Times,* August 23, 1936.

Dr. Murchison also asserted that Japanese wages were about one-sixth those in the United States and that total Japanese production costs for cloth were 30 to 40 per cent below American costs.

Although the Trade Agreements Act had passed in 1934, the administration in Washington was not deaf to complaints about imports. Secretary of State Hull and others had said they would administer the program so as to avoid injury to domestic interests. Under American pressure, Japan agreed to limit exports of cotton rugs and lead pencils to the United States and cotton cloth to the Philippines, then an American possession.[54] When in March 1935 the Senate expressed concern about rising imports of Japanese cotton goods, the Tariff Commission began an investigation. This was delayed while a Cabinet Committee made a "study of the cotton textile industry" [55] and the State Department made representations to Japan. In December 1935 the Japanese Ambassador reported that Japanese manufacturers and exporters had decided to restrict their shipments to the United States.[56]

This unilateral decision did not suffice to check either the increasing flow of Japanese cotton cloth or the American protest. In April 1936 the Tariff Commission reported to President Roosevelt on the investigation started a year earlier. The President accepted the recommendation for tariff increases of about 42 per cent on bleached, printed, dyed, or colored cotton cloths of certain yarn counts (31 to 50).[57] The press said this decision was the "result of the collapse of negotiations with Japan looking to a 'gentlemen's agreement' by which Japan would restrict to moderate amounts her exports of these goods to the United States." [58] The "moderate amounts" suggested by the United States were reported to be about those of 1935 sales. The reported reason for Japanese refusal of a gentlemen's agreement on cotton textile exports to the United States was simply the difficulty of working out the details involved, including those of classification of products and control of transshipments through third countries. There was no objection in principle, for gentlemanly agreement to do what is necessary, no matter how unpleasant, is part of the Japanese tradition.

[54] Department of State Press Release, January 9, 1936 and May 26, 1936.

[55] U.S. Tariff Commission, *Twentieth Annual Report, 1936* (Washington: GPO, 1936), p. 35.

[56] Department of State Press Release, December 21, 1935.

[57] U.S. Tariff Commission, *Twentieth Annual Report, 1936,* cited p. 35. This was not a case under the escape clause which was only introduced into the trade agreements later. There was no trade agreement with Japan, and no significant tariff concessions on cotton textiles had been made to other countries. The President and the Commission were acting under a provision of the Hawley-Smoot tariff of 1930 authorizing tariff increases to equalize foreign and domestic costs of production. The tariff rates had ranged from 23.85 to 33.5 per cent ad valorem, according to yarn count, and were raised to a range of 34 to 47.5 per cent.

[58] *The New York Times,* May 22, 1936.

The new tariff rates became effective June 20, 1936 but they too did not stop the increase in the imports. In August Dr. Murchison said that the new tariff rates "fall far short of offsetting the cost disparity between American and Japanese goods." For this reason, and because they had been restricted to bleached and colored cloths, the tariff increases could not "be regarded as more than the first step in solving the problem of protection from Japanese competition." He advocated "a solution of our trade problems by voluntary and amicable agreement between the two governments, or perhaps, and more effective, between the two industries . . . the procedure should be one of private and voluntary negotiation." [59]

Private negotiation was in fact what followed. Dr. Murchison and his colleagues prepared the ground carefully, and in December 1936 he sailed for Japan to negotiate directly with representatives of Japanese cotton textile manufacturers in Osaka. The aim was to persuade the Japanese that negotiated quotas were better for them than the alternatives. "It is inevitable," Dr. Murchison said, "that steps be taken sooner or later to protect American industry from the effects of such a sudden onslaught, and we suggest that it is better that Japanese industrialists should make a gentlemen's agreement to regulate their exports than continue on a course that must lead to quotas or other restrictive measures." [60]

An agreement was reached on January 21, 1937 limiting Japanese shipments to the United States of all cotton fabrics (velveteen and corduroy were dealt with separately). Subject to some arrangements to permit flexibility, the Japanese agreed to limit their shipments to the United States in 1937 to the 155 million square yards already on order and in 1938 to 100 million.[61] In December 1938 the agreement was extended for a second two-year period. This quota arrangement was not formalized as a contract but remained as an informal, even if quite specific, "gentlemen's agreement." In return for limiting exports the Japanese obtained agreement, as summarized by a Japanese manufacturer, that "the representatives of the American cotton manufacturers . . . shall consider it unnecessary to seek any further governmental restriction on Japanese cotton textile imports into the United States. The American representatives also shall consider the application of this quota as the basis for a reciprocal trade agreement between the U.S. and Japan through which tariff adjustments may be made." [62]

The separate agreement on velveteen and corduroy limited annual

[59] Same, August 23, 1936.

[60] Same, January 10, 1937.

[61] Same, January 23, 1937. Twenty-five per cent of the 1938 quota could be switched to 1937. The arrangements for 1939 and 1940 permitted transfer from one year to another of as much as 20 million square yards. Same, December 20, 1938.

[62] Abe, *The Story of the Japanese Cotton Textile Industry*, cited, p. 5.

Japanese shipments to the United States to two million square yards of velveteen and 700,000 square yards of corduroy. The agreement was in effect for three years, starting March 1, 1937.

As it turned out, the American market for Japanese cotton textiles proved too small for sales to reach the quota levels. The recession of 1937–1938, together with a boycott movement expressing American resentment against Japan for aggression in China, kept sales to 124 million square yards in 1937, 16 million square yards in 1938, 72 million in 1939 and 50 million in 1940. (Table 9-4.)

Postwar "Discussions" Leading to Japanese Quotas

In many ways, the 1950s were very different from the 1930s. The United States market had grown greatly. The country was far more prosperous, even during its brief recessions, than in the 1930s. Things Japanese enjoyed unprecedented popularity in the United States, international relations were again strained but Japan was a peaceful ally, no longer the Asian protagonist of military aggression. But so far as American policy toward cotton textile imports is concerned, the two periods are remarkably similar.

Once again the American industry felt that tariff protection was not enough. It wanted direct controls placed on the trade but the U.S. government did not impose import quotas. The outcome was an arrangement with a behind-the-scenes element in it under which Japanese restricted their exports instead of the Americans restricting imports. There is an important difference though in the way this was done. Whereas comment about the 1937 quota agreement seems to have been universally laudatory, interpretation of the U.S. antitrust laws has since evolved to a point where it is now regarded as impermissible for direct discussions on the subject of trade restrictions to take place between Japanese and American cotton textile manufacturers, as the Japanese would still prefer. The textile industry in this country has had to make its formal approaches to the U.S. government, which has dealt with the Japanese government, which in turn has discussed quotas with the Japanese cotton textile producers.

Although both the Republican and Democratic administrations resisted the pressure of the textile industry to impose import quotas, they were willing to seek Japanese agreement to limit exports to the United States. Secretary of State John Foster Dulles said late in 1955: "I have personally advised representatives of the Japanese Government that they should exercise restraint in their exports and not attempt to capture so much of the American market that an American industry will be injured." [63] This

[63] Letter to Senator Margaret Chase Smith, December 1, 1955, reprinted in *The Department of State Bulletin,* December 26, 1955, p. 1064; and in the *Congressional Record,* v. 102, pt. 8, June 28, 1956, p. 11240.

generalized advice was made very specific in a series of exchanges between representatives of the American and Japanese governments. The U.S. government was very careful to call them "discussions," not negotiations. Subsequent Japanese action was pointedly labeled voluntary.[64]

Preliminary quota arrangements for 1956 had been announced by the Japanese government in December 1955. The U.S. government was officially notified the following May that the limits for the calendar year 1956 were 5 million square yards of velveteen, 145 million square yards of other cotton fabrics (of which 20 million square yards was permitted in print cloth) and 2.5 million dozen blouses.[65] These figures called for an increase in cloth sales above their all-time peak level of 140 million square yards in 1955. As it turned out, actual exports from Japan to the United States in 1956 were only 123 million square yards. (Table 9-4.) Sales of velveteens, on the other hand, which had reached 6.8 million square yards in 1955 rose to 6.9 million square yards in 1956, substantially above the quota of 5 million square yards (according to U.S. statistics, Table 9-6). In the case of blouses 4 million dozen had been shipped to the United States in 1955 and the actual exports for 1956 turned out to be 2 million. (Table 9-4.)

These quotas did not by any means satisfy American producers. The velveteen escape-clause action had already been started in January 1956 and was pressed despite the May quota announcement by the Japanese. In February escape-clause applications had been made covering blouses and pillowcases. The former was withdrawn in June, after the Japanese had lowered their blouse quota from 2.5 million dozen for 1956 to 1.5 million dozen for the Japanese fiscal year ending in March 1957. On the other hand, an escape-clause application on ginghams was made in June 1956.[66]

The Japanese became convinced that more restrictions were in prospect. In September 1956 a note from the Japanese Ambassador to the Secretary of State announcing the start of discussions on quotas for 1957 and subsequent years set out the general principles on which the new quotas were to be based. It went on to say that this restrictive ac-

[64] Until May 1956 the legal sanction for such approaches was somewhat shadowy. In that month the Agricultural Act of 1956 was passed which gave the President power to negotiate with the governments of other countries "to obtain agreements limiting the export from such countries and the importation into the United States of . . . textiles and textile products. . . . " (Public Law 540, 84th Cong., 2d sess., sec. 204.)

[65] Exchange of notes between the Secretary of State and the Ambassador of Japan, Washington, May 16, 1956.

[66] Table 8-3. U.S. Tariff Commission, *Investigations under the "Escape Clause" of Trade Agreements*, 10th ed., cited, pp. 43–45; also letter from Thorsten V. Kalijarvi, Acting Deputy Under Secretary of State for Economic Affairs, to Senator Harry F. Byrd, Chairman, Senate Committee on Finance, June 26, 1956.

tion was "based on the condition that all feasible steps will be taken by the U.S. Government to solve the problem of discriminatory state textile legislation and to prevent further restrictive action with regard to the importation of Japanese textiles into the United States." [67]

On the same day Sherman Adams, the Assistant to the President, explained the administration's position in an address to the Northern Textile Association in Portsmouth, New Hampshire. "It has seemed urgent to undertake to find some extraordinary means to provide a ready remedy for the misfortunes of the textile industry that stem from the import problem." Referring to the Japanese note he added: "There are certain (and somewhat numerous) details to be worked out and agreed to before the effect of this new plan will be fully realized." [68]

The Quota Program for 1957–1961

The resulting quotas, as announced in January 1957, are listed in Table 9-9, along with modifications made in 1959, the preceding 1956 quotas, and the later plan for 1962. The 1956 quotas for cloth in general and for velveteens were cut sharply; that for cotton blouses remained the same; and print cloth was dropped as a quota category, a number of specific constructions now being separately restricted. The new arrangement extended the quota system to many more products.

In addition the Japanese government undertook a general obligation to avoid disrupting markets and to enter into discussions. "In order to preserve the principle of diversification and avoid excessive concentration on any particular item, it is understood with respect to any item for which a specific ceiling has not been established, that the Japanese government will consult with the U.S. government to determine an appropriate course of action, whenever it appears that there is developing an excessive concentration of Japanese exports in a particular item or class of items, or if there are other problems (e.g., possible problems resulting from an excessive concentration of exports of end items made from a particular type of fabric, such as the use of gingham in the manufacture of an excessively large portion of exported blouses, sport shirts, etc.)" [69]

The new quotas largely calmed the storm of American producer protest. The gingham manufacturers withdrew their escape-clause application. The President announced that, in view of Japan's quotas, he had decided not to act on the Tariff Commission's recommendation for

[67] Department of State Press Release No. 509, September 27, 1956.

[68] White House Press Release, September 27, 1956.

[69] "Japanese Program for Export of Cotton Textiles to the United States," released by Departments of State, Commerce and Agriculture, January 16, 1957, with Department of Commerce Press Release, Office of the Secretary G-767. Also issued with Department of State Press Release No. 25, January 16, 1957.

TABLE 9-9. JAPANESE QUOTAS ON EXPORTS OF COTTON TEXTILES TO THE UNITED STATES

Group and Commodity [a]	Unit [b]	Quota Schedules			
		1956	1957 and 1958 [c]	1959, 1960 and 1961 [d]	1962 [e]
I. Cotton cloth	million sq. yds.	**150**	**113** [f]	**113** [f]	**125.5** [f,g]
Ginghams (including gingham stripes)	million sq. yds.		35	40 (44)	46.2
Velveteens	million sq. yds.	5	2.5	2.5	2.75
All other fabrics [h]	million sq. yds.	20 [i]	75.5 [j]	70.5 [j] (66.5)	76.55 [j]
(Sheeting)	million sq. yds.		(50)	(50)	(30)
(Shirting—80 × 80 type)	million sq. yds.		(20)	(20)	(20)
(Other shirting)	million sq. yds.		(43)	(43)	(32)
(Twill and sateen)	million sq. yds.		(39)	(39)	(39)
(Poplin)	million sq. yds.		(25)	(25)	(30)
(Yarn-dyed fabrics)	million sq. yds.		(24)	(24)	(29)
II. Made-up goods [k]	million sq. yds.		**30** [f]	**33** [f]	**35** [f,g]
Pillowcases	1,000 doz.		400	400	450
Dish towels	1,000 doz.		800	800	840
All other made-up goods [h]	1,000 lbs.[l]		1,875 [m]	2,527 [m]	5,573
(Handkerchiefs)	1,000 doz.		1,200	1,200	(1,260)
(Table damask)	1,000 sq. yds.		3,720 [n]	10,833	(11,375)
III. Woven apparel	million sq. yds.		**71** [f]	**78.1** [f]	**90.5** [f,g]
Blouses	1,000 doz.	2,500 [o] 1,500 [p]	1,500	1,500	1,575
Sport shirts	1,000 doz.		750	750	787.5
Shorts and trousers	1,000 doz.		600	600 (800)	1,000
All other woven apparel [h]	1,000 lbs.[l]		2,321 [q]	3,864 [q]	6,642
(Dress and work shirts)	1,000 doz.		300	300	(315)
(Brassieres and other body-supporting garments)	1,000 doz.		600	600	(800)
(Raincoats)	1,000 doz.		—	—	(60)
(Dressing gowns and robes)	1,000 doz.		—	—	(70)
IV. Knit goods	million sq. yds.		**12** [f]	**13.2** [f]	**14** [f,g]
Men's and boys' T-shirts	1,000 doz.		500	500	643
Knit shirts, other than T-shirts	1,000 doz.		—	—	809
Gloves and mittens	1,000 doz.		450	450	472.5
All other knit goods	1,000 lbs.[l]		1,477 [r]	1,738 [r]	397.4
V. Miscellaneous cotton textiles	million sq. yds.		**9** [f]	**9.9** [f]	**10** [f]
Floor coverings,[s] fish nets and netting, cotton thread, etc.					5
Total	million sq. yds.		**235**	**247.2**	**275**

[a] The breakdown of the five groups into articles is as finally evolved in the quota schedule of 1962. As a result, in certain isolated instances a special interpretation of the figures for "all other" categories is required, as indicated in the notes below.

[b] Wherever a specific ceiling for an article was established, the basis of control was the number of units (e.g., square yards, dozens, pounds) given as a ceiling in the table.

[c] The initial limits established in 1957 were to apply, unless renegotiated, to every year, 1957 through 1961, except that the limits for ginghams and velveteens were to apply only to the years 1957 and 1958.

[d] The renegotiated schedule of the initial five-year agreement increased the over-all total by 5.2 per cent and the ceilings of certain groups and articles. The additional figures in parentheses apply to 1961 only.

[e] The quota schedule of 1962 was for a period of only twelve months, beginning January 1, 1962.

[f] The quota schedule of 1957–1958 provided that, within the over-all annual total, the limit for any of the five groups could be exceeded by not more than 10 per cent. In 1959 the flexibility provisions were made much more restrictive for the remaining years of the five-year agreement. No shifts were permitted *from* Group I or *to* Group III, but otherwise shifts up to 5 per cent were permitted among groups within the annual total. In 1961 this figure was again raised to 10 per cent. In the 1962 schedule, group ceilings could be exceeded by 5 per cent provided that this provision for "flexibility" permitted increases only in the "all other" categories coming under each group.

[g] In 1962 it was further specified that within the over-all ceiling for each group any shortfall with respect to the main categories under that group might be transferred to the "all other" category, with the provision that the specific limits indicated for the various articles not be exceeded.

[h] The "all other" category was further broken down into articles with specific limits, as shown.

[i] Print cloth.

[j] Within the limit for "all other fabrics" the total exports of fabrics made from combed warp and filling were not to exceed 26 million square yards a year in the quota schedule of 1957 and 1958; 30 million square yards in 1959, 1960, and 1961; and 33 million square yards in 1962.

[k] Usually included in U.S. cotton broad-woven goods production.

[l] To provide a common statistical basis, whenever pounds are specified as the controlling limit, the conversion rate is 4.6 square yards per pound.

[m] This subtotal, expressed in 1,000 pounds, *excludes* handkerchiefs and table damask, whereas in the 1962 schedule these articles are included in "all other made-up goods."

[n] This figure is in 1,000 dollars, as provided for in the 1957 quota agreement; in 1958 it was estimated that this value represented 10,833,000 square yards, an amount that was then substituted for the dollar figure in the renegotiated schedule for 1959–1961.

[o] Announced in May 1956 for the calendar year 1956.

[p] Announced in June 1956 for the Japanese fiscal year 1956 (April 1, 1956 to March 31, 1957). (*Source:* Letter from Thorsten V. Kalijarvi, Acting Deputy Under Secretary of State for Economic Affairs, to Senator Harry F. Byrd, Chairman, Senate Committee on Finance, June 26, 1956.)

[q] This subtotal excludes dress and work shirts and brassieres and other body-supporting garments, which in the revised 1962 schedule are still listed separately but are included within "all other woven apparel," along with raincoats and dressing gowns and robes.

[r] This figure for all other knit goods, expressed in 1,000 pounds, *includes* knit shirts other than T-shirts, which in the 1962 schedule are specified separately.

[s] A specific limitation of 4 million square yards on floor coverings was imposed "entirely at their own accord" by the Japanese. This subquota was retained without change in 1959. (Information from the All Japan Cotton Spinners' Association.)

Sources: 1956—Exchange of notes between the Secretary of State and the Ambassador of Japan (Washington, May 16, 1956).
1957, 1958—"Japanese Program for Export of Cotton Textiles to the United States," released by the Departments of State, Commerce and Agriculture, January 16, 1957, with Department of Commerce Press Release, Office of the Secretary G-767; also issued with Department of State Press Release No. 25, January 16, 1957.
1959—"Japanese Program for the Export of Cotton Textiles to the United States for 1959," supplement to Department of Commerce Press Release of April 24, 1959.
1960, 1961—Department of Commerce; Embassy of Japan, Washington.
1962—"United States–Japanese Bilateral Textile Agreement," Department of State Press Release No. 631, September 13, 1961.

modification of tariff concessions on velveteens.[70] A spokesman for American producers said in December 1958, even while urging U.S. import quotas: "Most United States industry people feel that the Japanese arrangement brought a semblance of order to the import pattern and that it has worked reasonably satisfactorily so far." [71]

The total value of imports into the United States of Japanese cotton manufactures dropped sharply in 1957 and then fluctuated well below the 1956 peak level, as follows (figures are in millions of dollars, from Table 9-5):

1956	84	1959	77
1957	66	1960	74
1958	72	1961	69

Gingham imports, which had reached 77 million square yards in 1956 were never above 47 million in the following five years. Velveteens had reached 6.9 million square yards in 1956 but in the next five years remained below 3.2 million. (Table 9-6.)

The quotas announced in January 1957 were annual ceilings, to apply for five years, except for ginghams and velveteens, which were for 1957 and 1958 only. The announcement left room for quota changes after annual consultations. "Anticipating that changes may well occur in the United States textile market within the next five years, these ceilings shall be the subject of annual reviews in which the Japanese Government will consult with the United States Government for the purpose of arriving at such adjustments, upward or downward, in the quotas as may be warranted by changed conditions." [72] Consultations held late in 1957 made no changes for 1958. At the second annual consultations, which began in the fall of 1958, the Japanese proposed a 5.5 per cent increase in the total quota. American producers protested, but when the 1959 quotas were announced in April 1959 they permitted a 5.2 per cent increase in total shipments (as shown in Table 9-9) but other changes substantially reduced the flexibility. The same levels were kept for 1960 and only minor changes were made within the same total for 1961.

Japanese Administration of the Quotas

The quota program is administered jointly by the Japanese government and cotton textile trade associations. The quota for cotton cloth is allocated among individual firms by the Textile Bureau of the Ministry of

[70] U.S. Tariff Commission, *Investigations under the "Escape Clause" of Trade Agreements,* 10th ed., cited, pp. 43, 45.

[71] Robert C. Jackson, executive vice-president of the American Cotton Manufacturers' Institute, in Pastore Subcommittee Hearings, cited, p. 1255.

[72] "Japanese Program for Export of Cotton Textiles to the United States," cited, p. 1.

International Trade and Industry (MITI) and the Japan Cotton Textile Exporters' Association. Shares are based on exports in the period January 1953 through June 1955. Firms having quota allocations may lend them to others. When a firm wishes to fill an American order it applies through the Exporters' Association to MITI which issues an export license if the applicant has a large enough unused allocation.

Thirty per cent of the cloth export quota was, from the beginning of the program, reserved for new items, to encourage diversification. Any firm, large or small, old or new, that offered a new or special item could apply to MITI for an export license. Although this provision has given new firms a chance to enter the export market, in practice successful new items have come mostly from firms already holding quota allocations.

The most serious administrative difficulty with the quotas has concerned transshipments, especially through Hong Kong. The quotas are intended to cover all Japanese cotton textiles entering the United States no matter where they come from. Whenever a shipment of Japanese cotton textiles is known to be destined for the United States, even by an indirect route, it is charged against the quota. But unauthorized transshipments sometimes take place, despite Japanese efforts to control or prevent them. Then shipments arrive in the United States that have not been charged against the quota, but that go into U.S. import statistics as having come from Japan. Japanese statistics show these shipments as having gone to Hong Kong or elsewhere, and up to the present the Japanese have refused to charge them against the quotas to avoid further reductions in direct shipments to the United States. As a result of transshipments, and also of withdrawals of goods from bond, imports of some quota items, notably velveteens, have, according to U.S. statistics, substantially exceeded the quota, even though Japanese export statistics show no such excess. Transshipments also complicate the allocation of quotas among Japanese firms. One reason the government does not charge transshipments against the quotas is to avoid reducing allocations for other firms than the one which has violated the rules. But MITI punishes the offending firm by withdrawing certain rights or privileges concerning future exports.

Another problem became acute in 1958, when it came to light that the Japanese were not charging to the gingham quota certain fabrics that are regarded as gingham in the United States. This issue was settled by an increase in the amount of gingham permitted and agreement on a definition of what was to come in under this subquota.

The Results

The 1950s ended with Japanese–American commercial relations in a reasonable degree of prosperity and harmony. Cotton textiles had proved the most sensitive commodity, but Japanese acquiescence in restrictions had proved the key to keeping the flow within politically tolerable limits. The commercial policy implications of quotas will be discussed in the chapter that follows. What is important here is that the Japanese quotas provided a political answer to a politically difficult situation. As the decade ended in a national election in the United States, neither imports from Japan generally nor imports of Japanese cotton textiles specifically were of more than passing concern to American voters, most of whom were probably quite unaware of the matter.

Japan had succeeded in raising its total sales in the United States to levels that exceeded prior expectations on either side of the Pacific. Of this rising total, all fabrics and clothing together constituted 22 per cent in 1954, 30 per cent in 1956, the peak year, 21 per cent in 1960, and 19 per cent in 1961. To these substantial figures cotton manufactures contributed a significant part, although one that declined after quotas were established. The share of cotton textiles in total U.S. imports from Japan was 9, 15, 7, and 6 per cent, respectively, in the same four years.[73] American cotton manufacturers, while not satisfied in the face of rising imports from other areas, found relatively little fault with Japan. But the Japanese were unhappy that their sales were not larger. That both sides were dissatisfied to some degree is an indication of compromise. A political compromise it was, although in economic and commercial terms the Japanese had capitulated, holding back under U.S. pressure from making sales that could have been made and which would have been eminently sound on economic and business grounds.

In the process of making these arrangements the United States and Japan passed a milestone in their relations. Instead of the public acrimony and bitterness of the 1930s and war years, the two countries had succeeded in settling in reasonable harmony a potentially inflammatory issue. The formula for settlement, agreed quota restrictions, proved so effective that it is being used more and more widely, among other countries as well.

MULTILATERAL QUOTAS UNDER GATT AUSPICES

The Japanese quotas worked well, in the sense that they controlled the flow of trade about as intended. But the limited imports from Japan did not satisfy the American demand for low-price cottons, so the traders looked elsewhere. An American buyer in Japan explained to me that unless he maintained a certain volume of purchases he could neither meet his market nor justify his activities in Japan. If the quotas kept

[73] Percentages calculated from figures for total imports in Table 8-2 and textile imports in Table 9-5.

him from buying something he needed in Japan, he took a plane to Hong Kong and placed his order there. This process, and other forces at work in Hong Kong, brought about a rapid increase in American imports from that territory after 1956. Other suppliers, too, have expanded production and show greater interest in the American market. After the recession of 1957–1958, U.S. imports boomed, as the following figures show (in millions of dollars):

	1956	*1957*	*1958*	*1959*	*1960*	*1961*
Total U.S. imports of cotton manufactures	**154.3**	**136.2**	**150.0**	**201.3**	**248.3**	**203.3**
Japan	84.1	65.8	71.7	76.7	74.1	69.4
Hong Kong	0.7	5.8	17.4	45.8	63.5	47.0
Other Asian countries	15.3	13.0	14.3	24.0	34.0	25.0
Egypt	0.4	0.5	0.3	0.3	5.9	1.0
Spain	0.3	0.3	0.4	1.6	7.2	3.2
Portugal	0.0	0.1	0.3	1.0	5.2	2.3

A similar expansion took place in imports of other textile products as well. (Table 9-5.) The reaction of American producers to the intensification of foreign competition was sharpened by the decline in their domestic activity in 1960. In that year, production of cotton cloth in the United States was lower than in any of the preceding six years except 1958 when there was a recession. The fall in production, like the relative size of imports, was fairly small in percentage terms, but still it was keenly felt.

Naturally, attention focused on Hong Kong. In Washington it seemed logical to ask the British colony to do as Japan had done and adopt export quotas, especially since exports to the United Kingdom were already restricted. But in Hong Kong the issue looked different and the requests from Washington were rebuffed in early 1959. On a trip to Hong Kong toward the end of the year Assistant Secretary of Commerce Henry Kearns reportedly warned that the administration might be forced to impose import restrictions. While opinion in Hong Kong was split, some of the important garment manufacturers thought it prudent to offer a plan for limiting sales of several of the most sensitive items. American producers felt the levels proposed were too high and the coverage too limited. Their rebuff produced not a better offer from Hong Kong but a refusal to apply any restrictions, with the result that shipments reached a new high in 1960.

As might have been expected, American producers undertook new steps to get import quotas. This time textile and apparel unions joined in with new force. Despite what appears to have been a tacit understanding, at least on the part of the Japanese, that in return for the Japanese quotas American producers would not make escape-clause applications, the typewriter ribbon cloth case was brought and won by the industry, and the appeal for quotas under agricultural price programs was made and lost (pp. 312–313). The clamor affected not just cotton goods but many other textile products as well. For instance, the Amalgamated Clothing Workers union threatened to ban work on Japanese cloth by its members because imports of men's suits had risen greatly, but canceled the plan before it was put into effect.

Strong pleas were made in the February 1961 hearings of the Pastore Subcommittee by representatives of manufacturers and of labor unions in the textile, apparel, and textile machinery industries.[74] The manufacturers mainly reiterated their previously declared positions:

> 1. The findings and recommendations made by this committee on February 4, 1959, were sound and prophetic as the last two years have clearly demonstrated.
> 2. Had the recommendations made in that report been fully carried out, the American textile industry, from fibers through apparel, would not be in the plight it is today.
> 3. The present situation is critical and unless immediate relief is provided, the domestic textile industry will be destroyed by foreign textile imports.
> 4. There is only one satisfactory solution: the establishment of import quotas by country and by category.
> 5. Quotas must be provided by the Government in 1961 to preserve the American textile industry and protect the general economy of the United States.[75]

Union representatives also reiterated previously expressed views. For present purposes the most important of these concerns tariff quotas on imports:

> *Textile industry historic levels of production should be safeguarded.* The TWUA [Textile Workers Union of America] has previously presented to your committee its conviction, and support for its position, that there should be safeguarded levels of national production with tariff rates adequate to assure the continuance of this volume of output. Such trade as we develop beyond this level may be subject to lower ad valorem rates.[76]

President Kennedy's Program for the Textile Industry

The new administration that took office at the beginning of 1961 was thus confronted in its first weeks with intense pressure to do something

[74] *Problems of the Domestic Textile Industry,* Hearings before a subcommittee of the Senate Committee on Interstate and Foreign Commerce, 87th Cong., 1st sess., February 6 and 7, 1961 (Washington: GPO, 1961), pp. 9–14, 61–76, 285–297, 323–340, 361–382.

[75] J. M. Cheatham, president of the American Cotton Manufacturers' Institute, before the Pastore Subcommittee, February 6, 1961. Same, p. 10.

[76] Statement of Solomon Barkin, Director of Research, Textile Workers Union of America, in same, p. 292.

for the textile industry, preferably by limiting imports. What the industry and labor people wanted was not new, but their mood was unusually belligerent. President Kennedy moved promptly. In mid-February he appointed a Cabinet-level committee under Secretary of Commerce Luther H. Hodges, a former textile manufacturer, to recommend action. While the committee was deliberating, the President made several moves, one of which was to dissuade the clothing workers from their threatened boycott of Japanese fabrics. In announcing his balance-of-payments policy the President made clear that he wanted to avoid import restrictions for a number of reasons, not least that they invite retaliation. The question remained whether the President could adhere to this preference and at the same time do something effective about textiles.

At the beginning of May the President announced a seven-point plan based on the report of his Cabinet Committee:

1. The Department of Commerce was to expand its research on textile products, processes, and markets.
2. The Treasury Department was to review its depreciation allowances (for tax purposes) on textile machinery, with a view to stimulating modernization of the industry through more rapid depreciation of equipment.
3. The Small Business Administration was to assist cotton textile firms to obtain financing for modernization.
4. The Department of Agriculture was to explore means to eliminate "the adverse differential in raw cotton costs between domestic and foreign textile producers."
5. The President planned to send Congress proposals for federal assistance to industries injured or threatened with serious injury as a result of increased imports.
6. The Department of State was to arrange an early conference of the principal textile exporting and importing countries, for the purpose of avoiding "undue disruption of established industries."
7. Applications by the textile industry for action under the escape clause or the national security provision of the Trade Agreements Act were to be "carefully considered on their merits." [77]

This program attacked the problem from several sides and seemed to suggest that the President wanted to find a way to help the industry without resorting to unilateral import restrictions. But the last point left that course open as well, if the others did not produce acceptable results. By May the textile industry filed an extensive brief with the OCDM under the national security clause of the Trade Agreements Act. The application called for an elaborate and comprehensive system of import quotas regulating U.S. purchases of all kinds of textiles and products, country by country. Although this application was never granted, the possibility

[77] White House Press Release, May 2, 1961.

that the OCDM might recommend to the President that he act on some of these proposals remained a significant factor behind the negotiations that followed, domestic and foreign.

The first major step under the new program was taken by the State Department. George W. Ball, Under Secretary of State for Economic Affairs, held a series of preliminary conversations in Europe, Hong Kong, and Washington to explore the possibilities of international action along the lines of Part 6 of the program. In mid-July 1961 a sixteen-nation conference assembled in Geneva under GATT auspices to discuss international trade in cotton textiles.[78] In one week of discussions this conference agreed on the text of an agreement for submission to participating governments for approval. It set forth specific short-term arrangements along with principles and procedures for an agreement of longer duration.

The agreement provided that during the twelve-month period, October 1961 through September 1962, importing countries could call upon exporting countries to limit exports in any of 64 listed categories of cotton textiles. Failing bilateral agreement, the importing countries could take unilateral action to limit imports to a level not lower than that of the twelve months, July 1960 through June 1961. The rationale of such restrictions was avoidance of market disruption as it had been defined by the GATT Contracting Parties on November 19, 1960.[79]

No long-term arrangement was spelled out at Geneva but a Cotton Textiles Committee of GATT was agreed upon. The committee was instructed to hold its first meeting in October, to report as appropriate from time to time to the other two GATT committees most concerned (the Market Disruption Committee and the Committee on Expansion of Trade), and to produce by April 30, 1962 recommendations for a "long-term solution" of the problems of cotton textile trade.

The short-term arrangement constituted a major innovation in trade policy. For the first time quotas were openly and formally discussed among the governments of countries concerned with international trade in cotton textiles. Conflict with the GATT obligations of participating governments was averted by having the conference held under GATT auspices. In the process, the substance of the agreement may possibly have been made less restrictive than might otherwise have been the case. But American cotton manufacturers got a large part of what they wanted. The new quotas were far more finely divided than the Japanese export

[78] The nations represented were Australia, Austria, Canada, India, Japan, Pakistan, Portugal, Spain, Sweden, the United Kingdom, the United States, and five members of the European Economic Community: Belgium, France, West Germany, Italy, and the Netherlands. The EEC, OECD, some governments, and industrial interests were represented informally by observers.

[79] This paragraph and the one below are based mainly on Department of State Press Release No. 531, July 26, 1961.

quotas had been, thus making it far more difficult for the over-all quota to be filled. The base period was so set as to provide a relatively low starting point, since imports of cotton goods into the United States had dropped sharply during the first part of 1961. Perhaps most significant of all, import quotas were authorized as a last resort.

While the main impact of the short-term arrangement was plainly restrictive, it had some other features. Countries that already had quotas on imports of cotton goods, and notably the expanding economies of Western Europe, were to "significantly increase access to their markets" after January 1, 1962. The GATT auspices and some broad statements about the orderly expansion of international trade also held out the prospect that the new arrangement could be something more than a multilateral blessing for familiar restrictive policies. But the test of these possibilities would plainly depend on the drafting and operation of the long-term agreement.

Bilateral Japanese–American Agreement for 1962

Armed with the Geneva draft short-term arrangement, even though it had not been formally approved by the various governments concerned, the United States promptly sent a delegation to Japan to negotiate the Japanese quotas on cotton textile exports to the United States in 1962. Producers in Japan were still smarting from what they considered a serious setback in Geneva. They persuaded their government to seek a 30 per cent increase over the 1961 level. The Americans were thinking in far smaller terms, even though the United States had kept reassuring the Japanese informally at Geneva that they "would be taken care of" in the bilateral negotiations. The Japanese wanted a reward for their restraint during the period of "voluntary" quotas. To satisfy textile producers in the United States, even partially, American negotiators were under pressure to assure that total textile imports into the United States would be lower in 1962 than in the recent past. To achieve that result Japanese quotas would have to rise less than Hong Kong shipments would fall.

What emerged from the negotiations in Japan, after vigorous bargaining, was a total quota for 1962 of 275 million square yards, an increase of 11.2 per cent over the 1961 level. (The details are shown in the last column of Table 9-9.) This 1962 quota was 17 per cent higher than the initial 235-million-yard level set in the "voluntary" quotas of 1957. The increase did not please American producers, but Japanese textile men thought it far too little to be a fair reward for past restraint. Japanese–American relations seem to have been strained more by this negotiation than by the "discussions" preceding the announcement of Japanese quotas in January 1957.

Even at these limited levels Japanese exports to the United States caused difficulty. After a large part of the 1962 quota for certain products had been used up by midyear, the United States approached the Japanese government and induced it to suspend entirely the export to the United States of blouses, shorts, and trousers after August 31, 1962 pending discussions on these items. The Japanese also agreed to reduce "greatly" shipments of ginghams, poplins, and pillowcases.[80]

The Long-Term Cotton Textile Arrangement

The GATT Cotton Textiles Committee blazed a further trail when in February 1962 it produced a draft long-term arrangement for approval by the governments. This agreement sanctions restraint of cotton textile trade, but within strict limits and only under specified circumstances. Countries without import controls are permitted by Article 3, as in the short-term arrangement, to request exporting countries to impose restraints under certain conditions; failing agreement on such restraints, the importing country may impose controls of its own. Requests for restraint can be made only if there has been market disruption as defined by GATT. If import controls are imposed they must allow at least as much to enter in the first year as actually entered during the twelve-month period ending three months before the request for restraint was made. If an import quota is continued beyond a year, it *should* rise for the second year, if possible by 5 per cent. If retained after the second year it *must* rise by at least 5 per cent a year. A quota imposed at the beginning of the long-term arrangement, October 1, 1962, and continued throughout the five-year period, would therefore have to rise by at least 5 per cent at the end of the second, third, and fourth years, thus being no less than 15.8 per cent higher in the fifth year than in the second, when it may or may not have been higher than in the first. Thus increase is mandatory at a rate that in five years falls slightly short of the 17 per cent increase in Japanese quotas between 1957 and 1962.

Countries already having import quotas on cotton textiles agree in Article 2 of the long-term arrangement to "relax those restrictions progressively each year with a view to their elimination as soon as possible." Details of this commitment were not published with the draft agreement, and there was some delay in reaching agreement as to how great the increases would be. Eventually it was announced that by the termination of the long-run agreement, in 1967, the European Economic Community would permit the importation of 88 per cent more cotton goods than in 1962, while the Scandinavian countries would increase their imports by 15 per cent and Austria by 95 per cent. While the higher figures offer

[80] Department of State Press Release No. 520, August 24, 1962.

Japan useful new markets, it must be remembered that the increases are less impressive than they sound because the starting place was low.

Over and above these formulas and operating provisions, there are two features of the long-term textile agreement that are important innovations. One is the preamble in which the signatories profess the aims of facilitating economic expansion by enlarging opportunities for underdeveloped countries to sell their manufactures abroad. Market disruption is to be avoided but is a problem that should be dealt with "in such a way as to provide growing opportunities for exports of these products. . . . " The second, related, feature is the creation of a continuing committee on which all the signatory governments are represented which will review the operation of the agreement and hear discussion of differences in view about its interpretation or application. Staffed by GATT and meeting under its auspices, the committee is a potentially major innovation in international trade negotiations. It will undoubtedly be looked on by exporting countries and others as the place where the principles of the preamble—and other language in the agreement—can be appealed to against the persistence of restrictive practices in the importing countries. The initial acceptability of the agreement to the exporters undoubtedly depended to an important degree on these innovations. It remains to be seen which will win out: the progressive approach of these features or the restrictive drive that led to the agreement in the first place.

The long-term arrangement promised enough protection to cause a group of 75 interested Congressmen to thank President Kennedy. But their satisfaction with what had been done for cotton manufactures did not prevent them from adding, "We hope that the Administration will now promptly move on wool, man-made fiber, silk and other fibers, which are in an even worse position." [81] (The Kennedy Administration had made it clear it did not want to follow such a course. The first article of the agreement itself spoke of the "special problems of cotton textiles" and said that the measures agreed on "are not to be considered as lending themselves to application in other fields.")

The Japanese reaction to the new agreement itself was limited and mild. Along with other exporting countries Japan gained something by the escalation provision and the promised increased access to European and other markets that had been restricted by import quotas. But Japanese were disappointed that the arrangement was for as long as five years and that the decision as to whether market disruption occurs in a given instance is left to the importing country alone.[82] The agreement

[81] *The New York Times,* February 16, 1962.
[82] *The Oriental Economist,* March 1962, p. 151.

also frees the hands of the United States to impose import quotas under certain conditions.[83]

The multilateral agreement provides a new status for American requests to Japan to restrict exports of cotton textiles but subjects them to new rules. It has not, however, put an end to bilateral negotiation.[84] At the beginning of 1963, the United States proposed that Japan agree to export ceilings on a number of the products listed in the agreement. The Japanese complained that if they accepted the American proposal trade would fall below its 1962 level. There was talk of the dispute being taken to the GATT committee but the negotiations continued, with proposals and counterproposals, until in late August a new bilateral "arrangement" was signed.[85]

The agreement limited trade in the items covered to 287,500,000 square yards for 1963, but observers said that because of new methods of calculating the totals, and especially of converting pounds into square yards, this amount was really little if any higher than the 275,000,000 square yards permitted in the 1962 agreement. More products were restricted than before and some categories were subdivided, each new group having a separate ceiling. It was reported that the Japanese gave assurances that they would make only limited use of their rights to switch quotas from one category to another. These features of the agreement and the limitations on some products in which trade had recently expanded, notably corduroys, were presumably what the Japanese Minister of International Trade and Industry had in mind when he said that the agreement contained "some unsatisfactory points that will make this country's cotton textile exports to the United States somewhat tight. . . . "[86] The Japanese were promised some improvement in the future, however. The agreement provided that in 1964 the ceiling on Japanese exports covered by the agreement should increase by 3 per cent, to 296,100,000 square yards (on the new basis of calculation). The increase in 1965 was to be another 5 per cent, to 310,900,000 square yards. The same percentage increases were to apply to all categories. There

[83] While Japan has not, at this writing, been subjected to such measures, the United States has acted against imports from several countries. Imports of 8 of the short-term arrangement's 64 categories from Hong Kong were stopped in March 1962. (Department of Commerce, Office of the Secretary, Press Release G 62-45, March 19, 1962.) Imports from Portugal were subsequently banned when they exceeded the limits agreed on.

[84] Article 4 of the agreement permits bilateral arrangements that are "mutually acceptable" to the parties and "not inconsistent with the basic objectives" of the agreement.

[85] The text and related documents appear in *The Department of State Bulletin*, September 16, 1963, pp. 440–449.

[86] *The New York Times*, August 28, 1963. Quotations that follow come from the same source and the issues of August 29 and September 10, 1963.

were also provisions concerning the action to be taken if Japanese sales of cotton textile products not covered by the agreement should lead to disruption in the American market.

When he signed the agreement, the Japanese Ambassador in Washington spoke of "the enormous sacrifices the Japanese industry must suffer to observe the new arrangement." *The New York Times* called it a "new favor for textiles." But the president of the American Textile Institute said, "We are disappointed that the Japanese have been given an increased share of the United States market for cotton textile products." And Jacob Potofsky, president of the Amalgamated Clothing Workers of America predicted "further disruption and unemployment in the United States as low-wage countries drive for an ever larger share of the United States apparel market." He discerned in Japan not the spirit of give and take that had made possible five years of voluntary quota agreements but "an insatiable militancy."

Perhaps the conflicting views of the bilateral agreement indicated that it was a real compromise. Certainly the comprehensive long-range multilateral agreement seems to offer something for virtually every interested group. American cotton manufacturers have a strong expectation, even if not assurance, that cotton textile imports will remain well under 10 per cent of total domestic demand. American producers of other products, especially textiles other than cotton, are encouraged to hope for similar restrictive arrangements. European and other producers disturbed by import competition are similarly encouraged. American importers, and their suppliers in Japan, Hong Kong, and elsewhere, are assured of a place in the U.S. market and of growth, even if at a slow pace, in the amount of imports to be admitted. Parallel assurance is given for other import markets in Europe and elsewhere. The opportunity for new foreign suppliers is probably too limited to stimulate much if any additional construction of new cotton textile manufacturing capacity in developing countries, but that is how American textile men want it, and few people anywhere seem to have expected the American market for imported cotton textiles to be much larger than it will be during the life of the long-term arrangement. And even those who, like the writer, think the arrangement excessively restrictive, can take some heart from the language of trade expansion in the agreement, from the room left for import growth beyond the minimum guaranteed, from the fact that restrictions must be explained to the Cotton Textiles Committee of GATT, and from the full-dress review required before the end of the five-year period. The implications of the agreement for American trade policy will be discussed in the next chapter.

Other Parts of President Kennedy's Program for Textiles

While international negotiations provided the main arena for the discussion of the textile problem, something was done under the six other points of President Kennedy's program of May 2, 1961. The Treasury moved promptly to modify tax regulations so as to permit faster write-off of assets in textile and apparel firms. The period of depreciation for machinery and equipment was shortened by about 40 per cent, thus giving a boost to modernization. Initial provisions affected spinning and weaving in October 1961; later actions in January and February 1962 affected apparel and knitwear respectively.[87] Before results could be assessed, however, similar provisions were extended to industry generally in July 1962. The proposal for adjustment assistance was covered by the more general provisions in the Trade Expansion Act of 1962 (p. 262) and was not greeted with great enthusiasm by textile men.

More interest has been shown—in Japan as well as in the United States—in the President's request to the Department of Agriculture to explore means to eliminate the price differential between the American cotton bought by domestic American mills and that bought by foreigners. The Secretary of Agriculture decided that the best solution would be to use powers under Section 22 of the Agricultural Adjustment Act to impose an equalization fee of 8½ cents a pound on imports of cotton textiles. When the matter was heard by the Tariff Commission in February 1962, the Department of Agriculture, represented by the Director of the Cotton Division, presented a comprehensive statement and also a substantial amount of supplementary material.[88] This was reported to have seemed so impressive to the representative of the cotton growers and manufacturers that he spoke only briefly, resting his case on what the Department of Agriculture had presented.[89]

The Japanese protested strongly against the new approach. The chairman of the All Japan Cotton Spinners' Association closed a letter to *The New York Times* with a threat: "Such restrictive action would force us, however reluctantly, to review and reconsider our position as the largest buyer of American raw cotton on the world market." [90] The correspondent in Japan of the same newspaper contributed a dispatch from a small textile town, Nishiwaki, showing that Japanese feeling ran high, but deny-

[87] White House Press Releases, January 15, 1962, and February 1962.

[88] U.S. Department of Agriculture, *Articles of Materials Wholly or in Part of Cotton,* statement submitted to the U.S. Tariff Commission at a public hearing, Investigation No. 22-25, *Cotton Products,* instituted under Section 22 (a) of the Agricultural Adjustment Act, as Amended, February 13, 1962 (mimeographed).

[89] *The New York Times,* February 14, 1962.

[90] Kichihei Hara, December 27, 1962.

ing the validity of the threat that Japanese mills might shift from American cotton. Among other things the dispatch reported:

> Everyone says it [the proposed 8½-cent tax] will put the town out of business. . . . Nishiwaki produces 350,000,000 square yards of textiles a year, all of it under subcontract to big Osaka concerns. About 60 per cent of the town's textile income comes from exports to the United States.
>
> "The tax will add 20 per cent to our costs," said a manufacturer. "How can we absorb this? . . . We cannot. Americans will not pay more. We will lose 60 per cent of our business."
>
> . . . .
>
> He waved away the question [of switching to non-American cotton]. "Too expensive; we are geared to American cotton." [91]

It is clear that this possible method of eliminating the artificial price differential on raw cotton was proving very troublesome, even without actual imposition of an equalization fee. To the Japanese it looked like a tariff, and any American tariff is worse than undesirable. Somehow this issue stirred emotions that had appeared calmer during the more important discussions relating to quotas. Japanese excitement boiled, despite the fact that the United States had given generalized assurances to Japan that if the equalization fee were imposed the United States would "consider steps to ease the burden on the Japanese economy." [92]

The outcome was anticlimatic. When the Tariff Commission acted in September 1962, it rejected the application, again on essentially technical grounds, as it had when the Secretary of Agriculture had recommended action under Section 22 in 1959 (p. 313). Its 3–2 decision said Section 22 applied specifically to agriculture and was not intended by Congress to be used to protect from import competition a domestic industry that processes an agricultural raw material.[93] Having taken this position, the Commission had only to decide whether the two-price situation in cotton was interfering with any programs of the Department of Agriculture. As one would expect, no such interference could be found, since present price arrangements push out a large volume of raw cotton on to world markets. Even the cotton that comes back in manufactured form may be increasing total cotton consumption over what it would be otherwise. An import fee that raised American prices of cotton

[91] A. M. Rosenthal, "Tax is Nightmare to Town in Japan," *The New York Times,* January 28, 1962.

[92] A. M. Rosenthal, "U.S. Tells Japan of Intentions to Offset Textile Duty," *The New York Times,* December 16, 1961.

[93] U.S. Tariff Commission, *Cotton Products,* Report to the President on Investigation No. 22-25 under Section 22 of the Agricultural Adjustment Act, as Amended, TC Publication 69 (Washington: Author, 1962), pp. 8–9.

manufactures "would clearly result in a reduction in the aggregate consumption of such articles." [94]

The textile industry did not respond to the President's virtual invitation to start escape-clause action but, as already noted, applied to the OCDM under the national security clause of the Trade Agreements Act. Ten organizations representing cotton, wool, silk and man-made fiber manufacturers and merchants presented a case running about as follows:

1. The industry is significant in the national economy, as generator of income, as employer, and as taxpayer.
2. It will be called on in time of national emergency for sharply expanded deliveries to the military forces, to defense-supporting industries, and to allied foreign countries.
3. Imports of competing goods cause the domestic industry to shrink and thus reduce its capacity to meet such emergency demands.
4. Much of the new foreign competition is from Asia and other faraway sources, but those areas are too distant to be counted on to provide necessary textiles in time of emergency.
5. Domestic producers' flexibility is further reduced by the current practice in the industry of working facilities on a three-shift basis, around the clock.
6. Further loss of flexibility results from the decline in textile and apparel exports. Having less export business, the industry has less leeway to shift from exports to military supply.
7. In addition to a declining labor force and decreasing productive capacity, the industry, including specifically the cotton textile industry, faces shortages of capital for modernization, as a result mainly of inadequate earnings. Earnings are substantially below those of all manufacturing industries in the United States.
8. Therefore the "industry is threatened with an absolute incapacity to meet projected national defense requirements by the overpowering influence of excessive imports. . . ." [95]

Such a case could be made for virtually every industry, large or small, that supplies necessities. It does not follow that national security requires enough peacetime capacity to permit the industry to meet war or

[94] Same, p. 12. In the spring of 1964 Congress sought to put American textile manufacturers on the same basis as their foreign competitors by providing a subsidy on the use of cotton.

[95] Before the Office of Civil and Defense Mobilization, *Application for Investigation,* In re: Application of the Textile Industry for an Investigation Under Sec. 8 of the Trade Agreements Extension Act of 1958 concerning Imports of Textiles and Textile Manufactures. American Cotton Manufacturers' Institute, Inc., National Association of Wool Manufacturers, Northern Textile Association, Apparel Industry Committee on Imports, Clothing Manufacturers' Association of the United States of America, American Silk Council, Inc., Association of Cotton Textile Merchants of New York, Man-Made Fiber Producers' Association, Inc., American Carpet Institute, Inc., Boston and Allied Wool Trade Associations (May 15, 1961), pp. 54, 103–105.

emergency needs, apparently without seriously reducing normal civilian consumption. At least the case stands unproven. Without demonstration that imports are the prime source of products that will be needed in an emergency, without consideration of stockpiling or information on how fast capital and labor requirements might be met in an emergency situation, with imports less than 10 per cent of total cotton textile production, and on the basis of other information presented in this chapter, the case is very unlikely to be provable. Until imports should displace far more cotton textile production than has yet occurred in the United States, it hardly seems necessary to limit imports as a means of strengthening national defense.

Far better would be a policy that stimulated strength and flexibility in the economy generally and specifically in a smaller and more agile textile industry, together with a textile machinery industry. Protection hampers flexibility and strength by preserving activities that cannot meet the test of the free market. The United States should be very cautious of moves in this direction in the name of national security. The high price of such protection would, if it had to be paid in other industries, buy not greater security but greater economic rigidity and greater vulnerability to economic stagnation and strategic danger.

Part III

Policy Needs and Possibilities

Chapter 10

Quotas and Low-Wage Imports

Behind the protection of cotton textile production in the United States lie questions of broad American trade policy. Are quantitative restrictions necessary? Does the international cotton textile agreement mark a significant innovation in the regulation of trade? Is it a useful model for other products? Or should it be regarded as an undesirable exception to basic American liberal trade principles, and one that should not be repeated? This chapter considers some of these questions in two main groups: first, those pertaining to whether protection is necessary at all, and second, those about the special problems of export quotas.

JAPANESE COMPETITION IN THE AMERICAN MARKET

Because most of the Japanese goods that appear in the American market are highly competitive with domestic products, they raise in particularly acute form a number of basic questions concerning American policy toward imports. Many Americans who are honestly troubled by the kind of competition domestic producers face from Japan and other low-wage countries question both the economic value of this trade and its political necessity. More than Japanese trade is involved. American makers of a growing number of products are being faced with low-priced imports made possible by the combination of modern machinery and low wages. Japanese producers have for some time been able to leap over tariffs that have long stopped producers in Europe and elsewhere from selling much here. Now goods are coming in from Hong Kong and other newer sources where wages are even lower than in Japan.

Why Don't the Japanese Sell Noncompetitive Goods?

An American businessman affected by import competition is not likely to be persuaded by generalizations about Japan's needs to export and the benefits to the American economy from importing at low prices. His belligerence rises as his sales fall. He asks whether there is not some other way for Japan to meet its export needs than by selling the particular competitive product in question. Why shouldn't the Japanese sell noncompetitive goods in the United States? If they did there would be no pain in purchasing from Japan.

The answer is not far to seek. The Japanese and other suppliers offer whatever they can make, old or new, native or American, that can be sold in the American market. There are some noncompetitive goods, like raw silk or manufactures of a distinctively Japanese character, but only a small fraction of the trade is made up of things essentially different from those produced in the United States. The great bulk of the Japanese products sold in the United States are goods in common use here, things that American firms are quite able to produce and, in many cases, have been producing much longer than the Japanese. This will not change. The United States *can* produce almost any kind of manufacture. The reason for foreign trade is seldom complete inability to produce certain things. At a price, American businessmen and farmers could produce a large number of the products now imported. We import because that is better business. The imports are cheaper, and American land, labor, capital, and technology can be devoted more productively and profitably to lines in which foreigners cannot undersell Americans.

It does not seem likely that goods embodying Japanese artistic or craft traditions but designed especially for the American market will ever come to dominate the list of Japanese goods sold in the United States. Nor can we expect the presently underdeveloped countries to offer more than a small fraction of their eventual manufactured exports in the form of things unique to the place of origin. To be sure, some countries with richer natural resources may not have to rely so heavily as Japan on exports of manufactured goods, but there is little doubt that cheap manufactured goods, at first mainly light-industry products, will become major exports of many newly industrialized countries. Like Japan they will have the advantage of low wages, which can often serve as a basis for low labor costs. Japan itself and especially Japanese cotton goods are already feeling sharp effects of new competition as Hong Kong and other suppliers provide the United States with products Japan could supply. The reason thus far is not so much price as Japanese export quotas, although price will become more of a factor as Japanese wages and labor costs rise.

When new foreign makers succeed in selling in the United States a product already widely used here, the imports displace American sales unless the market is expanding as much as imports. Some American productive facilities may be put out of operation, as happened in the case of velveteens for a while in the middle 1950s. Expansion of production abroad often means creation of surplus capacity, and it may be American capacity that is made idle. That is a normal way for shifts in production, domestic and foreign, to take place, unless demand is rising fast enough to permit the old suppliers—whether they are American or Japanese—to go on working, losing only relative position.

Should Not American Producers Have Prior Claim to the American Market?

The assumption of many American businessmen faced with foreign competition is that they have a prior right to the American market. Owners who have invested in factories and workers who make a living in them feel abused at losing sales and jobs to foreigners. An American firm having sunk large sums in developing a market, it seems unfair for someone else, especially a foreign competitor, to reap the advantage, particularly when he does it by offering lower prices. The American producer regards the market as in some significant sense his, and the customers as peculiarly his own. And if the best-known advantage of the foreign intruder is low wages, there is a particular edge to the feeling of the owner, manager, or worker that something he has worked hard to create is being taken away by unfair means. To unions, the word *unfair* in this connection has a meaning similar to that used in charges against employers of nonunion help.

In economic terms there is little, if any, justification for this proprietary attitude toward a market or for giving American producers preference over foreign producers. An exception would be justified if the disruptive effects of foreign competition threatened to equal or exceed the advantages offered by importing foreign goods, especially if the foreign producer's advantage seemed likely to be temporary, so that a lasting adjustment of the domestic industry would not be warranted. This is not the case, generally speaking, with the ability of Japan and others to sell a growing range of light products in the American market.

The economic interest of the United States is, with a few exceptions, to take advantage of existing and emerging possibilities for international specialization. But the national interest comprehends political and strategic considerations as well. In large measure these reinforce the economic argument since they call with compelling urgency for closer ties between the United States and other countries. Noneconomic arguments are, however, often used to support the case for more protection against foreign goods. Military dangers are perhaps the most commonly cited. Wartime experience, including the disruption of sea transportation and the loss of overseas supplies, has led to the stipulation of certain levels of productive capacity as the necessary mobilization base in strategic industries. Among these industries are electronics, many branches of machinery production, cotton textiles, and others. Various measures are taken to be sure that capacity does not fall below the level judged necessary for defense.

One cannot quarrel with the idea of a mobilization base if it is really a military necessity. It is hard for anyone not privy to defense plans to judge this necessity, though he may be entitled to some skepticism as to whether this is not preparation against today's and tomorrow's dangers by yesterday's methods. If defense justifies restricting imports, this is a very different matter from giving preference to American producers for their own benefit or because they feel some inherent right to the market. Moreover, defense of the United States today is by no means either wholly military or wholly American. To achieve such security as is possible in a world of grave tensions and spreading nuclear potential, Americans need far more than their military strength and the means to produce military and civilian supplies in time of emergency. They also need allies. To contribute to the strength of these allies, the United States must give them a fair chance to sell what they produce. To keep relations good they must be convinced that they will be fairly treated by the United States and can rely on it to help meet their economic needs. Defense policies that ignore these requirements are likely to be worth very little in the years ahead.

The political support for the prior claim of American producers to the domestic market depends not on logic but on fact. Since the United States has a representative government that is highly responsive to wishes expressed by even limited segments of the population, appeals for protection always command respect. The less capable a firm or industry is in meeting foreign competition, the more vigorous its political efforts are likely to be and the more costly the provision of protection. Lower foreign wage rates provide a politically attractive argument by suggesting that competition is unfair, while no mention is made either of the generally lower productivity and limited employment opportunities that make foreign wages low, or of the many foreign products that cannot compete successfully here in spite of low wages. There is also political effectiveness in the proposition that American production should not be "sacrificed" to imports or "given away." Where the idea of permitting some competitive imports is accepted by domestic producers, the amounts regarded as a "fair share" for foreigners are likely to be very small. Arguments about alternative uses of resources, even arguments about consumer advantage in buying at lower prices, carry relatively little weight when the immediate issue is threatened loss of a going plant or enterprise. The advantage is far away, long run, "theoretical," while the cost is visible and immediate to those concerned.

It is also geographically centered while the benefits are diffused throughout the country.

It seems remarkable that in this age, when change is often sought for its own sake, Americans could be so far misled by the idea that industries should be preserved because they exist. As consumers we are bombarded by appeals to discard quite usable clothing, cars, and other products for new models. It is commonly assumed that many products are purposely made to wear out more quickly than necessary, in order to promote resales. The word *new* has a strong appeal and occurs in a vast amount of advertising. Often what lies behind this label represents no change at all except in package or some other superficial feature. Yet a great deal of important change does take place, and at a rapid rate, in products, in uses, in adaptations, and in productive processes. It is a reflection of the capacity of human beings to act illogically and inconsistently that so many people who are attracted to new products and fashions should succumb to the false notion that the producer who is first in the market thereby gains some sort of claim to protection against competitive change.

From such ideas and the natural tendency in a political system to protect the domestic producer sprang the peril-point and escape-clause provisions that have long been part of the price necessary to obtain congressional approval for successive renewals of the Reciprocal Trade Agreements Act. But there is another kind of political pressure that has to be taken into account, that of foreign policy. It is most difficult to achieve the right balance between domestic and foreign interests or among the interests of countries all over the world, many of them conflicting. Highly responsive as the U.S. government inevitably is to domestic pressures, it would be folly to believe, as some Americans have done in the past, that "the tariff is a domestic issue." Complaints and retaliation over tariff action may be only the beginning. They often create political friction. Protectionist actions by the United States impede American efforts to lead the free world toward the kinds of trading arrangements that are needed for economic strength and welfare and for political harmony as well.

American producers have a preferred status in the American market and will no doubt continue to have it. Much of this represents the natural advantages of being near customers and knowing their tastes. To the extent that the preferred position results from political interference with market forces, it constitutes a drag on the productivity, flexibility, and vigor of our economy and also on our foreign relations. In the future there will be increasing need to weigh the domestic political considerations against economic, military, and diplomatic factors. A reasonable balance in our progressively more interdependent world can be found through liberal trade policies, discussed and agreed upon with other nations.

"How Much of Our Market Must We Give Up?"

American businessmen, despite their traditional vigor and the dynamism of the economy, share with their counterparts everywhere a yearning for security and certainty. They call for a policy that will "let them know where they stand." American textile and clothing men, whose markets are competitive to an unusual degree, are particularly vociferous on this point. Labor has joined management in demanding import quotas. As a clothing manufacturer put it:

> The apparel industry will go along with the State Department's belief that we must give up a share of the American market to our friends in the low-wage countries; however, what we urgently need right now is for this administration to decide how much of the American textile and apparel market they intend to give away. We need to know the total fixed amount, or percentage, that they believe should go to all our foreign friends in all low-wage countries.
>
> If the government will make this urgently needed decision, the textile and apparel industries would, in my opinion, be glad to cooperate with them in their efforts to work out an equitable plan of spreading the burden among the various segments of the two industries. This was done when our government officials were working out the Japanese quota system.[1]

The present international quota arrangement for cotton products comes close to doing what this manufacturer requested. It permits a ceiling to be put on the amount foreigners can ship here and if they can undersell domestic producers, the latter may have to bear most or all of the consequences of a drop in demand. But the import share of the total market for cotton goods is so small that the arrangement gives the domestic industry a substantial amount of market security. Other schemes have been proposed that would somewhat increase the security of domestic producers, by limiting imports to a designated percentage of total domestic sales. A third group of schemes for allocating the market would fix a minimum production level for the domestic industry and permit imports freely, or according to some formula, above that level. This kind of arrangement would give most security to American pro-

[1] From address by E. A. Morris, president of Blue Bell, Inc., before the Charlotte Textile Club, Charlotte, N.C., May 9, 1960, as reported in *America's Textile Reporter*, June 23, 1960, p. 39. A similar view was expressed by William F. Sullivan, secretary of the Northern Textile Association, before the Pastore Subcommittee in July 1958, *Problems of the Domestic Textile Industry*, Hearings before a subcommittee of the Senate Committee on Interstate and Foreign Commerce, 85th Cong., 2d sess. (Washington: GPO, 1958), pt. 1, p. 223.

ducers and least to foreigners but would, if adhered to, permit the latter to expand sales as fast as the market grew.

All such schemes involve interference with market forces. What producer or seller is to have access to American customers would be determined in part by government decision or international negotiation rather than wholly by the seller's ability to please through quality, design, price, service, or otherwise. The amount to be imported, either absolutely or as a share of the market, would be similarly limited. It seems most unlikely that businessmen who seek greater certainty appreciate how large a volume of imports of these troublesome products might be justified on economic grounds, or seem a "reasonable share" of the market to low-cost foreign producers. Yet if trade is to be regulated by political considerations, then foreign policy as well as domestic pressures must be taken into account. If a market-sharing arrangement prevents a country like Japan, which lives by exporting, from expanding sales here, then American relations with Japan will be damaged and that cost must be weighed against satisfying political demands at home.

Economically as well we must be wary of schemes that, to let American producers "know where they stand," actually impede desirable shifts of American resources into new and economically better activities. Advocates of market-sharing are rarely if ever prepared to contemplate the possibility—let alone accept the desirability—that segments of certain domestic industries might disappear, leaving the workers, managers, owners, suppliers, and others to find their fortunes elsewhere, while the United States became wholly dependent upon imports for the goods in question. Suggestions such as "spreading the burden among the various segments of the two industries" imply no thought of letting the domestic production of, say, velveteen, flatware, or umbrellas give way before imports that cost consumers less than domestically produced articles. Yet, progress in any economy and in the world at large requires change, including at times decline or total loss of particular kinds of production. Japanese hand spinners of cotton were wiped out soon after the opening of foreign trade in the nineteenth century. Wheat farming disappeared in New England when the Plains States proved cheaper sources of supply. We have virtually stopped production of harnesses, carriage whips, and surreys since the advent of automobiles, and there are few village blacksmiths left. But each of these losses has been more than made up by other, newer, economically more productive activities. Japanese factory spinning of cotton is in many aspects the cheapest in the world. New England has moved from grain farming through several subsequent economic phases. One was a textile phase, and the decline of textiles in New England has been long and painful. But now electronics and tourism and other newer activities hold far more promise than could be found in subsidized maintenance of cotton textiles or other declining industries.

We must expect a continual falling away of old productive activities and the appearance of new ones. Economic health and vigor are reflected in innovation and change. Artificial respiration for declining activities is far more costly than is usually evident. Perhaps the greatest cost of all to the domestic economy lies in the loss of vigor that goes with an expectation of protection from competition when the going is rugged. In today's divided and uncertain world, with communism attracting converts in developing nations, who is to be persuaded of the desirability of private enterprise and competition if the United States does not set an example to contrast with Communist statism?

American producers should expect, as a general principle, to relinquish any market they cannot hold through open competition with the best producers anywhere in the world. A few rare exceptions are admissible when they can be shown to benefit the national interest. This principle involves no "giving away." Foreign producers would get nothing except what they could earn in competition with the best American business performance. No major lines of production need be given up suddenly. A sound approach would emphasize the guidance of new investment away from activities that require protection against imports and toward export industries and others that can hold their own in world competition while still meeting American standards of wages, fringe benefits to workers, and all the rest.

It is certainty, or general reliability, of American policy that is needed, not certainty about particular products, quantities, or prices as so many businessmen seem to want. Healthy private enterprise is in significant part a contest, in which certainty applies only to the rules of the game, and definitely not to its outcome. Producers should know the ground rules and be able to rely on them. What is to be produced and in what quantities, and what prices are to be charged should not normally be matters for government decision. The certainty that is appropriate in an economy dedicated to private enterprise should be assurance that the government will *not* step in except where matters of genuine public interest are involved. When an American industry is losing out to imports, the proper role for government does not relate to how much is lost—except where security or other national concern is clearly involved—but to the pace at which the shift takes place and the means for making adjustments and relieving human suffering.

What Will Happen to Labor and Facilities Displaced by Imports?

If imports should displace American production, workers and managers may lose their jobs, factories may close, and investors lose money.

These hazards are much in the minds of industry and labor representatives when they protest imports and demand protection. The traditional view of American economists has been that the forces of the market should be allowed to work themselves out with a minimum of interference. In recent years there has been growing interest in government assistance to ease the adjustment. In the future, part of the burden that results from displacement by import products may be transferred from the individuals, firms, and localities directly affected to the whole body of taxpayers. The benefits of low-cost imports accrue to consumers in lower prices and wider choice, and to the whole nation in more productive resource allocation as well as in healthier relations with foreign countries. In the circumstances, it seems eminently reasonable that the cost of transferring workers and facilities to other activities should be assumed in part by the national budget. While government programs seem unlikely in practice to bear the full cost of such readjustments, the new proposals reflect modern concepts of welfare and promise to reduce the harshness of the market forces without creating a serious or permanent limitation on the extent to which they are allowed to work themselves out.

The United States and other industrial countries have already had experience with some types of readjustment programs. When the economy has been in recession, Presidents Eisenhower and Kennedy have sponsored temporary measures to extend unemployment benefits for longer than normal periods. Federal designation of labor-surplus areas has for a number of years led to special assistance in the forms of preference in awarding federal contracts, supplementary distribution of surplus agricultural commodities, special efforts by the U.S. Employment Service to assist in finding new jobs for the unemployed, and assistance in the development of new productive activities.[2] Proposals for increased efforts along these lines have received growing support during recent years until in 1961 a depressed-areas bill was passed by Congress and signed by President Kennedy.[3] It provides federal funds for loans and grants for machinery and equipment, for rebuilding outmoded industrial buildings or constructing new ones, or for modernizing or constructing public facilities such as water systems, for assessing needs and preparing plans for new development, for occupational training, and for subsistence payments to workers being retrained. The adjustment assistance provisions of the Trade Expansion Act of 1962—geared specifically

[2] U.S. Interdepartmental Committee to Coordinate Federal Urban Area Assistance Programs, *Federal Programs of Assistance to Labor Surplus Areas* (Washington: GPO, 1960).

[3] Public Law 87-27, approved May 1, 1961. In 1959 and 1960, depressed-areas legislation passed Congress but was vetoed by President Eisenhower.

to the effect of imports—add substantially to the government's ability to move in this direction.

For a number of years several European countries have had programs to relieve distress in areas of high unemployment, both by bringing employment to the areas and by moving workers to jobs elsewhere.[4] Both the European Coal and Steel Community and the European Economic Community provide assistance to firms and workers that are adjusting to new conditions of trade and competition. The most significant program is probably the British one for reorganizing and strengthening the Lancashire cotton industry. The cotton textile industry in Britain is declining, not only because of imports but also largely because of shrinking exports. The British government has fostered and in large part financed the scrapping of excess capacity, compensated displaced workers, and assisted in re-equipping and modernizing the remaining producing units.[5]

One great advantage of readjustment assistance is its one-time character. Tariffs tend to go on forever, and often quotas do too. Every unit of domestic production protected by these devices costs something, and the cost does not end as long as protection goes on. But public contributions to get people and facilities out of high-cost activities continue only until the transfer is successfully made. Although transfer is rarely easy and may be very slow and difficult, once it has taken place and the bills have been paid, the matter can be regarded as closed. The greatest part of the gain is the improved allocation of resources permitting more goods and services to be produced more efficiently here and abroad.

To have adjustment, one does not have to have government assistance. It is hard to judge from the present evidence how effective government programs are in inducing or speeding adjustments or reducing their social cost. The legal recognition of the government's possible role, the setting up of procedures and the provision of resources are, however, important steps in pointing a direction in which the economy should move.

"Won't Foreigners Get All Our Market?"

After a congressional hearing at which the writer had testified in favor of permitting imports to enter the American market in open competition with goods produced domestically, a reporter came up and asked, "But won't imports end up taking our whole market? Where else can all this end?" These questions, often heard, concern concepts and principles

[4] See, for instance, *Aid to Labor Surplus Areas in Great Britain, Belgium, the Federal Republic of Germany, and Sweden, Foreign Labor Information* (Washington: U.S. Department of Labor, Bureau of Labor Statistics, 1960).

[5] Great Britain, Board of Trade, *Reorganization of the Cotton Industry*, Cmnd. 744 (London: HMSO, 1959).

that are fundamental to all trade, domestic as well as foreign. They need an answer that applies to the case at hand, imports from Japan, and also to other imports that would flow in from elsewhere under the policies I am advocating.

The Japanese plan for doubling the national income during the 1960s sets targets for total exports in 1970 and for the share going to the United States. These are, to be sure, only projections, subject to substantial error. The official estimators have probably tried to be cautious by projecting imports and exports somewhat higher than the absolute minimum they might regard as necessary, but the human imagination has repeatedly underrated Japan's capacity for economic growth and the present plan may well prove to be another such case. The figure for 1970 exports set in the income-doubling plan is $9,320 million. Of this 29.9 per cent or $2,786 million would go to the United States.[6] This is almost exactly double the figure for 1962. The rate of increase called for during the remaining years of the plan is about 9 per cent a year, less than half the actual average annual increase between 1952 and 1962. The gross national product of the United States could reasonably be expected to increase by perhaps $200–300 billion between 1962 and 1970, making the $1.4 billion figure for added imports from Japan look very small indeed. It should be possible to absorb such an increase with only a little displacement of existing American productive activities, even though the Japanese hope to sell larger quantities of textiles, sundries, and other products that have aroused opposition in the United States. My own expectation is that the actual increase in imports from Japan will be a good deal more than the Japanese projections suggest, but that, as in the 1950s, the resultant economic difficulties in the United States will be very minor.

Imports from Hong Kong, Taiwan, India, Pakistan, Korea, and all the other countries that are trying to industrialize, often with U.S. aid, are harder to predict. The exports of such countries have generally grown more slowly than those of Japan and, in some cases, so slowly as to cause concern about the ability of these countries to sustain their own economic development. However, after the Japanese textile quotas were put into effect in 1957, Hong Kong and some other countries very rapidly expanded sales to the United States. Will the process go on, spreading from one product to another?

For the most part the newly industrializing countries have proved unable to export more than a few manufactured goods to the United

[6] Japan, Economic Deliberation Council, *Long-Range Trade Plan of Japan (1961–1970)*, Report of the Trade Committee, Translation Series No. 17, translated for the Indian Statistical Institute (Tokyo: Translation Unit, Economic Planning Agency, 1960), p. 32. See pp. 370–372 for a fuller account of the plan.

States. Their producers are likely to have only limited information, except as aided by American buyers who can provide samples, specifications, and other help. Capital is likely to be very scarce, so the export products first offered will tend to be labor-intensive; but skills too are limited and low wages often do not compensate for low productivity. The spread of skill to new workers is likely to be most rapid in activities already started, where the new worker can learn from one more experienced. Consequently, a new exporting country may offer only a narrow range of products that can meet the standards of the American market. If several new countries at once concentrate on the same few products only a small part of the American economy is affected. This could lead to some disruption of markets in the United States, but how serious the problem is likely to be depends on the quantity of competitive goods foreign producers can offer. It is quite likely that for some time to come these quantities will be limited but eventually the economic development of these countries will require a substantial increase in their exports. That is a situation for which the industrialized countries should be prepared, and for which they should equip themselves with flexible, progressive policies, permitting them to absorb larger quantities of cheap manufactures, to their own as well as the exporters' advantage.

While imports, from Japan as elsewhere, might completely displace American production of a few items, this is not likely to happen very frequently. The domestic producer usually has important advantages arising from closeness to the market. If no import barriers whatsoever were to impede the flow of imports into the United States, it seems most unlikely that foreign sources would soon, or ever, supply all U.S. consumption of, for instance, cotton blouses, men's shirts, slacks, transistor radios, toys, cameras, flashlights, or baseball gloves. An equilibrium would probably be reached with substantial production in the United States, although imports might take over the low-price end of product lines, or occasionally the bulk of the line.

Those concerned with the effects of imports on American economic activity must also take account of the uses foreigners make of the dollars they acquire from selling to the United States. Most of them will probably be spent for American products, thus sustaining employment and investment in the United States. The gains are likely to be in the types of production that the United States carries on best. A shift from protected industries to such output is beneficial to the national economy. It is unlikely then that even unhampered foreign trade would cause the kind of trouble feared by people who see no end to destruction of American jobs. And no one is seriously proposing that all U.S. import barriers be removed or that such reductions as are adopted should necessarily be applied all at once.

The probability that things will not be as bad as people fear and the positive advantages of increasing the efficiency of the American economy give us the response to the question posed at the beginning of this chapter: Are quantitative restrictions necessary? There are two answers: economically, no, except as temporary measures to permit adjustment; politically, often yes. On the recognition of this conflict depends much of the case for the supposed advantages of export quotas and multilateral agreements embodying them.

QUOTAS: NEW INSTRUMENT OF AMERICAN POLICY

Out of the long contest between the Japanese drive to expand sales in the American market and the efforts of American producers to limit those sales, there appeared in the middle 1950s a peculiar commercial policy device: the "voluntary" export quota. For some time its main significance lay in the cotton textile trade between Japan and the United States. In recent years, however, the technique has tended to spread. The international cotton textile agreement has opened a new phase, giving the use of export quotas multilateral sanction. It becomes important, then, to look closely at such quotas and their place in commercial policy.

For a long time, American policy has opposed the use of quantitative restrictions on imports of manufactured goods. Always subject to some exceptions, this principle is still adhered to and is embodied in the rules of GATT. Yet in recent years the United States has urged first Japan, then Hong Kong, and now other countries as well to impose export quotas on cotton goods being sent to the United States. Since their introduction in 1956 and 1957, export quotas spread to more than a dozen items exported from Japan to the United States, to exports from Japan to other markets, especially Western Europe, and then, in the multilateral agreements negotiated in 1961 and 1962, to a large part of world trade in cotton manufactures. Subsequently, pressure has been exerted by American woolen manufacturers and others for similar arrangements. In short, a pattern may be emerging, under American leadership, in which important segments of world trade are being directly controlled, despite all the postwar efforts of the United States to eliminate quantitative restrictions, including those that Japan and most other countries were forced to impose to deal with wartime and postwar shortages of foreign exchange.

How wise is this new approach? Is it a reversal of previous American policy, or is there an essential difference between unilateral import quotas and export quotas agreed to internationally? Is their international and voluntary character a fiction rooted in fear on one side and hypocrisy on the other? Are the new developments victories for protectionism that have to be done away with at the earliest possible moment by governments professing to follow liberal trade policies? Or are the quotas a recognition of realities, an inevitable development in bringing trade policy and practice up to date? Are they a constructive answer to the special problems of finding markets for cheap manufactured goods from low-wage countries? Are there ways to make export quotas useful instruments of trade policy, not unduly restrictive, but responsive to the reasonable needs and interests of both importing and exporting countries?

The Case for Export Quotas

The case for export quotas as they have been used in American–Japanese trade is largely pragmatic. Some call the action of the U.S. government in securing the imposition of Japanese quotas in 1956 and 1957 mediation. In effect, American officials told the Japanese what volume of exports of cotton textiles would probably prove tolerable to the United States, in the sense that it would largely remove the danger of unilateral action to limit imports. In one official's words, if American producers were to apply to the Tariff Commission for relief under the escape clause in respect to any product on which Japan specifically limited exports, "they would not have a leg to stand on." Just how much or what kind of study or consultation preceded the U.S. government's decision on levels to suggest to the Japanese is not clear. But there is no doubt that this expression of opinion must have carried weight with the Japanese, just as they would expect it to carry weight with the President when faced with recommendations from the Tariff Commission.

American producers preferred the Japanese export quotas to escape-clause action with its uncertainties and delays, as well as its requirement that injury be shown. This preference seems to have been justified. Quotas reduced imports more quickly, more certainly, and to a lower level than was to be expected through the established procedures of the escape clause. Moreover, the American producers suspected that Japanese goods could cross most tariff walls. They liked to know precise amounts and got a sense of security from "an understanding that no unilateral action can be taken in changing the quotas during the five-year period." [7] As industry men on both sides of the Pacific Ocean have said, the American producers, using the facilities and assistance of the U.S. government, in effect outbargained the Japanese.

In Japan, on the other hand, "Textile manufacturers and exporters . . . accepted the quota figures . . . with unhappiness verging on bitterness. There is no attempt to conceal the feeling that the textile industry here is getting the short end of the deal for political expediency—

[7] Henry Lesesne, *The Christian Science Monitor,* February 20, 1957.

to preserve friendly trade relations with the United States—and under pressure from the Foreign Ministry."[8] Even so, the outcry was perhaps no more than would have attended a single increase in import barriers through the escape clause. And without the Japanese quotas there would probably have been a series of escape-clause actions, accompanied by a far larger amount of publicity strongly adverse to the United States.

The quotas checked the import rise and for some time quieted the clamor of American producers. The cotton textile industry's very belligerent mood of 1956 disappeared. No escape-clause applications were made for almost three years after the quotas were announced in January 1957 even though velveteen imports in 1957 reached 3.2 million square yards, well above the quota of 2.5 million square yards. This kind of success in meeting a domestic political problem encouraged a new administration in Washington to follow the same approach in 1961 when imports from Hong Kong and elsewhere brought very heavy pressure from textile and apparel producers and labor unions. This time the activities of the U.S. government were frankly acknowledged to be negotiations. They were broadened to include other countries and led to a multilateral agreement under GATT auspices regulating a large part of international trade in cotton textiles.

A second line of argument in the case for export quotas rests on their diplomatic and to some extent economic advantages over unilaterally imposed import quotas. The fact that they are internationally "discussed" or negotiated before imposition and are even in a limited sense "voluntary" means that they are less likely to be met by reprisals than unilateral quotas. They also avoid direct violation of GATT rules. The Japanese, although they had to act under American pressure, had a chance to negotiate and the result included some element of compromise. Moreover, the possibilities of raising quota levels are greater under negotiated export quotas than under unilateral import quotas. Even though they were not free to act without prior consultation with the United States, and did not dare propose changes that were too drastic, the Japanese were better off than if any change had required American initiative, probably involving lengthy procedures. Under the "voluntary" system, quota levels were not completely rigid or fixed; the Japanese retained some initiative and used it to enlarge the quotas a little.

Combining these two sets of considerations, we can see a third argument for export quotas, one that holds them to be the least bad alternative in difficult circumstances. The power of protectionist forces in the United States in 1956 was so great that it seemed something had to be done. Without extraordinary measures, new import barriers might well

[8] Sheldon Wesson, *The Japan Times,* January 18, 1957, p. 6.

have been thrown up through escape-clause action, national security action, or perhaps even legislation. Any of the alternatives might well have been worse both for Japan and for American liberal trading principles than resort to export quotas. The export quotas evaded rules and obligations but without directly and formally violating them. The basic elements of American commercial policy remained formally intact, even if somewhat compromised in fact. Total U.S. imports from Japan, as well as from other manufacturing countries, have been higher since 1956 than ever before. In 1958 the Reciprocal Trade Agreements Act was extended for four years, the longest period in its history. And in 1962 a giant step forward was taken in enactment of the Trade Expansion Act, with its five-year trade agreement authority, its extensive tariff-cutting provisions, removal of the peril-point limitation, and provision for adjustment assistance. It is quite possible that without special arrangements for textiles the latter bill would not have passed; that at least appears to have been part of the calculation made by the Kennedy Administration in 1961 and early 1962 when it pressed for an international cotton textile agreement.

A quite different sort of argument has been advanced, less to make a case for the quotas than to explain that they were not as bad as they seemed. Cotton textile manufacture is not one of the most expansive and promising parts of Japanese industry. By the end of the 1950s textile mills were experiencing difficulty in finding enough labor. The young girls who for years had staffed much of the industry by working several years before marriage were finding many other opportunities. It is better for Japan to use scarce labor, as well as capital and other inputs, in newer industries with more rapidly growing markets than in cotton manufacturing. Therefore, runs this argument, the quotas in a sense moved in the same direction as market forces and accelerated the process of adjusting Japan's allocation of resources in the direction of its future needs.

The case for export quotas, with its pragmatic emphasis, has carried a great deal of weight in American politics and therefore in international affairs. Though the starting place is a politically significant set of pressures for protection of American producers, the outcome is something more complicated. The American producers do get greater assurance about market prospects and shares but foreign suppliers also get some assurance of their place in the market and a better chance to take advantage of opportunities than when access to markets is regulated by import quotas. Under the international agreement the exporters get something more: an assurance of at least slowly rising ceilings on sales volume and an international forum. But the international agreements and their potentialities represent a second stage of the argument, to be examined after reviewing the case against export quotas.

The Case Against Export Quotas

The first objection to quotas is that their imposition conflicts with the U.S. aim of reducing barriers to international trade. Quantitative controls imposed by administrative action have been regarded as more offensive than tariffs. These views have been embodied in the rules of GATT and other U.S. commitments. Because they were technically voluntary and unilateral on the part of the Japanese the export quotas did not violate these rules. The Japanese were penalizing their own trade, so to speak, not someone else's. But the U.S. pressure that led to the Japanese action violated the spirit of GATT and created measures that are economically as objectionable as import quotas.

Closely related is a second and perhaps even more serious objection. As means of evading rules of international trade the Japanese export quotas were worked out in discussions behind the scenes and, so far as American officials were concerned, without normal legal processes. There were no Tariff Commission investigations, public hearings, or other steps such as would normally permit public discussion and ensure orderly procedures within the framework of laws and international agreements. There was no invocation of the rules concerning injury which provide the legal basis for escape-clause action. Nor was Japan given concessions to which it would be entitled under GATT rules to compensate for the withdrawal of benefits by the United States. The evasiveness continued when the major European countries granted Japan nominally full rights in GATT but avoided the full substantive consequences of the move by understandings about export quotas on "sensitive" items. The damage to the position of the United States was particularly great because it was trying to persuade other countries, including Japan, to work toward the progressive reduction and removal of trade barriers while at the same time it was known to be the instigator of the evasive export quotas.

A third highly objectionable feature is the implicit discrimination involved in the U.S. pressure that led to Japan's export quotas. The discrimination took several forms. Despite all the increases of imports of manufactured goods into the United States in the 1950s—some of them particularly sharp, as in the case of small automobiles—the United States did not respond by urging European countries to limit exports.[9] Yet great pressure was put on Japan and then afterwards on Hong Kong. The difference can be attributed to many factors, including the greater sensitivity to imports on the part of U.S. textile and clothing manufacturers,

[9] An exception was the undertaking by Italy in 1957 to limit exports of velveteens to the United States. *The Department of State Bulletin,* February 11, 1957, p. 220.

the political strength of these widespread industries, the exceptionally rapid rate of increase of imports of some products, and the vulnerability of Japan to this kind of American pressure. Special weight must be given, however, to that old stand-by of protectionists, low wages. Wage differences between the United States and Asia are, of course, greater than those between the United States and Europe. There is a widespread feeling in Europe as well as in the United States that the very low wages constitute a valid reason for restricting imports from Asian countries, and perhaps from underdeveloped countries elsewhere as well. This view divides the world into two areas, one with which trade relations are normal, the other which requires special trade restraints because its low wages make it not a proper source of imports, at least of manufactured goods, and especially not in large and rapidly increasing quantities. That these latter, second-class areas happen to be non-Western and their populations non-white may be wholly incidental, but I have gained the impression, from Asians, Americans, and others, that racial differences are sometimes an important factor in thinking about trade barriers. Whatever relations there may be between race, wage levels, and other factors in the minds of individuals, the fact is that there is a kind of discrimination against Japan and other Asian countries in the quotas, which is potentially a serious source of friction.

The 1957–1961 quotas also discriminated specifically against Japan, the biggest exporter of manufactured goods among the "low-wage" countries. Only Japanese exports were restrained and the Japanese share of American imports of affected products declined markedly. During the five-year period Americans imported from Hong Kong, Taiwan, and elsewhere large quantities of cotton textiles that might otherwise have originated in Japan. These countries reaped the benefits of the restraint the Japanese imposed on themselves to oblige the United States. Hong Kong producers, who gained most, rebuffed American pressure to adopt export quotas. The Japanese, by being agreeable, had lost out to competitors who did not cooperate with the U.S. government. Of course, Hong Kong, too, had a case. Its textile production would perhaps have grown rapidly, even without Japan's quotas. What was more natural than that it should expand sales to the United States? There was no magic or justice in the relative shares of the American market that Japan and Hong Kong had had in some earlier period. The issue gives a taste of a whole series of problems that will flow from continued use of bilaterally negotiated export quotas. Once the government has intervened to prevent market forces from determining the pattern of trade, who is to say what is a fair allocation of U.S. imports among exporting countries? Is it fair to Japan if later arrivals are permitted to increase their share of the U.S. market? Would it be fair to shut out countries only beginning to be able to compete in the U.S. market, thus giving Japan special privileges?

A fourth fundamental weakness of export quotas is their tendency toward rigidity. The healthy expansion of production and trade, not their maintenance at past levels, is the great desideratum. For Japan, export expansion is essential to economic growth but quotas are roadblocks. They limit sales of some of the things Japan can most easily produce and export in larger amounts, products in which Japan has a clear, often very large, comparative advantage and the capacity to produce far more than it needs at home. To place rigid limits on exports of such goods is to interfere with international trade at just those points where its potential returns are greatest. Fixed export quotas like fixed import quotas create more of an obstacle than even high tariffs to the adjustments that would make it possible for the United States and other countries gradually to take more advantage of international differences in costs of production. Quotas may also stimulate investment in facilities to produce goods that could be imported more cheaply, thus tending to perpetuate the situation that gave rise to them.

A fifth drawback of the Japanese export quotas from the standpoint of U.S. policy springs from some of their secondary effects in Japan. Besides tending to confirm in many Japanese minds a picture of the United States as unwilling to buy from Japan in enough volume and on a sufficiently dependable basis to meet Japan's needs, U.S. pressure for quotas has worked to strengthen both the cartel organization of the cotton textile industry in Japan and government control of this and other industries. The administration of the cotton textile quotas is largely in the hands of the exporters' associations, in which the large firms dominate (p. 322). Japanese deny that these associations are cartels, but concede that their function is to restrain trade. Even in 1956, when only a few limitations were in force, an American newspaper correspondent in Japan reported:

> [The] quota device is being used by large trading firms who dominate the field as a means of freezing out their smaller competitors. . . . since the Japanese government is on record as favoring the concentration of more export business in the hands of "reliable" firms, the weight of the government is also behind the manipulation of "stabilization" devices to swing an increasingly large share of the trade to a handful of trading firms.[10]

By its pressure for export quotas, the United States, which imposed antimonopoly legislation on Japan early in the Occupation, has been strengthening the forces that resist change and inhibit the liberalization of economic life in Japan. It must be admitted, however, that while the quotas

[10] Sheldon Wesson, *The Japan Times,* August 13, 1956, p. 6.

have fostered cartelist tendencies in the Japanese textile industry, trade liberalization has had the same effect in other cases, for instance steel.

A New Way of Using Quotas?

The practical political advantages of export quotas are obtained at the cost of grave economic drawbacks and dangers. As this review of the arguments for and against quotas has indicated, there are conditions under which some of the economic and diplomatic disadvantages of the export quotas can be reduced. This suggests that it might be possible to work from the present employment of quotas toward arrangements that offer greater benefits and fewer disadvantages. Up to a point, the international cotton textile agreement moves in this direction—or at least offers the possibility of doing so.

To become constructive instruments of commercial policy export quotas should meet three main conditions. First, they should be regarded as temporary, transitional policy instruments. A quota level should not remain fixed for a long period of time; it should either rise fairly rapidly or be open for renegotiation at fairly frequent intervals, or both. Renegotiation is not in itself, however, a sufficient safeguard, unless the bargaining power of the parties involved is somewhere near to being equal. Second, quotas should be set by international agreement or at least after international negotiations. Third, all quotas, even those that are technically unilateral and voluntary, should be subject to review by the Contracting Parties of GATT. For this purpose new GATT rules covering quotas would have to be developed. These rules would have to be reviewed with great care, lest they permit freezing of trade and production patterns or reflect simply the political power of the GATT members participating. If quotas are to be internationally sanctioned, it is important that they take account of larger interests than those of the protected producers. The provisos and rules embodied in the long-term cotton textile arrangement are a good start for GATT rules, but their administration and elaboration require constant concern for protecting the public interest.

Economically, the key condition is the first, and the other two, aside from providing more equity along the way, are economically valuable mainly as they contribute to the first condition. Export quotas become economically far less objectionable if the volume of goods that may be shipped each year rises fairly rapidly. Within a few years they may no longer restrain trade. Even while a quota is actually limiting, its uneconomic effects are minimized if all concerned can depend on substantial increases according to a known schedule. Under such circumstances investment decisions in both the exporting and importing countries can be made in ways that promote desirable change instead of inhibiting it. This will also reduce one of the large economic wastes that rigid quotas encourage: investment to produce goods that could be imported more cheaply. If quotas or other trade barriers permit existing American facilities to be used for a reasonable period but do not encourage construction of new capacity unless it is able to compete with the output of low-cost countries, then the American consumer would be able to reap progressively more advantage from economic growth abroad, and American investors and workers would not be forced to more violent adjustments later on.

The international cotton textile arrangements worked out in 1961 and 1962 partially meet these three criteria. The agreements were the product of international negotiation but the great reluctance of some of the parties suggests that compliance will not be willing in many cases and may not be complete. GATT's sponsorship of the cotton textile arrangements, the declarations about expanding trade, and the safeguards for exporting countries are all advantages. The agreement promises progressive expansion of existing and future quotas; it lays down standards for the imposition of new quotas. None is sanctioned unless market disruption occurs or threatens, but there is a loophole in that the importing country is the sole judge of disruption.

If one is not disturbed, as Japanese exporters are, about unilateral declaration of market disruption by the importing country, and if one regards the escalation requirement as adequate, as I do not, then he may view the long-term arrangement as not very protectionist. In fact, if one favors protection of the American textile industry, he may think the arrangement's terms permit too large a flow of imports. How soon quotas can legally be imposed depends on the quickness or slowness of the U.S. government in deciding whether market disruption is occurring or threatening. Moreover, the agreement could be administered to permit imports of cotton textiles into the United States to grow far faster than the 5 per cent a year by which quotas are required to grow after the first two years. American textile men object to this possibility of large imports and suspect that the international agreement will give them far less protection than they wanted from national action.

Although exporting countries would prefer no trade barriers at all, they gain some advantages from the multilateral agreement. Its rules give them firmer, even if narrower, ground than the terms of GATT for opposing restrictions. While no longer free to condemn quotas on general principles, they can protest if quotas are imposed in circumstances that seem not to meet the GATT definition of market disruption. (By the kind of informal or unseen influence at which the Japanese government has long been expert, it may prove possible to hold exports to a level that will prevent market disruption, at least when Japan is the main supplier.) A potentially very great gain for the exporting countries would be real acceptance of the idea that the international cotton textile agreement should be a vehicle for an orderly transition in international trade. On the one hand the importing countries would limit the protection they give domestic producers but would be assured that there would be no disruption of markets. On the other hand the exporters would accept some restraint on exports as the price of assured easier access to foreign markets. In such circumstances one could regard trade expansion without disruption as being in important respects an advance over completely unrestrained competition.

Conflicting Forces

Whether the new ways of using quotas come close to living up to the statements of purpose in the international cotton textile agreement or instead prove to be just another phase of protectionism will depend on the interplay of a number of forces.

Textile protectionism in the United States may be expected to diminish somewhat in significance, even if not in intensity, during the years ahead. One of the leading protectionist interests in the country, the textile industry is a large employer in enough states to attract the attention and support of a good many Congressmen. But the number of workers on the industry's payroll, especially in cotton manufacturing, is dropping, while the total American labor force is rising. As time passes, the political influence of the textile industry, especially of cotton manufacturing, can be expected to decline as a result of the industry's loss of relative importance. The very existence of an international agreement assuring some degree of protection has some effect on the political strength of the industry because it may reduce the support given by political leaders and public opinion outside the industry itself.

Other, smaller industries start from lower levels of political power. While they are likely to remain protectionist for a long time, the possibility is now open to erode away such islands not only by normal economic progress but by conscious readjustment. Vigorous national economic growth with little unemployment could ease the problem substantially. If this kind of adjustment proves successful, even the textile problems may prove less difficult, and perhaps the gap can be substantially narrowed between the size of the textile industry in being and the sector of the industry that is able to hold its own in open competition.

There is also a good chance that exporting countries will have a greater influence than in the past. Newly independent and industrializing countries are growing in number; their interest in the future export of manufactured goods is increasingly recognized. Their influence can be expected to grow in GATT and to affect American foreign policy in other ways. Under multilateral agreements exporting countries, including the established ones like Japan, have more opportunity than in the past to hold out against unacceptable conditions and to influence the administration of the international trading arrangements. Taken all together these circumstances seem to warrant some optimism about the effect of the international agreement.

In contrast to these tendencies are some disturbing initial experiences in the negotiation and application of the agreement. The high-sounding multilateral agreement exists because the protectionist forces in the U.S. textile industry are very powerful. Negotiation of the international arrangements involved American diplomatic pressure of types and degrees that seem unbecoming to the most powerful nation on earth, especially when our basic policies are professedly liberal. The United States brought much of its influence to bear in extracting questionable bargains from weaker nations in contravention of important principles. What is worse, the long list of restrictions reportedly urged on Japan in the 1963 bilateral negotiations on cotton textiles (see p. 332) and the reported strong-arm tactics used in these negotiations suggest far less American concern for the trading principles involved than for arranging special privileges in behalf of a politically powerful producer group in the United States. These dangerous precedents augur ill, both for American policy and for the actions of other countries that may find themselves able to elbow their way internationally without regard for basic policy principles.

The basic views of American cotton manufacturers are firmly protectionist, not only with respect to the present and a transition period, but for the indefinite future as well. As one of them put it:

> We could welcome imports which were improvements on our own; our objection is to import of imitations of our own products coming in only because they are lower in price because they are made under cheaper foreign wages and standards. . . . We are looking for no temporary adjustment. Therefore we want permanent protection, whether by tariff or quota or both, that will maintain our American standards today, tomorrow and forever.[11]

This is a wish that cannot be honored by the international agreement, which limits protection and proclaims the goal of expanded markets for foreign exports, or by existing American commercial policy, which looks to the further reduction of barriers to foreign trade and the adjustment of production to conditions of international competition. But it is out of

[11] Letter from Donald Comer, former textile executive, *The New York Times,* March 24, 1961.

the conflict between the political strength of such group interests and broader national aims that the practical aspects of policy emerge.

As the discussion in the second part of this chapter has shown, the arguments about the possible uses of export quotas concern such conflicts. They do not lead to absolute conclusions, applicable in all circumstances. The basic American position against the use of quantitative trade controls remains the correct one. But if there have to be direct controls, it is probably better that they should take the form of export quotas than of import quotas—because it may prove easier to remove them. And if export quotas are to be used extensively it is better that they should be internationally negotiated and made the subject of open agreement than that they should be imposed as ostensibly "voluntary," unilateral measures—for equity and in the hope of establishing international standards for judging national action. And if there are to be such agreements, their provisions should meet tests like escalation of quotas, limitation on national restrictive action, clear commitments to an eventual enlargement of export markets, and supervision of the operation of the agreement by GATT. They must, in short, serve as vehicles for international adjustment.

The possibility that it can be used in this way is the main justification for the international cotton textile agreement, closely followed by the argument that any realizable alternative would be less liberal. Like other possible international agreements of this sort, the cotton textile arrangements have the marked disadvantage that the very forces that make them the least bad alternative may prevent their being used as true instruments of adjustment. Because of these risks, I see no reason to regard the cotton textile agreement as a highly desirable model for international trade in other cheap manufactured goods. There are other disadvantages; such agreements are likely to be cumbersome to administer and difficult to negotiate; the trade pattern for many products is likely to prove unsuitable for this kind of agreement. While multilateral agreements along the lines of the cotton textile arrangement are potentially means of bringing about major adjustments in international trade, our experience is too limited to warrant advocating their widespread application. Rather the device is something to be resorted to only when a pattern of economic and political pressure makes it likely that the sum total of national actions without an international agreement will prove more restrictive.

Chapter 11

Japanese Foreign Economic Policy in the 1960s

Japan has at long last found a place in the world economy that provides a satisfactory living without threatening the peace. Events have largely answered the basic question posed in 1945 by defeat and the enforced end of imperialism: How, if at all, could an overcrowded, defeated, island nation lacking essential resources make its way in the world and achieve an acceptable standard of living for its people? The period when American help was crucial has ended; for over a decade Japan has paid its way internationally without substantial foreign aid. Its prospects are excellent for continuing to do so in the future at progressively higher levels of production, trade, and income. Without the special privileges that before the war were thought essential to its position, Japan is competing successfully in foreign markets. Prosperity has been achieved with diminishing reliance on special sources of income, despite the virtual cessation of trade with the potentially large and politically significant China market. No longer is there any serious question about Japan's ability to pay in goods and services for the things it needs. Nor is there very much question about the existence in world markets of rich opportunities for Japan to buy, sell, borrow, and lend.

Other questions remain unanswered, especially two: Will Japanese trade grow fast enough to permit the economy to expand adequately? How will Japan conduct its international economic affairs? Only part of the answers will be found within Japan. Events and forces abroad will decide the rest. This chapter deals with the Japanese side of these questions and the next takes up the principal external issue: the place and policy of the United States.

JAPAN'S POSITION IN THE EARLY 1960s

Since 1945 the Japanese people have applied their traditional energy, skill, and intelligence to the enormous task of rebuilding, modernizing, expanding, and running their nation's economy. But without powerful external factors, mostly unforeseen, recovery and growth would have been substantially slower than they were. Again as in the past Japan has made progress by a combination of hard work and effective exploitation of opportunities.

A most important, unexpected element aiding recovery and growth was the strong support Japan received from the United States, the principal enemy in the Pacific war and the dominant power in the Occupation. American support was in part the result of another unforeseen factor, the cold war, which, on balance, has been very favorable to Japanese economic recovery and growth. Although Communist control of the Chinese mainland has thus far made it impossible for Japan to trade on a large scale with its huge neighbor, other results of the cold war have more than offset this handicap. The presence of large American military forces in Japan and elsewhere in Asia, and some of the U.S. procurement in Japan of aid goods for third countries, result from the cold war. Soviet intransigence, a major factor delaying the Japanese peace treaty, helped make its terms far more favorable to Japan than they would probably have been if imposed earlier. And many forms of American support for Japan, from sponsorship in international organizations to acceptance of Japanese goods and the GARIOA settlement, have probably been substantially more generous than they would have been but for the cold war.

The Korean War provided a great boost to the Japanese economy and did not put a heavy arms burden on Japan. Protected by an American military commitment, Japan has very light defense expenditures that leave most of the fruits of economic growth for consumption or investment. Foreign capital, much of it from the United States, has also contributed to investment while foreign technology, mostly American, has played a key role in Japanese growth. As in the Meiji era, borrowing has been extraordinarily successful; new products, technology, ideas, and machinery from abroad have been adapted and modified to fit Japanese circumstances.

The internal factors that have been of greatest importance in the evolution of Japanese economic growth and self-support have been the phenomenal rebuilding, modernization, and expansion of the productive plant and the generally very successful management of the national economy. The Japanese authorities have shown flexibility and skill in keeping prices reasonably stable, in stimulating extremely rapid economic growth, and in effectively managing the country's limited foreign exchange resources. Although their handling of balance-of-payments crises has left something to be desired, the record of Japanese financial policy is a commendable one. Production has risen very rapidly and a growing proportion of it has been reinvested in further expansion of facilities.

As output has risen, Japanese producers have found themselves able to compete in foreign markets more and more successfully. A widening range of goods has been exported to markets everywhere. Foreign import restrictions have not proved nearly so much of a deterrent as many people had feared. Japanese exports to the United States and the world at large have grown rapidly and with remarkably few major reverses, despite the virtual loss of the China market and the sluggishness of trade expansion in Southeast Asia.

Formal diplomatic relations have been re-established with most countries alienated by World War II—with the principal exception of Mainland China. Relations are being opened with new nations as they reach independence. Japan has joined nearly all the international organizations of interest to it, and in addition to benefiting from them is beginning to assume the responsibilities of its new economic strength.

Some of the reforms introduced by the Occupation—such as the dissolution of the military caste and the improvement in the status of farmers, workers, and women—have been effective in reducing the pressures within Japanese society, but tensions still remain and are complicated by the pace of change. Marxist ideas affect much of the thinking of students, teachers, unions, and left-wing political parties. Both the majority party and their main opponents, the Socialists, are riven by factional strife. Further tension results from a lack of cooperation, let alone of consensus, between government and opposition. Still, Japanese politics has shown remarkable stability. Except for a brief period early in the Occupation the conservatives, now led by the Liberal-Democratic Party, have dominated national politics. They consistently hold a majority in the Diet which is ample for many purposes but falls short of the two-thirds needed for revision of the Occupation-sponsored constitution.

Japanese policy makers and the people generally have been slow to acknowledge the great improvement in the nation's fortunes. Their thinking has not caught up with the actualities of recent achievements. Prosperity of present dimensions seems to make some Japanese uncomfortable, and they can hardly bring themselves to believe that it will last. At the same time ambitious economic plans are being carried out on the assumption that the present momentum can be maintained. The conflict between caution and optimism is discernible in the Japanese approach to economic policy.

CHANGING ATTITUDES ABOUT JAPAN'S POSITION AND PROSPECTS

While the economic doers in Japan were performing with tremendous success, observers, both in Japan and abroad, were until recently pessimistic about Japanese economic prospects. The pessimism was so widespread that Japan might almost be said to have backed into prosperity. That the people worked very hard—as they always had—was clear, but virtually nobody expected them to arrive at the economic level where they have recently found themselves.

Pessimism was fostered by the grim facts of economic life in Japan during the early postwar years, by the views of Western observers, and by the residues of the former propaganda of the imperialists who had claimed that to be prosperous Japan had to control Asian territory beyond its narrow islands. The most extreme pessimists in recent years were the numerous Marxists in the Japanese universities, who taught and believed such stereotypes as the inevitability of increasingly more destructive depressions, a growing disparity of incomes under "monopoly capitalism," and the utter unwillingness of the United States and other industrial countries to buy Japanese goods in adequate quantities. Perhaps the nearest thing to optimism before 1955 was to be found among Japanese businessmen. They paid close attention to immediate problems and prospects, varying their views with the ups and downs of the economy. But generally Japanese business was expansionist, investing all funds available and borrowing up to the hilt—and beyond at times—to expand facilities and raise production.

Much of the pessimism concerned foreign trade. In 1956, when Japan was enjoying a boom that was widely nicknamed *Jimmu Keiki,* the greatest prosperity since Jimmu, the legendary first emperor, an astute American reporter noted:

> . . . both Government officials and businessmen are already talking in terms of export ceilings. Many seem resigned to what they consider the inevitable—little or no further increase in foreign sales. . . .
>
> The trouble lies in the widespread, and mistaken belief that world trade has certain relatively fixed limits and that Japan merely wins a larger or smaller slice of the pie. The concept of an ever-expanding market is still far too new in Japan to enjoy wide acceptance.
>
> Most Japanese regard the current world trade boom, and Japan's consequent high level of exports, as abnormal and transitory. As soon as it subsides, the apologists predict direly, Japan will face a new crisis.[1]

[1] Igor Oganesoff, a correspondent of the *Wall Street Journal,* in *The Japan Times,* September 19, 1956, p. 11.

When the recession of 1957–1958 proved short and far less painful than many had anticipated, the pessimism was partly dissipated. Some Japanese at last escaped from the traditional feeling that theirs is a second-class economy because it depends on foreign raw materials, and from clichés about the inevitability of deep economic depressions in the capitalist world. Japanese exports did not fall at all during the 1957–1958 setback but only hesitated in their growth. When domestic and foreign business then surged forward, pessimism seemed more and more unrealistic. Not everyone modified his views, but a new tone became evident in Japanese discussion of the nation's economic situation and prospects.[2]

One of the first political leaders to reflect the change was Hayato Ikeda, who in early 1959 began to press for a program to double the national income in ten years. In June of that year he became Minister of International Trade and Industry and in July 1960 Prime Minister. After he returned to office following the Lower House elections of November 1960, a plan to double the national income by 1970 was adopted by the cabinet.

Plan for Rapid Economic Growth in the 1960s

Before Prime Minister Ikeda publicly announced his ambitious ideas for the Japanese economy, the Director of the Planning Bureau of the Economic Planning Agency (EPA) made the first public statement by a Japanese official indicating a shift toward the optimistic view Nobutane Kiuchi had expressed earlier. Saburo Okita, after a trip around the world in 1958, declared:

> It has often been said that Japan is too small, is lacking in natural resources, and has too large a population. There is no escaping the consequences of these three circumstances, it is claimed: the future is grim for the Japanese economy. However, after visiting a number of other countries and considering the likely future course of the world economy, this writer is of the strong impression that these three features of the Japanese economy are today by no means as unfavorable or significant as is commonly held.[3]

At this time Japan was in the early part of an economic plan calling for an average growth in national income of 6.5 per cent a year during

[2] A prophetic voice had been raised by Nobutane Kiuchi in *Foreign Affairs* in April 1956 ("False Assumptions about the Japanese Economy," p. 459), when, after reviewing all the usual arguments for pessimism, he said: "Individually these points are valid, but my reason for not taking them too seriously is my belief that the problems presented can all be solved in time. In fact, they are in a large measure being solved now." Very few others were ready to accept this view before the remarkably successful recovery that occurred after mid-1958.

[3] "A Reappraisal of Japan's Economy," *Japan Quarterly*, July–September 1959, p. 282.

the five years ending March 31, 1963.[4] This plan had replaced an earlier one calling for only 5 per cent annual growth in national income during the fiscal years 1956 to 1960.[5] The reason for this premature replacement was that actual expansion in 1956 was so rapid that the 1960 targets were nearly reached, and it became clear the plan was far too modest.

The Economic Planning Agency was already at work on long-range projections to 1970 and 1980 when Ikeda's idea of doubling the national income in ten years gained prominence. Publication of the EPA projections was delayed, and after Ikeda became Prime Minister his idea was adopted and worked into a ten-year plan for the fiscal years 1961 through 1970. This calls for national income to rise at an average annual rate of 7.8 per cent; per capita national income is projected to rise 6.9 per cent a year.[6] (Table 11-1.)

This is indeed very rapid growth, but slower than that achieved in the postwar years. The annual rate of increase in real gross national product averaged 11.5 per cent from 1947 through 1952 (fiscal years, as are all these figures), 8.3 per cent from 1953 through 1958 (including two recessions). The next three years were even higher: 17.7 per cent in 1959, 11 per cent in 1960, and 15 per cent in 1961. In 1962 the figure dropped to 5.2 per cent as a result of restraints imposed in 1961.[7] Some economists have regarded much of this expansion as catching up, both in the sense of reconstruction and in the sense of Japan's making up for lack of attention to civilian and welfare needs after the mid-1930s. If this idea is valid, then perhaps Japan may be said to have caught up now in varying degrees—depending on the indicators used—and it is reasonable for future growth to be slower than in the 1950s.[8] In any case, the planned doubling

[4] The rate of increase based on the actual national income of fiscal year 1956 was 5.8 per cent a year. But the 1956 level was regarded as above the norm in "base value" used by the EPA. From this lower level the annual increase called for in national income during the period FY 1958–FY 1962 was 6.5 per cent. Japan, Economic Planning Agency, *New Long-Range Economic Plan of Japan (FY 1958–FY 1962)* (Tokyo: Author, 1957), p. 28.

[5] Japan, Economic Planning Board (predecessor of present EPA), *Economic Self-Support 5-Year Plan,* decided by the cabinet on December 23, 1955; tentative translation (Tokyo: Author, 1956, mimeographed), p. 5.

[6] Doubling in ten years requires an annual increase of 7.2 per cent. The Japanese plan thus provides for slightly more than doubling total income, slightly less than doubling per capita income.

[7] Japan, Economic Planning Agency, *New Long-Range Economic Plan of Japan (1961–1970): Doubling National Income Plan* (Tokyo: The Japan Times, 1961), p. 3; Economic Planning Agency, *Economic Survey of Japan* (1960–1961) (Tokyo: The Japan Times, 1961), p. 2; same (1961–1962), p. 2; same (1962–1963), p. 12. The 1962 figure, from the last listed source, is referred to as real gross national expenditure, for which figures are also given (p. 328) in 1955 prices for the years 1957 through 1962.

[8] See, for instance, Shigeto Tsuru, "Growth and Stability of the Postwar Japanese Economy," *American Economic Review,* Papers and Proceedings, May 1961, especially pp. 406 and 411.

TABLE 11-1. JAPANESE ECONOMIC PROJECTIONS TO 1970

Economic Indicator and Unit	*Average FY 1956–1958*	*Target FY 1970*	*Total Increase (per cent)*	*Annual Average Increase (per cent)*
Population (millions)	91.1	102.2	12	0.9
Population, 15 years and older (millions)	62.2	79.0	27	1.9
Gross national product ($ billions)	27.1	72.2	167	7.8
Gross national product per capita ($)	297	707	138	6.9
National income ($ billions)	22.2	59.2	167	7.8
Primary production ($ billions)	4.2	6.0	44	2.8
Secondary production ($ billions)	7.4	22.9	209	9.1
Tertiary production ($ billions)	10.6	30.3	185	8.4
National income per worker ($)	535	1,216	127	6.5
National income per capita ($)	244	579	138	6.9
Employment (millions)	41.5	48.7	17	1.2
Primary sector (millions)	16.5	11.5	−30	−2.1
Secondary sector (millions)	10.1	15.7	56	3.5
Tertiary sector (millions)	15.0	21.5	43	2.8
Paid employees (millions)	19.2	32.3	68	4.1
Self-employed (millions)	9.9	9.0	−9	−0.6
Family workers (millions)	12.4	7.4	−41	−2.7
Imports, c.i.f. ($ millions)	3,126	9,891	216	9.3
Exports, f.o.b. ($ millions)	2,701	9,320	245	10.0

Note: All values are in 1958 prices.

Source: Japan, Economic Planning Agency, *New Long-Range Economic Plan of Japan (1961–1970): Doubling National Income Plan* (Tokyo: The Japan Times, 1961), pp. 11, 14, 16.

of income in the 1960s will require continuation of an extremely high rate of saving, above 30 per cent of gross national product, to provide not only the production capacity required but also vast investments in public services, including railways, highways, harbor, and urban facilities, and a growing volume of welfare services and social security expenditures. It will not be easy to meet these goals.

Jobs, which have traditionally been scarce in Japan, are, somewhat surprisingly, expected to increase less rapidly than the population of working age. The ratio of employed to the total population fifteen and more years old is expected to decline from 66.8 per cent in the base period (FY 1956–FY 1958) to 61.6 per cent in the target year (FY 1970). This decline reflects expected increases in the proportion of persons continuing their education beyond the age of fifteen, reduced need for work by family members, and substantial shifts from farming and other occupations involving much low-paid or unpaid labor. Family workers on farms are expected to decline from 10 million in the base period to 5.5 million in the target year, an average drop of 2.9 per cent a year.

At the same time the number of petty traders and other self-employed persons is expected to decline slowly. The number of employed workers, especially those in modern firms above the smallest size, is expected to increase rapidly, the total going up by over 4 per cent a year. Thus unemployment and underemployment are expected to decline in severity. Workers will be producing more, as a result both of these structural shifts and of rising productivity in particular jobs. National income per worker is expected to rise from $535 a year in the base period to $1,216 in the target year, an average increase of 6.5 per cent a year.[9]

Growth like this will make the Japanese economy even more dependent than it now is on foreign trade, since domestic sources of raw materials and fuels cannot grow so fast. Imports are projected to rise 9.3 per cent a year on the average, reaching nearly $10 billion, or 16.7 per cent of national income, in 1970. Since Japan also has other obligations such as interest, reparations, and GARIOA repayments, exports must grow faster than imports; 10 per cent a year is projected, bringing the total to $9.3 billion by 1970, over half a billion dollars below imports. If export growth should lag, then imports will have to be checked. And if imports fall short of projected levels, then the whole growth plan stands in danger of being retarded. Now as always foreign trade is potentially a limiting factor in Japanese economic growth.

If the announced targets are achieved, Japan will become substantially more prominent in world trade. Japanese goods will appear in individual markets in larger volume, and Japanese trade will constitute a larger share of world trade. Some Japanese products may be expected to lose position, as Japanese cotton textiles have declined in the American market while imports from other sources rose. But other Japanese goods will probably come to dominate both individual markets and total world trade as Japanese transistor radios have in recent years.

The unexpected degree of acceptance of Japanese goods abroad, especially in the United States, has been an important element in Japan's recent economic success. Will that acceptance continue through the 1960s? The answer may depend to an important degree on whether Japan will alter its own trade policy. This possibility seems to be far less fully anticipated in Japanese plans than the expansion of exports. But changed circumstances create new requirements. Japan was a follower, not a leader, in the postwar reconstruction of world trade. The country's weak and discredited position made leadership impossible; so Japan had to find its way to a new role and a new policy in an international economy that it had not helped to design. It did very well, but for the future Japan must expect to play a fuller part in shaping the free world economy.

[9] *New Long-Range Economic Plan of Japan (1961–1970): Doubling National Income Plan,* cited, pp. 11, 16–18.

CHANGING APPROACHES TO INTERNATIONAL TRANSACTIONS

Traditional Japanese skepticism about the world economy and pessimistic estimates of Japan's prospects held full sway in the early 1950s. When the Japanese once again took full charge of their national affairs in 1952, they retained the machinery for control of foreign trade and payments set up under the Occupation. The general principles of the Foreign Exchange and Foreign Trade Control Law of 1949 were that residents of Japan had to surrender to the Ministry of Finance any foreign currency they acquired, that imports were subject to licensing, and that other expenditures of foreign currency also required specific permission. Despite progressive relaxation in administration, the basic policy through 1958 was control, not freedom.

The recessions of 1953–54 and 1957–58 made it necessary to tighten temporarily the restrictions on foreign payments, although in each case credit limitation rather than exchange control was the main means of checking outpayments. These experiences demonstrated the value of having ready instruments of control for the protection of Japan's volatile balance of payments. With the second of these experiences very fresh in their minds, Japanese were surprised to learn in December 1958 that the pound sterling and the major currencies of continental Europe had been made convertible for nonresidents. Unlike the Europeans, who had been working toward this event for some years, most Japanese had not realized that the time was near when a large measure of liberalization of international payments would be restored. Japan had too recently emerged from defeat and occupation to feel fully confident in international affairs, whether economic, political, or military, and therefore few Japanese regarded liberalization as the desirable and relatively near aim it was for many Europeans. A member of one of the leading Japanese trading companies said at the time:

> One thing I do not understand is the reason why these European countries decided to restore the convertibility of their currencies in a hurry, for some of them may even suffer from the step they took. I think the step was motivated by the spirit of free enterprise which underlies European civilization. Japan lacks such a spiritual foundation.[10]

Liberalization since 1958

Soon after the European action, some Japanese began to call for extensive liberalization. Ever since then Japan's policy has been pulled strongly in two opposite directions: toward retention of direct controls

[10] Ninichi Nakagawa, Mitsubishi Shoji K. K., in *Economist* (in Japanese), January 31, 1959, as quoted in American Embassy, Tokyo, *Summaries of Selected Japanese Magazines,* February 16, 1959, p. 22.

and toward their relaxation and removal. The latter policy has, however, made a good deal of headway since 1959, largely as the result of pressure from abroad. At the meetings of the World Bank and International Monetary Fund in October 1959 and at the GATT meeting in Tokyo a few weeks later, many governments urged Japan to ease restrictions against all kinds of imports, both of goods and services, while the United States pressed particularly for the end of discrimination against dollar imports.

In June 1960 the Japanese cabinet adopted a "Plan for Trade and Exchange Liberalization" (pp. 135–137). An accelerated schedule announced during the annual IMF consultations in Tokyo in 1961 called for 90 per cent of Japan's imports to be liberalized by October 1, 1962; what was actually attained by that date was 88 per cent. By September 1963 the figure had risen to 92.2 per cent. This means that for items making up 92.2 per cent of the value of Japan's imports in the base year 1959 foreign exchange permits were granted more or less automatically. Items not imported in 1959 do not count in calculating the 92 per cent.

Noncommodity transactions were also liberalized to a large extent but not completely. Most current transactions are unrestricted, foreign-owned funds in free-yen accounts can be withdrawn at any time, and, since April 1963, most kinds of capital can also be withdrawn without the waiting periods formerly required. The controls that remain, notably the requirement of government permission for foreign investment and the limitation on the extent of foreign ownership, reflect the caution with which the Japanese approach liberalization. Japan held back as long as possible from changing its status in the IMF from that of a country falling under the transitional rules of Article 14 to that of a nation assuming full normal obligations under Article 8. Part of the reason for this caution is the commendable aim of making sure that obligations can be honored and that Japan's standing in foreign capital markets remains high. In part, however, the remaining controls reflect fear, a preference for controls, a good deal of protectionism, and also a strong element of nationalism.

As a result of the steps toward liberalization, it seemed clear that for the first time since the middle 1930s the tariff was to become the principal means of limiting imports into Japan. Hence, all the protectionist forces in the country would come to bear on it. This was apparent before liberalization was far advanced when, in the process of revising the tariff schedule, emphasis was put on the height of the duties on products to be freed from quotas and exchange controls.

The Economic Planning Agency said in 1961 that liberalization would bring changes in Japan's industrial structure and that tariff policy should be used to help ensure an orderly transition. "While it is advisable to give protection to those incipient industries which have potentialities for development from the standpoint of comparative advantage for a limited period of time, the Government should refrain from giving relief to declining ones. Attention should be paid rather to unemployment problems in the declining industries. Such Government attitude as outlined above would be felt as rather severe on industries and enterprises. But only by going through such a phase will Japan be strong enough to compete in the world market and gain a solid basis for economic growth." [11]

This recognition of the connection between import liberalization and Japan's export needs is exceptional. It embodies, however, an argument for liberalization that has a better chance of carrying weight with the pragmatic Japanese people than an appeal to the ideals of free trade, for which they lack a tradition. A more typical reaction was *The Oriental Economist's* comment on the original decision to liberalize. It called the government's announcement "unexpectedly early" and concluded gloomily: "Every fear exists that a lot of troubles will come to the fore in the course of realization, even if enforced with utmost caution." [12]

In the ensuing years while liberalization was put progressively into effect, two changes took place. Some fears were reduced by protective measures introduced to replace direct controls; tariffs have been raised and cartel arrangements have strengthened the hold of some Japanese producers on their domestic market. The second change was in the attitudes of Japanese toward liberalization. More and more of them have come to accept it as not only inevitable but in many ways good for Japan. One reason for this added confidence is that tremendous investments have been made in new technology and new productive facilities during recent years. Japanese factories can now produce more goods more efficiently than ever before. The measures of liberalization already taken have not brought disaster; the economy continues to flourish. And yet, there remains a good deal of doubt and reluctance about liberalization.

Reservations about Liberalization

Some of the Japanese reluctance to accept liberalization wholeheartedly is attributable to fairly specific worries related to recent experience. Some stems from deeply rooted characteristics of Japanese culture and society.

One inhibiting factor is continuing fear of huge deficits in the balance of payments. Three times in ten years the payments situation proved to be the main weak point and limiting factor in periods of economic diffi-

[11] *New Long-Range Economic Plan of Japan (1961–1970): Doubling National Income Plan*, cited, pp. 72–73.

[12] August 1960, p. 449.

culty. To many Japanese the recurrence of these crises means that the authorities should always be equipped, as they are now, to deal with the situation by whatever measures appear appropriate, including quantitative controls. Drawing rights under IMF procedures have not seemed to provide enough scope for emergency action. Yet the main device that has been used to check outpayments in times of foreign exchange crises has been credit restriction, and liberalization need not impede the use of this tool.

Another difficulty is that in the past Japan's direct controls on the use of foreign exchange have been strict enough to provide a large measure of protection to domestic high-cost producers. In fact, according to the Japanese bank that does the most foreign exchange business, the most important role of import controls has been "the protection of domestic industries and the adjustment of production quantities." [13] Only when sharp reduction of direct controls was begun did their highly protective effect become fully evident. Threatened with removal of this protection, Japanese producers have urged postponement of liberalization and, alternatively, increases in tariffs. Their cause has been strongly supported by the Ministry of International Trade and Industry.

Japan, we must remember, is a highly protectionist country. For a hundred years the government has found means to stimulate and give support to favored industries and firms, through purchase orders, subsidies, other favors, tariffs, or direct import controls. Now a major shift in method is taking place as direct controls disappear, but it would be rash to predict that a substantial reduction in the degree of protection will follow. Though the income-doubling plan calls for a relatively large increase of imports of finished manufactures other than machinery, they are scheduled to amount to only 6.0 per cent of total imports in 1970.[14] Since this category includes a vast range of goods which Japanese consumers could be expected to buy in even greater quantity if permitted to do so, some form of restraint on demand, and perhaps on imports, may be contemplated.

The urgent need to export has somewhat limited Japan's protectionist tendencies. Forced to trim costs and improve their products in order to export, Japanese producers have had to take whatever opportunities were available to buy cheaply from abroad. Bilateral trade agreements intended to break down foreign barriers to Japanese exports entailed some easing of Japanese import controls. These gains have been maintained

[13] Bank of Tokyo, *Semiannual Report,* October 1959–March 1960 (Tokyo: Author, 1960), p. 22.

[14] They were 2.6 per cent of the total in 1959. The projected absolute increase is from $105 million to $595 million. *New Long-Range Economic Plan of Japan (1961–1970): Doubling National Income Plan,* cited, p. 80.

as multilateral trade and currency convertibility have spread and bilateral agreements have declined in importance. Though little of Japan's trade is now financed through clearing agreements, bilateral trading arrangements remain popular. Many Japanese businessmen, accustomed at home to close ties among firms, find a sense of security in this kind of trade.

Security and related considerations play an important part in Japanese attitudes regarding liberalization as well as other things. The physical environment of Japan, for all its productive farms and natural beauties, is harsh in many ways. Life has long been hard; fluctuations between good times and bad have been extreme and often sudden. Earthquakes, typhoons, floods, and fires may occur at any time. The proper attitude is traditionally a combination of obedience, courage, determination, and hard work along with caution. The tradition permits Japanese to enjoy their present prosperity, but they are not yet ready to count on its continuation. What is more, they are not widely convinced that Japan is in a position to do much about the international circumstances that would foster continuation of the prosperity. The outside world has always been viewed as basically hostile and uncontrollable, even though at times presenting opportunities that may be turned to Japanese advantage by cleverness or hard work.

Crowded into narrow islands, the Japanese people have through the centuries evolved customs that rely on strict observance of detailed rules to make human contacts peaceable and effective. Duty and discipline are central features of life in a society so intricately interwoven as to be called "the web society." In Japanese eyes self-expression can easily tear the fabric, and social pressure is extreme for maintenance and reinforcement of the web. The harsh environment reduces the scope for individual action and enhances reliance on the group. And it is in group, rather than individual, activity that the Japanese people have been most outstanding. No other Asian people have been able to cooperate so effectively in large private firms or government civil or military organizations. Japanese objection to what is called "excessive" and "destructive" competition seems to reflect discomfort at "undisciplined" conduct as well as a feeling that the nation's interests are less well served by impersonal market forces than by conscious decisions on the part of leaders, accepted and followed by others.

The tradition of control from the top through strong governmental leadership has not been weakened by the vitality and success of private business and the complex interactions of government and business. In foreign economic policy a great deal of initiative lies with the executive arm of the government rather than with the Diet or with business, labor, or farm groups. Today's political opposition in Japan is mainly Socialist, with a minority of Communists and ultrarightists. None of these groups is pressing for a reduction in government control over international economic affairs.

Bureaucracy has a long and successful history in Japan. Government personnel are no longer so officious as in the ultranationalist days that ended in 1945, but there remains more than a trace of the feudal concept of authority. Government officials are not the public servants we Americans like to think ours should be, but rather members of an elite group, well trained, conscientious, usually efficient, but generally less concerned with public attitudes than with what they—and their superiors—think is desirable. While large Japanese firms have usually developed effective approaches to officialdom high and low, the individual businessman, especially the little man, may often be given less than sympathetic attention. The Japanese bureaucracy has tremendous power and knows it. Controls over foreign transactions are administered in ways that reflect this power.

So, in many ways the psychology and habit of control are deeply ingrained in Japan, while the counter forces pressing for freer competition are less deeply rooted. Without a strong philosophical basis for liberal trade policies, suspicious of "selfish" motives in businessmen as well as politicians, and used to bureaucratic control, the Japanese have not since 1931 known freedom in international economic relations. Those who remember the 1920s do not look on that period with satisfaction.

Although as dependent as any nation in the world on access to foreign markets and on the chance to compete freely, Japan shows marked reluctance to permit foreigners to compete in its own market. There is only limited domestic pressure to make the country a living example of the kind of commercial and financial policies that would most benefit Japan if followed by other nations. In this regard, Japanese psychology is that of a small country—pressing other countries for favorable treatment without demonstrating a sense of responsibility for the general character of international economic relations or the rules and practices involved.

Japan conforms to the international rules that prevail but does very little to strengthen or improve them, even when that would benefit Japan directly. The multilateral trade that contributes so much to Japan's unprecedented prosperity is accepted for what Japanese traders can gain. But much Japanese thinking has not yet caught up with the facts of Japan's trade position today, let alone pictured an improved world trading pattern that would benefit Japan.

In spite of all these factors causing them to prefer controls and security, the Japanese have gone far in liberalizing their foreign trade and payments. But they have done so with less than whole hearts, largely in response to foreign pressure, and have much left to do.

FUTURE JAPANESE POLICY

This study has shown that Japan can earn enough to pay for what it needs from abroad and can manage its economy in a way that enables it to live within its means. This has been done by following a policy that has been essentially cautious and conservative. Throughout the post-war period, the Japanese have been chiefly concerned with immediate issues and have given little thought to the broad outlines of the world economy. Expanding markets for essential exports and a variety of means of improving Japan's international position have preoccupied them. This practical—even opportunistic—concentration on the near and immediate has served the country well. Japan's experience has belied domestic and foreign pessimism and even sober analyses that not so many years ago seemed to lead to the conclusion that Japan's special problems would put a brake on economic progress and leave the country in a continuously precarious position. Now Japan finds itself in an unexpectedly favorable situation.

Since the unwritten prescription has worked so well, why should Japan not go on as in the past, adapting to new circumstances and pressures as they appear? The answer is that this approach may well prove inadequate in the years ahead. It is not in keeping with the rapidly changing international economy or with the potentialities in Japan's bold plan for doubling domestic income by 1970. Present policy is still an adaptation of that of the impoverished early 1950s and is not suitable for the vigorous Japan of the 1960s. The outlook and needs of the people have changed profoundly. The power of the Russians and Chinese has grown, and the relative strength of the United States has declined. The dollar shortage has ended, and with it the commanding position of the United States as a dispenser of economic favors. Special dollar expenditures in Japan continue, but at a declining rate, and soon they are likely to be no more than a minor factor in Japanese international payments. Economic growth and a degree of unification have increased Western Europe's power. The emergence of many new states, especially in Africa, and the economic development that is taking place in many parts of the world are bringing about changes in patterns of trade and capital flow. At home public investment needs are enormous, for housing, roads, public utilities. And there is a great deal of room for increasing consumer expenditures, especially among the poorer classes. These domestic outlets for new production require increasing attention.[15]

[15] *The Economist* in its brilliant survey of the Japanese economy, September 1, 1962 (pp. 787–824) and September 8, 1962 (pp. 907–936), discusses pointedly both possible means of supplementing insufficient demand (p. 815) and the pos-

So far, Japanese thinkers and leaders have given very little indication of the direction they think their country's policy should take to anticipate the changing world of the 1960s. If Japan is to keep on improving its fortunes, reach domestic goals, and win recognition as a leading nation in the world, it must embark on a more vigorous and imaginative foreign economic policy than it has had in the past. It seems to me clearly within Japanese capabilities to influence the shape and trend of international economic affairs in ways that advance the interests of Japan and of the world at large. To see how this might be done, one must look first at the outstanding feature of Japan's foreign economic relations since the war: the predominance of the United States.

Economic Ties with the United States

Would a significant loosening of Japan's economic ties with the United States be possible or desirable? Some Japanese think so. Not all members of this group are leftists. There are others as well who press most vigorously for reduction in Japan's "overdependence" on the United States. On one of the few occasions when I have been able to discuss trade with a Japanese leftist, I objected to his comments about American import barriers against Japanese exports, contending that he, like many other Japanese, exaggerated the extent and importance of these barriers. He did not deny my contention. In fact, he said, exaggeration is good if it proves an effective means for reducing Japanese dependence on the United States; this dependence is making Japan soft, and Japan thus loses more than it gains from trade with the United States, or from the various forms of American support of Japan. This view is symptomatic of the uneasiness felt by many Japanese because of the continued American "presence" long after the end of the Occupation and what they regard as their limited freedom of action.

Japan has depended so heavily on the United States in trade, financial, and military matters that the choices made by Japanese governments since 1952 have not in fact always originated in Japanese initiative. Rather, too many policies have obviously resulted from American and other foreign pressures. One result has been that even when the Japanese government has been quite content with the substance of American views, for instance on China trade, suspicion of foreign influence and foreign interests has stirred doubt in the minds of the Japanese and given the political opposition much to criticize. A most unpopular decision taken by the Japanese government in response to American pressure was the acceptance of export quotas on sales to the American market. The fact that Japan then lost sales when other exporting coun-

sibilities of Japan's greatly increasing aid and investment abroad, especially in Southeast Asia (pp. 930, 932), but does not relate the second subject to the first.

tries gained them by being less obliging introduced new strains in relations with the United States and inside Japan as well. In the matter of liberalization, too, Japan has undoubtedly acted largely in response to outside pressure.

Of course the policies of all countries are in part a response to the wishes of others. American influence was strong because of Japan's substantial strategic and economic dependence on the United States. An additional factor, in all probability, was the persistence of a Japanese view of patron-ward relationships carried over from feudal times. Inside Japanese society employers and employees, fathers and families, professors and favored students, politicians and their supporters, as well as many other leader-follower groupings, tend to be bound to each other by numerous and tight ties. Since World War II, to one thinking in such terms, Japan has had to accept inferior international status as a ward, and to conduct itself accordingly. After the end of the Occupation the relationship between the United States and Japan did not suddenly lose this quality, and the patron-ward relationship probably contributed to the unusual degree of Japanese amenability to American initiatives. It has probably been of more moment to the Japanese that their country stood well with the United States than that their policy followed a particular principle.

By now the patron-ward relationship should be at an end. Japan is no longer under any great compulsion to follow the lead of the United States. If Japanese policy appears to be made largely in deference to the wishes of other countries, resentment against foreign influence will increase. The longer the nation waits to formulate its own policy, the greater the danger of one's emerging without due thought in a moment of stress. In Japan's interest and in the interest of friendly countries there is need for a recognizably Japanese policy, based on a Japanese view of the world and of Japan's role in it.

It does not follow that such a policy will seriously weaken economic links with the United States. Japan needs export markets and the United States has proved to be its best. The other trading and financial relations of the two countries are also based on common interests more than on artificially fostered special relations. As Japan intensifies its economic relations with Europe and other parts of the world, the relative position of the United States is likely to be somewhat reduced, but it would be to the disadvantage of both countries if Japan, to prove its independence, deliberately destroyed or distorted the main economic links between the countries.

Economic Ties with China

One way to reduce dependence on the United States is to expand trade with Communist China, a course persistently sought by many Japanese. Chapter 7 showed that China trade has important, though often exaggerated, economic potentialities but also entails serious dangers. The unreliability of this trade is a strong argument for limiting it to an amount that Japan could afford to lose if the Peking regime chose to stop trade, as it has done in the past, or exact a political price for its continuance. Japan would also have to weigh against the benefits of expanding China trade the political risks of unfavorable American reactions.

The Chinese leaders would like very much to wean Japan away from the West and if possible bring it into the Communist camp, a sequence that is probably not contemplated by those Japanese who want a shift in Japan's orientation. But the hazards of China trade might be obscured if Peking should soften its attitude toward Japan and undertake tactical shifts in domestic affairs similar to the New Economic Policy and other expedients adopted by Russia in the early post-revolution period. The Chinese rulers have had to retreat a long way from the extremes of the 1958 "Great Leap Forward" and if they seriously wish to woo Japan they may offer attractive trade inducements. The five-year agreement concluded in late 1962 suggests some sort of return to more normal trade. The Chinese appear to have made two important concessions to the Japanese, by agreeing that contracts may not be canceled except by mutual agreement, and dropping their earlier stipulation that they would deal only with "friendly firms" in Japan. Although the agreement provides for the largest volume of Sino–Japanese trade in recent years, the amount is a very small proportion of total Japanese trade. And some of the stumbling blocks that have interfered with commercial relations in the past are still there—Chinese inability to pay and Japanese reluctance to offer China better credit terms than those extended to regular customers.

By giving official blessing to the private Japanese delegation that signed the trade agreement the Japanese government decided to risk the displeasure of the United States and Taiwan. Presumably it did so because it watched Canada, Australia, and Western European countries increase their trade with the Chinese without suffering serious disapproval by the United States. The Europeans, at least, have sold products that the Japanese could profitably have supplied. If China proves able to pay and willing to trade more, the proposed $100-million annual level may prove to be low. Then the Japanese government will once again have to choose between pursuing the country's commercial advantage in China and risking displeasure and possible pressure from the United States.

Even if the United States were to follow a strictly hands-off policy, a major consideration for Japan would be the degree of uncertainty it was prepared to accept in its trade. The Japanese have already had enough experience with politically motivated economic relations, both with Russia and with China, to be wary of entrusting too large a proportion of their trade to the vagaries of state-controlled commerce. On the other hand, many Japanese have doubts about the dependability of their trade with the West. It may be that if the Japanese felt freer to expand trade with China and did it on their usual businesslike basis, they would find, not the almost infinite expansion some seem to envisage, but relatively modest possibilities and that they would then see their total trading interest in a more realistic perspective. The existing large trade with the free world can serve as a kind of insurance covering a degree of experimentation in trade with China. Having these other rich markets, Japan is in a better bargaining position as it enters negotiations than if it were desperate and also has possibilities to fall back on if the Chinese try to exert pressure through trade or again interrupt the exchange for reasons of their own. Since Japan is not faced with all-or-nothing alternatives, it would be in the nation's best interests to adopt a flexible policy with regard to China, safeguarding its own position by arrangements that minimize the vulnerability of its traders, while exploring the commercial possibilities to determine whether the Chinese are more willing than in the past to trade on a reasonable basis.

A Trading Bloc for Japan?

A regional common market or some other special economic arrangement with Southeast Asia has attracted many Japanese in postwar years. As Chapter 7 showed, a grouping of Japan and Southeast Asia would not be a satisfactory economic unit; both Japan and Southeast Asia depend too much on trade with outside areas. Furthermore, the idea has not yet escaped from the bad heritage of the Co-Prosperity Sphere; even if it did, there is little political cohesion to be found in the area.

Perhaps the attraction for the Japanese of an Asian grouping is more psychological than economic. The Japanese are eager for recognition, they are active and successful joiners at home, they may feel the need to be members of a group in the world. But as a nation Japan does not fit easily into any grouping. Most of the industrial countries of the West are not yet ready to accept Japan fully as one of them, and the geographic and cultural gulf is still too wide to be bridged by existing ties. Among Asian countries, only Japan has achieved a modern, industrial society, and it looks upon its rural neighbors as country cousins. So Japan stands uncertainly in between, closer to the top of the scale of achievement than to the bottom.

Some regional arrangement might commend itself as a second-best course of action if the trade of Japan and Southeast Asia with the rest of the world were greatly hampered. If, for instance, the policies of the European Common Market impeded exports of manufactured goods from Japan and gave preference to Africa over Southeast Asia in the supply of raw materials, then the Asians might find their mutual interests served by closer economic relations. If they were joined by some of the British Commonwealth countries, like Australia and New Zealand, and perhaps India and Pakistan, the potential gain from the grouping would be greater. As a means of adapting to a world economy composed of large, protective trading blocs, an Asian market would be preferable to a wholesale retreat by its members into protection on a national basis. Much would depend on the policies of the United States, Canada, and Britain. But it is unlikely that an Asian regional grouping could be for Japan anything more than a poor substitute for wider trading opportunities.

Canada, Australia, and New Zealand have already proved to be partners with whom Japan can do a thriving trade. Japan hopes to expand its sales to Western Europe if growth continues in that area and barriers to imports from Japan are reduced. Trade with the U.S.S.R. presents many of the same problems as trade with China, though perhaps in less intense form. Some expansion of Japanese–Soviet trade seems likely. But even if all these developments take place, the United States is not likely to be displaced in the foreseeable future as the country with which Japan has the largest volume of commercial and financial transactions. There will be a gain, however, if there is some increase in the importance of other countries.

Aid and Trade

Japan may have a particularly valuable role to play in relations with underdeveloped countries. Here Japan is clearly on the same side of the table as the advanced countries of Europe and North America, facing a similar set of challenges, responsibilities, and opportunities. It is well to remember that Japan's route to the OECD lay through the Development Assistance Committee, of which it was a charter member.

Aside from technical assistance activities, economic aid by Japan has been chiefly in the form of reparations deliveries to four Asian countries. There have also been loans from the Japanese Export–Import Bank and private Japanese investment in developmental projects. There is justification, however, for the American view that Japan is capable of a larger effort.[16] In some of its technology, both adapted and indig-

[16] The Japanese do not disagree. Their long-range plan contemplates $1.5 billion in government and private foreign credit in fiscal 1970, plus $630 million of direct

enous, Japan may in fact be more helpful to the developing countries than the most advanced industrial countries. In international and regional organizations concerned with development programs it would be appropriate for Japan to begin to exercise responsible leadership. Effective use can be made of its experience in agriculture, industry, and commerce, and fuller participation by Japan in joint development planning will expand the scope of Japanese influence and enhance Japanese standing in international councils. A problem will remain in dissociating Japanese involvement in the affairs of underdeveloped countries from the imperialist past. There is hope in the fact that that past is now beyond the personal experience of a majority of the people in the developing countries. Their rapidly multiplying populations are predominantly youthful and many are ready to view Japan favorably if given good reason to do so.

There is another important respect in which Japan stands in a special place between the underdeveloped countries and the industrial centers of North America and Western Europe. In the long run, the underdeveloped countries must finance their growth more by export earnings than by aid. Now, and probably for some time to come, the largest part of these exports will be foodstuffs and raw materials. The export of manufactured goods from less developed countries is still exceptional, but cotton goods from India and a range of products from a few industrial enclaves, such as Hong Kong and Singapore, are already important in world trade. As time passes some underdeveloped countries are bound to try to increase greatly their exports of manufactured goods. Inevitably cheapness will be one of their main advantages; they will seek the large markets of the industrialized countries; consequently, there will be complaints from established producers against their new foreign competition.

Japan has been through all this, and the rest of the world with her. Perhaps something can be learned from that experience. It would certainly be desirable in the interests of the whole free world to avoid repetition of Japan's export frustrations during the prewar period which contributed so much to the economic and political troubles of the whole world. There is encouragement in the fact that eventually Japan found markets in North America and Europe for its manufactured goods. Japan's experience is not directly applicable to countries so different and so much less well developed but there are probably some relevant lessons, perhaps about export quotas, perhaps about international agree-

investment. When expenditures on technical assistance, educational aid to foreigners, and contributions to international organizations are added, nearly 3 per cent of Japan's gross national product in 1970 might go for international economic cooperation. In calendar 1961 Japan's aid to underdeveloped countries, as calculated by DAC, came to $376 million, about 1 per cent of GNP, plus reparations. OECD, *Development Assistance Efforts and Policies in 1961* (Paris: Author, 1962), p. 17.

ments, like that for cotton textiles, perhaps about concepts of market disruption. But whatever way the problem is handled, and however rapidly it develops, its solution will require a progressive opening of markets in the industrial countries to new lines of cheap imports of manufactured goods—and this time Japan will be on the receiving end. This fact is in itself an indication of one kind of trade policy problem Japan now faces.

A Trade and Payments Policy for the Future

Japan's economic successes in recent years have grown out of an ever-spreading network of relationships that spell interdependence with other parts of the world. It is clearly to Japan's advantage to strengthen the threads of this international network. The Japanese have not hesitated to press their case in some ways, by trying to gain freer entry for their goods in foreign markets and seeking full membership in bodies like GATT and the OECD. They have been much less energetic—perhaps even less clear—about providing the kind of treatment for foreigners that they ask for themselves. Free competition abroad is looked upon as a good thing, but few Japanese believe in wholly free competition in Japan; in domestic activities and in dealing with foreigners they show a strong preference for controls. They have done very well internationally but their commitment to multilateral trade is not complete; they appear to be distrustful of world markets and often give the impression that they do not fully accept the implications of policies that seem, to the outside observer, necessary to success in Japan's new role. By their own standards they have made enormous strides in the liberalization of trade and payments, but to the rest of the world the program seems inadequate and, what is perhaps worse, halfhearted; the Japanese appear to be going along with an essentially alien idea in which they do not really believe.

Japanese reluctance to move too far too fast is understandable. It may be somewhat diminished by the fact that the steps taken so far have not brought disaster. The continuation of prosperity through the period of liberalization has helped. To the pragmatic Japanese the fact that a system—no matter how reluctantly adopted—has proved to be workable may offer a sounder basis for continued adherence to it than belief in its theoretical desirability.

Several developments in the rest of the world have supported and supplemented the Japanese movement toward liberalization. The expansion of world trade, though proceeding erratically, has been steady enough to lend substance to long-range plans for Japanese exports. The ease with which Japan has been able to borrow abroad and the enthusiasm of foreigners for long-term investments in Japan have reduced the dangers of adverse capital movements. Most important, perhaps, is the gradual change in the attitudes of the other industrial countries toward Japan. They are being obliged to discard the convenient stereotypes of the past in the face of Japan's extraordinary industrial progress, the high quality of the goods it has for sale, and the rising wage levels and standard of living of the people.

By the spring of 1964 the cumulative effect of all these factors became apparent. Japan was admitted to the OECD; a series of trade agreements promised wider European markets; several European countries had at last granted Japan equal treatment in GATT, while others were seriously considering the removal of their restrictions. The Japanese government in turn agreed to accept the responsibilities required by the IMF's Article 8 and GATT's Article 12 prohibiting the use of quantitative restrictions on trade and payments, and indicated that virtually all foreign goods would soon be freely admitted.

This is an impressive list of accomplishments. Credit for it is due in many places. The fact that in adopting liberalization measures Japan has acted in response to foreign prodding does not detract from what has been achieved, nor does it carry the implication that foreign pressure will be needed in the future to maintain Japan on a course of liberalization. Japan has no bloc of its own to retire to for shelter. Confronted with a growing number of preferential systems, Japan needs policies that will keep open export markets and encourage the strengthening of multilateral relationships.

With Europe Japan has a special need to develop more trade. Most, if not all, of Western Europe may eventually become a single-market area, as rich a market as the United States and with a population half again as large. Many Europeans fear Japanese competition. If this fear is permitted to dominate their policies and tariff levels the consequences for Japanese trade could be very costly. In addition to being a potentially large market, Europe is also an expanding source of capital for Japan, and as Japanese exports rise Japan's borrowing capacity and import capacity also rise. These need not be balanced geographically but increased exports to Europe are likely to help Japan's credit standing there.

The challenge of Europe has parallels in Japan's opportunities and tasks in other high-income countries—Canada, Australia, New Zealand, and, of course, the United States. Economic activity per head in these countries—and consequently Japan's economic opportunity—is far greater than in the less developed areas of Asia, Africa, and Latin America. Although Japanese trade is already fairly well developed in the high-income areas, it has room to expand further; how much and how fast will depend in part on Japanese efforts and skill in pursuing its liberalization program. Although discrimination against Japanese goods persists and cannot be disregarded, the high-income countries have been able to point to Japanese discrimination against their exports. A continued paring down of Japan's own barriers would be the surest indication of its willingness to accept the obligations of GATT and the most persuasive argument for its claim to equal treatment in other markets.

Japan faces a special problem in determining its policy toward the international cotton textile agreement. Having signed the agreement, however reluctantly, it should see what can be made of it. It is clearly to Japan's interest to press, in GATT debate and elsewhere, for steps that will make the high principles of the agreement a reality. Japan should certainly be one of the leaders in moving toward stricter standards and closer supervision of quotas. In this it will naturally get the backing of other exporting countries, but it should try to win support from the importing countries as well. This might be done by accepting the idea that market disruption creates a problem that needs special attention; this approach is written into the agreement and Japan's earlier "voluntary" quotas tacitly accepted the same view as a practical necessity. Now that there is a chance to get away from the purely bilateral tests of strength that set some of the earlier quotas, Japan might gain if it sought imaginative and practicable ways of making the market disruption formulas meaningful and effective. An effort of that sort by Japan might elicit cooperation from the importing countries that would be reflected in their acceptance of reasonable compromises in applying the agreement. The results might go well beyond the cotton textile agreement. Workable methods for judging and handling "market disruption" could provide guidance for bilateral negotiations and would set standards to which countries could appeal in a variety of cases. In time Japan might even be able to get rid of some of its present export quotas that almost certainly hold trade well below any level approaching market disruption. One does not have to look that far ahead, however, to see that Japan stands to gain if the cotton textile agreement really carries out the principle that a limited but steady expansion of trade will permit exporters to keep markets they might lose to protectionist forces abroad if they pushed in too fast. While we still have much to learn about how the cotton textile agreement will work, it seems likely that Japan can have more influence on its operation if it accepts the system as a whole and does not concentrate exclusively on pushing exports. At least the approach seems worth a trial.

In its commercial relations with the industrial countries Japan's job is to live up to the rules they have set—a job that the others also need to work at more diligently. In its relations with the underdeveloped countries Japan has even more to do. Apprehensions of Japanese aggression have for the most part disappeared in Asia, where Japan is no longer a military power and where other powers and menaces now loom large. But Japanese investments and trading methods cause a good deal of concern. In the Philippines, for instance, there have been more than occasional mutterings about what the Japanese may be up to in their lumbering and mining operations in the outer islands. In trade relationships there is a fear of Japanese competition, especially in the traditional industries, like textiles, in which Japan can still undercut domestic prices. The result has been an increase in the import restrictions of the underdeveloped countries, partly to protect their own industries and partly to conserve their meager supplies of foreign exchange.

What kind of initiative might Japan take? It is already providing capital to the underdeveloped countries for the development of raw materials resources. To help countries industrialize it will have to extend assistance to manufacturing as well. And, like other manufacturing countries, Japan will face the problem of buying competitive products. The Japanese government at present sees the expansion of trade with the developing countries hampered by the limited amount of their raw materials needed by Japan and by their inability to pay for what Japan can supply. A policy that permits Japanese purchases of manufactured products as well as raw materials would remove a major impediment to large-scale trade once production in the underdeveloped countries reaches an adequate level. If the developing countries diversify their economies and then find outlets for the products of their young industries, they will be better customers for the heavy industrial goods that Japan can offer. The opportunity to export should stimulate the development of manufacturing that can produce competitively for world markets, in contrast to the very high-cost production in many developing countries today.

In dealing with this new competition Japan would be grappling with the very problems that make it hard for the United States to admit cotton textiles and other "sensitive" Japanese products. Although Japan has far less capacity than the United States for absorbing competitive factory products, it has the great advantage of extraordinarily rapid economic growth. It may be that Japan can blaze new paths in finding ways to adjust to heavy inflows of competitive goods. At least one voice has been raised in Japan to say that Japan should concentrate on the production of high-quality textiles and permit imports of lower-quality textiles. Professor Kiyoshi Kojima, with other experts of the Institute of Asian Economic Affairs (Tokyo), included this proposal in a series of recommendations for Japanese policy in Southeast Asia.[17] Part of Japan's challenge is to gain a larger acceptance at home of this

[17] Reported on in *The Economist,* September 8, 1962, p. 930. Unfortunately some of the other proposals seem far less appropriate, and opposition to them may add to the protectionist resistance to be expected for this one.

minority point of view. A Japanese policy of helping the less developed countries by accepting their competitive factory products might also help persuade other industrial countries to admit more of these products not only from the underdeveloped countries but also from Japan. In the treaty of commerce and navigation signed with the United Kingdom in late 1962 Japan agreed to extend to goods from Hong Kong the same treatment Britain agreed to give to Japanese goods. Triangular arrangements of this kind offset the hazards to Japanese producers of more foreign competition by the assurance of greater access to foreign markets. Since all the industrial countries profess an interest in the advancement of the underdeveloped areas, Japan might offer a liberalization of its imports from those areas in exchange for concessions to Japan on the part of the industrial countries.

THE PROSPECTS

The proposals in these pages call for large efforts by the Japanese. Ideally, constructive measures adopted by Japan should evoke a willingness in other countries to reciprocate. But what assurance is there that the rest of the world is ready to respond? Are the Japanese people willing to accept the risks of unilateral steps? Can they afford to expose their economy to the vagaries of other nations' commercial policies?

In spite of the extraordinary rate of growth in the last decade Japan is still not a rich country. Its 96 million people live in an economy that produces only about a tenth as much as the American, and in many places the margins are too small to provide a comfortable cushioning. Nearly a sixth of the national income is spent on imported commodities, many of them essential to the functioning of the economy. The dual structure of the economy, with technologically advanced factories side by side with cottage industries, makes for a lopsided pattern of growth that can be altered only slowly. Meanwhile some of the strongest opposition to the liberalization of foreign economic relations comes from the agricultural and small industrial groups that are outside the modern economy.

Memories are as long in Japan as they are anywhere else, and the extreme and often sudden fluctuations between good times and bad are not forgotten. Since so much of domestic activity is intimately related to the nation's international balance, the recurring drains on foreign exchange reserves have kept alive the fear of depending on any self-adjusting mechanism in international trade. Yet, if the balance of payments has proved three times in ten years to be Japan's weakest point, the government has also found in credit controls a way of dealing with each crisis. In the future it will be a major responsibility of government to anticipate cyclical swings in the balance of payments and act more promptly than in the past by imposing effective credit restraints before a crisis develops. If the government concerns itself with maintaining fairly stable prices and moderating the extremes in domestic demand, it may have no reason to resort to restrictions on foreign transactions in order to safeguard the international balance.

If necessary, therefore, Japan can make the often painful internal adjustments that fluctuations in its foreign policy may require. But this is essentially a counteractive procedure. To rely on it may mean a cutting back in those sectors of the economy that have the largest potentialities for growth and that would suffer the most from uncertain financing. The plans for 1970 call for an increasing modernization of Japan's industrial structure, a strengthening of research activities, and an acceleration in the shift from light to heavy industry. It seems unlikely that Japanese products will face any difficulty abroad so far as quality is concerned, but to produce them Japan will need an uninterrupted flow of supplies from foreign sources. Hence the projections are postulated on a progressive relaxation of both foreign and Japanese trade restrictions.

In this critical matter Japan will have an advantage it has not had before. It will participate as a regular member in the industrial club, the OECD. With credentials that include a commitment to a liberal trade policy, it will have more effective bargaining power than it had as an outside supplicant. There will be a greater opportunity to find acceptable solutions to problems that must be met by concessions on both sides. For Japan the major problems will be the matter of market disruption and the new external tariff wall of the Common Market. As to the first, the GATT arrangement for expanding quotas on Japanese exports of cotton textiles was an improvement on bilateral agreements or unilateral action by an importing country. Since the agreement came into force its provisions have been applied more restrictively than the stated purposes warrant. If it is dissatisfied, however, Japan can appeal to GATT for a more liberal interpretation by the importing countries, and especially the United States. A guarantee of a hearing does not ensure the redress of grievances, but it is a large step forward from a situation in which there was no court of appeal. In the OECD Japan will have additional opportunities to press for adherence by others to the principles of the organization but will be exposed to the same pressure in return.

As for the prospects for trade with the Common Market, Japan will have powerful allies. The United States, Canada, Britain, and the rest of the EFTA countries will all be working to secure freer entry for their goods and will welcome Japan's help. Japan and the United States in particular have basic common interests in restraining the impact of regionalism on trade and in broadening the scope of multilateralism. Each has domestic pockets of protection, entrenched enough to require some demonstration of government solicitude during an interim period. Both countries recognize, and their national policies reflect, the need for measures of adjustment for those segments of the economy that will be unable to compete with imports. But on a national scale each country can accommodate its domestic industrial structure to the impact of foreign competition provided foreign markets are open to its products.

With these interests in common Japan and the United States have the basis for a partnership that can exert a strong influence on international trading patterns. Their goals are the same; for Japan, however, there is a greater urgency. The American economy can continue to function, without disastrous consequences, in a world of rising trade barriers, but Japan's cannot, at least it cannot if it is to preserve any semblance to a free economy. The fact that there is really no acceptable alternative increases Japan's vulnerability and reinforces misgivings about the program it has embarked on. Shuzo Inaba, who has fought hard for free-trade principles, has boldly said: "Though the freeing of trade will cause a certain amount of domestic friction, Japan must not allow the trade balance to deter her. She must admit foreign products, use them to improve her own industries, and increase her own exports with goods of high quality and fair price. If Japan creates conditions under which foreign goods can be imported freely, the other nations will do the same for Japan. So have we believed, and so have we argued again and again. . . ." [18] He then goes on to voice the concern he felt after a trip to Europe and the United States and his fear that other nations will fail to act in accordance with the principles he had been urging his countrymen to accept.

The United States has played many roles in the reconstruction and development of postwar Japan. It is no longer a nursemaid or patron or economic underwriter. The new part is more complicated and calls for a certain amount of rethinking of U.S. policy.

[18] "The Freeing of Trade: The Problems of a Semi-Advanced Nation," *Japan Quarterly,* January–March 1962, p. 18.

Chapter 12

United States Foreign Economic Policy and Japan

Americans can take a great deal of satisfaction in the tremendous economic successes Japan has achieved in the postwar period. The United States has contributed much to these successes and has gained much from them. To a significant degree, the American role was the result of a set of policies based on recognition of the importance to the United States of an economically strong and politically stable Japan. Now that Japan has proved it can make its own way in the world and need no longer be treated as if its economy were sickly, the two countries can look at their relations in a new light. They continue to have important interests in common but each faces some new questions of policy. Japan's were the subject of the previous chapter, those of the United States are the subject of this one.

UNITED STATES POLICY AND JAPAN'S POSTWAR ECONOMY

The United States has had a greater part than any other foreign country in the postwar life of Japan. During the Occupation, as during the Pacific war, the role of the United States was so prominent as to make the participation of other Allied nations very minor on most matters. Americans initiated and directed the reforms of the Occupation—demilitarization, encouragement of labor unions, land reform, the breakup of the *zaibatsu,* the economic purges, the fiscal reforms, and the rest. It was American policy, American tax money, and, for the most part, American commodities that provided economic aid to an extremely needy Japan from 1946 through 1951.

The Occupation was not, however, the most important period of American influence on Japan's economy. The essential question about Japan's economic future remained unanswered when the Occupation ended in April 1952: How was the country to pay its way in the world economy, if, indeed, it could? American aid was disappearing from the balance of payments, but Japan gained even larger amounts of dollars through other forms of special income from the United States (and to a very small extent from other countries). Though the Japanese authorities could spend this new income as they chose, it provided no lasting solution to the country's basic problem of earning a living in the world economy. That was found only when exports rose to unprecedented levels, beginning in the late 1950s. Extraordinary income dropped, both absolutely and in its importance to Japan's balance of payments. Japan began to earn enough from exports to pay for a reasonable amount of imports. By taking the lead in accepting Japanese goods, the United States has continued to be Japan's chief supplier of foreign exchange. The United States has stood first also in providing the capital and invisible income Japan has obtained from abroad. Its military expenditures in Japan remain significant, though they have lost their past great importance.

The trade expansion was not just the product of governmental policies. Businessmen in the two countries took the opportunities that were offered. While Japanese observers were still dreaming of Asian markets, and Japanese prime ministers were seeking American help to finance Japanese ventures and exports there, Japanese products were attracting customers all over the United States and Japanese components were appearing in more and more sewing machines, cameras, radios, and other products of nominally American origin. Japanese sales in the United States rose by an average of over 20 per cent a year between 1952 and 1962. In 1962 about 30 per cent of Japanese exports were taken by the United States. The greatest part governmental policy played in this phenomenal trade increase was in the United States where successive administrations resisted pressures to check the import of Japanese goods.

The progressive freeing of international trade has been an essential condition of Japan's economic recovery. Other favorable developments have gained much in force and significance from the fact that the United States has accepted a vast and expanding flow of Japanese goods. The bond created by this trade is a major element in Japanese–American relations; it is marked by reciprocity and balance of interests and has a reasonable prospect of surviving (albeit with ever-changing elements) in an unstable and troubled world. Without such sales, Japanese–American relations would still have the unhealthy one-sidedness of the early 1950s, a patron-ward character that would not only give the lie to American protestations about the equality and sovereignty of nations but also cast a cloud over American friendship for Japan. Without this development of trade, Japan might not yet have found a reasonably promising role in the world economy, nor the United States a strong ally in the Far East.

The United States has helped Japan in many other ways. It has been the source of a large fraction of Japanese imports of goods and of much of the technology and capital Japan has received in growing volume. American defense measures have protected Japan while at the same time the Japanese budget has been spared the necessity of heavy military expenditures. American friendship and forbearance have fostered national self-respect in Japan; a less tolerant policy would have multiplied feelings of overdependence and probably neutralist and anti-American sentiment in Japan. Entirely apart from public policy, Americans have been showing unprecedented interest in things Japanese, especially Japanese culture. The United States and the world are a long way from being as hostile to Japan as used to be thought. One indication of the attention Washington was giving Japanese matters was the inauguration in November 1961 of a Committee on Trade and Economic Affairs in which Cabinet members from both countries could discuss major issues, thus assuring the Japanese that their viewpoints would be known at the highest levels in Washington. (The only other country with which the United States has a comparable arrangement is Canada.)

Japan has been a beneficiary of American leadership in efforts to rebuild the world economy. Institutions like the World Bank and the International Monetary Fund have helped Japan directly. The United States recommended Japanese membership in these and other bodies, such as the General Agreement on Tariffs and Trade (GATT), the United Nations, and the Organization for Economic Cooperation and Development (OECD). This kind of sponsorship might be expected of the power that had the principal part in the Occupation, but American support of Japan has gone far beyond the formalities. The United States has shown a genuine concern for Japan's economic welfare, for the continuing success of the steps toward democratization taken during the Occupation, for Japan's return to the family of nations and its becoming, and being accepted as, a member of that small group of industrial nations which have the economic power and political willingness to carry the burden of free world defense and of aid to the underdeveloped countries. This American role has been accepted by successive Japanese governments with gratitude, and they on their part have cooperated closely with the United States.

Japan today is the only highly industrial, urban, middle-class society in Asia or, indeed, in the whole non-Western world. Japan's evolving democracy and private enterprise economy provide a model that, while too remote from the realities of other Asian countries to be easily copied, nevertheless stands as a living and vigorous refutation of many Communist dogmas. "Capitalist monopolies" are not making the Japanese poor any poorer; rather, vigorous private enterprise is spreading the growing prosperity rapidly to an ever-larger majority of the population. Japanese business, big and small, is showing a notable lack of interest in military activities, and "war-mongers" are scarcer in Japan than in Communist countries, especially China. Cylical business downturns are not getting progressively worse, as Marx predicted, but remain mild and are consistently and effectively countered. Japanese saving and investment have shown that authoritarianism is not essential to rapid growth; in fact no Communist countries, in their various stages of development, have equaled the pace of Japan's growth, let alone the advance in the welfare of its people.

Despite a strong leftist minority and occasional anti-American demonstrations—most notably the riots when the U.S.-Japanese Security Treaty was up for revision by the Diet in June 1960—Japan today is politically stable and a partner of the United States. Factional strife within the dominant Liberal-Democratic Party has not prevented conservative governments from consistently following policies friendly to the United States and cooperating in international organizations. The smallness of the Japanese defense effort is disappointing and costly to the United States, but what forces there are offer significant support and cooperate effectively with U.S. military commands.

To appreciate what exists, one has only to suppose that in the stead of this kind of Japan there was an impoverished nation, unstable and resentful. Then it would take powerful military repression to keep the country from exploding internally, perhaps by way of a rightist or Communist coup, or something reminiscent of the military take-over during the 1930s. Even as early as the weeks following the Japanese surrender in 1945, General MacArthur foresaw such a danger and requested President Truman to send grain or else more troops. Then and later the United States chose grain. At best, troops could have provided only control. A resentful Japan would have added vastly to the world's insecurity.

Another possibility would be a Japan moderately well fed and industrially developed but committed to policies either neutralist or distinctly hostile to the United States. Such a Japan would greatly increase the defense burden of the United States and perhaps make U.S. positions in Okinawa and other bases in that part of the world untenable or, at best, far less valuable. By playing the United States and other Western countries off against Russia or China or both, Japan could have proved a most expensive neighbor for the United States.

THE COST TO THE UNITED STATES

To pursue policies that have helped create a prosperous, stable Japan has cost the United States something: in resources, in adjustments in its own economy, and in subordination of some domestic interests to a broader conception of the national interest. Have the gains outweighed the losses? Most of the answer to that question lies in the comparison just made between the Japan that is and the Japans that might have been. Compared to the alternatives, the reality of a flourishing Japan can fairly be said to justify the large transfer of American resources that helped bring it about. Judged on that basis the cost to the United States certainly looks modest.

The most easily measurable of the various forms of American contribution is direct economic aid: some $2.1 billion spent during the Occupation to restore Japan, of which $490 million is to be repaid. Aid valued at $847 million under the Military Assistance Program (plus $886 million under other military programs) and the much larger expenditure on the costs of the Occupation and the U.S. military establishment in Japan have had an important effect on the Japanese economy although they were undertaken primarily for strategic reasons. The $6.5 billion spent in Japan to support U.S. military forces and the $774 million worth of goods procured there for aid to third countries up to the end of 1962 represented purchases of goods and services. If not obtained from Japan, they would probably have cost more elsewhere. So while the stimulation to Japan's economy and the support of its balance of payments were welcome and intended results, these special dollar payments were not primarily aid, but expenditures that would have been heavier burdens on the U.S. taxpayer if made elsewhere.

Did these expenditures, however necessary, damage the U.S. balance of payments? The answer is complex. No single item can be isolated from the whole cluster of transactions to be blamed for the deficit. If Japan had not had special dollar income, would it have reduced imports from the United States or held back from building up its foreign exchange reserves? The relatively small deficits in the U.S. balance of payments before 1958 were the essential counterpart of a strengthening of the international economic position of Japan and of European countries as well. Inevitably, aid and special expenditures contributed to this net outflow of dollars but without them American policy would have failed. They were already declining by the time the balance-of-payments deficit became a serious problem for the United States in 1958. Nevertheless through these and other channels, notably capital movements, Japan has continued to draw more dollars from the United States than it has spent there.

In trade as in finance it is hard to strike a clear balance of gain and loss. Rising production and income are transforming Japan into a far more profitable market for American businessmen and farmers than was believed possible only a few years ago. Americans, like Japanese, are learning the lesson that trade among industrial countries has more potential than trade between an industrial nation and an area that specializes in one or a few primary products and whose population is mostly very poor. While the imports that have come from booming Japan have been far less damaging to American business than many Americans feared, the opportunities offered by the expanding Japanese market have far exceeded all predictions.

In 1961 and 1962, as in 1957 and 1959, Japan stood in second place as a customer for U.S. commodity exports. Only Canada bought more, and neither it nor any third country was growing as fast as Japan. Japan is, in fact, what a public relations man might call a land of opportunity for the American businessman. There he finds not only a prosperous market but also a private enterprise economy, made more attractive and productive by honest and remarkably effective government, by strong cooperation between government and business, and by government economic leadership at many points. The possibilities for trans-Pacific trade, investment, company tie-ups, patent licensing, and other business associations had never been so promising when Japan was poorer or when Japanese policy was aimed at privileged trading and investment in Japanese-controlled areas of Asia.

From 1945 through 1962, United States statistics showed exports to Japan of over $12 billion, imports from Japan of $8.2 billion, the latter comprising commodities ranging from toys to heavy electrical equipment. While raw silk, pearls, and a few other products were not available in the United States and would have been hard to obtain elsewhere, most of the imported Japanese products competed with domestic American production, even though not always in the same price and quality ranges. The U.S. economy gained through lower prices, new designs, or specialized models, as in the case of transistor radios, which came in from Japan before being widely and cheaply available from American sources, or the miniature, truly portable television sets offered for the first time from Japan alone. Clearly the American consumer is getting something he wants from the Japanese goods, which he buys more of year after year.

The obverse of the consumer's advantage is the problem faced by some American producers. Many American firms have been forced by Japanese competition to lower their prices. Some have shifted to other products or other methods of production. Others have failed to make the adjustment to foreign competition and have been forced to close down. The displacement of workers in vulnerable industries like textiles, chinaware, and glass has added to the unemployment in depressed areas where there are few opportunities for alternative employment. It is impossible to determine with any precision the economic and social costs of this process. Owner and worker protests sometimes make the cost seem high, but the evidence of this study is that Japanese competition has cost the United States remarkably little. In only ten escape-clause cases, most of them very minor, did the Tariff Commission find that American industries had suffered or were threatened with serious injury from Japanese competition. Compared to the vast number of producers in the United States, to the total output of the economy, or to the effects of domestic competition or changing habits of consumption, Japanese competition is an extremely small element. For a few kinds of production, however, the competition has been significant enough to lead the U.S. government to press Japan to impose export quotas. The Japanese have agreed, rather than risk harsher restrictions by the United States. American manufacturers of cotton textiles, the most sensitive and largest item on the list, now benefit—without any official determination of injury under normal escape-clause procedures—from a far more ambitious international arrangement establishing export quotas in a number of countries besides Japan.

Whatever benefits may have accrued to American producers from these protective measures must, of course, be set off against presumed disadvantages for American consumers. There can also be no doubt that pressure of competition from Japan has caused a retreat from professed American trade principles. We do not yet know how much violence has been done to these principles, to the GATT and other international trade agreements, and to the leadership of the United States in moves to build a healthy international economy. But it is clear that the extensive application of quotas to exports from Japan and other "cheap labor" countries constitutes a retreat, led by the United States, from the standards the United States has set for itself and others. Nevertheless, the whole quota matter remains a somewhat limited exception to an over-all U.S. trade policy that is generally hospitable to imports, even of competitive manufactures, and that has benefited Japan substantially.

Then too, the long-term cotton textile arrangement has in it some elements that justify treating it as, at least potentially, a compromise rather than an abandonment of principles. The professed aim of the agreement is to liberalize markets. Though it permits importing countries to act almost unilaterally, it limits the trade restrictions they may impose. Each year permissible imports should increase. The multilateral character of the arrangement may prevent it from becoming as restrictive as unilateral (or bilateral) quotas might be. Exporting countries have an international forum in which to air their grievances. The technique of using the quotas to retard, but not stop, the growth of international trade in sensitive products can, if there is sufficient will, be turned to advantage. Under the agreement the United States and Western Europe could over the years take increasing amounts of textiles from Japan and other producers, but at a rate that would permit equitable and orderly adjustments within the importing countries. Meanwhile, as the expansion in other U.S. industries continues to exceed that in cotton textile manufacturing, the political influence of this powerful producer group is likely to decline.

The experience under the quota system has not been a particularly satisfactory one for the Japanese, but the alternatives seemed to them even less desirable. By agreeing to limitations on their exports they have provided two American administrations with an acceptable means of meeting the pressure of domestic textile producers and have opened the way to the development of procedures for "orderly marketing" in other markets and other products. These procedures could be used to expand world trade more than they restrict it but only if the United States firmly commits itself to that course.

Taken all in all, the great improvement in Japan's position over that of 1945 is a gain not only for itself but for the United States. The American policies that have assisted Japan along the path to recovery, economic growth, and political stability have served the purposes for which they were adopted. The costs, so far as one can see, have not been exorbitant in terms of the national interests of the United States. Some of the costs fell on specific American interests, notably the producers of goods who lost markets to Japanese competition. How their disadvantages are to be weighed against the specific advantages other Americans gained, as consumers or exporters, is difficult to say. Nor is it easy to calculate the total effect of this trade on the American economy. The competition is not only in the American market but also in third markets and in Japan itself; it is not only in trade but in transportation, services, and other kinds of activity. Balance-of-payments difficulties and an unsatisfactory level of unemployment have increased American sensitivity to whatever damage there may have been, but a full assessment has also to take account of the benefits of competition as well as its costs. The gains from political stability and improved free world security, while they cannot be measured, must be added to the balance.

For the Japanese economy to grow rapidly enough to support the population of Japan at rising standards of living and to provide the basis for political stability, there must be a great increase in production and exports of Japanese goods and services. One cannot have one without the other. Inevitably some American producers will face greater competition, and some degree of adjustment and adaptation in the American economy will be necessary. These disadvantages—if that is what they are—are themselves reflections of the advantages the United States has gained from Japan's postwar performance. They are the inescapable counterpart of the success of American policy toward Japan.

FUTURE UNITED STATES POLICY

The policies that brought Japan and the United States to the early 1960s served both countries well. More benefits can be expected from continuing in the direction set during the past decade. But since the conditions of the 1960s are far different from those of the earlier postwar period, especially for Japan, some new policies may be called for and the emphasis shifted in those that continue. While Japanese–American relations, both political and economic, are at present closer and more harmonious than ever before, the two countries will inevitably be faced with problems that could impair these good relations if handled badly.

Japanese Competition in the American Market

Trade will continue to be the largest problem. The competition of Japanese products in the American market continues to raise more difficult issues than do imports from any other country. Most Japanese goods compete directly and actively with American goods. The United States imports more from Japan than from any other country except Canada, whose products are to a considerable extent not directly competitive with domestic production. The flow of Japanese goods into the American market has been increasing faster than total U.S. imports, faster than U.S. national income, and faster than the growth in world trade. It is evident that some American producers will continue to voice their unhappiness about Japanese competition. Their complaints will pose political problems for the U.S. government and sometimes their situation will present real problems of economic policy as well.

The guiding principle for U.S. policy should be to adhere as closely as is practicable to liberal import policies. Naturally the domestic economy, the balance of payments, and the condition of protesting industries or firms cannot be ignored. To the government official or politician, foreign and domestic considerations will often appear to conflict. As in the past, we can expect a tendency to compromise in the executive branch and in Congress. Also, as in the past, political leaders will tend to favor domestic interests. Here are votes as well as more familiar people, firms, industries, and problems. On the side of foreign relations there are no votes for Americans, the individuals and firms affected are far off and for the most part unknown, and their problems too are more remote. Intellectual arguments about U.S. national interests, especially when they favor the foreign as against the domestic party to a debate, are likely to be regarded suspiciously by politicians and "practical" people. Still, there is need to identify the national interest of the United States and to follow policies calculated to advance it, as against merely balancing the pressures exerted on the U.S. government by interested parties.

The evidence of this study is that U.S. national interests will be served by permitting the rapid increase of imports from Japan and other "low-wage" countries to continue. To serve that interest realistically, that is, to have a policy that works effectively, the United States has to judge, within reasonable limits, how great a flow of imports can be tolerated without undue damage to some part of the domestic economy or the generation of irresistible political pressures for import restriction. It should refrain from restricting imports before this limit has been reached and make sure that, if imports have to be checked, this is done in such a way as to minimize difficulties abroad and interferences to world trade. When this kind of lapse from liberal treatment is politically unavoidable, the restrictive measures should be only temporary. A major task of American policy is to foster the transfer of productive resources from less competitive and profitable activities in the United States to others that are more competitive and therefore more profitable, thus making room for more imports and assisting American industries to compete effectively abroad.

In the Trade Expansion Act of 1962 the United States has a promising instrument for accomplishing these tasks. To make it work effectively will require strong leadership by the administration in Washington in negotiating with foreign governments to expand trade. If it is to resist pressures from domestic producers the administration will also have to work hard to make a success of the act's path-breaking authority to assist American labor, management, and capital to move out of import-competing industries.

The generally excellent records of both the Eisenhower and Kennedy Administrations in limiting the use of the escape clause were marred not so much by the relatively few cases in which tariffs were raised as by the decision to put pressure on Japan to establish export quotas. To maintain a liberal policy during the 1960s, the United States must make it increasingly evident that restrictions of this sort are only exceptions; to do that, it must limit the creation of new exceptions and reduce the number of present ones. While one may hope for the ultimate elimination of such exceptions, that is far less important in the near future than firm adherence to generally liberal policies and convincing demonstrations that exceptions will not grow but rather shrink. Not so much an ideal world as evident progress in the real world is what we should aim for. The Japanese are at least as practical.

An important first step would be to establish standards of due process for determining whether to ask a foreign country to impose export restrictions. There is due process now in the use of the escape clause. The Tariff Commission makes investigations in accordance with law; interested parties have a voice; the Commission makes public its recommendations; the President makes the decision, taking into consideration not only the recommendations but other factors he deems pertinent. No such orderly processes apply when foreign governments are pressed to impose quotas on their exports to the United States. It would be logical, however, and I believe wise, to decide that the U.S. government should not request a foreign country to impose export quotas on goods destined for the American market before the Tariff Commission investigates the facts and recommends action.[1] The same principle could be applied to the long-term cotton textile arrangement. The United States should normally require a Tariff Commission investigation before declaring that market disruption has occurred or threatens. An emergency procedure could be set up for extreme cases, but any restrictions imposed under it should be valid only until the Tariff Commission has had time to make an investigation and recommendation and the President has acted.

The philosophy of the Trade Expansion Act of 1962 is that when domestic producers are suffering from foreign competition the President should examine the possibilities of domestic action to deal with the problem before limiting imports. This would still be the first step under my proposal. Then, if some increase in import restrictions seemed necessary, the Commission should consider all possible methods and in its recommendation should, where feasible, give the President a choice of different measures. Tariff increases should be preferred to quotas. If quantitative restrictions seemed necessary, the use of import quotas imposed by the United States should be compared with the possibility of asking one or more foreign governments to impose export quotas (which have certain advantages, as we saw on p. 354). If either kind of quota was employed, it should normally apply for only a limited period, say a year. At the end of this period every quota should either expire or escalate; those that continued should permit entry of a larger quantity of goods each year. All quotas now in effect should be subject to immediate review by the Tariff Commission, to discover the possibilities of modification or termination or, if necessary, substitution of other measures. Where there were widespread and persistent difficulties, the exploration of possibilities should include the consideration of a multilateral agreement. The characteristics of some products or the pattern of some kinds

[1] Perhaps a different procedure would be appropriate for agricultural quotas or those based on considerations of national security which involve quite different kinds of criteria.

of trade would make it difficult to devise workable agreements. In other cases lack of balance in bargaining strength between exporting and importing interests will make it impossible to negotiate an acceptable agreement. Our limited experience of the cotton textile arrangements makes me reserved about the benefits of this approach and suggests that it will rarely prove to be the most desirable alternative.

What is being recommended here is that a heavy burden of proof be put on any proposal to increase restrictions on imports into the United States. The burden should be especially heavy for quotas, American and foreign, existing and proposed, not just initially, but periodically as long as they last. If new restrictions are to be acceptable only after careful scrutiny, and if quotas are to expire after a period, then other measures must also be available to deal with problems arising from the competition of goods from Japan and other countries. Congress and voters will need to be convinced that American producers are not being abandoned to foreign competition. Tariff Commission investigations will have to continue to command respect for objectivity in research and analysis, as well as fairness in conclusions and recommendations. Their speed will have to be sufficient to convince doubters that American firms are not being unduly exposed to "unfair" competition from abroad. Relief and assistance in other forms than import restrictions will have to be prompt and effective enough to carry weight with Congress. And the President will need to remind Congress and the public repeatedly of the advantages to the United States of a trade policy that puts pressure on weak sectors of the American economy in favor of strong sectors.

If such policies as these are followed, Japan should be able to sell in the United States a sufficiently large and expanding volume of exports to meet reasonable needs. The groundwork would be laid for receiving imports of manufactured goods from a growing number of developing countries without repeating the disturbing history of the barring and harassing of Japanese goods in Western markets. Hopefully also, Japanese and others would come to feel they could depend on the receptivity of the American market for imports of competitive products, the limits being those made necessary by the practical prospects of moving American labor, management, and capital out of affected industries and into more profitable activities. If these things happen, measures to provide for "orderly marketing" will have become, not just a new means and excuse for trade barriers, but a positive force for trade expansion as well as order.

The U.S. Balance-of-Payments Deficit

Imports affect not only domestic production but the balance of payments, a matter the United States has had to be concerned about since

1958. This study does not provide the basis for extensive conclusions about a question that affects the whole range of American transactions with the rest of the world but we can put policy toward Japan in a reasonable perspective in relation to the larger problem.

The United States has a favorable trade balance with Japan but, because of aid and military expenditures, the United States paid more dollars to Japan between 1951 and 1962 than came back. Since 1958 special payments have declined (except in 1960) but except in 1961 they more than offset Japan's deficit on current account. Between 1958 and 1962 Japan's gold and foreign exchange reserves rose about $1 billion. Substantial short-term capital movements to Japan have also contributed to the deficit in the U.S. balance of payments. The strengthening of Japan's international financial position has been a significant part of the improvement of its economy. The added responsibility that goes with this improvement was marked by Tokyo's participation in the arrangement worked out in 1962 to provide additional stand-by resources for the International Monetary Fund.

Both the Eisenhower and Kennedy Administrations made a point of abjuring import restriction as a means of rectifying the balance of payments. This is the right approach and an essential one if the United States is to persist in its broad aims of expanding world trade. Of course, if the removal of trade barriers works only one way, resulting in a heavy increase in American imports and no gain in exports, and if other elements in the balance of payments remain unfavorable, the position might prove to be untenable. But if freer importation into the United States is part of a more general removal of trade barriers, including liberalization of imports into Japan, and if adjustments in the American economy move resources to more efficient uses (thus strengthening the country's competitive position), there is no incompatibility between the program advocated here and a proper management of the balance-of-payments problem.

What the right formula for that is, goes beyond the scope of this book. In the series of measures already taken by the United States to help its balance-of-payments position, there are a number which, while falling far short of trade restriction, have had an impact on Japan. Limitations on military expenditures abroad, on the use of American aid funds outside the United States, and on the value of goods tourists can bring back to the United States duty-free have reduced to some extent Japan's opportunities to earn foreign exchange. Whether that result has been justified by the gain to the dollar position of the United States is problematical. Some of the more drastic measures that have been suggested, such as restrictions on foreign investment, would certainly damage Japan and would reduce U.S. exports as well. President Kennedy's proposal of July

1963 for a special tax on foreign securities caused great concern in Japan and brought the Foreign Minister to Washington in a vain effort to get an exemption. While there is no reason for the United States to exempt Japan from measures it is forced to take to meet balance-of-payments needs, it seems likely that the requirements of an effective policy toward Japan do not in themselves greatly worsen the basic American problem, nor do they offer especially significant opportunities for attacking it.

Although the rectification of the balance of payments is ultimately the responsibility of the United States, the problem has given impetus to a significant series of measures of international financial cooperation. Japan should be expected to continue to cooperate in these measures, in accordance with the capabilities and responsibilities that go with its improved international position. This is not only for the benefit of the United States; it is an important step in the process of Japan's becoming fully accepted among the advanced nations of the world.

Employment and Economic Growth in the United States

Like the balance of payments, the slow growth of the U.S. economy in recent years, accompanied by unemployment and the underutilization of productive capacity, may work against a liberal foreign economic policy. For instance, people will ask whether expanding imports from Japan and other countries will not make it more difficult to stimulate rapid economic growth in the United States. Will not imports create more unemployment, perhaps in the very places where it is already highest and most difficult to reduce? Might not a liberal import policy permit excessive human suffering at these points, to gain advantages for export industries that may not particularly need a boost?

Actually, the attack on lagging economic growth is more likely to be helped than hindered by rapidly increasing imports of competitive products. Economic growth results from a vitality, an *élan,* associated with active investing in new productive facilities, with vigorous competition, and with a general feeling among businessmen that change and growth are necessary and desirable. The mood is one of actively looking forward to new opportunities. This is the very opposite of the tone of most protectionist pleas. These reflect generally a backward-looking determination to hold on to existing products, methods, and markets instead of moving forward to better ones. One of the greatest benefits of a liberal trade policy can be to reduce the tendency to hang on to the bitter end, and to encourage—or force—the seeking out of new products, new ideas, and new methods. The effect should be to discourage preservation of investments in high-cost protected industries and to emphasize low-cost competitive activities.

The United States, if it is to be strong and to succeed in its basic policies, must be a leader in the world economy. One of the tasks of the leader is to be first with new and better products and processes. Japan is treading on American heels in some industries, and even the newly developing countries are beginning to do so in a few restricted cases. The proper reaction for American business is to speed the pace of its forward motion, not to contest the rear areas with the foreign producers who are catching up.

Japan's two-way trade with the United States gives an excellent illustration of the American interest. There is ample evidence of Japan's competitive strength and vigor in selling textiles, toys, radios, steel products, and all the lengthening list of other things in the American market. Japan buys American cotton, wheat, coal, turbines, generators, calculators, and other machinery, up to the practical limit of what the nation can afford. Japanese will also in the 1960s buy a greatly expanded volume of American consumer goods—prepared foods, cosmetics, household fixtures, and so forth—if only the foreign exchange is available and the Japanese authorities will permit such things to come in. A liberalizing of this trade will stimulate economic growth in the United States. The export industries that will gain are by no means all concentrated in one sector of the economy or in one region of the country. Moving labor and facilities out of industries that cannot meet Japanese competition will not always require geographical shifts or great losses of skill or investment. What is required is that the workers and businessmen in threatened industries accept the fact that they must choose between competing effectively with imports or shifting to other work. They should not long entertain the possibility of basing their effective competition on substandard wage rates.

Imports will affect some areas and industries, such as parts of the textile industry, which have serious problems of long-term unemployment. These may need special treatment. Tariffs, or even quotas, may be justified for a few years while readjustment is carried out. Readjustment efforts must be stepped up by industries, by localities, by state governments, and by the federal government. One of the most effective ways to stimulate this acceleration is to make it clear that import limitations, especially quotas, are very temporary. Some American cotton textile men evidently do not believe this of present quotas and so are hardly likely to bend their best efforts to getting rid of lines that are not fully competitive, and to move vigorously into activities, perhaps outside textiles, that promise profits in the new, internationally more competitive situation.

In sum, a liberal import policy will in itself do much to stimulate vigorous economic growth in the United States. In addition, specific measures are called for to help those most seriously hurt by imports—to help them move, not stay put. Other measures that effectively stimulate the economy as a whole—such as President Kennedy's tax cut, which was enacted only after his death—will also tend to ease the problem of those adversely affected by imports.

Leading or Pushing Japan?

Both the general tone of Japan's foreign economic policy and many specific measures leave Americans dissatisfied. The reluctance with which the Japanese approach liberalization and the incompleteness of what they have done give rise to complaints. Sometimes American firms receive less favorable treatment than they deem reasonable or the U.S. government thinks justified. Americans think that Japan could do a good deal more for the less developed countries. In dealing with imports from Japan, the United States will continue to face the familiar alternatives of accepting the intensified competition, asking for Japanese export restraints, or, in the end, imposing import restrictions.

On these and other matters the U.S. government has in the past sought to persuade the Japanese of its point of view or to put pressure on them. They have been generally agreeable up to a point, but at times they proved themselves extremely tough negotiators, as, of course, the Americans were too. In the 1960s, the status and relations of the two governments are different from what they were in the 1950s, so one of the questions about U.S. policy that needs exploration is the proper approach to Japan.

How much influence can the United States exert on Japan in the future? How can the United States make the most of this influence, considering the political situation in Japan, and particularly the widespread feeling that there is already too much American influence on Japanese policy? One of the strengths of the liberal American import policy I am urging is that it gives a basis for pressing Japan and other countries to do likewise. There are two aspects of this advantage. One is that of example, which may be especially important in relation to Japan. The other is that of bargaining. So long as the United States is prepared to move toward greater liberalization in its own trade policies it can properly ask other countries to reciprocate. The larger the prospective market the United States is prepared to offer, the greater its leverage on other countries. In political and psychological terms reciprocal concessions have the great advantage of enabling each country to show advantages gained for its exports as the counterpart of the import concessions it has granted.

Although the emphasis in American tariff bargaining under the Trade Expansion Act of 1962 may well be on Europe,[2] Japan has a great inter-

[2] This would be particularly the case if the provision of the law could be widely used that empowers the President to eliminate duties on products for which the United States and the European Economic Community account for 80 per cent of

est in this matter because the law requires that whatever tariff reductions the United States makes should be extended on a most-favored-nation basis to all but the Communist countries (and those who discriminate against American exports). But the United States will not be willing to have Japan receive such advantages without giving comparable concessions. If American negotiations with Europe should result in substantial tariff reductions for a wide range of products, then Japan will get much and be expected to give much in return. Some of what it has to give will be determined by direct bargaining between the United States and Japan. There will also be more bilateral bargaining between Japan and European countries of the sort that led to a series of significant agreements in late 1962 and early 1963. While the United States may not be directly involved, the most-favored-nation clause will to some extent link all these sets of negotiations.

The immediate purpose of trade negotiations will, of course, be to improve the Japanese market for American goods but one can imagine that considerations of the treatment of capital and other aspects of policy will also be taken into account. Moreover the United States will want to induce the Japanese to play a more liberal part in international economic affairs generally. There is not very much the United States can do to persuade Japan to follow a liberal policy toward the rest of the world, notably Europe, if those countries do not respond in kind. And the United States will almost certainly not have any trade bargaining power to spare that it can use on Japan's behalf in Europe. Still, it is an important objective of American policy to keep Europe and Japan moving in the same direction.

American influence on Japan's foreign economic policy remains large, and it is proper for the United States to press Japan in ways that benefit both countries as well as world trade. But American influence in Japan has diminished greatly since the Occupation, and the United States needs to be careful not to be—or to appear—too overbearing in its approaches. Japan is moving in the right direction, even if too slowly and reluctantly. U.S. interests as well as U.S. hopes for Japan and for the world economy call for Japan to go further and possibly faster. The main feature that is lacking from Japan's trade and payments liberalization so far seems to be a deep Japanese confidence in that kind of policy. U.S. pressure will not generate such confidence. Only as the Japanese develop their own commitment to liberal foreign economic policies can one be sure that each of their specific measures will be sufficiently well rooted to last.

free world exports. General de Gaulle's refusal to agree to British entry makes this provision applicable to very few products unless the law is amended to count United Kingdom exports in the 80 per cent, even though Britain remains outside the EEC.

In the circumstances it is not easy to say just how the United States can best approach these matters. Sometimes overt direct pressure will be helpful. Often the Japanese will do better if allowed to decide for themselves without pressure. Sometimes the U.S. example may help to lead Japan in the desired direction. But until Japan has evolved a home-made policy of its own, American approaches must be more circumspect than may be the case once it becomes clear that Japan is no longer susceptible to undue influence from the United States.

An essential requirement of that state of affairs is that the rest of the free world should come to accept Japan on better terms than in the past. As long as they were denied the full benefits of membership in GATT, the Japanese could not be expected to embrace wholeheartedly the principles of liberal trade policy embodied in that agreement. Progress in relations with Europe in 1962 and 1963 coupled with membership in OECD are important steps forward. They reflect an approach to the end of the period of Japanese dependence on American sponsorship. Increasingly Japan can and should rely on its own performance and on the general rules of the free world's economic organizations. Others as well as the United States should have progressively less reason to regard Japan as a special problem.

Closely related is the decline in American ability to influence third countries in Japan's behalf. As Europe has increased its economic strength in the world, the United States has had to mobilize its bargaining power primarily to advance its own interests. What it can do for Japan is a good deal less than before—but Japan can do more for itself. The most promising course for both countries is to cooperate to support principles of international economic relations that hold long-run advantage for all countries. As matters now stand, the liberal principles I have in mind are being given less ardent support than they deserve by either Japan or the United States, and it is no cause for surprise that other countries tend to show more interest in immediate advantages than in principles that yield their benefits mostly over a long period of time.

Japanese Trade with Communist Countries

Japan's trade with Communist countries—and especially China—is a subject of potentially serious disagreement between Japan and the United States. Japanese wishes to expand that trade spring only in part from the normal business interests of a vigorous and eager group of manufacturers and traders. The feeling is widespread that Japan needs new trading opportunities and that China in particular is a natural market of great promise that will be exploited by others if Japan holds back. Underlying these economic considerations are strong feelings that Japan and China should maintain close ties, no matter what the nature of Chinese politics and government. Other Communist countries hold less fascination for the Japanese, but someone in Japan is unhappy whenever an opportunity for any kind of trade slips away.

As Japan's foreign economic policy becomes progressively more independent, it is likely to reflect these feelings, perhaps to an extent that will cause serious concern in the United States. If the Socialists come to power in Tokyo, this development may become politically serious in the American view. Even without this development, the problem is difficult. Most Japanese have far less fear of the Communist menace than Americans have. Many Japanese regard the cold war as a contest between the United States and Russia, or to some extent a contest between the United States and China, in which Japan need not necessarily be involved. These Japanese may feel that trade with Communist countries is politically desirable as a mark of independence or noninvolvement. For persons with such views, especially those who are eager to demonstrate freedom from American dominance, expanding trade with China, and to a lesser extent with Russia and other Communist countries, takes on a good deal of positive merit.

American concern about Japanese trade with the Communist countries is not based on fear of economic damage through the loss of export markets. Of course, if the trade expanded substantially, some American soybeans, coal, petroleum, and other products might be displaced by products from Russia and China. This is, however, a secondary consideration; the basis of U.S. concern about Japan's trade with the Sino–Soviet bloc is strategic and political. The concern is real but Japan's China trade could expand a good deal without serious danger.

The first condition is continued Japanese adherence to the strategic trade controls agreed on among the free world countries. This will minimize risks, even though some Americans wish the list of prohibited exports were larger. If the Japanese should try to violate or eliminate these controls, one would have to give credence to the view that they would be giving undue support to Communist military preparations.

Even within the strategic controls, Japanese trade with Communist areas still presents problems. For the most part, though, Japanese and American interests are not far apart, even with regard to the touchy matter of credit terms. Japan's refusal to treat the U.S.S.R. and China more favorably than other countries reflects a sound view of Japanese national interest. When it comes to credit, the Export–Import Bank of Japan can be expected to be careful about getting repaid and about the political leverage Moscow or Peking would gain by owing large sums to Japan. While a private businessman might be concerned only about what he could sell, it is difficult to see the normally wary and highly nationalistic Japanese officials permitting themselves to become excessively vulnerable in this fashion.[3] While one could imagine a Socialist government in Tokyo taking a different view of this matter, one should be cautious about assuming that once in power Socialist leaders will let ideology guide them more than nationalism or political astuteness in defending national interests.

Given the conditions of the early 1960s, it appears that any Japanese government looking out for its own national interests in trade with the Communist countries should give the United States little to worry about. Matters would be quite different if Japan were unable to find thriving markets for its exports in the Western world, or if Japan's balance of payments ran into severe deficit, or if there were a serious drop in domestic economic activity. Then pressure to export to any markets might well drive Japan to make dangerous concessions to Communist countries or to disregard the risks of becoming dependent on sales to them. In those circumstances the Communist countries could be expected to make attractive offers for the sake of ultimate political gain.

It is to Japanese and American interest alike to prevent such a situation from arising. To keep Japan from being squeezed in this way the United States and other Western countries should be prepared to provide markets for a volume of Japanese goods rising above the levels of recent years. Beyond this the United States should permit the Japanese to feel they are making their own policy about trade with the Communist areas. Up to now they do not have this feeling—and they are right. Over and above the agreed-on strategic export controls, they have to cope with American pressure on specific matters, as in the case of oil pipe for the Soviet Far East. At some point in Japan's economic resurgence and political evolution, the costs to Japanese–American relations and to Japanese self-esteem of this kind of thing will exceed any advantages the United States gains through such pressure. This point may be reached soon, if indeed it has not already been passed.

Cooperation Toward a Better World Economy

The interests of Japan and the United States are sufficiently close to warrant cooperation between the two countries on many matters beyond those discussed in this book. As I see them, their interests are virtually identical in many economic matters, generally consistent in most of the rest, and clearly conflicting only within a relatively narrow range.

Both countries will gain most in the long run if world trade is generally unfettered, competitive, and predominantly in private hands. Both countries will gain from rapid economic growth in the world at large, in both

[3] Normally conservative, Japanese financial policy has at times turned adventuresome, as in the case of the Nishihara loans which were essentially a political speculation on China during World War I. (See p. 99.)

primary producing areas and industrial regions. The two countries will lose if economic growth is generally sluggish in large areas of the world or if political interferences widely affect international trade. Where Japanese and American interests clash is usually in specific competitive situations. Whose airlines or ships will get what trans-Pacific business? What price shall be charged in a certain transaction? What should the terms be on a given loan or patent licensing arrangement? These are not fundamental conflicts of interest but matters that can be bargained out and compromised. How easy or difficult these dealings may be will depend in part on the level of prosperity of both countries.

The most obvious conflicts of interest are those between exporters in one country and producers in the other who feel damaged by the volume or price of imports. A somewhat comparable situation exists when Japanese resent American investments in their country. Numerous as such cases are, they often do not involve conflicts of real interest between Japan and the United States. The conflict is principally between particular interests within each country, such as producers and consumers, between protection for the one and more and cheaper imports for the other. Or the conflict may be between short-run and long-run national interests of either country. In the past, Japan and the United States have shown a remarkable capacity to work out solutions or compromises, and I believe that capacity is growing.

Having successfully resolved some sensitive and difficult issues between them, Japan and the United States should be able to cooperate in broader matters, like the improvement and expansion of world trade. The collapse of efforts to bring Britain into the European Economic Community has opened possibilities and, indeed, put a premium on cooperation among a number of countries to lower trade barriers. GATT and the OECD provide forums in which the United States and Japan can work together.

There are a number of less obvious possibilities. GATT has taken under its wing an ugly duckling—the cotton textile quotas—never thought of previously as part of the brood of a parent devoted to liberalization and expansion of trade. A good deal can be done to improve the duckling's looks, and one can even conceive of its emerging as a beautiful swan—a major new means of expanding trade in sensitive products. Japan can be expected to take the lead, with help from other interested exporting countries, in pushing for strict standards and closer supervision of the quotas. If Japan also accepted the idea that market disruption should be avoided (see p. 388), it would have a strong claim on American support for its position. As importer and exporter the two countries would naturally find themselves arrayed on opposite sides of some issues. While there is a limit to how far any Washington administration can go in opposing so powerful a group as the cotton textile industry and all its supporters, U.S. officials can properly insist that the United States must adhere to international standards of good conduct. Japanese pressure may help them do so.

The American interest in orderly marketing is not wholly that of a reluctant importer. American automobiles and a long list of consumer goods still have only restricted entry into Japan and many other markets—partly because local producers fear fierce competition. Perhaps refinement of GATT rules and procedures concerning market disruption could help the American cause. In any case, unless a conscious effort is made to devise orderly marketing procedures that work but are no more severe than necessary and that are compatible with expanding rather than restricting trade, protectionist forces will use the fear of market disruption as an excuse for maintaining and increasing trade barriers.

Readjustment and re-employment of displaced human and material resources, while remaining primarily a national responsibility, may be improved by some international cooperation. The field is a new one, especially for the United States and Japan; Europe has a little more experience. Something could be gained from international study and exchange of experience. GATT would seem the logical instrument for studies that might go as far back as the Anglo–French trade treaty of 1860 when France provided a sum to assist industries adversely affected by the removal of trade barriers.

There may also be room for a good deal of Japanese–American collaboration in positive trade expansion. In private enterprise economies like those of Japan and the United States, finding as well as exploiting of export opportunities is mainly a job for private businessmen. But in the less developed countries, most kinds of entrepreneurs are much less numerous and tend to be ill informed, especially about the outside world. There may be a place for assistance or collaboration, involving Japan, the United States, possibly the OECD, GATT, or the United Nations. Again a likely starting point would be research, or possibly an information service, that would relate surplus capacity and unused factors of production to shortages and bottlenecks elsewhere. Price information might also be helpful.

In aiding the newly developing countries, the United States has been the leader in the quantity and variety of aid given. Japan is gradually doing more, but not enough, judged either from the point of view of fair shares or from Japan's hope to win friendship and markets in the countries concerned. U.S. pressure on Japan may be able to induce more aid-giving than in the past. But perhaps what would evoke more Japanese response would be an imaginative proposal calling for Japanese–American cooperation. From time to time both countries have a good deal of unutilized industrial capacity, as they did in 1962. There is probably a way that more of it could be made useful to the developing countries. A cooperative program might be less vulnerable to short-range political considerations than direct U.S. aid has sometimes proved to be. Japanese have long wanted cooperative developmental activities in Southeast Asia. Perhaps this long-standing wish can be realized, even without the complete American financing Prime Ministers Yoshida and Kishi seemed to have in mind in 1954 and 1957, respectively.

One could go on, enumerating common interests and areas of potential cooperation between Japan and the United States. A certain number would be peculiar to the special circumstances of the two countries and their relations to one another; for the most part these have already been mentioned and the others are the rest of the problems on which all of the economically strong countries of the free world can profitably cooperate. That in itself is significant because it reminds us once again of a point that has emerged frequently from these pages: Japan is no longer a country with special difficulties and disadvantages but has advanced to a position of economic strength nearer that of the major industrialized nations than it has ever been before.

That advance is at once a great achievement and a promise of future achievement. It has removed Japan from a category in which it seemed to require special treatment on almost every count because of its economic vulnerability; it has opened the prospect that a strong Japan can begin to make a substantial contribution to the proper functioning of the free world economy and to its defense and development.

American policy played a great part in this evolution. The United States' aims were not just economic, but economic policy played a large part in the American effort to move Japan away from aggressive, authoritarian, and militarist ways toward greater freedom, welfare, and democracy. American policies played a crucial part in aiding Japanese recovery, in providing markets in which Japan could earn its own way, and in helping the Japanese to find an acceptable place in the world economy and in free world cooperative arrangements. They will continue to be essential to Japanese economic growth.

Naturally things will be different in the period ahead—but not entirely different. For the Japanese to succeed in their ambitious but not unrealistic plans, they will have to continue to find growing export markets. If they are to do so the United States will have to continue to follow much the same policies it has been following—not those of the first postwar decade when Japan needed special help, but those of the late 1950s and early 1960s that consisted very largely of accepting growing imports from Japan without throwing up new barriers in sufficient number, or of sufficient height, to do serious damage to Japan's growth. Naturally there will again be problems and friction, especially about trade and competition. Much of this will repeat the experience of the last decade and a half, though probably with other products, but some of it may be significantly different—because, for instance, of the international cotton textile arrangements and the Trade Expansion Act with its adjustment provisions, to name two major factors.

Among all the changes the most important is in Japan's capabilities. Because Japan now has the economic strength to do more than before, it will be expected to exercise the responsibility that goes with this power. To be fully accepted by the other countries it will have to carry its share of the load. This new strength also implies reduced dependence on the United States. Inevitably, and properly, Japan will act more and more independently. Cooperation will more often have to be won by the United States through a clear demonstration of advantages to Japan; there will be more times when the two governments will see matters differently and act accordingly. The forces in Japan that make a virtue of not agreeing with the United States may have more influence and may from time to time be in command.

But strong common interests will remain. Whatever course it follows, Japan needs satisfactory foreign trade; its main trading partner is and will almost certainly continue to be the United States. The commercial and financial links that bind the two countries can exercise a steadying influence if the two governments continue to recognize and cultivate them. Since 1945 Japan and the United States have done very well in finding methods, both old and new, to cope with common problems. The problems that can be foreseen look no more difficult, in fact generally less difficult, than some that have been encountered. To reverse a well-worn Japanese phrase, the future *can* be viewed with optimism, by both Japanese and Americans.

Appendixes and Bibliographic Note

Appendix A

Statistics on Japan's Balance of Payments, Foreign Exchange Movements, and Foreign Exchange Reserves

Like other members of the International Monetary Fund (IMF), Japan submits to the IMF periodically a balance of international payments. This is prepared in the Foreign Department of the Bank of Japan in accordance with the IMF *Balance of Payments Manual* (Washington: Author, 3d ed., July 1961). Both the Bank of Japan and the IMF publish a good deal of this material. The fullest information made public by each agency is issued on an annual basis, and interim reports are less complete. Table A-1 below is based mainly on the IMF's *Balance of Payments Yearbook,* and supplementary information comes from the Bank of Japan's annual *Balance of Payments of Japan.*

Having had detailed foreign exchange control throughout the postwar period, the Japanese authorities also gather a great deal of information about foreign exchange movements. Much of this is published in the Bank of Japan's *Foreign Exchange Statistics Monthly.* In addition, the Ministry of Finance reports frequently on the level of foreign exchange reserves, for which it is easy to find monthly figures in published sources.

Although the balance of payments is a preferable basis for much analytical work, and is the main source of information used in this study, the foreign exchange statistics are far more widely used by Japanese policy makers and by writers, both Japanese and foreign, chiefly because they are published frequently and promptly. But there has grown up a habit among many writers of using foreign exchange statistics as though they were the same as the balance of payments, in fact often applying the balance-of-payments label to foreign exchange statistics. The result is that reports on this subject are often unclear and must be used with considerable caution.

Differences Between the Balance of Payments and Foreign Exchange Movements

The distinctions between these two sets of accounts are well established among economists and are clear, both conceptually and in Japanese original sources. Essentially, the balance of payments is a statement, as complete and orderly as possible, of all Japan's foreign economic transactions, while the foreign exchange statistics refer to only those transactions that involve actual transfers of foreign exchange, and reports are made not according to rigorous definitions but on the varying bases used by businessmen in the actual transactions. The principal differences are of three kinds,[1] as follows:

Coverage. While the balance of payments is as complete as possible a report on the transactions between the residents of Japan and the outside world, the Japanese foreign exchange statistics omit transactions that do not involve transfers of foreign exchange. Among the more important items left out are reparations, investments made by assignment of patent rights rather than in cash, unremitted profits, and other accruals not reflected in actual financial transfers.

Valuation (and classification). In Japan as elsewhere the balance of payments follows the careful and detailed classification prescribed by the IMF, but Japanese foreign exchange statistics follow the foreign exchange documents themselves, and these vary from one transaction to another. The most significant case here concerns the valuation of commodity trade, with consequent effects on the transportation and insurance accounts. The balance of payments values both exports and imports at f.o.b. prices. The foreign exchange statistics use varying values. Fortunately, an indication of what these values include is provided, and one can thus get at least a rough idea of how much transportation and insurance cost is included with commodity trade in the foreign exchange statistics. In the Japanese fiscal year, April 1962–March 1963, the foreign exchange statistics reported commodity trade ("visible transactions") in the following ways, expressed as percentages of total value of exports or imports: [2]

Price terms	*Exports*	*Imports*
f.o.b.	37	35
c.i.f.	37	27
c.&f.	25	36
c.&i.	1	2

These figures say that freight charges are shown as part of the value of 62 per cent of Japan's exports, and 63 per cent of imports, in FY 1962. But not all of the exports so listed were carried in Japanese ships and not all the imports so listed arrived on foreign ships. Thus, a good deal of adjustment is necessary in the transportation account, and neither the goods account nor the transportation account actually shows what it may seem to the unwary to show. The transportation account is further than the goods account from being clear and complete. The balance of payments attempts to show only goods in

[1] These are explained by the Bank of Japan in the first two pages of every issue of *Foreign Exchange Statistics Monthly,* and in the "Introduction" to each issue of *Balance of Payments of Japan* (annual). The latter explanation is fuller than the former. A more detailed statement applying generally, not to Japan alone, is contained in the IMF *Balance of Payments Manual,* 3d ed., pp. 14–15. A standard textbook explanation is given in Charles P. Kindleberger, *International Economics* (Homewood, Ill.: Irwin, revised ed., 1958), pp. 39–42.

[2] Bank of Japan, *Foreign Exchange Statistics Monthly,* June 1963, pp. 11 and 13.

TABLE A-1. JAPAN'S BALANCE OF PAYMENTS, BY YEARS, 1945–1962

(In millions of dollars)

Line	Item	*1945–1946* [a]			*1947*		
		Credit	*Debit*	*Balance*	*Credit*	*Debit*	*Balance*
1	**Goods and services (ordinary)**	**69.0**	**322.2**	**−253.2**	**184.8**	**542.8**	**−358.0**
2	Merchandise trade	65.3	285.6	−220.3	181.6	449.0	−267.4
3	Services	3.7	36.6	−32.9	3.2	93.8	−90.6
4	Transportation }	0.5	36.6	−36.1	1.0	89.0	−88.0
5	Insurance }						
6	Travel	—	—	—	—	—	—
7	Investment income	—	—	—	—	3.4	−3.4
8	Government transactions, n.i.e.	—	—	—	—	—	—
9	Miscellaneous services	3.2	—	3.2	2.2	1.4	0.8
10	**Extraordinary items**	**192.7**	—	**192.7**	**404.4**	—	**404.4**
11	U.S. economic aid	192.7		192.7	404.4		404.4
12	U.S. military expenditures [b]	—		—	—		—
13	Reparations		—	—		—	—
14	**Errors and omissions (net)**			**−2.6**			**13.6**
15	**Capital and gold movements (ordinary)**	**113.6** [c]	**50.5** [d]	**63.1**	**−17.6** [c]	**42.4** [d]	**−60.0**
16	Private capital	—	—	—	—	—	—
17	Long-term assets	—	—	—	—	—	—
18	Long-term liabilities	—	—	—	—	—	—
19	Direct investment	—	—		—	—	
20	Other	—	—		—	—	
21	Short-term assets	—	—	—	—	—	—
22	Short-term liabilities	—	—	—	—	—	—
23	Official and banking capital	113.6 [c]	48.9 [d]	64.7	−17.6 [c]	40.6 [d]	−58.2
24	Long-term assets	—	—	—	—	—	—
25	Long-term liabilities	4.9	—	4.9	5.5	—	5.5
26	Short-term assets	—	48.9	−48.9	—	40.6	−40.6
27	Payments agreements	—	—		—	—	
28	Other	—	48.9		—	40.6	
29	Short-term liabilities	108.7	—	108.7	—	23.1	−23.1
30	To IMF and IBRD	—	—		—	—	
31	Payments agreements	—	—		—	—	
32	U.S. Revolving Fund Credit	—	—		—	23.1	
33	Other	108.7	—		—	—	
34	Monetary gold	—	1.6	−1.6	—	1.8	−1.8

[a] September 1945–December 1946.

[b] Includes small amounts spent in Japan by third countries, mostly during the Korean War by units and personnel of the United Nations Command.

[c] Change in Japanese liabilities abroad, calculated by adding increase in liabilities (in credit column) and subtracting reduction of liabilities (in debit column).

[d] Change in Japanese assets abroad, calculated by adding increase in assets (in debit column) and subtracting reduction of assets (in credit column).

[e] The 1958 reparations account here includes $176.9 million granted by Japan to Indonesia through cancellation of a commercial debt. Although this action was, in effect, part of Japan's reparations settlement with Indonesia in January 1958, neither the Japanese government nor the International Monetary Fund includes this sum in reparations; both list it among "other official donations."

Notes: A dash (—) indicates that a figure is zero or less than $500,000.
Minor inconsistencies result from rounding.

TABLE A-1 (cont'd)

Line	*Item*	*1948* *Credit*	*1948* *Debit*	*1948* *Balance*	*1949* *Credit*	*1949* *Debit*	*1949* *Balance*
1	**Goods and services (ordinary)**	**268.5**	**673.5**	**−405.0**	**556.8**	**907.8**	**−351.0**
2	Merchandise trade	262.3	546.6	−284.3	533.3	728.1	−194.8
3	Services	6.2	126.9	−120.7	23.5	179.7	−156.2
4	Transportation	3.0	123.2	−120.2	9.4	173.4	−164.0
5	Insurance						
6	Travel	—	—	—	7.2	—	7.2
7	Investment income	—	2.2	−2.2	—	1.3	−1.3
8	Government transactions, n.i.e.	—	—	—	—	—	—
9	Miscellaneous services	3.2	1.5	1.7	6.9	5.0	1.9
10	**Extraordinary items**	**479.8**	—	**479.8**	**583.3**	**18.4**	**564.9**
11	U.S. economic aid	461.0		461.0	534.7		534.7
12	U.S. military expenditures [b]	18.8		18.8	48.6		48.6
13	Reparations		—	—		18.4	−18.4
14	**Errors and omissions (net)**			**26.9**			**−17.7**
15	**Capital and gold movements (ordinary)**	**−58.1** [c]	**43.6** [d]	**−101.7**	**1.7** [c]	**197.9** [d]	**−196.2**
16	Private capital	—	—	—	—	—	—
17	Long-term assets	—	—	—	—	—	—
18	Long-term liabilities	—	—	—	—	—	—
19	Direct investment	—	—		—	—	
20	Other	—	—		—	—	
21	Short-term assets	—	—	—	—	—	—
22	Short-term liabilities	—	—	—	—	—	—
23	Official and banking capital	−58.1 [c]	41.0 [d]	−99.1	1.7 [c]	195.0 [d]	−193.3
24	Long-term assets	—	—	—	—	—	—
25	Long-term liabilities	3.6	—	3.6	—	17.5	−17.5
26	Short-term assets	5.0	46.0	−41.0	—	195.0	−195.0
27	Payments agreements	—	—		—	—	
28	Other	5.0	46.0		—	195.0	
29	Short-term liabilities	—	61.7	−61.7	19.2	—	19.2
30	To IMF and IBRD	—	—		—	—	
31	Payments agreements	—	—		—	—	
32	U.S. Revolving Fund Credit	—	61.7		19.2	—	
33	Other	—	—		—	—	
34	Monetary gold	—	2.6	−2.6	—	2.9	−2.9

[a] September 1945–December 1946.

[b] Includes small amounts spent in Japan by third countries, mostly during the Korean War by units and personnel of the United Nations Command.

[c] Change in Japanese liabilities abroad, calculated by adding increase in liabilities (in credit column) and subtracting reduction of liabilities (in debit column).

[d] Change in Japanese assets abroad, calculated by adding increase in assets (in debit column) and subtracting reduction of assets (in credit column).

[e] The 1958 reparations account here includes $176.9 million granted by Japan to Indonesia through cancellation of a commercial debt. Although this action was, in effect, part of Japan's reparations settlement with Indonesia in January 1958, neither the Japanese government nor the International Monetary Fund includes this sum in reparations; both list it among "other official donations."

1950			*1951*			*1952*			
Credit	*Debit*	*Balance*	*Credit*	*Debit*	*Balance*	*Credit*	*Debit*	*Balance*	*Line*
945.9	**984.3**	**−38.4**	**1,541.1**	**1,991.5**	**−450.4**	**1,449.1**	**2,017.6**	**568.5**	1
821.5	822.1	−0.6	1.353.6	1,645.4	−291.8	1,288.7	1,701.3	−412.6	2
124.4	162.2	−37.8	187.5	346.1	−158.6	160.4	316.3	−155.9	3
16.5	134.5	−118.0	41.0	255.7	−214.7	71.4	223.4	−152.0	4
0.1	3.4	−3.3	3.7	15.6	−11.9	5.5	15.4	−9.9	5
21.3	0.9	20.4	8.9	4.4	4.5	8.2	5.0	3.2	6
0.3	5.9	−5.6	1.1	6.4	−5.3	6.1	11.0	−4.9	7
0.1	0.3	−0.2	1.0	2.0	−1.0	3.7	6.0	−2.3	8
86.1	17.2	68.9	131.8	62.0	69.8	65.5	55.5	10.0	9
513.9	—	**513.9**	**779.5**	—	**779.5**	**793.2**	—	**793.2**	10
360.3		360.3	155.3		155.3	5.4		5.4	11
153.6		153.6	624.2		624.2	787.8		787.8	12
	—	—		—	—		—	—	13
		−16.7			**8.6**			**0.7**	14
−25.6 [c]	**433.2** [d]	**−458.8**	**33.3** [c]	**371.0** [d]	**−337.7**	**138.7** [c]	**364.1** [d]	**−225.4**	15
5.4 [c]	—	5.4	43.9 [c]	9.7 [d]	34.2	42.1 [c]	4.7 [d]	37.4	16
—	—	—	—	0.3	−0.3	—	0.5	−0.5	17
4.1	—	4.1	24.6	—	24.6	16.3	—	16.3	18
4.0	—		22.0	—		10.8	—		19
0.1	—		2.6	—		5.5	—		20
—	—	—	—	9.4	−9.4	—	4.2	−4.2	21
1.3	—	1.3	19.3	—	19.3	25.8	—	25.8	22
−31.0 [c]	429.4 [d]	−460.4	−10.6 [c]	356.9 [d]	−367.5	84.7 [c]	359.4 [d]	−274.7	23
—	—	—	—	—	—	—	113.5	−113.5	24
0.5	—	0.5	—	2.4	−2.4	—	3.2	−3.2	25
—	429.4	−429.4	—	356.9	−356.9	—	245.9	−245.9	26
—	30.0		—	46.2		—	12.7		27
—	399.4		—	310.7		—	233.2		28
11.6	43.1	−31.5	25.0	33.2	−8.2	96.4	8.5	87.9	29
—	—		—	—		45.0	—		30
—	—		—	33.2		10.8	—		31
—	43.1		—	—		39.7	—		32
11.6	—		25.0	—		0.9	8.5		33
—	3.8	−3.8	—	4.4	−4.4	11.9	—	11.9	34

Notes: A dash (—) indicates that a figure is zero or less than $500,000.
Minor inconsistencies result from rounding.

TABLE A-1 (cont'd)

Line	Item	*1953* Credit	*1953* Debit	*1953* Balance	*1954* Credit	*1954* Debit	*1954* Balance
1	**Goods and services (ordinary)**	**1,411.9**	**2,420.3**	**−1,008.4**	**1,801.5**	**2,454.7**	**−653.2**
2	Merchandise trade	1,257.8	2,049.6	−791.8	1,611.3	2,040.6	−429.3
3	Services	154.1	370.7	−216.6	190.2	414.1	−223.9
4	Transportation	76.6	247.0	−170.4	89.7	255.9	−166.2
5	Insurance	4.8	17.7	−12.9	8.5	19.9	−11.4
6	Travel	10.0	7.0	3.0	11.2	6.8	4.4
7	Investment income	11.8	34.9	−23.1	8.2	47.0	−38.8
8	Government transactions, n.i.e.	7.6	8.8	−1.2	12.1	11.1	1.0
9	Miscellaneous services	43.3	55.3	−12.0	60.5	73.4	−12.9
10	**Extraordinary items**	**803.3**	—	**803.3**	**602.3**	—	**602.3**
11	U.S. economic aid	—		—	—		—
12	U.S. military expenditures[b]	803.3		803.3	602.3		602.3
13	Reparations		—	—		—	—
14	**Errors and omissions (net)**			**1.4**			**17.7**
15	**Capital and gold movements (ordinary)**	**326.9**[c]	**123.2**[d]	**203.7**	**156.8**[c]	**123.6**[d]	**33.2**
16	Private capital	−15.7[c]	2.1[d]	−17.8	47.9[c]	34.5[d]	13.4
17	Long-term assets	—	0.7	−0.7	—	2.5	−2.5
18	Long-term liabilities	20.1	—	20.1	25.2	—	25.2
19	Direct investment	11.0	—		18.6	—	
20	Other	9.1	—		6.6	—	
21	Short-term assets	—	1.4	−1.4	—	32.0	−32.0
22	Short-term liabilities	—	35.8	−35.8	22.7	—	22.7
23	Official and banking capital	342.6[c]	118.7[d]	223.9	108.9[c]	86.4[d]	22.5
24	Long-term assets	—	191.1	−191.1	—	3.0	−3.0
25	Long-term liabilities	—	8.4	−8.4	1.9	—	1.9
26	Short-term assets	130.3	57.9	72.4	127.0	210.4	−83.4
27	Payments agreements	—	20.5		—	91.2	
28	Other	130.3	37.4		127.0	119.2	
29	Short-term liabilities	351.0	—	351.0	138.6	31.6	107.0
30	To IMF and IBRD	249.9	—		—	—	
31	Payments agreements	73.0	—		—	31.6	
32	U.S. Revolving Fund Credit	0.3	—		35.5	—	
33	Other	27.8	—		103.1	—	
34	Monetary gold	—	2.4	−2.4	—	2.7	−2.7

[a] September 1945–December 1946.

[b] Includes small amounts spent in Japan by third countries, mostly during the Korean War by units and personnel of the United Nations Command.

[c] Change in Japanese liabilities abroad, calculated by adding increase in liabilities (in credit column) and subtracting reduction of liabilities (in debit column).

[d] Change in Japanese assets abroad, calculated by adding increase in assets (in debit column) and subtracting reduction of assets (in credit column).

[e] The 1958 reparations account here includes $176.9 million granted by Japan to Indonesia through cancellation of a commercial debt. Although this action was, in effect, part of Japan's reparations settlement with Indonesia in January 1958, neither the Japanese government nor the International Monetary Fund includes this sum in reparations; both list it among "other official donations."

1955			*1956*			*1957*			
Credit	*Debit*	*Balance*	*Credit*	*Debit*	*Balance*	*Credit*	*Debit*	*Balance*	*Line*
2,247.9	**2,517.5**	**−269.6**	**2,840.1**	**3,364.3**	**−524.2**	**3,306.9**	**4,310.9**	**−1,004.0**	1
2,006.4	2,060.9	−54.5	2,481.8	2,612.8	−131.0	2,854.0	3,256.4	−402.4	2
241.5	456.6	−215.1	358.3	751.5	−393.2	452.9	1,054.5	−601.6	3
127.4	276.0	−148.6	209.8	513.0	−303.2	260.6	761.8	−501.2	4
10.4	19.1	−8.7	12.0	24.8	−12.8	16.8	34.0	−17.2	5
14.3	8.1	6.2	16.5	12.3	4.2	21.8	14.5	7.3	6
14.1	55.5	−41.4	27.3	66.1	−38.8	33.7	82.4	−48.7	7
18.6	13.3	5.3	25.9	19.3	6.6	36.1	19.6	16.5	8
56.7	84.6	−27.9	66.8	116.0	−49.2	83.9	142.2	−58.3	9
517.9	**23.9**	**494.0**	**510.3**	**19.8**	**490.5**	**459.8**	**75.9**	**383.9**	10
12.7		12.7	12.3		12.3	10.4		10.4	11
505.2		505.2	498.0		498.0	449.4		449.4	12
	23.9	−23.9		19.8	−19.8		75.9	−75.9	13
		−101.5			**14.1**			**4.7**	14
206.4[c]	**329.3[d]**	**−122.9**	**249.8[c]**	**230.2[d]**	**19.6**	**192.6[c]**	**−422.8[d]**	**615.4**	15
94.3[c]	9.0[d]	85.3	65.5[c]	67.9[d]	−2.4	114.2[c]	49.5[d]	64.7	16
—	31.8	−31.8	—	75.6	−75.6	—	54.4	−54.4	17
14.5	—	14.5	16.2	1.9	14.3	41.7	—	41.7	18
5.7	—		16.2	—		29.9	—		19
8.8	—		—	1.9		11.8	—		20
22.8	—	22.8	7.7	—	7.7	4.9	—	4.9	21
79.8	—	79.8	51.2	—	51.2	72.5	—	72.5	22
112.1[c]	318.7[d]	−206.6	184.3[c]	161.9[d]	22.4	78.4[c]	−472.8[d]	551.2	23
—	—	—	—	2.4	−2.4	—	0.1	−0.1	24
49.1	—	49.1	23.0	—	23.0	32.3	—	32.3	25
—	318.7	−318.7	—	159.5	−159.5	478.2	5.3	472.9	26
—	42.2		—	17.7		—	5.3		27
—	276.5		—	141.8		478.2	—		28
168.7	105.7	63.0	168.1	6.8	161.3	155.9	109.8	46.1	29
—	62.4		—	2.4		125.0	7.3		30
—	10.4		—	4.4		—	31.5		31
—	32.9		29.1	—		30.9	—		32
168.7	—		139.0	—		—	71.0		33
—	1.6	−1.6	—	0.4	−0.4	—	0.5	−0.5	34

Notes: A dash (—) indicates that a figure is zero or less than $500,000.
Minor inconsistencies result from rounding.

TABLE A-1 (cont'd)

Line	Item	1958 Credit	1958 Debit	1958 Balance	1959 Credit	1959 Debit	1959 Balance
1	**Goods and services (ordinary)**	**3,300.6**	**3,208.9**	**91.7**	**3,924.9**	**3,874.3**	**50.6**
2	Merchandise trade	2,870.8	2,501.4	369.4	3,413.3	3,052.2	361.1
3	Services	429.8	707.5	−277.7	511.6	822.1	−310.5
4	Transportation	240.1	406.0	−165.9	287.9	466.6	−178.7
5	Insurance	22.2	32.1	−9.9	24.2	39.4	−15.2
6	Travel	24.3	15.9	8.4	32.6	20.1	12.5
7	Investment income	27.0	66.9	−39.9	47.8	85.1	−37.3
8	Government transactions, n.i.e.	22.8	23.7	−0.9	14.3	27.4	−13.1
9	Miscellaneous services	93.4	162.9	−69.5	104.8	183.5	−78.7
10	**Extraordinary items**	**413.9**	**241.2**	**172.7**	**380.8**	**70.1**	**310.7**
11	U.S. economic aid	10.2		10.2	0.3		0.3
12	U.S. military expenditures[b]	403.7		403.7	380.5		380.5
13	Reparations		241.2[e]	−241.2[e]		70.1	−70.1
14	**Errors and omissions (net)**			**71.6**			**57.1**
15	**Capital and gold movements (ordinary)**	**−81.4[c]**	**254.6[d]**	**−336.0**	**476.4[c]**	**894.8[d]**	**−418.4**
16	Private capital	73.0[c]	37.0[d]	36.0	43.1[c]	125.4[d]	−82.3
17	Long-term assets	—	43.9	−43.9	—	118.6	−118.6
18	Long-term liabilities	83.5	—	83.5	96.7	—	96.7
19	Direct investment	11.5	—		18.5	—	
20	Other	72.0	—		78.2	—	
21	Short-term assets	6.9	—	6.9	—	6.8	−6.8
22	Short-term liabilities	—	10.5	−10.5	—	53.6	−53.6
23	Official and banking capital	−154.4[c]	187.2[d]	−341.6	433.3[c]	649.2[d]	−215.9
24	Long-term assets	—	1.1	−1.1	—	269.2	−269.2
25	Long-term liabilities	57.2	—	57.2	76.8	—	76.8
26	Short-term assets	171.2	357.3	−186.1	7.4	387.4	−380.0
27	Payments agreements	171.2	—		7.4	—	
28	Other	—	357.3		—	387.4	
29	Short-term liabilities	0.8	212.4	−211.6	405.4	48.9	356.5
30	To IMF and IBRD	—	144.1		192.8	—	
31	Payments agreements	—	6.2		—	—	
32	U.S. Revolving Fund Credit	—	18.7		—	47.3	
33	Other	0.8	43.4		212.6	1.6	
34	Monetary gold	—	30.4	−30.4	—	120.2	−120.2

[a] September 1945–December 1946.
[b] Includes small amounts spent in Japan by third countries, mostly during the Korean War by units and personnel of the United Nations Command.
[c] Change in Japanese liabilities abroad, calculated by adding increase in liabilities (in credit column) and subtracting reduction of liabilities (in debit column).
[d] Change in Japanese assets abroad, calculated by adding increase in assets (in debit column) and subtracting reduction of assets (in credit column).
[e] The 1958 reparations account here includes $176.9 million granted by Japan to Indonesia through cancellation of a commercial debt. Although this action was, in effect, part of Japan's reparations settlement with Indonesia in January 1958, neither the Japanese government nor the International Monetary Fund includes this sum in reparations; both list it among "other official donations."

1960			1961			1962			
Credit	*Debit*	*Balance*	*Credit*	*Debit*	*Balance*	*Credit*	*Debit*	*Balance*	*Line*
4,577.0	**4,777.6**	**−200.6**	**4,848.2**	**6,134.2**	**−1,286.0**	**5,637.6**	**5,994.9**	**−357.2**	1
3,981.5	3,710.7	270.8	4,148.6	4,707.1	−558.5	4,860.3	4,458.7	401.6	2
595.5	1,066.9	−471.4	699.6	1,427.1	−727.5	777.3	1,536.2	−758.8	3
318.5	587.2	−268.7	354.7	830.4	−475.7	388.1	799.9	−411.8	4
32.0	48.7	−16.7	44.1	61.8	−17.8	49.8	73.2	−23.4	5
39.7	40.5	−0.8	47.4	52.5	−5.1	48.3	47.9	0.4	6
80.3	113.3	−33.1	95.8	144.0	−48.2	107.2	199.1	−91.9	7
12.3	30.9	−18.6	18.7	38.8	−20.1	14.6	41.6	−27.0	8
112.7	246.4	−133.7	139.0	299.5	−160.6	169.3	374.5	−205.1	9
412.6	**68.6**	**344.0**	**389.2**	**85.6**	**303.6**	**376.9**	**68.4**	**308.5**	10
—		—	—		—	—		—	11
412.6		412.6	389.2		389.2	376.9		376.9	12
	68.6	−68.6		85.6	−85.6		68.4	−68.4	13
		32.6			**19.0**			**5.7**	14
679.9[c]	**855.9**[d]	**−175.9**	**1,158.2**[c]	**194.8**[d]	**963.4**	**761.4**[c]	**718.3**[d]	**43.0**	15
44.0[c]	143.1[d]	−99.1	260.1[c]	280.3[d]	−20.2	535.7[c]	280.4[d]	255.3	16
—	144.7	−144.7	—	265.8	−265.8	—	291.7	−291.7	17
61.4	—	61.4	224.6	—	224.6	439.3	—	439.3	18
6.4	—		58.7	—		58.2	—		19
55.0	—		166.0	—		381.1	—		20
1.6	—	1.6	—	14.5	−14.5	11.3	—	11.3	21
—	17.4	−17.4	35.5	—	35.5	96.4	—	96.4	22
635.9[c]	712.3[d]	−76.4	898.1[c]	−111.1[d]	1,009.2	225.7[c]	437.4[d]	−211.7	23
—	26.3	−26.3	—	43.9	−43.9	—	18.3	−18.3	24
74.7	19.0	55.7	73.6	—	73.6	42.4	—	42.4	25
15.5	701.5	−686.0	394.2	239.3	154.9	—	419.1	−419.1	26
—	—		—	—		—	—		27
—	—		—	—		—	—		28
596.0	15.8	580.2	887.0	62.5	824.5	183.3	—	183.3	29
—	—		—	—		—	—		30
—	—		—	—		—	—		31
—	—		—	—		—	—		32
—	—		—	—		—	—		33
—	0.5	−0.5	—	25.6	−25.6	—	0.5	−0.5	34

Notes: A dash (—) indicates that a figure is zero or less than $500,000.
Minor inconsistencies result from rounding.

Sources: 1945–1960—International Monetary Fund, *Balance of Payments Yearbook* (1945–1946 figures from v. 2; 1947–1949 figures from v. 5; 1950–1954 figures from v. 8; 1955–1959 figures from v. 12; 1960 figures from v. 13).
1961–1962—Bank of Japan, *Balance of Payments of Japan*, 1961, 1962.

the merchandise account, only transportation in that account, only insurance in that account, etc.

Timing. The balance of payments attempts to report all transactions as of the time they occur, but the foreign exchange statistics are affected only when payment takes place in foreign exchange. On a great many transactions these two events are separated by several months. What is more, the lag between the movement of goods and the payment varies from time to time, greatly affecting foreign exchange flows, even without changes in the volume of transactions. For example, in November 1960 the Japanese Finance Ministry extended the maximum term permissible for "usance" borrowing from abroad from 90 to 120 days, thus reducing apparent "visible" imports, according to the foreign exchange statistics, mainly in February and March 1961. For noncommodity transactions the gap is different, probably smaller in most cases than for commodity transactions.

Thus, the balance of payments is a far more precise report of what happened. But in order to achieve the necessary precision, more time and effort is needed to compile the report. This is probably the reason why the Japanese publish the foreign exchange statistics much sooner and more often. And that is a good reason why the foreign exchange statistics are much more widely used. But how fully these statistics displace the actual balance of payments in Japanese policy making was indicated sharply when I asked a high official of the Ministry of Finance about interpreting something in the *Balance of Payments of Japan.* He exclaimed that he'd never seen the publication before. He had for years been in the very midst of the policy discussions of his government on balance-of-payments issues, but the published report in IMF terms had escaped him. He had been used to relying mainly on foreign exchange statistics, both what the public sees and supplementary information that is not made public.

While there seems no danger that such officials will be misled by using whatever statistics they choose, the distinction between the balance of payments and foreign exchange movements is being lost in a good deal of the writing dealing with Japan's international economic relations. The unwary reader runs the danger of being misled. The terms *surplus* and *deficit* have come to mean foreign exchange net inflows or outflows, whether the account being discussed is a foreign exchange account or a balance of payments, and as often as not the term *balance of payments* is used as a label for information about foreign exchange flows.[3]

[3] Perhaps some examples of recent usage will be useful. Although the International Monetary Fund warns about the adjustments that must be made if a foreign exchange account is used as a basis for balance-of-payments figures (*Balance of Payments Manual,* cited), the IMF's own *International Financial News Survey* (*IFNS*) frequently quotes press articles that speak of a balance of payments when it is foreign exchange movements that are being reported. The careful reader can spot such usage in various ways, including references to monthly figures and to fiscal year movements. These must be foreign exchange figures, since the balance of payments is not compiled on these bases. *IFNS,* October 12, 1962, p. 331, speaks of an estimate of the balance of payments for the current fiscal year. The issue of August 3, 1962, p. 243, refers to a shift in the balance of payments from deficit to surplus in

Recent Changes in Foreign Exchange Statistics

Since 1950 the basic report on Japan's foreign exchange receipts and payments has been the Bank of Japan's *Foreign Exchange Statistics Monthly*. Although this report has never included the level of foreign exchange holdings or reserves, it has presented a vast array of statistics on exchange flows, and the movements underlying them. Movements were long reported by the foreign currency involved as well as in total. Commodity movements, as reflected by foreign exchange receipts and payments, were reported by commodity, currency, and country. Noncommodity transactions were reported in great detail. Besides monthly figures for these movements, the report also presented many useful summaries, including quarterly and annual totals for many tables. Annual totals were shown for both calendar and fiscal years.

In April 1960 a major revision of the publication was made. The amount of detail presented was sharply reduced, and figures for earlier months were not shown. (Each earlier issue had shown some figures going back to 1950 or 1951.) Since then the time series shown in any issue goes back only to April 1960. Movements are no longer shown by individual foreign currency; the number of acceptable currencies became too great. Calendar year totals are no longer given.

But several changes were made to bring the form of the foreign exchange statistics closer to that of a balance of payments. Capital movements are now shown more fully than before, and net movements of short-term capital are shown separately. And the account is divided to show current and capital transactions separately.

Table A-2 below presents the major components of foreign exchange statistics by quarters. Short-term capital movements are omitted, being available only since April 1960 and only in net form. The figures for exports financed by U.S. aid funds (along with the small UNKRA shipments) are not included with other merchandise exports but among invisibles. Both these peculiarities are necessitated by the available information before April 1960.

June 1962. Robert F. Emery, economist of the Board of Governors of the Federal Reserve System in Washington, speaks of "substantial deficit in the international balance of payments beginning in May 1961." ("The Japanese Measures to Restore Economic Equilibrium," *Asian Survey*, June 1962, p. 33.) The Bank of Japan, in its *News Survey* for April 30, 1962, speaks of a balance-of-payments surplus in March.

The Oriental Economist, April 1960, p. 173, has a table entitled "Actual Balance of International Payments," the main columns of which are "Exchange Receipts for Exports" and "Exchange Payments for Imports." The Bank of Tokyo, in its *Weekly Review*, October 1, 1962, p. 265, presents a detailed foreign exchange report under the heading "Balance of Payments in August." The Ministry of Finance in Tokyo also publishes foreign exchange statistics under the heading "Balance of Payments" (e.g., in *Quarterly Bulletin of Financial Statistics*, March 1963, p. 71). But the Ministry also publishes "Balance of Payments (based on IMF method)" (e.g., same, p. 72).

Thus the key is the label IMF. In most writing coming out of Japan today a balance of payments needs to have the IMF label. Without that the statistics given are likely to be foreign exchange statistics. But not all sources are so careful as the Ministry of Finance, and the reader must be on his guard.

TABLE A-2. JAPAN'S FOREIGN EXCHANGE RECEIPTS AND PAYMENTS, BY QUARTERS, 1950–1962
(In millions of dollars)

		Merchandise [a]			*Invisibles* [a]			*Long-term Capital*			*Total* [c] (*except short-term capital*)		
Year	*Quarter*	*Receipts*	*Payments*	*Net*	*Receipts*	*Payments*	*Net*	*Receipts*	*Payments*	*Net*	*Receipts*	*Payments*	*Net*
1950	1st	134	155	−21	10	3	7		[b]		144	158	−15
	2d	166	132	34	54	8	46				220	140	80
	3d	198	161	37	64	4	60				262	165	97
	4th	275	197	78	108	16	92				383	213	170
1951	1st	281	471	−190	163	27	136		[b]		444	498	−54
	2d	373	516	−143	224	38	186				597	553	44
	3d	323	398	−75	257	51	206				580	448	132
	4th	321	340	−19	299	70	229				619	410	209
1952	1st	388	405	−17	230	18	212	3	10	−7	621	433	188
	2d	344	419	−75	271	29	242	7	28	−21	622	475	147
	3d	271	402	−131	215	33	182	6	28	−22	493	463	30
	4th	286	493	−207	225	58	167	4	3	1	514	553	−39
1953	1st	268	476	−208	205	39	166	7	7	—	479	521	−42
	2d	289	574	−285	232	49	183	12	6	6	532	630	−97
	3d	285	464	−179	250	49	201	9	7	2	544	519	25
	4th	315	587	−272	244	48	196	5	8	−3	564	643	−79
1954	1st	356	617	−261	161	58	103	4	7	−3	580	682	−162
	2d	353	517	−164	198	50	148	5	5	—	557	572	−16
	3d	377	440	−63	219	56	163	6	10	−4	601	506	95
	4th	447	387	60	180	55	125	4	7	−3	631	449	183

1955	1st	425	423	2	150	60	90	2	12	−10	577	495	82
	2d	453	483	−30	165	80	85	11	7	4	628	570	58
	3d	525	469	56	188	63	125	3	9	−6	716	541	175
	4th	551	474	77	190	83	107	4	10	−6	746	567	179
1956	1st	566	531	35	180	82	98	3	13	−10	749	626	124
	2d	612	569	43	201	105	96	3	16	−13	816	691	125
	3d	605	682	−77	204	99	105	4	26	−22	814	807	6
	4th	620	688	−68	216	109	107	10	10	—	845	807	38
1957	1st	658	843	−185	198	126	72	5	24	−19	861	993	−132
	2d	658	991	−333	229	154	75	6	16	−10	894	1,161	−268
	3d	711	1,015	−304	202	126	76	12	10	2	926	1,152	−226
	4th	754	723	31	196	128	68	11	19	−7	962	869	92
1958	1st	696	618	78	158	114	44	3	20	−17	856	752	104
	2d	660	620	40	172	120	52	13	16	−3	846	757	89
	3d	647	592	55	177	105	72	35	16	19	858	713	145
	4th	725	638	87	196	124	72	30	16	14	950	778	173
1959	1st	696	638	58	173	121	52	50	22	28	920	781	139
	2d	749	665	84	183	134	49	25	22	3	956	821	136
	3d	831	743	88	189	142	47	35	84	−49	1,056	969	87
	4th	889	810	79	199	157	42	26	28	−2	1,114	995	119
1960	1st	844	827	17	188	155	33	33	18	15	1,065	1,000	65
	2d	867	930	−63	212	181	31	29	34	−5	1,108	1,145	−37
	3d	978	918	60	222	188	34	47	50	−3	1,246	1,156	91
	4th	1,037	954	83	239	204	35	31	43	−11	1,307	1,201	107
1961	1st	891	1,114	−223	198	224	−26	49	29	21	1,138	1,367	−228
	2d	923	1,282	−359	232	233	−1	102	41	62	1,257	1,556	−298
	3d	1,002	1,281	−279	205	229	−24	69	41	28	1,275	1,551	−275
	4th	1,103	1,247	−144	223	251	−28	98	46	52	1,424	1,544	−120

TABLE A-2 (cont'd)

Year	Quarter	Merchandise [a]			Invisibles [a]			Long-term Capital			Total [c] (except short-term capital)		
		Receipts	Payments	Net	Receipts	Payments	Net	Receipts	Payments	Net	Receipts	Payments	Net
1962	1st	1,049	1,177	−128	190	229	−40	114	83	31	1,354	1,490	−136
	2d	1,155	1,192	−37	204	260	−56	95	33	62	1,454	1,484	−30
	3d	1,230	1,064	166	213	251	−38	133	32	101	1,577	1,348	229
	4th	1,342	1,112	230	216	277	−61	116	48	68	1,674	1,437	237

[a] Procurement based on U.S. foreign economic aid funds and UNKRA funds is included in invisibles rather than in merchandise exports. This was the practice in published statistics until March 1960. Later published figures show these receipts with merchandise. To make this table consistent, the following sums have been shifted from visible to invisible receipts:

1960	2d quarter	$36 million	1961	1st quarter	$31 million	1962	1st quarter	$2.6 million
	3d quarter	38 million		2d quarter	30 million		2d quarter	2.7 million
	4th quarter	42 million		3d quarter	10 million		3d quarter	1.6 million
				4th quarter	3.2 million		4th quarter	2.7 million

[b] Long-term capital is included in invisibles for 1950 and 1951.

[c] Short-term capital movements were not reported in the foreign exchange statistics until April 1960, and since then only as net movements. Consequently, the total figures shown here are incomplete, with short-term capital omitted throughout. Net figures, including short-term capital movements, are shown since April 1960 in Table A-3 below.

Source: Bank of Japan, *Foreign Exchange Statistics Monthly*, various issues.

TABLE A-3. JAPAN'S FOREIGN EXCHANGE MOVEMENTS AND RESERVES, BY QUARTERS, 1956–1962

(In millions of dollars)

	Net Movements			*Reserves*		*Discrepancy*
Year and Quarter	*Without short-term capital (as in Table A-2)*	*Short-term capital*	*Total, including short-term capital*	*Total at end of quarter*	*Change*	*Change in reserves minus net movement*
1956						
1st	124					
2d	125			868		
3d	6			874	6	0
4th	38			941	67	29
1957						
1st	−132			738	−203	−71
2d	−268			511	−227	41
3d	−226			455	−56	170
4th	92			524	69	−23
1958						
1st	104			629	105	1
2d	89			718	89	0
3d	145			759	41	−104
4th	173			861	102	−71
1959						
1st	139			974	113	−26
2d	136			1,105	131	−5
3d	87			1,209	104	17
4th	119			1,322	113	−6
1960						
1st	65			1,361	39	−26
2d	−37	128	91	1,451	90	−2
3d	91	111	202	1,658	207	6
4th	107	54	161	1,824	166	5
1961						
1st	−228	383	155	1,997	173	19
2d	−298	226	−72	1,912	−85	−12
3d	−275	−7	−282	1,610	−302	−20
4th	−120	8	−112	1,486	−124	−12
1962						
1st	−136	229	93	1,561	75	−18
2d	−30	146	115	1,623	62	−53
3d	229	−126	103	1,720	97	−6
4th	237	−77	160	1,841	121	−39

Sources: Bank of Japan, *Foreign Exchange Statistics Monthly*, various issues; Japan, Ministry of Finance, *Quarterly Bulletin of Financial Statistics*, March 1959, p. 70, March 1963, p. 73.

TABLE A-4. BALANCE OF PAYMENTS OF JAPAN WITH THE UNITED STATES, BY YEARS, 1951–1962

(In millions of dollars)

	1951			*1952*		
Item	*Credit*	*Debit*	*Balance*	*Credit*	*Debit*	*Balance*
Goods and services (ordinary)	**683**	**691**	**−8**	**307**	**752**	**−445**
Merchandise trade	405	556	−151	222	626	−404
Services	278	135	143	85	126	−41
Transportation and insurance	5	68	−63	34	79	−45
Travel	6	2	4	6	3	3
Investment income	1	5	−4	3	7	−4
Private donations	21	10	11	25	6	19
Other	245	50	195	17	31	−14
Extraordinary items	**782**		**782**	**789**		**789**
U.S. economic aid to Japan	155		155	5		5
U.S. aid procurement in Japan	12		12	16		16
U.S. military expenditures [a]	615		615	768		768
Errors and omissions (net) [b]			**28**			**−3**
Capital and gold movements (ordinary) [c]	d	d	**−118**	**47**	**228**	**−181**
Private capital [c]				15	4	11
Long-term [c]				15	1	14
Short-term [c]				—	3	−3
Official and banking capital [c]				32	179	−147
Long-term [c]				36		36
Short-term [c]				−4	179	−183
Monetary gold				—	45	−45
Multilateral settlements			**−684**			**−160**

[a] Until 1960, estimated by Bank of Japan from figures showing total foreign military expenditures in Japan

[b] Beginning in 1959, includes "regional adjustments"; beginning in 1960, includes merchandise transactions abroad, which had previously been treated as an adjustment to commodity trade.

[c] In the capital account credits reflect changes in Japanese liabilities to U.S. residents, debits reflect changes in assets in the United States and in claims on residents of the United States.

[d] For 1951, details of the capital account and of gold movements, if any, are not known.

A second move to make the foreign exchange account look more like a balance of payments was made in April 1962, when a new item was introduced called "errors and omissions." This figure for the first time makes possible a reconciliation of reported foreign exchange movements with reported foreign exchange holdings.

Statistics on Foreign Exchange Reserves

Foreign exchange holdings or reserves have been reported by the Japanese Ministry of Finance quite separately from the reports of the Bank of Japan on foreign exchange movements. Until 1958 a series of figures on foreign ex-

1953			*1954*			*1955*			*1956*		
Credit	*Debit*	*Balance*	*Credit*	*Debit*	*Balance*	*Credit*	*Debit*	*Balance*	*Credit*	*Debit*	*Balance*
290	**755**	**−465**	**337**	**856**	**−519**	**475**	**784**	**−309**	**578**	**1,067**	**−489**
218	642	−424	257	716	−459	379	632	−253	413	856	−443
72	113	−41	80	140	−60	96	152	−56	165	271	−46
29	54	−25	24	67	−43	29	68	−39	68	110	−42
8	4	4	9	3	6	11	4	7	13	4	9
10	16	−6	7	19	−12	9	24	−15	20	26	−6
17	1	16	26	1	25	26	1	25	25	—	25
8	38	−30	14	50	−36	21	55	−34	39	71	−32
795		**795**	**595**		**595**	**575**		**575**	**621**		**621**
—		—	—		—	13		13	12		12
17		17	15		15	57		57	111		111
778		778	580		580	505		505	498		498
		−15			**7**			**−25**			**−55**
20	**68**	**−48**	**103**	**−146**	**249**	**117**	**216**	**−99**	**238**	**381**	**−143**
12	—	12	29	8	21	55	−5	60	72	85	−13
15	—	15	22	2	20	14	3	11	63	20	43
−3	—	−3	7	6	1	41	−8	49	9	65	−56
8	68	−60	74	−154	228	62	221	−159	166	296	−130
−6	2	−8	30	—	30	4	—	4	42	1	41
14	66	−52	44	−154	198	58	221	−163	124	295	−171
—	—	—	—	—	—	—	—	—	—	—	—
		−267			**−332**			**−142**			**66**

Notes: A dash (—) indicates that a figure is zero or less than $500,000.
Minor inconsistencies result from rounding.

change "holdings" was published, and its figures were very inclusive. In 1958 a more restrictive definition was adopted for a new series called "reserves," which omitted bilateral (open) account balances, working balances held by Japanese banks, and certain other items. The new series has continued down to the present.

Comparison of the old and new series was possible for about five years, since certain figures of the new series were published, going back to 1952. The relation between the two series varied sharply. At one extreme, March 31, 1953, "reserves" were actually above "holdings" by $110 million. At the other extreme, "holdings" exceeded "reserves" by $679 million, on March 31, 1955.[4]

[4] Ministry of Finance announcement, May 23, 1958 (processed).

TABLE A-4 (cont'd)

Item	1957 Credit	1957 Debit	1957 Balance	1958 Credit	1958 Debit	1958 Balance
Goods and services (ordinary)	**680**	**1,466**	**−786**	**793**	**1,120**	**−327**
Merchandise trade	469	1,197	−728	582	878	−296
Services	211	269	−58	211	242	−31
Transportation and insurance	82	132	−50	92	111	−19
Travel	17	5	12	18	5	13
Investment income	25	39	−14	19	34	−15
Private donations	26	1	25	28	—	28
Other	61	92	−31	54	92	−38
Extraordinary items	**577**		**577**	**505**		**505**
U.S. economic aid to Japan	10		10	10		10
U.S. aid procurement in Japan	118		118	91		91
U.S. military expenditures [a]	449		449	404		404
Errors and omissions (net) [b]			**1**			**−10**
Capital and gold movements (ordinary) [c]	**70**	**−436**	**506**	**15**	**413**	**−398**
Private capital [c]	79	45	34	65	12	53
Long-term [c]	37	21	16	73	16	57
Short-term [c]	42	24	18	−8	−4	−4
Official and banking capital [c]	−9	−481	472	−50	370	−420
Long-term [c]	26	—	26	1	1	—
Short-term [c]	−35	−481	446	−51	369	−420
Monetary gold	—	—	—	—	31	−31
Multilateral settlements			**−298**			**230**

[a] Until 1960, estimated by Bank of Japan from figures showing total foreign military expenditures in Japan.
[b] Beginning in 1959, includes "regional adjustments"; beginning in 1960, includes merchandise transactions abroad, which had previously been treated as an adjustment to commodity trade.
[c] In the capital account credits reflect changes in Japanese liabilities to U.S. residents, debits reflect changes in assets in the United States and in claims on residents of the United States.
[d] For 1951, details of the capital account and of gold movements, if any, are not known.

Foreign Exchange Movements vs. Foreign Exchange Reserves

The trouble with both series on foreign exchange balances was that neither agreed with the published statistics on foreign exchange movements. In fact, whereas the cumulative movement reported for the five fiscal years 1952 through 1957 showed net receipts of $310 million, the "holdings" of foreign exchange were reported at the end of the period to be $1,060 million, exactly the same as at the beginning of the period. Foreign exchange "reserves," on the other hand, were reported to have declined from $930 million to $629 million, or by $301 million.[5] For a country that has had to control its foreign exchange as tightly as Japan has, such discrepancies are remarkable.

[5] Same, and Bank of Japan, *Foreign Exchange Statistics Monthly.*

1959			*1960*			*1961*			*1962*		
Credit	*Debit*	*Balance*	*Credit*	*Debit*	*Balance*	*Credit*	*Debit*	*Balance*	*Credit*	*Debit*	*Balance*
1,153	**1,259**	**−106**	**1,220**	**1,730**	**−510**	**1,309**	**2,252**	**−943**	**1,701**	**2,076**	**−375**
925	957	−32	930	1,318	−388	985	1,704	−719	1,351	1,442	−91
228	302	−74	290	412	−122	324	548	−224	350	634	−284
102	138	−36	116	171	−55	123	220	−97	131	248	−117
26	12	14	31	27	4	35	35	—	35	30	5
36	45	−9	63	64	−1	67	88	−21	73	132	−59
34	1	33	44	1	43	46	2	44	44	3	41
30	106	−76	36	149	−113	53	203	−150	67	221	−154
489		**489**	**560**		**560**	**463**		**463**	**387**		**387**
—		—	—		—	—		—	—		—
111		111	147		147	74		74	10		10
378		378	413		413	389		389	377		377
		−182			**−45**			**−297**			**50**
238	**547**	**−309**	**554**	**652**	**−98**	**1,019**	**−165**	**1,184**	**589**	**481**	**108**
78	40	38	65	25	40	219	19	200	424	—	424
82	32	50	52	29	23	190	8	182	353	9	344
−4	8	−12	13	−4	17	29	11	18	71	−9	80
160	323	−163	489	612	−123	800	−184	984	165	481	−316
29	−3	32	−4	2	−6	18	3	15	32	1	31
131	326	−195	493	610	−117	782	−187	969	133	480	−347
—	184	−184	—	15	−15	—	—	—	—	—	—
		108			**93**			**−407**			**−170**

Notes: A dash (—) indicates that a figure is zero or less than $500,000.
Minor inconsistencies result from rounding.

Source: Bank of Japan.

Since 1958 these discrepancies have been generally much smaller. Still they persist, despite the detail in which the Japanese continue to control receipts and payments of foreign exchange. Table A-3 shows quarterly figures for seven years ending in 1962. During this period the discrepancies varied a good deal, but for the six and one-half years (from mid-1956 through 1962) reported foreign exchange movements indicate $206 million more of income than do reported changes in reserves. During the period from mid-1958 through 1962 the cumulative discrepancy came to nearly $353 million.

These discrepancy figures are what are now being reported in *Foreign Exchange Statistics Monthly* as errors and omissions. With this figure now published, we have an easy means of reconciling foreign exchange movements with announced reserves. It may be that with progressive liberalization of foreign exchange receipts and payments this discrepancy will tend to rise.

Appendix B

Commodity Groupings in Basic Trade Tables

The basic tables[1] on the commodity composition of Japanese foreign trade have been built up by selecting what appear to be the most significant export and import products. Japanese customs statistics do not perform this function well but do provide detailed information on the basis of which the student can make almost any grouping he might wish.[2]

The commodity categories chosen cannot be indicated precisely by short labels such as are used in the tables herein. Some readers may wish at times to have a more accurate and complete description of the categories. The code numbers by which items are designated in the customs statistics provide the best answer to this need. These codes gained increased importance in 1963 when the *Trade of Japan* (Annual Return) for 1962 appeared with no headings in English or Japanese, only code numbers to indicate which item is which.

The 1962 trade figures present other, more difficult problems for the analyst. A major revision of certain commodity categories was adopted, along with a modification of the notation system used in code designators. For this reason the 1962 code numbers are often different from those used in 1961 and earlier years. There had been minor code changes every year, but not until 1962 were the changes very extensive.

The 1962 changes, for instance, especially in the rapidly evolving field of machinery exports, have produced a number of new categories that I have not been able to fit precisely with categories for earlier years. In places where this problem seems serious enough to be worth the reader's attention, I have provided footnotes in the tables themselves and similar indications in the listings below.

[1] Table 5-2, Japan's Imports by Commodity, 1954, 1957, 1960, 1961, 1962; Table 6-2, Japan's Exports by Commodity, 1954, 1957, 1960, 1961, 1962; Table 7-4, Japan's Imports from the United States, by Commodity, 1954, 1957, 1960, 1961, 1962; and Table 8-1, Japan's Exports to the United States, by Commodity, 1954, 1957, 1960, 1961, 1962.

[2] See the Bibliographic Note below for a discussion of the customs statistics, how they are organized, and the forms of their publication.

The two tables that follow show code designators separately for 1961 and 1962. In general the 1961 codes apply also to the earlier years covered in the four basic tables (1954, 1957, and 1960). Where minor changes occurred in commodity grouping or code number between 1954 and 1961, the grouping used for earlier years has been as close as feasible to that of 1961.

TABLE B-1. JAPANESE IMPORT CODES
(Used in Tables 5-2 and 7-4)

Commodity	*1961* [a]	*1962*
Food, beverages, and tobacco	**0, 1**	**0, 1**
Wheat	041–01	041–0
Rice	042	042
Barley	043–01	043–0
Corn	044–01	044–0
Sugar	061–01, –02	061–1, –2
Animal feedstuffs	081	081
Unmanufactured tobacco	121	121
Raw materials, except fuel	**2**	**2**
Hides and skins (except furs)	211	211
Soybeans	221–04	221–4
Other oilseeds	221 less 221–04	221 less 221–4
Crude rubber and latex	231–01	231–1
Synthetic rubber	231–02	231–2
Logs and lumber	242, 243	242, 243
Pulp and waste paper	251	251
Raw wool (sheep's and lambs')	262–01	262–1
Raw cotton and linters	263–01, –02	263–1, –2
Phosphate rock	271–03	271–3
Crude salt	272–0510	276–320
Iron ore and concentrates	281–01	281
Iron and steel scrap	282	282
Nonferrous metal ores and concentrates	283	283
Nonferrous metal scrap	284	284
Mineral fuels and lubricants	**3**	**3**
Coal	311–01	321–4
Crude petroleum	312–01	331
Heavy oil	313–0330, –0340, –0350	332–4
Lubricating oils and greases	313–04	332–5
Fats and oils	**4**	**4**
Beef tallow	411–0210	411–321
Chemicals	**5**	**5**
Inorganic chemicals	511	513, 514, 515
Organic chemicals	512	512
Medicinal and pharmaceutical products	541	541
Potassic fertilizers	561–03	561–3
Synthetic plastic materials	599–01	58

TABLE B-1. (cont'd)

Commodity	*1961* [a]	*1962*
Manufactured goods classified by material	**6**	**6**
Pig iron	681–01	671–1, –2, –3
Steel plates, sheets, shapes, rails, etc.[b]	681–04, –05, –06, –07, –08	673, 674, 675, 676
Other iron and steel	(Total steel is 681)	(Total steel is 67)
Nonferrous metals	682, 683, 684, 685, 686, 687, 689	68
Machinery and transport equipment	**7**	**7**
Power-generating machinery	711	711
Office machinery	714	714
Machine tools and other metal-working machinery	715	715
Machinery for conveying, mining, and road construction [b]	716–03	718–4, 718–511 through –549, 719–311 through –349
Textile machinery	716–08	717–1
Electrical machinery and appliances	721	72
Automotive vehicles and parts	732	732
Aircraft and parts	734	734
Miscellaneous products and transactions	**8, 9**	**8, 9**
Scientific, etc., instruments and apparatus	861	861

[a] Codes for 1954, 1957, and 1960 are generally the same as for 1961. Where changes have occurred, the grouping for earlier years has been made to conform as closely as possible to that of 1961.

[b] Because of the extensive reorganization of the components of this item in 1961, coverage differs somewhat as between 1962 and earlier years.

TABLE B-2. JAPANESE EXPORT CODES

(Used in Tables 6-2 and 8-1)

Commodity	*1961* [a]	*1962*
Food, beverages, and tobacco	**0, 1**	**0, 1 (plus 512–710)**
Fish and fish products	031, 032	031, 032
Mandarin oranges (preserved)	053–0111	053–911
Tea	074–01	074–1
Monosodium glutamate	099–0960	512–710
Raw materials, including fuel, fats, and oils	**2, 3, 4**	**2, 3, 4**
Lumber	243	243
Raw silk	261–03	261–3
Synthetic fibers	266	266
Petroleum products	313	332
Fats and oils	4	4
Chemicals	**5**	**5 (less 512–710)**
Inorganic chemicals	511	513, 514, 515
Organic chemicals	512	512 less 512–710
Medicinal and pharmaceutical products	541	541
Manufactured fertilizers	561	561
Synthetic plastic materials	599–01	58
Manufactured goods classified by material	**6**	**6 (plus 897)**
Rubber manufactures	629	62
Wood manufactures	63	63
Plywood	631–02	631–2
Paper, pulp, and manufactures	64	64
Textiles	65	65
Woolen yarn	651–02	651–2
Cotton yarn	651–03, –04	651–3, –4
Other yarn and thread	651–01, –05, –06, –07, –09	651–1, –5, –6, –7, –8, –9
Cotton fabrics	652	652
Silk fabrics	653–01	653–1
Woolen and worsted fabrics	653–02	653–2
Synthetic fiber fabrics	653–05	653–4, –5, –6
Cordage and manufactures, incl. fishnets	655–06	655–6
Blankets, sheets, towels, etc.	656	656
Floor coverings	657	657
Nonmetallic mineral manufactures	66	66
Cement	661–02	661–2
Tiles and other clay construction materials	662–02	662–4
Glass and glassware	664, 665	664, 665
Pottery	666	666
Gems, jewelry, etc.	67	667, 681, 897
Pearls	672–03, –04	667–1
Costume jewelry	673–02	897–2
Iron and steel products	681	67
Nonferrous metals and products	682 through 687, 689	682 through 687, 689

TABLE B-2. (cont'd)

Commodity	*1961* [a]	*1962*
Manufactured goods classified by material (cont'd)		
Metal manufactures	69	69
Wire nails of iron and steel	699–0711	694–111
Hand tools and implements	699–12	695
Cutlery	699–16, –17	696
Machinery and transport equipment	**7**	**7**
Internal combustion engines (excl. aircraft engines)	711–05	711–5
Office machinery	714	714
Industrial machinery (incl. for mining and construction) [b]	716	717, 718, 719
Conveying, mining, and road machinery [b]	716–03	718–4, 718–511 through –520, 719–311 through –349
Textile machinery	716–08	717–1
Sewing machines	716–11	717–3
Ball and roller bearings and parts	716–14	719–7
Electrical equipment	72	72
Heavy electrical equipment	721–01	722–1
Electric light bulbs	721–03	729–2
Radio receivers	721–0412, –0413, –0414	724–2
Insulated wire and cable	721–13	723–1
Automotive vehicles and parts	732	732
Bicycles and parts	733–01, –02	733–1
Ships and boats	735	735
Miscellaneous products and transactions	**8, 9**	**8, 9 (less 897)**
Clothing	841	841
Underwear and nightwear	841–02, –04	841–1, 841–431 through –449
Outerwear	841–03, –05	841–0, 841–451 through –479
Gloves [c]	841–12	841–251, 841–320 through –339, 841–411 through –419
Shawls, comforters, and mufflers	841–192	841–221 through –229
Footwear	851	851
Instruments (optical, scientific, etc.)	861	861
Binoculars	861–0131, –0132, –0133	861–313, –314
Cameras and parts	861–0211 through –0239	861–410 through –480, 861–511, –512, –513
Sporting goods [c]	899–14	894–4
Toys	899–1511 through –1529	894–231 through –259

[a] Codes for 1954, 1957, and 1960 are generally the same as for 1961. Where changes have occurred, the grouping for earlier years has been made to conform as closely as possible to that of 1961.

[b] Because of the extensive reorganization of the components of this item in 1962, coverage differs somewhat as between 1962 and earlier years.

[c] Gloves for baseball and other sports are classified under gloves, not under sporting goods.

Bibliographic Note

From the opening of foreign trade in 1854 the language of Japan's foreign trade has been English. Much is published in English about Japanese foreign trade by the Japanese government, by Japanese banks, and by others. Japanese academic economists have published a good deal about foreign economic relations, some in English but much only in Japanese. The student of Japanese foreign trade who does not use the Japanese language will therefore have difficulty, as I have had, in following fully the Japanese academic work concerned.

This difficulty has been somewhat reduced in importance by the fact that the present work is focused on policy issues, while much Japanese academic study of international trade has focused on theoretical questions. In fact one Japanese professor who had devised a method for predicting certain trends in Japanese exports, when consulted about his results, declared, "It's not the results that interest me but the method."

To take account of thinking, especially academic, that is not reflected fully in English-language publications, I have relied mainly on Japanese specialists, along with other persons whose positions or command of the Japanese language qualify them to know about thinking in Japan. I have visited Japan four times since the end of the Occupation, in 1955, 1958, 1959, and 1963. In 1958 I devoted somewhat more than two months specifically to the present study, and I gave a good deal of attention to international economic questions during the other visits. Japanese of various schools of thought were consulted, along with other informed persons. In addition I had important assistance from a graduate student who worked with me at the University of Rochester in 1957 and 1958, Akira Takayama, now Assistant Professor of Economics at the International Christian University in Tokyo, who ably surveyed for me important Japanese-language sources. During the prolonged course of the writing and revision of this book I have consulted frequently with Japanese and American officials stationed in Washington, with visitors from Japan, and with others concerned with the issues involved. My visit to Japan in the summer of 1963 was made when the manuscript was virtually complete, and I was able to take new soundings and check my thinking against what I found in the high-income, mass-consumption Japan of today.

I. GENERAL SOURCES ON JAPANESE ECONOMIC AFFAIRS

A large volume of material is published on Japanese economic life. Much is available in English. Some reports, especially statistical periodicals, are printed in English and Japanese together. Other English reports are translations (frequently poor and carelessly printed) of Japanese originals. Original works in English are fewer and many of these, naturally enough, are produced in the United States.

Official Statistics and Reports

Aside from the specialized materials mentioned in appropriate places below, there are a number of worthwhile general statistical sources on Japanese economic affairs. Some of these publications are widely circulated and also easily obtainable from Japan. Two of the most valuable statistical publications come from the Statistics Department of the Bank of Japan; they are *Economic Statistics of Japan* (English and Japanese; Tokyo: Author, annual) and *Economic Statistics Monthly* (English and Japanese; Tokyo: Author). Each covers a wide range of subjects, the former more than the latter, with heavy emphasis on finance. Their tables are unusually reliable, not only in their structure and content, but also in their usual typographical accuracy (which contrasts sharply with some of the other Japanese publications in English). The annual gives mainly yearly figures, often in tables covering a long time span. Original source is shown for every table in both publications, and footnotes are frequent enough to be helpful, although far less full than in many American publications.

The Economic Planning Agency of the Japanese government produces an indispensable annual report and a useful statistical monthly. *Economic Survey of Japan* (English translation of Japanese original; Tokyo: The Japan Times, annual) is a large (453 pages for FY 1960–1961), detailed analytical study covering a fiscal year, with a vast amount of statistical information, both in the body of the survey and in a statistical annex. This source is essential to any serious study of Japan's economy in recent years. Much of its statistical information is different from that available elsewhere; for instance, where its tables and charts cover familiar ground they often refer to fiscal years while other sources refer to calendar years. Unfortunately, the English edition contains so many mechanical errors that statistical information, and even at times the text, cannot be wholly relied on. EPA's *Japanese Economic Statistics* (English; Tokyo: Author, monthly) parallels in large part the Bank of Japan's *Economic Statistics Monthly* but is much briefer on finance and puts more stress on industry and trade, and many tables show a longer time series. An unusual feature of *Japanese Economic Statistics* is that many tables give historical data in monthly averages rather than annual or monthly totals. This publication has changed form, but not title, since its origin in the early days of the Occupation. The author agency, on the other hand, has changed its name several times without essential change in the nature of its work.

Another basic statistical source is Japan, Office of the Prime Minister, Bureau of Statistics, *Japan Statistical Yearbook* (English and Japanese; Tokyo: Japan Statistical Association, annual since 1949). Replacing the *Statistical Yearbook of the Empire of Japan* (1882–1941), this large compendium is the most comprehensive of Japan's official statistical annuals, somewhat comparable to the *Statistical Abstract of the United States*. The 1961 volume runs to 557 pages, divided into 31 chapters covering land area and use, population, a wide variety of economic phenomena, and certain other subjects, including education, health, justice, and some international comparisons. Exceptional accuracy combined with great detail and useful notes, including source indications for most tables, make this a fundamental tool for study of contemporary public affairs in Japan. But its completeness and thoroughness make it appear less promptly than other sources of most of the statistics used in this study.

Many of these same statistics are available on a monthly basis also, in Japan, Office of the Prime Minister, Bureau of Statistics, *Monthly Bulletin of Statistics* (English and Japanese; Tokyo: Author). This is the publication referred to as *Monthly Statistics of Japan* in the publication discussed in the following paragraph.

The fullest available description of Japanese official statistical organization, methods, and output is presented annually in Japan, Administrative Management Agency, Statistical Standards Bureau, *Supplement to the Monthly Statistics of Japan: Explanatory Notes* (English and Japanese; Tokyo: Author, annual). This new source (first published in 1962) should be extremely valuable to anyone first attempting to find his way in the vast array of Japanese statistical reports. The 1963 edition contains 163 double-page spreads, each consisting of one page in Japanese and one in English, explaining each table in the *Monthly Bulletin of Statistics* and describing methods of survey, statistical agencies, and their responsibilities. An introduction describes the Japanese government's statistical organization, personnel, legislation, classification systems, and related matters.

The Economic Research Institute of the Economic Planning Agency does important work, some of which is reflected in its *Economic Bulletin*, which began in February 1959 and of which ten issues had appeared by July 1962. Each issue is a substantial monograph. Each issue carries in an introductory statement the following paragraph:

> Although it is attached to the Economic Planning Agency of the Japanese Government, the Economic Research Institute, established in July 1958, conducts its activities independently of Government policies. It aims to carry out scientific and objective studies on problems of the Japanese economy with respect to its growth, cycles and structure so as to facilitate improvement of economic policies.

The Ministry of Foreign Affairs has been issuing for information purposes a *Statistical Survey of Economy of Japan* (English; Tokyo: Author, annual). In tables and charts this small (72 pages in 1962) volume gives a quick and vivid impression of the main features of the Japanese economy.

Japan Report, edited and published by the Japan Information Service,

Consulate General of Japan, New York, is a brief (8–15 pages), semimonthly, free information bulletin that contains some economic information and Japanese official commentary.

The following official reports on agriculture and labor are of value in connection with some of the subjects discussed in this study:

Japan. Ministry of Agriculture and Forestry. Statistics and Survey Division. *Abstract of Statistics on Agriculture, Forestry, and Fisheries.* Tokyo: Author, annual since 1922 (excepting years 1937 to 1952).

———. ———. *Japan's Agriculture and Forestry White Paper.* Tokyo: Author, 1957. 80 p. (This is the only one in this series to be published in English up to the present.)

———. Ministry of Labor. *Japan Labor Year Book.* Tokyo: Author, 1955, 114 p.; 1956, 69 p.; 1957, 86 p.

———. ———. *Monthly Labor Statistics and Research Bulletin.* Tokyo: Author, issued since January 1948.

———. ———. Division of Labor Statistics and Research. *Year Book of Labor Statistics and Research.* English and Japanese; Tokyo: Author, issued since 1948.

Japanese Bank Reports on Economic Affairs

Japanese banks publish in English a large amount of useful economic reporting and analysis. Their publications reflect strong research departments and the importance of foreign business to leading Japanese banks. All the publications are furnished upon request without charge.

The leading bank publications in English, other than the statistical publications mentioned above, are listed below:

Bank of Japan. Economic Research Department. *Monthly Economic Review.* English version of Japanese original; Tokyo: Author. Each issue, of 10 to 16 pages, contains a section, "General Economic Conditions," and a page of "Selected Economic Indicators." Usually there is also an interpretive article on an aspect of Japanese finance. Valuable mainly for these articles and as a check on other reporting.

———. ———. *News Survey.* English; Tokyo: Author, appears about twice a month. A single sheet with about a half dozen news items, mostly from the Japanese press. One issue each month has on the back a series of statistical indicators. Comes promptly and consequently is sometimes the first source to arrive with news or statistics.

Bank of Tokyo. *Weekly Review.* English; Tokyo: Author. Each issue has 7 pages of news items prepared by the bank's economic research department. Once a month a folding sheet of economic statistics is added. Reflecting the prominence of this bank in Japanese foreign trade and the strength of the bank's research activities, the review is a major source of news about Japanese foreign trade, and also about investment and technology flows and important features in the domestic economy. The frequency and promptness of this review, as well as its focus and large volume of reporting, make it an unusually valuable source for the student of Japan's foreign economic relations.

———. *Semiannual Report.* English; Tokyo: Author. Each issue contains a business report on the bank itself, an article, usually on an aspect of Japan's foreign economic relations, and a statistical section. The articles are significant research reports and have proved very valuable in this study.

The Dai Ichi Bank, Ltd. *Monthly Report on Business Conditions in Japan.* English; Tokyo: Author. Each 4-page issue contains a section on current economic affairs and an article on a particular industry.

The Fuji Bank, Ltd. *Fuji Bank Bulletin.* English; Tokyo: Author, quarterly. Contains articles on domestic and international economic subjects, along with reports on the bank's own operations and statistical tables. Most issues have about 40 pages of text, but in 1961 a special issue (v. 11, no. 4) on *Banking in Modern Japan* ran to 245 pages.

The Industrial Bank of Japan, Ltd. Research Department. *Survey of Japanese Finance and Industry.* English; Tokyo: Author, quarterly. Through 1962 it appeared bimonthly, with each issue usually 12–16 pages but occasionally up to 30 pages, containing two or more review articles, usually on particular industries, and tables showing foreign investments in Japan. The first 1963 issue was labeled January–March 1963 and marked "Published Quarterly." It contained 30 pages of reviews of trends in major Japanese industries, covering mainly the period April–September 1962, but including charts and a few tables that cover longer periods.

The Mitsui Bank, Ltd. Research Department. *Monthly Review.* English; Tokyo: Author. Eight pages each issue, mostly devoted to a leading article.

The Nippon Kangyo Bank, Ltd. Foreign Department. *NKB Research Monthly.* English; Tokyo: Author, issued approximately every month. Eight pages each issue, devoted to a selected Japanese industry.

Sumitomo Bank, Ltd. Information Department. *Sumitomo Bank Review: Economic Conditions in Japan.* English; Osaka: Author, monthly.

Journals, Newspapers, and Other Periodicals

The leading unofficial economic journal in the English language is *The Oriental Economist* (Tokyo: The Oriental Economist, monthly since 1934. Its articles and notes cover the whole range of subjects concerned with Japanese economic affairs, as well as a few other subjects. Each issue contains a small but useful statistical section. The Oriental Economist's *Japan Economic Yearbook* (Tokyo: Author) contains brief reviews on a wide range of subjects, along with statistical tables.

The Mitsubishi Economic Research Institute publishes a useful *Monthly Circular,* subtitled *Survey of Economic Conditions in Japan* (Tokyo: Author). Its size, content, and organization are much like the larger of the bank reports mentioned earlier.

A good deal of the daily news about Japan refers to economic affairs, and one can follow events in a general way in *The New York Times.* English-language daily newspapers in Japan are *The Japan Times, Asahi,* and *The Mainichi Daily News.* These and other Japanese papers publish weekly or other summary editions in English, including *The Japan Times Weekly* and *The Mainichi Daily News, Monthly International Edition.* A notable new development took place in December 1962 when the *Nihon Keizai Shimbun* (*Japan Economic Journal*) started publication of its *Weekly International Edition.* Volume 1, no. 1 of this new weekly, dated December 4, 1962, bears the legend "Japan's Oldest and Most Influential Economic Daily." This boast seems to be true, for this paper, in its morning and evening editions published in Tokyo and Osaka, commands attention and respect from businessmen and from officials concerned with economic affairs.

Some items from Japanese-language newspapers and magazines are summarized elsewhere. In addition to the Bank of Japan's *News Survey,* cited, the International Monetary Fund's *International Financial News Survey* (Washton: Author, Weekly) has recently had an item on Japan in nearly every issue, especially from *Nihon Keizai Shimbun,* cited.

The American Embassy in Tokyo issues two especially valuable mimeographed reports: *Daily Summary of the Japanese Press* and *Summaries of Selected Japanese Magazines* (weekly since 1953). These rich sources on Japanese sentiment are available at the Department of State in Washington, and copies are provided free to those scholars lucky enough to be included in the limited distribution.

The United Nations Economic Commission for Asia and the Far East in Bangkok publishes a number of reports touching on Japan. The basic dilemma for ECAFE is that Japan is so different from other countries in the region that it is difficult to make meaningful comparisons and aggregates that include Japan, while ECAFE is not much interested in studying a single country without comparison with others in the region. Nevertheless the *Economic Survey of Asia and the Far East* (Bangkok: Author, annual since 1948) does contain a good deal of information on Japan. In a smaller degree so does the *Economic Bulletin for Asia and the Far East* (Bangkok: Author, quarterly since 1950, including as one of its issues the annual *Survey*).

Other periodicals frequently refer to Japanese economic affairs. *The Economist* (London) is particularly perceptive. *The Wall Street Journal* has had a reporter stationed in Japan for a number of years, and its occasional articles are of high quality. *The Journal of Commerce* (New York) frequently publishes useful articles on Japanese economic affairs. *The Far Eastern Economic Review,* a weekly published in Hong Kong, carries something about Japan in every issue. This journal's *Far Eastern Economic Review Yearbook* contains round-up articles that include a good deal on Japan.

Books

Three books stand out among general sources on Japan's economy since World War II. Two were published in 1958. Each of these is a short but comprehensive, readable, and perceptive report and interpretation by a leading Western student of Japanese economic affairs. They are:

Allen, George Cyril. *Japan's Economic Recovery.* Issued under the auspices of the Royal Institute of International Affairs. London, New York, Toronto: Oxford University Press, 1958. 215 p.

Cohen, Jerome B. *Japan's Postwar Economy.* Bloomington: Indiana University Press, 1958. 262 p.

The third is a reprint of the brilliant interpretation that appeared as a special supplement in two issues of *The Economist* (London), September 1 and 8, 1962 (pp. 787–824 and 907–936). Attention is focused mainly on the forces affecting economic growth, the prospects for continued growth and the policy lessons to be drawn. The book version bears the same title as the supplements: *Consider Japan* (London: Duckworth, 1963, 121 p.).

Another unusually valuable item is the following report, which will be mentioned again below in connection with materials on Japan's balance of payments and also on policy:

Committee for Economic Development. *Japan in the Free World Economy.* A statement on national policy, including a statement by the Japan Committee for Economic Development. New York: Author, 1963. 58 + 45 p.

A number of books, or parts of books, deal with specific aspects of the economy. Those that relate to particular parts of the present study are indicated in appropriate places below. One of more general interest is Shigeto Tsuru, *Essays on Japanese Economy,* Institute of Economic Research, Hitotsubashi University, Economic Research Series No. 2 (Tokyo: Kinokuniya Bookstore Co., 1958; 241 p.). Six of Tsuru's essays were written between 1949 and 1957 with respect to current conditions; these provide a record of the views of an informed Japanese observer. More recent and closer to the present study is the little volume of the Economist Intelligence Unit, *The Japanese Economy,* a survey prepared for the Federation of British Industries (London: Federation of British Industries, 1962; 126 p.). In four chapters this survey covers the economy generally, the inflow to Japan of foreign capital and techniques, Japan as a market, and the prospects for British exports, licensing agreements, and investments.

The books listed below are other sources dealing broadly with Japan's postwar economy, or some major aspect thereof:

Abegglen, James C. *The Japanese Factory: Aspects of Its Social Organization.* Glencoe, Ill.: The Free Press, 1958. 142 p.

Ackerman, Edward A. *Japan's Natural Resources and Their Relation to Japan's Economic Future.* University of Chicago Press, 1953. 655 p.

Cohen, Jerome B. *Economic Problems of Free Japan.* Princeton: Center of International Studies, 1952. 92 p.

Japan F.A.O. Association. *An Introduction to Technical Development in Japanese Agriculture.* Tokyo: Author, 1959. 127 p.

Kirby, E. Stuart. *Japan's Economic Future.* United Kingdom Paper No. 1. London: Royal Institute of International Affairs, 1947. 50 p.

Levine, Solomon B. *Industrial Relations in Postwar Japan.* Urbana: University of Ilinois Press, 1958. 200 p.

Matsuo, Takano. *Rice and Rice Cultivation in Japan.* Tokyo: Institute of Asian Economic Affairs, 1961. 180 p.

Mitsubishi Economic Research Institute (MERI). *Mitsui-Mitsubishi-Sumitomo: Present Status of the Former Zaibatsu Enterprises.* Tokyo: Author, 1955. 360 p.

Sapir, H. Michael. *The Economics of Competitive Coexistence: Japan, China, and the West.* Washington: National Planning Association, 1959. 79 p.

Tobata, Seiichi. *An Introduction to Agriculture of Japan.* Tokyo: Agriculture, Forestry, and Fisheries Productivity Conference, 1958. 74 p.

Yamanaka, Tokutaro, and Yoshio Kobayashi. *The History and Structure of Japan's Small and Medium Industries–with Two Specific Surveys.* Tokyo: Science Council, 1957. 89 p.

Articles

Articles about Japan's economy appear in journals all over the world. Of the few selected for inclusion here, some seem to me to contribute new information or unusual insights; others, by contrast, state widely held views.

Drucker, Peter. "Japan Tries for a Second Miracle," *Harper's,* March 1963, pp. 72–78.

Lockwood, William W. "'The Socialistic Society': India and Japan," *Foreign Affairs,* October 1958, pp. 117–130.

Nakayama, Seiki. "The Rice Diet," *Japan Quarterly,* April–June 1961, pp. 226–233.

Ohkawa, Kazushi. "Significant Changes in Japanese Agriculture since 1945," *Journal of Farm Economics,* December 1961.

Okita, Saburo. "Japan's Economic Prospects," *Foreign Affairs,* October 1960, pp. 123–131.

———. "A Reappraisal of Japan's Economy," *Japan Quarterly,* July–September 1959, pp. 282–290.

Olson, Laurence. "A Japanese Small Industry: A Letter From Kyoto," *Explorations in Entrepreneurial History,* April 1956, pp. 233–244.

Ono, Kazuichiro, and Heitaro Namba. "The Growth of Iron and Steel Industry in Japan and the Problem of Raw Materials," *Kyoto University Economic Review,* April 1955, pp. 11–45, and October 1955, pp. 50–69.

Ota, Kaoru. "The Productivity Movement in Japan and Its Problems; The Sohyo Viewpoint," *Japan Quarterly,* July–September 1956, pp. 296–301.

Rockefeller, John D., 3rd. "Japan Tackles Her Problems," *Foreign Affairs,* July 1954, pp. 577–587.

Tsuru, Shigeto. "Growth and Stability of the Postwar Japanese Economy," *American Economic Review,* May 1961, pp. 400–411.

Materials on the Occupation and Earlier Periods

Allen, George Cyril. *A Short Economic History of Modern Japan, 1867–1937.* London: Allen & Unwin, 1946. 200 p.

Barnett, Robert W. "Occupied Japan: The Economic Aspect," in Seymour E. Harris, *Foreign Economic Policy for the United States.* Cambridge, Mass.: Harvard University Press, 1948. Pp. 104–133.

Cohen, Jerome B. *Japan's Economy in War and Reconstruction,* with a foreword by Sir George Sansom. Minneapolis: University of Minnesota Press, 1949. 545 p.

Ehrlich, Edna E., and Frank M. Tamagna. "Japan," in Benjamin H. Beckhart, ed., *Banking Systems.* New York: Columbia University Press, 1954. Pp. 517–572.

Fearey, Robert A. *The Occupation of Japan. Second Phase: 1948–56.* New York: Macmillan, 1950. 239 p.

Fine, Sherwood. "Japan's Postwar Industrial Recovery," *Contemporary Japan,* v. 21, 1952–53, pp. 165–216.

Japan. Economic Stabilization Board. Research Section. "Over-all Report on Damages Caused by the World War II," in *Analysis of Post-War Japanese Economy.* Tokyo: Author, 1950. 84 p.

Johnston, Bruce F., M. Hosoda and Y. Kusumi. *Japanese Food Management of World War II.* Stanford University Press, 1953. 283 p.

Lockwood, William W. *The Economic Development of Japan: Growth and Structural Change, 1868–1938.* Princeton University Press, 1954. 612 p.

Martin, Edwin M. *The Allied Occupation of Japan.* Stanford University Press, 1948. 155 p.

Ohkawa, Kazushi. *The Growth Rate of the Japanese Economy since 1878.* Tokyo: Kinokuniya Bookstore Co., 1957. 250 p.

Orchard, John E. *Japan's Economic Position: The Progress of Industrialization.* New York: McGraw-Hill, 1930. 504 p.

Rosovsky, Henry. *Capital Formation in Japan, 1868–1940.* Glencoe, Ill.: The Free Press, 1961. 358 p.

Schumpeter, Elizabeth Boody, and others. *The Industrialization of Japan and Manchukuo, 1930–1940: Population, Raw Materials and Industry.* New York: Macmillan, 1940. 944 p.

Supreme Commander for the Allied Powers. Economic and Scientific Section. *Mission and Accomplishments of the Occupation in the Economic and Scientific Fields.* Tokyo: Author, 1949. 30 p. (Processed.)

U.S. Strategic Bombing Survey. Over-all Economic Effects Division. *The Effects of Strategic Bombing on Japan's War Economy.* Washington: GPO, 1946. 244 p.

II. JAPAN'S BALANCE OF PAYMENTS AND FOREIGN EXCHANGE STATISTICS

(Chapter 3 and Appendix A)

The primary sources of public information on Japan's balance of payments and foreign exchange movements are, as indicated in Appendix A, the following:

Bank of Japan. Foreign Department. *Balance of Payments of Japan.* English and Japanese; Tokyo: Author, annual since 1954.
———. ———. *Foreign Exchange Statistics Monthly.* English and Japanese; Tokyo: Author, since October 1950.
International Monetary Fund. *Balance of Payments Yearbook.* Washington: Author, since 1947.

Most of the balance-of-payments figures used in this study come from the third of these publications. The first has been used as a supplement. The second is the source of figures on foreign exchange movements.

Foreign exchange reserves, including gold holdings, are reported officially by the Ministry of Finance, mainly in the form of announcements to the press. Perhaps the most official of the English-language sources in which those figures are published is the *Quarterly Bulletin of Financial Statistics,* issued by the Ministry of Finance (Tokyo: Author, three times a year with 2d and 3d quarters covered in a single issue). But this publication appears so late after the issuance of reserve figures that for most purposes newspapers and other secondary sources are used not only in this study but generally.

Secondary sources of basic information on Japan's balance of payments are numerous but of varying value, often low. Among the more useful is a summary table in Bank of Japan, *Economic Statistics of Japan.* In the 1962 issue, for instance, on pages 261 and 262 the main items in the balance of payments are shown, with both debits and credits, for each of the years 1957 through 1961 and for January–June 1962. A briefer and less useful summary appears in the Ministry of Finance's *Quarterly Bulletin,* cited. In the March 1963 issue, for 4th quarter, 1962 fiscal year, on p. 72 there are figures for January–September 1962. In the preceding issue, labeled 2d and 3d quarter, 1962 fiscal year, December 1962, p. 72 gives preliminary figures for 1961.

Two other useful secondary sources are the *Japan Statistical Yearbook* and the *Monthly Bulletin of Statistics,* both issued by the Office of the Prime Minister. The user of these has available the excellent explanations in *Supplement to the Monthly Statistics of Japan: Explanatory Notes,* issued by the Statistical Standards Bureau of the Administrative Management Agency. (In the issue dated January 1963 a clear explanation on balance-of-payments and foreign exchange statistics and tables appears on pages 97 and 98.)

Mainly because of the confusion and imprecision in secondary sources on Japan's balance of payments, as described in Appendix A, such sources have not often been found useful in this study. Even the two sources cited above, one issued by the Bank of Japan, which actually compiles balance-of-payments statistics, the other issued by the Ministry of Finance, which is officially responsible for figures supplied to the International Monetary Fund, have not proved helpful here. And, as an illustration of Japanese problems with the English language, we may note that in both of the cited issues of the *Quarterly Bulletin* debit columns are entitled "Debt."

Secondary sources on foreign exchange movements and reserves are, by contrast, generally consistent, reliable, and prompt in appearance. The problems of definition and consistency discussed in Appendix A cause less difficulty when the reader wants foreign exchange movements than when he wants the balance of payments, even though the latter term is frequently applied to the former information. If it is available, the easiest and most satisfactory source of summary information on foreign exchange movements and reserves is the Bank of Japan's *Economic Statistics Monthly,* although for one interested in details the primary source, *Foreign Exchange Statistics Monthly,* is available just about as promptly (in the United States about three months after the end of the latest month covered).

For information on both the balance of payments and foreign exchange an excellent source is *International Financial Statistics* of the International Monetary Fund (Washington: Author, monthly since 1948). For a small but useful selection of news items, mainly from the Japanese press, the IMF's *International Financial News Survey* (Washington: Author, weekly) has recently been a valuable source.

The general sources on the Japanese economy, discussed in the preceding section of this Bibliographic Note, are likely to provide as much on these subjects as the nonspecialist will usually require.

Reports, analyses, and interpretations of Japan's balance of payments are a normal part of many discussions on Japanese economic affairs. But detailed and careful analyses are remarkably few. Probably the main reason is that persons with the competence and need for such analyses are mostly officials whose most detailed work is not shared with the public.

The items listed below include the major works and a selection of other material on the subjects indicated.

Japan's International Accounts Before World War II

Furuya, Seikow Yoshisada. *Japan's Foreign Exchange and Her Balance of International Payments, with Special Reference to Recent Theories of Foreign Exchange.* New York: Columbia University Press; London: King & Son, 1928. 208 p.

Gordon, Margaret S. "Japan's Balance of International Payments, 1904–1931," in E. B. Schumpeter and others, *The Industrialization of Japan and Manchukuo, 1930–1940.* New York: Macmillan, 1940. Pp. 865–925.

Horie, Yasuzo. "Japan's Balance of International Payments in the Early Meiji Period," *Kyoto University Economic Review,* April 1954, pp. 16–34.

Hunsberger, Warren S. *The International Financial Position of Japan,* Yale Ph.D. Dissertation, 1937. 374 p. (Typewritten.)

———. "Japan's Position in International Payments," *Far Eastern Survey,* June 15, 1938, pp. 133–139.

———. "The Yen Bloc in Japan's Expansion Program," *Far Eastern Survey,* November 9, 1938, pp. 251–258.

Inouye, Junnosuke. *Problems of the Japanese Exchange, 1914–1926.* London: Macmillan, 1931. 263 p.

Moulton, Harold G. (with the collaboration of Junichi Ko). *Japan: An Economic and Financial Appraisal.* Washington: Brookings Institution, 1931. 645 p.

Schumpeter, E. B. "Manchukuo, the Key to Japan's Foreign Exchange Problem," *Far Eastern Survey,* May 12, 1937, pp. 107–112.

———. "Politics and the Yen," *Far Eastern Survey,* May 26, 1937, pp. 117–122.

Selected References on Japan's Basic Payments Problem After World War II

This listing omits Japan's economic plans from 1955 on, but includes several of the studies that preceded these later plans. References to the plans will be made below in the section on Japanese foreign economic policy.

Cohen, Jerome B. "The International Aspects of Japan's Economic Situation," in Hugh Borton and others, *Japan Between East and West.* New York: Harper, for the Council on Foreign Relations, 1957. Pp. 108–152.

Committee for Economic Development. *Japan in the Free World Economy.* A statement on national policy, including a statement by the Japan Committee for Economic Development. New York: Author, 1963. 58 + 45 p.

Horie, Shigeo. "Japan's Balance of Payments," *Japan Report,* August 1, 1960, pp. 8–10.

Hunsberger, Warren S. *Japan in United States Foreign Economic Policy.* Study prepared for the Subcommittee on Foreign Economic Policy of the U.S. Joint Economic Committee, 87th Cong., 1st sess. Washington: GPO, 1961. 27 p.

Institute of World Economy. *The Conditions of Japan's Economic Self-Support—With Respect Mainly to External Relations.* Tokyo: Author, 1950. 47 p.

Irvine, Reed J. "Japan's Balance of Payments Prospects," *Far Eastern Survey,* December 31, 1952, pp. 196–203.

Japan. Self-Supporting Council. *Report on Economic Self-Supporting Program,* Submitted to the President of the Economic Stabilization Board. Tokyo: Author, January 20, 1951. 35 p.

Kiuchi, Nobutane. "False Assumptions About the Japanese Economy," *Foreign Affairs,* April 1956, pp. 459–468.

Okita, Saburo. "A Reappraisal of Japan's Economy," *Japan Quarterly,* July–September 1959, pp. 282–290.

Foreign Exchange Problems, Procedures and Rates

Bank of Japan. Foreign Exchange Control Department. *Guidance for Preparation and Submittal of Reports on Foreign Exchange Transactions.* Tokyo: Author, 1952. 21 p.

———. ———. *Manual of Foreign Exchange and Foreign Trade System in Japan.* Tokyo: Author, 1955. 38 p.

Bank of Tokyo. "Foreign Exchange Budget: Compilation and Operation," *Semiannual Report,* September 1956, pp. 5–32.

———. "Gold in Japan," *Semiannual Report,* September 1953, pp. 6–41.

———. "Postwar Development of Japan's Foreign Exchange System," *Semiannual Report,* September 1953, pp. 42–71.

Japan. Ministry of Finance. Financial Commissioner's Office. *Guide to Economic Laws of Japan.* Tokyo: Kobunsha Co., 1950. 876 pp.

——. ——. *Japan. Laws, Ordinances and Other Regulations concerning Foreign Exchange and Foreign Trade.* Tokyo: Foreign Exchange Study Association, annual.

McDiarmid, Orville J. "The Japanese Exchange Rate," *Far Eastern Survey,* June 15, 1949, pp. 133–135.

Tatemoto, Masahiro. "Exchange Depreciation, National Income and the Balance of Trade," *The Economic Science* (Economic Society of Nagoya University), July 1955, pp. 1–10.

Watanabe, Tsunehiko, and Ryutaro Komiya. "Findings from Price Comparisons, Principally Japan vs. the United States," *Weltwirtschaftliches Archiv,* no. 1, 1958, pp. 81–96.

Cycles in the Balance of Payments and Foreign Exchange Position

Emery, Robert F. "The Japanese Measures to Restore Economic Equilibrium," *Asian Survey,* June 1962, pp. 33–39.

Fuji Bank. "Recent Developments in Japan's International Payments Balance," *Fuji Bank Bulletin,* June 1960, pp. 9–18.

Narvekar, P. R. "The Cycle in Japan's Balance of Payments, 1955–58," *Staff Papers* (IMF), December 1961, pp. 380–411.

——. "The 1954–55 Improvement in Japan's Balance of Payments," *Staff Papers* (IMF), November 1957, pp. 143–169.

Patrick, Hugh T. "Monetary Policy in Japan's Economic Growth, 1945–1959," *Far Eastern Survey,* May 1959, pp. 65–71.

Reparations

Bennett, Martin T. "Japanese Reparations: Fact or Fantasy," *Pacific Affairs,* v. 21, no. 2 (1948), pp. 185–194.

Chang, Hsiu-hai. "The Treaty with Japan: A Chinese View," *Foreign Affairs,* April 1948, pp. 504–514.

Itagaki, Yoichi. "Reparations and Southeast Asia," *Japan Quarterly,* October–December 1959, pp. 410–419.

Japan. "Reparations Agreement between Japan and the Republic of the Philippines Signed at Manila, May 9, 1956," *Contemporary Japan,* v. 24, nos. 4–6 (1956), pp. 362–369.

Miyata, Kiyozo. "Reparations and Japan's Economy," *Asian Affairs,* September 1956, pp. 233–245.

Overseas Consultants, Inc. *Report on Industrial Reparations Survey of Japan to the United States of America, February 1948.* New York: Author, 1948. 224 p. + exhibits.

Ozawa, Takeo. "Japanese Foreign Debts and Reparations Problems," *Asian Affairs,* September 1956, pp. 274–289.

Pauley, Edwin W. *Report on Japanese Reparations to the President of the United States, November 1945 to April 1946.* Washington: GPO, 1946. 52 p.

Reday, Joseph Z. "Reparations from Japan," *Far Eastern Survey,* June 29, 1949, pp. 145–151.

Yamamoto, Noburo. "Reparations and Economic Cooperation–Influence of Japan's Reparations on the Economic Development of Southeast Asia," *Asian Affairs,* September 1956, pp. 246–259.

III. CAPITAL AND TECHNOLOGY MOVEMENTS
(Chapter 4)

The principal public sources, in English, of information on these interconnected subjects are indicated in the footnotes to Chapter 4. Far more information is available in Japanese than in English.

The Foreign Capital Research Society at the Bank of Japan for a number of years issued two principal annual publications, one to attract potential foreign investors, the other to report the cases of actual investment. The first, called *Japanese Industry,* is a slick 156 pages (1962 edition) of text, tables, and beautiful color pictures, mainly on industries. Tables on foreign capital and technology imported into Japan were a regular feature of each volume through 1961 (pp. 151–154 in the 1961 issue), but in the 1962 issue these have been reduced to one brief table (on p. 30). The other annual publication, *Statistical Data and List of Principal Cases of Foreign Capital Investment in Japan,* ceased publication with the issue that gave information as of March 31, 1960. That issue, following the general form of its predecessors, gave 89 pages of detailed information, case by case and industry by industry, of technology import, foreign direct investments in Japanese firms, and foreign private loans (other than short-term commercial credits) to Japanese firms.

More abbreviated statistical reports are made in other sources, for example, the Bank of Japan's *Economic Statistics of Japan,* and Industrial Bank of Japan's *Survey of Japanese Finance and Industry.* The latter publication, in issues published before the end of 1962, usually included two pages of statistics on capital and technology import, but for odd dates. The issue for September/October 1962, for example, presented statistics as of October 14, 1962.

Certain kinds of capital movements affecting Japan are reported very fully. The World Bank and the Export–Import Bank of Washington issue detailed reports on the status of all their loans; Japan is a prominent customer of each bank.

The most comprehensive and authoritative statistics on Japan's public obligations to foreign creditors are contained in the Prospectuses filed with the Securities and Exchange Commission in Washington whenever a bond issue of the Japanese government, or one carrying a government guarantee, is floated in the United States. Some of these are referred to in footnotes to Chapter 4.

Several sources offer information to prospective foreign investors in Japanese business, both to firms that might make direct investments and to a firm or individual possibly interested in the Japanese stock market. Japanese securities dealers provide a growing volume of information. An example is *Investors Digest,* published monthly in Tokyo by the Yamaichi Securities Company, Ltd. since 1951. The U.S. Department of Commerce provides a wide range of services and publications aimed at helping Americans who might be interested in doing business in Japan.

Sources dealing with Japanese policy on international movements of capital and technology will be discussed below, along with sources on policy related to commodity trade.

IV. JAPANESE COMMODITY TRADE

(Chapters 5, 6, 7, parts of Chapters 8 and 9; Appendix B)

Primary Sources of Statistics on Trade Movements

Two publications of customs statistics, one monthly, one annual, serve as the basis of most reports on Japanese foreign trade. Additional information may be obtained, on payment for the cost of necessary work, directly from the Research and Statistics Section, Customs Division, Ministry of Finance, Tokyo. The amount of detail made available is phenomenal, but these primary statistics are of limited use if one is not prepared to do a vast amount of adding to obtain meaningful groupings.

Monthly figures of commodities exported and imported appear in Japan, Ministry of Finance, *Trade of Japan* (English and Japanese; Tokyo: Japan Tariff Association, monthly plus cumulative issues for January–June and January–December). Through 1961 the English title of this publication was *Monthly Return of the Foreign Trade of Japan,* and its organization was somewhat different from that adopted with the new title in January 1962. Most references in this study are necessarily to issues appearing before 1962, usually to the January–December cumulative issue for a particular year. To make certain of identification when the new title is cited, I refer to it as *Trade of Japan* (Monthly Return). I sometimes refer simply to *Monthly Return* for either title.

This basic publication lists in two long tables, for exports and imports respectively, every commodity that flows out of or into Japan, insofar as the Customs Bureau can tell. Exports are shown at f.o.b. values, imports at c.i.f. values, both in thousands of yen. In addition, physical quantities are shown, usually in metric units since Japan now officially uses the metric system. Often two physical measures are given, e.g., both square meters and kilograms of cloth exported.

Commodity categories are described in three ways: in Japanese, in English, and in code numbers. The codes, like the statistical classifications they represent, follow the United Nations Standard International Trade Classification. These codes are presented separately in Japan, Ministry of Finance, *Statistical Classification of Commodities for Japanese Foreign Trade* (English and Japanese; Tokyo: Japan Tariff Association, annual). In this system the major commodity groupings are given one-digit code designators, from 0 through 9. Up through 1961, the progressively smaller categories had two, three, five, or seven digits in their designators; there were no codes of four or six digits. In 1962 the five- and seven-digit codes were dropped in favor of four- and six-digit codes.

The *Monthly Return* lists all of the smallest categories and shows any trade that may have taken place in each. Aside from the grand total, only one-digit and five-digit (in 1962, four-digit) subtotals are included. No subtotals are given for the important three-digit and two-digit groupings; the headings are there, and in bold type, but the quantity and value columns are simply left blank. The Japanese Customs Bureau reports that its statistical machines have been able to produce simultaneously only the three kinds of totals now published. New machines were being installed in 1963, however, and it was expected that beginning with the September 1963 issue totals would be published for every code level.

Each issue of the *Monthly Return* also contains two valuable summary tables, entitled "Principal Export by Country" and "Principal Import by Country," taking 41 and 11 pages respectively in the January–December 1960 issue, which totaled 409 pages. These useful tables have been cut down in size with the changed format introduced in 1962. The issue for January–December 1962 devotes only 13 pages to showing where 24 categories of exports went, 6 pages to showing the main sources of 20 categories of imports. For the user satisfied with the groupings presented there, the *Monthly Return* is a very handy source. Other tables list total value of imports and exports for a number of preceding months and years, and the value of trade with each foreign country; in addition there are unit value and quantum indices, a table showing the nationality of ships and airplanes carrying Japanese trade, and a few other incidental statistics.

The *Monthly Return* is a necessary, even if somewhat frustrating, source for serious study of Japanese trade. Its main tables are generally accurate, and some of the errors that inevitably creep in are corrected in an errata sheet inserted in each copy. The English headings sometimes contain remarkable typographical errors, but these are usually apparent and any ambiguities can be cleared up by reference to different issues. In addition to the omission of important group totals and subtotals, the *Monthly Return* is sometimes marred by poor binding. Some copies literally fall apart on first opening.

The second primary source is Japan, Ministry of Finance, *Trade of Japan,* but it appears only once a year. Through 1960 its title was *Annual Return of the Foreign Trade of Japan* [1] (English and Japanese; Tokyo: Japan Tariff Association). For a number of years, ending in 1961, this return consisted of three volumes, two of which were huge and expensive. For 1960 they were as follows: Commodity by Country (2252 p.); Country by Commodity (Import) (764 p.); Country by Commodity (Export) (2976 p.). Thus the total was 5992 closely printed pages, for which the total purchase price was 21,000 yen, equal to $58.33. The second and third of these volumes contain for every country the same small commodity details that the *Monthly Return* (cumulative January–December issue) shows for the world as a whole. The

[1] Although the covers and title pages now use the English title, *Trade of Japan,* the explanatory notes continue to use the longer title. To avoid confusion when it is necessary to refer to this new title, I call it *Trade of Japan* (Annual Return). For any year, I sometimes use the abbreviated title, *Annual Return,* where that seems sufficient.

first volume contains a long export section (1734 p.) and a shorter import section (484 p.) plus several small miscellaneous tables. The export and import sections repeat the details shown in the *Monthly Return* (cumulative January–December issue) and add complete information as to the destination of every bit of each export item and the origin of each import item. The second and third volumes present mainly the same information, organized by countries rather than commodities. The reason the country-by-commodity information takes up more than half again as many pages as the commodity-by-country information is that country names are far shorter than the names of the many commodity categories. In the first volume it is country names that are repeated as fully as necessary, after the listing of each commodity. But in each of the other two volumes a country is listed only once, after which every commodity category in which there was trade is listed in seven-digit detail.

Extremely few subtotals are shown in the *Annual Return.* The two country volumes show only country totals and one-digit code subtotals. The commodity volume provides no subtotals at all in its two main tables. But, for instance in 1960, this volume had two introductory tables (30 and 34 pages long, respectively, for exports and imports), repeating the five-digit-code subtotals shown in the January–December 1960 issue of the *Monthly Return.*

The format of the *Annual Return* was revolutionized with the 1962 edition. All descriptions of countries and commodities in English or Japanese are confined to a listing at the back of each volume. This listing is the same as the one appearing in *Statistical Classification of Commodities for Japanese Foreign Trade,* except that in the *Annual Return* tariff classification numbers are also included. As before, the *Annual Return* has four main tables. In one volume, imports are shown by commodity and country, then by country and commodity (601 p., appendices 255 p.). In the other volume, exports are shown by commodity and country, then by country and commodity (2211 p., appendices 219 p.). But all commodity and country references in these four tables are by code only, and the figures must be decoded as well as combined to be useful. At the same time there were a number of changes in commodity classifications.

The retreat from English and Japanese into codes is associated with an increased use of machines for tabulating the customs figures. The elimination of words and characters has abbreviated the listings, especially the country by commodity tables, so much as to reduce the bulk of one year's return to two volumes. But the old curse of these returns remains: useful subtotals are simply omitted. In its present form the *Annual Return* is more than ever a tool for the specialist alone.

In addition to yen values the *Annual Return* shows two indicators of the physical volume of many movements, for example in the case of ships exported both the number and the gross tonnage. In both *Annual Return* and *Monthly Return,* re-exports and re-imports are shown separately from exports and imports. Both publications have valuable detailed explanatory notes at the front of each volume.

The *Annual Return* is a higher quality product than the *Monthly Return,* especially in the quality and type of binding. Apparently the *Annual Return* is regarded as a more permanent record than the *Monthly Return,* although the latter also contains information of lasting value.

Secondary Sources

Most of the economic and statistical publications mentioned at the beginning of this Bibliographic Note and a substantial proportion of the books treat foreign trade in one way or another. Because trade looms large in Japanese economic life, it also occupies much space in publications on general economic trends and problems. For statistics, when primary sources are not necessary, I have often found it convenient to use the Bank of Japan's *Economic Statistics of Japan* and *Economic Statistics Monthly.* The Ministry of International Trade and Industry, International Trade Bureau, publishes *Monthly Foreign Trade Statistics,* mostly in Japanese but with enough English to make this secondary source useful for following new trade trends and comparing them with figures for past years. Values are given in dollars, and there is more information than in the Bank of Japan's *Economic Statistics Monthly.*

The leading secondary source is the Ministry of International Trade and Industry's annual white paper on trade, a book-length report in Japanese. Much, but not always all, of this report is translated into English and published as *Foreign Trade of Japan* (Tokyo: Japan External Trade Organization (JETRO), annual). This essential source (215 large printed pages in the issue dated 1962) gives statistics and comment, mainly for the three calendar years preceding publication, on all major movements, by commodities, by countries, by commodities and countries, and by countries and commodities. The 1962 edition, giving figures for 1959, 1960, and 1961, contains 369 tables. Unlike the jungle overgrowth of small numbers in the customs returns, the MITI white paper presents meaningful groupings. And values are given in thousands of dollars, a great convenience for readers used to thinking in dollar terms.

This most valuable report has some disadvantages. The English-language version is not available in the United States until nearly a year after the latest statistics that are included. Thus this is not a report for following late developments. The very selection process that makes tables short and simple means that minor items are left out, and the careful student finds himself frequently driven back to the primary sources. And the fact that this material has gone from primary sources through publication in Japanese before translation into English provides many opportunities for typographical and other errors. Inaccuracies are, however, not usually a serious problem.

The U.S. Tariff Commission's *Postwar Developments in Japan's Foreign Trade,* Report No. 201, Second Series (Washington: GPO, 1958; 195 p.) is the most substantial survey of the subject produced in the United States. One of a series the Tariff Commission has produced through the years on Japanese trade, this study is authoritative and careful and contains much information, especially on tariffs, not easily available elsewhere. The substantial statistical appendix is reduced in value by the fact that prewar figures are shown without adjustment for postwar changes in Japan's boundaries.

Trade journals have sprouted almost like weeds in the fertile ground of Japan's expanding prosperity. Many of these contain information—like company names, addresses, and product listings—that is essential for businessmen. But for the economic analyst such publications seldom are very helpful.

Analyses of Japanese trade in the postwar period, other than the Tariff Commission study cited, have been mostly very general, with trade usually only one subject touched, or very narrow, dealing with one or a few particular commodities, markets, or problems. By contrast, the half dozen years just preceding the attack on Pearl Harbor saw the appearance of several broad studies of Japanese trade. Partly the difference is a reflection of the much lower level of acrimony and acuteness in Japanese trade problems today. Still, there is a short supply of comprehensive studies, and the inquirer often fails to get his question answered.

The listings below include major separate sources. Most of the individual short articles in the indispensable *The Oriental Economist* and other frequently used sources are not included here.

Statistical problems are not fully discussed in English-language sources. But two articles of value in pointing up some of these problems are:

Hollerman, Leon. "The Interpretation and Use of Japanese Foreign Trade Statistics," *Economic Development and Cultural Change*, v. 8, no. 1 (1959), pp. 69–78.

Minobe, Ryokichi (Chief, Statistical Standards Division, Administrative Management Agency). "Real Scale of Foreign Trade," *The Oriental Economist*, May 1956, pp. 235–237.

Materials on Japanese Trade Before 1945

Farley, Miriam S. *The Problem of Japanese Trade Expansion in the Post-War Situation.* New York: International Secretariat, Institute of Pacific Relations, 1940. 93 p. (IPR inquiry series.)

Hersey, Arthur, and Steffie Browne. *The Place of Foreign Trade in the Japanese Economy.* U.S. Department of State Intelligence Research Report OCL-2815, 2 v. Washington: U.S. Department of State, 1946. V. 1, 153 p.; v. 2, 128 p. of tables.

Lockwood, William W. *Trade and Trade Rivalry Between the United States and Japan.* Study prepared for the sixth international conference of the Institute of Pacific Relations, held at Yosemite, California, August 15–29, 1936. American Council Papers, no. 6. New York: American Council, Institute of Pacific Relations, 1936. 66 p.

Mitsubishi Economic Research Bureau, Tokyo. *Japanese Trade and Industry, Present and Future.* London: Macmillan, 1936. 663 p. (After World War II, the Bureau changed its name to Mitsubishi Economic Research Institute.)

The Oriental Economist. *Foreign Trade of Japan, A Statistical Survey.* Tokyo: Author, 1935. 708 p.

Shotwell, James T., general ed., Baron Yoshiro Sakatani, Japanese series ed. *Economic and Social History of the World War. The Effect of the World War upon the Commerce and Industry of Japan,* prepared by Kakujiro

Yamasaki and Gotaro Ogawa. New Haven: Yale University Press, for the Carnegie Endowment for International Peace, 1929. 345 p.

Supreme Commander for the Allied Powers. General Headquarters. Economic and Scientific Section. Programs and Statistics Division. *Japanese Trade Patterns, 1930–1934.* Tokyo: Author, 1952. 138 p. + appendices.

U.S. Department of Commerce. Bureau of Foreign and Domestic Commerce. Far Eastern Unit. *Civil Affairs Handbook–JAPAN. Section 8B: Commerce.* Washington: Headquarters, Army Service Forces, 1944. 99 p.

U.S. Tariff Commission. *The Foreign Trade of Japan: A Study of the Trade of Japan with Special Reference to That of the United States.* Washington: GPO, 1922. 229 p.

———. *Japan: Trade during the War; A Study of the Trade of Japan, Particularly during the Years 1913 to 1917 and with Special Reference to the Trade with the United States.* Washington: GPO, 1919. 147 p.

———. *Japanese Trade Studies: Annotated Tabular Survey of the Trade of Japan Proper (including That with Korea and Formosa).* Washington: GPO, 1945. 228 p. + index.

———. *Recent Developments in the Foreign Trade of Japan, Particularly in Relation to the Trade of the United States.* Report No. 105, Second Series. Washington: GPO, 1936. 207 p.

———. *United States Imports from Japan and Their Relation to the Defense Program and to the Economy of the Country.* Washington: Author, 1941. 239 p.

Vakil, Chandulal N., and D. N. Maluste. *Commercial Relations between India and Japan.* Studies in Indian Economics No. 12. New York: Longmans, Green, 1937. 210 p.

Japan—Postwar Trade and Export Industries

Books and Booklets

Asia Kyokai. *Japanese Fisheries: Their Development and Present Status.* Tokyo: Author, 1957. 253 p.

———. *The Smaller Industry in Japan.* Tokyo: Author, 1957. 148 p.

Fujii, Shigeru (Professor of Economics, Kobe University). *Japan's Trade and Her Level of Living.* Economic Series No. 6. Tokyo: The Science Council of Japan, Division of Economics and Commerce, 1955. 76 p.

Institute of Asian Economic Affairs. *Asian Trade Statistics: Statistics on Foreign Trade between Asian Countries and Industrial Nations Classified by Commodities, 1956–58.* Tokyo: Author, 1961. 506 p.

Japan. Ministry of Foreign Affairs. *A Statistical Survey on Trade Between Japan and Asian Countries.* Tokyo: Author, 1955. 52 p.

———. Ministry of International Trade and Industry. *The Inspection System of Japan's Exports and Law Governing Her Exports.* Tokyo: Institute of Foreign Exchange and Trade Research, 1956. 51 p.

Leng, Shao Chuan. *Japan and Communist China.* Foreword by Kenneth S. Latourette. Kyoto: Doshisha University Press, 1958. 169 p.

Meade, J. E. *Japan and the General Agreement on Tariffs and Trade.* The Joseph Fisher Lecture in Commerce, given in Adelaide, August 8, 1956. Adelaide, Australia: Griffin Press, 1956. 27 p.

Minobe, Ryokichi. *Japan's Foreign Trade.* Tokyo: Japanese Ministry of Foreign Affairs, 1956. 19 p.

Miyashita, Tadao (Professor of Economics, Kobe University). *Development of the Trade between Japan and Communist China: Its Present Problems and Its Future.* Japanese Paper No. 1. Tokyo: Japan Institute of Pacific Relations, 1958. 56 p. + appendix. (Processed.)

Okita, Saburo. *The Rehabilitation of Japan's Economy and Asia.* Tokyo: Japanese Ministry of Foreign Affairs, Public Information and Cultural Affairs Bureau, 1956, 16 p.

Takeuchi, Ryuji (Minister Plenipotentiary of Japan). *Memorandum on Japan's Economy and Foreign Trade—to The Honorable Clarence B. Randall, Chairman, Commission on Foreign Economic Policy.* Washington: Embassy of Japan, October 27, 1953. 15 p.

United Nations. Economic Commission for Asia and the Far East. *Problems and Prospects of Accelerated Economic Development in the ECAFE Region through Trade with Japan.* Lake Success: Author, 1950. 238 p.

U.S. Department of State. Office of Intelligence Research and Analysis. *Japan's Bilateral Trade and Payments Agreements.* Intelligence Report No. 7663. Washington: Author, 1958. 31 p.

Wang, K. P. *Minerals in Japan's Industrial Economy.* Washington: U.S. Department of the Interior, Bureau of Mines, 1962. 37 p. + bibliography.

Yankelovich, Daniel, Inc. *Strengthening the Japanese Trade Position in the United States: A Pilot Study.* Washington: United States–Japan Trade Council, 1959. 71 p. (Processed.)

Articles, Papers, and Portions of Books

Bank of Tokyo. "Japan's Trade with South and Southeast Asia," *Semiannual Report,* December 1958, pp. 13–41.

———. "Japanese Exports to the United States," *Semiannual Report,* June 1959, pp. 13–43.

———. "Structure of Japan's Foreign Trade—Before and After the War," *Semiannual Report,* March 1956, pp. 5–29.

Cohen, Jerome B. "Japan's Foreign Trade Problems," in Edwin O. Reischauer and others, *Japan and America Today.* Stanford University Press, 1953. Pp. 121–131.

———. "Problems in Foreign Trade and Investment," *Annals of the American Academy of Political and Social Science,* November 1956, pp. 95–101.

Duxbury, D. "Japan's Resurgence in Perspective," *The Banker,* November 1958, pp. 722–726.

Fujiyama, Ai-Ichiro. "United States-Japan Economic Relations," *Contemporary Japan,* v. 22, nos. 1–3 (1953), pp. 30–37.

Hattori, K., and J. Fujii. "Japanese Trade With the United States and Communist Areas: Comparison of Pre-war and Post-war Developments and Future Prospects," *Monthly Circular, Survey of Economic Conditions in Japan* (Mitsubishi Economic Research Institute), May 1957, pp. 10–24.

Hiraoka, Kentaro. "Japan's Trade with Communist China," *Contemporary Japan,* v. 21, nos. 10–12 (1953), pp. 648–653.

Hollerman, Leon. "The Logistic View versus the National Income View of Foreign Trade Dependence, with Special Reference to Japan," *Hitotsubashi Journal of Economics,* October 1960, pp. 52–58.

———. "What Does 'Dependence' Mean in International Trade?," *Kyklos* (Basel), no. 1, 1960, pp. 102–109.

Hunsberger, Warren S. "Japanese Exports and the American Market," *Far Eastern Survey,* September 1957, pp. 129–140.

Ishibashi, Tanzan (Minister of International Trade and Industry). "Trading with China," *The Oriental Economist,* August 1956, pp. 396–397.

"Japan Upgrades Its Old Label. Nippon is banking on quality rather than cheapness of exports to win its way back into the markets of the West," *Business Week,* September 7, 1957, pp. 154, 157–158.

"Japan's Economic Role in Asia," *Pakistan Horizon* (Pakistan Institute of International Affairs), September 1958, pp. 184–192.

Kojima, Kiyoshi. "Economic Development and Import Dependence in Japan," *Hitotsubashi Journal of Economics,* October 1960, pp. 29–51.

Mendel, Douglas H., Jr. "Japan and the Two Chinas," *The Japanese People and Foreign Policy.* Berkeley: University of California Press, 1961. Pp. 215–244.

Morozumi, Yoshihiko. "Ten Years of Reconstruction and Development. Part II. Trade and Industry Reviewed," *Contemporary Japan,* v. 24, nos. 1–3 (1956), pp. 55–67.

Nagano, Shigeo (President, Fuji Iron & Steel Company). "Raw Materials for Iron and Steel," *The Oriental Economist,* September 1957, pp. 472–474.

Okita, Saburo. "Post-war Structure of Japan's Foreign Trade," *Economia Internazionale,* February 1960, pp. 83–102.

Olson, Lawrence. " 'In Ten Years, in Fifty Years': Comments on China Trade," in *Dimensions of Japan.* New York: American Universities Field Staff, 1963. Pp. 335–346.

Ota, Kaoru. "The Productivity Movement in Japan and Its Problems; The Sohyo Viewpoint," *Japan Quarterly,* July–September 1956, pp. 296–301.

Piquet, Howard S., and Elden E. Billings. "Japan Still Has a Trade Problem," *World Affairs,* Summer 1960, pp. 52–54.

"Russian Market—A Hope for Japan," *Eastern World,* October 1958, pp. 34–35.

Sasaki, Kyohei. "Quantitative Effect of the United States Economy on Japan's Foreign Trade Between 1950 and 1956," *The Review of Economics and Statistics,* August 1959, pp. 320–324.

Trezise, Philip H. "The Place of Japan in the Network of World Trade," *American Economic Review, Papers and Proceedings,* May 1963, pp. 589–598.

United Nations. Economic Commission for Latin America. "Recent Developments and Prospects in Trade between Latin America and Japan," *Economic Bulletin for Latin America,* February 1957, pp. 68–85.

Ushiba, Nobuhiko. "Possibility of Expanding Trade with the Communist Bloc," *Asian Affairs,* March 1958, pp. 71–79.

Waldstein, George. "Showdown in the Orient," *Harvard Business Review,* November–December 1954, pp. 113–120.

A fairly new trade association, the United States–Japan Trade Council in Washington, has since 1956 issued nearly one hundred pamphlets reporting on trade movements between Japan and the United States, urging liberal American trade policies, and opposing restrictions on Japanese exports. Reportorial pamphlets include the following:

"Japan: A Growing Market for U.S. Exports," June 1960, 11 p.

"Japan, the American Farmer's Best Export Market," June 1962, 16 p.

"Texas, the Nation's Top Exporter to Japan," October 1961, 6 p.

"Trade through Hampton Roads," October 1962, 6 p.

"U.S. Exports to Japan, 1955–1959–A Commodity Analysis," August 1960, 16 p.

"U.S. Trade with Japan, 1961," August 1962, 6 p.

"Where Are Japan's Best Export Markets?," March 1958, 9 p.

V. COTTON TEXTILES

(Chapter 9, part of Chapter 10)

The high degree of tension that cotton textile problems create in Japan, the United States, and other countries is reflected in a large flow of words and statistics. The factual and analytical material is discussed here. Policy material will be taken up in the sections that follow.

In both Japan and the United States information comes mainly from a combination of government and industry sources. The Ministry of International Trade and Industry in Tokyo has a strong Textile Bureau. This agency and other parts of the Japanese government compile, with industry help, many of the statistics of Japanese cotton manufacturing. Few analytical reports, however, are available from the Textile Bureau in English.

In Osaka the powerful All Japan Cotton Spinners' Association maintains, as part of its headquarters, a strong and well-staffed economic research department. Economic research staffs are also to be found in individual textile companies, especially the big spinners. (The Kureha Spinning Company of Osaka, for instance, has issued its *Kureha Textile Review* quarterly since 1951.) More useful for this study are reports on issues, for instance: Toyo Spinning Company, Ltd., Institute for Economic Research, *Cotton Industrial Wages in Japan* (Osaka: Author, Toyobo Economic Series 2, 1955; 36 p.). The Spinners' Association has been helpful in the present study, but less through its regular publications than in its answers to inquiries. The most valuable of its periodical publications is the *Monthly Report of Japanese Cotton Spinning Industry* (Osaka: Author, monthly). An example of a useful separate report from this association is *Labour Situation of the Cotton Spinning Industry in Japan* (Osaka: Author, 1958; 32 p.).

Of even more use in the present study have been two volumes on cotton manufacturing in Japan. The first, Keizo Seki's *The Cotton Industry of Japan* (Tokyo: Japan Society for the Promotion of Science, 1956, 417 p.) lists its author as chairman of the board of directors of the Toyo Spinning Company. The second, published less than a year later, is in a way a short supplement to the first. Entitled *The Story of the Japanese Cotton Textile Industry,* this volume has a preface signed by Kojiro Abe on behalf of the All Japan Cotton Spinners' Association, the Japan Cotton Textile Exporters' Association, and the Japan Textile Products Exporters' Association. These associations are all listed as publishers of the book (Osaka, 1957, 90 p.). I have taken the easy way and listed Abe as author in my references to this volume, which was written mainly in the research department of the spinners' association, of which Abe was then president.

In the United States also, the main textile trade association publishes economic information about the industry. The American Textile Manufacturers' Institute (before October 1962 called the American Cotton Manufacturers' Institute) publishes *Textile Hi-Lights* (prepared and published quarterly by the Institute's Economic Research Division in Washington). Like its Japanese counterpart, this Institute has contributed more to the present study through conversations and answers to inquiries than through its publications. A good deal of the output of the Institute has more pertinence to policy, however, than to economic inquiry.

The U.S. government produces a remarkably large volume of reports related to American trade in cotton and its manufactures. Taking segments of the government alphabetically, we find in the Department of Agriculture not only the agencies that handle the programs for the production and marketing of raw cotton but also a staff that keeps abreast of developments in cotton textile manufacturing. One of the best summaries of the cotton textile problem to come from any source is by Beatrice M. Hornbeck of the Cotton Division, entitled "U.S. Cotton Textile Imports—Perspective on a Complex Problem" (Washington: Department of Agriculture, Foreign Agricultural Service FAS M-125, 1962, 14 p.). Another valuable report is L. D. Howell's *Changes in American Textile Industry: Competition, Structure, Facilities, Costs,* Agricultural Marketing Service, Technical Bulletin No. 1210 (Washington: GPO, 1959; 337 p.). Among the other individual and serial publications of the Department of Agriculture that include material pertinent to this study are:

Economic Research Service. *The Cotton Situation.* Bimonthly.

———. *Statistics on Cotton and Related Data, 1920–1956.* Statistical Bulletin No. 99. Washington: Author (then called Agricultural Marketing Service), revised 1957. 256 p. + annual supplements.

Foreign Agricultural Service. *Foreign Agriculture Circular.* Washington: Author, irregular. (In 1962, 22 issues were devoted to cotton—production, yields, trade, demand, etc.)

———. *Prospects for Foreign Trade in Cotton.* March 1963. 24 p.

The Department of Commerce's Census Bureau is, of course the primary source of American published statistics on foreign trade. Since July 1957 a special Census Bureau report has been issued monthly on cotton textile imports (*United States General Imports of Cotton Manufactures,* Report FT 130). On the basis of these and other statistics the Bureau of International Commerce has been publishing each summer since 1960 a particularly valuable report, "U.S. imports of textiles, apparel, and related manufactures and comparisons with U.S. production and exports," the title of the issue published in August 1962 ending, "1957–61" (*World Trade Information Service,* pt. 3, no. 62-24, Washington: Author, 1962; 12 p.). Other noteworthy publications of the Department of Commerce include:

Business and Defense Services Administration. *Textile Outlook for the Sixties.* Washington: GPO, 1960. 54 p.

———. *Comparative Fabric Production Costs in the United States and Four Other Countries.* Washington: GPO, 1961. 59 p. The four other countries in this comparative study are Italy, the United Kingdom, India, and Japan.

The Department of Commerce has also kept Congress supplied with information. An example of a valuable report is "Japanese Program for Regulation of Export of Cotton Textiles to the United States," in U.S. House, Committee on Ways and Means, *Foreign Trade Policy,* compendium of papers collected by the staff for the Subcommittee on Foreign Trade Policy (Washington: GPO, 1957, pp. 621–628). A recent report published by the Department of Commerce was *Economic Effect of Textile Mill Closings, Selected Communities in Middle Atlantic States,* prepared by George Perazich and W. T. Stone of Galaxy, Inc. (Washington: GPO, 1963; 58 p.).

The Department of Labor is concerned mainly with matters affecting wages and employment. Statistics and reports are published in the *Monthly Labor Review;* an example of a report with special reference to Japan is Boris S. Yane's *Japanese Wage Structure and Wages in Japanese Mining and Manufacturing Industries, 1953* (Washington: U.S. Department of Labor, Bureau of Labor Statistics, 1954; 17 p.). A number of reports on the U.S. domestic situation are also issued, notably:

U.S. Department of Labor. Bureau of Labor Statistics. *Factory Workers' Earnings in Selected Manufacturing Industries, June 1959.* Bulletin No. 1275. Washington: GPO, 1960. 47 p.

———. ———. *Wage Structure: Cotton Textiles, August 1960.* BLS Report No. 184. Washington: GPO, 1961. 62 p.

———. ———. *Wage Structure: Women's and Misses' Dresses, August 1960.* BLS Report No. 193. Washington: GPO, 1961. 30 p.

The Department of State has had a great deal of concern for Japanese cotton textiles during the past quarter century. Most of its publications relate to policy, but the following reports also were consulted during the present study:

U.S. Department of State. *The Japanese Textile Industry, 1928–36.* OIR Report No. 4529. Washington: Author, 1947. 65 p.

———. *The Textile Mission to Japan.* Department of State Publication 2619, Far Eastern Series 13. Washington: GPO, 1946. 39 p.

The Tariff Commission is on the front lines whenever escape-clause or other Commission proceedings occur. The most significant reports and actions for purposes of this study are indicated in the footnotes to Chapters 8 and 9, and in the list of escape-clause cases in Table 8-3. Two earlier reports affecting Japan are:

U.S. Tariff Commission. *Cotton Cloth.* Report to the President on the Differences in Costs of Production of Cotton Cloth in the United States and in the Principal Competing Country as Ascertained Pursuant to the Provisions of Section 336 of Title III of the Tariff Act of 1930, with Appendixes. Report No. 112, Second Series. Washington: GPO, 1936. 163 p.

———. *The Japanese Cotton Industry and Trade: Recent Developments and Future Outlook (with Special Reference to Comparative Costs and Competition between Japan and the United States).* Washington: GPO, 1921. 162 p.

A recent report that has significant bearing upon Japan is:

U.S. Tariff Commission. *Cotton Products.* Report to the President on Investigation No. 22-25 under Section 22 of the Agricultural Adjustment Act, as Amended. TC Publication 69. Washington: Author, 1962. 209 p.

Among the mass of other materials available on the subject of cotton textiles and international trade, with special reference to Japan and to implications for the American economy, those listed below are noteworthy:

Books

Arthur D. Little, Inc. *Diversification: An Opportunity for the New England Textile Industry.* A report to the Federal Reserve Bank of Boston, the Massachusetts Department of Commerce, the Rhode Island Development Council, the Business Development Company of Rhode Island. Boston: Federal Reserve Bank of Boston, 1955. 109 p.

Canada. Royal Commission on the Textile Industry. *Report of the Royal Commission on the Textile Industry.* Ottawa: Author, 1938. 308 p.

Copeland, Melvin T., and Edmund P. Learned. *Merchandising of Cotton Textiles: Methods and Organization.* Business Research Studies No. 1. Boston: Harvard Graduate School of Business Administration, 1933. 96 p.

Cox, Reavis. *The Marketing of Textiles.* Washington: The Textile Foundation, 1938. 367 p.

Great Britain. Board of Trade. *Reorganization of the Cotton Industry.* Cmd. 744. London: H. M. Stationery Office, 1959. 10 p.

Hague, Douglas C. *The Economics of Man-made Fibres.* London: Duckworth, 1957. 315 p.

———, and Peter K. Newman. *Costs in Alternative Locations: The Clothing Industry.* National Institute of Economic and Social Research, Occasional Papers No. 15. Cambridge, Eng.: University Press, 1952. 73 p.

Harris, Seymour E. *The Economics of New England: Case Study of an Older Area.* Cambridge: Harvard University Press, 1952. 335 p.

——. *New England Textiles and the New England Economy.* Report to the Conference of New England Governors, February 1956. 197 p.

Japan. Ministry of Labor. *Working Conditions in the Japanese Textile Industry.* Tokyo: Author, 1955. 15 p. + tables.

Kroese, W. T. *The Japanese Cotton Industry.* Leiden: H. E. Stenfert Kroese's Uitgeversmij N. V., for the Association of the Netherlands Cotton, Rayon and Linen Industry, 1950. 158 p.

Ludwig, Mario, ed. *The Cotton Industry in a World Economy.* Manchester, Eng.: International Federation of Cotton and Allied Textile Industries, 1958. 286 p.

Michl, H. E. *The Textile Industries: An Economic Analysis.* Washington: The Textile Foundation, 1938.

Miernyk, William H. *Inter-Industry Labor Mobility: The Case of the Displaced Textile Worker.* Boston: Bureau of Business and Economic Research, Northeastern University, 1955. 158 p.

Moser, Charles K. *The Cotton Textile Industry of Far Eastern Countries.* Boston: Pepperell Manufacturing Co., 1930. 144 p.

Pearse, Arno S. (General Secretary, International Federation of Master Cotton Spinners' and Manufacturers' Associations, Manchester, England). *The Cotton Industry of Japan and China.* Manchester: Taylor, Garrett, Evans, 1929. 254 p.

——. *Japan's Cotton Industry, 1955,* with chapter on "Hong Kong and Shanghai Cotton Mills. [Stockport?], Eng.: Cloister Press, 1955. 135 p.

Primary Textiles Institute (Toronto). *The Textile Industry in Japan.* Report of a Visit by a Group of Three from the Canadian Textile Industry to Japan. Toronto: Author, 1956. 129 p.

Shindo, Takejiro. *Labor in the Japanese Cotton Industry.* Tokyo: Japan Society for the Promotion of Science, 1961. 276 p.

Stewart, John R. *Japan's Textile Industry.* New York: Institute of Pacific Relations, 1949. 82 p. (Processed.)

Utley, Freda. *Lancashire and the Far East.* London: Allen & Unwin, 1931. 395 p.

Articles

Cohn, David L. "Southern Cotton and Japan," *Atlantic Monthly,* August 1956, pp. 55–57.

Ellinger, B. and H. "Japanese Competition in the Cotton Trade," *Journal of the Royal Statistical Society,* v. 93, no. 2 (1930), pp. 185–231.

"Labour Problems of Modernisation in the Textile Industry," *International Labour Review,* June 1960, pp. 527–556.

Mitsubishi Economic Research Institute. *International Structure of the Manufacturing Industries with Special Reference to the Textile Industry,* November 1955.

Nehmer, Stanley. "The Future of Japanese Textiles," *Far Eastern Survey,* August 28, 1946, pp. 261–264.
Torrens, James G. "Japan's Textile Industry," *Far Eastern Survey,* June 4, 1947, pp. 124–127.
"Wage Differentials Only Part of Competitive Textile Import Situation," *America's Textile Reporter,* October 1, 1959, pp. 51–54.

VI. JAPANESE FOREIGN ECONOMIC POLICY

(Chapters 2 and 11, parts of Chapters 4, 5, and 6)

Materials on Japanese policy are generally the same as those already mentioned in connection with one or another aspect of Japan's foreign economic relations. Writers on policy matters usually combine policy discussion with reporting, analysis, and interpretation. On the historical development of policy the footnotes in Chapter 2 indicate the sources used in this study.

Recent years have seen the development of three major themes in Japanese economic policy. One is the shift from cautious and inadequate planning and modest expectations to the optimistic and ambitious plans and thinking epitomized by Prime Minister Ikeda's income-doubling plan for the 1960s. The second theme is liberalization of Japanese foreign economic policy, a process that has lagged behind the emergence of official optimism about Japan's capabilities and prospects. The third theme is "voluntary" or negotiated Japanese export restraints, most especially those affecting cotton textiles. This theme is associated, of course, with the abiding need to expand Japanese exports.

The plans, in their English versions, are as follows:

Japan. Economic Planning Board. *Economic Self-Support Five-Year Plan,* Decided by the Cabinet Meeting on 23 December 1955. Tentative translation. Tokyo: Author, 1956. 36 p. (Processed.) With separate volume entitled *Economic Self-Support Five-Year Plan Tables.* 30 p. (Processed.)
———. Economic Planning Agency. *New Long-Range Economic Plan of Japan (FY 1958–FY 1962).* Tokyo: Author, 1957. 196 p.
———. ———. *New Long-Range Economic Plan of Japan (1961–1970): Doubling National Income Plan.* Tokyo: The Japan Times, 1961. 128 p.

Comments on the plans are to be found in much of the literature of the past ten years. The traditional, pervasive pessimism about Japan's prospects was even more apparent in comment on the plans than in the plans themselves. Part of the reason is that, in scrutinizing the assumptions behind each plan, analysts can easily challenge many of them. Two noteworthy commentaries are:

Kitamura, Hiroshi. "Long-Run Projection of the Japanese Economy—A Critical Evaluation," *Kyklos* (Basel), no. 2, 1956, pp. 135–163.
Fujioka, Masao. "Appraisal of Japan's Plan to Double Income," *Staff Papers* (IMF), March 1963, pp. 150–185.

Of greater concern to the present study are Japanese approaches to foreign economic policy, as represented dramatically in debates over liberalization and over barriers to Japanese exports, notably the quotas on textiles. As one might expect, Japanese writers advert often to the latter subject, seeking ways to reduce or remove barriers. But the pressure for Japanese liberalization has been less from Japan than from abroad. In an unusually well-balanced statement covering both points, the Committee for Economic Development in March 1963 felt it necessary to speak strongly in urging Japan to admit foreign goods, foreign capital, and foreign management more liberally. The report, already mentioned in this Bibliographic Note, is entitled *Japan in the Free World Economy,* a statement on national policy, including a statement by the Japan Committee for Economic Development (Keizai Doyukai) (New York: Author, 1963; 58 + 45 p.).

In its section of the report the Keizai Doyukai makes an unusually vigorous statement, for a Japanese group, on freedom of trade and Japan's need to liberalize, but the statement has a strong current throughout of the great need for Japan to have freer access to export markets abroad.

A general awareness of Japanese policy issues, trends, and positions may be gained from *The Oriental Economist,* English-language Japanese newspapers, translations of Japanese press and magazines, and the American press. My own work has relied in part on such sources, in part on specific materials listed in these pages, and in part on discussions through the years with informed persons.

The items mentioned below do not represent the whole literature on Japanese foreign economic policy, but instead are items that generally focus more on policy than on economic reporting and analysis. There is a little repetition of outstanding articles already mentioned above, but a large percentage of the works on Japanese economic affairs would need to be repeated to provide reasonably full coverage on Japanese policy concerning trade with specific areas, on the Marxist element in Japanese intellectual life and its impact on foreign policy issues, on the specific issues related to cotton textiles, on Japanese suspicions of the intentions of Americans and others, and on other issues.

Books

Borton, Hugh, and others. *Japan between East and West.* New York: Harper, for the Council on Foreign Relations, 1957. 327 p.

The Economist Correspondents. *Consider Japan.* London: Duckworth, 1963. 121 p.

Mendel, Douglas H., Jr. *The Japanese People and Foreign Policy.* Berkeley: University of California Press, 1961. 269 p.

Morley, James W. *Soviet and Communist Chinese Policies toward Japan, 1950–1957.* Study prepared for the thirteenth international conference of the Institute of Pacific Relations, held at Lahore, Pakistan, in February 1958. New York: International Secretariat, Institute of Pacific Relations, 1958. 46 p.

Articles and Papers

Akashi, Yasushi. "Japan's Foreign Policy," *Yale Review,* Winter 1958, pp. 198–218.

Bronfenbrenner, Martin. "Economic Thought and Its Application and Methodology in the East: The State of Japanese Economics," *American Economic Review, Papers and Proceedings,* May 1956, pp. 389–398.

Ishizaka, Taizo. "Japan's Role in World Economy," *Contemporary Japan,* v. 24, nos. 4–6 (1956), pp. 266–272.

Kase, Toshikazu. "Japan's New Role in East Asia," *Foreign Affairs,* October 1955, pp. 40–48.

Kiuchi, Nobutane. "False Assumptions about the Japanese Economy," *Foreign Affairs,* April 1956, pp. 459–468.

Lockwood, William W. " 'The Socialistic Society': India and Japan," *Foreign Affairs,* October 1958, pp. 117–130.

Morley, James W. "Japan's Image of the Soviet Union, 1952–61," *Pacific Affairs,* Spring 1962, pp. 51–58.

Ohira, Zengo, and Terumichi Kuwahara. "Fishery Problems between Japan and the People's Republic of China," *The Japanese Annual of International Law,* no. 3, 1959, pp. 109–125.

Okita, Saburo. "Japan's Economic Prospects," *Foreign Affairs,* October 1960, pp. 123–131.

———. "A Reappraisal of Japan's Economy," *Japan Quarterly,* July–September 1959, pp. 282–290.

Takagaki, Katsujiro (President, Mitsubishi Trading Company, and a board member of the Federation of Economic Organizations). "Trade Measures," *The Oriental Economist,* March 1956, pp. 131–133.

Takahashi, Ryutaro. "Trade Policies of the New Japan," *Foreign Affairs,* January 1952, pp. 289–297.

VII. U.S. POLICY RELATING TO JAPAN'S ECONOMY

(Chapters 1 and 12, parts of Chapters 8 and 10)

The body of published material dealing specifically with American economic policy toward Japan is not very large, especially by contrast to what there is with regard to Europe. Most of the materials that I have found to be directly pertinent to this work, aside from congressional documents and partisan appeals, are discussions of Japanese problems, of general Japanese–American relations, or of general economic policy. Many of the works already cited contain some reference to policy or some ideas bearing on policy issues.

U.S. government publications provide the largest mass of specific material. *The Economist* (London) has enough reporting and comment on Japan to be an important current source, and its consistently high quality contrasts sharply with the extremely varied quality of congressional documents. There are so many short articles on Japan in *The Economist* that I have omitted reference to specific articles. *Foreign Affairs* has published during the past ten years a remarkable series of articles bearing on many of the policy issues treated in this volume. Other sources of material are newspapers and news magazines, and, of course, the special pleaders of one sort or another.

There are very few books on U.S. economic policy toward Japan since the end of the Occupation in 1952. An important short one is the March 1963 policy statement of the Committee for Economic Development (*Japan in the Free World Economy,* cited). Jerome Cohen's various cited writings devote some attention to policy. G. C. Allen's cited writings, like Cohen's, deal with Japan's economic problems and performance, but Allen, being British, has had less to say about American policy.

U.S. Government Publications

The greatest volume of policy material I have used has been published by the U.S. government, especially the Congress and the Tariff Commission. For a decade now, Japan has had a prominent place in congressional discussions on foreign trade policy and related matters, including such varied subjects as the domestic American textile industry, problems of unemployment in the United States, the deficit in the U.S. balance of payments, and foreign aid. Let us look first at what congressional documents have to offer.

The Committee on Ways and Means in the House of Representatives has been a particularly productive source, especially in its consideration of tariff legislation. Hardly any aspect of U.S. trade policy has been neglected, or any point of view left unexpressed, in its publications. Of course, some policy positions have been stated over and over again, especially in hearings before the committee or one of its subcommittees. Perhaps the most valuable single document put out by the committee was published in 1957 by a subcommittee headed by Congressman Hale Boggs, in preparation for the 1958 renewal of the Trade Agreements Act: *Foreign Trade Policy,* compendium of papers collected by the staff for the Subcommittee on Foreign Trade Policy (Washington: GPO, 1957, 1157 p.). Its thirteen parts dealing with the major aspects of the subject are made up of papers by individual authors or, in some cases, by government agencies. Implications for Japan and specific references to Japan are to be found throughout the volume, but three parts are especially worth noting because they focus on problems and measures in which Japan is particularly important: Pt. 6, "Quantitative Regulation of Imports—Advantages and Disadvantages—United States and Foreign Experience," pp. 593–642; Pt. 9, "Foreign Trade Policy in Relation to Wages and Employment—Problems in Adjustment," pp. 761–822; and Pt. 10, "United States Cotton and Cotton Textiles in Relation to International Trade," pp. 823–1027.

An earlier product of the same subcommittee (with an earlier name) also stands out for bringing to light commercial issues between Japan and the United States. A series of hearings were held in Washington in September and October 1956 and overseas conferences in Europe and Japan in November and December of that year. The Ways and Means Committee published reports that included not only digests of oral testimony but also written statements provided to the subcommittee. Valuable material on Japan appears on pages 1974–2138 in Pt. 4 (Overseas Conferences). The document is listed as:

Administration and Operation of Customs and Tariff Laws and the Trade Agreements Program. Overseas Conferences. Hearings before the Subcommittee on Customs, Tariffs and Reciprocal Trade Agreements, 84th Cong., 2d sess. Washington: GPO, 1957. Pt. 4, pp. 1765–2138.

Other useful documents of the Ways and Means Committee include the hearings and reports published in connection with consideration of the 1955 and 1958 extensions of the Trade Agreements Act and of the Trade Expansion Act of 1962.

The Senate Committee on Finance is the counterpart of the Ways and Means Committee in the House of Representatives. The Finance Committee has also produced hearings and reports on the trade bills. But no special subcommittee comparable to that of Mr. Boggs has produced material specifically on Japan.

The Senate Committee on Interstate and Foreign Commerce in 1958 established a special subcommittee under Senator John O. Pastore of Rhode Island to investigate the problems of the domestic textile industry in the United States. This subcommittee has produced the series of published hearings and reports listed below. These documents have proved a rich source of information on the problems, attitudes, and issues involved, with protectionist views given particular prominence.

Problems of the Domestic Textile Industry. Hearings before the subcommittee, 85th Cong., 2d sess. Washington: GPO, 1958–59. 4 parts; 2067 p.

Problems of the Domestic Textile Industry. Report of the Committee on Interstate and Foreign Commerce made by the subcommittee. Senate Report No. 42, 86th Cong., 1st sess. Washington: GPO, 1959. 28 p.

Problems of the Domestic Textile Industry. Hearings before the subcommittee, 87th Cong., 1st sess. Washington: GPO, 1961. 577 p.

Problems of the Domestic Textile Industry. Supplementary Report of the Committee on Interstate and Foreign Commerce made by the subcommittee, 87th Cong., 1st sess. Washington: GPO, 1961. 22 p.

Study of the Domestic Textile Industry. Hearings before the subcommittee, 87th Cong., 2d sess. Washington: GPO, 1962. 197 p.

Problems of the Domestic Textile Industry. Second Supplementary Report of the Committee on Commerce made by the subcommittee, 87th Cong., 2d sess. Washington: GPO, 1962. 16 p.

The House Foreign Affairs Committee and the Senate Foreign Relations Committee have had to pay attention to economic matters concerning Japan, and there are some hearings and reports, including those related to the Senate's concurrence in treaties. An example of an ad hoc proceeding is *Imports of Cotton Textiles from Japan,* Hearings before a subcommittee of the Senate Foreign Relations Committee, 84th Cong., 2d sess., on Green amendment to Mutual Security Act of 1956 (Washington: GPO, 1956; 29 p.).

The House Committee on Education and Labor has also been involved in matters concerning Japan, primarily through hearings conducted by the Subcommittee on the Impact of Imports and Exports on American Employment, headed by Congressman Adam C. Powell. Some eloquent expressions of both liberal and protectionist views can be found in *Impact of Imports and Exports on Employment,* A Fact-finding Investigation of Foreign Competition and Its Effects upon Domestic Employment, Hearings before the subcommittee, 87th Cong., 1st and 2d sess. (Washington: GPO, 1961, 1962; 8 parts).

Among other congressional committees that have had occasion to deal with matters affecting the Japanese economy, the Armed Services Committees of both houses have been concerned with military expenditures and so have the Appropriations Committees.

The Department of Agriculture has contributed relatively little policy material, except in connection with attempts to use agricultural programs and legislation for the protection of cotton manufacturers in the United States, as reported in Chapter 9.

The Department of Commerce, although at the forefront of foreign trade operational activities, has not published much on American foreign economic policy affecting Japan. It has, however, made a valuable contribution to both analysis and policy discussion in *U.S. Commodity Exports and Imports as Related to Output, 1959 and 1960,* prepared by the Bureau of the Census, Series ES2, No. 3 (Washington: GPO, 1962; 46 p.).

The Department of Labor is involved in matters of wage rates and labor costs, subjects that often arise in Japanese–American economic relations. This department, like other executive departments, generally follows administrative guide lines, but it also tends to work closely with the AFL-CIO in developing policy positions. The department's approach to foreign trade policy is indicated in "Role of Labor Cost in Foreign Trade," *Monthly Labor Review,* May 1963, pp. 485–490.

The Department of State publishes a stream of materials bearing on policy related to Japanese foreign economic affairs. Among these materials are treaties, notably the 1953 Treaty of Friendship, Commerce and Navigation between Japan and the United States, and also less formal agreements, such as the short-term and long-term arrangements on cotton textiles. In the category of documents related to the GATT a notable report is *General Agreement on Tariffs and Trade: Analysis of Protocol (including Schedules) for Accession of Japan; Analysis of Renegotiations of Certain Tariff Concessions Negotiated at Geneva, Switzerland, February–June 1955,* Department of State Publication No. 5881, Commercial Policy Series 150 (Washington: GPO, 1955; 125 p.). Press releases and items in *The Department of State Bulletin* constitute a continuing flow of new material, for example the communiqués of the first and second meetings of the cabinet-level U.S.–Japan Committee on Economics and Trade:

"Cabinet Members Attend Economic Meeting," *The Department of State Bulletin,* November 27, 1961, pp. 891–893.

"Joint U.S.–Japan Committee Concludes Second Meeting," *The Department of State Bulletin,* December 24, 1962, pp. 559–561.

The Tariff Commision publishes reports on its numerous investigations, and many of them have information about Japan. The escape-clause cases involving Japan are listed in Table 8-3; for each case in which a formal finding was made, the Commission issued a Report to the President on Investigation No. –, under the Provisions of Section 7 of the Trade Agreements Extension Act of 1951, as Amended (or, since October 11, 1962, under the successor statute, the Trade Expansion Act of 1962). Information about Japan may also be found in other Tariff Commission publications, such as its *Annual Report,* the yearly summary entitled *Operation of the Trade Agreements Program,* the reports on investigations under Section 22 of the Agricultural Adjustment Act, and the reports on the status of investigations (in two volumes, one permanent and one revised periodically). There have also been special reports bearing on U.S. policy concerning Japanese trade, notably:

U.S. Tariff Commission. *Memorandum for the Senate Committee on Finance on Senate Resolution 236, 84th Congress.* A Study of the Effect of Imports of Textiles and Textile Products upon the Domestic Textile Industry. Washington: Author, 1955. 14 p. + 84 p. of tables. (Processed.)

———. *Postwar Developments in Japan's Foreign Trade.* Report No. 201, Second Series. Washington: GPO, 1958. 195 p.

Books and Booklets

The discussion of U.S. foreign trade policy and the analysis of the issues involved in it rest on a literature much too large to cite here. The list in this and the following sections includes only those sources that deal primarily with U.S.–Japanese relations or with some specific problems treated in this book.

Bidwell, Percy W. *What the Tariff Means to American Industries.* New York: Harper, for the Council on Foreign Relations, 1956. 304 p.

Hunsberger, Warren S. *Japan in United States Foreign Economic Policy.* Study prepared for the Subcommittee on Foreign Economic Policy of the U.S. Joint Economic Committee, 87th Cong., 1st sess. Washington: GPO, 1961. 27 p.

Thorp, Willard L. *American Interest in Asian Development.* Washington: Brookings Institution, 1956. 117 p. + 49 tables.

U.S. Commission on Foreign Economic Policy (Randall Commission). *Minority Report,* by Daniel A. Reed and Richard M. Simpson. Washington: GPO, 1954. 20 p.

———. *Report to the President and the Congress.* Washington: GPO, 1954. 94 p.

———. *Staff Papers.* Washington: GPO, 1954. 531 p.

Wright, Philip G. *The American Tariff and Oriental Trade.* University of Chicago Press, for the Institute of Pacific Relations, 1931. 177 p.

Articles, Papers, and Portions of Books

Abegg, Lily. "Japan Reconsiders," *Foreign Affairs,* April 1955, pp. 402–415.

Allen, G. C. "The Present Economic Situation in Japan," *International Affairs,* July 1955, pp. 291–299.

America's Textile Reporter. This journal, a weekly published in Boston since 1887, said of itself: ". . . no other weekly newspaper published has been so consistently protectionist, pro-right-to-work, anti-inflationist and pro-South." (Front cover, v. 75, no. 12, 1961.) In articles like the following it takes a strong stand on U.S. import policy: "U.S. Economy Is Being Bled White by Giveaways and Cheap Imports. Efforts to Put into Practice the Daydreams of the One-Worlders and Free Traders Can Only Spell Ruin, Business Executive Warns," December 17, 1959, pp. 45–50; "Free Trade Theory Amounts to Importing Foreign Slave Labor. American Industrial Economy Is Being Destroyed as Poorly Advised Leaders Persist in Suicidal Trade Policies, Says N.Y. Manufacturer," by Herman C. Jones, December 10, 1959, p. 31.

Armstrong, Hamilton Fish. "Japan at Cross-Purposes," *Foreign Affairs,* January 1956, pp. 227–244.

Bidwell, Percy W. "The Tariff in Transition," *Foreign Affairs,* April 1954, pp. 450–472.

Borton, Hugh, and others. "Economic and Political Position of Japan," *Proceedings of the Academy of Political Science,* January 1955, pp. 71–115.

Braibanti, Ralph. "The United States and Japan: A New Century Begins," *Virginia Quarterly Review,* Summer 1955, pp. 383–400.

Finn, D. "What the Japanese Intellectuals Are Thinking," *American Scholar,* Fall 1955, pp. 443–455. Reply by G. Z. Bereday.

Hunsberger, Warren S. "Japanese Exports and the American Market," *Far Eastern Survey,* September 1957, pp. 129–140.

"Japanese Intellectuals Discuss American-Japanese Relations," *Far Eastern Survey,* October 1960, pp. 145–160.

Kravis, Irving B. "International Trade and Domestic Employment," in William Haber and others, *Manpower in the United States: Problems and Policies.* New York: Harper, 1954. Chapter 9.

Ladejinsky, Wolf. "Agrarian Revolution in Japan," *Foreign Affairs,* October 1959, pp. 95–109.

Lebergott, Stanley. "Wage Structures," *Review of Economic Statistics,* November 1947, pp. 274–284.

Leiter, R. D. "Organized Labor and the Tariff," *Southern Economic Journal,* July 1961, pp. 55–65.

Morris, I. I. "Foreign Policy Issues in Japan's 1958 Elections," *Pacific Affairs,* September 1958, pp. 219–240.

———. "Japanese Foreign Policy and Neutralism," *International Affairs,* January 1960, pp. 7–20.

Neal, Alfred C. "New Economic Policies for the West," *Foreign Affairs,* January 1961, pp. 247–258.

Petit, Thomas A. "Impact of Imports and Tariffs on the American Tuna Industry," *American Journal of Economics and Sociology,* April 1960, pp. 275–288.

Reischauer, Edwin O. "The Broken Dialogue with Japan," *Foreign Affairs,* October 1960, pp. 11–26.

Rockefeller, John D., 3rd. "Japan Tackles Her Problems," *Foreign Affairs,* July 1954, pp. 577–587.

Scalapino, Robert A. "Japanese Socialism in Crisis," *Foreign Affairs,* January 1960, pp. 318–328.

Seidman, B. "Organized Labor's Answer to International Competition," *American Federationist,* November 1959, pp. 8–9.

Williams, Faith M., and Edgar I. Eaton. "Payments for Labor and Foreign Trade," *American Economic Review,* September 1959, pp. 584–601.

The following is a sampling of the many policy pamphlets issued by the United States–Japan Trade Council in Washington. Copies of such pamphlets may be obtained, free of charge, from this trade association.

"Japan: Ally and Trading Partner," March 1963, 6 p.

"Japan, the United States, and the Common Market," October 1962, 10 p.

"Japan's Trade Liberalization and American Exports," May 1963, 10 p.

"The Trade Expansion Act: Problems and Prospects," February 1963, 14 p.

Index

Note: The words "Japan" and "Japanese" have in most instances been omitted from the index, and it should be understood that "Economic policy," for example, means "Japanese economic policy" unless otherwise described. Data in the tables have not been indexed; for their contents see the list of tables in the front matter.

Publications of the Council on Foreign Relations

FOREIGN AFFAIRS (quarterly), edited by Hamilton Fish Armstrong.

THE UNITED STATES IN WORLD AFFAIRS (annual). Volumes for 1931, 1932 and 1933, by Walter Lippmann and William O. Scroggs; for 1934–1935, 1936, 1937, 1938, 1939 and 1940, by Whitney H. Shepardson and William O. Scroggs; for 1945–1947, 1947–1948 and 1948–1949, by John C. Campbell; for 1949, 1950, 1951, 1952, 1953 and 1954, by Richard P. Stebbins; for 1955, by Hollis W. Barber; for 1956, 1957, 1958, 1959, 1960, 1961, 1962 and 1963, by Richard P. Stebbins.

DOCUMENTS ON AMERICAN FOREIGN RELATIONS (annual). Volume for 1952 edited by Clarence W. Baier and Richard P. Stebbins; for 1953 and 1954, edited by Peter V. Curl; for 1955, 1956, 1957, 1958 and 1959, edited by Paul E. Zinner; for 1960, 1961, 1962 and 1963, edited by Richard P. Stebbins.

POLITICAL HANDBOOK AND ATLAS OF THE WORLD (annual), edited by Walter H. Mallory.

FOREIGN AFFAIRS BIBLIOGRAPHY, 1952–1962, by Henry L. Roberts.

THE DOLLAR IN WORLD AFFAIRS, An Essay in International Financial Policy, by Henry G. Aubrey.

ON DEALING WITH THE COMMUNIST WORLD, by George F. Kennan.

FOREIGN AID AND FOREIGN POLICY, by Edward S. Mason.

THE SCIENTIFIC REVOLUTION AND WORLD POLITICS, by Caryl P. Haskins.

AFRICA: A Foreign Affairs Reader, edited by Philip W. Quigg.

THE PHILIPPINES AND THE UNITED STATES: Problems of Partnership, by George E. Taylor.

SOUTHEAST ASIA IN UNITED STATES POLICY, by Russell H. Fifield.

UNESCO: ASSESSMENT AND PROMISE, by George N. Shuster.

THE PEACEFUL ATOM IN FOREIGN POLICY, by Arnold Kramish.

THE ARABS AND THE WORLD: Nasser's Arab Nationalist Policy, by Charles D. Cremeans.

TOWARD AN ATLANTIC COMMUNITY, by Christian A. Herter.

THE SOVIET UNION, 1922–1962: A Foreign Affairs Reader, edited by Philip E. Mosely.

THE POLITICS OF FOREIGN AID: American Experience in Southeast Asia, by John D. Montgomery.

SPEARHEADS OF DEMOCRACY: Labor in the Developing Countries, by George C. Lodge.

LATIN AMERICA: Diplomacy and Reality, by Adolf A. Berle.

Publications of the Council on Foreign Relations

The Organization of American States and the Hemisphere Crisis, by John C. Dreier.

The United Nations: Structure for Peace, by Ernest A. Gross.

The Long Polar Watch: Canada and the Defense of North America, by Melvin Conant.

Arms and Politics in Latin America (Revised Edition), by Edwin Lieuwen.

The Future of Underdeveloped Countries: Political Implications of Economic Development (Revised Edition), by Eugene Staley.

Spain and Defense of the West: Ally and Liability, by Arthur P. Whitaker.

Social Change in Latin America Today: Its Implications for United States Policy, by Richard N. Adams, John P. Gillin, Allan R. Holmberg, Oscar Lewis, Richard W. Patch, and Charles W. Wagley.

Foreign Policy: The Next Phase: The 1960s (Revised Edition), by Thomas K. Finletter.

Defense of the Middle East: Problems of American Policy (Revised Edition), by John C. Campbell.

Communist China and Asia: Challenge to American Policy, by A. Doak Barnett.

France, Troubled Ally: De Gaulle's Heritage and Prospects, by Edgar S. Furniss, Jr.

The Schuman Plan: A Study in Economic Cooperation, 1950–1959, by William Diebold, Jr.

Soviet Economic Aid: The New Aid and Trade Policy in Underdeveloped Countries, by Joseph S. Berliner.

Raw Materials: A Study of American Policy, by Percy W. Bidwell.

NATO and the Future of Europe, by Ben T. Moore.

African Economic Development, by William Hance.

India and America: A Study of Their Relations, by Phillips Talbot and S. L. Poplai.

Japan Between East and West, by Hugh Borton, Jerome B. Cohen, William J. Jorden, Donald Keene, Paul F. Langer and C. Martin Wilbur.

Nuclear Weapons and Foreign Policy, by Henry A. Kissinger.

Moscow-Peking Axis: Strength and Strains, by Howard L. Boorman, Alexander Eckstein, Philip E. Mosely and Benjamin Schwartz.

Russia and America: Dangers and Prospects, by Henry L. Roberts.

Foreign Affairs Bibliography, 1942–1952, by Henry L. Roberts.